A PRACTITIONER'S GUIDE
TO THE
EUROPEAN CONVENTION
ON HUMAN RIGHTS

AUSTRALIA
LBC Information Services
Sydney

CANADA and USA
Carswell
Toronto

NEW ZEALAND
Brooker's
Auckland

SINGAPORE and MALAYSIA
Thomson Information (S.E. Asia)
Singapore

A PRACTITIONER'S GUIDE TO THE EUROPEAN CONVENTION ON HUMAN RIGHTS

BY

KAREN REID

LONDON
SWEET & MAXWELL
1998

Published in 1998 by Sweet & Maxwell Limited
100 Avenue Road
London NW3 3PF
(http://www.smlawpub.co.uk)

Typeset by Dataword Services Ltd of Chilcompton
Printed and bound in Great Britain by Butler & Tanner Ltd, Frome and London

No natural forests were destroyed to make this product;
only farmed timber was used and replanted.

ISBN 0 421 54730 8

A CIP catalogue record for this book is available
from the British Library

ACKNOWLEDGMENTS

To Sebastian and Joshua, for their patience and tolerance in respect of time spent on a book, which does not involve a story, or even any pictures.

To all the members of the Secretariat of the European Commission of Human Rights, without whose combined energy and efforts none of the applications under the European Convention of Human Rights would reach a meaningful determination, with a particular mention for the indispensable work of Mieke Pijnenberg, Gail FitzGerald and Dympna Swanton, the leadership (sadly moved elsewhere) of Chris Krüger, the infectious idealism and humour of Sally Dollé and the unobtrusively dedicated professionalism of Stephen Phillips.

DISCLAIMER

CONTENTS

TABLE OF CASES

TABLE OF CASES BEFORE THE
EUROPEAN COURT OF HUMAN RIGHTS

TABLE OF CASES BEFORE THE
EUROPEAN COMMISSION OF HUMAN RIGHTS

TABLE OF LEGISLATION

l

Council Resolutions

INTRODUCTION

PURPOSE OF THIS BOOK

This is intended to be a practical book. It will not offer solutions or theories or an exhaustive study. It will, hopefully, indicate the range of situations and legal problems which may fall within the scope of the European Convention of Human Rights ("the Convention") and its Protocols. And it aims to explain the what, when, how and why of a particular procedure, that of introducing applications before the Convention organs, currently the European Commission of Human Rights ("the Commission") and the European Court of Human Rights ("the Court"), soon to be replaced by a single permanent Court.

WHAT

The basic subject matter of this procedure are human rights. This is a concept which is trammelled with popular misconceptions, false expectations and knee-jerk prejudices. In this book, the term means solely those rights and freedoms expressly guaranteed under the Convention and its Protocols. The competence of the Commission and Court is defined by the Convention. Every complaint must base itself squarely on the Convention's provisions and comply with its requirements. Essentially, the provisions of the Convention cover classic civil and political rights: economic and social rights are only covered indirectly, if at all. Part II: Problem Areas highlights the situations and disputes which fall, or may fall, within the ambit of the Convention rights.

HOW

An application begins, simply, with a letter to the Commission, setting out the substance of the complaints.

The procedures that follow do require some explanation (see Part I: Practice and Procedure). However, there are the minimum of formalities and no fees which reflects the fact that the system is intended to be open to everyone, legally represented or not and that a significant number of cases are pursued by individuals who have no access to, no means to pay or no inclination to use lawyers.[1]

WHEN

A strict time-limit applies. An application must be made within six months of the final decision relating to the subject-matter of the complaint where domestic remedies exist or within six months of the event or act complained of where no domestic remedies exist. Limited exception arises where there can be said to be a continuing situation of violation (see Part IB: Admissibility Checklist).

---

[1] In 1996, 4% of applications were introduced by lawyers; in 1991, 51%.

1

WHY

The responsibility of Governments to adhere to minimum standards of fair and proper conduct in exercising their powers in respect of their own citizens and any others within their jurisdiction is acknowledged on domestic and international level. In ratifying the Convention, the United Kingdom Government has expressly pledged by way of treaty obligation to ensure the observance of the fundamental rights and freedoms guaranteed in that instrument. It has, as a result, accepted the right of individuals, groups of individuals, non-governmental organisations and private companies to introduce complaints against it (and all public authorities and institutions under its responsibility) under the implementation system provided by the Convention organs in Strasbourg. Since this is a supranational instance, it offers the possibility of remedies where a domestic system cannot. No national legal system is free from lacunae, historical anomalies, cultural biases or blindspots. While the United Kingdom, sometimes unfairly, seems to be subject to unfavourable scrutiny in Strasbourg, it is a compliment to the Government, which allows free, unhindered access to the system and co-operates fully and fairly in the procedures; to the applicants, who are prepared to fight for justice against the weight of the State and to the lawyers who bring a common law approach and British-trained legal expertise to the process.

In the proceedings, applicants can obtain a limited but not negligible range of remedies. It is possible that the Government will offer to settle the case: providing specific reparation (for example, right of entry to the United Kindom, grant of planning permission); or a change of legislation or administrative practice; *ex gratia* payment of compensation and reasonable legal costs.

Before the Court, a binding judgment may make public declaration of the State's violation accompanied by a monetary award of just satisfaction and payment of legal costs (Part III). Following such judgment, the State is required to comply with the Court's findings which may also lead to a specific result such as change in legislation or other step necessary to remedy whatever failing has been identified.[2]

Besides rendering a successful outcome for a particular individual, an application can be seen in a wider context. It is a method of achieving law reform and improving or maintaining civil liberty standards. It participates in furnishing a system of model standards contributing to worldwide developments. In that context, practitioners, prepared to represent applicants, play a significant and creative role in identifying those cases which can usefully be dealt with by the Strasbourg organs and in developing the case law of the Convention by the arguments and principles which they advocate in presenting those cases.

YES, BUT . . .

There are drawbacks. The admissibility threshold is high: approximately only one in ten cases succeeds in crossing it (see Part IB: Admissibility Checklist). But it is possible to be selective and successful. Some practitioners from the United Kingdom have a high success rate in reaching the admissibility stage, and subsequent friendly settlement or findings of violation by the Court.

There is delay. Ironically, for institutions which sit in judgment on allegations that domestic courts fail to decide cases within a reasonable time, it takes about five years for a successful case to conclude before the Court. (Less successful cases are generally disposed of more summarily and often as quickly as within three to six months.) The reasons for the

---

[2] If the case is not referred to the Court but dealt with by the Committee of Ministers, there may be a finding of violation with award of compensation and legal costs: see Part IA: Procedure and Part III: Just Satisfaction.

delay are several: the backlog of cases which increases with every new country that ratifies, shortage of staff and resources, the semi-permament nature of the Commission and Court, the duplication in procedures before the two organs, and the inbuilt delays in the system. While the Commission in particular is sensitive to these problems, constantly reviewing its procedures, introducing such improvements as are compatible with its powers and resources, the position has long been unsatisfactory. Further fundamental reforms are very imminent in the form of a new single permanent Court to replace the current two-tier system once the Eleventh Protocol comes into force on November 1, 1998. Meanwhile, those who consider the possible outcome worth the exercise must reconcile themselves to a certain lack of expedition, save in those cases involving threat to life and limb (Part IA: Procedure, Interim Relief).

There are also flagrant inequalities as regards the position of the applicant. Governments enjoy procedural advantages in addition to obvious superiority of resources.

No international system can be perfect, immune to error. All who have worked in the Commission have had experience of cases that were, in their view, disappointing, regrettable, if not worse. But these are on the whole outweighed by the successes. The Convention system is a tool of remarkable possibilities. While the continuing rise in the volume of cases has practical disadvantages, it has also contributed to dynamic trends in interpretation as the case law extends into new areas and adapts to changing climates and perceptions. As a final and hopefully persuasive illustration, the following changes in U.K. legislation and practice resulted from, or were contributed to, by cases dealt with in Strasbourg: Security Service Act 1989; Interception of Communications Act 1985; end of blanket censorship of prisoners' letters; change in practice regarding grant of legal aid on appeal in Scotland; Children Act 1989; end of criminalisation of homosexual relationships between consenting adults over 21; regular review by a tribunal of the continued detention of mental health patients and life sentence prisoners (excluding adults sentenced for murder); end of corporal punishment in state schools and birching in Isle of Man; contempt of court rules changed; and, revision of the system of military court martials.

PART I: PRACTICE AND PROCEDURE

A. PROCEDURE

1. THE NEW EUROPEAN COURT OF HUMAN RIGHTS

Protocol No. 11, which comes into force on November 1, 1998, abolishes the Commission and Court and creates a new single permanent European Court of Human Rights.[1] The new Court will have full jurisdiction, the right of individual petition will be automatic and the role of the Committee of Ministers will be restricted under former Article 54 to monitoring compliance with Court judgments.[2]

Membership

The qualifications for judges remain the same as the old Court, namely, that they must be of high moral character and possess the qualifications required for appointment to high judicial office or be jurisconsults of recognised competence.[3] However the Protocol introduces the age limit of 70 at which their office will expire. The judges are also under an obligation not to engage in any activity incompatible with a full-time office, the intention being that the judges should live in Strasbourg.

Organisation of the Court

There are four compositions: committees of three, chambers, the Grand Chamber and the Plenary Court.

Committees of three may reject or strike out cases by unanimous vote in the same manner as the committees of the Commission currently do.

Chambers consist of seven judges. There is no quorum and substitute judges will sit to maintain the number. It is currently envisaged that there will be four chambers. Cases not dealt with in committee will be examined by a Chamber. Where a Chamber considers that the case raises a serious question affecting the interpretation of the Convention or protocols, or where the resolution of a question might have a result inconsistent with a judgment previously delivered by the Court (Article 30), it may relinquish jurisdiction to the Grand Chamber, unless one of the parties to the case objects. After the Chamber gives judgment, the parties may within three months in exceptional cases request that the case be referred to the Grand Chamber (Article 44). A panel of the Grand Chamber (five judges) shall accept the request if the case raises a serious question affecting the interpretation and application of the Convention or a serious issue of general importance (Article 43).

The Grand Chamber (17 judges including the President, Vice-Presidents of the Court and Presidents of the Chambers and a national judge[4]) will thus deal with cases where the

---

[1] The Commission and Court had sat only for short sessions during the year. The Commission continues in existence for one further year to dispose of the admissible cases still pending before it.

[2] In the previous system it had a decision-making function on cases which the Commission did not refer to the Court.

[3] A judge for each Contracting State will be appointed by the Parliamentary Assembly, from three candidates proposed by each State.

[4] Either a sitting judge or one appointed ad hoc.

Chambers have relinquished jurisdiction and those referred on the request of a party after decision of the Chamber.[5]

Procedure

Subject to the adoption by the new Court of its Rules and Procedure, it is envisaged that the procedure will follow in outline the current procedure before the Commission.[6] There is expected to continue a separation of stages of admissibility and merits,[7] a stage of friendly settlement between admissibility and merits and the use of a *judge rapporteur*. Admissibility criteria, powers to strike out and grant just satisfaction remain essentially unchanged.

Proceedings will be more public than hitherto, the presumption being that hearings and documentation lodged with the Registrar shall be public, unless decided otherwise.[8]

Approach to case law

It is to be anticipated that even though the new Court is not formally bound by pre-existing case law it will rely heavily on the past experience of the Commission and Court, past case law continuing to be highly relevant for at least some time to come. It will have an opportunity, however, if it wishes, to change practice and adopt different approaches.[9]

Outline of procedure

(as set out in the Explanatory Report to Protocol No. 11 concerning cases which proceed to judgment on the merits)

- Lodging of application — Note 1
- Preliminary contacts with the Court's Registry — Note 2
- Registration of application — Note 3
- Assignment of application to a Chamber
- Appointment of *judge rapporteur* by the Chamber — Note 4
- Examination of the application to the respondent Government — Note 5
- Communication of the application to the respondent Government — Note 6
- Filing of observations and establishment of facts — Note 7
- Oral hearing[10] — Note 8
- Admissibility decision by the Chamber — Note 9
- Possibility of friendly settlement negotiations — Note 10
- Judgment by the Chamber — Note 11

---

[5] It also has competence to issue advisory opinions.

[6] Explanatory Report to Protocol No. 11, para. 52.

[7] Art. 29: save in exceptional cases where a separate admissibility decision might not be found necessary. For example, possibly where the Government waives admissibility.

[8] Art. 40.

[9] See "Opinion: The Legacy of the Commission to the New Court under the Eleventh Protocol" by Nicholas Bratza, Q.C. and Michael O'Boyle, European Human Rights Law Review 1997, Issue 3, which *inter alia* identifies those points of difference between the Commission and Court on which the new body could decide anew, *e.g.* transsexuals, effectiveness of judicial review as a remedy under Art. 13, exclusion of issues relating to access to the public service.

[11] It is unlikely however that oral hearings can be held in more than a small percentage of cases, given the volume of work that the new Court will inherit.

2. PREVIOUS PRACTICE OF THE CONVENTION ORGANS

The procedure of the new Court is likely to take over many features of the procedures of the old Convention organs, in particular, those of the Commission. The sections below refer to previous practice.

Note 1. Lodging of applications

According to the practice of the Commission, introduction of an application may be done by letter or fax. To stop time running for the purposes of the six-month rule, any preliminary letter, pending submission of a detailed application, must contain a brief outline of the facts and complaints such that the substance of the application is apparent.[10]

A full application contains all the information set out in the Commission's application form (see Appendix 5). An application must be accompanied by all relevant documents (copies *not* originals, in particular, copies of the domestic decisions relating to the remedies process).

A period of six weeks is usually indicated as the time within which an application form should be returned. This is not a formal rule derived from the Convention but a practice to prevent long lapses in time in registering a case: it is possible if necessary and not unreasonable in the circumstances for longer time to be taken (see Part 1B: Admissibility, Six months).

A legal representative must provide a letter of authority signed by the applicant authorising the lawyer to represent him before the Commission.

Note 2. Preliminary contacts with the Registry

The new Court will be staffed by a Registry, initially combined from lawyers from the old Commission Secretariat and old Court Registry. Currently, the Secretariat manage applications as follows.

A provisional file is opened with each new complaint/letter. It is allotted to a unit of case lawyers with relevant linguistic and legal expertise. The Secretariat inform the applicant of any outstanding items and as a general rule will not register the case until all documents are provided. The Secretariat are authorised to draw to applicants' attention any apparent problems as to admissibility. This will allow any errors, omissions to be remedied and indicate difficult points which need further attention. The points raised, even if disagreed with, should be answered. Since clearly inadmissible cases can be rejected in summary fashion (committees of three), it is advisable to establish that the case does not fall into that category.

Note 3./4. Registration of the application and appointment of Rapporteur

Once the case is registered, it becomes a pending case before the Commission. The speed with which it receives its first examination will depend largely on the current state of the backlog (3 months–18 months). Cases may be given priority (*e.g.* where serious health issues or children are involved) and treated urgently.[11] The case is also allotted a *rapporteur* — a member of the Commission charged with presenting it to the Commission when it is listed for examination. The identity of the *rapporteur* is never disclosed. It is the *rapporteur*, with the assistance of the case lawyer from the Secretariat, who makes proposals to the

---

[10] See rr.43 and 44, para. 4 of the Commission's Rules of Procedure.
[11] r.33.

Commission as to the procedure, decisions and reports to be adopted in respect of a case. Whether the new Court will adopt a system of *judge rapporteur* is one of the matters to be settled in the adoption of the new Court's rules.

Note 5. Examination by Committee

Previously, the Commission used *Committees of three* to examine cases put forward by the *rapporteur* as clearly inadmissible or which might be struck out on clear grounds.[12] The procedure was introduced to allow the Commission to reject, expeditiously, hopeless cases and to fight its ever increasing backlog. The members of the Committee must agree unanimously for the proposal to be adopted. If a Committee rejects a proposal, it is re-presented before the Chamber or Plenary. The Plenary, on objection raised by a member of the Commission, may refer a Committee case before the Chamber or Plenary for decision.

Note 6. Examination by Chambers

Before the new Court, cases which are not rejected in Committee will be examined before one of the four Chambers.

According to previous practice, while cases could be declared inadmissible by a Chamber of the Commission or the Plenary on first examination, any case which raised an issue meriting further examination was communicated to the respondent Government. No case was declared admissible without first inviting the Government's response.

Communication to the respondent Government

Pursuant to Commission procedure, when a case is communicated to the respondent Government, questions are usually put. These indicate the areas of concern to the Commission. The parties may be directed that no submissions need be made on a particular point, which will generally be an indication that it is regarded as inadmissible. The questions put should be addressed or risk going by default.

The applicant receives the Government observations in order to reply. It is essential to counter any Government argument raised on inadmissibility, whether non-exhaustion, six months, or manifestly ill-founded. While the Commission is perfectly capable of rejecting Government arguments on its own knowledge of domestic and Convention case law, well-prepared argument by applicants is of valuable assistance to a thorough examination of the issues.

Note 7. Establishment of the facts

As with the old Commission and Court, the new Court will have powers to take evidence and hear witnesses.

It is rare that the Commission is unable to sufficiently determine the factual basis of an application for the purpose of the complaints before it on the documentary material provided by the parties. Where a matter has been adjudicated in a domestic system it is likely that the crucial facts have become common ground between the parties or the differences between them unlikely to be resolved further. The Commission has occasionally carried out fact-finding missions where the location was of particular relevance, for example, conditions of detention.[13] Where there has been no apparent effective factual

---

[12] See Art. 20, para. 3 of the Convention.
[13] See *e.g. A. v. UK*, 6840/74, (Rep.), July 6, 1980, 20 D.R. 5 (concerning conditions in Broadmoor); *Dhoest v. Belgium* 10448/83, (Rep.), May 14, 1987, 55 D.R. 5.

investigation at domestic level and disagreement as to the basic facts, it has also been forced to take on the role of hearing witnesses in cases from the state of emergency region in Turkey.[14]

Note 8. Oral hearings

Oral hearings are an exception before the Commission, the majority of admissible cases being decided on the basis of written submissions from the parties. Hearings tend to occur in cases raising difficult or new issues or which may, in the view of the Government, have fundamental effects in an important area of law or practice. It is unlikely, in view of the new Court's inheritance of a large backlog, that it will be able to afford to be generous in the scheduling of hearings. Many cases are likely therefore to be declared admissible or inadmissible without a hearing.

When an oral hearing on admissibility is decided, the Commission sends the parties a list of questions to be addressed. This indicates its concerns and other issues are addressed at the risk of being regarded as irrelevant. An opportunity is provided for a written brief to be submitted ten days before the hearing — this is sent to the other party. This may be useful for providing relevant background information, further factual developments or subsidiary arguments.

Parties are also requested to provide a copy of their speech in advance. This is solely to assist the interpreters. Amendments may be made to the speech as required. Speakers should bear in mind the interpretation process and avoid talking fast. Commission hearings are *in camera*.

The procedure for the hearing is notified to the parties beforehand, the timing being subject to strict regulation. The standard hearing held in a morning consists of 30 minutes each for Government and applicant, questions from members, a 20–30 minute adjournment, a final round of 15 minutes each for Government and applicant, to address questions and make final points (including answering the other sides' arguments). The average hearing is over in two hours. Exceptionally, complex cases, or cases joined and being heard together, will be allocated further time but this generally does not exceed 90 minutes total for each party.

Hearings before the old Court were similarly limited in time, rarely taking more than a morning or afternoon. Hearings before the new Court will be in public and may be expected to be more formal than the Commission proceedings. Before the old Court, lawyers made their submissions standing and did not wear robes.

When Commission hearings close, the parties agree a brief press release summarising facts and arguments with the Secretariat. The Commission proceeds directly to deliberate and generally reaches a decision as to admissibility the same day. The text of the decision is adopted shortly afterwards. Where the case is declared admissible, it is the Commission's practice also to deliberate on a preliminary basis the merits as far as may be possible. If it reaches a meaningful provisional opinion, it may be notified to the parties as a tool in assisting friendly settlement (see below). This provisional opinion is *strictly confidential*.

Note 9. Decisions on admissibility

As with the Commission, where the new Court declares the case inadmissible, there is no provision for appeal. Where admissible, the settlement and merits stage of the proceedings follow.

---

[14] *e.g. Akdivar v. Turkey*, September 16, 1996, R.J.D., 1996–IV, No. 15, the first of a series of cases which are being investigated by way of fact-finding missions.

Note 10. Friendly settlement procedure

The Commission informs both parties when it sends the decision of admissibility that it is at their disposal to assist a friendly settlement. Where it has been a position to reach a provisional view on the merits, this is communicated to the parties on a strictly confidential basis. This is only provisional and is only likely to encourage a settlement where the Government is forewarned of a tendency to a finding of violation.

Either party may send settlement proposals to the Commission which acts as conduit. Where it appears that there is a basis or will to settle, the Commission may intervene to make its own recommendations. However, it rarely, if ever, indicates to a Government what laws, practices or policies should be amended or repealed, since it is generally for States to choose the appropriate domestic measures to put right any violation of the Convention.

Pressure is more likely to be exerted on an applicant to settle than on a Government, particularly in a case which is unlikely to be sent to the Court, for example, where there is established case law on the Convention issue. As a means of encouraging applicants to settle, the Commission adopted a practice, where an applicant has rejected its recommended proposal for settlement, of proposing a lesser sum of compensation when consulted by the Committee of Ministers in its proceedings on just satisfaction.[15] It may arrange a meeting between the parties and a Delegate of the Commission and the Secretariat where such would be useful in bringing parties to agreement by breaking an impasse.

If an agreement is reached, the Commission adopts a report which is sent to the Committee of Ministers and made public. The parties are generally left to arrange payment of compensation and assessment of reasonable costs between themselves.

If an agreement is not reached, the negotiations are never made public and the case continues.

Note 11. Judgment on the merits

The Chamber of the new Court will have the same options as the old Commission and Court to request further written observations, hold hearings on the merits or take evidence. Since it will have the competence to make awards of just satisfaction, a procedure requiring the applicant to make his claims for just satisfaction will be necessary. Pursuant to old Court procedure, this had to be contained in the memorial, or if he did not submit a memorial, at least one month before the hearing.[16] The heads of claim had to be covered e.g. pecuniary loss, non-pecuniary loss and/or legal costs and expenses.[17]

Before the old Court, non-governmental organisations or human rights bodies could apply to submit written submissions by way of filing an amicus curiae brief. If granted permission, they were to address points of national or international law and not argue the facts or law of the particular case.[18] They did not become parties to the proceedings thereby.

---

[15] Where the case was not sent to the Court.

[16] Failure to submit claims by the time-limit resulted in claims being dismissed as out of time e.g. Ferrantelli and Santangelo v. Italy, R.J.D. 1996–III, No. 12.

[17] This does not automatically require the fine detail of legal expenses or for pecuniary loss to be narrowed down to the last centime, since this may be affected by the extent of the breach found. Failure to quantify claims in good time however, may result in no award being made e.g. Ausiello v. Italy, 1996–III, No. 10.

[18] e.g. Amnesty International in Soering v. U.K. 11 E.H.R.R. 439; July 7, 1989, Series A, No. 161; Liberty, Committee on the Administration of Justice in McCann and others v. U.K., 21 E.H.R.R. 97; September 27, 1995, Series A, No. 324.

Under its Rules of Procedure, the old Court was able to strike a case from its list without proceeding to a determination of the merits, where there was an agreed settlement, or even where the applicant had rejected an offer of settlement, the Court was satisfied that the steps taken by the Government were such as to furnish a solution of the matter.[19]

The old Court's judgment was delivered orally on average six months to one year later in open court in Strasbourg. If the applicant did not attend, a copy was faxed at that time. The Chambers of the new Court, sitting permanently, may hopefully be more expeditious.

Where the old Court found that the question of just satisfaction was not ready for decision, it had a practice of reserving all or part of the applicant's claims. The parties were encouraged to agree where possible. The subsequent judgment on just satisfaction (Article 50) recorded the terms of their agreement or gave the Court's decision on the applicant's claims.

A State Party or the Commission, on behalf of an applicant, was able to request *interpretation of a judgment* within three years of the delivery of a judgment. This was an exercise of inherent jurisdiction, limited to clarifying the meaning and scope which the Court intended to give to a previous judgment, specifying if need be what it thereby decided with binding force.[20]

A State Party or the Commission, on behalf of an applicant, could also request *revision of a judgment* within six months from the date it acquired knowledge of a fact which might by its nature have a decisive influence and was unknown both to the Court and to that Party or the Commission.[21]

Monitoring compliance

Pursuant to Article 54 (to be replaced by Article 46, para. 2), the Committee of Ministers[22] supervises execution of Court judgments. Its role is to oversee what action is taken by Governments in response to a finding of violation. When the case is placed on its agenda, it invites the State to inform it of the measures taken, and the matter is automatically recalled on the agenda at intervals of not less than six months. When it is satisfied that a Government has complied, it issues a resolution recording the position and declaring that it has exercised its functions. Since the old Court rarely hinted at what steps would remedy a violation, the Committee of Ministers operates largely independently. It has received considerable criticism not only for the length of time taken to issue a resolution and complete the execution process but also in respect of its position in accepting a lack of positive action by a Government in response to a finding of violation.[23]

---

[19] Rule 49, para, 2, Rules of Court A, *e.g. Paez v. Sweden*, October 30, 1997, R.J.D. 1997–III, No. 56 (an expulsion case), where the Government granted the Peruvian applicant permanent residence, lifting the expulsion order. The applicant had also claimed compensation and refused to settle. The Court struck the case out as resolved.

[20] *Ringeisen v. Austria (No. 3)*, June 23, 1973, Series A, No. 16, para. 13; 1 E.H.R.R. 513; *Allenet de Ribemont v. France* (Interpretation), August 7, 1996, R.J.D., 1996–III, No. 12, where the Commission's question whether Article 50 meant that any sum awarded must be paid to the injured party personally without attachment (the sum awarded to the applicant had been attached pursuant to an earlier domestic court finding) was a general abstract point of interpretation and outside the bounds of its rules. As regarded the question as to what sums the Court awarded for non-pecuniary and pecuniary damage in its total awarded to two million FF, it did not so distinguish in its judgment, did not have to do so and had no intention of doing so and therefore its judgment was clear. To hold otherwise would modify not clarify.

[21] Rule 58(A); revision was granted in *Pardo v. France (revision-recevabilite)*, July 10, 1996, R.J.D., 1996–III, No. 11, on the basis that the applicant had produced two letters, previously unobtainable, one of which had been referred to expressly by the Court in the context of lack of substantiation of his complaint.

[22] The Committee of Ministers consists formally of the Foreign Ministers of the Member States of the Council of Europe, but they are generally represented by Deputies who meet in Strasbourg.

[23] See, *e.g.* "The Committee of Ministers" by Adam Tomkins, European Human Rights Law Review Launch Issue 1995.

Thus, in *Brogan and Others v. United Kingdom*,[24] the Committee of Ministers accepted the United Kingdom's derogation under Article 15 as complying with the judgment and in other cases, it has found it enough for the State to publicise the judgment and draw it to the attention of the relevant authorities.

Under its rules an applicant may make communications to it about failure to receive compensation awarded by Court or any other matter relating to execution.

3. INTERIM RELIEF

Protocol No. 11 has not made any changes by way of providing the new Court with any power to order interim or injunctive relief. Commission practice is as follows.

Under Rule 36 of the Commission's Rules of Procedure, the Commission may *request* that a measure be taken in the interests of the parties or the proper conduct of the proceedings. The Commission relies on the goodwill and co-operation of Contracting States and will not abuse this procedure by intervening in domestic affairs unless there is an apparent real and imminent risk of irreparable harm. It may be said that as a result there is a very high compliance rate by Contracting States. In practice, this means Article 2 and Article 3 treatment — typically expulsion to a country where there is a fear of serious ill-treatment.[25] For example, the Commission has applied it to an alleged Sikh terrorist facing expulsion to India, a drug trafficker facing expulsion to Iran, etc. It has also been applied where the risk derives from the effect on health of the measure *per se*, for example, where the applicant facing expulsion was in the later stages of a difficult pregnancy with a medical history of miscarriages[26] and where the applicant AIDS sufferer would have no access to treatment on deportation from the United Kingdom to St Kitts.[27]

While it has on occasion been invoked in the context of other measures, *e.g.* adoption of children, which may arguably be of an irreparable nature, Rule 36 has not been applied. Matters of detention, interference with property rights, are generally not covered.[28]

If an applicant intends to request a measure, it is necessary to submit the facts of the case in an outline application, detailing the complaints. It should be shown that domestic remedies have been exhausted (Rule 36 may not be applied if there are any pending procedures unless these do not have suspensive effect) — copies of these decisions should be provided.[29] The expulsion must also be *imminent* — the date should be provided or the fact that it can legally take place without further warning. Any materials substantiating alleged risk to life or of ill-treatment should be provided or referred to, such as, medical reports concerning past incidents of torture, up-to-date reports on conditions in the receiving country (Amnesty, UNHCR, U.S. State Department country reports) details substantiating that the individual applicant faces a real risk.

Rule 36 requests are dealt with urgently. Outside a Commission session the President or acting President will be contacted. As much time as possible should be given to allow the necessary steps to be taken by the Secretariat. It is wise to fax, with "Rule 36 — Expulsion" prominently on the letter, and to telephone the Secretariat to warn of the

---

[24] November 29, 1988, Series A, No. 145-B; E.H.R.R. 117: Resolution DH (90) 23.

[25] While there is a certain presumption that Contracting States provide the necessary guarantees against ill-treatment, the Commission has applied Rule 36 to an expulsion from France to Spain of an ETA member and to an expulsion of a Kurd from the Netherlands to Turkey (see section Immigration and expulsion).

[26] *Poku v. U.K.* 26985/95, May 15, 1996, unpublished.

[27] *D. v. U.K.*, May 2, 1997. R.J.D. 1997–III, No. 37.

[28] See, however, Sweden 25849/94, (Dec.) November 16, 1994 where Rule 36 was applied to a woman allegedly faced with a risk of strict house arrest, and other ill-treatment from her husband's family on return to Lebanon.

[29] In U.K. expulsion cases, the Secretary of State's decision(s), Adjudicator and Immigration Appeal Tribunal decisions, judgments of courts in judicial review proceedings, etc.

arrival of the fax or other documents. If the request is granted, the Government is immediately informed. Often the case is at the same time registered and communicated to the Government for observations to allow for the utmost speed in dealing with the case. If the Rule 36 request is rejected, the case may nonetheless continue in the normal manner.

Rule 36 requests are generally granted for limited but renewable periods. Since they rely on the continued existence of the risk, they will not be renewed if that risk disappears. Measures may be applied to the applicant. This is rare but has occurred in hunger strikes where the Commission has requested an applicant to give up the strike until the proceedings have been resolved.

4. LEGAL AID AND LEGAL REPRESENTATION

Procedure

Legal aid only becomes available when a case is communicated by the Commission to the respondent Government. At that stage, declaration of means forms will be sent where legal aid is requested. The declaration of means form must be certified by the relevant domestic authority. This is a formality required by the Commission's and Court's rules of procedure and insisted on rigidly by some Contracting States. The DSS in the United Kingdom apply the standard of eligibility for civil legal aid — which is not strictly relevant to the Convention organs.

When the Commission receives the means form and certification, it sends copies to the Government for comment. Once the Government's observations have been received, or the time limit expired, the Commission proceeds to decide the legal aid application. If granted, offers of legal aid are sent at each stage of the proceedings. The applicant's lawyer must sign and return them. When the work covered by the offer has been done, a claim form is sent to the lawyer, requiring bank details. On its return, the Secretariat forwards details to the Council of Europe finance division, which has the amounts sent by bank transfer.

The conditions for the grant of legal aid

The Commission's rules of procedure impose the criterion of financial necessity (*i.e.* insufficient means). Though there is another criterion, that it is necessary for the discharge of the Commission's functions, provision of legal aid to financial needy applicants is generally regarded as axiomatic. Exceptionally, in cases which form part of long series on identical issues, legal aid has not been considered necessary, or has been granted at a lower rate. There are no written guidelines as to what insufficient means are and the Commission takes a flexible approach. It is aware that the cost of legal representation is likely to be prohibitive to any person of moderate income and that, where an applicant is pursuing a human rights issue, it is in the general interest that it be facilitated. A person on income support and a prisoner with no income is certainly covered. Low-middling salaries may also attract legal aid, as in the case of Goodwin, a working journalist. The extent to which other family members' income and means is taken into account is also not subject to written guidelines. It is only likely to be relevant where the parent/spouse is of liberal means and can be reasonably expected to contribute.

In practice, it is rare for the United Kingdom Government to comment negatively on applications and rare for the Commission to refuse.

The conditions for legal aid before the old Court were similar.

Level of legal aid

In the vast majority of cases, a standard grant of legal aid is made by way of set contributions for particular items of fees and expenses (see Annex 1998 to Legal Aid Rates). The figures given are generally the maximum and may be reduced for submissions which are of particular brevity. The amounts are not generous compared with the level of United Kingdom professional fees and are intended rather to be a contribution towards fees and expenses.

Hearings

For representation at hearings, generally a fee and expenses for one lawyer are paid. Exceptionally for the U.K., the accepted practice is to grant expenses for counsel and solicitor, though still only one fee. Applicants will generally be granted expenses for attending. Additional counsel/legal advisers may attend, uncovered by legal aid, if permission is obtained from the Commission. Since proceedings are confidential, all persons present must have a legitimate concern in the case and their presence must be relevant and necessary (no sightseers).

Additional items

Legal aid is not given in respect of any work done without specific request by the Commission. Any specific items, e.g. obtaining transcripts; fees for translations; medical opinions *must obtain prior approval*.

Legal aid does not take local VAT levels into account.

Unrepresented applicants

Applicants who represent themselves will only be reimbursed expenses. No claim can be made for hours worked by analogy to legal fees.

Legal representation

Before the Commission, an applicant may be represented by a lawyer or any other person resident in a Convention country, unless the Commission decides otherwise.[30] Legal aid may be granted, however, only to a qualified legal practitioner resident in a Contracting State (solicitor, counsel or equivalent professional qualifications, which in practice may include academics of university standing).[31] Other persons may be able to represent an applicant but will not qualify for legal fees as opposed to expenses. The Commission retains the power to rule on who may act and may refuse to accept change of representation, e.g. at a late stage.

Before the old Court, an applicant could be represented by an advocate authorised to practice and resident in a Member State. Others could be authorised by the President.[32] Also unless authorised by the President, the representative had to have adequate knowledge of an official language (French and English).[33]

[30] Art. 32(2) of the Commission's Rules of Procedure.
[31] Art. 4 Legal Aid Addendum.
[32] Art. 30 of the Rules of Court A.
[33] Court hearings were rarely in other languages whereas Commission hearings may often involve other languages.

Length of proceedings before the old Convention organs

The new Court will inherit a pending caseload of approximately 4–5,000 cases. It is not anticipated that it will be able, in the early stages, to improve on the delays before the old organs.

A. Before Commission:

Committee case:	3–12 months
Chamber/Plenary inadmissible case:	9 months–3 years
Case considered on the merits:	2–4 years

B. Before the old Court

From reference to judgment:	1–2 years

Average time taken for case reaching a judgment before the Court:	4–5 years[35]

C. Before the Committee of Ministers:

Article 32 procedure — cases not referred to the old Court	6–18 months[36]
Article 54 procedure — monitoring compliance:	up to 8½ years

[35] Less than a year could be taken in urgent cases, *e.g. Soering v. U.K.* July 7, 1989, Series A, No. 161; 11 E.H.R.R. 439.
[36] Up to 5½ years has occurred, *e.g. Biondi v. Italy*, February 26, 1992, Series A, No. 226–C.

B. ADMISSIBILITY CHECKLIST

Cases must comply with the grounds of admissibility identified below. A case may also be struck out before or after admissibility under Article 30 (see below).

1. Six months[1]

Principle of rule: legal certainty and avoidance of stale complaints[2]

The rule cannot be waived, either by the Commission or a respondent Government.[3] Even if a Government does not raise it, the Commission must do so of its own motion.

1. When time runs from

(a) *Where there are domestic remedies*

- Time begins running from the day after the final decision in the process of exhaustion of effective domestic remedies in respect of each complaint (see below).

The date of the final decision is that when the judgment is rendered orally in public, or where it is not pronounced in public, the date on which the applicant or his lawyer are informed of the final decision.[4] The date is however taken from notification of the lawyer, even if the applicant becomes aware later[5] and where the reasons for the decision are relevant for the application to the Commission, time runs from the date on which the full text is received, rather than the serving of the operative parts of the decision.[6]

(b) *Where there are no domestic remedies*

- Where the complaint relates to a specific act or omission:
  from the date of the act or omission, or from the date of knowledge of that act or its effect or prejudice on the applicant.[7]
- Where there is a sequence of events linked in time and place:
  from the end of the episode, depending on whether it is practical to expect complaint earlier.[8]

---

[1] Art. 26 of the Convention becoming Art. 35, para. 1 when Protocol No. 11 comes into force on November 1, 1998.

[2] *e.g. Kelly v. U.K.*, 10626/83, (Dec.) May 7, 1985, 42 D.R. 205.

[3] *e.g. K v. Ireland*, 10416/83, (Dec.) May 5, 1984, 38 D.R. 158.

[4] *e.g. Netherlands*, 21034/92 (Dec.) January 9, 1995, 80–A D.R. 87.

[5] *Netherlands* 14056/88, (Dec.) May 28, 1991, 70 D.R. 208.

[6] *P v. Switzerland* 9299/81, (Dec.) March 13, 1984, 36 D.R. 20. See also cases where decisions only become final at a later date: *e.g. Italy*, 12077/86 (Dec.) December 9, 1991, 71 D.R. 13.

[7] *e.g.* see *Christians against Racism and Fascism v. U.K.* 8440/78, (Dec.) July 16, 1980, 21 D.R. 138 (actual effect of the measure); *Hilton v. U.K.*, 12015/86, (Dec.) July 6, 1988, 57 D.R. 108 (date of knowledge).

[8] *Demir v. Turkey*, 22280/93, (Dec.) January 9, 1995, where the six-month time limit ran from the end of the raid on the village (which took place over a three-day period).

- Where there is a continuing situation, act or omission or state of affairs: *e.g.* a state of legislation which continously affects the exercise of a guaranteed right or freedom,[9] the six-month time limit does not apply.
- Where the applicant makes use of a remedy which later proves to be ineffective for the purposes of exhaustion of domestic remedies: from the moment that he becomes aware or should reasonably have become aware of this situation.[10]

2. When time stops running

- Date of introduction of the application before the Commission — this is in general that communication[11] which sets out, even summarily the object of the application.[12] In practice to introduce an application, a qualifying communication must identify the applicant, the factual basis of each complaint and the violations of the Convention alleged to result.[13]

The date taken is:

- the date written on the letter (an undue gap between this date and arrival will be regarded with caution);
- where the letter is undated, from the postmark on the envelope;
- if postmark illegible, date of arrival at the Commission (stamped in registry);
- the date of arrival of the fax version at the Commission.

3. Effect of undue delay

- An unreasonable or unexplained delay in communications after the original letter may result in the first letter ceasing to be regarded as introducing the application.[14] The date of introduction in such cases is taken from the next communication in which the applicant re-affirms his intention to revive or continue the case.

A holding introductory letter will only serve its purpose if the application is pursued actively. If there are intervening domestic events which render the case premature, it is only possible to keep the file active in the Commission for a limited period. It will either have to be pursued regardless or where there are effective domestic remedies being exhausted, be reintroduced within six months of the final effective decision in those proceedings.

---

[9] *e.g. Dudgeon v. U.K.*, October 22, 1981, Series A, No. 45; 4 E.H.R.R. 149; a distinction must be drawn between a situation disclosing a situation of ongoing violation and the after-effect or consequences of a particular breach which occurred and ended at a particular point in time; *e.g.* 25681/94 (Dec.) April 1, 1996, 86–A D.R. 134, p. 134, where the traumatic personal suffering of the families of victims of "Bloody Sunday" did not constitute a continuing situation; *Loizidou v. Turkey*, March 23, 1995, Series A, No. 310; 23 E.H.R.R. 513.

[10] *Laçin v. Turkey*, 23654/94, (Dec.) May 15, 1995, 81–A D.R. 76, where the events took place in December 1992 and the application was introduced in March 1994. While the applicant applied to the public prosecutor in May 1993, he had received advice that this remedy was ineffective and he should have introduced his complaints when he became aware of this situation.

[11] Although the word used in Rule 44, para. 4 is "communication" the Commission has not held in a decision that an application may be introduced by telephone. It is unlikely that this would be the case, save in an extreme urgency excluding the possibility of written notification. See *Rosemary West v. U.K.*, 34728/97, (Dec.) October 20, 1997, 91–A D.R. 85, where a claimed introduction of an application by telephone was not accepted.

[12] Rule 44, para. 4 of the Commission's Rules of Procedure; *e.g. B v. U.K.* July 8, 1987, Series A, No. 121; 10 E.H.R.R. 87.

[13] There is a certain flexibility, *e.g.* a reference to interference with freedom of expression is enough without mentioning Art. 10.

[14] *e.g. Kelly*, above n.2. See Rule 44, para. 4 in fine referring to "good cause" for changing the date of introduction: this practice is to prevent an application lying dormant and thus bypassing the spirit and purpose of the six-month rule.

4. Special circumstances suspending the period

Only very limited circumstances of *force majeure* are regarded as suspending the running of the period:

- illness and mental incapacity have not yet been accepted in any case[15];
- detention is not sufficient in itself, unless it is proved that outside contact with others was totally barred;
- ignorance of the Convention or its case law is not enough. In particular, time is not suspended by applications to non-effective remedies such as the Parliamentary Commissioner of Administration or applications for discretionary or exceptional remedies (*e.g.* requests to the Home Secretary for a reference to the Court of Appeal and *ex gratia* criminal injuries compensation funds).

2. Exhaustion of domestic remedies[16]

1. Principle of the rule

Before an international jurisdiction decides whether a State has violated a human right, the State should have the opportunity to remedy the matter itself. The Strasbourg organs should primarily be a supervisory last resort and the main business of enforcing human rights should be conducted by domestic authorities who are in the best position to do so.[17]

2. Application of the rule

- The burden is on the Government invoking the rule to prove the existence in theory and practice of available and sufficient remedies at the relevant time.[18] However, once this burden of proof has been satisfied it falls to the applicant to establish that the remedy was in fact exhausted, was for some reason not effective or adequate in the circumstances of the case or there existed special circumstances absolving him from the requirement.[19]
- A Government may not use arguments which are incompatible with those which it relied on in domestic court proceedings.[20]
- A Government must generally invoke the rule prior to the Commission's decision on admissibility. Failure by the Government to respond to communication of complaints may result in the matter going by default and any issues as to effectiveness of remedies being dealt with on the merits, where relevant.[21]

---

[15] *X v. Austria*, 6317/73, (Dec.) July 10, 1975, 2 D.R. 87: mere reference to a bad state of health was insufficient; *Germany*, 25435/94 (Dec.) February 20, 1995, where the applicants both suffered from mental illness but this did not prevent them from complying with the six-month time limit given the fact that they were able to pursue domestic proceedings at that time.

[16] Art. 26, above.

[17] *Akdivar v. Turkey*, September 16, 1996, R.J.D., 1996–IV, No. 15.

[18] *e.g. Deweer v. Belgium*, February 27, 1980, Series A, No. 35; 2 E.H.R.R. 439; *U.K.* 13590/88, (Dec.) November 8, 1989, 63 D.R. 174; *U.K.* 17579/90, (Dec.) January 13, 1993, 74 D.R. 139.

[19] *Akdivar*, para. 68, above n.17, where the total passivity of the national authorities in the face of serious allegations of misconduct by State agents was given as such a factor and shifted the burden of proof rendering it incumbent on the Government to show what they had done in response to the scale and seriousness of the matters complained of. See also *Aksoy v. Turkey*, December 18, 1996, R.J.D., 1996–IV, No. 26; 23 E.H.R.R. 553 where the applicant was exempted in view of the failure of the State prosecutor to react to his injuries incurred during a period in custody.

[20] *e.g.* 23892/94, (Dec.) October 16, 1995, D.R. 83–A, p. 57 (citing *Kolompar v. Belgium*, September 24, 1992, Series A, No. 235; 16 E.H.R.R. 197).

[21] *e.g. Ergi v. Turkey*, 23818/94, (Dec.) March 2, 1995, 80–A D.R. 157.

The Commission has nonetheless on occasion relied on an argument of non-exhaustion which has not been raised by the Government.[22]

- The applicant is generally required to raise in substance in the domestic proceedings the complaints made in Strasbourg and in compliance with the formal requirements and time limits imposed by domestic law.[23] This includes any procedural means which might have prevented a breach of the Convention.[24] It is sufficient for the substance of the Convention complaint to be put before the domestic courts, even if it is not formulated expressly.[25]
- The rule does not apply to a State administration practice of violation.[26]

3. Convention approach

- Remedies must be real and practical and not theoretical or illusory,[27] *e.g.* genuine fear of reprisals, intimation.
- Account will be taken not only of the personal circumstances of the applicant, but the general legal and political context in which the alleged remedies operate.[28]
- An unduly formalistic approach is not to be taken by the Convention organs which will apply a certain degree of flexibility.[29]

Remedies must be:

- Effective: *i.e.* capable of providing redress for the complaint (*i.e.* power to recommend is not enough as in the old Parole Board for discretionary lifers, the Board of Visitors,[30] ombudsmen[31]; the speed of the procedure may also be relevant to its effectiveness[32]; the remedy must be capable of remedying directly the state of affairs[33];

---

[22] *Veenstra v. U.K.* 20946/92, (Dec.) August 8, 1994, where the applicant had not applied for judicial review in respect of complaints of opening of letters from his solicitor in a Scottish prison, following the Court of Appeal decision in an English case holding *ultra vires* a prison rule allowing such interference on wider grounds than merely to ascertain if they were in truth bona fides communications. Also, on the first examination of an application, clear cases of non-exhaustion will be rejected by the Commission of its own motion.

[23] *Cardot v. France*, March 3, 1991, Series A, No. 200; 13 E.H.R.R. 853 — see procedural mistakes 18079/91, December 4, 1991, 72 D.R. 263.

[24] *e.g. Barbera, Messegue and Jabardo v. Spain*, December 6, 1988, Series A, No. 146; 11 E.H.R.R. 360.

[25] *e.g. Gasus Dosier-und Fördertechnick GmbH v. Netherlands*, February 23, 1995, Series A, No. 306–B; 20 E.H.R.R. 360: where the applicant company had not relied on Article 1 of Protocol No. 1 expressly before Dutch courts, relying rather on Art. 6, the Court was not impressed by the fact that the applicant had not invoked the former provision since in any event it did provide the courts with the opportunity of preventing or putting right the alleged violation of that provision. The purpose of the rule is to allow the Contracting States the opportunity of putting right violations (para. 48).

[26] *e.g. Donnelly v. U.K.* 5577–5583/72, (Dec.) December 15, 1975, 4 D.R. 4. See Part IIB: Torture, inhuman and degrading treatment.

[27] *Akdivar*, (Dec.) October 19, 1994. See n.17.

[28] *Akdivar*, para. 69. See n.17.

[29] *Cardot*, para. 34. See n.23.

[30] Applying for leave to appeal or appealing on grounds or circumstances where the court has no competence to entertain the matter is not effective, *e.g.* applying for leave to appeal to the House of Lords against a decision of the Court of Appeal refusing leave to appeal.

[31] *Denmark*, 8395/78, (Dec.) December 16, 1981, 27 D.R. 50; *Montion v. France*, 11192/84, May 14, 1987, 52 D.R. 227.

[32] *Turkey*, 15530–1/89, (Dec.) October 10, 1992, 72 D.R. 169.

[33] *Ireland*, 12742/87, (Dec.) May 3, 1989, 61 D.R. 206: *Purcell v. Ireland*, 15404/89, (Dec.), April 16, 1991, 70 D.R. 262.

- part of the normal process of redress and involving normal use of the remedy: *e.g.* not cover exceptional or discretionary remedies such as requests for *ex gratia* compensation or for re-opening of judicial proceedings[34];

- accessible[35]: it may be relevant if an applicant is barred from taking action due, for example, to lack of money or legal representation, where these are practically essential[36];
- offer reasonable prospects of success[37]: the Commission has long stated that a mere doubt as to the prospect of success in going to court does not exempt from exhaustion. Where case law is unclear, contradictory or in the process of ongoing interpretation, an applicant may be expected to pursue an action or appeal which allows the courts to rule on the issues.[38] Where a statute provides new provisions, it may be necessary to put them to the test even where their scope or application is untried and unknown. Counsel's opinion that there is no prospect of success may be enough to indicate that a remedy or appeal would not be effective.[39] The fact that an identical claim has been dismissed may be sufficient to indicate that there is no prospect of success;

Also:

- if there is more than one remedy available, an individual is not required to try more than one[40];
- an applicant is generally not required to try the same body again by way of a repeated request or application.[41]

(a) *Particular remedies in the United Kingdom*

Note: these are generally required but will always be subject to the principles above and to the provisions or practice of domestic law as it develops.

---

[34] *Agee v. U.K.*, 7729/76, (Dec.) December 17, 1976, 7 D.R. 164; *Switzerland*, 8850/80, October 7, 1980, 22 D.R. 232 (request for re-trial not included unless domestic law establishes that this provides an effective remedy; *Switzerland*, 19117/91, (Dec.) January 12, 1994, 76–A D.R. 70 or request for exercise of ministerial discretion to award compensation); *Byloos v. Belgium*, 14545/89, (Dec.) October 9, 1990, 66 D.R. 238; see also *Buckley v. U.K.*, (Dec.) May 3, 1994, where power of Secretary of State shown to have been rarely exercised. Normal use of remedies, *e.g. Turkey*, 16278/90, (Dec.) May 3, 1993, 74 D.R. 93; *Yagiz v. Turkey*, August 7, 1996, R.J.D. 1996–III, No. 13.

[35] *Byloos v. Belgium*, 14545/89, (Dec.) October 9, 1990, 66 D.R. 238; *Belgium*, 12604/86, (Dec.) July 10, 1991, 70 D.R. 125; *Kuijk v. Greece*, 14986/89, (Dec.) July 3, 1991, 70 D.R. 240 (where remedies brought to attention of foreign detainees in language applicant did not understand).

[36] However, the Commission has expected applicants to take proceedings themselves even where they have been refused legal aid; in complex proceedings, as in *Airey v. Ireland*, October 9, 1979, Series A, No. 32; 2 E.H.R.R. 305, lack of legal aid should presumably form a ground of exemption.

[37] *Akdivar*, para. 68. See n.17.

[38] *Whiteside v. U.K.*, 20357/92, (Dec.) March 7, 1994, 76A D.R. 80; concerning constitutional testing — *E.N. v. Ireland*, 18760/91, (Dec.) December 1, 1993.

[39] *e.g. U.K.* 10000/82, (Dec.) September 4, 1985, 33 D.R. 247; *Ireland*, 24196/94, (Dec.) January 22, 1996, 84–A D.R. 72 — where counsel advised no hopes of success and it was accepted that this indicated the remedy was ineffective; however *K, F and P v. U.K.*, 10789/84, (Dec.) 40 D.R. 298, where counsel's doubts did not absolve the applicant from applying to the House of Lords, especially where the Court of Appeal gave leave in a similar case shortly afterwards.

[40] *McCann, McCann and others v. U.K.*, 18984/91, (Dec.) September 3, 1993; *Yagiz v. Turkey*, August 7, 1996, R.J.D. 1996–III, No. 13; *Sargin and Yagci v. Turkey*, June 8, 1995, Series A, No. 319; 20 E.H.R.R. 505; *France*, 14838/89, (Dec.) March 5, 1991, 69 D.R. 286. Where there is a choice of remedies, the selection of the appropriate one is primarily for the applicant — *Airey, supra* n.36, para. 23.

[41] *Granger v. U.K.*, March 28, 1990, Series A, No. 174; 12 E.H.R.R. 469; *Agee v. U.K.*, see n.34.

(i) CRIMINAL:

- Application for leave to appeal against conviction and/or sentencing is to the Court of Appeal, renewing application from single judge to the full court; it is generally assumed that appeal to the House of Lords is an exceptional remedy though there might be in a particular case a point of law of general public importance which might be reasonably be expected to be pursued[42];

(ii) CIVIL:

- Generally, the highest avenue of appeal where there is a prospect of success is the Court of Appeal; whether it is necessary to go to the House of Lords may depend on the nature of the claims and the existing state of case law[43];
- child care cases:
  - appeal may not be required to the Court of Appeal due to its limited intervention on the assessment of facts but will depend, *inter alia*, on the nature of the complaints about the proceedings, counsel's opinion as to the existence of grounds of appeal, and whether the Court of Appeal has intervened in the exercise of the particular type of discretion by a first instance judge before.
- prisoners:
  - for matters of internal discipline and regulation, petition to the prison authorities/Secretary of State in relation to the application of norms is expected, also though not in respect of the content of those norms[44]; Board of Visitors generally is not effective as without binding powers of decision; judicial review may not be effective due to its limited scope of review, but this may depend on the nature of the claims made and the existence of case law showing the complaints disclose a prospect that the court will examine them in substance[45]; in respect of assault, ill-treatment, negligence, the appropriate civil proceedings are generally expected;
- planning:
  - appeal is from Inspectors and decisions of the Secretary of State to the High Court, notwithstanding the limited scope of review, where the matters of complaint may arguably be considered by the court in some manner[46];
- immigration and expulsion:
  - appeals to adjudicators, immigration appeal tribunal; judicial review may be required where risk to life or limb is concerned (see Part IIB: Immigration and expulsion) or in other cases, depending on whether the nature of the complaints falls within the scope of the limited review and having regard to previous precedents.[47]

---

[42] e.g. 10789/84, see n.39.

[43] e.g. *Leech v. U.K.* 20075/92, (Dec.) August 31, 1994 where there were conflicting decisions of the Court of Sessions and the Court of Appeal, which could have been ruled on by the House of Lords on appeal from the former.

[44] *Silver v. U.K.*, March 25, 1983, Series A, No. 61; 5 E.H.R.R. 347.

[45] e.g. *Veenstra*, see n.22.

[46] e.g. *Bryan v. U.K.*, November 22, 1995, Series A, No. 335–A; 21 E.H.R.R. 342.

[47] e.g. 14507/89, (Dec.) April 2, 1990, 65 D.R. 296, judicial review ineffective for discretionary decision refusing entry of non-national wife.

3. Manifestly ill-founded[48]

- Complaint unsubstantiated or unsupported by the material submitted.
- The facts complained of do not disclose an interference in the enjoyment of the right.[49]
- Interference or decision complained of prima facie an interference but justified on grounds contained in the provisions of the Convention, *e.g.* child removed from parents but the evidence supports the domestic court view that it is necessary to protect the rights of the child.
- The applicant has ceased to be a victim.[50]

4. Incompatibility

1. Incompatibility *ratione temporis*[51]

- Where the complaint relates to events which occurred before a Contracting State's acceptance of the right of individual petition under Article 25 (or for the Court before the acceptance of its jurisdiction under Article 46[52]) it must be rejected as incompatible *ratione temporis* where the State has specified that its ratification is prospective only. Without such stipulation it will be regarded as retrospective and the Convention organs will be competent to examine the complaints, subject to the other admissibility criteria.[53]

Note: where a complaint is about the length of proceedings covering a period before and after acceptance of jurisdiction under Articles 25 or 46, the prior period may be taken into account in assessing the reasonableness of the later period (see Part IIA: Fair trial, length of proceedings).

2. Incompatibility *ratione loci*[54]

- Where complaints are based on events in a territory outside the Contracting State and there is no link between those events and any authority within the jurisdiction of the Contracting State.[55]

3. Incompatibility *ratione personae*[56]

This includes:
- complaints against a State which has not signed the Convention or the relevant protocol[57];

---

[48] Art. 27, para. 2 of the Convention (Art. 35, para. 3 after November 1, 1998).

[49] *e.g.* U.K., 24875/94, (Dec.) September 6, 1996, 86–A, D.R. 74, where the operation of child maintenance assessment legislation was not of such a nature or degree to disclose any lack of respect for family life.

[50] *e.g.* there was unfairness at trial but there is acquittal on appeal; a measure constituting an interference has ceased to apply to the applicant. This head is to be distinguished from the head of incompatibility *ratione personae* below — where the applicant is found not to be a victim of the interference.

[51] Art. 27, para. 2 (Art. 35, para. 3 from November 1, 1998).

[52] *e.g. Yagiz v. Turkey*, August 7, 1996, R.J.D. 1996–III, No. 13.

[53] *e.g. De Varga–Hirsch v. France*, 9559/81, 33 D.R. 158; *Demicoli v. Malta*, August 27, 1991, Series A, No. 210; 14 E.H.R.R. 47 (Commission).

[54] Art. 27, para. 2 (Art. 35, para. 3 from November 1, 1998).

[55] This is likely to arise only where an applicant complains of matters within an overseas territory for which the Contracting State has not extended its acceptance of the right of individual petition under Art. 63.

[56] Art. 25.

[57] *e.g.* the United Kingdom has not ratified Protocols 4, 6 and 7 which include, *inter alia*, rights for aliens, abolition of the death penalty, equality of spouses and rights of appeal.

- complaints against an individual or body for which the State is not responsible[58];
- where the applicant is not a victim of the events or measures which base the allegations.[59] A person may claim to be a victim where he is directly affected by a measure — it is not necessary to show prejudice or damage.[60]

4. Incompatibility *ratione materiae*[61]

This includes;

- where a person invokes a right not included in the Convention[62];
- where the person's complaints fall outside the scope of particular rights invoked.[63]

5. Substantially the same[64]

- Where the complaints are substantially the same as a matter which has already been examined:
  - by the Commission; or
  - by another procedure of international investigation or settlement[65]; and it contains no new, relevant information.

New, relevant facts may include: further lapse of time in the length of proceedings already examined by the Commission[66]; continuation of a period in remand[67]; where an application

---

[58] *e.g.* lawyers (unless there is an issue that a State provided lawyer failed to assure the defence of an accused person in circumstances for which the domestic courts should have taken responsibility — see Part IIA: Fair Trial, Legal Representation in criminal proceeding) or, commonly, neighbours or private employers (assuming that it cannot be argued that the State failed in a positive obligation to prevent the interference by the private person).

[59] *e.g.* where a person complains on behalf of another without the necessary authority; where the person cannot claim to be affected by the measures (*e.g. Agrotexim v. Greece*, October 24, 1995, Series A, No. 330; 21 E.H.R.R. 250, where shareholders cannot claim to be victims of interferences with the rights of the company, in the absence of direct effect on their own property rights in the shares). Where organisations bring applications in their own name, it has to be their own rights which are affected, *e.g.* in *Purcell*, see n.33, the trade union was not affected by the broadcasting restrictions, though its members were.

[60] *e.g. Eckle v. Federal Republic of Germany*, July 15, 1982, Series A, No. 51; 5 E.H.R.R. 1; *Dudgeon v. U.K.*, see n.9, October 22, 1981, No. 45, para. 41, referring to continuous and direct effect on private life from the legislation prohibiting adult homosexual acts irrespective of the fact that he had not been subject to a measure of implementation; *Wassink v. Netherlands*, September 27, 1990, Series A, No. 185–A, No. 38: status of "victim" may exist even where there is no damage, which is relevant to the application of Article 50 (just satisfaction for pecuniary or non-pecuniary damage).

[61] Art. 27, para. 2 (Art. 35, para. 3 from November 1, 1998).

[62] *e.g.* right to a job, or to minimum wage or certain standard of living (*e.g. X v. Denmark*, 6807/75, (Dec.) December 10, 1975, 3 D.R. 153; *Andersson and Kullman v. Sweden*, 11776/85, (Dec.) March 4, 1986, 46 D.R. 251), to be granted a driving licence (*Germany*, 7462/76, March 7, 1977, 9 D.R. 112), to obtain a prosecution against another person, right to political asylum (*Sweden*, 21808/93, September 8, 1993, 75 D.R. 264), free choice of doctor (*Sweden*, 18998/92, August 30, 1993, 75 D.R. 223), right to conscientious objection (*Autio v. Finland*, 17086/90, 72 D.R. 245).

[63] *e.g.* where the unfairness alleged under Art. 6 concerns proceedings which do not involve the determination of criminal charges or civil rights and obligations; where there are no existing ties of family life for the purpose of Art. 8.

[64] Art. 27, para. 1(b) (Art. 35, para. 2(b) from November 1, 1998).

[65] *e.g. U.K.*, (Dec.) 11603/85, 50 D.R. 228 (where it was not the applicants who had brought the same complaints before the ILO); *Spain*, 16358/90, (Dec.) December 10, 1990, 73 D.R. 214 (where the complaints were substantially the same as those examined by an organ of the ILO); *Spain*, 17512/90, (Dec.) July 6, 1992, 73 D.R. 214 (applicants' complaints substantially the same as those brought by them before the UN Human Rights Committee).

[66] *X v. U.K.*, 8233/78, (Dec.) October 3, 1979, 17 D.R. 122.

[67] *Vallon v. Italy*, 9621/81, (Dec.) October 13, 1983, D.R. 33, p. 217.

was rejected for non-exhaustion and the applicant has terminated the domestic proceedings; the discovery of new factual information or evidence relevant to the previous complaints.[68] They do not include legal arguments concerning the interpretation of the Convention that the applicant did not submit in the prior application.[69]

6. Abuse of petition[70]

It may be applied in cases of:
- forgery; fraud; deliberate misrepresentation;
- vexatious and repeated applications of a similar nature[71];
- claims based on facts for which the applicant is himself responsible[72];
- deliberate, flagrant breach of the Commission's rules of confidentiality[73];
- abusive contents of submissions[74];

Political motivations:

The fact that applicants may be pursuing a political goal or purpose of some kind is generally not sufficient to disclose abuse. The Commission does not find it abusive for applicants to use the Strasbourg procedure as part of a pressure campaign or publicity to put pressure on a State or to influence public opinion subject to the proviso that the complaints are based on true facts, not unsupported by the evidence or concerning matters outside the scope of the Convention.[75]

7. Striking out

The Commission may proceed to strike a case from its list under Article 30[76] where:
- the applicant does not intend to pursue his petition.[77] This includes withdrawal by the applicant where there has been an informal settlement with the Government[78] or where the applicant has lost interest in pursuing the case[79];

---

[68] *e.g. U.K.*, 23956/94, (Dec.) November 28, 1994, unpublished, concerning where new information about the applicant prisoner's security status in prison, relevant to his previous complaints of transfer/visiting restrictions.
[69] *X v. U.K.*, 8206/78, (Dec.) July 10, 1981, 25 D.R. 147.
[70] Art. 27, para. 2 (Art. 35, para. 3 from November 1, 1998).
[71] *e.g. M v. U.K.*, 13284/87, (Dec.) October 15, 1987, 54 D.R. 214 abuse found on the fifth application. The Commission held that it was not its function to deal with a succession of ill-founded, querulous complaints, which created unnecessary work incompatible with its function of ensuring the implementation of the Convention and which hindered it in that function.
[72] *e.g.* where the applicant complained of the length of extradition proceedings, the Commission considered that this was largely the result of the applicant jumping bail on the failure of his appeal and hiding to avoid arrest (*Ireland*, 9742/82, (Dec.) March 2, 1982, 32 D.R. 251).
[73] *e.g.* revealing to the press pleadings (observations of the parties to the Commission), correspondence between the parties and the Commission. Minor inadvertent breaches will generally receive only a warning.
[74] *Stamoulakatos v. U.K.*, 27567/95, (Dec.) April 9, 1997 (unpublished).
[75] *e.g. McFeeley and others v. U.K.*, 8317/78, (Dec.) March 15, 1980, 20 D.R. 44 and *McQuiston and others v. U.K.*, (Dec.) 11208/84, 46 D.R. 182, where the Government alleged the complaints were part of a concerted campaign to get political status; *Akdivar* No. 21983/93, (Dec.) October 19, 1994: confirmed by the Court in its judgment para. 54 (above, n.17), where the Turkish Government alleged that the application was abusive as being part of a separatist propaganda campaign by the PKK to undermine the Turkish State, the Commission found that the complaints were based on genuine grievances and allegations of human rights violations which were not proved to be without factual basis.
[76] Art. 37, para. 1 from November 1, 1998.
[77] Art. 30, para. 1(a) (Art. 37, para. 1(a) from November 1, 1998).
[78] *e.g. Abbott v. U.K.*, 15006/89, December 10, 1990, 67 D.R. 290. Where a friendly settlement is negotiated between the parties and the Commission after admissibility, the case is dealt with in a report under Article 28.
[79] *e.g.* has failed to respond to requests for information, failed to observe time limits without reasonable explanation, failed to provide a forwarding address or loss of contact with legal representative (*e.g. U.K.*, 10239/83, (Rep.), April 11, 1989, 60 D.R. 71).

- where the matter has been resolved, for example, by a settlement between the parties[80];
- where for any other reason the Commission finds it no longer justified to continue the examination of the application[81]; where, for example, the applicant has been given adequate redress in the domestic system but nonetheless persists in pursuing the application which ceases to have legal interest[82]; or where the circumstances are such that the Commission is unable to continue an effective examination[83]; or, where there has been deliberate and manipulative breach of confidentiality rules.[84]

In theory, the Commission may nonetheless continue the examination of a case in any of the above where respect for Human Rights requires such a course. In theory, an applicant cannot be bought off by a Government leaving a situation where similar violations may continue to occur. However there has been no recent case[85] where the Commission has insisted on continuing a case where the applicant has wished to withdraw, with the exception of certain cases where the Commission was not satisfied that the applicant's expression of intention to withdraw was genuine.[86]

8. Appeal against admissibility decisions or re-opening

There is no appeal by an applicant against a decision declaring his application or part of his application inadmissible.[87] Pursuant to Article 30, paragraph 3, the Commission may restore an application to the list. The practice is only to do so where the Commission has made a factual error in the decision which is of relevance to its conclusions, for example, where it overlooked a letter introducing the application which affected the calculation of the six-month time limit or where it relied in its reasoning on a fact which was not correct. It might also be possible that re-opening occurs where it appears that the Government had failed to comply with a settlement[88]; or where new circumstances arose enabling the Commission to resume its examination.[89]

9. Standing

- An individual, group of individuals or non-governmental organisation claiming to be a victim of a violation of the Convention or other person (friend, relative,

---

[80] Art. 30, para. 1(b) (Art. 37, para. 1(b) from November 1, 1998), this overlaps with settlement solutions under Article 30, para. 1(a) above. See *e.g. Germany*, 14261/88, October 13, 1990, 66 D.R. 228.

[81] Art. 30, para. 1(c) (Art. 37, para. 1(c) from November 1, 1998).

[82] *U.K.*, 22382/93, January 19, 1995, 80 D.R. 132 where legislation on the age of consent in issue had changed.

[83] *Turkey*, 22057/93, (Dec.) January 13, 1997, 88–A D.R. 17.

[84] *e.g. Familiapress v. Austria*, 20915/92, (Rep.) March 3, 1995, 80 D.R. 74: the lawyer of the applicant company had submitted to the Supreme Court in support of his appeal the letter from the Commission informing him on a confidential basis of its provisional opinion on the merits. The Commission found this a serious breach of its rules for which there was no justification and struck the case from its list.

[85] *cf. Tyrer v. U.K.*, April 25, 1978, Series A, No. 26; 2 E.H.R.R. 1, where the applicant informed the Commission after it had declared his complaint about birching admissible that he wished to withdraw but the Commission pursued the case without his participation, as the case raised general questions of a general character affecting the observance of the Convention.

[86] *e.g. Kurt v. Turkey*, 24276/94, (Dec.) May 22, 1993, 81–A D.R. 112 (now pending before the Court).

[87] See, however, Art. 29 which allows a Government to raise fresh admissibility arguments after a case has been declared admissible — no such provision in Protocol No. 11 in force from November 1, 1998.

[88] *e.g. Aldrian v. Austria*, (Dec.) 16266/90, May 7, 1990, 65 D.R. 337.

[89] *e.g.* an applicant who failed to maintain contact with his lawyer renewed his complaints, with a convincing reason for the lapse (*e.g.* substantiated claims of intimidation); where an application was struck off as premature and events had subsequently culminated.

etc., as well as lawyer, NGO representative) who has authority to act (by means of signed letter of authority specifying that the applicant wishes him to act in the proceedings before the Commission) may present an application.[90]

- Municipal bodies or public law corporations performing official duties cannot bring an application.[91]
- An application cannot be brought in the name of a deceased person. A person with required standing as next-of-kin or as heir of the estate may bring the application in his own name as a victim.[92] Where an applicant dies during the proceedings, it may continue in principle where a spouse or appropriate close relative with a legitimate interest adopts it. This happens in most cases.[93] However, when the applicant in the *Scherer v. Switzerland*[94] case died, the Court proceeded to strike the case out, where there was no close relative wishing to continue, only an executor, and it found, in light of change in legislation and case law, that there was no reason of public policy to examine the case further.

---

[90] Where children are concerned, parents may act unless there is a conflict of interest or lack of legal standing, *e.g. Hokkanen v. Finland*, September 23, 1994, Series A, No. 299–A; 19 E.H.R.R. 139 where the father no longer had the standing to represent his child under domestic law.

[91] 26114/95 and 26455/95, (Dec.) June 28, 1995, 82 D.R. 150; *Ayuntamiento de M v. Spain*, 15090/89, (Dec.) January 7, 1991, 68 D.R. 209; 25978/94, (Dec.) January 18, 1996, 84–A D.R. 129 the status of the BBC has been left open.

[92] *e.g.* in *Yasa v. Turkey*, 22495/91, (Rep.) April 8, 1997, not yet published, pending before the Court, the Commission accepted that the applicant could complain as a directly affected victim on behalf of his uncle who had been killed in a similar attack to the one which injured the applicant. While the Government objected that he had no standing in domestic law to represent his uncle, this was not found decisive, in the absence of any indication of a more appropriate and closer relative. Also there was no conflict of interest and the complaints were closely related.

[93] *e.g. Deweer v. Belgium*, February 27, 1980, Series A, No. 35; 2 E.H.R.R. 439; *X v. France*, March 31, 1992, Series A, No. 234–C the parents of the deceased AIDS sufferer (length complaint); *Lukanov v. Bulgaria*, March 20, 1997, R.J.D. 1997–II, No. 34, the wife of the deceased applicant (unlawful arrest and detention); *Laskey, Jaggard and Brown v. U.K.*, February 19, 1997, R.J.D. 1997–I, No. 29; the father of deceased applicant (private life complaints — conviction for sado-masochism).

[94] *Scherer v. Switzerland*, March 25, 1994, Series A, No. 287; 18 E.H.R.R. 276.

29

C. CONVENTION PRINCIPLES AND APPROACH

Applying the Convention involves a special perspective distinct from national law. There is a set of interlocking principles governed by its international and human rights context. The Convention organs intend to lay down certain minimum international standards.[1] They are not seeking to identify the most appropriate way to protect human rights, recognising the diversity in the Contracting States. They identify at most the minimum which a particular legal system should attain.

1. Subsidiarity

The Convention organs are primarily a supervisory body and subsidiary to the national systems safeguarding human rights.[2] Pursuant to Article 1 of the Convention the Contracting States undertook to "secure to everyone within their jurisdiction the rights and freedoms" set out in the Convention. It is therefore first and foremost the role of the State to protect human rights. Article 13 imposes the obligation on the State to provide a remedy to all those who claim, arguably, that their rights under the Convention have been violated, while Article 26 requiring the exhaustion of domestic remedies as a precondition reflects the fact that coming to Strasbourg is meant to be very much the last resort.[3]

2. Fourth instance

The Convention organs are not, as the Commission is fond of saying, a court of appeal from domestic courts and cannot intervene on the basis that a domestic court has come to the "wrong" decision or made a mistake. Their role is to ensure compliance with the provisions of the Convention by the Contracting States.

The Convention organs will generally not rehear cases, except to the extent that factual or legal issues arise under the Convention similar to those in domestic proceedings. Their fact-finding function is limited. While the Commission is under an obligation to find the facts in admissible cases, its examination is almost entirely limited to the written submission of the parties and the documents provided. Its hearings are generally on points of applicable domestic law and the scope of Convention rights: it only rarely hears witnesses or even sees the applicant, its procedures being largely in writing. In the vast majority of cases, where a case has been thoroughly examined on the domestic level, the facts have been thrashed out and the Commission cannot hope to do any better in resolving disputed elements.[4] In most cases, the essential facts are not in dispute or do not

---

[1] *Belgian Linguistics Case (No. 1)*, February 9, 1967, Series A, No. 5; 1 E.H.R.R. 241.

[2] *e.g. Handyside v. U.K.*, December 7, 1976, Series A, No. 24; 1 E.H.R.R. 737, para. 48; *Akdivar v. Turkey*, September 16, 1996, R.J.D., 1996–IV, No. 15, para. 65; *Eckle v. Federal Republic of Germany*, July 15, 1982, Series A, No. 51; 5 E.H.R.R. 1, para. 61 where it stated that it would not be compatible with the subsidiary character of the Convention machinery to admit complaints where the national authorities had expressly or in substance acknowledged a breach and afforded redress.

[3] There is also the practical consideration that the Commission has neither the time nor resources to decide on the merits itself all cases referred to it. Nor is it particularly geared to do the fact-finding tasks commonly fulfilled by domestic courts, with no compellable powers over witnesses or discovery of documents.

[4] *Stocke v. Germany*, March 19, 1991, Series A, No. 199; 13 E.H.R.R. 839, where the applicant alleged connivance by police officers with an informer who tricked him onto a plane which came to Germany where he was arrested. The Commission heard witnesses including the police officers but was not able to come to any different conclusion than the domestic courts.

have to be resolved since the examination undertaken by the Convention organs often focusses on the procedural safeguards, the decision-making procedure, the applicable standards.[5] If it is alleged that the Convention organs rely too heavily on domestic courts' findings, this is a reflection of the nature of the exercise that is being undertaken. The Convention organs will not re-decide whether or not a decision to remove children was in fact the correct decision, but will assess whether the manner of decision-making and implementation failed in some way to protect the parents' rights. In a case of suspicious killing by an unknown assassin, the Commission cannot seriously attempt to identify the culprit and thereby whether the State was directly responsible as alleged. What it can do is examine whether the victim was sufficiently protected beforehand — by the standards imposed by law, or, if applicable the necessary safeguards — and whether afterwards the incident was properly investigated in such a way as to indicate the rule of law is in force.[6] Consequently, much of Convention case law turns on procedural considerations.

That said, there is a general overview of the merits taken in the Court's requirement that decisions and measures taken are supported by "relevant and sufficient" reasons[7] and in the context of Article 14, objective and reasonable justification. This is a means both of verifying that decisions are in fact in pursuit of the alleged aims and that they are not arbitrary or in abuse of power.

3. Margin of appreciation

The domestic authorities are recognised by the Convention organs as generally being in the best position either to reach a decision in a particular case or to decide on the measures necessary in a particular area, whether it be expropriation of property to build a new road, banning blasphemous videos or the sale of sex education books.[8] In this context frequent reference is made to the "margin of appreciation" to be accorded to Contracting States. This is a term which is not subject to, or perhaps capable of, precise definition and smacks somewhat of a "let out" to Governments, particularly in those cases where there is a prima facie interference with a right, arguments either way as to whether such interference is necessary and the case is resolved by pulling the term "margin of appreciation" out of the hat.[9]

The fact that customs, policies and practices vary considerably between Contracting States is sometimes used to support the existence of a margin of appreciation. Where there is no uniform conception, for example, of morals, there is accepted to be a number of possible solutions or approaches in such areas.[10] In *Dudgeon v. United Kingdom*[11] the Court referred to differing moral and social conditions which can apply in different areas, noting that because a restriction is not seen as necessary elsewhere does not mean it is unacceptable in one particular area. However, in that case the Court considered that

---

[5] There is also the frequently used technique of reaching conclusions "even assuming" a particular state of affairs, to avoid the necessity of settling doubtful factual issues.

[6] *Yasa v. Turkey*, 22495/95, (Rep.), April 8, 1997, pending before the Court.

[7] In the context of the necessity for measures, *e.g. Olsson v. Sweden*, March 24, 1988, Series A, No. 130; 11 E.H.R.R. 259 (Article 8) the reason must be pertinent to the interference and justify the extent or nature of the interference; *Lingens v. Austria*, July 8, 1986, Series A, No. 103; 8 E.H.R.R. 103 (Article 10). See n.71 below.

[8] *e.g. Müller v. Switzerland*, May 24, 1988, Series A, No. 133; 13 E.H.R.R. 212, para. 35; as being in direct and continuous contact with the vital forces of their countries.

[9] *Handyside v. U.K.*, December 7, 1976, Series A, No. 24; 1 E.H.R.R. 737, paras. 48, 54 and 57 (seizure and forfeiture and conviction in relation to "Little Red Schoolbook"); *Stubbings and others v. U.K.*, October 22, 1996, R.J.D., 1996–IV, No. 18, para. 74 (different time limits imposed on persons claiming injuries); *Buckley v. U.K.*, September 25, 1996, R.J.D., 1996–IV, No. 16, para. 84 (refusal of planning permission to gypsy family); *Wingrove v. U.K.*, November 25, 1996, R.J.D., 1996–V, No. 23 (banning of a video film as blasphemous).

[10] *Handyside*, para. 48. See n.9.

[11] October 22, 1981, Series A, No. 45.

notwithstanding the margin of appreciation, it was for the Convention organs to make the final evaluation and it came to the conclusion that the prohibition of adult homosexual activities was not necessitated in the conditions of Northern Ireland to maintain moral standards or protect vulnerable members of society. The cost was disproportionately high on the individual with correspondingly little concrete gain for the community.

In other controversial areas, the Court has relied on the lack of consensus or common ground as indicating that it cannot act to impose obligations on Contracting States.[12] This shows a more cautious approach, since it might be argued that it is in such difficult areas that the Convention areas should assist a consensus to emerge. On the other hand, where there is a wide agreement in Member States as to particular standards to apply, this will generally be a material consideration, as in the case of judicial corporal punishment in *Tyrer v. U.K.*[13]

The scope of the margin of appreciation will differ according to the context.[14] It has been held by the Convention organs to be particularly wide in the areas of national security[15]; planning policies[16]; matters such as transsexualism or AID (artificial insemination by donor) perceived to be controversial. As regards the area of the protection of morals, the Court in *Dudgeon*[17] did not accept that the margin was wide as a general proposition, stating that it was not only the aim of the measures which affected the scope of the margin of appreciation but the nature of the activities involved. Since *Dudgeon* concerned interference with an imtimate area of priate life, the balance tipped towards applicants in requiring "particularly serious reasons" for interferences.

In practice, the margin of appreciation operates as a means of leaving a State freedom of manoeuvre in assessing what its society needs and the best way to achieve those needs, and even the timing of polices.[18] There is not only one way of protecting children from abuse or fighting drug-trafficking. In multicultural Europe, with its morasse of local traditions, the Convention cannot and should not attempt to impose uniformity or detailed and specific requirements.[19] In its supervisory capacity however, the Convention organs can require legitimate aims and that the State does not step beyond certain boundaries. For example, in the field of nationalisation and expropriation, where issues of the national economy may be in play, the Court gives the general and public interest a wide meaning and will respect the State's assessment unless manifestly without reasonable foundation.[20]

---

[12] This is notably in the area of transsexuals in the United Kingdom. See *Rees v. U.K.*, October 17, 1986, Series A, No. 106; 9 E.H.R.R. 56, para. 37; *Cossey v. U.K.*, September 27, 1990, Series A, No. 184; 13 E.H.R.R. 622, para. 40; *B v. France*, March 25, 1992, Series A, No. 232–C; 16 E.H.R.R. 1, para. 48 where there is reference to insufficient scientific, medical, legal and social consensus of the phenomenon. See also *X, Y and Z v. U.K.*, April 22, 1997, R.J.D., 1997–II, No. 35, where there was no common ground as to parental and family rights of transsexuals, in particular in relation to children born by artificial insemination by donor, where matters of filiation were not subject to any clear consensus.

[13] April 25, 1978, Series A, No. 26; 2 E.H.R.R. 1, paras. 31 and 38: vast majority of States had not used such methods for years; reference to the "commonly accepted standards". See also *Dudgeon v. U.K.*, above n.11, para. 60 concerning the prohibition of adult homosexual acts, where the majority of States no longer considered it appropriate to apply criminal sanctions to such acts.

[14] *Sunday Times v. U.K.*, April 26, 1979, Series A, No. 30, para. 59; *Dudgeon, ibid.* n.11, para. 52.

[15] *Leander v. Sweden*, March 26, 1987, Series A, No. 116; 9 E.H.R.R. 433.

[16] *Buckley*, see n.9, para. 75: in the planning area, the authorities have to exercise a discretion involving a multitude of local factors.

[17] At para. 52. See n.11, above.

[18] *e.g. Lindsay v. U.K.*, 11089/84, (Dec.) November 11, 1986, 49 D.R. 181, where the Commission noted that the margin of appreciation applies to when a State decides to change a system. The fact that the United Kingdom changed its tax system did not indicate that a previous lack of objective and reasonable justification since goals can legitimately change from time to time.

[19] *e.g. Sunday Times, supra*, n.13, para. 61.

[20] *e.g. Lithgow v. U.K.*, July 8, 1986, Series A, No. 102 (nationalisation); *James v. U.K.*, February 21, 1986, Series A, No. 98 (sweeping leasehold reform); *Pressos Compania v. Belgium*, November 20, 1995, Series A, No. 30 (legislation intervention in pending tort claims).

Nonetheless, generally, provision should be made with regard to compensation of the persons affected. In the field of education, though without express mention of the margin of appreciation, the Court referred to limits which should not be exceeded. Thus, while the setting and planning of a school curriculum falls in the first place for the State to settle and the State is not prevented from imparting information or knowledge of a religious or philosophical kind, it cannot step over the line into indoctrination.[21]

The limits are set in the content of the general themes described below.

4. Autonomous concepts

When it comes to interpreting the extent or application of the substantive rights and freedoms under the Convention, the Commission and Court look very much to the substance of the right protected. They are not to be distracted by how a Contracting State chooses in domestic law to interpret a term or principle. Whatever the domestic label, the Convention organs will examine the matter in form, substance and procedure before reaching their own decision.

The Court thus maintains that the terms contained in the Convention are autonomous concepts and that it is free to assess their application to particular situations in domestic systems. This covers the concepts of "civil rights and obligations", "criminal charge", "witness", etc. It will determine the scope of the rights guaranteed under the Convention and Contracting States cannot limit or redefine them by formal classifications and definitions in domestic law. But even where it does not refer to autonomous concepts, it approaches notions of "family" and "private life" by looking at the substance of what is at stake without being governed by the meaning given to the term in the particular State.

5. Effectiveness

The Convention is a system for the protection of human rights. This renders it of crucial importance that it is interpreted and applied in a manner which renders these rights practical and effective, not theoretical and illusory.[22] A State cannot therefore escape its obligations by protecting a right in a superficial or self-defeating manner. For example, it is not enough for an accused to be provided with a lawyer but the assistance given must be effective[23]; a State cannot disclaim responsibility in expelling an individual to a country where he faces a real risk of treatment contrary to Article 3[24] and the use of deliberate lethal force by State agents must be subject to the most careful scrutiny, and attract some form of effective official investigation.[25]

6. Strict limitations

Exceptions to the rights guaranteed under the Convention are to be strictly construed.[26] Thus, case law indicates the importance of physical freedom or liberty and emphasises that exceptions are exhaustively limited to those set out in the sub-paragraphs of Article 5,

---

[21] *Kjeldsen, Busk, Madsen and Pedersen v. Denmark*, December 7, 1976, Series A, No. 23; 1 E.H.R.R. 711.

[22] *Artico v. Italy*, May 13, 1980, Series A, No. 37; 3 E.H.R.R. 1, para. 33.

[23] *Artico, ibid.*, para. 33; *Campbell and Fell v. U.K.*, June 28, 1984, Series A, No. 80; 7 E.H.R.R. 165 access by a prisoner to a lawyer is not effective where consultations must be conducted within hearing of prison officers.

[24] *Soering v. U.K.*, July 7, 1989, Series A, No. 161; 11 E.H.R.R. 439.

[25] *McCann and others v. U.K.*, September 27, 1995, Series A, No. 324; 21 E.H.R.R. 97. See n.19 on p. 12.

[26] *e.g. Van Mechelen v. Netherlands*, April 23, 1997, R.J.D., 1997–III, No. 36, para. 58: limits to defence rights must be restricted to those "strictly necessary".

paragraph 1. If the detention does not fall within any of these categories then it cannot be justified under Article 5, paragraph 1, however useful the aim might be.[27]

7. Essence of the right

The Convention organs in assessing the impact of restrictions or interferences sometimes have regard to the "essence" of the right, whether it has been effectively destroyed or an acceptable scope for its exercise remains. This is applied in cases of access to court where limitations even if proportionate and pursuing reasonable aims must not impair the essence of the right.[28] In the cases of *CR* and *SW v. United Kingdom*, where the applicants challenged the decision of the House of Lords as retrospectively abolishing the marital immunity to rape, the Court found that the decisions, having regard to the manifestly debasing character of rape, could not be said to be at variance with the object and purpose of Article 7, which was to prevent arbitrary prosecution, conviction and punishment.[29]

8. Lawfulness

The rule of law is one of the key principles underlying the Convention. It implies that an interference by the authorities with an individual's rights should be subject to effective control, especially so where the law bestows on the executive wide discretionary powers.[30] Where in *Stran Greek Refineries v. Greece* there was legislative interference with judicial process, the Court emphasised several times the idea of rule of law which Greece undertook to respect in joining the Council of Europe and ratifying the Convention.[31]

A State may interfere with citizens' rights or regulate their freedom to act for specified legitimate aims but if it does so it must do so by law, and a norm cannot be classified as a law unless it is accessible and also foreseeable to a reasonable degree in its application and consequences.[32] This is the approach generally taken wherever the word "law" or "lawful" appears as a requirement.[33] Article 2 in addition makes references to protection by law,[34] while Article 6 provides a detailed procedural code for the operation of courts of law and Article 7 expressly prohibits retrospective imposition of criminal offences and heavier penalties. The requirement of effective access to court, and the scrutiny of any attempt to remove court jurisdiction over claims, can be said to derive from this fundamental concept.[35]

Lawfulness has been interpreted to refer to two elements. Firstly, the measure in issue must have some basis in domestic law[36] and secondly, that it possesses the quality of law,

---

[27] *e.g. Ciulla v. Italy*, February 22, 1989, Series A, No. 148, 13 E.H.R.R. 346, para. 41: arrest and detention pending the order of preventive measures fell outside the permitted exceptions of Art. 5 despite the acknowledged importance of the fight against the mafia. See also the *Engel v. Netherlands*, June 8, 1976, Series A, No. 22 case, para. 57, where the claim of special exclusion for military discipline was not accepted.

[28] *Ashingdane v. United Kingdom*, May 28, 1985, Series A, No. 93, para. 57; under Art. 12; the essence of the right to marry should not be hampered by national laws (Part IIB: Marriage); *Osman v. U.K.*, 23452/94, (Rep.), August 1, 1997, para. 92, pending before the Court: in the context of positive obligations to protect life.

[29] November 22, 1995, Nos. 335–B–C.

[30] See, *e.g. Silver v. U.K.*, March 25, 1983, Series A, No. 61; 5 E.H.R.R. 347, para. 90.

[31] Also *Hornsby v. Greece*, March 19, 1997, R.J.D., 1997–II, No. 33, para. 40 where the Court emphasised the rule of law in the effective implementation by the authorities of judicial decisions.

[32] *e.g. Sunday Times*, above n.14.

[33] "In accordance with law" (Art. 8) "prescribed by law" (Arts. 9, 10 and 11); procedure prescribed by law (Art. 5, para. 1); "lawful" as precondition for every sub-para of Article 5; conditions provided for by law (Art. 1 Protocol 1 first paragraph).

[34] *McCann and others* Comm. Rep., para. 92, see n.25: reference to rule of law requiring effective oversight of the use of force by agents of the State to avoid the arbitrary abuse of power.

[35] *Fayed v. U.K.*, September 21, 1994, Series A, No. 294–B; 18 E.H.R.R. 393.

[36] See, *e.g. Malone v. U.K.*, August 2, 1984, Series A, No. 82; 7 E.H.R.R. 14 (see Part IIB: Interception of communications).

namely, that it is accessible and enables the individual to foresee with reasonable degree of certainty the consequences of his actions or the circumstances in which, and the conditions on which, authorities may take certain steps.[37] These elements are applied with a view principally to ensuring that safeguards against arbitrary abuse of power are in place in the domestic law itself. Powers to interfere with the rights of individuals must be subject to defined limitations as to their subject-matter, duration, methods of implementation, having regard to the practical consideration that absolute certainty is neither possible or desirable and that many laws are inevitably couched in terms which are to some extent vague and whose interpretation and application are questions of practice.[38] The Convention organs are interested in ensuring certain minimum standards and a wide discretion, or partially defined concepts, will not necessarily offend.[39]

Matters of interpretation and application of domestic law itself are primarily for the national courts, and the Convention organs are not likely to contradict their findings.[40] Nonetheless since compliance with domestic law is an integral part of the obligations of Contracting States, the Court has stated its competence to satisfy itself of such compliance where relevant, subject to the inherent limits in the European system of protection.[41] In particular, where deprivation of liberty is concerned, it may verify that domestic law is not interpreted or applied in an arbitrary manner, since no arbitrary detention can ever be regarded as "lawful".[42] In practice, this gives a certain leeway to domestic systems but might also be said to avoid breaches which are technical and lacking in merit.[43]

9. Democratic values

In addition to the rule of law, reliance in interpretation and application of Convention rights is placed on "democratic values".[44] These involve recognition of the importance of rights of the defence to a fair trial and the fundamental rights guaranteed by Article 2 (right to life) and Article 3 (prohibition of torture and inhuman and degrading treatment).[45] States are required to adopt a certain tolerance and broadmindedness and to accept a certain pluralism and diversity.[46] States must also afford protection to the media, which acts in democratic society as a "watchdog" (see, Part IIB: Freedom of expression), and must expect to bear more criticism than others and react with restraint.[47]

---

[37] General principles — *Sunday Times*, see n.14, para. 49; *Malone*, above, n.36, paras. 67–68; also findings of violation: *Kruslin v. France*, April 24, 1990, Series A, No. 176–B; 12 E.H.R.R. 547; *Huvig v. France*, April 24, 1990, Series A, No. 176–B; 12 E.H.R.R. 528; *Amuur v. France*, June 25, 1996, R.J.D., 1996–III, No. 11.

[38] *Sunday Times*, see n.14, para. 49; changes in case law through judicial development are compatible with "lawfulness" criteria where reasonably foreseeable, if necessary with the assistance of a lawyer (see Part IIA: Retrospectivity).

[39] See Part IIB: Surveillance and Interception of Communications.

[40] e.g. *Casada Coca v. Spain*, February 24, 1994, series A. No. 285; 18 E.H.R.R. 1, para. 43.

[41] *Lukanov v. Bulgaria*, March 3, 1997, R.J.D., 1997–II, No. 34, para. 41 where on examination of the provisions of Criminal Code relied on, the Court found that the applicant ex-minister's participation in a collective decision to send aid to the Third World did not constitute a criminal offence under Bulgarian law at the time.

[42] *Winterwerp v. Netherlands*, October 24, 1979, Series A, No. 33; 2 E.H.R.R. 387, paras, 39 and 45.

[43] e.g. *Germany*, 9997/82, (Dec.) December 7, 1982, 31 D.R. 145.

[44] e.g. *Soering*, see n.24, para. 87: "any interpretation of the rights and freedoms guaranteed had to be consistent with the general spirt of the Convention, an instrument designed to maintain and promote the ideals and values of a democratic society" citing *Kjeldsen*, above n.20, para. 53.

[45] *Soering, ibid.*, para. 88; *McCann*, see n.25, para. 147; *Young, James and Webster v. U.K.*, June 26, 1981, Series A, No. 44; 4 E.H.R.R. 38, para. 63; a democracy does not mean that the majority always prevails: a balance must be achieved which endures the fair and proper treatment of minorities and avoids abuse of a dominant position.

[46] *Dudgeon*, see n.11, para. 53 concerning homosexual acts but see *Laskey, Jaggard and Brown v. U.K.*, February 19, 1997, R.J.D., 1997–I, No. 29 where the applicants' plea for toleration and broadmindedness was not successful in relation to group sado-masochistic activities of a certain severity.

[47] e.g. *Castells v. Spain*, April 23, 1992, Series A, No. 236; 14 E.H.R.R. 445, para. 46.

10. Necessity

Where interferences under the Convention may be justified in pursuit of specified legitimate aims, the requirement that these interferences nonetheless be "necessary" appears to place a burden on the State. The Court has laid down the element that an interference with a right has to be justified by "a pressing social need".[48] However, in practice, this is not applied in such a manner as to require a Government to establish, for example, that the measure is of any particular urgency or unavoidable, or that there is no other way of achieving the goal with lesser impact on individual rights. The findings of the Convention organs are phrased less demandingly in terms that having regard to the various relevant factors, the interference may be considered as necessary in a democratic society.[49] The principle of proportionality is more decisive (see below).

11. Proportionality

Proportionality is a dominant theme underlying the whole of the Convention. It is an ingredient of the requirement of the necessity of measure under provisions Articles 2, and 8–11 and has been imported into other provisions — in the context of objective and reasonable justification for difference in treatment under Article 14, as regards restrictions on access to court under Article 6, and the framework of property rights under Article 1 of Protocol No. 1, as well as the basis for finding positive obligations on the State to act. It requires a reasonable relation between the goal pursued and the means used.[50] It is also used in the sense of finding a balance between the applicant's interests and those of the community.[51] Many issues centre on the conflict between an individual's position and the good of the general amorphous mass of society: roads; taxes; airports; preservation of the countryside are objectively to everyone's benefit. Proportionality examines whether providing them places an excessive burden on certain individuals. Whether this burden has been mitigated by procedures or forms of relief will be relevant to whether the State has struck the right balance.

The question of whether the State could achieve the goal in another way may be asked under proportionality but can only go so far.[52] Since the Convention is not setting ideal standards, it is not enough to establish a violation that, for example, other methods are used in another State.[53] The method used must fail the proportionality test and fall outside the margin of appreciation having regard to the particular circumstances of the case.

12. Positive obligations

The provisions of the Convention impose primarily negative obligations on States, namely, to refrain from taking steps infringing fundamental rights and freedoms. Increasingly,

---

[48] *Handyside*, see n.9, para. 48; *Sunday Times*, n.14, para. 59; "necessary" identified as less than "indispensable" but not as flexible as "useful" "reasonable" or "desirable".

[49] *e.g. Laskey*, see n.46, para. 50 "the national authorities were entitled to consider the prosecution and conviction of the applicants were necessary in a democratic society for the protection of health . . ."

[50] *James v. U.K.*, see n.19.

[51] *Sporrong and Lonroth v. Sweden*, September 23, 1982, Series A, No. 52; 5 E.H.R.R. 35, para. 69.

[52] *Inze v. Austria*, October 28, 1987, Series A, No. 126; 10 E.H.R.R. 394 — the fact that the law about inheritance changed did not show that there had been a violation but did indicate that there were other ways of achieving the Government's aim of maintaining farms.

[53] *Hewitt and Harman No. 2.* 20317/92, (Dec.) September 1, 1993; see, however, 21825/93–23414/94 *McGinley and E v. U.K.*, (Rep.) November 26, 1996, pending before the Court, concerning access to court and information for nuclear test veterans, where the Commission referred to the public enquiries which were set up in the United States and Australia; *Chahal v. U.K.*, November 15, 1996, R.J.D, 1996–II, No. 22 where the Court referred to the method applied in Canada to permit courts to review sensitive security material.

however, rights are being interpreted in such a manner as to impose positive obligations on States to take steps to protect the enjoyment of rights from interferences from other sources (see Part IIB: Private life). In this area, limitations on the imposition of obligations derive from the consideration of the factors identified above in the context of the margin of appreciation dominated by the perception that this trespasses more acutely in matters of State policy, priorities and allocations of resources.[54] In assessing whether the State is under an obligation to take a particular step, the Court examines whether a fair balance has been struck between the interests of the individual and those of the community. Where Article 8 is concerned for example, in striking the balance, the legitimate aims adverted to in the second paragraph may be relevant. The interests of the general community perhaps start out heavier in the balance, with a certain burden on the individual to establish that his interests clearly predominate.[55] The cases indicate that where an important individual right is at stake, the applicant suffering significant effects, a positive obligation may arise. However, where the individual interest is not perceived as suffering material prejudice, or an important State interest is at stake, this is less likely.[56]

13. Individual rights

The Convention is based on the right of individual petition. An applicant must claim to be a victim of a violation of one of the guaranteed rights. The Convention organs will not entertain complaints by way of *actio popularis* or *in abstracto*. Their examination will generally be restricted to the measures as they affect the individual in his situation. They will not respond with enthusiasm to an invitation to look at the global position, as in the case of gypsies, who may well be suffering from the social and legal developments of the last fifty years but can only complain with any hope of success to the Convention organs of matters which can be shown to effect them personally and concretely.[57] Arguments which focus on the general injustice or unfairness of a policy or measure will be of limited assistance unless relevant to explaining or setting in context the impact on the individual applicant.

14. Living instrument

The Convention is seen as a living instrument, to be interpreted in light of present day conditions.[58] As a result, notwithstanding the possible intentions of the drafters of the Convention fifty years ago, the Convention organs will have regard to developments in Contracting States in applying the rights guaranteed in the Convention. Thus changing attitudes to homosexuality,[59] children born out of wedlock,[60] equality of the sexes[61] have

---

[54] *Abdulaziz and others v. U.K.*, May 28, 1985, Series A, No. 94; 7 E.H.R.R. 471, para. 67; *Osman*, see n.27, para. 91.

[55] See *e.g. X, Y and Z*, see n.12 where the Court in para. 47 stated that while it had not been shown that recognition of the filiation of a child born by AID was contrary to the interests of the community, it had not been established as necessary to the welfare of the child either.

[56] *e.g. Abdulaziz*, see n.54 (immigration policy); transsexuals in *Rees* and *Cossey* and *XYZ*, see n.12, not considered to suffer significant hardship such as would require the State to change its entire registration system whereas in *B v. France*, the applicant suffered daily humilation and the civil register system did not require radical alteration.

[57] *e.g.* see Part IIB: Gypsies; the Commission resisted examining the designation system as applied to gypsies since the individual applicants could not establish that it had been applied to them directly.

[58] *e.g. Tyrer v. U.K.*, April 25, 1978, Series A, No. 26, 2 E.H.R.R. 1, para. 31; *Johnston v. Ireland*, December 18, 1986, Series A, No. 112; 9 E.H.R.R. 203, para. 53; *Inze*, see n.52, para. 41.

[59] *e.g. Dudgeon*, see n.11.

[60] *e.g. Johnston*, see n.58, *Inze*, see n.52.

[61] *Schuler-Zgraggen v. Switzerland*, June 24, 1993, Series A, No. 263; 16 E.H.R.R. 405, para. 67; *CR v. U.K.*, see n.29, para. 60.

played a role in decision-making. There must, however, apparently be a general acceptance of the changing conditions before this can be decisive, as shown by the transsexual cases, where the Court, although allegedly aware of the difficulties facing transsexuals, does not consider a consensus to have been reached and has adverted to the need to keep the matter under review. The contents of domestic and constitutional law, Council of Europe texts, other international treaties and human rights jurisprudence may be of relevance in establishing trends and developments or accepted principles. This cannot however extend so far as to create rights not intended to be included in the Convention.[62]

As part of this theme, the notion of flexibility can be identified. The Court and Commission case law develops progressively and has overruled earlier decisions.[63] In the area, particularly, of domestic remedies, they intend to apply the Convention flexibly, avoiding excessive formalism.[64]

15. Convention approach to evidence and burdens of proof

There are no rules of admissibility of evidence. Parties may present such documentary evidence as they think appropriate and are not bound to comply with required domestic forms of presentation or content.[65] In the hearing of witnesses, there is no prohibition of hearsay. Nor is there any formalised theory of burden and standard of proof. The Convention organs take the approach of a free assessment of the available evidence, including matters taken *proprio motu*.

In practice, however, an applicant must present an application which provides prima facie substantiation of an interference with his rights and an arguable basis for eventual violation. It will only be in exceptional cases, complaints raising serious issues against a background that provides justification for failure to present factual substantiation, that the application will be considered as meriting further examination by communication to the respondent Government.[66]

As regards admissibility, the Government bears a burden of establishing the existence of available and effective remedies (see Part IB: Admissibility Checklist). In other contexts, it may be seen that once an interference with rights is established, the burden shifts practically onto the Government to provide convincing justification.[67] However, where public and individual interests are more finely balanced, due either to the nature of the claims or the fact that a positive obligation is in issue, it appears that the applicant faces the onus of substantiating the degree of prejudice alleged.

In relation to disputed factual situations, where there are allegations of torture, inhuman and degrading treatment contrary to Article 3, the Court has used the standard of proof beyond a reasonable doubt. This was, however, in an interstate case, where dozens of witnesses were heard concerning practices used in interrogation in Northern Ireland. It was rarely used again until the Commission undertook witness hearings in Turkey

---

[62] Where later provided in the protocols (*ne bis in idem*, freedom of movement) or otherwise, *e.g. Johnston*, para. 53, concerning the Court's refusal to evolve interpretation of Article 12 to include a right to divorce clearly not intended by the drafters. There is therefore a distinction to be drawn, possibly fine, between the creation of new rights and the extension by interpretation of existing ones.

[63] *e.g. Borgers v. Belgium*, October 30, 1991, Series A, No. 214; 15 E.H.R.R. 92, para. 24 overruling *Delcourt v. Belgium*, January 17, 1970, Series A, No, 11; 1 E.H.R.R. 355, in light of growing recognition of the importance of maintaining public confidence in administration of justice.

[64] *Akdivar*, para. 69.

[65] Though it is not infrequent for parties to submit statements by way of affidavit and this may be taken into account as part of the weighing of the credibility of the evidence.

[66] *e.g.* the cases brought by villagers from South-East Turkey, where serious allegations were made and no documentary substantiation was allegedly possible due to the ineffective nature of domestic remedies. There was independent confirmation of village destruction in other international texts and NGO reports.

[67] *Dudgeon*, see n.11; freedom of expression cases.

concerning allegations under Articles 2 and 3, about ill-treatment and deaths at the hands of security forces.[68] Outside this context, the Commission's establishment of the facts is generally carried out without any reference to standards and burden of proof.

It is perhaps worth mentioning that there is a certain presumption in practice that Governments act in good faith, that the authorities comply with important domestic rules and that legal processes work in the way laid down by law. For example, judges are presumed very strongly to abide by their oaths and duties[69] and statutory systems of protection to function as intended.[70] Any allegations alleging abuse or misuse of power tend to require a certain level of substantiation.

16. Structured approach

In any complaint of substance, the Convention organs analyse the application of the invoked provision with regard to each ingredient. This involves generally an examination of whether the complaint falls within the scope of the right claimed (applicability) and whether any interference with the right conforms with its conditions (compliance). While this may vary concerning the subject-matter, the general approach for the most commonly-invoked provisions is set out below:

Article 5, para. 1

- is there a deprivation of liberty?
- is it in conformity with lawfulness considerations?
- is it for a ground permitted under para. 1? Does it comply with its conditions?

Article 6

Criminal:

- do the proceedings relate to a criminal charge? (see Part IIA: Fair trial, criminal charge);
- if so, have the guarantees been complied with?

Civil:

Applicability:
- do the proceedings concern a right or obligation recognised in domestic law?
- is there a genuine and serious dispute ("*contestation*") about the right or obligation (which includes the consideration whether the proceedings are directly decisive for that right or obligation)?
- is the right or obligation "civil" in character?
- have the guarantees under paragraph 1 been complied with?

---

[68] *e.g.* Comm. Rep. *Diaz Ruano v. Spain*, April 26, 1994, Series A, No. 285–B; 19 E.H.R.R. 555 struck off before the Court. Concerning recent cases involving fact-finding *e.g. Aydin v. Turkey*, September 25, 1997, Reports 1997–VI, No. 50; *Tekin v. Turkey*, (Rep.) April 17, 1997, pending before the Court.

[69] See *Kraska v. Switzerland*, April 19, 1993, Series A, No. 285–B, 18 E.H.R.R. 188 (where a judge announced that he had not read the applicant's documents).

[70] See *e.g.* Part IIB: Interception of communications, and Surveillance and secret files; *Goddi v. Italy*, April 9, 1994, Series A, No. 76; 6 E.H.R.R. 457, para. 76, in the absence of substantiation of a factual point from either side, the Court was not prepared to find the Government at fault.

Articles 8–11

First paragraph:
- applicability: whether the complaint falls within the scope of the right;
- existence of an interference: whether the matters complained of infringe the right.

Second paragraph — justification for any interference:
- lawfulness critieria;
- legitimate aim;
- necessity, including considerations of "pressing social need", margin of appreciation, proportionality, procedural safeguards and relevant and sufficient reasons for any decisions involved.[71]

Where positive obligations are concerned the examination does not extend into the second paragraph but the considerations of aim and proportionality are transposed into a general balancing exercise as to the existence of the obligation.

Article 13

- is the claim in relation to an alleged violation of a substantive provisions?
- is it arguable?
- is there any effective remedy?

Article 14

- is there a substantive right in issue?
- is there a difference in treatment?
- between persons in relevantly similar positions?
- based on grounds of personal status?[72]
- without objective and reasonable justification (including consideration of legitimate aim and proportionality, margin of appreciation)?

Article 1 of Protocol No. 1

- are "possessions" involved which fall within this provision?
- if so, does the measure consistute a deprivation, a control of use or an interference with peaceful enjoyment?
- compliance: Legitimate aim (whether specified as general or public interest); lawfulness; margin of appreciation and proportionality (including procedural safeguards, compensation) are relevant to all heads in some degree.

---

[71] So far the latter criterion has been almost wholly applied in Article 8 and 10 cases, though now applied to Article 11, *inter alia*, in *Sidiropulos v. Greece*, (Rep.) April 11, 1997 pending before the Court.
[72] See Part IIB: Discrimination; this criterion is of dubious validity.

1. Court judgments

Available:

- on the internet (http://www.dhcour.coe.fr — from 1996);
- provisional blue copies on request from the Court;
- official series: texts of judgments:
  - until 1996 Series A Nos. 1–338;
  - from 1996, yearly volumes of Reports published as "Reports of Judgments and Decisions".
    (These contain the entire text of the court judgment with any separate opinions and also save in early volumes, the "Opinion" part of the Commission report on the merits.)[1]

There is no formal doctrine of precedent binding either Court or Commission. As a matter of general practice and practical necessity, the Commission regards the Court's binding judgments as the final authority on the interpretation of the Convention. It has been known, however, to resist a line of authority, or to follow with reluctance.[2] The Court obviously pays attention to relevantly similar cases decided by itself but may choose if it considers it appropriate or timely to depart expressly or impliedly from previous positions.[3] Therefore authority from the Court in support of an argument is one of the most convincing arguments, although not necessarily conclusive before either the Commission or Court.

2. Commission cases

Principal source:

- *Decisions and reports:* from 1974, the principal publication of Commission cases published in numerical volumes (D.R. 1–90 and rising.[4] Volumes 1–75 contained each extract in English and French. To diminish the time taken for publication, there are now A and B versions of each volume: volume A contains the text in the original language, and volume B produced later contains the

---

[1] There is no official index for Series A. The Court registry has provided a survey of activities for 1959–1991 with annual supplements in following years. There is a Council of Europe publication, "Judgments of the European Court of Human Rights 1959–1995", which gives useful reference charts of findings but which is becoming increasingly out of date.

[2] *e.g.* the Commission's approach in transsexual cases (see Part IIB: Transsexuals); the Court's rejection of Commission's approach to "arguable claim" under Art. 13 (see Part IIB: Remedies).

[3] Procedurally, however, any change in case law should be conducted by a Grand Chamber. A Chamber should not depart from the previous cases since this is a ground on which the case should be ceded to a Grand Chamber (Rule 51(1) of Rules of Court A).

[4] These are selected by the Secretariat from the mass of Commission output on the basis of significance and relevance, generally including Commission reports on the merits (Art. 31) which are not sent to the Court, friendly settlement reports (Art. 28), strike out reports (Art. 30) admissibility decisions and Committee of Ministers' resolutions. The summary form committee cases are never published. They are roughly chronological, varying as to the times the texts were adopted or made public. There is a time lag at present of six months in publishing cases.

translation into the other official language. Indexes, by name, number and summaries by article and keyword, are produced at intervals for every 20–15 volumes;

Supplementary sources:
- *Collection of Decisions* consists of 46 volumes covering 1955–74, including selected decisions, with indexes for 1–30 and 32–43 only. These includes cases of interesting historical significance *e.g.* Commission decisions in *Ireland v. U.K.* interstate case;
- *Yearbook of the European Convention of Human Rights* published annually, containing general institutional information and statistics and the cases which tend to reproduce those in D.R., although some material may be included which is not published elsewhere. There is no complete index to the Yearbook;
- *Digest of Strasbourg case law* (1982) (arranged by chunks of relevant texts of decisions and reports under each Article of the Convention in five volumes). It is not regarded as an official source of published case law and it is not cited as a source as a matter of practice. Looseleaf supplements have brought it up to 1990 for decisions and reports and up to 1992 for judgments;
- Commission cases (reports on the merits which have been made public) are to be accessible on the internet (http://www.dhcommhr.coe.fr).

There is a gap between decisions being made and their publication. Press releases are issued after each Commission session and after hearings.[5] As a last resort the Secretariat are available to provide up-to-date information about recent cases or to assist in identifying relevant precedents. Where an important decision or report does not appear in a published collection, it may also be requested from the Secretariat.

The Commission endeavours to maintain consistency in its decisions and opinions, subject to case law deriving from the Court. Reference to its decisions and reports may be useful in the proceedings before the Commission. Indeed the Commission can be seen to prefer to cite its own reports in a number of cases, relying on its own sometimes more detailed analysis, particularly where the Court has, with more refined judicial economy, reached conclusions without finding it necessary to refer to particular points or issues.[6]

It is only recently that the Court has openly given weight to Commission precedent. It is therefore not irrelevant to refer the Court to Commission case law which is particularly persuasive or based on its special expertise.

3. Procedure

Both the Commission and Court have rules of procedure, copies of which can be obtained from the respective bodies and the current versions are annexed to this book.

There is no equivalent of practice notes, with the result that there is no official published source of authority for Commission and Court practice in granting Rule 36 requests, legal aid, rights of audience or delays in providing written pleadings or documents. Basic notes are given for guidance at Commission and Court hearings and explanatory letters sent by the Secretariat or Court Registry with each procedural step. As a result, the main source of information about procedural matters is generally the lawyers working at the institutions. Enquiry by letter or telephone is possible.

[5] These can be obtained from the Council of Europe Press Service FAX + 33/(0)3.88.41.27.89.
[6] The evolution of the Commission's case law is such that very old volumes should be cited with care, it being preferable to find more recent support for any principle or interpretation.

4. Institutional and statistical information

The Court and Commission publish annual surveys of statistical information, and summaries of principal case law. Information about judges and Commission members is available on the internet. See also the Yearbooks (Section 2, above).

5. Journals and periodicals

- *European Human Rights Reports* (Sweet and Maxwell);
- *European Human Rights Law Journal* (Sweet and Maxwell): bi-monthly, which includes bulletin of information and pending hearings and judgments and provides case notes of judgments and decisions reached in the previous two or three months.

6. Relevant external sources of human rights materials

The following may be relevant, in particular as indicative of existing or emerging international human rights standards:
- the state of law in other Contracting States on certain points (with a view to indicating any European consensus on a particular standard or approach);
- Council of Europe materials: Parliamentary Assembly, Committee of Ministers, Committee for the Prevention of Torture;
- case law of the European Court of Justice;
- European Parliament recommendations;
- other European or international treaty provisions;
- United Nations sources, *e.g.* General Assembly, Convention and treaty provisions (*e.g.* I.C.C.P.R.), cases from the Human Rights Committee, reports from the UNHCR, ILO;
- Inter-American reports and judgments;
- constitutional law material from outside Europe, *e.g.* United States Supreme Court.

Index of Articles

PART II: PROBLEM AREAS

PART II PROBLEM AREAS

A. FAIR TRIAL GUARANTEES

General Principles: Fairness

Key provisions:

Article 6, paragraph 1 (fair and public hearing in the determination of criminal charges and civil rights and obligations, within a reasonable time, before an independent and impartial tribunal); paragraph 2 (presumption of innocence) and paragraph 3(a) (information about the charge); paragraph 3(b) (adequate time and facilities for preparation); paragraph 3(c) (right to be present and represented); paragraph 3(d) (right to call and examine witnesses); paragraph 3(e) (right to interpretation).

Key case law:

Artico v. Italy, May 13, 1980, Series A, No. 37; 3 E.H.R.R. 1; *Barbera, Massegué and Jabardo v. Spain*, December 6, 1988, Series A, No. 146; 11 E.H.R.R. 360; *Colak v. Germany*, December 6, 1988, Series A, No. 147; 11 E.H.R.R. 513; *Kamasinski v. Austria*, December 19, 1989, Series A, No. 168; 13 E.H.R.R. 36; *Kraska v. Switzerland*, April 19, 1993, Series A, No. 254–B; 18 E.H.R.R. 188; *Kerojärvi v. Finland*, July 19, 1995, Series A, No. 322.

1. General principles

Complaints about court proceedings form a major percentage of the cases before the Convention organs, reflecting that it is in court that most people are likely to come into contact, in a significant manner, with the power and authority of the State as it administers civil and criminal justice. However, justice is not the word that is highlighted by the Convention or the Convention organs. The key principle governing Article 6 guarantees is fairness. Paragraphs 2 and 3 are constituent elements, or specific aspects of the fair trial guaranteed in paragraph 1.[1] Further, while the sub-paragraphs 3(a)–(e) exemplify the notion of fair trial in typical procedural situations, their intrinsic aim is always to ensure or contribute to ensuring the fairness of the proceedings as a whole.[2] Though they are expressed as applying to criminal proceedings, they have also been considered by the Court to be implicit requirements in fairness outside the criminal sphere, applying *mutatis mutandis*.[3] While the "fairness" guarantee applies to both criminal and civil proceedings, a special importance is attached to the rights of the defence in criminal proceedings and it has been held by the Court that where civil litigation is involved national authorities enjoy greater latitude.[4] Nonetheless, in general the same principles of

---

[1] *e.g. Kamasinski*, para. 62; *Hadjianastassiou v. Greece*, December 16, 1992, Series A, No. 252-A; 16 E.H.R.R. 219, para. 31; *Hamer v. France*, December 17, 1996, R.J.D. 1996–III, No. 13.
[2] Thus, sub-paragraphs are often considered in conjunction with paragraph 1 see, *e.g. Can v. Austria*, (Rep.) July 12, 1984, Series A, No. 96; 8 E.H.R.R. 121.
[3] *Albert and Le Compte v. Belgium*, February 10, 1983, Series A, No. 58; 5 E.H.R.R. 533.
[4] *Niderost-Huber v. Switzerland*, February 18, 1997, R.J.D. 1997–I, No. 29, para. 28: where failure to allow the applicant to see and comment on submissions made by the Cantonal Court to the Federal Court on appeal disclosed a violation of Article 6, para. 1.

equality of arms, adversarial proceedings, etc., described below apply, if not with the same force, in civil cases.

The right to a fair trial is seen as holding so prominent a place in democratic society that the Court has stated that there is no justification for interpreting Article 6, paragraph 1 restrictively.[5]

As to "fairness", it is perhaps simpler to say what it does not mean. The Commission and Court frequently state that they are not courts of appeal from domestic courts and they cannot examine complaints that a court has reached the wrong decision or that a person was, for example, wrongly convicted. They will not enter into the merits of decisions. For this reason, complaints concerning miscarriages of justice are unlikely to succeed before them.[6]

Domestic courts are in the best position to assess the evidence before them, to decide what is relevant or admissible. Matters of interpretation of domestic law and the categorisation of claims in domestic law are also primarily for the appreciation of domestic courts.[7] In this area the Convention organs exercise only a limited supervisory jurisdiction, guided by the overriding principle of fairness. While more recently developments have indicated that Convention organs will require that reasons be given and that a lack of reasons on key points may disclose unfairness, it is unlikely that they will intervene on substantive matters, *i.e.* the decision itself, unless in the Commission's words there is some gross unfairness or arbitrariness. This would appear to mean that there is something striking and palpable on the face of the decision.

From the Convention point of view it is not so much the result that is in question but the process of "hearing". An applicant should be "heard", given an adequate and effective opportunity to be present at his case. Domestic courts are under a duty to conduct a proper examination of the submissions, arguments and evidence adduced by the parties, without prejudice to their assessment of whether they are relevant to its decision.[8] Basing a decision on a clearly inaccurate finding may disclose a failure by the court to ensure an applicant receives a fair hearing.[9]

2. Aspects of fairness

A number of subsidiary principles have been identified. *Equality of arms* between the parties, or a "fair balance" must be achieved. This means that each party must be afforded a reasonable opportunity to present his case — including his evidence — under conditions which do not place him at a substantial disadvantage *vis-à-vis* his opponent.[10]

Proceedings should also be *adversarial* in character, with an opportunity for the parties to a criminal or civil trial to have knowledge of and comment on all evidence adduced or observations filed even by an independent member of the national legal service with a view to influencing the court's decision.[11]

---

[5] *Moreira de Azevedo v. Portugal,* October 23, 1990, Series A, No. 189, para. 66.

[6] See, *e.g. Birmingham Six case,* U.K. No. 14739/89, May 9, 1989, 60 D.R. 296. The applicants' complaints focussed on the failure to hold a jury trial to rehear the new evidence rather than a reference to the Court of Appeal. These matters could not in Convention terms reveal unfairness since juries are not standard features of criminal trials in Europe as a whole and there is no right to a re-trial contained in the Convention. In essence they were arguing miscarriage of justice, that their conviction was wrong, based on flawed evidence and they were trying to prove it. Fortunately for them, they eventually succeeded on a domestic level, if belatedly.

[7] *e.g.* 10153/82 Austria, October 13, 1986, 49 D.R. 67.

[8] *e.g. Barbera,* para. 68; *Kraska,* para. 30.

[9] *Fouquet v. France,* (Rep.) October 12, 1994, R.J.D., 1996–I, No. 1, (settled before the Court), where the *Cour de Cassation* based itself, erroneously, on the finding that the applicants had admitted fault in their pleadings.

[10] *Dombo Deheer BV v. Netherlands,* October 27, 1993, Series A, No. 274, para. 33.

[11] See, *e.g. Ruiz-Mateos v. Spain,* September 12, 1993, Series A, No. 262, para. 63. It may apply to proceedings ancillary to the main proceedings, *e.g.* in *Mantovanelli v. France,* March 18, 1997, R.J.D., 1997–II, No. 32, concerning the procedure whereby the court appointed expert produced his report. (See below, Part IIA: Equality of arms).

The importance of ensuring *the appearance of the fair administration of justice* is adverted to in a number of contexts. Foremost, there are the objective requirements of independence and impartiality but there is also the importance of public hearings which allows for public scrutiny of the processes of justice and maintains confidence in the administration of justice.[12]

An accused, and in civil proceedings the parties, must be able to *participate effectively* in proceedings. Measures taken in the conduct of a trial must be reconciliable with an *adequate and proper exercise of the rights of the defence*.[13] The importance of securing defence rights in criminal proceedings has been identified as a fundamental principle of democratic society and in this respect Article 6 must be interpreted to render them practical and effective rather than theoretical and illusory.[14] States are expected to exercise diligence in ensuring defence rights[15] and any measures restricting them should be strictly necessary.[16] Thus while an applicant's own conduct will be relevant domestic courts must still ensure the requirements of Article 6, paragraph 1 are met.[17]

The standard applied, however, is not one of perfection. The proceedings are looked at as a whole and the restriction on the defence may be insufficient to render the proceedings as a whole unfair. The Commission and Court will examine whether any other opportunities were offered to remedy or make up for some shortcoming. Defects in a trial may be remedied by subsequent procedures before appeal courts.[18] They also have a pragmatic approach to difficulties of criminal justice, in particular to drug-trafficking, organised mafia-type crime and terrorism, and where good reasons exist to keep witnesses anonymous or where circumstances make it impossible for the authorities to act otherwise, allowance is generally made notwithstanding the undesirable effects on defence rights.[19]

Whether or not the "unfairness" alleged has an effect on the outcome of the proceedings is a factor which generally is not, or should not be of relevance.[20] However, occasionally, it is taken into account whether some factor had the possibility of effecting the course of proceedings or outcome and whether the applicant has shown whether it was capable of such effect to distinguish material factors from extraneous or trivial ones.

---

[12] *Bulut v. Austria,* February 22, 1996, R.J.D. 1996–II, No. 3, para. 47; *Borgers v. Belgium,* October 30, 1991, Series A, No. 214–B, para. 24.

[13] *e.g. Ludi v. Switzerland,* June 15, 1992, Series A, No. 238; 15 E.H.R.R. 173.

[14] *Artico,* para. 33.

[15] See, *e.g. Colozza v. Italy,* February 12, 1985, Series A, No. 89; 7 E.H.R.R. 516, para. 28; *Hamer v. France,* See n.7, December 17, 1996 para. 28 where Court found that the French appeal system putting the onus on convicted appellants to find out when an allotted period of time starts to run or expires was not compatible with diligence which States must exercise to ensure rights guaranteed under Article 6 are enjoyed in an effective manner.

[16] *Van Mechelen v. Netherlands,* April 23, 1997, R.J.D., 1997–III, No. 36, para. 58 — anonymous witness case. If a less restrictive measure can suffice then that measure should be applied.

[17] *Barbera,* para. 75; lack of fair trial notwithstanding the applicants' lawyers own failure to make objections to documents in the file not being read out which led to a drastically brief trial; *Kerojärvi,* para. 42; it was irrelevant that the unassisted applicant made no complaint about non-communication of documents — the Supreme Court should have made them available, since it knew they had not been transmitted to him by the lower court, which practice the applicant would have been unaware of.

[18] See, *e.g. Edwards v. U.K.,* November 25, 1992, Series A, No. 247–B; 15 E.H.R.R. 417 where failure to disclose evidence at trial remedied by a reference to the Court of Appeal which examined the new evidence and heard argument as to whether the conviction should be quashed.

[19] See, *e.g. Ferrantelli and Santangelo v. Italy,* August 7, 1996, R.J.D. 1996–III, No. 12, where the applicants were unable to question a key witness who had died before opportunity had been given; *Baegen v. Netherlands,* October 27, 1995 Series A, No. 327–B (inability to question abuse victim) *Doorson v. Netherlands,* March 26, 1996, R.J.D. 1996–II, No. 6, (drug trafficking).

[20] *Artico,* para. 35; a requirement to show actual prejudice from a lack of legal representation would deprive the guarantee of its substance.

3. Aspects of conduct of the proceedings

(a) *Conduct of the judge*

Besides the requirements of independence and impartiality, the conduct of the judges in the proceedings must in principle comply with the standard of fairness. However, the cases have so far revealed a certain reluctance to find judges at fault. In *Colak v. Germany*, the Court found no unfairness in an alleged assurance to defence counsel from the President of the Assize Court that the only basis for conviction would be grievous bodily harm although subsequently his client was convicted of attempted murder.[21] While in *Kraska v. Switzerland*, where in appeal proceedings in a fraud case, one of the five judges had stated in open court that he had been unable to read the file, the Court, even while noting the importance of appearances in the administration of justice, found that the applicant's standpoint was not decisive and any misgivings must also be objectively justified. It found that there was no evidence to suggest that the members of the court failed to examine the appeal with due care before taking their decision and although the judge's comments were open to criticism it did not give rise to any reasonable misgivings.[22]

A failure by a court to comply with domestic procedural rules will not necessarily be fatal either. Where a judge failed as required by law to record his comments to the jury during its deliberations, the Commission noted that Article 6 did not lay down any requirements regarding internal court procedures which were primarily a matter for the domestic courts, although it did not exclude that non-observance of such national rules could raise an issue.[23]

(b) *Appearances and incidents in the conduct of the proceedings*

While the conformity of a trial with the requirements of Article 6 must be assessed on the basis of the trial as a whole, a particular incident may assume such importance as to constitute a decisive factor in the general appraisal of the trial overall. In this context there have been occasional incidents where witnesses have been arrested in open court, a dramatic intervention which might be considered to influence the views of juries in particular.[24] In a Swiss case,[25] the applicant's main witness was ordered to be arrested by the prosecution as an accomplice, the arrest being carried out during the hearing. The Commission noted that the matter of the arrest had been debated before the jury which considered that it did not feel influenced and was able to continue and that the applicant had not been prevented from questioning the witness by the action taken.

Complaint has been made of the adverse effect of the handcuffing of defendants during criminal trials. The Commission has criticised the practice as undesirable in public but not

---

[21] The Court noted that the formal position was clear as to the charge before the court, the court had never stated that it did not intend to deal with the charge and counsel should have known that the court would only rule after its deliberations. Further he should have verified that the President's appraisal of the case indeed reflected the views of the court itself.

[22] See the minority led by President Ryssdal who stressed that in a democratic society the courts must inspire confidence in the public and above all the parties. They agreed with the Commission's opinion to the effect that from his comments the judge had indicated that he wanted to read the memorial which he regarded as pertinent and the proceedings had raised a doubt that applicant's observations had not been properly considered by one member of the court. This doubt should have been decisive. The Commission majority had found that a party cannot be effectively heard where a judge participates in the case without having acquainted himself with all the material which he regards as possibly relevant to the outcome of the case.

[23] *Denmark* 13926/88 October 4, 1990, 66 D.R. 209: though the Commission noted sound reasons for the rule, having regard to the proceedings as a whole, it concluded that they were not conducted so as to place the applicant at any disadvantage *vis-à-vis* the prosecution.

[24] See Part IIA: Fair trial guarantees, Juries.

[25] *Switzerland*, 9000/80, (Dec.) March 11, 1982 28 D.R. 27.

yet found the issue decisive. In the *Campbell v. United Kingdom* case, where the applicant was handcuffed during his appeal, no problem of appearances arose and Commission did not consider that it prevented him presenting his own appeal adequately.[26] Where defendants sat in a glass cage, the Commission did not accept this stigmatised them before the court and jury, having regard to the fact that it was a permanent security feature and since the applicant was able to communicate with the lawyer freely, he was not put in an unfavourable position in relation to the court or jury or at a disadvantage in relation to the prosecution.[27] In *Welch v. United Kingdom*, where there was a heavy security presence at the applicant's trial, which was alleged to overdramatise his dangerousness, the Commission considered that the security arrangements had not been shown to be unnecessary or to have been stage-managed, and referring to the practical view that no trial could otherwise be held in security-risk cases, held that the precautions may have led a jury to deduce that the police considered an accused to be dangerous but that this was not the same as a presumption of guilt.

4. Extent of the applicability of fairness

Fairness applies not only to the immediate conduct of proceedings before the domestic courts *inter partes* but to the proceedings as a whole. Thus the intervention of the legislature to determine the outcome of pending proceedings by passing a law may violate the principle of equality of arms.[28] Execution of judgments also falls within the notion of "trial".[29]

---

[26] *U.K.* 12323/86, (Dec.) July 13, 1988, 57 D.R. 148.
[27] *France* 11837/85, (Rep.) June 7, 1990 69 D.R. 126.
[28] *Stran Greek Refineries v. Greece*, December 9, 1994, Series A, No. 301–B, para. 49.
[29] *Hornsby v. Greece*, March 19, 1997, R.J.D. 1997–II, No. 33 (failure to implement for 5 years a final judicial decision — civil).

General Principles: Criminal charge

Key provisions:

Article 6, paragraphs 1, 2 and 3.

Key case law:

Engel v. Netherlands, July 8, 1976, Series A, No. 22; 1 E.H.R.R. 706; *Ozturk v. Germany*, February 21, 1984, Series A, No. 73; 6 E.H.R.R. 409; *Campbell and Fell v. U.K.*, June 28, 1984, Series A, No. 80; 7 E.H.R.R. 165; *Agosi v. U.K.*, October 24, 1986, Series A, No. 108; 9 E.H.R.R. 1; *Weber v. Switzerland*, May 22, 1990, Series A, No. 177; 12 E.H.R.R. 508; *Demicoli v. Malta*, August 27, 1991, series A, No. 210; 14 E.H.R.R. 909; *Société Stenuit v. France*, February 27, 1992, Series A, No. 232–A; 14 E.H.R.R. 509; *Ravnsborg v. Sweden*, February 21, 1994, Series A, No. 283–B; 18 E.H.R.R. 38; *Raimondo v. Italy*, February 22, 1994, Series A, No. 281–A; 18 E.H.R.R. 237; *Bendenoun v. France*, February 24, 1994, Series A, No. 284; 18 E.H.R.R. 54; *Air Canada v. U.K.*, May 5, 1995, Series A, No. 316; 20 E.H.R.R. 150; *Gradinger v. Austria*, October 23, 1995, Series A, No. 328–C; *Putz v. Austria*, February 22, 1996, R.J.D., 1996–I, No. 4; *Garyfallov AEBE v. Greece*, September 24, 1997 to be published in R.J.D. 1997; *Pierre-Bloch v. France*, October 21, 1997 to be published in R.J.D. 1997.

1. General considerations

In determining the existence of a "criminal charge" for the purposes of applying Article 6, paragraphs 1–3, *Engel v. Netherlands* established the three criteria to be read in light of the autonomy of the concept under the Convention — the classification of the offence in domestic law, the nature of the offence and the severity of the penalty. It suffices that the offence in question is "criminal" by its nature from the Convention perspective or that the person is liable to a sanction which is of a nature or severity to fall within the "criminal' sphere. However, where the separate analysis of each criterion does not make it possible to reach a clear conclusion, the Court may adopt a cumulative approach.[1]

2. Autonomous concept

The Convention organs will not allow the Contracting States to recategorise offences at will to avoid the application of Article 6 guarantees. They reserve supervisory jurisdiction over whether an offence is properly designated as disciplinary but the Court commented that a State would be free to designate as a criminal offence an act or omission not constituting the normal exercise of one of the rights that the Convention protects since such a choice renders applicable Articles 6 and 7.[1a] Although in *Ozturk v. Germany* the Court was not in theory opposed to decriminalisation of traffic offences to "regulatory" matters, it considered that it must nonetheless ensure that States do not act against the object and purpose of Article 6. Similarly, notwithstanding the special context of military or prison discipline, the guarantee of a fair hearing under Article 6 is one of the fundamental principles of a democratic society and any dividing line between the "disciplinary" and "criminal" sphere has to be consistent with that provision.[2]

[1] *Bendenoun,* para. 47; *Garyfallov AEBE*, para. 33.
[1a] *Engel, para. 81; Société Stenuit,* para. 60–61 where domestic law was alleged to exclude fines on corporate bodies from being criminal.
[2] *Engel*, paras. 81–82; *Campbell and Fell*, para. 69.

3. The *Engel* criteria

(a) *Classification of the offence in domestic law*

This has not proved an important criterion in practice and is only a starting point.

(b) *Nature of the offence*

The Convention organs have regard to factors such as how the offence is regarded in other Contracting States, the procedures applied, their connection or similarity to criminal offences and procedures[3] and whether the subject-matter constitutes an offence because of its context or because of general prohibition in the public interest.[4]

Regarding "disciplinary" offences, a distinction is drawn between offences applicable to persons under a specific regime and those affecting potentially the whole population. For example, criminal offences were at stake in *Weber v. Switzerland*, where contempt of court applied to a journalist unconnected with the trial was not regarded as part of the internal functioning of the court and in *Demicoli v. Malta*, where breach of privilege applied to a journalist for a publication about a member of the legislature was not a matter of internal parliamentary discipline. In *Ravnsborg v. Sweden*, however, the Court noted that the applicant was fined as a party in the domestic proceedings, which contempt provisions did not apply to persons making statements outside those proceedings. Sanctions imposed on persons participating in proceedings pursuant to court powers to ensure the orderly conduct of the proceedings are therefore likely to fall outside the criminal sphere[5] unless where the penalty is severe enough to attract the guarantees of Article 6 nonetheless.

The lack of seriousness of minor offences, as in careless driving in *Ozturk*,[6] may not divest offences of their criminal character. In *Ozturk*, the Court considered the character of rule, noting that it was still criminal in other countries and aimed at the public generally.

(c) *Severity of the penalty*

Regard is had to the nature and purpose of the penalty, in particular whether it is intended to be deterrent and punitive.[7]

---

[3] *e.g. Gradinger*, where the terminology of administrative "criminal" offences was noted.

[4] In *Campbell and Fell*, the Court examined whether the conduct was only an offence because committed in prison or whether it was also prohibited by the criminal law, (mutiny and incitement was akin to conspiracy, gross personal violence to a prison officer was akin to assault) which could give a "certain colouring" beyond that of a purely disciplinary matter; *Société Stenuit*, (Rep.) para. 62, where the ministerial imposition of a heavy fine on a company was for infringement of economic legislation which affected the general interests of society normally protected by criminal law; *Bendenoun*, where tax penalties applied to all citizens under a general rule. Conversely, *Eggs v. Switzerland*, 7341/76, (Dec.) March 4, 1978, 15 D.R. 35 a refusal to obey an order (fatigues) was clearly a disciplinary matter, based on internal organisation rules as was 5 days' isolation as punishment of a soldier for late return from leave (*X v. Switzerland*, 7754/77, (Dec.) May 9, 1977, 11 D.R. 216).

[5] *Putz*, para. 33; fines imposed on applicant by court for disrupting the proceedings, which proscribed conduct in principle fell outside Article 6.

[6] See also *Schmautzer v. Austria*, October 23, 1995, Series A, No. 328–A (fine for not wearing seatbelts); *Umlauft v. Austria*, October 23, 1995, Series A, No. 328–B (refusal to give breath sample); *Malige v. France* (27812/95, (Rep.) May 29, 1977, pending before the Court (loss of points on driving licence).

[7] *Ozturk*, para. 53; *Steel and others v. U.K.* 24838/94, (Rep.) April 9, 1997, pending before the Court, where proceedings for breach of the peace leading to binding over were found to be criminal in nature, due to their deterrent nature (requiring the person to keep the peace) and punitive (since if person does not agree he will be imprisoned).

Deprivation of liberty as a penalty (excepting measures which by length or nature are not appreciably detrimental[8]) generally belongs to the criminal sphere, bearing in mind the seriousness of what is at stake and the importance attached to physical liberty.[9] The threat of imprisonment may also be decisive. In *Engel*, the fact an applicant received a penalty not occasioning deprivation of liberty did not affect the Court's assessment since the final outcome of the appeal could not diminish the importance of what was initially at stake.[10] In *Campbell and Fell v. United Kingdom*, loss of remission of almost three years, even though remission was a privilege rather than a right, was taken into account since it had the effect of extending the expected period of detention and came close to deprivation of liberty. The Court found that the object and purpose of the Convention required that imposition of a measure of such severity attracts guarantees of Article 6.

Where fines are concerned, consideration is given to whether they are intended as pecuniary compensation for damage or essentially as a punishment to deter re-offending.[11] In *Ozturk*, where the applicant was only fined 60 DM, the Court referred to the purpose of the penalty being to deter and punish. In other cases, where considerations as to the nature of the offence weigh more heavily, larger fines have not been decisive.[12] Forfeiture measures have not been regarded as criminal penalties[13] nor have preventive measures or the application of personal security measures.[14] Confiscation orders, which are conditional on criminal convictions, and are deterrent in nature and purpose, rather than preventive, have been found to constitute "penalties" under Article 7, which prohibits retrospective criminal penalties.[15] A payment order imposed on an electoral candidate for exceeding the limit set on campaign expenses was found by the Court to be by way of a payment to the community of the sum by which the candidate improperly took advantage to seek votes and thus not to be a "criminal" penalty akin to a fine.[16]

4. Proceedings excluded from Article 6 "criminal aspect"

The following have not been found "criminal":

- proceedings relating to issues of lawfulness of detention where the *lex specialis* is Article 5[17];

---

[8] *Engel*, where for one applicant a risk of two days strict arrest for absence without leave was considered too short a duration and for another, four days light arrest did not constitute deprivation of liberty.

[9] *Engel*, para. 82; *Campbell and Fell*, p. 37, para. 72.

[10] *Engel*, where three applicants faced risk of 3–4 months committal to disciplinary unit; *Demicoli*, where the applicant, though only fined for breach of privilege, risked imprisonment of 60 days; *Weber*, where the applicant was at risk of fine for contempt of 500 Swiss francs convertible in certain circumstances into a period of imprisonment; *Gradinger*, a fine for drink driving with prison in default.

[11] See *e.g. Bendenoun*, para. 47, where tax penalties were not intended as compensation for pecuniary damage but as punishment to deter re-offending; *Société Stenuit*, para. 64, where sanctions were imposable on a company up to five per cent of its turnover which indicated that it was intended to be deterrent.

[12] *Ravnsborg*, which involved three fines of 1000 kroner for contempt, convertible to imprisonment by District Court in limited circumstances in which case the applicant would be summoned to an oral hearing in separate proceedings. Also the fines were not registered on police files as other criminal "fines" were; in *Putz*, fines were convertible but only up to 10 days, not entered on the record and appeals were possible; *Benedoun*, where the substantial fines of 400,000–500,000 FF were not decisive in themselves.

[13] *Agosi* (seizure and forfeiture of the applicant's kruegerrands by Customs); *Air Canada* (customs seizure of the applicants company's aircraft, released on payment of £50,000). Where property or pecuniary rights are concerned. Art. 6 in its civil aspect is likely to apply.

[14] *e.g. Raimondo*, para. 43 concerning special supervision, including confiscation of property of the applicant on grounds of suspicion of membership in a mafia-type organisation, *Guzzardi v. Italy*, November 6, 1980, Series A, No. 39, para. 108, concerning compulsory residence requirements.

[15] *Welch v. U.K.*, February 9, 1995, Series A, No. 307–A; 20 E.H.R.R. 247.

[16] *Pierre-Bloch v. France*, para. 58.

[17] *e.g.* review of an order for detention on remand 6541/74, (Dec.) December 18, 1974, 1 D.R. 82.

- decision to deport an alien[18];
- decisions by courts on extradition requests, even where there is an assessment as to whether there is a case to answer[19];
- decision to classify prisoner as a "Category A" dangerous prisoner[20];
- restrictions placed by Secretary of State on applicant's activities in running insurance business.[21]

Cross-reference

Part IIA: Length of proceedings (duration of "criminal charge")
Part IIA: Retrospectivity (penalties)

---

[18] *e.g. Agee v. U.K.* 7729/76, (Dec.), December 17, 1976, 7 D.R. 64.
[19] *U.K.* 10479/83, March 12, 1984, 37 D.R. 158.
[20] *X v. U.K.* 8575/79, (Dec.), December 14, 1979, 20 D.R. 202.
[21] *U.K.* 7598/76, (Dec.), July 17, 1980, 21 D.R. 5.

General Principles: Civil rights and obligations

Key provision:

Article 6, paragraph 1.

Key case law:

Le Compte, Van Leuven, and De Meyere v. Belgium, June 23, 1981, Series A, No. 43; 4 E.H.R.R. 1; *Sporrong and Llonroth v. Sweden*, September 23, 1982, Series A, No. 52; 5 E.H.R.R. 35; *Benthem v. Netherlands*, October 23, 1985, Series A, No. 97; 8 E.H.R.R. 1; *Feldbrugge v. Netherlands*, May 29, 1986, Series A, No. 99; 8 E.H.R.R. 425; *Deumeland v. Germany* May 29, 1986, Series A, No. 100; 8 E.H.R.R. 448; *Van Marle v. Netherlands*, June 26, 1986, Series A, No. 101; 8 E.H.R.R. 483; *W v. U.K.*, July 8, 1987, Series A, No. 121; 10 E.H.R.R. 29; *Pudas v. Sweden*, October 27, 1987, Series A, No. 125; 10 E.H.R.R. 380; *H v. Belgium*, November 30, 1987, Series A, No. 127; 10 E.H.R.R. 339; *Tre Traktorer v. Sweden*, July 7, 1989, Series A, No. 159; 13 E.H.R.R. 309; *Allan Jacobsson v. Sweden*, October 25, 1989, Series A, No. 163, 12 E.H.R.R. 56; *Hakansson and Sturesson v. Sweden*, February 21, 1990, Series A, No. 171; 13 E.H.R.R. 1; *Mats Jacobsson v. Sweden*, June 28, 1990, Series A, No. 180–A; 13 E.H.R.R. 79; *Skarby v. Sweden*, June 28, 1990, Series A, No. 180–B; 13 E.H.R.R. 90; *Fredin v. Sweden*, February 18, 1991, Series A, No. 192; 13 E.H.R.R. 784; *Oerlemans v. Netherlands*, November 27, 1991, Series A, No. 219; 15 E.H.R.R. 561; *Kraska v. Switzerland*, April 19, 1993, Series A, No. 254–B; 18 E.H.R.R. 188; *Ruiz-Mateos v. Spain*, June 23, 1993, Series A, No. 262; 16 E.H.R.R. 505; *Schuler-Zgraggen v. Switzerland*, June 24, 1993, Series A, No. 263; 16 E.H.R.R. 405; *Massa v. Italy*, August 24, 1993, Series A, No. 265–B; 18 E.H.R.R. 266; *Zander v. Sweden*, November 25, 1993, Series A, No. 279–B; 18 E.H.R.R. 175; *Ortenberg v. Austria*, November 25, 1994, Series A, No. 295–B; 19 E.H.R.R. 524; *Beaumartin v. France*, November 24, 1994, Series A, No. 296–B; 19 E.H.R.R. 485; *Schouten and Meldrum v. Netherlands*, December 9, 1994, Series A, No. 304; 19 E.H.R.R. 432; *Procola v. Luxembourg*, September 28, 1995, Series A, No. 326; 22 E.H.R.R. 193; *Masson and Van Zon v. Netherlands*, September 28, 1995, Series A, No. 327; 22 E.H.R.R. 491; *Sussman v. Germany*, September 16, 1996, R.J.D., 1996–IV, No. 15; *Neigel v. France*, March 17, 1997, R.J.D., 1997–II, No. 32; *Georgiadis v. Greece*, May 29, 1997, R.J.D., 1997–III, No. 38; *Rolf Gustafsson v. Sweden*, August 1, 1997, R.J.D., 1997–IV, No. 41.

1. General considerations

Outside the criminal sphere, the guarantees of fair trial under Article 6, paragraph 1 apply only to proceedings which involve the determination of "civil rights and obligations". This includes a number of considerations: the rights or obligations must at least on arguable grounds exist in domestic law; there must be a dispute or "contestation" about those rights and obligations of a "genuine and of a serious nature",[1] and the rights claimed must be "civil" in nature.

Interpretation has been progressive in this area. Matters which once were considered as outside the scope of Article 6, paragraph 1, such as welfare benefits, now generally fall inside the concept of "civil rights and obligations". The principles applied are wide and capable of application to almost any type of significant dispute.

2. Basis in domestic law

Article 6 does not guarantee any particular content for "rights and obligations" in the substantive law of Contracting States. There must at least on arguable grounds be a basis

---

[1] *Benthem*, para. 32.

for the right in doemstic law.[2] A number of cases, from the United Kingom, have raised issues as to the effect of privileges, immunities or certificates from the Secretary of State which arguably limit the scope of rights. There is an objection in principle to allowing the State to remove categories of claim from the civil courts and the Convention organs applying the *Ashingdane v. United Kingdom* criteria of legitimate aim and proportionality may verify whether this has the effect of depriving an applicant of the essence of the right to court (see Part IIA: Access to court).

Where in childcare cases the Government claimed that on the issuing of parental rights resolutions, parental rights of access ceased in domestic law, the Court noted that the effect of the measures did not extinguish all parental rights in respect of a child, which in any event would hardly have been compatible with fundamental rights of family life under Article 8, and having regard to statutory recognition that parental access was desirable, found that there was at least on arguable grounds a right of access in domestic law. It would seem that where parent-child relationships are concerned the Convention organs are reluctant to find no right existing in domestic law, on an underlying assumption that such matters are of fundamental importance.[3] Similar considerations might apply where proceedings concern serious interferences with other fundamental rights guaranteed under the Convention.

3. Dispute or "contestation" concerning rights and obligations

This element which is derived from the French text of Article 6 is not to be construed too technically, and is to be given a substantive rather than formal meaning.[4] A tenuous connection or remote consequences between the dispute and the right does not suffice.[5] Civil rights or obligations must be the object or one of the objects of the dispute and the result of the proceedings must be directly decisive for such a right.[6] A dispute can for these purposes concern not only the actual existence of the right but the scope of the right or its manner of exercise.[7] It may concern both questions of fact and law.[8]

The dispute must also be of a "genuine and serious nature". For example, in *Logan v. United Kingdom*,[9] where the applicant made complaints about the amount of child maintenance imposed by the Child Support Agency, the Commission noted that there was no provision for the costs of access visits to be taken into account under the applicable formulae as the applicant argued and that the applicant did not deny that the assessment had been correctly made under the legislation. Thus there was no dispute, or any dispute of a genuine or serious nature about any civil right or obligation. In *Van Marle v. Netherlands*, the Court found no dispute, where the applicant accountants had been refused registration as certified accountants on the basis of an examination of their competence. It considered that there were no claims of irregularity in the procedure and that assessments

---

[2] See where subject-matter of the claim is at the discretion of the authorities, *e.g. Masson and Van Zon*, where awards for costs incurred in criminal proceedings ending in an acquittal were at the discretion of the courts; 16484/90, (Dec.) January 17, 1991 where the applicant could not claim a right to obtain a licence in Gibraltar to operate a fast launch, where the applicable regulation did not impose any duty on the Captain of the Port to grant a licence; *B v. Netherlands*, 11098/84, (Dec.) July 1, 1985, 43 D.R. 198 where compensation for criminal injuries was *ex gratia*; see, however, *Rolf Gustafsson v. Sweden* where the Court found domestic law conferred a right to compensation where certain conditions were fulfilled.

[3] *Price v. U.K.*, No. 12402/86, (Dec.) July 14, 1988, 55 D.R. 224: no rights in domestic law were found for grandparental access to children.

[4] *Le Compte*, para. 45.

[5] *ibid.*, para. 47.

[6] *ibid.*, para. 47. *Balmer-Schafrorn and others v. Switzerland*, August 26, 1997, R.J.D. 1997–IV, No. 43, para. 32.

[7] *e.g. Le Compte*, para. 49: thus Art. 6 applied even though the right to practise medicine was not removed but only briefly suspended.

[8] *e.g. Pudas*, para. 31.

[9] *U.K.* 24875/94, (Dec.) September 9, 1996 86–A D.R. 74.

involving the evaluation of knowledge and experience for carrying on a profession were akin to school or university examinations and as such were removed from normal judicial functions. Conversely in *H v. Belgium*, where the applicant had been struck off from the Bar and refused reinstatement, the Court found a dispute capable of judicial assessment, having regard to the terms of the regulations which allowed reinstatement in "exceptional circumstances" which left scope for a variety of interpretations and under which the applicant could arguably claim the right to practise at the Bar since he fulfilled the conditions.

The Court has stated that Article 6, paragraph 1 can be relied on where an applicant claims that an interference with the exercise of a civil right is unlawful.[10] Thus in cases where notwithstanding the wide discretion imposed on public authorities in the imposition of measures, applicants who are able to challenge the lawfulness of the measures in the most general sense may claim a dispute. This was where the authorities' discretion was not unfettered since they were bound by generally recognised legal and administrative principles.[11]

4. Civil nature of the right or obligation

The concept of "civil rights and obligations" is not to be interpreted solely by reference to the respondent State's domestic law but is an autonomous notion based on the character of the right.[12] Article 6, paragraph 1 also applies irrespective of the status of the parties, the character of the legislation which governs how the dispute is to be determined and the character of the authority which is invested with jurisdiction in the matter, the key point being whether the outcome of the proceedings is decisive for private rights and obligations.[13]

The Court has regard to the private and personal nature of the right, whether it is connected with contractual relationships,[14] connected with the exercise or enjoyment of property rights[15] or the exercise of commercial, business or professional activities,[16] the subject-matter of the action is pecuniary in nature and founded on infringement of rights of a pecuniary nature.[17] For example, in *Pudas v. Sweden*, where the applicant taxi-driver's

---

[10] *Le Compte*, para. 44.

[11] *Pudas*, para. 34; *Allan Jacobsson*, para. 69; *Mats Jacobsson*, para. 32; *Skarby*, para. 28, *Tre Traktorer*, paras. 39–40. Where for example the applicants alleged improper motives by the authorities, departure from longstanding practice, failure to take their interests into account, discrimination, abuse of power, which was regarded as raising issues of lawfulness.

[12] *e.g. Konig v. Germany*, June 28, 1978, Series No. 27, paras. 88–89; *Baraona v. Portugal*, July 8, 1987, Series A, No. 122, paras. 42–43 where it was not decisive that Portuguese law distinguished between acts of private and public administration, where the right in issue was a personal property right.

[13] *Ringeisen*, para. 94; *Editions Periscope v. France*, March 26, 1992, Series A, No. 234, para. 40, where it was not decisive that the dispute originated in the State's functions in imposing tax and was dealt with in the administrative courts.

[14] *Le Compte*, para. 48, where a profession is conducted by means of private relationships with clients on a contractual or quasi-contractual nature, regardless of whether the profession is exercised in the public interest with special duties, *e.g.* medical profession.

[15] *e.g. Baraona*, para. 44; Swedish property restriction cases, *e.g. Sporrong and Llonroth* (imposition of expropriation permit on the estate), para. 79; *Hakansson and Sturesson* (refusal to grant permit to retain property bought at auction), para. 60; *Mats Jacobsson* (amendment to building plan preventing construction on his property), para. 34; *Fredin* (revocation of permit to exploit gravel pit), para. 63; *Oerlemans* (restrictions on certain farming activities, *e.g.* using herbicides), para. 48.

[16] *Benthem*, para. 36, concerning refusal to the owner of a garage of a licence to install LPG storage tank to supply motor vehicles; *Tre Traktorer*, para. 43 finding that revocation of a restaurant license to serve alcohol had adverse effects on the goodwill and value of the business run and that the serving of acohol was a private commercial activity based on the earning of profits and contractual relationships. *H v. Belgium* right to practise as an advocate.

[17] *e.g. Editions Periscope*. However, this is to be distinguished from proceedings which merely have an economic aspect *e.g. Pierre-Bloch v. France*, para. 51.

taxi licence was revoked, the right involved was clearly civil, having regard to its connection with his business activities, carried out with the object of earning profits and based on contractual relationship with customers. State regulation of activities in the public interest, *e.g.* transport or sale of alcohol or the practice of law, may bestow features of public law but will not suffice to exclude private commercial activities from the category of civil rights.[18]

Proceedings for compensation generally have a private law character even where derived from public law or criminal proceedings.[19] Where the outcome of constitutional or public law proceedings may be decisive for civil rights and obligations, such proceedings, even if before the Constitutional Court, will fall within the scope of Article 6, paragraph 1. In *Ruiz-Mateos v. Spain*, the Court noted that the constitutional proceedings challenging a law were the sole means available to the applicants to complain of an interference with their property rights by an expropriation decree. Application to the *Conseil d'Etat* for the annulment of orders fixing milk quotas in *Procola v. Luxembourg* was closely connected by its possible outcome to the pecuniary rights and economic activities of the applicant agricultural association.[20]

In the area of social security, the Court has adopted the approach of examining whether the private law or public law features are of greater significance.[21] Particular weight has been given to the similarity between social security schemes and private insurance as lending a private law character. Links with contracts of employment have also been emphasised. In the cases before the Court, these private law features have tended to outweigh the public law elements present, such as the character of the legislation, assumption of responsibility by public authorities, and compulsory nature of the schemes.[22] In *Schuler-Zgraggen v. Switzerland* the Court stated that as a general rule Article 6, paragraph 1 applied in the field of social insurance and that the most important consideration militating in favour of applicability was that the applicant has suffered an interference with her means of subsistence and was claiming "an individual, economic right flowing from the specific rules laid down in domestic law".[23] While this approach was stated not to apply automatically to obligations to pay contributions as opposed to claims to entitlements, Article 6 was still found to apply to disputes about the amount of contributions to be paid in *Schouten and Meldrum v. Netherlands*. (See Part IIB: Welfare benefits.)

The status of European community "rights" for the purpose of Article 6, paragraph 1 has been considered in a few cases. The Commission has found that "civil rights" includes rights arising under directly applicable European community law.[24] However, where the character of the right is public, Article 6 has been excluded.[25]

---

[18] *e.g. Pudas*, para. 37; *Tre Traktorer*, para. 43; *H v. Belgium*, where advocates were part of the judicial system and subject to public law regulation, they still exercised an independent professions and their chambers and clientèle constituted property interests.

[19] *e.g. Georgiadis*, para. 35; claim was for compensation for detention following acquittal in criminal proceedings; *Beaumartin*, where the applicant's claim to compensation for expropriation of property in Morocco derived from an international agreement between France and Morocco — notwithstanding the treaty and State prerogative aspects, French nationals could claim a share pursuant to a decree, and the right was pecuniary in nature based on property rights.

[20] See also *Kraska* (public law proceedings concerning practice of the medical profession); *Sussman* (Constitutional Court proceedings concerning amendments to civil servants pension schemes); *Ortenberg* (public law objections to planning permission granted by the authorities to owner of neighbouring land).

[21] *e.g. Schouten and Meldrum*, paras. 40–60.

[22] *e.g. Feldbrugge; Deumeland; Salesi v. Italy*, February 26, 1993, Series A, No. 257–E.

[23] para. 46.

[24] *Greece* 24960/94, (Dec.) January 11, 1995 where nonetheless the applicant *avocat stagiaire* in Rome did not enjoy the status under EEC provisions to claim the right to practise law in Greece.

[25] *Adams and Benn v. U.K.*, 28979/95 and 30343/96, (Dec.) January 13, 1997 where applicants claimed rights of freedom of movement within European Union under Maastricht, the Commission noted the origin and general nature of the provision, and the lack of personal, economic or individual aspects which are characteristic to the private law sphere.

Areas falling outside Article 6 are principally issues of deprivation of liberty which fall under the *lex specialis* of Article 5[26]; proceedings relating to asylum, expulsion and nationality.[27] The Court also considers that matters of access to the public service fall outside Article 6.[28] In *Neigel v. France*, where a shorthand typist employed by a town council claimed but was refused reinstatement after a leave of absence, the Court, overruling the view of the Commission,[29] referred to the basic distinction in many Member States between civil servants and employees governed by private law and considered that as this complaint essentially concerned her claim to reinstatement it fell outside Article 6, paragraph 1. It did not refer to the element of her claim concerning payment of her salary.

Matters relating to the obligation to pay tax will generally fall outside the scope of civil rights, save where relating to pecuniary claims with a foundation in private law (see Part IIB: Tax). Claims relating to electoral or political matters will be excluded (see Part IIB: Electoral rights).

Commission cases have also held Article 6, para. 1 inapplicable to a right to report on a public trial[30]; refusal to issue a passport[31]; right not to be denied elementary education[32]; unilateral decision of the State to compensate the victims of a natural disaster.[33]

Cross-reference

Part IIA: Access to court
Part IIA: Costs
Part IIA: Pensions
Part IIA: Tax
Part IIA: Welfare benefits

---

[26] *e.g.* 6541/74 (Dec.) December 18, 1974 1 D.R. 82.

[27] *Omkarananda v. Switzerland*, 8118/77, (Dec.) March 19, 1981, 25 D.R. 105; *Bozano v. France*, 9990/82, (Dec.) May 15, 1984, 39 D.R. 119.

[28] *e.g. Massa*, para. 26, where it stated that disputes relating to the recruitment, careers and termination of service of civil servants were as a general rule outside the scope of Art. 6, para. 1, though it did apply in that case to a dispute about the applicant's rights as the surviving spouse of a civil servant to a reversionary pension. The Commission has applied the same exclusion to recruitment and career disputes by employees of international organisations (*Germany*, 26991/95, (Dec.) April 12, 1996, concerning European Patent Office).

[29] The Commission considered due to her claim for salary that her claims were at least partly pecuniary in nature and that the dispute was akin to ordinary employer-employee relationship. Also the special factor of public service should depend on the job-content; while there were certain public service posts with responsibilities affecting matters of general interest, or involving the exercise of official authority, which the Member States were entitled to fill at their discretion, this was not the case for shorthand typists.

[30] *Switzerland*, 23868–23869/94, (Dec.) February 24, 1995 80 D.R. 162.

[31] *Finland*, 19583/92, (Dec.) February 20, 1995 80 D.R. 38.

[32] *U.K.*, 14688/89, (Dec.) December 4, 1989 64 D.R. 188.

[33] *Sweden*, 14225/88, (Dec.) December 3, 1990 69 D.R. 223.

Access to court

Key provision:

Article 6, paragraph 1.

Key case law:

Golder v. U.K., February 21, 1975, Series A, No. 18, 1 E.H.R.R. 524; *Campbell and Fell v. U.K.*, June 28, 1984, Series A, No. 80; 7 E.H.R.R. 165; *Ashingdane v. U.K.*, May 28, 1985, Series A, No. 93; 7 E.H.R.R. 528; *Powell and Rayner v. U.K.*, February 21, 1990, Series A, No. 172; 12 E.H.R.R. 355; *Philis v. Greece*, August 27, 1991, Series A, No. 209; 13 E.H.R.R. 741; *Hennings v. Germany*, December 16, 1992, Series A, No. 251–A; 16 E.H.R.R. 83; *Geoffre de la Pradelle v. France*, December 16, 1992, Series A, No. 253; *Zumtobel v. Austria*, September 21, 1993, Series A, No.' 268–A; 17 E.H.R.R. 116; *Fayed v. U.K.*, September 21, 1994, Series A, No. 294–B; 18 E.H.R.R. 393; *Air Canada v. U.K.*, May 5, 1995, Series A, No. 316; 20 E.H.R.R. 150; *Tolstoy v. U.K.*, July 13, 1995, Series A, No. 323; 20 E.H.R.R. 442; *Bellet v. France*, December 4, 1995, Series A, No. 333–B; *Bryan v. U.K.*, November 22, 1995, Series A, No. 335–A; 21 E.H.R.R. 342; *Stubbings and others v. U.K.*, October 22, 1996, R.J.D., 1996–IV, No. 18; *Hornsby v. Greece*, March 19, 1997, R.J.D., 1997–II, No. 33; *Canea Catholic Church v. Greece*, December 16, 1997, to be published in R.J.D. 1997.

1. General considerations

The interpretation of Article 6, paragraph 1 to confer an effective right of access to court in the determination of civil rights and obligations is one of the most significant and creative steps taken by the Convention organs. In *Golder v. United Kingdom*, where a prisoner had been refused permission to contact his solicitor with a view to bringing a civil action for libel against a prison officer, the Court, faced with the question whether Article 6, paragraph 1 was limited to guaranteeing the right to a fair trial to pending legal proceedings or whether in addition it secured a right of access to court for persons wishing to bring an action concerning their civil rights and obligations, found in favour of the latter. The Court noted that otherwise a Contracting State would be free to abolish its courts or remove jurisdiction over particular classes of action, which would bring in the danger of arbitrary power and the denial of the principles of justice.

The right of access to court is not absolute but subject to limitations. By its very nature, the Court has said, it calls for regulation by the State, which may vary in time and in place according to the needs and resources of the community and individuals.[1] The State has a margin of appreciation in making such regulations but the limitations applied must not restrict or reduce the access left to the individual in such a way that the very essence of the right is impaired. In addition, a limitation will not be compatible with Article 6, paragraph 1 if it does not pursue a legitimate aim and if there is not a reasonable proportionality between the means employed and the aim sought to be achieved.[2] These criteria are sometimes referred to as the "Ashingdane principles".

2. Applicability

Access to court can only apply in respect of *contestations* (disputes) over civil rights and obligations which can be said, at least on arguable grounds, to be recognised under domestic law; it cannot in itself guarantee any particular content for those rights.[3]

---

[1] *Golder,* para. 38.
[2] *Ashingdane,* para. 57.
[3] See, *e.g. W v. U.K.* July 8, 1987, Series A, No. 121; 10 E.H.R.R. 29.

An applicant's complaint of denial of access must relate to a right which has a basis in domestic law. In *Powell and Rayner v. United Kingdom*, where a statute provided that nuisance and trespass would not lie in respect of the ordinary incidents of flights of aircraft which conformed with reasonable height requirements and navigation regulations, the Court found that as a result of this exclusion of liability the applicant houseowners could not claim to have a substantive right under English law to obtain relief for exposure to aircraft noise in those circumstances.[4]

Whether a limitation on a claim constitutes a procedural bar restricting access to court or forms part of the substantive definition of the right in domestic law may in some cases be difficult to distinguish and the matter has been left open by the Court in a number of cases. The Commission has tended to find that where an existing right of action is subject to special defences, privileges and immunities, there is an arguable basis for a right in domestic law and the restriction must be examined for conformity with the *Ashingdane v. United Kingdom* principles (see section 4: Defences, privileges and immunities, below).

3. Procedural and practical restrictions

Procedural and practical impediments may contravene the Convention where they operate to bar effective access to court.[5]

(a) *Obstacles in obtaining access*

Refusal of permission to a prisoner to contact his solicitor with a view to suing a prison officer in libel deprived him of access to court: it was not for the Secretary of State to take the role of determining whether or not such a claim had prospects of success.[6] Inability for a prisoner to have confidential out of hearing consultations with a solicitor also was considered to deny effective access to court.[7]

Lack of access by the applicant veteran servicemen to their service records and other relevant records for the purposes of establishing that their health problems derived from their exposure to Pacific nuclear tests has been found by the Commission to be a disproportionate restriction on their access to the tribunal which adjudicates on disability pensions.[8] It was no answer that the applicants could possibly institute civil proceedings and through discovery obtain the documents, since, insofar as Article 6, paragraph 1 guaranteed effective access to court, it presupposed that the access was effective without the necessity for instituting separate legal proceedings.

(b) *Limitations on categories of litigant and legal standing*

Limitations on access as regards minors, persons of unsound mind, bankrupts and vexatious litigants have been acknowledged as pursuing legitimate aims. However, the

---

[4] *Sweden*, 12810/87, (Dec.) January 18, 1989, 59 D.R. 172; *Spain*, 14324/88, (Dec.) April 19, 1991 69 D.R. 227.

[5] *Golder*, para. 26. More extreme examples are illustrated in the Turkish cases pending before the Court in which it is alleged that the situation in the south-east emergency region is such as to render access to court practically ineffective, having regard, *inter alia*, to the powers of the emergency governor and the security forces, intimidation and fear of reprisals, the vulnerability of the applicants etc. *e.g. Akdivar v. Turkey*, September 16, 1996, R.J.D., 1996–IV, No. 15.

[6] *Golder, ibid.*

[7] *Campbell and Fell v. U.K.*; *McComb v. U.K.*, 10621/83, (Dec.) March 11, 1985, where complaints of opening of legal correspondence between a prisoner and solicitor were declared admissible under Art. 6 (alleged denial of effective access to court) but settled on change of practice. Restrictions on prisoners' correspondence with domestic courts was in issue in *Hodgson v. U.K.*, (11392/85, (Dec.) March 4, 1987 dismissed when the restrictions were removed by amendment to prison regulations.

[8] *McGinley and E. v. U.K.*, 21825/93 and 23414/94, (Rep.) November 26, 1996 pending before the Court.

Ashingdane principles still apply, though so far restrictions examined have generally not been found incompatible with them.[9]

Where a claim belonging to an individual may only be pursued by another person or body, in the absence of any incapacitating feature as those above, it may be harder for the restriction to be justified. In *Philis v. Greece*, the applicant engineer's claims for remuneration for work done could only be pursued by the Technical Chamber of Greece. While this procedure might have provided engineers with the benefit of experienced legal representation for little expense, the Court found it insufficient to justify removing the applicant's capacity to pursue and act in his own claim.

The removal or denial of legal capacity to take proceedings may also impair the substances of the right to a court, as in *Canea Catholic Church v. Greece*, where a court ruling that the applicant church did not have legal personality led to the dismissal of actions brought to assert its property rights.

(c) *Time bars and prescription periods*

Time limits imposed on the bringing of claims are acceptable in the interests of good administration of justice, pursuing the legitimate aims of preventing stale claims and injustice to defendants faced with evidential difficulties in contesting allegations relating to distant events and of promoting legal certainty.[10] The Convention organs have accepted final time limits which cannot be waived, even when new facts have arisen after the expiry of the time limit[11] or where knowledge of the cause of action only arose after the time limit.[12] A three-year time limit was found to be reasonable for paternity proceedings[13] and six years for assault and trespass to the person, including sexual abuse.[14]

Possibly if a time limit was so short as to render it practically impossible to act within time this might be found to impair the essence of the right of access to court.[15] However, short procedural time limits will not offend where the inability to act derives from the applicant's conduct. In *Hennings v. Germany*, where the applicant complained of the one-week notice given by the prosecution notice, the Court found that his main excuse for not reacting to the notice was the claim that he had no key to his mailbox, which he could reasonably have been expected to obtain and for which failure to do so the authorities were not responsible.

---

[9] *cf. Winterwerp v. Netherlands*, October 24, 1979, Series A, No. 33, paras. 73–76 where there was a breach of Art. 6 para. 1 where proceedings by which a person committed to mental detention had the automatic effect of divesting him of all capacity to administer his property but did not afford him the opportunity to appear or be represented.

[10] *Stubbings*, para. 51.

[11] *X v. Sweden*, 9707/82, (Rep.) October 6, 1982, 31 D.R. 223 where the applicant had three years from the birth of the child to contest paternity but did not discover that he could not be the father until 24 years after the birth.

[12] In *Stubbings*, the applicants, sexual abuse victims, complained that they were subject to an inflexible time-limit which they were unable to comply with (suppressed memories; delayed awareness that health problems derived from the abuse). The Court found under Art. 6 that a six year time-limit from the age of majority did not impair the essence of right of access to court, noting no general principle of flexibility in time-limits (*i.e.* from date of knowledge) accepted in Contracting States. Under Art. 14, contrary to the Commission which found no reason for treating the applicants differently from personal injury victims who enjoyed a flexible time-limit, the Court found that assuming that different categories of claimants for injuries were in analogous positions, there was objective and reasonable justification for the difference in that the categories had evolved separately in domestic law and civil claims were less obvious to victims of negligently inflicted harm than those injured by deliberate actions.

[13] No. 9707/82, see n.11.

[14] *Stubbings*.

[15] See 28090/95, *M.P. v. Spain*, (Rep.) October 21, 1997 pending before the Court: where the applicants had a three day time-limit to bring an appeal, lodged it by sending it recorded delivery within that time but it was rejected since it was received by the court registry outside that time.

(d) *Coherent procedures*

Applicants may claim a right to procedures which are "coherent" and afford a clear, practical and effective opportunity to challenge administrative acts which affect their rights.[16] Thus where the law was considered to be extremely complex, and an applicant could not be expected to realise time for appealing ran from the official publication of the decree rather than the serving of the notice,[17] there was a denial of effective access to court. A court rejection of an applicant's claim for damages for HIV infection from a blood bank on the basis that he had accepted compensation from a special fund was found to constitute a restriction on access to court since the applicant reasonably relied on the wording of the applicable legislation in bringing his claim and the system was not sufficiently clear or sufficiently attended by safeguards to prevent misunderstanding as to the procedures for making use of available remedies and the restrictions stemming from the simultaneous use of them.[18]

(e) *Costs*

Prohibitive levels of court costs may raise issues of denial of access to court. See Part IIA: Costs in court.

(f) *Arbitration*

While it is compatible with Article 6 for parties to regulate their civil disputes by submitting them to arbitration proceedings in place of the courts, as this pursues the aim of encouraging non-judicial settlements and relieving the courts of an excessive burden, issues may arise where the procedure is not voluntary or part of a contractual arrangement to which the applicant can be considered to have agreed.[19]

(g) *Denial of legal aid*

Lack of legal aid may constitute a denial of access to court. See Part IIA: Legal representation in civil proceedings.

(h) *Lack of enforcement*

Execution of a judgment is an integral part of the "trial" for the purposes of Article 6, paragraph 1, the guarantees of which would become illusory if a domestic legal system allowed a final, binding judicial decision to remain inoperative to the detriment of one party. Failure by the authorities for more than five years to take the necessary steps to comply with a final enforceable judicial decision was therefore found in *Hornsby v. Greece* to deprive Article 6, paragraph 1 of all useful effect and disclose a violation.

---

[16] *De Geoffre de la Pradelle*, para. 34 where designation of land as conservation area affected the applicant's property rights.
[17] *i.e.* the time-limit expired the day before the Prefect served the notice of the decree on him.
[18] *Bellet*.
[19] *See e.g.* 11960/86, *Sweden*, (Dec.) July 13, 1990 where the applicants had entered into a private contractual relationship providing for arbitration; 23173/94, *Turkey*, (Dec.) October 22, 1996; 28101/95, *Netherlands*, (Dec.) November 27, 1996 where the Commission implied that some court review of arbitration was required but that arbitral bodies did not need to comply with Art. 6 para. 1 and strict conditions could be imposed for the quashing of an arbitral award.

4. Defences, privileges and immunities

Potential problems arise where an immunity or special defence exists effectively preventing an action taking place. This can be either set out specifically in statute or be the result of development of case law.

In *Ashingdane* (concerning an immunity in statute barring civil actions by mental patients against staff or health authorities without leave on grounds of bad faith or lack of reasonable care) and in *Fayed v. United Kingdom* (concerning the privilege of Department of Trade Inspectors from suit in defamation),[20] the Court found it unnecessary to decide whether these limitations defined the content of the right or imposed a restriction on access, since in any event the essence of the right to a court was not impaired nor the principle of proportionality transgressed. In *Ashingdane*, it found that the applicant could nonetheless take proceedings for negligence, whereas in *Fayed*, it found that any restriction pursued a legitimate aim (ensuring the proper conduct of the affairs of public companies) in a proportionate manner, noting that the applicants had brought their private lives into the public domain for their own purposes and that in producing their report the Inspectors were bound by a duty to act fairly and were subject to judicial review where they exceeded the bounds of their function.

Where public immunity certificates remove a court's jurisdiction to examine the applicant's claims on a particular point, this may deprive him of effective access to court. In *Tinnelly and McElduff v. United Kingdom*,[21] where statutory provisions conferring rights against discrimination in employment did not apply where an act was done for the purpose, *inter alia*, of safeguarding national security, the Commission found that the serving of a certificate by the Secretary of State as conclusive evidence that national security applied conferred a form of immunity from action. The applicants should, however, have been able to argue and present evidence to show that the act was not in pursuance of national security considerations and the court been able to freely appreciate the issue.

Immunities bestowed by the courts may also be found to bar effective access to court. In *Osman v. United Kingdom*,[22] which concerned the public policy immunity from suit in negligence for the police acting in an investigative or preventative capacity, the majority of the Commission found that this denied the applicants access to court for their claim in respect of police failure to prevent death and injury caused by an armed attack. The majority of the Commission considered that the concern to prevent police time being taken up in litigation or overcautious policing was not sufficient to justify removing the jurisdiction to consider serious claims of interferences with fundamental rights.

5. Limitations in the scope of review of the court

Where claims may be put before a court but the court does not have full jurisdiction over the facts and legal issues in the case, there may be a denial of access to court.[23] Relevant factors here relate to the subject-matter of the dispute, whether the court may, even with limited competence, adequately review the disputed issues; the manner in which that decision was arrived at; and the content of the dispute, including the desired and actual grounds of the action or appeal.[24]

---

[20] The Commission found the privilege operated as a limitation on access to court.
[21] 20390/92 and 21322/93, (Rep.) April 8, 1997 pending before the Court.
[22] 23452/94, (Rep.) July 1, 1997.
[23] Where a court appears to deprive itself of jurisdiction over crucial aspects of a dispute, it may also be regarded as depriving the applicant of access to a "tribunal" satisfying the requirements of Art. 6, para. 1 as having jurisdiction to examine all questions of fact and law relevant to the dispute before it, *e.g. Terra Woningen BV v. Netherlands,* December 17, 1996, R.J.D., 1996–VI, No. 25.
[24] *Bryan,* para. 45.

In childcare cases, where parents sought access or custody of their children in local authority care, judicial review, which was confined to issues of illegality, unfairness or irrationality, was not sufficient, the Court finding that Article 6, paragraph 1 required that local authority decisions be reviewed by a tribunal having jurisdiction to examine the merits.[25]

In administrative areas of a more technical nature, restricted review of decisions by courts has been accepted as a common feature in Contracting States. In *Zumtobel v. Austria* where there was dispute over expropriation of property and the appropriate compensation, with expert assessments of property values etc., the Court referred to a notion of expediency, *i.e.* that courts may legitimately restrict their review of decisions by the administrative authorities on grounds of expediency. In *Bryan v. United Kingdom*, concerning enforcement proceedings for breach of planning controls in respect of the applicant's "barns", appeal to the High Court restricted to points of law was not a problem even though its jurisdiction over the facts was limited. The Court emphasised the specialised character of planning, considered to be the typical example of the exercise of discretionary judgment in the regulation of citizen's conduct and this was found to render it reasonable to restrict the intervention of courts *vis-à-vis* the factual application of this discretion, the realm of the executive. The manner in which the decision that reached, in particular, that the planning enquiry beforehand was run on fair, adversarial lines, was also a relevant factor in finding the limited review compatible with Article 6.[26]

Cross-reference

Part IIA: Costs in court
Part IIA: Legal representation in criminal proceedings
Part IIA: Legislative interference in judicial process

---

[25] *e.g. W v. U.K.*, see n.3, para. 82.
[26] *e.g. Air Canada*, where H.M. Customs confiscated an aircraft and released it on payment of a sum of money, the Court rejected the applicant's arguments that the scope of judicial review would have been too narrow to allow any meaningful challenge of the very broad discretion bestowed on the Customs by statute; having regard to the special statutory context, judicial review was found to satisfy the requirements of Art. 6 for the complaints of a foster-carer about the proceedings before the social services fostering panel which resulted in his being de-registered No. 32788/96, *U.K.,* (Dec.) April 9, 1997.

Adequate time and facilities

Key provision:

Article 6, paragraph 3(b) (adequate time and facilities for preparation of defence).

Key case law:

Campbell and Fell v. U.K., June 28, 1984, Series A, No. 80; 7 E.H.R.R. 165; *Bricmont v. Belgium*, July 7, 1989, Series A, No. 158; 12 E.H.R.R. 217; *Hadjianastassiou v. Greece*, December 16, 1992, Series A, No. 252–A; 16 E.H.R.R. 219; *Melin v. France*, June 22, 1993, Series A, No. 261–A; 17 E.H.R.R. 1; *Kremzow b. Austria*, September 21, 1993, Series A, No. 268–B; 17 E.H.R.R. 322; *Domenchini v. Italy*, November 15, 1996, R.J.D. 1996–V, No. 22; *Vacher v. France*, December 17, 1996, R.J.D., 1996–VI, No. 25; *Foucher v. France*, March 18, 1997, R.J.D., 1997–II, No. 33.

1. General considerations

The provisions of Article 6, paragraph 3 depend on a criminal charge having been brought, though the Court has commented that these elements were implicit in the notion of fair trial in civil matters *mutatis mutandis*.[1] The case law indicates that they are aspects of the general principle of fairness guaranteed in the first paragraph, to be assessed not on the basis of an isolated incident or element but having regard to the proceedings as a whole. Thus while the sub-paragraphs of Article 6, paragraph 3 exemplify the notion of fair trial in typical procedural situations, their intrinsic aim is always to ensure or contribute to ensuring the fairness of the proceedings as a whole.[2] Frequently, therefore, complaints under Article 6, paragraph 3 are considered in conjunction with Article 6, paragraph 1.

Where non-criminal cases are concerned, questions of adequate time and facilities are dealt with under Article 6, paragraph 1, having regard to fairness and other applicable principles such as equality of arms, adversariality and the ability to practicipate effectively in the proceedings.[3]

Applicants' access to evidence, facilities and lawyers is restricted to what is necessary for the defence.[4] In *Lamy v. Belgium*, the applicant's inability to consult the investigation file for the first 30 days did not affect the preparation of his defence and the Commission found that Article 6, paragraph 3(b) was not applicable.[5]

2. Victim status

A person acquitted in criminal proceedings may not complain of alleged difficulties in preparing his defence.[6] An accused who declares that he will not take any further part of the proceedings cannot complain either.[7]

---

[1] *Albert and Le Compte v. Belgium* February 10, 1983, Series A, No. 58; 5 E.H.R.R. 533.

[2] *Canada v. Italy* (Rep.) July 12, 1984, Series A, No. 96 (settled before the Court).

[3] See Part IIA: Fair Trial Guarantees, General Principles: Fairness.

[4] *e.g.* 8463/78, (Dec.) July 9, 1981, 26 D.R. 24. No right to unrestricted access to lawyer for example; 11396/85 U.K., (Dec.) December 11, 1986 50 D.R. 179 where there were practical limits to what prison authorities can be expected to provide by way of legal research material to prisoners. The applicant had not been given all he had listed but prison had bought two books, and he had access to some others in library. The Commission noted that his grounds of appeal had covered relevant points and the court summarised his argument on nullity before rejecting it in line with authority.

[5] *Lamy v. Belgium* No. 10444/83 (Rep.) October 8, 1987, Series A No. 151.

[6] 8083/77, (Dec.) March 13, 1980, 19 D.R. 223 where applicant was no longer a victim when the Court of Appeal quashed the contempt charge.

[7] 8386/78, (Dec.) September 10, 1980, 21 D.R. 126 where counsel withdrew from the trial, embarassed by statements made by applicant contradicting his not guilty plea, the applicant refused offer of help from solicitors or to pursue questions himself or call witnesses.

3. Adequate time

Where time for the preparation of trial is concerned, short periods have been found acceptable. It is also expected that applications for adjournment are made where there is an alleged problem. Thus, in *Campbell and Fell v. United Kingdom*, concerning prison disciplinary proceedings, five-days notice of charges and notice of the report given the day before were found by the Court to be sufficient in the circumstances, noting that no request was made for an adjournment.[8] On that basis, the Commission has so far appeared to accept the practice of briefing counsel at short notice, presuming that by training they are able to cope with short delay and that if they cannot, they have the possibility to apply for an adjournment.

Where time limits are imposed which, either by their brevity or vagueness, render the right of any appeal or application ineffective, violations have been found.[9] The rules by which courts function must be "sufficiently coherent and clear".[10] The Court has emphasised that States must ensure that everyone charged with a criminal offence benefits from the safeguards of Article 6, paragraph 3. Putting the onus on convicted defendants to find out when an allotted time started to run or expire was not compatible with the diligence which the Contracting States must exercise to ensure that rights are enjoyed in an effective manner.[11]

4. Facilities: access to evidence

The Commission has held that everyone charged with a criminal offence should have facilities which include the opportunity to acquaint himself with the results of the investigations carried out throughout the proceedings for the purposes of preparing his defence. Although a right of access to the case file was not expressly guaranteed, such a right could be inferred. It went so far as to hold that it was irrelevant by whom or when the investigation was carried out — the applicant had the right for the purposes of exonerating himself or obtaining a reduction in sentence to access to all relevant elements that have been or could be collected by the competent authorities. The right was stated to be restricted to those facilities which assist or may assist in defence.[12]

While that principle seems far-reaching, in practice it has proved of narrow application. Where the applicant alleged lack of access to a special folder of the public prosecutor, the Commission, although stressing that refusal of access would breach Article 6, paragraph 3(b) if it contained anything enabling him to exonerate himself or reduce his sentence, found that there was no evidence from the applicant that it contained anything relevant and the Commission was not prepared to presume that the Government had not complied with its obligations.[13] This seems to put a difficult burden on applicants to prove the

---

[8] *Kremzow*; where the Attorney General served documents three weeks before an appeal hearing, and the applicant could also have consulted the file beforehand, no violation.

[9] *Hadjianastassiou*; where the time-limit for lodging grounds of appeal expired before the applicant knew the substance of the court's decision convicting him, there was a violation since he was as a result unable usefully to exercise his right of appeal. It was not enough, as the Government argued, for parts to be included in oral pronouncement and for him to deduce the rest from the proceedings beforehand. See *Vacher* below.

[10] *Melin*; para. 24, *Vacher*, para. 26.

[11] *Colozza v. Italy*, February 12, 1985, Series A, No. 89; 7 E.H.R.R. 516 para. 28. See *Melin* and *Vacher*, concerning the practice of the *Cour de Cassation* where the court did not inform appellants in person when the hearing of the appeal was to take place or set time-limits to lodge submissions. There was a violation where in *Vacher*, his appeal was dismissed eight days before he lodged his ground of appeals. There was no violation for *Melin*, who was a lawyer who had worked at the court of cassation bar. Also in *Melin* there was a four month 10 day delay before the dismissal of the appeal, whereas in *Vacher* it was two months days which was shorter than the average time usually taken.

[12] *Jespers v. Belgium* 8403/78, (Rep.) December 14, 1981, 27 D.R. 61.

[13] *Jespers, ibid.*

relevance of material they have not seen. In the same case, lack of access to a police report was accepted since the information was repeated in other documents on the basis that the defence knew of the conversation which the report recounted and could have taken steps to identify the police officer who was present. Where information is available elsewhere or within means of an applicant and lawyer to obtain, it appears that this is sufficient by way of facilities, even if it might be reasonably be expected (as well as quicker and more efficient) for the prosecution to provide the information.[14] Where there was a more fundamental lack of access to the case file, however, and no opportunity to make copies at first instance, then the possibility to make application for access at the appeal stage did not prevent a violation of Article 6, paragraph 3(b).[15]

Limitations on evidence disclosed to applicants has been found acceptable where there is a sound reason in the interests of the administration of justice, even though arguably the evidence was of significance to the defence.[16] The Commission has accepted the practice of *ex parte* applications by the prosecution to withhold evidence which are decided by the trial judge on sight of the material: it seemed to consider the review by the judge and the procedural check of the Court of Appeal's further review of all the materials and issues, and a lack of any appearance of arbitrariness was sufficient.[17]

5. Facilities: overlap with access to legal advice

There is overlap with the right of access to a lawyer, since representation by a lawyer is often meaningless unless some prior consultation is included in the "facilities" provided to the defendant.[18] In *Domenchini v. Italy*, monitoring of a prisoner's correspondence with his defence lawyer was a violation of Article 6, paragraph 3(b) since the delay resulting in forwarding a letter led to the filing of grounds after the statutory time limit.

6. Article 6, paragraph 3(a) — information about the charge

Where an applicant has not been promptly informed of the charge, this may prevent him from properly preparing his defence at the same time.[19] The Commission commented that the provision of information that an offence has been reclassified is not enough, since it has to be in good time and allow the opportunity to organise the defence on the basis of the reclassification.[20]

Cross-reference

Part IIA: General Principles
Part IIA: Legal representation in criminal proceedings
Part IIA: Information about the charge

---

[14] See also *Bricmont,* where there was no violation for failure of the authorities to produce an exhibit which the applicants said would have enabled them to rebut the charge, since they did not give details supporting this, nor violation from failure to obtain a special audit of accounts since the applicants had never asked for one.

[15] *Foucher,* para. 32.

[16] 11219/84, (Dec.) July 10, 1985, 42 D.R. 287 where defence lawyer was barred from discussing with the applicant the statements of anonymous witnesses which would allow him to identify them (even though he argued he could not be informed of important parts of the testimony for that reason).

[17] *e.g. U.K.,* 29335/95, (Dec.) January 17, 1997 where evidence relevant to the credibility of prosecution witnesses was not disclosed since it would uncover details of police informers.

[18] *Campbell and Fell.*

[19] *e.g. Chichlian and Ekindjian v. France,* November 28, 1989, Series A, No. 162–B; 13 E.H.R.R. 553.

[20] *Bulgaria* 24751/94, (Dec.) June 28, 1995, 82–A D.R. 85.

Appeals

Key provision:

Article 6, paragraphs 1–3 (fair trial).

Key case law:

Delcourt v. Belgium, January 17, 1970, Series A, No. 11; 1 E.H.R.R. 355; *Pretto v. Italy*, December 8, 1983, Series A, No. 71; 6 E.H.R.R. 182; *Axen v. Germany*, December 8, 1983, Series A, No. 72; 6 E.H.R.R. 195; *Sutter v. Switzerland*, February 22, 1984, Series A, No. 74; 6 E.H.R.R. 272; *Monnell and Morris v. U.K.*, March 2, 1987, Series A, No. 115; 10 E.H.R.R. 205; *Ekbatani v. Sweden*, May 26, 1988, Series A, No. 134; 13 E.H.R.R. 504; *Granger v. U.K.*, March 28, 1990, Series A, No. 174; *Kremzow v. Austria*, September 21, 1993, Series A, No. 268–B; 17 E.H.R.R. 322; *Brualla Gomez de la Torre v. Spain*, December 19, 1997, to be published in R.J.D. 1997.

1. General considerations

There is no right to appeal contained in the Convention itself (as opposed to the right provided for in Article 2 of Protocol No. 7). However, where a judicial system provides appeals, the Court had held since Delcourt[1] that the fundamental guarantees of Article 6 will apply. Having regard, however, to the fact that in many Contracting States, higher instances take differing forms, this is subject to the rider that the way in which Article 6 applies will depend on the special features of the proceedings. This includes consideration of the functions, in law and practice of the appellate body, its powers and the manner in which the interests of the parties are presented and protected.[2]

There can therefore be no right as such to any particular kind of appeal or manner of dealing with appeals. For example, Article 6 does not require that matters of new evidence raised on appeal should be remitted by the Court of Appeal for rehearing by a jury.[3] Access to a final instance may be regulated and include conditions such as the requirement to be represented by a lawyer or the imposition of fines for abusive appeals.[4]

2. Application of Article 6 guarantees

Where an appeal lies, the provisions of Article 6 generally will apply. However, there may be special features of the appellate body which will affect the way in which the guarantees apply.

One important distinction has been found to exist between appeal and leave to appeal proceedings in the United Kingdom. In *Monnell and Morris v. United Kingdom*, concerning leave to appeal proceedings where applicants may not necessarily be present or represented, the Court found that the nature of leave to appeal proceedings was such that this was not incompatible with fairness, as it did not involve the rehearing of witnesses or re-examination of the facts, the issue being whether there were arguably grounds which would justify the hearing of an appeal. The principle of equality of arms was respected since the prosecution did not appear and the applicants' interests were sufficiently safeguarded by receipt of legal advice as to their prospects of appeal, and the opportunity

---

[1] *Delcourt*, p. 14, paras 25–26.
[2] *Monnell and Morris* para. 56.
[3] *e.g.* 14739/89, *U.K.*, (Dec.) May 9, 1989, 60 D.R. 296.
[4] 16598/90, *Greece*, (Dec.) November 16, 1990 66 D.R. 260; 15384/89, (Dec.) May 9, 1994, 77–A D.R. 5.

to submit written submissions. Where applicants had already been represented by counsel at trial, this was considered sufficient to safeguard their interests. In contrast, in *Granger v. United Kingdom*, where an appeal hearing was in issue, the failure to provide the accused with legal representation did disclose a violation of Article 6, paragraph 3(c). The prosecution was present and the applicant could not be expected to present his case effectively.

Where appeal proceedings involve points of law or limited cassation procedure, the approach has been taken that lack of a public hearing at second or third instances may be justified by these special features.[5] Where, however, as in *Ekbatani v. Denmark*, a court of appeal has to examine both facts and law and could not fairly or properly determine the issues without hearing the applicant in person and the complainant, the denial of a public hearing or right to be heard in person may disclose a violation. Similarly, where an appeal raises issues as to the personality of the applicant, he may claim a right to be present and participate.[6] The Court has stated, however, that the personal attendance of accused does not take on the same crucial significance for an appeal hearing as it does for trial.[7]

The requirement for higher instance courts to render judgments publicly also has been interpreted in light of their role. Where their role is to confirm lower instances' judgments or give brief decisions, it has been considered sufficient if lower courts judgments were rendered publicly and "public" access is provided to the superior court's decisions for by way of, for example, access to court registry records.[8]

Presumption of innocence may also cease to apply in appeal proceedings, due to the nature of those proceedings, after an accused has been convicted at first instance. It has therefore not been successfully argued that the Court of Appeal in England fails to comply with this requirement in the test which it applies in deciding whether or not to quash a conviction in light of new evidence.[9]

The Court has also found that conditions of access to superior appeal courts, in particular Supreme Courts, may be stricter and more formal. It found no deprivation of access to court in *Brualla Gomez de la Torre v. Spain*, where an applicant's appeal to the Supreme Court was rejected due to an intervening change in the criteria for cases which it could deal with. The applicant has, it noted, received two full hearings in lower instance courts.

3. Curing effects at first instance

In criminal proceedings, the extent to which a higher court can cure defects in the trial is limited, though the possibility exists where the nature of the defect permits the effect of the shortcoming to be rectified.[10] An accused, however, has a right to a fair trial at first instance with its fundamental guarantees and it is no argument to state that, for example, the appellate body offers the independence lacking below.[11]

---

[5] *Axen; Sutter.*

[6] *Kremzow.*

[7] *Kamasinki v. Austria,* December 19, 1989, Series A, No. 168; 13 E.H.R.R. 36 para. 107; where the Court also noted the difficulties that attach to attendance of prisoners.

[8] *Pretto, Axen, Sutter.*

[9] 14739/89, above n.3.

[10] *De Cubber v. Belgium,* October 26, 1984, Series A, No. 86, para. 33; *Adolf v. Austria,* March 26, 1982, Series A, No. 49 paras. 38–41 where the Supreme Court cleared of any finding of guilt an applicant in respect of whom the lower court had respected the presumption of innocence; *Edwards v. U.K.,* November 25, 1992, Series A, No. 247–B; 15 E.H.R.R. 417 where it was found that the review of a conviction by the Court of Appeal in light of material which had not been revealed to the defence by the police at the trial did remedy the defects in the original trial.

[11] *Findlay v. U.K.,* February 25, 1997 R.J.D., 1997–I, No. 30 para. 79; *Foucher v. France,* March 18, 1997, R.J.D., 1997–II, No. 33, where denial of access to the file at first instance was not cured by the possibility of applying for access on appeal.

In civil proceedings, proceedings lacking in conformity with Article 6, paragraph 1 may be cured by subsequent review of the case by a tribunal offering the necessary guarantees and appropriate scope of review.[12]

---

[12] *Le Compte, Van Leuven* and *De Meyere v. Belgium,* June 23, 1981, Series A, No. 43; 4 E.H.R.R. 1: where the proceedings before the Appeals Council were not in public and not cured by a public hearing before the Court of Cassation since it could not take cognisance of the merits of cases; *Bryan v. U.K.,* November 22, 1995, Series A, No. 335–A; 21 E.H.R.R. 342 and *Zumtobel v. Austria,* September 21, 1993, Series A, No. 268–A; 17 E.H.R.R. 116 where restricted scope of review was accepted; 18874/91 *Switzerland,* (Dec.) January 12, 1994, 76–A D.R. 44.

Costs in court

Key provisions:

Article 6, paragraph 1 (access to court); Article 6, paragraph 2 (presumption of innocence); Article 1 of Protocol No. 1 (peaceful enjoyment of possessions).

Key case law:

Airey v. Ireland, October 9, 1979, Series A, No. 32; 2 E.H.R.R. 305; *Tolstoy v. U.K.*, July 13, 1995, Series A, No. 323; 20 E.H.R.R. 442; *Masson and Van Zon v. Netherlands*, September 28, 1995, Series A, No. 327; 22 E.H.R.R. 491; *Robins v. U.K.*, September 23, 1997, R.J.D., 1997–V, No. 49.

1. General considerations

Problems have principally arisen as to the compatibility with the presumption of innocence of costs orders against acquitted accused; in the procedural context, the extent to which the guarantees of Article 6, paragraph 1 apply, to the costs procedure following substantive litigation; and the impact which costs may have on effective access to court.

The obligation to pay "litigation costs" *per se* does not appear to involve any right under substantive provisions since they are "contributions" within the meaning of the second paragraph of Article 1 of Protocol No. 1 and escape detailed supervision.[1] The Commission has found the basic rule that costs follow the event in civil litigation is reasonable as such, acting as a disincentive to unnecessary litigation and providing for at least the recovery of some of the successful litigant's costs.[2]

2. Costs orders against acquitted accused

See Part IIA: Presumption of innocence.

3. Applicability of Article 6, paragraph 1 to costs procedures

(a) *Criminal proceedings*

Whether proceedings concerning reimbursement of legal costs incurred during criminal proceedings in which an applicant has been acquitted attracts the guarantees of Article 6 depends principally on whether there is a "right" to costs in domestic law. The grant to a public authority of a considerable measure of discretion may indicate that no right is recognised in domestic law, as in *Masson and Van Zon v. Netherlands*, where the courts made awards where "reasons in equity" existed.[3]

---

[1] 15434/89, *U.K.*, (Dec.) February 15, 1990 64 D.R. 232.

[2] *ibid.*

[3] The Commission had differed, finding there was a dispute which was pecuniary in nature and the fact a person was entitled under Dutch law to seek such damages indicated that it could be claimed on arguable grounds that there was right recognised under Netherlands law.

(b) *Civil proceedings*

Costs procedures following substantive proceedings were generally held by the Commission not to involve the civil rights of the individual.[4] Recently, this view was overruled by the Court in the *Robins v. United Kingdom* case. It now appears established that, where the substantive proceedings involve civil rights and obligations, the costs proceedings, even if separately decided, must be seen as a continuation of the substantive litigation and fall within the scope of Article 6, paragraph 1. Thus, four years taken in the costs proceedings in the *Robins* case disclosed a violation of the reasonable time requirement in Article 6, paragraph 1. Considering the limited or technical nature of the issues arising in costs proceedings, it is perhaps doubtful that the guarantees of Article 6 will apply with full vigour, for example, as regards the requirement for public hearings or the public rendering of decisions.

4. Access to court

Though there is no right to free proceedings or right to repayment of costs and fees in civil matters,[5] the high cost of proceedings may raise a problem with respect to right of access to court, if it can be shown to have a prohibitive effect depriving an applicant of the essence of the right having regard to the *Ashingdane v. United Kingdom* principles.[6]

For example, there was a lack of effective access to court in *Airey v. Ireland*, where the costs for representation (legal aid was not available) in a separation application were "very high" and the procedure so complex and the subject matter entailing an emotional involvement such that the applicant could not be expected effectively to present her own case.

Where a precondition for appeal is the payment into court of security for costs, the cases indicate that such orders which pursue the legitimate aim of protecting one party from being faced with an irrecoverable bill for legal costs if the party appealing is unsuccessful, will disclose no problem if there has been a full and fair hearing at first instance and the court gives a fair chance to the applicant to argue that the interests of justice require an appeal to go on.[7]

5. Penalty costs orders against lawyers

Wasted costs orders against lawyers in courts do not concern the determination of civil rights or obligations and thus do not attract guarantees of Article 6. Nor have they been

---

[4] 8569/79, *Ireland*, (Dec.) May 8, 1985, 42 D.R. 23 where the substantive action concerned public law; 21775/93 *Portugal*, (Dec.) May 25, 1995 81 D.R. 48 where the Commission found the question of costs was a subsidiary issue to the main civil proceedings and did not concern civil rights and obligations; majority Commission opinion in *Robins v. U.K.*

[5] *e.g.* 6202/73, *Netherlands*, (Dec.) March 16, 1975, 1 D.R. 66; 15488/89 *Italy*, (Dec.) February 27, 1995, 80–A D.R. 14.

[6] *i.e.* whether the essence of the right is impaired and whether the restriction pursues a legitimate aim in a proportionate manner, having regard to the proceedings as a whole. See Part IIA, Access to Court.

[7] See *Tolstoy,* where the applicant, the unsuccessful defendant in defamation proceedings (1.5 million pounds award) was required to pay £124,900 as security for costs in order to pursue his appeal. However the applicant had had a full hearing at first instance; there was no indication that the sum was not a fair reflection of the likely costs and the Court of Appeal considered in effect the merits of the case in deciding whether or not the measure would amount to a denial of justice, basing, thereby showing no arbitrariness but basing itself on a full and thorough evaluation of the relevant factors. If the matter had been decided purely by the registrar of the court, the result might not be so obvious.

found to involve the determination of a criminal charge.[8] Such orders are regarded as "contributions" within the meaning of second paragraph of Article 1 and not an interference with possessions.[9]

---

[8] 10615/83, (Dec.) July 3, 1984, 38 D.R. 213 where a solicitor was ordered to bear costs thrown away in his absence, the Commission found the matter was disciplinary in the context of the administration of justice and though it was imposed by way of a sanction, neither the penalty nor the nature of the proceedings were such as to involve a "criminal charge".

[9] 7544/76, *Germany,* (Dec.) July 12, 1978 14 D.R. 60 where counsel had to bear the costs of suspension of a criminal trial, these were contributions reasonably regarded as "necessary" within the meaning of the second paragraph; 7909/74, *Austria,* (Dec.) October 12, 1974 15 D.R. 160.

Double jeopardy

Key provisions:

Article 6, paragraph 1 (fair trial); Article 4 of Protocol No. 7 (no trial or punishment in same State for offence for which already acquitted or convicted).

Key case law:

Gradinger v. Austria, October 23, 1995, Series A, No. 328–C.

1. General considerations

The principle of "double jeopardy" or *non bis in idem* which prohibits that a person be tried twice for the same offence is not expressly contained in the Convention itself but subject to specific provisions in Article 4 of Protocol No. 7, which only came into force relatively recently for a number of Contracting States.[1]

2. Fairness

While it has not been clearly excluded that the trial of a person for the same offence in the same State could not raise separate issues of fairness under the Article 6, paragraph 1,[2] which would be of relevance where a State had not ratified Protocol No. 7, such a possibility would be difficult to reconcile with the existence of the specific right in Protocol No. 7, notwithstanding arguments as to widespread recognition of the fundamental principle.

The Commission has stated that in interpreting the Convention it may be useful to take into account provisions contained in other international legal instruments, including the Brussels Convention which barred prosecution of a person in one State in respect of whom a trial had been finally disposed of in another State concerning the same facts. However, there was no question of lending provisions of the Convention a scope which the Contracting Parties expressly intended to exclude by means of a Protocol No. 7 which applied only to prosecution of a person twice within the same State. Article 6 could not therefore be interpreted to imply a more extended right applying between States.[3]

3. Article 4 of Protocol No. 7

There has been one significant case, indicating that administrative proceedings which penalise the same conduct which was in issue in criminal proceedings will offend the prohibition, notwithstanding the differing designations and the allegedly different purposes of the proceedings. In *Gradinger v. Austria*, the applicant, who killed a cyclist while driving, was convicted of causing death by negligence rather than the more serious crime of being under influence of alcohol since his level was below the prescribed limit. The administrative authorities proceeded to fine him for driving under the influence of drink on the basis of a medical report which deduced that in fact he was over the limit. Since both decisions were based on the same conduct, there was a violation of Article 4 of Protocol No. 7.[4]

[1] November 1, 1988. The United Kingdom and Ireland have not ratified.
[2] 9433/81, December 11, 1981, 27 D.R. 233; 8945/80, *Germany,* (Dec.) December 13, 1983, 39, D.R. 43.
[3] 21072/92, *Italy,* (Dec.) January 1, 1995, 80–B D.R. 89; where the applicant had allegedly been tried in Denmark and Italy in respect of the same matters.
[4] The Commission had commented strongly that it would render Art. 4 of Protocol No. 7 ineffective if States could prosecute an individual under nominally different offences.

Entrapment and agents provocateurs

Key provision:

Article 6, paragraph 1 (fair trial); Article 8 (private life).

Key case law:

Ludi v. Switzerland, June 15, 1992, Series A, No. 238; 15 E.H.R.R. 173.

1. General considerations

The fine line between entrapment, incitement and undercover investigations is a well-known problem. There have been few cases. Issues arise as to the fairness of proceedings where a person becomes involved in a crime which would otherwise not have been contemplated but for the suggestion of the agent provocateur, as to whether the use of evidence gathered undercover is compatible with the rights of the defence and potentially, with respect for private life.

2. Relevance to fairness of trial

(a) *Incitement of offences*

The essential question appears to be whether the role played by undercover agents was determinative for the commission of the offence such that it affects the fairness of the subsequent proceedings. The Commission appears to give weight to the factor whether the conduct of the agents was the essential if not exclusive cause of the crime being committed.[1]

Where in *Teixeira de Castro v. Portugal*[2] the police agents were found by the domestic courts to have exerted "very great insistence" and to have acted as provocateurs, there was a violation whereas in *Radermacher and Pferrer v. Germany*,[3] where the Commission found on the facts that the police informer had not initiated the offence there was no violation, notwithstanding the active and important role of the police informer in the events leading to the delivery of counterfeit money. In the latter case, the Commission found no objection as such to the use of undercover agents or informers and had regard to procedural safeguards in the proceedings, namely, the possibility of challenging the conviction and that the involvement of undercover agents was seen as a mitigating factor in sentencing.

In the *Teixeira de Castro* case, the Commission appeared also to lend weight to the fact that the police agents were acting of their own initiative and not in the context of an operation to control drug trafficking under the supervision of a magistrate. The involvement of a magistrate would seem to reflect a perception that a controlled operation is less likely to provoke the commitment of offences which otherwise would not have occurred. Remark was also made to a lack of finding by the domestic courts that the applicant exhibited behaviour which might have lead to the conclusion that he was ready to commit the offence even without the intervention of the police officers.

(b) *Use of evidence from undercover agents*

The principal consideration is whether the evidence in a trial is put forward in such a way that the proceedings are fair as a whole, including an adequate opportunity for the defence

---

[1] *Teixeira de Castro v. Portugal*, 25829/94, February 25, 1997, (Rep.) pending before the Court, para. 46, referring to U.S. Supreme Court case law and the position in Germany.
[2] *ibid.*
[3] *Germany*, 12811/87, (Rep.) (1990) 34 Ybk of the E.C.H.R. 274.

to challenge any evidence before the court. In *Ludi v. Switzerland*, where evidence against the applicant included an undercover agent's report, the inability to challenge the evidence of the agent in oral proceedings disclosed a violation of Article 6, paragraph 3(d) taken together with Article 6, paragraph 1. The Court was not satisfied that a need for anonymity excluded all defence challenge of the agent, since matters could have been arranged in such a way as to protect the legitimate police interest in being able to use their agent again. Thus the rights of the defence were limited to such an extent that the applicant was deprived of a fair trial.

3. Invasion of privacy complaints

Deliberate intervention in the affairs of suspects, involving the striking up of relationships and personal contact, might appear to involve an invasion of privacy and to raise problems of respect for private life under Article 8.

In *Ludi*, where an applicant was convicted on drugs charges on the basis of evidence of an undercover agent and telephone tapping, the Commission found an interference with private life from the involvement of the undercover officer together with telephone tapping, since the words intercepted had resulted wholly or in part from the relationship which the officer established with the suspect, gaining entry by subterfuge to the suspect's private life. That aspect was not in accordance with the law required by Article 8, paragraph 2, as there was insufficient safeguards against arbitrariness, in particular, the legislation did not specify in which cases undercover work was allowed, on whose authority, for what duration or using which methods. The Court did not rule on this aspect, however, since it found that the use of an undercover agent alone or the telephone interception did not affect private life. It observed that the undercover agent's actions took place within the context of a large cocaine deal, that the applicant must have been aware that he was engaged in criminal acts and that he ran the risk of encountering an undercover police officer. There was apparently no interference with a Convention right on the basis that the conduct concerned related to criminal activities, which seems an unduly strict approach tailored to this case.

While the conformity with "law" of telephone tapping and secret surveillance has often been reviewed by the Convention organs, the only challenge to "lawfulness" of undercover activities has been *Ludi*. The nature of undercover work would, however, appear to render it less amenable than telephone tapping to detailed statutory regulation and it is arguable that the minimum would suffice.

Cross-reference

Part IIA: Evidence
Part IIA: Witnesses
Part IIB: Interception of communications
Part IIB: Surveillance and secret files

Equality of arms

Key provision:

Article 6, paragraph 1 (fair trial).

Key case law:

Delcourt v. Belgium, January 17, 1970, Series A, No. 11; 1 E.H.R.R. 355; *Bonisch v. Austria*, May 6, 1985, Series A, No. 92; 9 E.H.R.R. 191; *Monnell and Morris v. U.K.*, March 2, 1987, Series A, No. 115; 10 E.H.R.R. 205; *Brandstetter v. Austria*, August 28, 1991, Series A, No. 211; 15 E.H.R.R. 378; *Borgers v. Belgium*, October 30, 1991, Series A, No. 214; 15 E.H.R.R. 92; *Ruiz-Mateos v. Spain*, June 23, 1993, Series A, No. 262; 16 E.H.R.R. 505; *Schuler-Zgraggen v. Switzerland*, June 24, 1993, Series A, No. 263; 16 E.H.R.R. 405; *Dombo Deheer B.V. v. Netherlands*, October 27, 1993, Series A, No. 274–A; 18 E.H.R.R. 213; *Bendenoun v. France*, February 24, 1994, Series A, No. 284; 18 E.H.R.R. 54; *Van De Hurk v. Netherlands*, April 19, 1994, Series A, No. 288; 18 E.H.R.R. 481; *Hentrich v. France*, September 22, 1994, Series A, No. 296–A; 18 E.H.R.R. 440; *Stran Greek Refineries v. Greece*, December 9, 1994, Series A, No. 301–B; 19 E.H.R.R. 293; *Schouten and Meldrum v. Netherlands*, December 9, 1994, Series A, No. 304; 19 E.H.R.R. 432; *Lobo Machado v. Portugal*, February 20, 1996, R.J.D., 1996–I, No. 3; *Bulut v. Austria*, February 22, 1996, R.J.D., 1996–II, No. 3; *Vermeulen v. Belgium*, February 20, 1996, R.J.D., 1996–I, No. 3; *Ankerl v. Switzerland*, October 23, 1996, R.J.D., 1996–V, No. 19; *Mantovanelli v. France*, March 18, 1997, R.J.D., 1997–II, No. 32.

1. General considerations

Equality of arms, in the sense of "fair balance", is one of the long-established elements of fairness.[1] It is sometimes linked to considerations that proceedings must be adversarial. It implies that each party must be afforded a reasonable opportunity to present his case — including his evidence — under conditions which do not place him at a substantial disadvantage *vis-à-vis* his opponent.[2] This means in principle the opportunity for the parties to a criminal or civil trial to have knowledge of and comment on all evidence adduced or observations filed.[3] Particular importance is to be attached in this context to the appearance of the fair administration of justice.[4]

2. Aspects of equality of arms

(a) *Opportunity to receive and respond to submissions*

The right to adversarial trial has been held to mean that in a criminal case both prosecution and defence must be given the opportunity to have knowledge of and comment on the observations filed and the evidence adduced by the other party. While there are various ways by which national law may seek to achieve this, whatever method is chosen should ensure that the other party will know if observations are filed and will get a real opportunity to comment.[5] Where civil rights and obligations are concerned, even in

---

[1] *Delcourt*, para. 28.
[2] *Dombo Deheer*, para. 33.
[3] *Ruiz Mateos*, para. 63; *Lobo Machado*, para. 31.
[4] *Bulut*, para. 47; *Borgers*, para. 24.
[5] *Brandstetter*, para. 67: a violation was found in that the prosecutor's submissions were not communicated to the applicant nor their existence notified. It was not enough that in the Austrian system the applicant could have anticipated something might have been submitted and applied to see the complete file nor that there was indirect opportunity to answer the prosecutor's points which had been adopted in the appeal court's judgment.

the context of the special nature of Constitutional Court proceedings, parties must as a rule be granted free access to the observations of the other participants and a genuine opportunity to comment on them.[6]

Where legal officers, such as *procureurs-general*, participated in proceedings, the Court initially accepted that they could be regarded[7] as neutral or impartial and therefore no breach of equality resulted from failure to give parties or an accused the opportunity to know the content of and respond to their interventions. However, the Court has since found that where a legal officer has recommended that an application be rejected or accepted, such an officer can no longer be regarded as neutral.[8] The presence of such legal officers during court deliberations has also disclosed inequality of arms, since even if their role is limited to neutral points of law, which may be doubted, an accused may legitimately fear that the opportunity is used to bolster arguments to obtain a particular result.[9]

It is not necessary for identifiable prejudice to flow from a procedural inequality. In *Bulut v. Austria*, the Government's argument that the observations submitted by the Attorney-General to the Supreme Court (but not served on the applicant) merely recommended the court to deal with the case in a particular manner, was rejected. It was for the defence to assess whether a submission deserved a reaction and unfair for the prosecution to make submissions to a court without the knowledge of the defence.

(b) *Opportunity to present or give evidence*

Where a party is permitted to confine its submissions in a summary fashion which deprives the other party of an effective opportunity to counter the case against them, there may be a breach.[10] Generally, a party may claim the right to give evidence on his own behalf, despite technical domestic rules.[11]

(c) *Inequal status of witnesses*

The position of experts must be attended by a fair balance between the parties. The mere fact that official experts in expropriation proceedings worked for the administrative authority was not a ground in itself for justifying fears that they did not act with neutrality. Otherwise it would place unacceptable limits on the possibility to obtain expert advice.[12] In respect of court appointed experts, problems may arise where the expert has

---

[6] *Ruiz-Mateos:* violation where the Counsel for the State had filed observations concerning validity of impugned law and applicants not given opportunity to reply; conversely, in *Van de Hurk:* no violation where the minister changed his ground of objection to quota request before the Tribunal, since the applicant had a genuine opportunity to respond.

[7] *Delcourt.*

[8] *e.g. Bulut; Borgers,* while the Court still accepted the independence and impartiality of the procureur's department, it referred to the evolution in its case-law concerning the importance to be attached to appearances and to the increased sensitivity of the public to the fair administration of justice.

[9] *e.g. Lobo Machado; Borgers; Vermeulen.*

[10] *e.g. Hentrich,* where in the proceedings to challenge the pre-emption of the applicant's purchase of property by the Revenue, she was unable to challenge the Revenue's assessment by adducing evidence to show that she had acted in good faith and that the proper market price had been paid and, in addition the tribunals allowed the Revenue to confine its reasons for pre-emption to a summary and general statement.

[11] *Dombo Deheer;* violation found where the applicant company was in a civil dispute with a bank over an oral agreement but the applicant company director was barred from being a witness since he was identified with a party to the proceedings whereas the bank representative, who was involved in the transaction, could be a witness.

[12] *Zumtobel v. Austria* September 21, 1993, Series A, No. 268–A, 17 E.H.R.R. 116 para. 86: the applicants were free to submit their own private expert opinions, which if disregarded, could be subject to appeal.

been involved in the prosecution but whether a violation arises will depend on whether he in fact exercised a privileged role.[13]

Technical differences may be discounted, as in *Ankerl v. Switzerland*, where the wife was not allowed to take an oath, but her evidence was nonetheless before the Court.[14]

(d) *Procedural inequalities*

Potentially, issues might arise where one party enjoys by their position advantages over the conduct of the proceedings or access to material.[15] However, these may to some extent be unvoidable where State authorities are concerned and the Court seems to take a pragmatic approach to whether the applicant has in fact been disadvantaged. For example, there was no prejudice from the fact that a time limit was not imposed on the submission by the Attorney-General of his position paper to Supreme Court[16]; there was no inequality of arms where the applicant complained of not being given copies of the contents of the file held by tax authorities in tax evasion proceedings, where the Court found that those documents were not among those relied on by the tax authorities and he did not put forward any reasons for seeking disclosure.[17] As to an alleged ability by a State authority to delay the proceedings, the Court found no substance in the allegations that the authority could choose the order of cases, since no preceding case prejudged the applicant's claims or prevented him putting his arguments.[18]

(e) *Legislative interference*

Where a State intervenes by passing a law to ensure the favourable outcome of pending proceedings in which it is a party, there may be a striking inequality of arms. In those circumstances, it is not enough that in the proceedings before the domestic court a party is able to present all the arguments he wished, since fairness applies to the proceedings in their entirety, not merely the hearing *inter partes*. Such intervention infringes the principle that each party must be afforded a reasonable opportunity to present his case under conditions that do not place him at a substantial disadvantage *vis-à-vis* his opponent.[19]

Cross-reference

Part IIA: General Principles
Part IIA: Evidence
Part IIA: Witnesses
Part IIB: Review of detention, Equality of arms under Article 5, paragraph 4

---

[13] *Bonisch*; violation of Art. 6 para. 1, since the expert whose report had lead to the applicant's prosecution was appointed court expert with special status and powers to question whereas the applicant's expert had limited attendance possibilities; *Brandstetter*; no violation, since, even though the expert who initiated the proceedings was appointed court expert, there was no inequality as he did not question anyone and the defence, largely agreeing with the court expert, relied on matters on which he had made no submissions.

[14] *Ankerl.*

[15] e.g. *Mantovanelli*; violation as regarded the applicants' lack of effective involvement in the preparation of the court expert report whereas the defendant hospital staff were involved (framed as infringement of the adversarial principle).

[16] *Kremzow*, para. 75.

[17] *Bendenoun; Schuler-Zgraggen*, where there was no inequality of arms in relation to complaints of access to material — the applicant had access to the file and was able to make copies, while the report which she did not see was not part of the file, was summarised in another document she had seen and the courts did not have the full report either.

[18] *Schouten and Meldrum.*

[19] *Stran Greek*, para. 46.

Evidence

Key provision:

Article 6, paragraphs 1–3 (fair hearing guarantees).

Key case law:

Barbera, Messegue and Jabardo v. Spain, December 6, 1988, Series A, No. 146; 11 E.H.R.R. 360; *Schenk v. Switzerland*, July 12, 1988, Series A, No. 140; 13 E.H.R.R. 242; *H v. France*, October 24, 1989, Series A, No. 162; 12 E.H.R.R. 74; *Edwards v. U.K.*, November 25, 1992, Series A, No. 247–B; 15 E.H.R.R. 417; *Dombo Deheer B.V. v. Netherlands*, October 27, 1993, Series A, No. 274–A; 18 E.H.R.R. 213.

1. General considerations

The admissibility and assessment of evidence is, primarily, a matter for the domestic courts. Whether or not the courts have correctly assessed the evidence is largely outside the competence of the Commission and Court.[1] There is only a limited supervision by the Convention organs, having regard to their perception that they are neither a fourth instance nor in an appropriate position to overrule the opinion of the local courts who have first-hand knowledge and experience.

The Convention organs examine, in terms of the Convention, whether the requirements of Article 6, paragraph 1 as to fairness have been complied with, including the way in which evidence was submitted.[2] This means generally that any alleged evidential imbalance or unfairness will be looked at in light of the proceedings as a whole and as to whether an applicant has been deprived of an ability to participate effectively in the proceedings or the position of the defence significantly impaired.[3] In criminal cases, the whole matter of the taking and presentation of evidence must also be looked at in light of the guarantees of paragraphs 2 and 3. For example, in light of the presumption of innocence, when carrying out their duties, the members of a court should not start with the preconceived idea that the accused has committed the offence and the burden of proof is on the prosecution and any doubt should benefit the accused. It also follows that the prosecution must inform the accused of the case against him so that he may prepare and present his defence, and to adduce evidence sufficient to convict him.[4]

2. Presentation of evidence at trial

In principle, the evidence against the accused should be presented in court publicly, subject to an adversarial procedure. In *Barbera, Messegue and Jabardo v. Spain*, where a case of robbery and murder resulting in sentences of up to 36 years was examined in a trial lasting one day, the Court found a violation cumulatively on a number of defects but, particularly, in that very important pieces of evidence were not adequately adduced and discussed at the trial in the applicants' presence and under the watchful eye of the public. This included material evidence such as weapons relied on by the prosecution but not produced in court; confessions which the applicants stated were given under duress and in

---

[1] 6172/73, *U.K.*, (Dec.) July 7, 1975, 3 D.R. 77.
[2] *Barbera*, para. 68.
[3] *e.g. Dombo Deheer*, para. 33 (equality of arms): a party must have a reasonable opportunity to present his case, including evidence under conditions not placing him at a substantial disadvantage *vis-à-vis* his opponent.
[4] *Barbera*, paras. 76–77.

which respect the Court had reservations since they were obtained during a long period of incommunicado custody; and lack of attendance at the trial of witnesses whose statements incriminated the applicants and whom the applicants had no prior possibility of examining.

There is a duty on courts to ensure they have evidence properly and fairly presented. Thus in *Barbera*, the Court held that even though the prosecution and defence had agreed to waive having the documentary evidence read out and presented at trial, this did not dispense the court from complying with the requirements of Article 6, paragraph 1.

Regarding the methods of presentation of evidence, the Commission criticised the practice where, before an appeal court, the statement of a witness was read out and he was asked if he maintained it, noting that it may reduce the value of the statements of a witness if he is reminded of what he said before. However, since the parties were able to put further questions to the witnesses and to challenge the correctness of the evidence, the method was not of such a character that it rendered the hearing unfair.[5]

3. Admissibility of evidence

Article 6, paragraph 1 does not lay down any rules as to the admissibility of evidence which is primarily a matter for regulation under national law.[6] A failure by the applicant or his counsel to object to any evidence is an important, if not necessarily decisive factor, bearing in mind the courts' general duty to ensure the fairness of the proceedings of their own motion.[7] Also relevant are any aspects which might remedy or mitigate the alleged unfairness and where the matter was subject to careful scrutiny by the appeal courts.

(a) *Accomplices*

Issues of fairness may arise where an accomplice, who has been granted immunity, gives evidence against an applicant. However, where that fact was made known to the defence and the terms of the agreement explained to the jury, who were warned by the judge and the matter examined on appeal, no violation occurred.[8] Where a guilty plea of a co-accused to tax evasion charges was admitted as evidence at the applicant's trial, this did not render the proceedings unfair, given, *inter alia*, the judge's warning to the jury of its limited relevance.[9]

(b) *Indirect or documentary evidence*

The Commission has held that use of indirect evidence is not prohibited by the Convention. It has had regard however to whether it was the sole evidence. In a German case, where the applicant complained that the evidence before the court was largely written statements of alleged witnesses it noted that the conviction was based primarily on the accused's own statements made before the first instance court.[10] Also relevant is whether an applicant has had an opportunity to challenge at some stage a witness whose written evidence was used against him.[11] The Commission has also had regard to whether

[5] 10486/83, *Denmark,* (Dec.) October 9, 1986, 49 D.R. 86.
[6] *e.g.* 12505/86 *Germany,* (Dec.) October 11, 1988, 58 D.R. 106.
[7] *e.g.* 7306/75 *U.K.,* (Dec.) October 6, 1976, 7 D.R. 155; 8876/80 *Belgium,* (Dec.) October 16, 1980, 23 D.R. 233.
[8] 73605/75 *U.K.,* (Dec.) October 6, 1976, 7 D.R. 115; 17265/90 *Switzerland,* (Dec.) October 21, 1993, 75 D.R. 76 where the Commission commented that evidence of co-accused whose sentences had been reduced should be regarded critically but since there was other evidence and their evidence was subject to challenge, no unfairness disclosed.
[9] 28572/95 *U.K.,* (Dec.) January 17, 1997.
[10] 8945/80 *Germany,* (Dec.) December 13, 1983, 39 D.R. 43.
[11] See Part IIA: Fair trial guarantees, Witnesses.

the authorities made efforts to find or bring the absent witness and in the case of impossibility seems to regard it acceptable, even desirable, that the proceedings are not abandoned.[12]

(c) Hearsay

The Commission has held that the rule excluding hearsay evidence is legitimately based on the aim of ensuring the best evidence before the jury, who can evaluate the credibility of witnesses and avoid reliance on evidence untested by cross-examination. It is not, in principle, contrary to Article 6, paragraph 1.[13]

(d) Confessions

Where convictions are based on confessions allegedly obtained by coercion, the Convention organs still apply the principle that the assessment of the evidence is for the domestic courts. The Commission has held that the guarantee of a fair trial requires a procedure whereby the validity of such evidence can be examined. It found the process in English courts of a *voire dire* (adversarial trial-within-a-trial, including evidence and argument, before a judge in the absence of jury) ruling on admissibility and the probative value being left to the jury was sufficient safeguard and provided in that case a fair trial.[14]

In *Ferrantelli and Santangelo v. Italy*, where the applicants complained that they had been convicted on the basis of confessions obtained by coercion, the Court, noting that the question of ill-treatment was subject to specific investigation by the judicial authorities, who ruled no case to answer against the alleged perpetrators, found insufficient material before it depart from their findings. This appears to allow confessions to be used as long as the domestic courts investigate any allegations of ill-treatment. In the absence of this procedural guarantee, and where doubts arise due to the prolonged periods in police custody without being brought before a judicial officer, doubts as the confessions produced may disclose unfairness.[15]

(e) Unlawfully obtained evidence

The use of unlawfully obtained evidence is not excluded as a matter of principle. However, the way the evidence was obtained and the role played at the trial will be examined in the context of ascertaining whether the trial as a whole was fair.[16] In practice, alleged unlawful elements have not been found to disclose unfairness, where the conviction is not wholly or mainly based on the evidence and it has been subject to adversarial proceedings, with the applicant able to challenge it.[17] Thus, in *Schenk v. Switzerland*, the Court found that the use of a recording, unlawful insofar as it was not ordered by the investigating judge, did not render the trial automatically unfair or furnish a ground for violation *per se*. It examined the fairness factors, and it was sufficient that the applicant had knowledge of the tape and

---

[12] 20341/92 *Netherlands*, (Dec.) January 6, 1993, 74 D.R. 241.

[13] 12045/86 *U.K.*, (Dec.) May 7, 1987 52 D.R. 273, the applicant, convicted of buggery and murder, complained of the exclusion of hearsay evidence consisting of statements made by a third party to the police and others implicating another in the commission of the crime. The Commission considered the exclusion of the evidence was not unfair in the circumstances.

[14] 9370/81 *U.K.*, October 13, 1983, 35 D.R. 75.

[15] *e.g. Barbera* above; *Hazar and others v. Turkey* 16311–13/90 etc. (Dec.) November 11, 1991, 72 D.R. 200 settled (Rep.) December 10, 1992, 73 D.R. 111, where the applicants alleged numerous violations, torture in police custody, 14 days in police custody before being brought before a judicial officer and that the confessions obtained from the alleged torture were used to obtain convictions.

[16] 12505/86 *Germany*, (Dec.) October 11, 1988, 58 D.R. 106.

[17] 12505/86 *loc. cit.;* 13274/87, *Italy,* (Dec.) September 6, 1990, 66 D.R. 164.

circumstances in which it was recorded and was able to challenge its use. The Court also attached weight to the fact it was not the only evidence on which the conviction was based.

4. Weight given to evidence

The probative value of evidence also falls essentially for the domestic instance to determine.[18] Thus in an Italian case, where the applicant, accused of instigating a murder, complained that the conviction was based only on circumstantial evidence and presumptions, the Commission found it sufficient that the charges against him were presented and debated adversarially before the trial judges and the Court of Cassation. It did list the elements of indirect proof presumably implying that the "whole body of indirect evidence" on which the judges based their finding that he ordered the execution was not unfair.[19]

5. Failure to disclose evidence

There is a requirement for the prosecution to disclose to the defence all the material evidence for or against the accused.[20] Whether or not a failure to do so discloses objectionable unfairness will depend on an assessment of the proceedings as a whole. In *Edwards v. United Kingdom*, the failure to disclose that a witness had failed to identify the applicant from a police photograph album and the existence of fingerprints (not the applicant's) at the scene of the burglary, was a defect, but the Court found it was cured since when this was discovered there was an independent enquiry and the case was referred to the Court of Appeal where counsel had every opportunity to persuade the court to overturn the conviction, including the possibility to apply for police officers to be called as witnesses.

However, in a German case, where the appeal court upheld the prosecutor's appeal from the applicant's acquittal referring to reports obtained after the trial and which had not disclosed to the applicant, the Commission declared the case admissible and it was subsequently settled.[21]

There may also be occasions where courts approve the non-disclosure of evidence to the defence, for example on application by the prosecution authorities to protect informers or security interests. The extent to which *ex parte* review of the material by the trial judge or the Court of Appeal provides sufficient procedural guarantees of fairness, and lack of arbitrariness is under examination in cases pending before the Commission.[22]

6. Refusal to call expert evidence or take other investigative measures

The Commission has not excluded that the refusal by a court to order an expert, hear a witness or to accept other types of evidence might in certain circumstances render the proceedings unfair. Since, however, it was for the national courts to decide what was necessary or essential to decide a case, it has commented that only in exceptional circumstances would it conclude that a decision of a national court in such a matter violated the right to a fair hearing. It gave the example of where an applicant adduced

---

[18] e.g. 12013/86 *Italy*, (Dec.) March 10, 1989, 59 D.R. 100.

[19] 12013/86 *loc. cit.*

[20] *Jespers v. Belgium* 8403/78 (Rep.), December 14, 1981, 27 D.R. 61; *Edwards*, para. 36.

[21] 13467/87, (Rep.) December 11, 1989, 63 D.R. 156.

[22] e.g. *Rowe and Davis v. U.K.*, 28901/95; *Jasper v. U.K.*, 27052/95 and *Fitt v. U.K.*, 29777/96 (Decs.) September 15, 1997. However, no arbitrariness or unfairness was found in *U.K.* 29335/95, (Dec.) January 17, 1997 where the trial judge and the Court of Appeal reviewed the material concerned.

some evidence which the court rejected outright, refusing to allow verification of it and without giving sufficient reasons for its refusal.[23]

7. Admission of new evidence

Where new evidence following conviction appears, there is no right to retrial.[24] Nor where a case is re-opened, is there a requirement for a complete rehearing. In a case introduced by the Birmingham Six, the Commission rejected the argument that the new evidence adduced should have been put in front of a jury rather than reviewed by the Court of Appeal. The Commission noted that a jury trial was not essential to fairness[25] and it found the proceedings before the Court of Appeal fair, that court having stated that if there had been the least doubt that the verdicts were safe or satisfactory it would quash the convictions.[26]

8. Assessment of evidence

Notwithstanding the general statements above, the Commission has stated that it will intervene where the assessment of evidence discloses gross unfairness or arbitrariness.[27] What this means in practice has not been explored. It seems to indicate that there may be verification that there is some evidence to support the decision. The fact that a judge prefers particular evidence is unlikely to be sufficient, unless his stated reasons for doing so disclose a fundamental unsoundness.[28]

Cross-reference

Part IIA: Entrapment
Part IIA: Presumption of innocence
Part IIA: Witnesses
Part IIB: Interception of communications

---

[23] *H. v. France*, where the courts refused the applicant's application for a medical opinion for the purpose of proving the causal link between his medical treatment and the injury to his health. The Commission noted, *inter alia*, that there was medical and expert evidence in the file and it was evident that the decision was reached after fairly detailed examination of whether or not there was sufficient reason to presume the existence of a causal connection. The Court agreed, commenting adversely on the applicant's dilatoriness in taking proceedings. See however *Vidal v. Belgium*, April 22, 1992, Series A, No. 235, where appeal court overturned an acquittal without hearing witnesses requested by the applicant, and without giving reasons.

[24] 7761/77 (Dec.) May 8, 1978, 14 D.R. 171.

[25] Not all Contracting States rely on, or admire the institution.

[26] 14739/89 *U.K.*, (Dec.) May 9, 1989, 60 D.R. 296.

[27] *e.g.* 7987/77, *Austria*, (Dec.) December 13, 1979, 18 D.R. 31, where an applicant company complained of the assessment of compensation for expropriation of property, the Commission found that evaluation of the evidence was necessarily a matter within the appreciation of the courts and could not be reviewed by the Commission unless the judge has drawn grossly unfair or arbitrary conclusions from the facts before him. However the judge's findings of fact that the company had not intended to work the clay deposits and thus no loss of profit ensued were supported by the higher court and the reasons on which decisions based sufficient to exclude any arbitrariness; 22909/93, *Turkey*, (Dec.) September 6, 1995, 82–B D.R. 25.

[28] *e.g. mutatis mutandis, Schuler-Zgraggen v. Switzerland*, June 24, 1993, Series A, No. 263; 16 E.H.R.R. 405 No. 263, where the court relied on factors discriminatory on grounds of sex.

Independence and impartiality

Key provision:

Article 6, paragraph 1 (fair trial by "independent and impartial tribunal").

Key case law:

Ringeisen v. Austria, July 16, 1971, Series A, No. 13; 1 E.H.R.R. 455; *Le Compte v. Belgium*, June 23, 1981, Series A, No. 43; 4 E.H.R.R. 1; *Piersack v. Belgium*, October 1, 1982, Series A, No. 53; 5 E.H.R.R. 169; *Sramek v. Austria*, October 22, 1984, Series A, No. 84; 7 E.H.R.R. 351; *Campbell and Fell v. U.K.*, June 28, 1984, Series A, No. 80; 7 E.H.R.R. 165; *Belilos v. Switzerland*, April 29, 1988, Series A, No. 132; 10 E.H.R.R. 466; *De Cubber v. Belgium*, October 26, 1984, Series A, No. 86; 7 E.H.R.R. 236; *Hauschildt v. Denmark*, May 24, 1989, Series A, No. 154; 12 E.H.R.R. 266; *Langborger v. Sweden*, June 22, 1989, Series A, No. 155; 12 E.H.R.R. 416; *Oberschlick (No. 1) v. Austria*, May 23, 1991, Series A, No. 204; 19 E.H.R.R. 389; *Demicoli v. Malta*, August 27, 1991, Series A, No. 210; 14 E.H.R.R. 47; *Pfeiffer and Plankl v. Austria*, February 25, 1992, Series A, No. 227; 14 E.H.R.R. 692; *Sainte-Marie v. France*, November 24, 1992, Series A, No. 253–A; 16 E.H.R.R. 116; *Fey v. Austria*, February 24, 1993, Series A, No. 255; 16 E.H.R.R. 387; *Nortier v. Netherlands*, August 24, 1993, Series A, No. 267; 17 E.H.R.R. 273; *Saraiva de Carvalho v. Portugal*, April 22, 1994, Series A, No. 286–B; 18 E.H.R.R. 534; *Van de Hurk v. Netherlands*, April 19, 1994, Series A, No. 288; 18 E.H.R.R. 481; *Debled v. Belgium*, September 22, 1994, Series A, No. 292–B; 19 E.H.R.R. 506; *Diennet v. France*, September 26, 1995, Series A, No. 315–B; 21 E.H.R.R. 554; *Procolo v. Luxembourg*, September 28, 1995, Series A, No. 326; 22 E.H.R.R. 193; *Thomann v. Switzerland*, June 10, 1996, R.J.D., 1996–III, No. 11; *Ferrantelli and Santangelo v. Italy*, August 7, 1996, R.J.D., 1996–III, No. 12; *Findlay v. U.K.*, February 25, 1997, R.J.D., 1997–I, No. 30; *De Haan v. Netherlands*, August 26, 1997, R.J.D., 1997–IV, No. 44 .

1. General considerations

This core element of the notion of a fair trial has generated many cases. The two aspects are often interlocked, a lack of independence coinciding with a lack of objective impartiality. Thus the two notions are frequently treated together. The basic principles were established early. The cases tend merely to illustrate their application to a diverse number of factual and procedural circumstances.

2. Independence

The tribunal or court must be independent of the executive and the parties[1] and also of the legislature or Parliament.[2] As to whether it satisfies the condition of independence, regard is had to the manner of appointment of the members, the duration of their office, the existence of guarantees against outside pressure and the question whether the body presents an appearance of independence.[3]

---

[1] *Ringeisen*, para. 95.
[2] *e.g.* 8603/79, (Dec.) December 18, 1980, 22 D.R. 220; *Demicoli*, breach of privilege proceedings before the Maltese House of Representatives against a journalist for defamatory articles — the Commission found lack of independence, the Court found lack of impartiality.
[3] *Piersack*, para. 27.

Aspects and guarantees

(a) *Composition*

The presence of legally-qualified or judicial members is a strong indicator of independence, as in *Le Compte v. Belgium* where on the Appeals Council the members were made up equally of medical practitioners acting in personal capacity and members of the judiciary, being chaired by one of latter.[4] Where, in *Sramek v. Austria*, the regional authority in land disputes included three civil servants from the local government, which was a party in the proceedings, there was a legitimate doubt about their independence, since even though there was no indication that they were subject to instructions, they were subordinate in status to the officer acting for the local government in the proceedings. Where patents bodies were entirely made up of civil servants, who had no guarantees of irremovability and were appointed from a pool to act at first instance and on appeal, the Commission found problems of structural independence.[5]

(b) *Appointment and term of office*

The mere fact that a minister appoints members does not pose a problem since in many systems judges are so appointed on approval by ministers of justice. However, the irremovability of judges is in general a corollary of their independence although the lack of this guarantee is not necessarily fatal. For example, although there were no regulations or guarantees concerning Board of Visitors members, it was accepted that although the Home Secretary could require a member to resign this would be done in only the most exceptional circumstances.[6]

Fixed terms also tend to be regarded as a guarantee. In *Le Compte*, six-year terms for Appeals Council members was found to furnish a guarantee. Three-year terms for Board of Visitor members in *Campbell and Fell v. United Kingdom* were considered rather short but it was acknowledged that the posts were unpaid and it was difficult to get volunteers.

(c) *Appearances*

While weight is given to the proper appearance of independence, suspicions have to be to some extent objectively justified. In *Campbell and Fell*, the Commission thought that the Board of Visitors did not give an appearance of institutional independence, since it fulfilled a number of administrative roles in prison and was associated by prisoners with prison management. The Court, however, found that the fact the Board had administrative roles was not decisive and it could still be independent. It also took the view that in a custodial setting certain sentiments by prisoners were inevitable but there was no indication that they would be reasonably entitled to think that the Board was dependent on the prison.

Where a police board acting in a judicial capacity was concerned however, appearances were found to be decisive in the context of determining whether it acted as a "tribunal" for the purposes of Article 6, paragraph 1. In *Belilos v. Switzerland*, a member of the police sat in his personal capacity on the Police Board, was not subject to orders, took an oath and could not be dismissed. Since, however, he was a civil servant who would return afterwards to other departmental duties and would tend to be seen as member of the police force subordinate to superiors and loyal to colleagues, this disclosed a situation which could undermine the confidence which courts should inspire.

---

[4] *Campbell and Fell*, where the Board of Visitors' membership was generally half magistrates.
[5] *British American Tobacco v. Netherlands*, November 20, 1995, Series A, No. 331–A; 21 E.H.R.R. 409, No. 331.
[6] *Campbell and Fell*, para. 80; *McMichael v. U.K.*, (Rep.), Series A, No. 307–B, paras. 63 and 114, Comm.Rep. where the Commission had doubts concerning removability of members of the Children's Panel by the Secretary of State.

(d) *Subordination to other authorities*

The tribunal must not be subject to instructions in an adjudicatory role although it may be compatible for a minister to issue general guidelines.[7] Where a minister had the power to set aside the decisions issued by the tribunal deciding on milk quota disputes, the Court found that the tribunal lacked independence, even though it seemed that the power was not exercised in practice. The power to give a binding decision which could not be altered by a non-judicial authority was identified as inherent in the guarantees of Article 6, as confirmed by the use of the term "determination".[8]

3. Impartiality

The Court distinguishes between subjective impartiality — the existence of actual prejudice on the part of a judge or tribunal — and objective impartiality — whether a judge offers guarantees sufficient to exclude any legitimate doubt in this matter.[9] Personal impartiality of a judge is to be presumed, until there is proof to the contrary.[10] In practice, this is a very strong presumption, no claim of bias by a judge having been successful notwithstanding frequent complaints.[11]

In the context of *objective impartiality*, appearances are of a certain importance having regard to the confidence which the courts must inspire in the public in a democratic society and above all in criminal proceedings in the accused. The latter aspect was later qualified when the Court noted that the standpoint of the accused was important but not decisive. What was determinant was whether the fear can be held to be objectively justified.[12] The Court has also commented that any judge in respect of whom there is a legitimate reason to fear a lack of impartiality must withdraw.[13]

Major problems have arisen where a judge plays different procedural roles in the course of the proceedings; where the composition of a court coincides with a court which has been involved in some related aspect of the case or where the tribunal is not, as the traditional court, made up of trained legal or judicial members.

(a) *Differing roles of a judge*

This problem tends to arise on the Continent where judges can have an investigating role or there is overlap between the prosecution (*e.g. "procureur"*) and the trial court. The mere fact that a judge has been involved in decisions on remand is not sufficient to render him lacking in objective impartiality, special features being required beyond the judge's knowledge of the case file, the fact that he has looked at questions of risk on remand decisions or assessments of the existence of a prima facie case.[14] It is necessary for the

---

[7] *Campbell and Fell*; concerning the Board of Visitors.

[8] *e.g. Findlay*, where the convening officer had power to confirm the court martial decision.

[9] *Piersack*, para. 30.

[10] *Le Compte*, para. 58.

[11] Judicial comments, interventions have never been found, taken in the context of the proceedings as a whole, to disclose actual prejudice, even in one unpublished case, where a judge in his summing-up likened the accused to a rat leaving a sinking ship.

[12] *Hauschildt*, para. 48; *Fey*, para. 30.

[13] *Piersack*, para. 30; *Nortier*, para. 33: objective test even where applicant's apprehensions may be understandable.

[14] *Sainte-Marie; Fey; Nortier; Saraivo de Carvalho.*

judge to have been squarely involved in deciding issues relevant to those in the trial or to have been involved in a prosecution capacity.[15]

(b) *Specialist tribunals*

It is accepted that there may be good reasons in technical areas for opting for special adjudicatory bodies.[16] The mere existence of professional connections between an applicant and members of a tribunal is generally not sufficient to cast doubt on their impartiality, even if it may be assumed there is a potential for a conflict of interests.[17] More direct links between members and a party may be required to raise issues but once a legitimate doubt is raised, it may not be enough to point to the presence of judicial members or a judicial casting vote.[18] In the military area, hierarchical dependence between court martial members and superior officers has caused problems, even where judicial members sat and the Commission has considered that the use of military tribunals over civilians *per se* raises problems of independence and impartiality.[19]

(c) *Dual roles*

Where a body has dual roles, which conflict, its independence and impartiality as an adjudicating body may be undermined. In *Procolo v. Luxembourg*, concerning a milk quota dispute, four members of the *Conseil d'Etat* had performed successive advisory and judicial roles in the case. This was capable of casting doubt on the structural impartiality of the judicial committee, giving rise to fears which were objectively justified and a legitimate doubt however slight that members might feel bound by their previous opinion.[20]

(d) *Rehearings*

Where a first instance decision is quashed on appeal and returned for a fresh decision, the fact that the same body, with or without the same membership, decides the matter again

[15] See *Piersack*, where a judge had previously been the head of the public prosecutor's section responsible for instituting the prosecution; *De Cubber*, where one of the three judges in the criminal court had been the investigating judge; *Hauschildt*, where the presiding judge had taken decisions on pre-trial detention, subject to a special feature that on nine occasions in deciding on remand he referred to a "particularly confirmed suspicion" that the accused committed the offence, *i.e.* the judge had to be convinced of a very high degree of clarity as to guilt, the difference with the issue to be settled at trial was tenuous and an applicant's fears were objectively justified; *Ferrantelli and Santangelo*, where the presiding judge on an appeal court had been involved in convicting co-accused in a judgment referring to the applicants' participation in events and the appeal judgment cited extracts from that earlier judgment when it convicted the applicants; *Oberschlick No. 1 v. Austria*, where a judge who participated in the judgment at first instance particpated in the appeal hearing against that judgment; *De Haan v. Netherlands*, where Judge presided over a tribunal called to decide upon an objection against a decision for which he was responsible.
[16] *British American Tobacco*, concerning patents.
[17] Where, in *Le Compte*, medical appeals council was made up of half doctors and half judicial members, the Commission found that the former could not be deemed neutral since their interests were close to those of the parties. The Court disagreed, finding that the composition on and the presence of a judicial chairman with casting vote was a definite assurance of impartiality (contrast *Langborger* below). In *Debled*, where the applicant doctor complained of the medical members of the medical appeals structure, the Court took a pragmatic approach, finding that the system generally acceptable as regarded structural objectivity; that the applicant threatened to paralyse the whole system if challenged members were excluded from all decisions; his complaints were general and abstract and not based on specific material facts showing any member was hostile towards him.
[18] *Langborger*, concerning the Housing and Tenancy Court, made up of two professional judges and two lay assessors nominated by property owners and tenants associations, where the lay assessors had close links with the two associations which sought to maintain a clause the applicant was challenging — there being a legitimate fear that their interests were contrary to his own, it was not sufficient that the judicial president had the casting vote.
[19] *Mitap and Müftüğlu v. Turkey*, March 25, 1996, R.J.D., 1996–II, No. 6 (Rep.).
[20] Four of five members sat on the advisory panel which gave its opinion on the regulation in issue.

does not *per se* disclose legitimate fears of lack of impartiality.[21] Thus in *Diennet v. France*, where the decision of a medical appeal tribunal was quashed by the Cour de Cassation for a procedural error, the inclusion of three of the same members in the second hearing which reached the same conclusion, raised no ground for legitimate suspicion. Where in *Thomann v. Switzerland*, an applicant was retried by the court which had convicted him *in absentia*, the Court considered that the judges would be aware that they had reached their first decision on limited evidence and would undertake fresh consideration of the case on a comprehensive, adversarial basis.[22]

(e) *Juries*

These principles apply equally to juries (see Part IIA: Fair Trial Guarantees, Juries).

4. Curing defects on appeal

Problems of independence and impartiality may be curable where a higher instance body provides a hearing with the necessary guarantees and adequate rehearing of the issues in civil cases. In *Le Compte* and *Belilos*, the higher instances did not have jurisdiction to re-examine the facts or merits and therefore their undoubted independence and impartiality was not sufficient. Following judgments dealing with specialist administrative areas,[23] less appears to be required by way of review by the judicial instances on grounds of expediency and the exercise of discretionary powers. In criminal cases, it appears that an accused can claim to have the full guarantees of independence and impartiality present at first instance.[24]

5. Waiver

The extent to which an accused may waive his right to impartial tribunal by failing to challenge judges has not been clearly decided. To the extent that waiver may be possible, the Court has stated that this must be limited and that minimum guarantees remain which cannot depend on the parties alone. In any event, the waiver must be established in an unequivocal manner. A failure to object in *Pfeiffer and Plankl v. Austria* to two court judges who had been investigating judges and disqualified was not sufficient.[25]

The waiver argument also failed in *Oberschlick (No. 1) v. Austria* where the presiding judge of a Court of Appeal had participated in previous proceedings and was not under the Code of Criminal Procedure supposed to sit. While the applicant did not challenge his presence, he did not know that two other judges were similarly disqualified and he could not be said to waive his right to impartial tribunal. The Court appeared to give weight to the failure to abide by the domestic rules aimed at eradicating reasonable doubts as to impartiality.

---

[21] *Ringeisen*, para. 97.

[22] The Court commented that to require a newly constituted court would give an applicant tried in absentia an advantage over a defendant who appeared at trial since in effect it would mean a rehearing and would also place too great a burden on courts.

[23] *Zumtobel v. Austria*, September 21, 1993, Series A, No. 268–A, 17 E.H.R.R. 116; *Bryan v. U.K.*, November 22, 1995, Series A, No. 335–A; 21 E.H.R.R. 342.

[24] *Findlay*.

[25] In circumstances where one of the judges approached an applicant, in the absence of a lawyer, concerning his disqualification and where under Austrian law, the disqualified judges were under an obligation not to act in judicial capacity in the case and to inform the President of the Court of their disqualification.

Cross-reference

Part IIA: Appeals
Part IIA: Juries
Part IIA: Tribunal established by law

Information about the charge

Key provision:

Article 6, paragraph 3(a).

Key case law:

Albert and Le Compte v. Belgium, February 10, 1983, Series A, No. 58; 5 E.H.R.R. 533; *Campbell and Fell v. U.K.*, June 28, 1984, Series A, No. 80; 7 E.H.R.R. 165; *Brozicek v. Italy*, December 19, 1989, Series A, No. 167; 12 E.H.R.R. 371; *Gea Catalan v. Spain*, February 10, 1995, Series A, No. 309; 20 E.H.R.R. 266; *De Salvador Torres v. Spain*, October 24, 1996, R.J.D., 1996–V, No. 19.

1. Applicability

The context of Article 6, paragraph 3(a) is criminal and it is to be seen as a particular aspect of the right to fair trial.[1] Nonetheless, in *Albert and Le Compte v. Belgium*, concerning disciplinary proceedings against doctors, the Court commented that the civil and criminal aspects of Article 6, paragraph 1 were not mutually exclusive and that Articles 6, paragraphs 2 and 3 were aspects of the notion of fair trial contained within paragraph 1 in the civil context.

2. Information about the charge

The Commission held that this includes not only the cause of the accusation (the material facts which form the basis of the accusation) but the nature of the accusation (the legal classification of these material facts) in order that the accused may prepare his defence, this being a prerequisite for ensuring the proceedings are fair.[2]

Information must in fact be received by the person: a legal presumption of receipt is not enough.[3] No particular form of notification is required.[4]

Common sense and practicality is to be applied in examining complaints. Though the Commission in *Gea Catalan v. Spain* found a violation where the prosecution referred in its submissions to aggravating factor one and the domestic court convicted on aggravating factor seven, the Court agreed with the domestic courts that it was a mere clerical error. The material facts relied on by the prosecution were the same relied on by the domestic court and factor seven was referred to expressly by the investigating judge on committal. In *De Salvador Torres v. Spain*, though the offence of simple embezzlement had been in issue in the lower courts, the application by the Supreme Court of the aggravating factor of abuse of public office did not disclose a violation since it had been an underlying factual element throughout, the relevance of which the applicant could not claim to be unaware.[5]

---

[1] *F.C.B. v. Italy*, August 28, 1991, Series A, No. 208–B; 14 E.H.R.R. 909 para. 29; *Can v. Austria*, (Rep.) July 12, 1984, Series A, No. 96; 8 E.H.R.R. 121, para. 29 (settled before the Court).

[2] *Gea Catalan*, based on line of Commission case law, *e.g. Zimmerman v. Austria*, 8490/79, (Dec.) March 12, 1981, 22 D.R. 140 (admissible complaint where an applicant was convicted by a judge of an offence not in the indictment), (Rep.) 30 D.R. 15 (settled); *Chichlian and Ekindjian v. France*, (Rep.) March 16, 1989, para. 65, Series A, No. 162–B; 13 E.H.R.R. 553 (settled before the Court).

[3] Italy 10889/84 May 11, 1988, 56 D.R. 40 where notification by the investigating judge was delivered to address, was signed by someone else and the applicant claimed that he did not receive it.

[4] *e.g. Erdogan v. Turkey*, 14723/89, July 9, 1992, 73 D.R. 81 the applicant complained that he was not formally served with the arrest warrant or indictment but the Commission seemed to find that he was aware of the terms of the arrest warrant and the fact that he did not get the indictment was attributable to his own conduct (he failed to go to embassy or return to Turkey).

[5] Also *Campbell and Fell*: where the applicant Campbell knew that he was accused of "mutiny" following disturbances in prison, the Court rejected his claim that he was not able to understand precisely what this term meant.

Where, however, an offence has been reclassified in a substantive sense, and this possibility has not been brought to the attention of the accused, a violation is likely to arise. In *Chichlian and Ekindjian v. France*, the two applicants were acquitted of a currency offence charged under section 7 of a decree and then convicted on appeal of the offence under section 1. The Commission noted that the material facts had always been known to the applicants but there was no evidence that the applicants had been informed by the relevant authority of the proposal to reclassify the offence before the appeal hearing.[6]

3. Language

The information about the charge must be in a language the applicant understands. In *Brozicek v. Italy*, where the German applicant was not Italian or resident in Italy and had clearly expressed his language difficulties to the court, the Court found that the authorities should have had the notification translated unless they were in a position to establish that he knew adequate Italian, which was not the case.[7]

4. Promptly

Though the requirement for information being provided is of promptness, the Commission has not appeared unduly demanding. Thus in one case, where there was a delay in notification of proceedings, the Commission noted that the applicant was not affected immediately. Also he was served with a notice four months before trial which was in good time for the preparation of his defence, which was the principal underlying purpose of the safeguard.[8]

5. Relationship with Article 6, paragraph 3(b)

Where an applicant has not been promptly informed of the charge, it may well be that this has prevented him from properly preparing his defence at the same time, there being a logical connection between the two provisions.[9] Information about the nature and cause of the accusation must be adequate to enable a suspect to prepare his defence. In *Chichlian and Ekindjian*, the Commission commented that notification of the mere fact of reclassification of the offence is not enough, it has to be in good time and allowing the opportunity to organise the defence on the basis of that reclassification.

6. Relationship with Article 5, paragraph 2

Article 5, paragraph 2 concerning reasons for arrest and detention generally requires less detail and is not as rigorous as Article 6, paragraph 3(a).

Cross-reference

Part IIA: Introduction
Part IIA: Adequate time and facilities
Part IIB: Reasons for arrest and detention

---

[6] See n.2, above: though there were civil party submissions on the point lodged in the court file, they were apparently not brought to the attention of the applicants.

[7] The Government submitted that in the context it was clear he knew Italian.

[8] 10889/84 see n.3.

[9] *Erdogan, op. cit.*; *Bulgaria*, 24571/94; 24572/94, (Dec.) June 28, 1995, 82–A D.R.: where an appeal court upholding convictions relied on a provision which was not the ground for the conviction (concerning minister's failure to take measures following Chernobyl). The Commission found that the provision had been referred to in the first instance proceedings, that the same article of the Criminal Code was in issue throughout and that the applicants could and did defend themselves under this provision.

Interpretation

Relevant provision:

Article 6, paragraph 3(e) (free assistance of an interpreter).

Relevant case law:

Luedicke, Belkacem and Koç v. Germany, November 28, 1978, Series A, No. 29; 2 E.H.R.R. 149; *Kamasinski v. Austria*, December 12, 1989, Series A, No. 168.

1. General considerations

The ability to comprehend the proceedings in a criminal trial, guaranteed in Article 6, paragraph 3(e), may be seen as another aspect of the importance for an accused to participate effectively in the proceedings.

Issues as to the standard of the interpretation provided would only arise if it could be established as inadequate and damaging to the accused's effective participation in the proceedings. A failure to complain at the trial would probably be fatal to later claims before the Commission, since the domestic courts must be given an opportunity at the time to remedy any inadequacy.

2. Absolute nature of the right

The right is absolute, with no expressed qualifications to the right and none implied.[1] Interpretation costs cannot be reclaimed from defendants after conviction, as the Government argued in *Luedicke Belkacem and Koç v. Germany*. Similarly, the Commission found a violation even where an applicant who was required to pay costs of interpretation after conviction was covered by his legal insurance.[2]

The requirement for interpretation must, however, be genuine and necessary to the fair conduct of the proceedings. Where an applicant has sufficient understanding of the language of the proceedings, he cannot claim a cultural or political preference for another.

3. Translation of documents

Article 6, paragraph 3(e) has been held to cover documentary material and pre-trial matters but it does not extend to requiring translations of all documents in the proceedings.[3] It is sufficient if the applicant is assisted by interpreters, translations and the help of his lawyers so that he has knowledge of the case which enables him to defend himself, in particular by being able to put forward his version of events. If this standard is reached, a failure to provide all the translations an applicant might have wanted is not a problem.[4] An applicant would presumably have to indicate that the untranslated

---

[1] See, however, No. 11311/84 *Fedele v. Germany*, (Dec.) December 9, 1987 where the applicant failed to attend two hearings and was charged with the interpreters' fees, the Commission found that "assistance" referred to an accused who is present and that only someone who is present and cannot understand or speak the language used in court can be "assisted" by the interpreter; since the applicant was not present he could not claim free assistance of an interpreter.

[2] *Akdogan v. Germany*, 11394/85, (Rep.) July 5, 1988.

[3] *Kamasinski*, para. 74.

[4] See *Norway*, 14170/88, (Dec.) November 13, 1987; *Hayward v. Sweden*, 14106/88, (Dec.) December 6, 1991 where a British applicant tried in Sweden was unable to understand Swedish and complained that all the documents were in Swedish — the Commission noted that his Swedish lawyer understood English and there was no indication that an interpreter was refused when requested.

documents were material to his ability to defend himself and that he was refused or not permitted the necessary facilities.

Cross-reference

Part IIA: Adequate time and facilities
Part IIA: Information about the charge

Juries

Key provision:

Article 6 (fair trial by an independent and impartial tribunal).

Key case law:

Holm v. Sweden, November 25, 1993, Series A, No. 279–A; 18 E.H.R.R. 79; *Remli v. France*, April 23, 1996, R.J.D., 1996–II, No. 8; *Pullar v. U.K.*, June 10, 1996, R.J.D., 1996–III, No. 11; *Gregory v. U.K.*, February 25, 1997, R.J.D., 1997–I, No. 31.

1. General considerations

There is no right contained within Article 6, paragraph 1 to trial by jury, not surprisingly perhaps since some Contracting States do not use juries. The Commission accordingly dismissed an Irish case in which the applicant complained of the special courts presided over by judges without a jury which were introduced to deal with specific terrorist-related offences.[1] Similarly, in the United Kingdom, where the Birmingham Six argued that new evidence should not have been considered by the Court of Appeal, submitting that they could not receive a fair trial unless the evidence in its entirety was heard by a jury, the Commission found no reason why new evidence could not be fairly and properly assessed by an appellate body of professional judges.[2]

2. Undue influence on the jury

Concerns are sometimes raised as to the susceptibility of untrained, lay jurors to suggestions or inferences that an accused person is guilty contrary to the presumption of innocence as well as impinging on the fairness of the trial.

Old precedents indicate that a virulent press campaign may adversely affect the fairness of trial through its effect on the jury.[3] No finding of unfair trial has been found as yet on this ground. It would take more than close media interest in a case and it would be likely that the fact that the jurors took oaths, and would be warned to discount news coverage, would be regarded as offsetting prejudice. Other aspects of the proceedings, relating to security measures which appear to label the accused as "guilty" in advance, have also been examined. However, even where the Commission has expressed reservations, it has taken the attitude that juries can distinguish between security measures based on assessments of "dangerousness" and the examination of the merits in the trial.[4]

3. Independence and impartiality

This requirement of a fair trial applies equally to lay jurors as to judges (see Part IIA: Independence and impartiality).

---

[1] No. 8299/78, (Dec.) October 10, 1980, 22 D.R. 51.

[2] No. 14739/89, (Dec.) May 9, 1989, 60 D.R. 296.

[3] *e.g.* No. 8403/78, *Belgium*, (Dec.) October 15, 1980, 22 D.R. 100 dismissed on non-exhaustion since the applicant had not petitioned for the case to be transferred elsewhere.

[4] The Commission has been uneasy about the use of handcuffs before juries *e.g. Campbell v. U.K.* No. 12323/86, (Dec.) July 13, 1988; 57 D.R. 148; however glass cages for accused did not "stigmatise" the applicant in *Auguste v. France* No. 11837/85, (Rep.) June 7, 1990, 69 D.R. 126; while in *Welch v. U.K.* 17440/90, (Dec.) February 12, 1993, where the applicant complained of the intense security at his trial, the Commission did not find that it was unnecessary (one trial already abandoned due to attempt to influence a juror) or stage-managed, and did not consider that the effect on the jury would be such as to violate the presumption of innocence.

Convention organs will presume the subjective impartiality of a judge and apparently that of an unprofessional, untrained member of a tribunal. The Commission in *Holm v. Sweden* noted however that the unreasoned nature of a jury's verdict leads to a particular need for objective guarantees of impartiality and independence.

Objective independence and impartiality may be called in doubt by an exterior feature, for example, connection between a juror and a party to a civil case or a juror and prosecution witnesses. Regard is had to the nature of that connection and the safeguards in the system. In the *Holm* case, where five jurors out of nine in a libel case were members of the political party SAP, which was the dominant shareholder in the defendant company and political overtones were of relevance since the alleged libel related to the plaintiff applicant's activities in an organisation known as hostile to the SAP, the connection was of such a nature as to allow the applicant legitimately to fear that the jurors would be influenced by their political opinions. There was also the factor that there were no procedural ways of curing any defect in this case, the Court of Appeal having limited jurisdiction where as in this case the jury gave a verdict of acquittal.

However, in a Scottish case, *Pullar v. United Kingdom*, where the doubt arose from the discovery that one juror was an employee of a key Crown witness, the Court discounted the fact that the juror was disqualified in domestic law.[5] In its view it did not follow that because a member of a tribunal had personal knowledge of a witness he would be prejudiced in favour of that person's testimony. It was necessary rather to assess whether the familiarity was of such nature and degree to indicate lack of impartiality. Since the juror was a junior employee, unconnected with the events and under notice of redundancy, it was not certain that he would be inclined to believe his employer rather than defence witnesses. It also noted safeguards in the system, including the number of jurors (15), the sheriff's directions, and the oaths taken. This approach seemed to confuse considerations of the existence of actual bias with whether there were objective grounds for the applicant having doubts as to the impartiality of the jurors. The Commission found that it could legitimately be feared that the juror, even if ignorant of the facts of the case, would bring his own personal opinion of the credibility of the Crown witness to bear on his own and the other jurors' assessment of the case. The Commission noted that the High Court laid down rules to avoid future re-occurences.

Where racial bias has arisen, the Convention organs have had regard to the steps taken by domestic courts to counteract its influence. It would appear that if a court reacts in a firm manner the defect may be presumed cured. In *Remli v. France*, where a juror was overheard outside the courtroom saying "En plus je suis raciste", the applicant's lawyers brought it to the attention of the President of the Court who refused to take cognisance of it. Since domestic courts are under an obligation to verify their impartiality when a ground arises not manifestly without merit, the failure to take any steps disclosed a violation.

In *Gregory v. United Kingdom*, however, where a note was received from the jury "jury showing racial overtones one member to be excused", the judge consulted counsel and addressed the jury directing them as to their obligation to decide the case according to the evidence without prejudice. The Court admitted that there might be circumstances where a judge might have to discharge a jury but found that in this case a firmly-worded direction by an experienced judge who had observed the jury during the trial was sufficient to dispel doubts as to the impartiality of the tribunal.[6]

---

[5] *Oberschlick v. Austria*, May 23, 1991, Series A, No. 204; 19 E.H.R.R. 389 where it took a different view where a disqualified judge sat on a case, finding that the failure to abide by the domestic rules aimed at eradicating reasonable doubts as to impartiality left the proceedings open to doubt.

[6] The only dissenting judge found that a speech from a judge could not dispel racial prejudice within a jury if such existed and that it was not a question whether the judge had acted reasonably but whether the accused had received a fair trial as required by Art. 6, para. 1.

The fact that jurors take oaths to acquit their duties impartially was not considered a sufficient guarantee to outweigh the doubt on their impartiality in *Holm* deriving from their political affiliation, yet was mentioned as a guarantee in *Gregory*, which concerned apparent racial bias and in *Pullar*, concerning personal connections.

4. Secrecy of jury deliberations

The prohibition on publishing details of jury deliberations was found compatible with Article 10 of the Convention, where a newspaper and two editors were fined for contempt of court for revelations about the Blue Arrow trial.[7] The Commission noted that secrecy was the basis of the jury system in the United Kingdom and that the absolute nature of the offence could be regarded as necessary to protect jurors and prevent undue influence on their decisions by factors outside the jury room. While research into juries in fraud trials had been recommended by the Royal Commission on Criminal Justice, the Commission observed that research was not in issue in the case, which solely concerned revelations in one high profile trial.

Cross-reference

Part IIA: Independence and impartiality

---

[7] *Associated Newspaper Ltd and others v. U.K.*, 24770/94, (Dec.) November 30, 1994.

Legal aid in civil cases

Key provision:

Article 6, paragraph 1 (access to court).

Key case law:

Airey v. Ireland, October 9, 1979, Series A, No. 32; 2 E.H.R.R. 305.

1. General considerations

There is no right as such in the Convention to receive legal aid in cases concerning civil rights and obligations. Issues may however arise where lack of legal aid has the effect of depriving an applicant of effective access to court. The right of access to court is not unlimited. Limitations may be compatible where they do not restrict or reduce access to the extent that the very essence of the right is impaired, where they pursue a legitimate aim and disclose a reasonable relationship of proportionality between the means employed and the aim sought to be achieved.[1]

2. Lack of access to court

A denial of access to court in breach of Article 6, paragraph 1 was found in *Airey v. Ireland* in circumstances where, in the absence of legal aid for separation proceedings in the High Court, the applicant could not be expected to pursue proceedings herself. This was where the procedure was complex, raising complicated points of law and necessitating proof of adultery, unnatural practices of cruelty; it might involve expert evidence, the calling and examining of witnesses; and the subject-matter entailed an emotional involvement scarcely compatible with the degree of objectivity required by advocacy in court.

While the Court commented that the possibility of taking proceedings in person would permit effective access to court in some cases, the elements identified in *Airey* are likely to arise in many civil disputes, few of which would not be complex from the point of view of a lay litigant. The Commission has in practice confined the application of the *Airey* principles, giving weight to the reasons for refusal of legal aid. It has stated that due to limited resources States may legitimately restrict the grant of legal aid, imposing contributions or requiring a case to be well-founded, not vexatious or frivolous, in which case an applicant will bear the burden to bring the case some other way (by himself or obtaining assistance from another source), though it will have regard to whether the assessment by the authorities is arbitrary.[2] In such cases, the Commission generally finds that applicants may still enjoy reasonable access to court where they will have the opportunity to be heard under the proper and effective control of the fairness and conduct of the proceedings by the court.[3]

---

[1] *e.g. Ashingdane v. U.K.,* May 28, 1985, Series A, No. 93; 7 E.H.R.R. 528.

[2] No. 8158/78, July 10, 1980, 21 D.R. 95, refusal of legal aid to a prisoner on basis that his claims of ill-treatment lacked reasonable prospects of success was not a denial of access to court where the decision of the legal aid authority was shown not to be arbitrary, the Commission also finding the allegations unsubstantiated. There was also nothing to prevent the applicant obtaining assistance elsewhere as he had before the Commission (where he was represented by counsel).

[3] U.K. 9353/81, May 11, 1983, 33 D.R. 133, concerning refusal of legal aid for appeal from magistrates in affiliation proceedings, alleged to involve complex points of law, expert witnesses and emotional aspects. The Commission found no complex point of law, noting from the applicant's submissions that he fully understood the nature of the proceedings, was able to obtain evidence on his behalf and had the opportunity to be heard by a court, notwithstanding that the judge had stated that he considered legal assistance desirable. *Airey* was distinguished on the basis that the case involved appeal from the magistrates and not the High Court.

The mere fact that the other side is legally aided does not render the refusal of legal aid incompatible with Article 6, paragraph 1.[4]

Grounds for refusal linked to abuse of process may also be acceptable, as in a case where the Commission found that even though the applicant had prospects of success in suing for divorce it was compatible to refuse her legal aid in view of court findings that she had not intended to set up married life with her husband (marriage was to obtain him an entry permit) and that she had divorced before in similar circumstances. The Commission did not find unreasonable the court's view that she knew the position and did not require legal protection.[5]

3. Defamation

Even though defamation cannot, even in meritorious cases, be subject to a grant of legal aid in the United Kingdom, the Commission has nonetheless not found the blanket prohibition to disclose any violations of Article 6, paragraph 1. It held in *Winer v. United Kingdom*[6] that it could be legitimate to exclude certain categories of legal proceedings altogether from legal aid and that it had not been shown to be arbitrary to do so in that case (having regard to the fact that he secured a settlement and an apology by himself). While Commission did acknowledge the difficulties of defamation for a lay person in *Munro v. United Kingdom*,[7] it found that it was sufficient for the purposes of Article 6, paragraph 1 that the Industrial Tribunal hearing the applicant's case of unfair dismissal considered associated complaints about his employers' alleged malice and the Commission also commented, in indirect assessment of the merits, that there was no indication that he would have had better success in defamation proceedings.

4. Prohibition orders

The Commission has found it compatible for a prohibition order to be used to prevent application for civil legal aid where an applicant has made numerous applications. This is comparable to regulation of access for bankrupts, persons of unsound mind and vexatious litigants, where the aim is to prevent abuse of legal aid authorities.[8]

Cross-reference

Part IIA: Access to court
Part IIA: Legal representative in criminal proceedings

---

[4] 9353/81, above.
[5] 11564/85, (Dec.) December 4, 1985, 45 D.R. 291.
[6] 10871/84, (Dec.) July 10, 1986, 48 D.R. 154.
[7] 10594/83, July 14, 1987, 52 D.R. 158. See also, *Ian Stewart–Brady v. U.K.*, 27436/95 and 28406/95, (Dec.) July 2, 1997, 90–A D.R. 45.
[8] 27788/95 *U.K.*, (Dec.) January 27, 1996: the applicant could apply for the five year ban to be lifted.

Legal representation in criminal proceedings

Key provision:

Article 6, paragraph 3(c) (right to legal assistance of own choosing or where insufficient means to be given free when the interests of justice require).

Key case law:

Artico v. Italy, May 13, 1980, Series A, No. 37; 3 E.H.R.R. 1; *Pakelli v. Italy*, April 25, 1983, Series A, No. 64; 6 E.H.R.R. 1; *Kamasinski v. Austria*, December 19, 1989, Series A, No. 168; 13 E.H.R.R. 36; *Monnell and Morris v. U.K.*, March 2, 1987, Series A, No. 115; 10 E.H.R.R. 205; *Granger v. U.K.*, March 28, 1990, Series A, No. 174; 12 E.H.R.R. 469; *Quaranta v. Switzerland*, May 25, 1991, Series A, No. 205; *S. v. Switzerland*, November 28, 1991, Series A, No. 220; *Croissant v. Germany*, September 25, 1992, Series A, No. 237–B; 16 E.H.R.R. 135; *Imbrioscia v. Switzerland*, November 24, 1993, Series A, No. 275; 17 E.H.R.R. 441; *Maxwell v. U.K.*, October 28, 1994, Series A, No. 300–C; 19 E.H.R.R. 97; *Boner v. U.K.*, October 28, 1994, Series A, No. 300–B; 19 E.H.R.R. 246; *Poitrimol v, France*, November 27, 1993, Series A, No. 277–A; 18 E.H.R.R. 130; *Tripodi v. Italy*, February 22, 1994, Series A, No. 281–B; 18 E.H.R.R. 295; *Lala v. Netherlands*, September 22, 1994, Series A, No. 297–A; 18 E.H.R.R. 586; *John Murray v. U.K.*, February 8, 1996, R.J.D., 1996–I, No. 1.

1. General considerations

The provisions of Article 6, paragraph 3 depend on a criminal charge having been brought. The case law indicates that they are aspects of the general principle of fairness guaranteed in the first paragraph. As with the first paragraph, they are not to be assessed on the basis of an isolated incident or element but having regard to the proceedings as a whole.[1]

Article 6, paragraph 3(c) guarantees three rights; the right to defend oneself; where one does not wish to do so, the right to appoint a lawyer of own choosing; or where an applicant has insufficient means and interests of justice so require, the right to free legal assistance.[2]

2. Pre-trial representation

The right to legal representation applies not only to the trial, but to the pre-trial stages[3] but does not confer unlimited access to legal representation.

The case law indicates that any restrictions to free contact with defence counsel must remain an exception and must be justified by special circumstances, the accused's right to communicate with his advocate out of hearing of a third person being a basic requirement of a fair trial in democratic society.[4] Where a lawyer is bound by professional obligations, the Commission and Court are unlikely to be persuaded in the absence of objective justification that restrictions are necessary to prevent the risk of collusion through or with the lawyer.[5] Restrictions of three months on free unsupervised contact during the crucial

---

[1] *e.g. Can v. Austria*, (Rep.) July 12, 1984, Series A, No. 96; 8 E.H.R.R. 121: their intrinsic aim is always to ensure or contribute to ensuring the fairness of the proceedings as a whole — thus often the sub-paragraphs are considered in conjunction with para. 1.

[2] *Pakelli v. Italy*, para. 31.

[3] Citing ICCPR and Rule 93 of Standard Minimum Rules for the Treatment of Prisoners (Council of Europe Res. CM(73)5).

[4] *S v. Switzerland*, para. 48.

[5] *e.g. Can; S v. Switzerland*, where there were vague unsubstantiated doubts of collusion.

investigation stage disclosed a violation in *Can*. However, seven month surveillance of defence counsel visits in *S. v. Switzerland* disclosed a violation even though there was a two-year period without restrictions before trial, indicating that it is not necessary to show damage to the presentation of the defence at trial from the restrictions and that the right is to effective representation throughout the proceedings.

Whether an applicant can claim a violation from a refusal to allow access to a solicitor immediately on arrest will depend on the circumstances. Short periods of several days have been found not to infringe defence rights.[6] Where, however, in *John Murray v. United Kingdom*, the applicant, arrested for terrorist offences, was refused access to a solicitor for 48 hours there was a violation having regard to the special features of the procedures in the early interrogation stage in Northern Ireland where inferences could be drawn from silence or responses to police questions. Since the accused was in a position where his defence could be irretrievably prejudiced, restriction on access to legal advice was incompatible with Article 6, paragraph 3(c) without it being necessary to show the applicant would have acted differently if he had seen his solicitor. It might be argued that in any case where confessions may be obtained in the early stages of questioning in the absence of a solicitor that the position of the defence may also be irretrievably prejudiced. Given the acknowledgement in most Contracting States of the importance to defence rights of prompt legal advice and its contribution to providing safeguards against abuse, it is not inconceivable that the Convention organs will develop this line of case law further.

3. Legal representation of own choosing

The right to free legal assistance does not confer the right to choose legal aid counsel. There are no substantial cases where a paying applicant has been presented from having the counsel of his choice. Potentially issues could arise where a court barred counsel for lack of qualifications but the Commission and Court would be likely to accept domestic rules on eligibility which were not totally unreasonable or arbitrary. Courts may appoint defence counsel which an accused considers unnecessary or objectionable. Where in *Croissant v. Germany*, the applicant had appointed two counsel and objected to the third appointed by the courts, the Court found that the domestic courts' reasons were relevant and sufficient, namely, serving the interests of justice by avoiding interruptions or adjournments and that the counsel was properly qualified.

Where a court bars counsel from appearing on grounds that the accused has failed to appear or surrender to custody, the Court has not been convinced that this is a proportionate response having regard to the importance of assuring an accused's defence.[7] It is for the domestic courts to ensure that an accused is properly defended and that counsel who appears is afforded the opportunity to act. While it is important for an accused to be present, it was more important for him to be adequately defended. Even if properly summoned, this does not in absence of excuse justify depriving him of the right to be defended by counsel.

Where, however, a lawyer appointed by an applicant failed to attend a hearing in cassation proceedings because he was ill, the Court in *Tripodi v. Italy* appeared to find that the State could not be responsible for the shortcomings of a lawyer appointed by the accused,

---

[6] 11526/84, *France*, (Dec.) September 5, 1988, 57 D.R. 47: where an applicant's inability to consult for three days prior to appearing before the investigating judge did not infringe defence rights, where there was free consultation during the investigation period and the applicant was able to make full use of procedures and remedies; 12391/86, *U.K.*, (Dec.) April 13, 1989 60 D.R. 182 concerning two and a half days without access to a lawyer, where the reason to deny access was potential prejudice to enquiries (the solicitor's premises were being searched), there was no substantiation that the applicant had made any confessions, that he was unable to prepare defence over following year or use legal procedures concerning release.

[7] e.g. *Poitrimol v. France*, para. 38; *Lala v. Netherlands*, para. 33.

bearing in mind code provisions indicating that lawyers should provide replacements. President Ryssdal, dissenting, noted that the lawyer was required to rest completely so could not be expected to act, while the Commission had found that courts are not allowed to remain passive but must take steps to ensure an accused is properly defended. Indeed there seems no reason why the obligation by a court to ensure a proper defence should depend on the method of appointment of the accused's lawyer (see section 5 below).

4. Free legal assistance

Free legal assistance does not exclude liability to repay the fees later. It only has to be free at the time of trial and while the applicant's insufficiency of means continues. In *Croissant v. Germany*, the German system whereby convicted accused may be required to reimburse fees after trial was not found to be incompatible with Convention *per se*, and no violation was disclosed where the lawyers appointed by the court could be regarded as necessary and the amounts charged not excessive. According to Commission case law, a problem only arises if liability is enforced regardless of financial position.[8]

There are two conditions as follows.

(a) *Financial eligibility*

This aspect has been rarely disputed. In *Pakelli v. Germany*, where the Government contested that the applicant was indigent at the time of the appeal, though the ground for refusal of legal aid concerned the offence, the Court was satisfied by the documentary materials put forward by the applicant and the fact that he had been found to qualify for legal aid from the Commission.

(b) *Interests of justice*

The condition does not require it to be proved that legal assistance if provided would have altered the course of the proceedings, as the Government argued in *Artico v. Italy*, for example, by pleading a statutory limitation.[8a] This was impossible to prove and would render the guarantee ineffective. However, it may be that this principle is distinct from the need to establish that the interests of justice require representation by pointing to reasons why in a particular stage in proceedings the accused required the assistance of a lawyer, namely that there was potentially something of material value which a lawyer could contribute.

(I) FIRST INSTANCE

In deciding whether interests of justice require legal representation, the Court looks at the seriousness of the offences and the potential sentence imposable; complexity of the case is an additional factor, lack of which is not decisive. In *Quaranta v. Switzerland*, for example, where there were no special difficulties in establishing facts, the Court considered that issues arose concerning applicable measures as well as matters relating to the applicant's personal situation, foreign origin, underprivileged background and long criminal record, which seem more relevant to sentencing. It found his appearance unrepresented in court on minor drugs charges facing up to eighteen months did not enable him to present his case in an adequate manner.

(II) LEAVE TO APPEAL VERSUS APPEAL PROCEEDINGS

Appeal and leave to appeal proceedings on convictions and/or sentence concern the determination of a criminal charge and the guarantees of Article 6, paragraphs 1 and 3

---

[8] *e.g.* 9365/81, *Germany*, (Dec.) May 6, 1982, 28 D.R. 229.
[8a] Para. 35.

continue to apply though the manner of that application will depend on the nature and significance of the appeal or cassation proceedings, taking into account the powers of the court and the manner in which the applicant's interests were presented and protected.[9]

Leave to appeal and appeal hearings may be distinguished. Leave to appeal proceedings where the prosecution are not present may not require free legal assistance. In *Monnell and Morris v. United Kingdom* the applicants had representation at first instance and advice on the merits of an appeal with the possibility to put in written submissions. The Court found that they were able fairly and effectively to present their application and the interests of justice were met in their ability to make written submissions, taking into account the fact that counsel had advised there were no grounds of appeal.

Conversely, in the Scottish system where there is a general right to appeal, without leave, and applicants appear in person in oral proceedings at which the prosecution is represented and may address the court, it has been found that the nature of the proceedings will, where there is a serious matter at stake, require legal representation to be fair. This was found to be the case in *Granger v. United Kingdom* where difficult legal issues were at stake on which there was oral argument before the court by the Solicitor-General in which the applicant was unable to play effective part.[10] But subsequent cases have showed that where substantial sentences are at stake, that alone will render matters sufficiently serious for the interests of justice to require legal representation at the appeal hearing.[11] In these cases, the applicants had presented arguments on their own behalf, perhaps not inexpertly in some instances, but there has been no question of considering that this rendered the provision of legal assistance unnecessary in the interests of justice.

The Commission has rejected some cases concerning minor offences with low sentences where it was found that the interests of justice did not require legal representation, for example, nine months' sentence for assault where the Commission considered that there were no complex legal issues requiring assistance[12]; 60 days for failure to give a breath specimen, taking car, etc.[13]; conviction for breach of peace, one year suspended sentence.[14]

5. Scope of the obligation to provide legal assistance

The appointment of a legal aid lawyer does not exhaust the obligations of the State. Legal assistance provided must be effective and if the authorities are notified that a legal aid lawyer is unable to fulfill his duties the authorities are under an obligation to replace him.[15] Where appointment of a lawyer is made in circumstances that affect the effectiveness of his participation, issues may arise, as in *Goddi v. Italy*, where the court did not inform the applicant's lawyer of the hearing and the lawyer appointed in replacement

---

[9] e.g. *Monnell and Morris v. United Kingdom*.

[10] See also *Pham Hoang*, where the applicant, fined several million francs for drugs offences, was refused legal aid counsel for appeal in cassation — interests of justice required legal representation having regard to the serious consequences at stake, the complexity of issues he intended to raise, on inability to present and develop the appropriate arguments (e.g. only experienced counsel could seek to persuade the court to depart from its previous case law); *Pakelli v. Germany*, where the applicant could not respond to the judge rapporteur or contribute to the development of case law.

[11] Violations in *Maxwell v. U.K.* (5 years' sentence, with no complex issues in the case); and in *Boner v. U.K.* (8 years' sentence); before the Commission: *Wotherspoon* (22112/93, (Rep.) October 16, 1996, life imprisonment; relatively complex issues; *Murdoch* 25523/94, (Rep.) October 16, 1996 (2 years; relatively complex) *Robson* 25648/94, (Rep.) October 16, 1996 (appeal against sentence only; concurrent sentences of over 12 years: Commission noted lawyer still needed even if sentencing issues less complex) *Middleton*, 23934/94, (Rep.) October 16, 1996 (3 years' for housebreaking).

[12] U.K. 17120/90, (Dec.) December 3, 1990.

[13] U.K. 14001/88, (Dec.) January 19, 1989.

[14] U.K. 13098/87, (Dec.) May 6, 1988.

[15] e.g. *Artico v. Italy* where legal aid lawyer refused the appointment because of other commitments and the authorities failed to appoint a substitute.

knew neither the client nor the file. Failure to ensure the effective defence of an accused was found by the Commission in *Biondo v. Italy*, where a lawyer failed to appear at an appeal though notified and the interests of justice required the defence to be represented to answer the prosecution and expand the grounds of appeal.[16] Incompetence of a legal aid lawyer may also raise issues of lack of effective representation, where this is manifest and has a clear effect on the position of the defence.[17]

The State is not however liable for every shortcoming of a legal aid lawyer.[18] The conduct of the defence is essentially a matter between the lawyer and defendant and the competent authorities are only required to intervene if failure by legal aid counsel to provide effective representation is manifest or sufficiently brought to their attention in some other way.[19] The Court will have regard to the proceedings in their entirety and the mere fact that counsel in some respects acted against what applicants consider to be their best interests will not be sufficient to render the representation below the required standard.[20]

The Commission has so far had little sympathy for the accused who dismiss counsel during proceedings or failing to obtain an adjournment or fresh counsel continue the proceedings unrepresented.[21] Where the person has sacked numerous solicitors already, it is perhaps more obvious that the situation is of his own making and the domestic court may reasonably regard it as delaying tactics.[22] Where a person faces serious charges and loses confidence in inexperienced counsel, it would perhaps be harder to dismiss a complaint lightly. However, it would require gross or obvious failure on the part of the defence counsel, beyond difference of opinion between counsel and applicant as to tactics, before the Convention organs would be likely to find an obligation on the authorities to replace counsel.

Cross-reference

Part IIA: Legal aid in civil cases

---

[16] *Italy*, 8821/79 (Rep.) December 8, 1979. Resolution DH (89) 30.

[17] *Daud v. Portugal*, 22600/93, (Rep.) December 2, 1993 pending before the Court, where the court-appointed lawyer's grounds of appeal to the Supreme Court were declared inadmissible for inadequate presentation and failure to cite the provisions violated. A Commission majority found a violation of Art. 6, para. 3(c) having regard to the manifest nature of the failing, which resulted in barring access to the Supreme Court, also noting that since the applicant was a foreigner, it was incumbent on the courts to ensure the applicant's effective defence.

[18] *Artico v. Italy; Kamasinki v. Austria;* also *Imbroscia v. Switzerland* where the applicant's counsel was absent during initial interrogations with prosecutor but the Court noted the short period, lack of complaint by the applicant and the provision of replacement by the authorities.

[19] *Kamasinki v. Austria.*

[20] *e.g. Kamasinki v. Austria*, where the applicant criticised the brevity of visits of counsel, counsel's failure to inform him of all prosecution evidence, omitting to make motions, accepting certain written statements etc. *U.K.* 9728/82, (1983) (Dec.) July 7, 1983 6 D.R. 155: there was no problem where legal aid counsel limited unnecessary repeated, consultations to save costs to the legal aid fund; *e.g.* an accused is not entitled to require a lawyer to adopt a particular defense strategy: 9127/80. *Switzerland*, (Dec.) October 6, 1981, where the court appointed counsel had refused to maintain the applicant's not guilty plea. The Commission noted that the lawyer had found the plea impossible to maintain and that the applicant could have addressed the court himself. He was also able to appeal with lawyers whom he did not object to.

[21] *e.g.* 8386/78 *U.K.*, (Dec.) October 9, 1980 21 D.R. 126: where counsel withdrew but the judge refused to adjourn for new counsel, the Commission considered that the judge's view that other counsel would be similarly embarrassed was not unreasonable in light of the applicant's admissions in court and that since he was given the opportunity to defend himself and chose not to, there was no appearance of a violation; 13572/88, *Sweden*, (Dec.) March 1, 1991, 69 D.R. 198: where a *Sami* was unrepresented on appeal, due to his rejection of the court-appointed lawyer, whom the court had found had not failed to fulfil his functions. The Commission held that Art. 6, para. 3(c) did not give a right to choose official counsel or to change official counsel once appointed. Lack of representation at appeal was largely attributable to the applicant but Commission also had regard to the minor sentence imposed on conviction (1 month) and the fact that no further convictions were added.

[22] *France* (1996) 24667/94, May 20, 1996, 85–B D.R. 103 where the applicant dismissed the lawyer towards the end of the trial.

Legislative interference in judicial process

Key provision:

Article 6, paragraph 1 (fair trial).

Key case law:

Stran Greek Refineries v. Greece, December 9, 1994, Series A, No. 301–B; 19 E.H.R.R. 293; *Pressos Compania Naviera and others v. Belgium*, November 20, 1995, Series A, No. 322; 21 E.H.R.R. 301; *Papageorgiou v. Greece*, October 22, 1997, R.J.D. 1997–IV, No. 54; *National & Provincial Building Society and other v. U.K.*, October 23, 1997, R.J.D. 1997–VI, No. 55.

1. General considerations

Where the legislature passes a law which has direct and significant effect on the adjudication of pending civil claims, issues will arise under Article 6, paragraph 1. In *Stran Greek Refineries v. Greece*, the Court rejected the Government argument that the legislative action was outside the court proceedings, emphasising that fairness applied to the proceedings in their entirety. While there was no doubt that the appearances of justice before the courts were preserved, the principle of the rule of law and the notion of fair trial precluded any interference by the legislature with the administration of justice designed to influence the judicial determination of the dispute.[1]

2. Effect on the proceedings

In *Stran Greek Refineries*, the law which was passed effectively excluded any meaningful examination since it took away any enforceability of the domestic court's arbitration award. The Court in finding a violation also referred to the case law on equality of arms.[2] Where the State is a party in proceedings, use of its legislative powers may clearly place an opponent at a substantial disadvantage. Where the effect of a legislative measure, in conjunction with the method and timing of its enactment, is effectively to extinguish a pending claim, a violation of Article 6, paragraph 1, is likely to arise in that the applicant is thereby deprived of a fair hearing.[3]

The aspect of access to court, combined with lack of equality of arms, was the basis for violation of Article 6, paragraph 1 in the Commission's report in *Pressos Compania Naviera*, where the applicant shipowners with claims pending before the courts, complained of legislation which was passed to exempt the State and its pilots from liability for negligent acts. The intervention was an interference in access to court, which was not proportionate and deprived the applicants of the right to obtain a decision on their civil rights following a fair trial before a tribunal. The Court finding a violation of property rights (Article 1 of Protocol No. 1), having regard to the lack of any compensation and its view that State financial considerations and uniformity did not justify retrospective interference with fundamental rights, did not consider Article 6 further.

---

[1] *Stran Greek Refineries v. Greece,* para. 49: violations were found under Art. 6, para. 1 and Art. 1 of Protocol No. 1: interference with property rights.
[2] See Fair trial guarantees, Equality of arms.
[3] *e.g. Papageorgiou v. Greece*, October 22, 1997, R.J.D. 1997–VI, No. 54, paras 34–40.

3. Justifiable interventions

Whether legislative interference may, even if retrospective, be compatible with Article 6 has been raised in a third case. In *National & Provincial Building Society and others v. United Kingdom*,[4] where retrospective legislation intervened with the building societies' prospects of obtaining restitution of tax paid under invalid regulations, the Commission followed, by a narrow majority, the *Stran Greek Refineries* approach that intervention by the legislature influencing proceedings in the State's favour is *per se* objectionable. However, the Court held that Article 6, paragraph 1 could not be interpreted as preventing any interference with pending legal proceedings to which the State was a party, though respect for the rule of law and notion of a fair trial required the use of retrospective legislation to be regarded with great circumspection. While in *Stran Greek Refineries*, there was a nine-year-old private law dispute with the Government as a party to a contract where an arbitration award had been made and there was an inconsistency in the State position since the Government had originally requested arbitration, in this case there were special circumstances, namely, a clear intention of Parliament to tax the money from the beginning, with legislation swiftly introduced to prevent windfalls and the frustration of the legislative purpose by the fortuitious exploitation of technical defects in the original regulations.

In those circumstances, the Court found the applicant building societies could not justifiably complain of a denial of access to court.

Cross-reference

Part IIA: Access to court
Part IIA: Equality of arms
Part IIB: Property

---

[4] *U.K.*, 21319/93, etc. (Rep.), June 25, 1996 (11 votes to 9 on Art. 6), *e.g. Papageorgiou v. Greece*, see n.3.

Length of proceedings

Key provision:

Article 6, paragraph 1.

1. General considerations

The requirement that proceedings do not exceed a "reasonable time" applies to both the determination of criminal charges and civil rights and obligations. The principles are well-established in a series of cases dominated by Italy. The reasonableness of the length of proceedings is to be assessed in the light of the particular circumstances of the case, regard being had to three heads: the complexity of the case; the conduct of the applicant; and, the conduct of the authorities. On the latter point, what is at stake for the applicant may have to be taken into account. Thus criminal proceedings will generally be expected to be pursued more expeditiously than civil. Where time may play a role in determining the merits, such as childcare cases[1] or where time is pressing for other reasons, there may be special need for diligence on the part of the authorities.[2]

2. Period to be taken into consideration

Civil proceedings commence from the institution of the relevant court procedure which concerns the determination of a dispute relating to civil rights and obligations.[3] The proceedings terminate on the date of giving judgment in the final instance or, where later, the issuing of the written judgment to the applicant. Where a court decision only became final after a year, the Court took that date.[4] Subsequent costs and enforcement proceedings may be taken into account, where related to substantive proceedings concerning civil rights and obligations.[5]

Criminal proceedings commence from the moment that a formal charge is brought against the applicant. In cases where this is unclear, the test is from the date the defendant's situation has been substantially affected as a result of the suspicion against him.[6] The charge may be defined as the "official notification given to an individual by the competent authority of an allegation that he has commited a criminal offence which also corresponds to the test whether the situation of the suspect has been affected".[7] This may be the date of arrest,[8] the date the applicant was officially notified that he was to be

---

[1] The child may bond with his new carers, *e.g. H v. U.K.,* July 8, 1987, Series A, No. 120; 10 E.H.R.R. 95.

[2] *e.g.* claims by AIDS victims for compensation from contaminated blood banks, *i.e.* in *X v. France,* March 31, 1992, Series A, No. 234–C; 14 E.H.R.R. 483 where a period over two years was excessive; where the applicant has suffered injuries, special, even exceptional, diligence has been required — *Silva Pontes v. Portugal,* March 23, 1994, Series A, No. 286–A; 18 E.H.R.R. 156, para. 39 and *Martins Moreira v. Portugal,* October 26, 1988, Series A, No. 143; diligence has also been required in employment disputes — *Nibbio v. Italy,* February 26, 1992, Series A, No. 228–A.

[3] *Darnell v. U.K.* (15058/89) October 26, 1993, Series A, No. 272; 18 E.H.R.R. 205 settled before the Court — despite lengthy internal disciplinary enquiries, until the applicant was dismissed, there was no "dispute" as to civil rights or obligations.

[4] *Trevisan v. Italy,* February 26, 1993, Series A, No. 257–F.

[5] *Robins v. U.K.,* September 23, 1997, in R.J.D., 1997–V, No. 49, 1997 (costs); *Silva Pontes op. cit.* n.2. *Di Pede* and *Zappia v. Italy,* September 26, 1996, R.J.D., 1996–IV, No. 17 (enforcement).

[6] *e.g. Germany,* 9132/80, (Rep.) December 12, 1983, 41 D.R. 13: where the applicant was implicated in proceedings against another person, the date was taken from moment that the authorities searched his premises, when it became clear that a suspicion that he was an accomplice existed and this measure severely affected his position, becoming known to other people; *Ewing v. U.K.,* 11224/84, (Rep.) October 6, 1987, 56 D.R. 71: date when substantially affected, *i.e.* arrest.

[7] *e.g. Eckle v. Germany,* July 15, 1982, Series A, No. 51, para. 73.

[8] 9559/81, (Dec.) May 9, 1983, 33 D.R. 158.

prosecuted, the date preliminary investigations were opened, the date of opening of a criminal investigation,[9] or the request for an investigation following initial questioning of the applicant.[10] Where specific separate counts are added later, the dates are taken from those occurrences as relevant.[11] The proceedings end when the charges are finally determined or the sentence imposed becomes final.[12] This may be the date of the conclusion of last appeal or the issuing of the judgment.

Length complaints may be examined where the proceedings have not terminated if it is alleged that there has already been unreasonable delay.[13] Where the Commission or Court only become competent *ratione temporis* during the course of proceedings, the time already elapsed is taken into account in assessing the reasonableness of length of proceedings after that date.[14] Also, in cases where an applicant absconds during the proceedings (criminal), that period is deducted.[15]

3. Victim status

The fact that an applicant is acquitted does not deprive him of victim status for the purpose of a length complaint.[16] Where, however, national authorities have acknowledged the breach of the Convention expressly or in substance and afforded redress for the breach in circumstances where it would duplicate the domestic process to bring complaints to Strasbourg the applicant ceases to be a victim for purposes of an application.[17] This requires an acknowledgement in a sufficiently clear manner of the failure to observe the reasonable time requirement and redress is required, such as reducing the sentence in an express and measureable manner.[18]

The Commission has found that where a court fails to find, or expressly denies, a violation of the Convention, the applicant still may claim to be a victim but any action taken by the court in reducing the sentence in view of the length is to be taken into account in the assessment of the reasonableness of the delay.[19] The logic of this approach is not readily apparent since the applicant has suffered the delay whatever the result and without an express acknowledgement of the breach.

4. Complexity of the case

All aspects of the case may be relevant to the assessment of complexity of the proceedings, including the subject-matter, whether there are disputed facts, number of accused, international elements, number of witnesses, or volume of written evidence.

---

[9] *Mlynek v. Austria*, 11688/85, (Rep.) March 10, 1988, 62 D.R. 120.

[10] 13017/87 *Austria*, (Rep.) July 4, 1989, 71 D.R. 52.

[11] 9315/81 *Jesso v. Austria*, (Rep.) May 7, 1986, 50 D.R. 44.

[12] *Eckle*, para. 77, see, n.7.

[13] *e.g. Mylnek v. Austria* (settled before court) October 27, 1992, Series A, No. 242–C; 18 E.H.R.R. 581: period of three years nine months and still pending.

[14] *Mitap and Müftüğlu v. Turkey*, March 25, 1996, R.J.D., 1996–II, No. 6.

[15] *e.g. Girolami v. Italy*, February 19, 1991, Series A, No. 196–E.

[16] 13156/87, (Dec.) July 1, 1992, 76 D.R. 5.

[17] *Eckle*, see n.7, para. 66.

[18] *Eckle*, see n.7 9299/81 (Rep.) July 12, 1985 46 D.R. 5 where the Swiss authorities implicitly acknowledged the breach, finding that there had been considerable delays and reduced two-and-half years to 18 months and decided not to enforce expulsion order; 17669/91, (Dec.) March 31, 1993, 74 D.R. 156: reduction from two-years-six-months to eight months half suspended in light of excessive delay; *Neubeck v. Germany*, 9132/80, (Rep.) December 12, 1983, 41 D.R. 13, where the applicant remained a victim as the courts only referred to part of the excessive delay without quantifying the reduction, the Commission finding a vague reference to fact that sentence would have been longer was insufficiently clear.

[19] *e.g.* 18905/91, *R. B. v. Switzerland*, (Rep.), May 24, 1995 no violation in light of complexity of case and fact the domestic court reduced sentence from 24 months to 16 months.

The complexity of the case, balanced with the general principle of securing proper administration of justice, may justify a not inconsiderable length of time. In *Boddaert v. Belgium*,[20] the Court found that six years almost three months was not unreasonable since the case concerned a difficult murder enquiry, and the parallel progression of two cases. In a civil case, *Katte Klitsche v. Italy*,[21] the Court found that eight years disclosed no violation, notwithstanding three identified periods of abnormal delay, since the case, a land development matter, was complex on facts and law and having regard to its importance to environmental interests and Italian case law.

However, even where a case is complex, there is a point where this ceases to suffice.[22] In *Ferrantelli and Santangelo v. Italy*, where the applicants were convicted finally after 16 years, the Court agreed that the case concerned a complex, difficult murder trial, acknowledged the sensitive problems of dealing with juveniles and that the proceedings were generally active but when the case was looked at as a whole, the only possible conclusion was unreasonable delay.

5. Conduct of the applicant

Only delays attributable to the State may justify a finding of failure to comply with "reasonable time" requirement.[22a]

An applicant who stays outside the jurisdiction, for example failing to answer to an arrest warrant or who flees, cannot complain about length, even though the criminal proceedings remain pending indefinitely as a result.[23]

An applicant in principle cannot have it held against him that he has made full use of the procedures available to him under domestic law to pursue his defence.[24] An applicant is not required actively to co-operate with the judicial authorities but nonetheless his conduct may be taken into account as an objective factor for which the Government are not responsible.[25] The fact that an applicant has applied for expedition is often a factor in his favour but failure to do so is not necessarily crucial.[26]

The factor of the applicant's conduct was significant in *Monnet v. France*[27] (contested judicial separation lasting seven years one month) where the applicant contributed considerably to prolonging the proceedings by two requests for deferment and by delay in submitting documents and in setting down the hearing of the appeal. In *Ciricosta and Viola v. Italy*[28] concerning an application to suspend works likely to interfere with property rights and where the applicants had requested at least 17 adjournments and not objected to six others requested by other party, though 15 years on its face appeared unreasonable,

---

[20] *Belgium*, October 12, 1992, Series A, No. 235.

[21] *Italy*, October 27, 1994, Series A, No. 293–B.

[22] *e.g. Ferrantelli and Santangelo v. Italy*, August 7, 1996, R.J.D.–III, No. 12.

[22a] *e.g. Proszak v. Poland*, December 16, 1997, to be published in R.J.D. 1997.

[23] *e.g. A.P. v. Italy* 27679/95 (Dec.), June 24, 1996; *Erdogan v. Turkey*, 14723/89 (Dec.) July 9, 1992, 73 D.R. 81.

[24] *Eckle*, above, n.7, see para. 82.

[25] *e.g. Eckle*, above, n.7, there were allegations of deliberate obstruction but though the applicants slowed matters by numerous applications and appeals, the Court still found one of the main causes of the length of the proceedings to be the conduct of the judicial authorities, the length not accounted for by the conduct of the applicants alone.

[26] *e.g. Ceteroni v. Italy*, November 15, 1996, R.J.D. 1996–V, No. 21, where the judge had never refused any adjournments by liquidator and the Court accepted that applications by the applicant would have had no effect; however *M v. U.K.*, 13228/87, February 13, 1990, where the Commission took into account that the applicant consented to the steps which delayed proceedings; *Ewing v. U.K.*, 11224/84, (Rep.) October 7, 1987: where the Commission noted that the applicant could have applied for expedited hearing before House of Lords and found the overall period three years 10 months was not unreasonable overall.

[27] October 27, 1993, Series A, No. 273–B.

[28] December 4, 1995, Series A, No. 337.

the Court held that while the courts were responsible for some delay, they did not bear the primary responsibility and it did not accept that the judge was negligent in not putting an end to the applicants' dilatory conduct. However in *Beaumartin v. France*[29] where the applicants contributed to delay by bringing the case in the wrong court and in submitting pleadings four months after lodging their appeal, the authorities were more at fault, the court taking over five years to hold the first hearing and the respondent ministry taking 20 months to file its pleadings.

6. Conduct of the judicial authorities

The Court has had regard to the principle of the proper administration of justice, namely, that domestic courts are under a duty to deal properly with the cases before them.[30] Domestic court decisions concerning the taking of evidence, to join cases, adjourn for particular reasons, are therefore likely to be given some weight, at least up to a certain point. For example, in *Ewing v. United Kingdom*[31] the joining of three cases, which delayed the trial was not shown to be arbitrary or unreasonable, or as causing undue delay giving account to the due administration of justice. However the Commission in *Reilly v. Ireland*[32] noted that the decision taken to separate murder and burglary proceedings meant that the responsibility to ensure a speedy determination of the charges was more onerous given the potential impact on length of the proceedings.

However, excuses as regards backlog or administrative difficulties are not accepted since States are under an obligation to organise their judicial systems in such a way that their courts can meet the Convention's requirements.[33] A temporary backlog before a court will not entail liability provided the authorities take reasonably prompt remedial action to deal with the exceptional situation.[34] Where the state of affairs becomes prolonged or a matter of structural organisation, provisional methods, such as giving priorities, are no longer sufficient and the State cannot postpone further the adoption of effective measures.[35] However, the obligation on States to organise judicial systems to comply with the requirements of Article 6 does not apply in the same way to a Constitutional Court which has a role of guardian which may render it necessary to take other considerations into account, *e.g.* the importance of cases in political and social terms rather than chronological order.[36]

Where specific periods of delay are attributable to courts, *e.g.* delay in the transmission of a file or documents from one instance to another or delay in issuing judgment, violations may be found where the rest of the proceedings were otherwise not lacking in diligence.[37]

---

[29] November 24, 1994, Series A, No. 296–B.

[30] *e.g. Boddaert v. Belgium,* October 12, 1992, Series A, No. 235–D, para. 39.

[31] See n.26.

[32] *Ireland,* 21624/93, (Rep.) February 22, 1995.

[33] *e.g. Salesi v. Italy,* February 26, 1993, Series A, No. 257–E.

[34] *e.g. Bucholz v. Germany,* May 6, 1981, Series A, No. 42; 3 E.H.R.R. 597 (alleged economic recession causing backlog in labour courts: five years over three instances disclosed no violation, since the authorities showed consciousness of responsibilities and had made efforts; *Foti v. Italy,* December 10, 1982, Series A, No. 56 (troubles in Reggio causing unusual political and social climate taken into account but violation still disclosed).

[35] *Zimmerman and Steiner v. Switzerland,* July 13, 1983, Series A, No. 66; 6 E.H.R.R. 17 where there had been a steady increase in volume of administrative litigation since 1969, such that there was no temporary excess of work but a question of structural organisation to which the authorities had not given a satisfactory response. Since there were three and a half years during which the case was largely stationary, there was a violation.

[36] *Sussman v. Germany,* September 16, 1996, R.J.D. 1996–IV, No. 15. Given the unique circumstances of reunification and the serious social implications of the disputes, the Constitutional Court was entitled to give priority to 300,000 employment cases — no violation for proceedings lasting 3 years 4 months.

[37] *e.g.* in *Reilly v. Irelands,* see n.32 above, the Commission commented adversely on 12 months for the Supreme Court to render judgment and 14 months for the trial judge to approve the transcript of evidence; in *Bunkate v. Netherlands,* May 26, 1993, Series A, No. 248–B; 19 E.H.R.R. 477, the Court singled out fifteen and a half months for the court of appeal to send the casefile to the Supreme Court.

Presence in court

Key provision:

Article 6, paragraph 1 (right to a fair trial) and paragraph 3(c) (right to defend oneself in person).

Key case law:

Goddi v. Italy, April 9, 1984, Series A, No. 76; 6 E.H.R.R. 457; *Colozza v. Italy*, February 12, 1985, Series A, No. 89; 7 E.H.R.R. 516; *Monnell and Morris v. U.K.*, March 2, 1987, Series A, No. 115; 10 E.H.R.R. 205; *Kamasinski v. Austria*, December 19, 1989, Series A, No. 168; 13 E.H.R.R. 36; *F.C.B. v. Italy*, August 28, 1991, Series A, No. 208–B; 14 E.H.R.R. 909; *Kremzow v. Austria*, September 21, 1993, Series A, No. 268–B; 17 E.H.R.R. 322; *Poitrimol v. France*, November 23, 1990, Series A, No. 277–A; 18 E.H.R.R. 130; *Zana v. Turkey*, November 25, 1997, R.J.D. 1997–VII, No. 57.

1. General considerations

The applicant, generally, has a right to be present during criminal proccedings. The object and purpose of Article 6, paragraphs 1 and 3(c)–(e) presuppose the accused's presence. This is not an absolute right, as in special circumstances where witnesses are heard anonymously or where the accused is unruly.[1] The Commission in *Colozza and Rubinat v. Italy* stated, however, that the rights of the defence could not be said to have been respected if the applicant had not been given the "possibility" of attending. In this context, the authorities must show requisite diligence in ensuring the accused's right to be present in an effective manner, having regard to the prominent place which the right to a fair trial enjoys in democratic society.[2]

The most difficult problems have arisen in conviction *in absentia* cases where States retain the right to continue procecedings where an accused absconds or fails to appear.

2. Waiver

Waiver by an accused of his right to be present may be possible but must be unequivocal and attended by the minimum safeguards commensurate to the important of the right.[3]

In *Zana v. Turkey*, where the applicant was not present before the National Security Court which convicted him, the Court found that the procedural objection raised by the applicant on previous appearance in the Assize Court and his refusal to speak Turkish, rather than Kurdish, did not give rise to any implicit waiver of his right to appear.

Mere failure to appear is insufficient. In *FCB*, where the applicant was detained in the Netherlands, the Milan Court of Appeal held a retrial in his absence although informed by his counsel that he was detained abroad. The Court considered that the applicant had not expressed the wish to waive attendance and was not impressed by the argument that he had used deliberate delaying tactics in not providing the Italian authorities with his address. The crucial consideration was that the Italian authorities were aware that the applicant was subject to proceedings abroad and it was hardly compatible with the

---

[1] *Colozza and Rubinat v. Italy*, Com. Rep. para. 117, Series A, No. 89.
[2] *FCB v. Italy*, para. 35.
[3] *e.g. Poitrimol v. France*, para. 31.

diligence required in ensuring defence rights were effectively exercised to continue trial without taking further steps to clarify the position.[4]

Where there are difficulties in proving whether an applicant who knew of the date of trial was unable to attend, the Court has placed a certain burden on the applicant in substantiating his case. In *Goddi v. Italy*,[5] where the applicant placed in detention on other charges claimed that he had told the prison authorities of the hearing, the Government contested this. In absence of substantiation from either side, the Court considered that it could not be established that the Government were at fault.

3. Opportunity for rehearing on the merits

Proceedings *in absentia* may not be incompatible with the Convention if the person concerned can subsequently obtain a hearing complying with Article 6, namely, which provides a fresh determination of the merits of the charge.[6] Remedies which put the burden on the applicant to show that he had not tried to evade justice, been prevented from attending by *force majeure*, or that the authorities had not complied with applicable rules of service have been found insufficient.[7] The Commission appeared to take the view that the guarantee to "everyone" of a fair trial included those who deliberately absconded[8] though the Court in *Poitrimol v. France* expressed doubt as to whether the requirement for a rehearing would apply to an accused who unequivocally waived his right to appear.[9]

4. Exclusion from the hearing

Where proceedings concern only points of law, no issue may arise from the refusal to allow an accused to attend in addition to his lawyer. The Court considers that personal attendance of an accused at the appeal hearing does not take on the same crucial significance as it does for trial. In *Kremzow v. Austria*, where the applicant was excluded from a hearing on points of nullity (law), the Court found his presence not required by Article 6, paragraph 1 or 3(c), his lawyer being able to attend and make points on his behalf.[10] There was a breach however where the applicant was excluded from the hearing of the appeal on sentence, which involved an increase in sentence to life imprisonment and committal to special prison and a ruling on the motive for the crime which the jury had been unable to establish. Since the assessment of the applicant's character, state of mind and motivation were significant to the proceedings, and there was much at stake for the applicant, fairness required that he be present and able to participate as well as his lawyer.

In leave to appeal proceedings, absence of the accused and lawyer may be compatible where the nature of the issues are not such as to require presence and having regard to the prior proceedings (in particular previous legal representation and legal advice as to the prospects of appeal). In these circumstances the interests of justice and fairness may be met by the possibility of presenting written submissions to the court.[11]

---

[4] Also *Kremzow v. Austria:* a failure by the applicant to apply to attend the appeal hearing did not constitute a waiver, particularly as domestic procedures provided that, even without a request, the accused should attend where necessary in interests of justice and that there was a positive duty on the State to ensure his attendance.
[5] Para. 29.
[6] *Colozza*, para. 29; *Poitrimol*, para. 31.
[7] *Colozza; Stamoulakatos v. Gr.* Comm. Rep. May 20, 1992, Series A, No. 271.
[8] *e.g. Stamoulakatos* above, where the Commission considered that remedies for conviction *in absentia* which put the burden on the applicant to show that the authorities knew his address abroad or that they failed to comply with rules for service were insufficient to guarantee Art. 6, para. 1 rights.
[9] *Poitrimol*, para. 31.
[10] See also *Kamasinski*, para. 106.
[11] *Monnell and Morris v. United Kingdom.*

In *Kamasinski v. Austria*, in rejecting a complaint of discrimination in that accused persons at liberty were not excluded from appeal hearings, the Court appeared to give weight to the difficulties that attach to the attendance of prisoners which do not apply to accused persons at liberty or civil parties.[12]

Cross-reference

Part IIA: Legal representation in criminal proceedings
Part IIA: Public hearing and judgment

---

[12] The Commission had found no objective or reasonable justification for refusing to allow an accused prisoner to attend merely because of cost and administrative difficulties, attaching importance to his right to hear his case.

Presumption of innocence

Key provision:

Article 6, paragraph 2 (presumption of innocence).

Key case law:

Minelli v. Switzerland, March 25, 1983, Series A, No. 62; 5 E.H.R.R. 554; *Salabiaku v. France,* October 7, 1988, Series A, No. 141–A; 13 E.H.R.R. 379; *Schenk v. Switzerland,* July 12, 1988, Series A, No. 140; 13 E.H.R.R. 242; *Pham Hoang v. France,* September 25, 1992, Series A, No. 243; 16 E.H.R.R. 53; *Sekanina v. Austria,* August 25, 1993, Series A, No. 266A; 10 E.H.R.R. 182; *Allenet de Ribemont v. France,* February 10, 1995, Series A, No. 308; 20 E.H.R.R. 557; *John Murray v. U.K.,* February 8, 1996, R.J.D., 1996–I, No. 1; *Leutscher v. Netherlands,* March 26, 1996, R.J.D., 1996–II, No. 6.

1. General considerations

The presumption of innocence applies to persons charged with criminal offences.[1] The principle has had relevance in regard to the different ways domestic systems deal with factual presumptions and the evidentiary burden of proof, the way in which courts penalise defendants in costs or issue qualified acquittals and the prohibition of public statements of guilt by officials.

2. Burden of proof: evidential presumptions

Rules which impose presumptions of law or fact which act to place the burden on the defendant to rebut them are not *per se* contrary to Article 6, paragraph 2. They must however be confined within reasonable limits which take into account the importance of what is at stake and the rights of the defence. In particular, the operation of presumptions must not strip a trial court of any effective power of assessment of the facts or guilt.

Thus in *Salabiaku v. France,* where the applicant took delivery of a locked trunk which proved to contain drugs, he was subject to a presumption of responsibility. Since however the domestic courts maintained a freedom of assessment and gave attention to the facts of the case, quashing one conviction, the Court found no violation.[2] Where in *Pham Hoang v. France,* a presumption was applied to the driver of the car involved in a drugs deal who was convicted of possession, the Court found that it was not irrebuttable nor prevented the driver from raising a defence (*e.g. force majeure,* unavoidable mistake or necessity). Since the court refrained from any automatic reliance on the presumption but carried out an assessment of the facts, basing its finding of guilt on a cumulation of factors (the circumstances of the arrest, and his earlier involvement in the gang's activities), the presumption was not applied in a manner incompatible with Article 6, paragraph 2.

Similarly in a Maltese case, the Commission found that it was acceptable to impose liability on a company director for customs offences committed by the company unless he

---

[1] However, in *Albert and Le Compte v. Belgium,* February 10, 1983, Series A, No. 58; 5 E.H.R.R. 533, the Court held that the presumption of innocence applied to disciplinary proceedings against doctors, whether they were civil or criminal, the principles set out in paras 2 and 3 being implicit in para. 1.

[2] There was a defence of "unavoidable error" and the court gave weight to the fact that he had been warned by an official not to take the trunk unless he was sure it was his and therefore he had been put on notice and could have checked the contents.

could show that the offence was committed without his knowledge and that he exercised all due diligence to prevent the commission of the offence. This was not an irrebuttable or self-contradictory presumption and the courts retained a genuine freedom of assessment in determining whether an offence had been committed by the applicant.[3] In cases where owners of pit bull terriers and other dangerous breeds were faced with a statutory presumption that their dogs were of such a breed unless proved otherwise the Commission found no violation since there was the opportunity to disprove the assumption and courts retained an area of assessment, albeit limited, where the matter was put in issue.[4]

3. Orders on acquittal or termination of proceedings

Article 6, paragraph 2 applies to criminal proceedings in their entirety, not solely the part dealing with the merits. Thus, comments made by judges on the termination of proceedings or following acquittal which reflect the opinion that he is guilty will violate the presumption of innocence.[5] Thus, in *Minelli v. Italy*, where a court in declining to follow the normal rule of awarding costs to the accused, remarked that he "very probably" would have been convicted but for the termination of the proceedings because of rules of prescription, a violation was found. Where an applicant was acquitted by one court and refused costs by a different court, the presumption of innocence guarantee still applied to the second proceedings and was violated where the second court found that serious grounds for suspecting him still existed.[6] Some voicing of suspicion regarding an accused may be conceivable before the conclusion of the proceedings, as in the *Lutz v. Germany*[7] case but it was not permissible to rely on such suspicions after acquittal became final.

Where therefore a judge makes remarks which expressly or by clear implication attribute guilt to an acquitted defendant, there is likely to be a violation. In *Moody v. United Kingdom*[8] and *Lochrie v. United Kingdom*[9] the judge's comments on disallowing the costs for a failed prosecution for sale of obscene material which were to the effect that the material was obscene and that they should nonetheless be penalised for having been involved in dealings with it were found incompatible with the presumption of innocence. Conversely, in *D.F. v. United Kingdom* where the judge refused a full costs order when the applicant was acquitted commenting that the case stank of greed and that if ever a man brought a case upon himself it was the applicant who had not said anything to clear himself during the investigation,[10] the Commission found that the refusal of costs was not made on the basis of any continuing suspicion being harboured and that though the judge referred to greed his comments could not be interpreted as implying any finding of dishonesty which was an element of many criminal offences.

---

[3] 16641/90, (Dec.) December 10, 1991.

[4] *e.g.* U.K. *Bates* 26280/95; *Foster* 28846/95 and 26279/95 *Brock* (Decs.), January 16, 1996.

[5] *e.g. Minelli v. Italy,* para. 37.

[6] *Sekanina v. Austria.*

[7] The criminal proceedings had been stayed due to a time bar, and in refusing to order repayment of the applicant's costs, the domestic courts stated that he would most probably have been found guilty. The court considered that this statement of the existence of a suspicion did not disclose a violation.

[8] 22613/93, (Rep.) January 16, 1996.

[9] 22614/93, (Rep.) January 18, 1996.

[10] He waited until the trial for the case to be undermined by evidence proving allegedly that there was no deception exercised 22401/93 U.K., (Dec.), October 24, 1995.

4. Statements implying guilt by other state authorities

The presumption of innocence is binding not only on the court before which a person charged is brought but on other State organs.[11] In *Allenet de Ribemont v. France*, where the applicant, while in police custody, was described at a press conference by senior police officers as being the instigator of the murder under investigation, the Court rejected the Government argument that Article 6, paragraph 2 only applied to the judicial authority in the context of criminal proceedings ending in a conviction but held that it applied to other public authorities where an applicant was "charged with a criminal offence". Since the declaration of guilt was made without any qualification or reservation and encouraged the public to believe the applicant guilty, in prejudgment of the assessment of the facts by the competent judicial authority, there was a violation, which was not cured by the fact that the applicant was later released by a judge for lack of evidence.

Where issues related to criminal charges on which a person has been acquitted arise in civil cases, courts may deal with the aspect of civil responsibility arising from the same facts but must regard themselves bound by the finding of the criminal court with regard to criminal responsibility. Therefore no violation was found where labour courts dismissed a teacher who had been acquitted of the charge of supplying drugs to a boy who committed suicide under their influence. The domestic court referred to the factors in which the teacher failed to help the boy in appropriate ways without contradicting the findings of the criminal court.[12]

5. Penalties for failure to give information

In a number of contexts, liability involving fines or imprisonment may be imposed where a person fails to comply with a requirement to provide information. This has not been found a problem in traffic offences, where an owner of the car is liable if he does not give the name of the person who was driving it at the time, such presumption of responsibility having been found acceptable.[13]

Where the question of the right to silence or privilege against self-incrimination has been in serious issue however, the Convention organs have tended to treat the issue as a problem of fairness under Article 6, paragraph 1 rather than the presumption of innocence.[14]

6. Cure on appeal

It may be possible for a breach of presumption of innocence to be cured by a superior court making the matter clear where the person was acquitted or proceedings

---

[11] 7986/77, (Dec.) October 3, 1978, 13 D.R. 73, where the applicant complained that the Minister of Justice had made a statement on television to the effect that she had committed criminal acts although she had not yet been convicted, the Commission rejected the complaint, as although the statement could have been more carefully worded, in context the words could be taken as information given to the public about the basis of suspicion against the applicant and the announcement of a trial about to take place; *U.K.*, 20755/92, (Dec.) October 10, 1994 where the Commission found that the Parole Board as a public authority was bound by the applicant's acquittal on charges of rape and incest not to treat him as guilty of these offences (allegedly committed while he was on 48 hour pre-release scheme). It was not however precluded, in reaching a decision against release, from examining the circumstances leading up to the prosecution in its overall assessment of the applicant's risk to the public.

[12] 9295/81, (Dec.) October 6, 1982, 30 D.R. 227; 11882/85, (Dec.) October 7, 1987, 54 D.R. 162 where a janitor of a school was acquitted of theft but his dismissal upheld by an industrial tribunal.

[13] 23861/94, *Spain*, (Dec.) May 17, 1995 car caught by radar for speeding; owner refused to say who drove and fined 50,000 pesetas.

[14] See Part IIA: Right to Silence.

terminated.[15] This occurred in *Adolf v. Austria*[16] where in discontinuing proccedings for triviality, the Austrian court made ambiguous statements, which the applicant claimed were capable of suggesting that he had inflicted bodily harm on the complainant. However, the Supreme Court on the applicant's application clearly stated that discontinuance was not to include anything in the nature of a verdict of guilt and it would have been preferable if the lower court had stated this more explicitly. The Court found that the lower court judgment had to be read in light of the Supreme Court ruling and therefore the applicant was cleared of any finding of guilt and the presumption of innocence no longer called into question. Where the applicant was found guilty and the presumption of guilt occurred during the proceedings, it might be more problematic to cure without acquitting or sending back for re-trial.

Cross-reference

Part IIA: General principles
Part IIA: Right to silence

---

[15] *Austria v. Italy*, (1966) 788/60, 6 Ybk of the ECHR 740, where a breach is so gross as to distort the course of the proceedings, cure may not be possible.
[16] March 26, 1982, Series A, No. 49.

Public hearing and judgment

Key provision:

Article 6, paragraph 1 (right to public hearing and public pronouncement of judgment).

Key case law:

Albert and Le Compte v. Belgium, February 10, 1983, Series A, No. 58; 5 E.H.R.R. 533; *Pretto v. Italy,* December 8, 1983, Series A, No. 71; 6 E.H.R.R. 182; *Axen v. Germany,* December 8, 1983, Series A, No. 72; 6 E.H.R.R. 195; *Sutter v. Switzerland,* February 22, 1984, Series A, No. 74; 6 E.H.R.R. 272; *Campbell and Fell v. U.K.,* June 28, 1984, Series A, No. 80; 7 E.H.R.R. 165; *H v. Belgium,* November 30, 1987, Series A, No. 127; 10 E.H.R.R. 339; *Ekbatani v. Sweden,* May 26, 1988, Series A, No. 134; 13 E.H.R.R. 504; *Hakansson and Sturesson v. Sweden,* February 21, 1990, Series A, No. 171; 13 E.H.R.R. 1; *Helmers v. Sweden,* October 29, 1991, Series A, No. 212–A; *Jan-Ake Andersson v. Sweden,* October 29, 1991, Series A, No. 212–B; 15 E.H.R.R. 218; *Fejde v. Sweden,* September 26, 1991, Series A, No. 212–C; 17 E.H.R.R. 14; *Schuler-Zgraggen v. Switzerland,* June 24, 1993, Series A, No. 263; 16 E.H.R.R. 405; *Fredin (No. 2) v. Sweden,* February 23, 1994, Series A, No. 283-A; *Diennet v. France,* September 26, 1995, Series A, No. 315–B; 21 E.H.R.R. 554; *Botten v. Norway,* February 19, 1996, R.J.D., 1996–I, No. 2; *Bulut v. Austria,* February 22, 1996, R.J.D., 1996–II, No. 3; *Stallinger and Kuso v. Austria,* April 23, 1997, R.J.D., 1997–II, No. 35; *Werner v. Austria* and *Szucs v. Austria,* November 24, 1997, R.J.D. 1997–VII, No. 56.

1. General considerations

There are two hearing aspects — whether the proceedings are open to public and whether there is an oral hearing at which applicant may address the court.

2. Public hearing

The public character of proceedings before judicial bodies protects litigants against the administration of justice in secret without public scrutiny. It maintains public confidence in the courts and in rendering the administration of justice visible contributes to the achievement of a fair trial, a fundamental guarantee in a democratic society.[1] While practice varies in States, as regards hearings and pronouncement of judgments, the Court will look at the realities of the procedure, the purpose underlying the guarantee rather than at the formalities which are of lesser importance.[2]

Generally a public hearing is required before the court of first and only instance.[3] Lack of public hearing will not be cured by a public hearing before an appeal or cassation instance where that does not consider the merits of the case or is not competent to deal with all aspects of the matter.[4] Where a public hearing has not been provided at first instance, exceptional reasons will be required to justify refusal of one at second instance.[5]

---

[1] *Axen,* para. 25; *Werner,* para. 45.

[2] *Axen,* para. 26.

[3] However, see *Schuler-Zraggen v. Switzerland* below which suggests that in technical matters such as social security courts may dispense on grounds of expediency on systematic hearings.

[4] *e.g. Albert and Le Compte v. Belgium,* para. 37 where a public hearing in the Court of Cassation did not cure the lack of publicity before the professional jurisdictional organs; *H. v. Belgium,* where in reinstatement proceedings by a lawyer struck from Bar roll the proceedings were not heard in public or decision pronounced in public — there were no circumstances such as to warrant the proceedings being held in camera, no indication of waiver and this was not cured by later hearings as there was no appeal; *Diennet v. France,* no public hearing in disciplinary body, not cured by medical appeal body being in public since not judicial with full jurisdiction.

[5] *Stallinger and Kuso v. Austria,* para. 51.

3. Absence of a hearing

Hearings may not take place at all where a domestic court decides on the basis of written submissions. It generally flows from the notion of a fair trial that an accused person is entitled to attend a trial hearing in criminal matters. Where in civil proceedings, there is no hearing before the first and only judicial instance, and the proceedings raise issues of fact and law, it is likely that a violation will arise.[6] However, in *Schuler-Zgraggen v. Switzerland*, there was no oral hearing before the Federal Insurance Court in respect of a claim for invalidity insurance. While the Court found that the rules made provision for the possibility of hearing on application by a party or by the court's own motion and that there was unequivocal waiver from the applicant's failure to ask for a hearing, it also made reference to the nature of the proceedings, which were highly technical concerning private medical details and no issues of public importance, in which circumstances it considered domestic courts could have regard to reasons of expedition, efficiency and economy in avoiding holding hearings systematically.

A hearing is not automatic for appeal or later proceedings, the Court allowing for factors of dealing expeditiously with court caseloads. The question must be settled with regard to the nature of the proceedings, the scope of examination and powers of the domestic court and the manner in which the applicant's interests are presented and protected.[7]

In leave to appeal proceedings, appeal or cassation proceedings involving only questions of law the lack of hearing at second or third instances may be justified by their special features.[8] Leave to appeal in a criminal case, where the applicants were not able to be present at leave to appeal against conviction and to present argument, did not raise issues of such a nature as to require their presence and since they had received free legal advice as to appeal (they had been advised no grounds arose), were able to present written argument on all relevant issues, the interests of justice and fairness were satisfied.[9]

The fact that an appeal instance has jurisdiction over facts as well as law is not decisive, it being more relevant the nature of the issues to be decided in the particular case.[10] In *Ekbatani v. Sweden*, where the Court found that the court of appeal could not fairly or properly determine the issues without hearing the complainant or applicant in person, the crucial question appeared to be the credibility of the applicant and complainant. In *Helmers v. Sweden* (a private prosecution in defamation by the applicant), the court of appeal had to examine questions of fact and law and make full assessment of the defendant's guilt or innocence. The Court also had regard to the seriousness of what was at stake for the applicant's professional reputation and career though it is not apparent why this would require an oral hearing which was otherwise not warranted by the factual or legal issues to be decided.[11] The importance of what is at stake appeared to play a decisive role in two

---

[6] *Fredin (No. 2) v. Sweden*: concerning an application for annulment of revocation of a permit for a gravel pit where the Supreme Administrative Court was the only instance but refused a hearing. The court had jurisdiction not only over law but facts and the submissions in the case where capable of raising issues of fact and law shown by the minority of court who expressed opinion that it was necessary to obtain clarifications at an oral hearing.

[7] e.g. *Monnell and Morris v. U.K.*, para. 56.

[8] *Monell and Morris, Axen and Sutter*; see also *Bulut*, where no violation for lack of hearing when the Supreme Court rejected a plea of nullity in summary proceedings as manifestly lacking in merit, these being akin to leave to appeal proceedings and nature of grounds not such as to require a hearing.

[9] *Monell and Morris, ibid.*

[10] *Helmers v. Sweden.*

[11] The lack of particularly convincing elements which might require a further hearing is indicated by the large dissenting minority (11 votes to 9 for violation). The importance of what was at stake for the applicants in *Monnell and Morris* was not apparently relevant in the leave to appeal proceedings. See also *Botten v. Norway*, where the Supreme Court had full jurisdiction, and overturned the acquittal on its assessment of "neglect" and dealing with sentencing (issues of personality and character) without hearing the applicant — reference to the effect on the applicant's professional career in finding a violation.

other cases, *Jan-Ake Andersson v. Sweden* (a road traffic offence and small fine) and *Fejde v. Sweden* (illegal possession of firearm and small fine) where the Court referring to the minor nature of the penalties and the inability of the courts to increase them, found no violation for lack of oral hearing on appeal, since though the court had jurisdiction over facts and law, there were no issues which could not adequately be determined on the basis of the case file.[12]

4. Waiver

A public hearing may be waived by the applicant if by his own free will and unequivocal.[13] Waiver must however not run counter to any important public interest, which appears to suggest that in serious cases the appearances of justice will require a public hearing regardless of the applicant's views.[14] Where in *Hakansson and Sturesson v. Sweden*, the appeal court (the only judicial instance) had the power to hold an oral hearing[15] but the applicants did not ask for one, this was found to constitute an unequivocal waiver of their right to a public hearing and there were no questions of public interest which would have rendered one necessary.[16] On the other hand, in *H v. Belgium* there was no waiver although the applicant did not ask for public hearing, since there was no provision for it or practice in the procedures adopted, and little prospect of securing one.[17] In *Botten v. Norway*, where the applicant made no request to be present or any objection, the Court found that the Supreme Court was under a positive duty to take positive measures to ensure his presence as necessary to a proper assessment.

5. Exclusion of public

There are specified exceptions to the requirement that proceedings be open to the public *e.g.* morals, public order, national security, interest of juveniles, protection of private life of the parties or where strictly necessary in special circumstances where publicity would prejudice the interests of justice.[18] These have not been subject to considerable examination. In *Campbell and Fell v. United Kingdom*, while the Court found that criminal trials with security problems must almost always be open to the public, as regarded disciplinary hearing in prisons, the practical difficulties in admitting the public to prison precincts or problems of transportation if the Board of Visitors met outside would render a requirement of public hearings a disproportionate burden on the State.

6. Public pronouncement of judgment

The Court, faced with apparent absolute wording of this part of Article 6, noted in *Pretto v. Italy*, *Axen v. Germany* and *Sutter v. Switzerland* that domestic courts had a variety of ways of rendering decisions public. Assuming that the drafters of Convention could not

---

[12] The Commission found the cases indistinguishable from previous authorities, finding violations since the appeal court had jurisdiction over facts and law and had to reconsider guilt and innocence.

[13] *e.g. Albert and Le Compte*, para. 35: the Court found that there was nothing in the letter or spirit of Art. 6, para. 1 to prevent waiver of this aspect in medical disciplinary proceedings.

[14] *Hakansson and Sturesson v. Sweden*, para. 66.

[15] Even though the Commission found that practice mitigated against one being granted in such a case.

[16] See also *Zumtobel v. Austria*, September 21, 1993, Series A, No. 268–A; 17 E.H.R.R. 116 unequivocal waiver found where applicant represented by lawyer who did not request a hearing as was open to him and the nature of the proceedings not require hearing (no issues of public interest — expropriation proceedings).

[17] See also *Werner v. Austria*, para. 48, an applicant cannot be blamed for not making an application which had no prospect of success.

[18] The converse, that a party or accused, could claim a right to in camera proceedings, has not been examined substantively as yet.

have overlooked this, the Court refused a literal interpretation and held that the form of "publicity" to be given to the "judgment" in domestic law must be assessed in the light of the special features of the proceedings and by reference to the object and purpose of Article 6, paragraph 1. It may be sufficient for higher instances with limited reviewing functions to dispense with pronouncement in open court where provision is made for some form of scrutiny by the public via publications or registries.[19] At lower instances, the requirements are more stringent. Where there is no access to lower court judgments, there is likely to be a violation as in *Werner v. Austria* and *Szucs v. Austria*, in which the courts of first instance and courts of appeal did not give judgment in public nor were the full texts of their judgments openly available to the public in their registries, access limited to those with a "legitimate interest".

A violation was found in *Campbell and Fell*, since not only did the Board of Visitors not pronounce judgment publicly but also took no other steps to make their decisions public.

Cross-reference

Part IIA: Legal representation in criminal proceedings
Part IIA: Presence in court

---

[19] No violations in *Pretto, Axen* and *Sutter,* which concerned high instances of appeal or cassation, which had limited review powers, for example, being unable to alter the verdict but only to confirm or quash or render final. Regard was also had to whether there were public hearings and judgment at earlier stages. It was enough by way of publication in *Pretto* that the judgment of the *Cour de Cassation* was deposited in the registry and available on demand. In *Sutter,* it was acceptable that the full text of the judgment of the military court of cassation was available from the court and this case was published in an official collection, although a dissenting minority noted the considerable delay in publication and that access was only to persons who established an interest.

Reasons for decisions

Key provisions:

Article 6, paragraph 1 (fairness); paragraph 3(b) (adequate time and facilities).

Key case law:

H v. Belgium, November 30, 1987, Series A, No. 127; 10 E.H.R.R. 339; *Van de Hurk v. Netherlands*, April 19, 1994, Series A, No. 288; 18 E.H.R.R. 481; *Ruiz Torija v. Spain and Hiro Balani v. Spain*, December 9, 1994, Series A, Nos. 303–A; *De Moor v. Belgium*, June 23, 1994, Series A, No. 292–A; 18 E.H.R.R. 372; *Georgiadis v. Greece*, May 29, 1997, R.J.D., 1997–III, No. 38.

1. General considerations

Article 6, paragraph 1 has been interpreted as obliging courts to give reasons for their decisions though this does not require a detailed answer to every question.[1] The Convention organs' resistance to constituting a fourth instance leaves in practice little scope for attacking the adequacy of the reasons given in judgments. There has been no development under Article 6 as in the context of Article 8, 9 and 10 that decisions must necessarily be supported by relevant and sufficient reasons, which requirement only comes into play where it is established that there has been an interference with a protected right. Article 6 confers primarily procedural protection based on the paramount consideration of fairness. It does not guarantee as such the "right" result and on the current approach by the Convention organs, the quality of reasoning is only likely to disclose a violation where there is clear arbitrary or grossly unreasonable failure on the part of the domestic court concerned.

2. Lack of reasons

Lack of reasons in a decision was taken as an aspect of procedural safeguards in *H v. Belgium*. In that case, the Bar Council's procedure was open to criticism in two respects: lack of public hearing and the lack of precision in rules or case law as to the meaning of the "exceptional circumstances" condition required for reinstatement to the Bar. The imprecise nature of the statutory concept rendered it all the more necessary for impugned decisions refusing reinstatement to give sufficient reasons. Since the decision in the case merely said that no such circumstances existed without explaining why those relied on by the applicant did not qualify, there was found to be a breach of Article 6, paragraph 1, together with the aspect of lack of public hearing.

Juries in criminal cases rarely give reasoned verdicts. The relevance of this to fairness has been touched on in a few cases. Where in an Austrian case, the jury in a criminal case gave no reasons for their verdict, the Commission found no unfairness since they were given detailed questions to answer on which counsel could apply to make modifications and this specificity made up for lack of reasons. In addition, the applicant could and did file grounds of nullity on the basis that the judge wrongly explained the law.[2]

---

[1] *Van de Hurk.*

[2] 25852/94 *Austria*, May 15, 1996. See also 15957/90 *Belgium*, (Dec.) March 30, 1992, 72 D.R. 195, where the Commission noted that the extent to which reasons must be given depends on the circumstances of the case, particularly its nature and complexity — the applicant had been convicted of homicide by a jury on basis of simple "yes" answer — while an issue might arise where as here there was an appeal on the merits from the decision for which no reasons given it was not a problem in this case since the judge had put questions on the facts to the jury for their answer and the defence could contest the questions or request modifications, which compensated for the lack of reasoning and contest the questions or request modifications, which compensated for the lack of reasoning and formed the framework of the decision. (Same reasoning 20664/92 *Belgium*, (Dec.) June 29, 1994, 78 D.R. 97).

Lack of reasoning is likely to be more acceptable in the higher instances, in the same way that it may be compatible to dispense with oral or public hearings.[3] The Convention organs are unlikely to be demanding in the reasons given where the issues raised, from their nature or subject-matter, may legitimately receive short shrift. In a case dealing with the relatively trivial matter of a tax disc on a car,[4] the Commission found no violation where a fine was imposed by the *Cour de Cassation* without reasons when dismissing an appeal though it was impossible to deduce from the legislation or decision why the fine was imposed. It was enough for the Commission to note that the grounds of appeal appeared manifestly ill-founded and the *Cour de Cassation* rejected them after a thorough, amply reasoned examination.[5]

3. Omissions and reliance on inadequate reasons

While a court has to give reasons, the Court has held that it is not required to answer all points raised and that it was not the Court's role to examine whether arguments are adequately met.[6]

A violation may arise however where domestic courts fail to answer relevant submissions which are not ill-founded.

In *Ruiz Torija v. Spain* (an action against the applicant for breach in terms of lease of gaming machines) there was a total failure of the *Audencia Provincial* to address the applicant's clear and timely submission that the action was time-barred. The Court noted that it was not its role to rule if the objection was well-founded. It was enough that it was "relevant" in the sense that if the court had ruled in his favour the action would have been terminated. Conversely, the Court was not convinced that the objection was so ill-founded that it was unnecessary for the appeal court to refer to it. The first instance had allowed evidence on the point and in absence of mention in the judgment, it was not apparent whether it was impliedly rejected or whether the court had merely neglected to consider it. Since the point required an express reply not contained in a decision on the merits, there was a violation. A similar approach was adopted in *Hiro Balani v. Spain*, a trademark dispute in which the applicant's claim that her trademark had priority would have been decisive if upheld. There was no answer in the Supreme Court's judgment to this "clearly relevant" submission, and the Court did not consider that it could be assumed that it was impliedly rejected. It was not so clearly ill-founded that no reply was necessary and there was a violation in the absence of that reply.

---

[3] See Part IIA: Public hearing.

[4] 15384/89, (Dec.) May 9, 1994, 77–A D.R. 5.

[5] See, *e.g.* 12275/86 *France*, (Dec.) July 2, 1991, 70 D.R. 47, where the Commission held that absence of reasons in a judicial decision may raise a question as to fair hearing but that in this case where the *Conseil d'Etat* judgment in dismissing the appeal as vexatious and imposing a fine did not state exactly why it was vexatious, this was sufficiently shown by the fact that it went through all the appeal grounds in detail finding them groundless. It was not unfair that no opportunity was given to argue whether the appeal was vexatious or not, since the issue was closely connected to the disposal of the appeal on the merits as a whole.

[6] *Van de Hurk:* On the whole, in a general assessment of the judgment, the Court did not find it insufficiently reasoned. See also Commission's approach, *e.g.* 10153/82 *Austria*, (Dec.) October 13, 1986 49 D.R. 67: judges have to hear the arguments but are not bound to discuss each submission in detail or reflect the parties submissions explicitly. The applicants had complained that the courts did not deal with the case in the way they presented it and had distorted the legal assessment of their claims *i.e.* they had made claims under a specific provision and a more general provision and the court had referred only to the former. The Commission said that it was not its task to interfere with the legal assessment of claims made by national courts under domestic law, the application and interpretation of which was in principle reserved to them. Domestic courts were free to qualify a claim according to the criteria which they regard as legally relevant. Therefore a failure to discuss each submission or refer explicitly to them was not unfair as long as the court heard the parties and their pleadings were considered. The fact that the court may have considered them as irrelevant or unfounded and implicitly rejected them could not amount to a breach.

Lack of detailed explanation of the finding of "gross negligence" in *Georgiadis v. Greece* disclosed a violation since the lack of precision of the concept, which was decisive for the applicant's claim for compensation, required more detailed reasoning.

By way of guidance, the Court stated in these cases that the extent of the obligation to give reasons may vary according to the nature of the decision. It was necessary to take into account also the diversity of submissions that a litigant may bring into a court and the differences in Contracting States with regard to statutory provisions, customary rules, legal opinion, and the presentation and drafting of judgments — in other words, all the circumstances of the case.

Failure to give reasons based on the applicable law may also disclose a lack of fairness. In *De Moor v. Belgium*, the refusal of the Bar Council to admit the applicant as a pupil advocate disclosed a violation since it did not base itself on one of the grounds in the applicable code but held that it rejected the application in line with the practice not to admit persons who had fulfilled a full career outside the Bar (which did not automatically disclose any unfitness or incompatibility under the Code). The Court phrased its finding to the effect that the Bar Council did not give the applicant a fair hearing since the reason which it gave was not legally valid.[7]

4. Effective access to appeal procedures

Lack of reasons may raise problems under Article 6, paragraph 3(b) or access to court, where it prevents effective use of appeal procedures. For example, issues may arise from lack of access to the judgment itself[8] or from insufficient detail as to the grounds of the first instance decision.[9] In the latter context, courts must indicate with sufficient clarity the grounds on which they base their decisions, since this is essential for the effective exercise of available rights of appeal.

---

[7] In addition to not providing a public hearing.

[8] *e.g.* where the appeal to Supreme Court was dismissed although the applicant had been unable to obtain copies of the judgments he was appealing against: 15553/89 *Netherlands*, (Rep.) January 17, 1995 settled after admissibility.

[9] *Hadjianastassiou v. Greece*, December 16, 1992, Series A, No. 252–A: the judgment of the Court Martials Appeal court made no mention of the questions as they appeared in the record of the hearing (*i.e.* only gave the brief answers affirmative or negative) and by the time the applicant received the full text he was barred from expanding his grounds of appeal. Therefore the defence was subjected to such restrictions that deprived the applicant of the benefit of a fair trial.

Retrospectivity

Relevant provision:

Article 7 (prohibition of restrospective criminal offences or imposition of heavier penalties).

Relevant decisions:

The Sunday Times v. U.K., April 26, 1979, Series A, No. 30; 2 E.H.R.R. 245; *Welch v. U.K.* February 9, 1995, Series A, No. 307–A; 20 E.H.R.R. 247; *Kokkinakis v. Greece*, May 25, 1993, Series A, No. 260–A; 17 E.H.R.R. 397; *Jamil v. France*, June 8, 1995, Series A, No. 320; 21 E.H.R.R. 65; *G v. France*, September 27, 1995, Series A, No. 325–B; 21 E.H.R.R. 288; *C.R. v. U.K.* and *S.W. v. U.K.*, November 22, 1995, Series A, Nos. 335–B and 335–C; *Cantoni v. France*, November 15, 1996, R.J.D., 1996–V, No. 20.

1. General considerations

Article 7, an essential element of the rule of law, aims at the provision of effective safeguards against arbitrary prosecution, conviction and punishment.[1] Its importance is indicated by the fact that no derogation is possible under Article 15. It embodies the general principle that offences must be based in law, and that an individual must be able to know from the wording of the relevant provision, and if need be, with the assistance of the courts' interpretation of it, what acts and omissions will make him criminally liable.[2] That generally entails that the law must be adequately accessible — an individual must have an indication of the legal rules applicable in a given case — and he must be able to foresee the consequences of his actions, in particular, to be able to avoid incurring the sanction of the criminal law.[3]

In terms of the standard of foreseeability, absolute certainty cannot be required, and indeed may be undesirable, entailing the risk of excessive rigidity, since the law has to be able to keep pace with changing circumstances. A standard of "reasonable foreseeability" is sufficient.[4] The Court in *S.W.* and *C.R. v. United Kingdom* noted that judicial interpretation of criminal law provisions was a widespread and even necessary feature. Article 7 could not be read as prohibiting the gradual clarification of the rules of criminal liability through judicial interpretation from case to case, but the resultant development must be within the bounds of reasonable foreseeability and not alter the "essence" of the offence.[5] Changes which are not to the accused's detriment escape the prohibition.[6]

Retrospective measures in other spheres are not expressly prohibited under the Convention and whether they offend will generally depend on the aims pursued and the proportionality of the effects.[7]

---

[1] *S.W.* para. 34.

[2] *e.g. Kokkinakis*, para. 52, *S.W.*, para. 35.

[3] See, *e.g. G v. France*, para. 25, where notwithstanding changes in legislation leading to reclassification of the sexual offences of which the applicant was accused, these fell within the scope of the Criminal Code provisions, which were accessible and foreseeable.

[4] *Sunday Times*, para. 49.

[5] *S.W.* para 36; *C.R.* para. 34. See also Commission earlier formulation, *e.g.* 8710/79, (Dec.) May 7, 1982, 28 D.R. 77, which excluded that an act not previously punishable be made a criminal offence by the courts or that a definition be extended in such a way as to include acts not previously a criminal offence.

[6] *Kokkinakis*, para. 52; *G v. France*, para. 26 where it was noted that to the extent the law applied retrospectively it mitigated the seriousness of the offence.

[7] See Fair trial guarantees, Legislative interference in proceedings; Tax.

2. Retrospective criminal offences

The complaints brought tend to raise issues less of new statutes or laws being introduced with retrospective effect but of the alleged uncertainty or lack of precision of those unarguably in existence. In these cases, the issues depend on the analysis of whether or not in a particular jurisdiction at a particular time a legal provision complied with the requirement of reasonable foreseeability. In assessing this, the Commission considers that knowledge of specialised or technical provisions may be assumed amongst those persons who work in a particular field.[8]

The Convention organs have also qualified the reasonable certainty test with reference to the hypothetical person seeking appropriate legal advice.[9] In *Cantoni v. France*, where there was allegedly inconsistent case law on the application of the term "medicinal product", the Court noted that a law may still satisfy the requirement of foreseeability, even if the individual has to take appropriate legal advice to assess the consequences of a given action. This was particularly so in respect of persons engaged in professional or commercial activities entailing a certain degree of risk.

The borderline between reasonable and unreasonable development is an uneasy one. Clarification of an element of an offence may not infrequently extend the criminal law to conduct previously thought to be excluded. In a German case,[10] where the courts interpreted an offence of coercion as extending to the applicant's participation in a sit-in in a public road, the Commission commented that extensive interpretation with a view to adapting an offence to the developments in society was acceptable if it could be reasonably brought under the concept of the offence and was foreseeable by the citizen. It concluded that this example of judicial creativity was compatible with Article 7.

In marital rape cases from the United Kingdom which concerned the domestically controversial judicial abolition of an exemption from rape previously accorded to husbands, the Court had no difficulty accepting that the step was reasonably foreseeable, as part of a discernable trend of judicial interpretation.[11] The Court also had regard to the nature of the conduct, namely, rape which was essentially degrading, as showing that the development could not be said to be contrary to the purposes of Article 7 and was in fact in conformity with the fundamental objectives of the Convention, the essence of which was respect for human dignity and freedom. This would seem to indicate that judicial developments which are otherwise in conformity with the spirit of the Convention or relate to inherently objectionable conduct will be more readily found to be reasonably foreseeable.

3. Retrospective imposition of heavier penalties

Where rules regarding procedures and consequences of convictions have changed, this may operate to the significant detriment of persons awaiting trial or already convicted. This is where the second sentence of Article 7, paragraph 1 comes into operation, prohibiting the

---

[8] *e.g.* in the context of criminal prosecution in Austria of a butcher for failure to comply with food standards legislation — 8141/78, (Dec.) December 4, 1978, 16 D.R. 141.

[9] 8710/79, see n.5 where the applicants convicted for blasphemous libel alleged that the law lacked clarity, in particular that the lack of any intention to blaspheme was not established until their own case. The Commission observed that courts could clarify existing elements and adapt to new circumstances. The findings of the courts in the applicants' case was held to be an acceptable clarification and reasonably foreseeable to the applicants with appropriate legal advice.

[10] 13079/87, (Dec.) March 6, 1989, 60 D.R. 256.

[11] There was a line of cases whittling away at the purported immunity. See however the substantial Commission minority who dissented: they saw the abolition of what was a defence to husbands in circumstances in which it had previously been available went too far and was something which should be done by legislation and not retrospectively by the courts, a view shared by the Law Commission.

imposition of a heavier penalty in respect of an offence than that applicable at the time the offence was committed.

It does not apply where on appeal a sentence is increased within the applicable statutory maximum.[12] Where an offence is reclassified to allow it to be tried in a different court where the powers of sentencing are different, the applicant may be sentenced more heavily than he might otherwise anticipated but if the sentence is still within the statutory maximum applicable at the time of the offence the provision is not breached.[13]

A significant impact on punishment was felt by life prisoners when the practice in parole changed to exclude the possibility of release before a minimum of 20 years for certain categories of murderers and other serious offenders. However since the harsh effect related rather to the execution of the penalty than its imposition, the measure was compatible with Article 7.[14]

The notion of "penalty" has been considered in a number of cases.[15]

For the Court the starting point is whether the measure in question is imposed following conviction for a criminal offence.[16] It referred to the other relevant factors in identifying a "penalty" as being the nature and purposes of the measure; its characterisation under domestic law; the procedures involved in its making and implementation and its severity. In *Welch v. United Kingdom*, the retrospective imposition of confiscation orders on persons convicted of drugs offences was found to concern penalties having regard to its integral part of the conviction and sentencing process and the punitive nature of the measure.[17]

A distinction has also been drawn between preventive confiscation measures and punitive confiscatory measures, retrospectivity being prohibited only in respect of the latter. In *M v. Italy*,[18] where a suspected participant in organised crime was subject to confiscation measures imposed retrospectively by an administrative tribunal separate from the criminal proccedings against him, the Commission distinguished between penal measures and measures with a preventive aim, such as the judicial investigation of the probable source of revenue of a person and its removal to prevent its future use in organised crime.

Imposition of imprisonment ordered by a criminal court in default for non-payment of fines where it is intended to be a deterrent and where the applicant remained liable to pay has also been found to involve a penalty. Article 7 was accordingly violated where a drug trafficker on conviction was subject to a retrospective law which increased the period of imprisonment in default of payment replacing the previous maximum of four months with a two year period.[19]

---

[12] See, *e.g.* 12002/86, (Dec.) March 8, 1988, 55 D.R. 218.

[13] 14099/88, (Dec.) April 14, 1989, where the sentencing powers of the Sheriff in Scotland in particular cases increased between the applicant's conviction and sentence — the Sheriff had always had powers to refer to a high court if he considered his own powers inadequate.

[14] 11653/85, (Dec.) March 3, 1986, 41 D.R. 231: the applicant after 13 years was strongly recommended for release and preparing for release in an open prison. After the announced change of policy by the Home Secretary he was returned to closed prison, prospects of parole ended. The Commission found no violation of Article 7 — he had been convicted of an offence for which life imprisonment was provided, that was the sentence received, which under law he remained liable to serve and which was the "penalty" for the purpose of Art. 7, para. 1.

[15] See Part IIA: Fair trial, Criminal Charge (penalties).

[16] See *e.g. Jamil*, para. 31.

[17] *e.g.* the sweeping assumptions imposed by statute that all money in the possession of a convicted trafficker was to be considered as proceeds of crime unless proved otherwise; that measures extended not merely to elements of unjust enrichment but to all proceeds; the way in whch the judge could take into account culpability in allotting confiscation between various co-accused and the possibility of imprisonment in default of payment.

[18] 12386/86, (Dec.) April 15, 1991, 70 D.R. 59.

[19] *Jamil,* where the Court rejected the Government's argument that the measure that could be likened to the seizure of immovable or immovable property to indemnify and compensate the damage suffered through the illegal import of prohibited goods.

4. The exception: general principles of law of civilised nations

There is no decision on the point. The trial judge in *S.W. v. United Kingdom* had been of the opinion that even assuming Article 7, paragraph 1 had been breached, the case fell within the exception in the second paragraph as concerning conduct (rape) which at the time it was committed was criminal according to the general principles of civilised nations. The Court and Commission's majority did not comment. Mr Loucaides in his dissenting opinion to the Commission noted from the *travaux preparatoires* that this provision was intended to cover prosecution of crimes against humanity in the context of the Nuremberg trials. While he did not exclude that other conduct might fall within the meaning of the phrase, a similar common law immunity of rape in the marital area existed or had existed until recently in a number of common law jurisdictions and he was not prepared to find sufficient international consensus on marital rape. However, with the apparent use of rape as a weapon of deliberate policy in some areas, it is perhaps less obvious that rape falls outside this exception or should be excluded because of some local peculiarities.

Right to silence

Key provisions:

Article 6, paragraph 1 (right to a fair trial); Article 6, paragraph 2 (presumption of innocence).

Key case law:

Funke v. France, February 25, 1993, Series A, No. 256–A; 16 E.H.R.R. 297; *John Murray v. U.K.*, February 8, 1996, R.J.D., 1996–I, No. 1; *Saunders v. U.K.*, December 17, 1996, R.J.D., 1996–VI, No. 24; *Serves v. France*, October 20, 1997, R.J.D., 1997–VI, No. 53.

1. General considerations

The right to silence has made a recent appearance in the case law dealing with procedural fairness in criminal trials. It appears to achieve more prominence in the Anglo-Saxon systems, with the formalised system of cautions and the importance attached to oral evidence. There is however all over Europe an increase in the type of criminal/fiscal provisions which place defendants in the position whereby they are required to provide information on pain of a penalty.

In *Funke v. France*, the Court laid down the general principle that Article 6, paragraph 1 contains the right to anyone charged with a criminal offence to remain silent and not to incriminate himself. The right to remain silent under police questioning and the privilege against self-incrimination were found in *John Murray v. United Kingdom* to be generally recognised international standards lying at the heart of the notion of a fair procedure and by providing an accused with protection against improper compulsion contributed to avoiding miscarriages of justice.

2. Coercion to provide incriminating documents or oral testimony

In *Funke*, the Court found that the imposition of fines by the French customs on the applicant for failing to disclose documents concerning his financial transactions violated Article 6, paragraph 1 as offending the principle against self-incrimination. The Commission had reached a different opinion, considering that the protection of a State's vital economic interests legitimately and reasonably required individuals to produce documents relating to matters within customs and fiscal control. It was to be viewed, not as a means of facilitating prosecutions, but as essential for the implementation of the legislation in question and as a reasonable corollary of the trust reposed in citizens generally, allowing the State to forgo more restrictive measures of control and supervision.

The Commission had in mind fiscal powers common everywhere in Europe which require disclosure of income which can be used as the basis of tax evasion proccedings. The Court found, without elucidating, that the special feature of customs law did not justify the coercion applied in this case. The case has attracted criticism.[1]

In *Saunders v. United Kingdom*, where the applicant complained of the transcripts of oral testimony obtained under compulsory powers of DTI inspectors being used in his criminal trial, the Court identified the essence of the privilege against self-incrimination as requiring the prosecution to prove their case without resort to evidence obtained through coercion or oppression against the will of the accused. This objectionable method was to be distinguished from the use of material obtained through compulsory powers, such as blood

---

[1] *e.g.* S. H. Naismith, "Self-incrimination: Fairness or Freedom", [1997] 3 E.H.R.L.R.

or other physical samples, documents, which have an existence independent of the will of the accused. While the Government argued that the statements to the DTI inspectors were in fact exculpatory, the Court found that use of an accused's admissions of knowledge, which were relevant to credibility or contradicted other evidence, could be used by the prosecution to incriminatory effect in violation of Article 6.

As to whether there may be legitimate restrictions on the right against self-incrimination, the Court in *Saunders* rejected the Government's argument that the complexity of corporate fraud and the vital public interest justified the measures applied, even with alleged procedural safeguards. The right applied in criminal proccedings without distinction.

Following the approach of the Court in *Saunders* rather than *Funke v. France*, the Commission has found no infringement of Article 6, paragraph 1 in the context of blood samples obtained under threat of prosecution[2]; requirement to provide information to the tax authorities[3] or due to conviction for speeding offences or parking offences.[4]

Where however a person is fined for failure to give evidence in proccedings in which he is a witness, the approach has been unclear. In *K v. Austria*,[5] the fine was treated by the Commission as interference with freedom of expression, Article 6 not being applicable to proceedings in which he was not subject to a criminal charge. In *Serves v. France*, however, where the applicant refused to take the oath to appear as a witness before an investigating judge in a murder case, the Court found that the applicant could be considered to be subject to "criminal change" for the purposes of Article 6. However, the fines imposed on him for his refusal did not constitute measures compelling himself to incriminate himself. The applicant had, on his account, refused since he did not wish to answer incriminating questions. The Court took the rather narrow view that the fines were imposed on him for refusing to take the oath, a requirement to ensure truthfulness which did not force witnesses to answer specific questions.[6]

3. Drawing of inferences from silence

In *John Murray*, the Court held that the right to silence is not absolute and while it may be incompatible to base a conviction solely or mainly on an accused's silence or on a refusal to answer questions, it is equally obvious that the privilege does not prevent an accused's silence being taken into account in situations which clearly call for an explanation. It had been alleged that the inferences which could be drawn from the failure of a suspect in Northern Ireland either to give explanations to the police for his presence at the scene of a crime or to give evidence at trial amounted to violations of both the right to fair trial and presumption of innocence. However, in this case, the applicant had not been coerced into incriminating himself as in *Saunders*. Nor had he been subject to direct coercion of the type in *Funke* and *Saunders*, being neither fined nor threatened with imprisonment. Having

---

[2] *U.K.*, 30551/96, (Dec.) April 9, 1997.

[3] *e.g. Netherlands*, 27943/95, (Dec.) February 26, 1997, 88–A D.R. 120 where the information was used in tax fraud and evasion proceedings.

[4] *e.g. Spain*, 23816/94, May 17, 1995, 81, D.R. 82 where a car owner was fined when his car was caught in a speed trap and he alleged coercion, either to be convicted himself or inform on another. The Commission saw no problem of the right to silence, since the car used to commit the offence was registered in the applicant's name and he had the overall responsibility for the use to which the car was put.

[5] 16002/91 (Rep.) October 13, 1992, Series A, No. 255–B (settled before the Court).

[6] The Court minority and Commission majority found that the fines were penalties attracting the guarantees of Art. 6 and a violation arose from the imposition of the fines without taking the privilege against self-incrimination properly into account. Other Commission members found a violation because the coercion applied *per se* prejudiced the proceedings which were later taken against him (though they were still pending at the time). Mr Trechsel considered that he could not claim to be a victim of a breach of Art. 6 in his own regard, the facts rather disclosing a breach of Art. 10.

regard to position in other Contracting States where the conduct of the accused can be freely taken into account in the assessment of the evidence, the Court found that the use of inferences was an expression of the common sense implication drawn where an accused fails to provide an innocent explanation for his actions or presence at the scene of a crime. There were sufficient safeguards to comply with fairness and the general burden of proof remained with the prosecution who had to establish a prima facie case before the inference could be brought into play by the judge.[7] The Court's reasoning relies on the facts of the case, where the applicant was found at a house where an IRA kidnap victim was being held and there was other evidence implicating the applicant in the crime.

The use of inferences in Northern Ireland will be examined further in pending cases. These cases involve, *inter alia*, inferences drawn from failure to mention matters to the police later relied on in their defence and arguably are less compatible with the rights of the defence since in effect an accused will be penalised if he gives evidence in court or not. The cases may also indicate whether the Convention organs would find a conviction which relied more heavily on the inferences than in *John Murray* would conform with the requirements of fairness.[8]

Cross-reference

Part IIA: General principles
Part IIA: Legal representation in criminal proceedings
Part IIA: Presumption of innocence

---

[7] The Court discounted the applicant's arguments that it was unfair to draw inferences from his silence at a time before he had received legal advice in the context of Art. 6, para. 1 but dealing with lack of access to a solicitor separately under Art. 6, para. 3(c) found a violation since due to the operation of the provisions in question denial of access at this stage of police questioning might well irretrievably prejudice the rights of the defence. This perhaps achieves the compromise position of permitting States to draw inferences but insists that the suspects receive legal advice as to the consequences of their silence. The Commission had particular regard to one factor in the safeguards to the fair functioning of inferences: the fact that it was a judge who drew them. Mr Bratza in a separate opinion further emphasised this point. A jury would in his view be less equipped to draw justifiable (and subtle distinctions) inferences and did not produce a reasoned judgment which could be appealed.
[8] 22348/93 K.S.M., *Hamill* 21656/93, *Quinn* 23496/94 (Decs.) October 21, 1996, pending before the Commission, while in John Murray, the accused was found at the house where the police found an IRA kidnap victim and might be expected to produce an explanation, in Quinn, inferences were drawn from the accused's failure to talk to the police before the arrival of his solicitor.

Sentencing

Key provisions:

Article 6 (fair trial); Article 3 (inhuman and degrading punishment).

Key case law:

Weeks v. U.K., March 2, 1987, Series A, No. 114; 10 E.H.R.R. 293; *Hussain v. U.K.*, February 21, 1996, R.J.D., 1996–I, No. 4; *Prem Singh v. U.K.*, February 21, 1996, R.J.D., 1996–I, No. 4.

1. General considerations

Matters of sentencing generally fall outside the scope of the Convention.[1] It is irrelevant whether a burglar is sentenced to five years or ten or whether a suspended sentence is granted for mitigating circumstances. There have been a few hints that a sentence may be so disproportionate that it could disclose a violation. For example, in *Hussain v. United Kingdom* and *Prem Singh v. United Kingdom*, the Commission and Court agreed with the applicants that a true life sentence imposed on children even for murder would raise problems under Article 3. Indeterminate sentences for adults have been found compatible with the Convention where there is sufficient link between the original conviction and continuing detention.[2]

2. Discrimination

However, a measure which might not in itself offend, may do so if applied in a discriminatory manner. Regarding sentencing policies or practices, this has been touched on in a number of cases but no findings of violation made as yet. In *P v. United Kingdom*, complaints concerning the different regimes applicable to boys and girls were settled.[3] In *Nelson v. United Kingdom*,[4] a juvenile offender in Scotland claimed that he was not able to benefit from remission in sentence unlike adults or children in England and Wales. The Commission commented that while complaints about length of sentence, passed after due process of law by a judge in possession of the facts of the case, will not generally fall within the scope of the Convention, a settled sentencing policy which affects individuals in a discriminatory fashion might raise issues of Article 14 in conjunction with Article 5. However in the actual case, any difference with adults was justified since different considerations applied in relation to children and any difference between the regime in Scotland and that in England and Wales was based on geographic grounds and not on personal status.

In *Grice v. United Kingdom*,[5] the Commission also commented that discriminatory release procedures would be problematic but did not find that the applicant AIDS sufferer had substantiated his complaint that prisoners suffering from other illnesses were better treated than he was as regarded compassionate release.

[1] *Weeks*, para. 72.
[2] *Weeks*, Comm. report 9787/82, December 12, 1993, para. 72; 7994/77, *Kotalla v. Netherlands*, 7994/77, (Dec.) May 6, 1978, 14 D.R. 239. A life sentence without any possibility of release might conceivably, notwithstanding the fact that there is no right to parole, raise issues of inhuman treatment.
[3] *U.K.*, 15397/89, (Dec.) January 8, 1992.
[4] *U.K.*, 11077/84, (Dec.) October 13, 1986, 49 D.R. 170.
[5] *U.K.*, 22564/93, (Dec.) April 14, 1994, 77–A D.R. 90; also *U.K.*, 22761/93, (Dec.) April 4, 1994, 77–A D.R. 98 where R.M., an AIDS sufferer, claimed that AIDS was not taken into account as mitigating factor in sentence unlike other illnesses but specifically excluded. However no discrimination was made out of the facts of the case.

3. Fair trial

Procedural rights under Article 6 apply equally to criminal proceedings dealing with sentence. Thus failure to conform with fairness guarantees prior to the passing of sentence may lead to violation.[6]

Cases are currently pending before the Commission as to whether the tariff[7] system applied discretionary lifers, custody for life or detainees during Her Majesty's pleasure offends either Article 5 or 6. If the trial judge recommends one figure for minimum sentence and the Home Secretary increases it, it is arguable that this is an assumption by the Executive of a role in fixing detention not subject to control of the courts or the determination of part of a criminal charge by a non-judicial body.

Cross-reference

Part IIA: General principles
Part IIA: Legal representation in criminal proceedings
Part IIA: Retrospective imposition of heavier penalties

---

[6] *e.g.* lack of legal aid on sentencing appeal *Murdoch v. U.K. (No. 2)*, 5523/94, (Rep.) October 16, 1996; independence and impartiality *Findlay v. U.K.,* February 25, 1997, R.J.D., 1997–I, No. 30.
[7] The term applied to the period of imprisonment fixed for punishment and deterrence before release may be considered.

Tribunal established by law

Key provision:

Article 6, paragraph 1 (fair trial).

Key case law:

Le Compte v. Belgium, June 23, 1981, Series A, No. 43; 4 E.H.R.R. 1; *Campbell and Fell v. U.K.*, June 28, 1984, Series A, No. 80; 7 E.H.R.R. 1; *Sramek v. Austria*, October 22, 1984, Series A, No. 84; 7 E.H.R.R. 351; *H v. Belgium*, November 30, 1987, Series A, No. 127; 10 E.H.R.R. 339; *Belilos v. Switzerland*, April 29, 1988, Series A, No. 132; 10 E.H.R.R. 466; *Demicoli v. Malta*, August 27, 1991, Series A, No. 210; 14 E.H.R.R. 47; *Pfeiffer and Plankl v. Austria*, February 25, 1992, Series A, No. 227; 14 E.H.R.R. 692; *Van de Hurk v. Netherlands*, April 19, 1994, Series A, No. 288; 18 E.H.R.R. 481; *Beaumartin v. France*, November 24, 1994, Series A, No. 296–B; 19 E.H.R.R. 485; *Procola v. Luxembourg*, September 28, 1995, Series A, No. 326; 22 E.H.R.R. 193; *Bulut v. Austria*, February 22, 1996, R.J.D., 1996–II, No. 5.

1. General considerations

Civil rights and obligations or criminal charges must be determined by a "tribunal established by law".

A tribunal does not have to be a court of the "classic" kind integrated with the standard judicial machinery[1] but the fact that it fulfills judicial functions is not enough.[2] Even a court which generally fulfills the ordinary conception of a judicial organ may in certain circumstances lose this classification. According to case law it must be a body independent of the parties, in particular of the exective, and impartial, upon which national legislation confers a power of binding decision in a particular area.[3] This is sometimes expressed as involving substantive aspects, namely its judicial function in determining matters within its competence on the basis of rules of law and after proceedings conducted in a prescribed manner, and procedural aspects, *inter alia*, independence, impartiality, duration of members' terms of office.[4] There is an obvious overlap with the separate requirements of independence and impartiality contained in Article 6, paragraph 1.

2. Plurality of roles

The mere fact that a body has a plurality of functions (administrative, regulatory, adjudicative, advisory or disciplinary) does not exclude it from being a tribunal, Thus in *H v. Belgium*, the Court considered that the *Conseil de l'ordre d'avocats* could be considered a tribunal, as it was exercising a judicial function in deciding on applications for readmission and its impartiality and independence were beyond dispute.[5] However, in *Procolo v. Luxembourg*, in the context of structural impartiality, the Court found that the fact that

---

[1] *Campbell and Fell*, para. 76.

[2] *Le Compte*, para. 55.

[3] Commission in *Pudas v. Sweden*, (Rep.) Series A, No. 125–A, para. 51 citing *Sramek*, para. 36; *Le Compte*, para. 55; Commission report, para. 114 in *McMichael v. U.K.*, February 24, 1995, Series A, No. 307–B concerning the Children's Panel which it considered was not a tribunal having regard *inter alia* to the fact that it was intended not to be a court but to deal with children's cases in a non-contentious manner.

[4] *Belilos*, para. 64.

[5] It did find the fairness of the procedures lacking in two aspects — no reasons for the decision and no public hearing — finding a violation of Art. 6, para. 1 on those grounds whereas the Commission had stated robustly that it was not a tribunal due to the nature of its functions, constitution and lack of procedures.

four out of five members of the *Conseil d'Etat* acted in both advisory and judicial functions in the same case was capable of casting legitimate doubt.[6]

3. Disqualified judges

The Court has held that the right to be tried by a court whose composition was in accordance with law was a right of essential importance, whose exercise did not depend on the parties alone. There was a violation therefore in *Pfeiffer and Plankl v. Austria*, where two disqualified judges sat in circumstances where domestic law did not permit waiver. Where however in *Bulut v. Austria*, there was a disqualified judge who sat but counsel waived objection during the proceedings, the Court found that domestic law permitted waiver and that the matter was examined by higher courts which found the composition of the lower court complied with the law.[7]

4. Power to decide

The power to render a binding decision, which may not be altered by a non-judicial authority to the detriment of a party, is a basic attribute of a tribunal. In *Van de Hurk v. Netherlands*, the tribunal deciding milk quota disputes was subject to a legislative provision which gave the Government the power to deprive judgments of their effect. There was a violation therefore, notwithstanding the Government's argument that the power was never used. In *Beaumartin v. France*, the character of "tribunal" was not satisfied where the *Conseil d'Etat* referred the question of interpretation of the treaty to the Foreign Minister and thus had neither full jurisdiction nor independence from the executive.

5. Procedural guarantees

Lack of independence and impartiality may operate to deprive a body of the necessary character of "tribunal" or disclose a violation *per se*. In *Belilos v. Switzerland*, where a police officer sat in a judicial function deciding cases on a Police Board, the Court referred to its case law on the characteristics of a "tribunal" but its finding of a violation of Article 6 centred on the legitimate doubts as to the independence and organisational impartiality of a civil servant who would return to other departmental duties and would tend to be seen as a member of the police force subordinate to superiors and loyal to colleagues. Similarly, the Court in *Demicoli v. Malta* found that the House of Representatives played a judicial function in determining the applicant journalist's guilt of breach of privilege but it was not impartial since two members impugned in the publications participated throughout proceedings. The Commission had doubted whether part of the legislature could by its very nature be considered a court, having regard to its links with the executive.

Cross-reference

Part IIA: Access to court
Part IIA: Independence and impartiality

---

[6] It found it unnecessary to decide if it was an independent tribunal — paras. 43–45.
[7] Para. 29 citing *Casado Coca v. Spain*, February 24, 1994, Series A, No. 285; 18 E.H.R.R. 1.

Witnesses

Key provision:

Article 6, paragraph 3(d) (right to examine and have cross-examined witnesses).

Key case law:

Unterpertinger v. Austria, November 24, 1986, Series A, No. 110; 13 E.H.R.R. 175; *Kostovski v. Netherlands*, November 20, 1989, Series A, No. 166; 12 E.H.R.R. 434; *Brandstetter v. Austria*, August 28, 1991, Series A, No. 211; 15 E.H.R.R. 378; *Windisch v. Austria*, September 27, 1990, Series A, No. 186; 13 E.H.R.R. 281; *Isgro v. Italy*, February 19, 1991, Series A, No. 194; *Delta v. France*, December 19, 1990, Series A, No. 191–A; 16 E.H.R.R. 574; *Asch v. Austria*, April 26, 1991, Series A, No. 203–A; 15 E.H.R.R. 597; *Vidal v. Belgium*, April 22, 1992, Series A, No. 235–B; *Saïdi v. France*, September 20, 1993, Series A, No. 261–C; 17 E.H.R.R. 251; *Ludi v. Switzerland*, June 15, 1992, Series A, No. 238; 15 E.H.R.R. 173; *Edwards v. U.K.*, November 25, 1992, Series A, No. 247–B; 15 E.H.R.R. 417; *Baegen v. Netherlands*, October 27, 1995, Series A, No. 327–B; *Doorson v. Netherands*, March 26, 1996, R.J.D., 1996–II, No. 6; *Ferrantelli and Santangelo v. Italy*, August 7, 1996, R.J.D., 1996–III, No. 12; *Van Mechelen v. Netherlands*, April 23, 1997, R.J.D., 1997–III, No. 36.

1. General considerations

Courts are allowed a fair measure of discretion in governing their proccedings. Judges may assess to what extent a requested witness may provide admissible or relevant testimony and intervene to prevent, for example, time-wasting or irrelevant questioning.[1] While the exercise of this discretion is subject to the overriding fairness principle, fairness is judged in relation to the proceedings as a whole and it will be rare that isolated, limited interventions by a judge will exceed that margin however annoying or frustrating to the defence. Since matters of the assessment of evidence are primarily for judges and courts, decisions that a proposed witness's testimony is irrelevant will not disclose a violation unless clearly arbitrary, unreasonable or it is substantiated that the witness was essential to the fair conduct of the proccedings or to secure the rights of the accused.[2]

"Witness" as used in the Convention is an autonomous term, not governed by domestic law classifications, and will cover situations where statements by a person are used by a court or read out at trial.[3]

The most difficult problems arise where witnesses are not available for cross-examination even though their statements are admitted in evidence for the prosecution, whether by reason of vulnerability to threats (organised crime, terrorism) lack of compellability (wives etc.) security of undercover policemen, or where the witness has died or disappeared. The Court is also alert to the inherent dangers of anonymous witnesses. While it states that it does not underestimate the importance of fighting organised crime, the right to fair administration of justice holds so prominent a place in democratic society that it cannot be sacrificed to expediency. A series of sometimes contradictory Court judgments deals with the problems arising in different situations.

---

[1] *Vidal*, para. 33 referring to "appropriate"; *Bricmont*: "necessary" or "advisable".

[2] See, *e.g. Bricmont*, para. 89 referring to "exceptional circumstances" being required to find domestic courts' decisions in this area incompatible with fairness. Also *Barbera v. Spain*, December 6, 1988, Series A, No. 146; 11 E.H.R.R. 360, finding that it was not for the Convention organs to assess whether or not evidence was correctly admitted and assessed but to ascertain whether the proceedings as a whole, including the way in which evidence was taken were fair.

[3] *e.g. Isgro*, para. 33.

2. Use of anonymous witnesses or written evidence from unexamined witnesses

A number of principles have been established[4]:

- in principle all evidence must be produced in the presence of the accused at a public hearing with a view to adversarial argument;
- use of statements in absence of oral testimony is not *per se* incompatible with Article 6, paragraphs 1 and 3(d) but must be compatible with the rights of the defence;
- this rule generally means that the accused must be given a proper and adequate opportunity to challenge and question a witness against him either when the witness makes the statement or later[5];
- it is generally not compatible, where there has been no opportunity to challenge the evidence given by witnesses, for a conviction to be based solely or to a decisive extent on their statements.[6]

Any measure restricting the defence should be strictly necessary and if a less restrictive measure can suffice then that measure should be applied.[7] The Court does not consider that genuine fear of reprisals or of revelation of the identity of undercover police officers can be decisive or overrule the interests of fairness to the defence.[8] Domestic courts also must make proper assessment of any alleged threat to witnesses.[9] While in *Ludi v. Switzerland* there was a legitimate interest in maintaining the anonymity of the undercover policeman the Court was not persuaded that this rendered it impossible to arrange an opportunity for a confrontation or opportunity to question him in such a way as would preserve that anonymity. In *Van Mechelen v. Netherlands*, where the undercover policemen gave evidence in a room separate from the defence but connected by a sound link, the Court was not convinced that these extreme limitations had been shown to be necessary in that case and they were not counter-balanced by the fact that the investigating judge who had ascertained the agents' identities had in a detailed report for the court stated his opinion as to their reliability and credibility.

The Court has found it insufficient to respect the rights of the defence that an accused is only able to put written questions to an anonymous witness, since this deprives him of the opportunity to demonstrate the unreliability or prejudice of the witness.[10] Reference has been made to the importance that the trial court itself should hear the anonymous witness

---

[4] *e.g. Kostovski, Unterpertinger.*

[5] *e.g. Isgro*, where the opportunity to confront a witness, not available at the earlier stage before the investigating judge, and to put questions was sufficient to respect the rights of the defence though the witness had also been questioned by the judge in the applicant's absence.

[6] *e.g. Unterpertinger*: a violation was found where a conviction for assault was mainly based on the complainants' written statements; *Windisch*: the conviction was based largely on anonymous witness statements; *Ludi*, however, where a violation was found, the conviction was not based solely on the written statements of the undercover agent but these played a role in establishing the facts leading to conviction; *Doorson*, where the Court seemed to suggest that even in presence of counterbalancing features (*e.g.* possibility of counsel questioning the witnesses) a conviction should not be based solely or to decisive extent on anonymous witness evidence; *Asch*, where the Commission found the case indistinguishable from *Unterpertinger* but the Court found no violation concerning a conviction where the alleged victim refused to give evidence, seeming to rely on the fact that the conviction was not solely based on her statement.

[7] *Van Mechelen*, para. 58.

[8] *Kostovski; Saidi*, where the Government argued that the witness drug addicts were fragile psychologically, but the Court found that notwithstanding the ravages of drugs etc. and difficulties in obtaining evidence, such a restriction on rights of the defence was not justified (*i.e.* conviction solely based on anonymous statements of the drug addict witnesses).

[9] *Van Mechelen*, para. 61.

[10] *Kostovski*, para. 42; *Van Mechelen*, para. 62.

to be able to judge reliability.[11] In *Baegen v. Netherlands* however, the Commission narrowly found no violation where an accused was able to confront the alleged victim of sexual abuse but did not have the opportunity to question her. The Commission had regard to special features of rape and sexual offences trials and accepted that in criminal proceedings concerning sexual abuse measures may be taken to protect the victim provided such are reconcilable with an adequate and effective exercise of the rights of the defence. Since the accused had not used his opportunity to put written questions or applied to the court to hear her and he had the opportunity to contradict her evidence by submitting to blood or other tests, it was not established that he was unable to challenge the victim's credibility.

In several cases, the Court seemed to accept that the applicant may claim a right to "confront" the witnesses against him, namely, to be physically present and question the persons who have identified him as a suspect.[12] But there may be circumstances where it is sufficient for counsel to confront and question a witness in the absence of the accused, as in *Doorson v. Netherlands*, where the Court found that there were relevant and sufficient reasons for the anonymity of the drug addict witnesses and the domestic court knew the identities of the witnesses and was able to assess their credibility.[13]

Where a witness is no longer available due to death or disappearance, the Court appears to give weight to whether the authorities are at fault in failing to produce him. In *Isgro v. Italy*, the Court noted that the authorities had attempted to find the missing witness.[14] In *Ferrantelli and Santangelo v. Italy*, where the applicants complained that there was no confrontation with a witness who died, the Court noted that the Government was not responsible for the death and that the statement was found by the domestic courts to be corroborated by other evidence.[15]

3. Refusal to call witnesses for the defence

Article 6, paragraph 3(d) does not require the attendance and examination of every witness for the defence.[16] Its essential aim is to ensure equality of arms in examining witnesses, though considerations of equality do not exhaust the provision. A violation was found in *Vidal v. Belgium* where the Court of Appeal heard no witnesses for the prosecution or defence, refusing to call the four witnesses requested by the defence. Since however it overturned the acquittal on basis of the co-accused's statement and case file and increased sentence without giving reasons for rejecting the defence's request, the Court found that this was inconsistent with the notion of fair trial and that the rights of the defence were restricted in breach of Article 6. Where, as in *Brandstetter v. Austria*, a court appoints an expert, the fact that he issues a report unfavourable to the defence will not require the court to appoint another on request of the defence. Where there was no reason to challenge the objectivity of the expert, there was no breach of equality of arms otherwise the procedure would continue ad infinitum. In *Doorson*, the Court found no problem where

[11] See, *e.g. Isgro* where the investigating judge saw the witness (no violation); *Delta*, where the court did not (violation); in *Van Mechelen*, the Commission dissenters (8) considered it insufficient that the investigating judge saw the anonymous witnesses since the trial court had no opportunity to assess their demeanour and there was no pressing reason why the court of appeal when requested by the applicant should not have heard the witnesses itself. The Court did not expressly advert to this element.

[12] *e.g. Saidi*, where the conviction was based solely on the statements of witnesses identifying him to police as drug dealer and he wished a "confrontation" with them.

[13] Paras. 70–73: however the conviction was not solely or decisively based on the statements; contrast *Saidi*, above.

[14] Also *Doorson*, para. 80, where despite the court's efforts it was impossible to secure the attendance of a witness, there was no unfairness in relying on his statement, especially since it was corroborated by other evidence.

[15] The Commission found a violation since it was the Government's fault that they had not acted more speedily (the death occurred 20 months after the arrest) and the statement had, as in *Ludi*, played an important role in establishing the facts leading to conviction.

[16] *Vidal*, para. 33.

the domestic court refused to call a defence expert to give general evidence that drug addicts were not reliable witnesses, noting that it was a matter for the domestic court which could consider that the evidence did not as such elucidate the facts of the case and would not contribute much since similar evidence had already been given by other experts.

B. OTHER

Abortion

Key provisions:

Articles 2 (right to life), 3 (prohibition on torture and inhuman treatment), 8 (respect for family and private life), 9 (freedom of conscience and religion), 10 (freedom of expression) and 11 (freedom of peaceful assembly).

Key case law:

Open Door Counselling and Dublin Well Woman v. Ireland, October 29, 1992, Series A, No. 246; 15 E.H.R.R. 244.

1. General considerations

Abortion continues a controversial subject in European States generally and reveals widely differing approaches, ranging between liberal freedom of choice to women in Norway and almost total prohibition in Ireland. Sensitive to the difficult moral and ethical issues involved and to the lack of consensus, the Commission has been reluctant to intervene and condemn any particular State policy that has been adopted, with the result that no cases on the practice of abortion have even reached the Court. Nonetheless there have been peripheral issues arising around the abortion, in particular, the steps taken, publicly, to support or criticise the practice, which have given rise to case law in the context of Article 10.

2. Who can complain?

Only a person directly affected by the measure or legislation in question may bring a complaint. This includes any woman of child-bearing age (it is not required for a woman to be pregnant)[1]; the husband of a woman who intends to have an abortion[2]; the putative father of a foetus carried by an unmarried mother.[3] It does not include a minister who considers that domestic legislation permitting abortion is wrong[4] or a man (husband and father of children) who objects to legislation on principle.[5]

3. Right to life of the unborn child

The Commission tends to the view, without deciding, that the foetus or unborn child is not protected by Article 2.[6] It refers to the terms of Article 2 as not appearing to apply to

---

[1] 6959/75, *Brüggeman and Scheuten v. FRG,* (Dec.) May 19, 1976, 5 D.R. 103.
[2] 8416/78, *U.K.,* (Dec.) May 13, 1990, 19 D.R. 244.
[3] *H v. Norway,* 17004/90, (Dec.) May 19, 1992, 73 D.R. 155.
[4] *Norway,* 11045/84, (Dec.) March 8, 1985, 42 D.R. 247.
[5] 7045/75, *Austria,* (Dec.) December 12, 1975, 7 D.R. 87.
[6] 6959/75, *Brüggeman and Scheuten v. FRG,* (Rep.), July 12, 1977, 10 D.R. 100. In *Open Door Counselling,* the Court left open whether the restriction on abortion information could be considered as pursuing the aim of protecting the rights of others in the sense of the unborn child.

an unborn child. It does not necessarily exclude the application of the Convention in other circumstances, perhaps outside the medical context of abortion.[7]

4. Inhuman treatment

In *H v. Norway*, the potential father raised the issue of the pain possibly caused to the 14-week-old foetus by the abortion procedure. The Commission found this allegation to be unsubstantiated by the material before it.

5. Rights of a potential father

A potential father cannot derive a claim to be consulted in advance of any abortion. While his rights to potential family life may be interfered with by an abortion, they have to be weighed against the rights of the mother. Where the abortion was on grounds of medical welfare of the mother, the rights of the mother have been found to outweigh those of the father.[8] Where the abortion was not on health grounds but social hardship in *H v. Norway*, the Commission still found that the rights of the woman, as the person primarily concerned by the pregnancy and its termination, prevailed over the father, notwithstanding that the couple had planned to marry and had together planned the pregnancy.

6. Rights of the woman

Availability of abortion

As indicated above, where domestic legislation allows abortion, whether on health or non-health related grounds, the woman's rights prevail over the putative father's. The position is different where the legislation restricts abortion and it is the woman who claims a wider right under domestic law. In a German case,[9] a law was struck down by the Constitutional Court as unconstitutional, which permitted abortion within 12 weeks without a particular ground of necessity. Abortion was subsequently limited to particular grounds. The Commission found that this legislation did not constitute an interference with the applicant women's rights to respect for private life. It had regard to the fact that abortion was permissible, that the health and distress of the mother were taken into account (albeit in restricted scope) and that the criminal provisions did not penalise women excessively (*i.e.* a pregnant woman was exempt from punishment if the abortion was performed by a doctor within 22 weeks and had made use of counselling).

There has as yet been no case introduced by a woman alleging that she has been prevented from having an abortion because of either a blanket prohibition or because she fell foul of restrictive conditions. The Commission's reaction would be likely to be cautious. In the *H v. Norway* case, it referred to the fact that laws on abortion differed considerably between the Contracting States and that "assuming that the Convention may be considered to have some bearing in this field" it found that in such "a delicate area" States must have a certain discretion. Varying restrictions are therefore acceptable. Even if the

---

[7] 23186/94, *Mentes and others v. Turkey*, (Dec.) January 9, 1995 where the Commission declared admissible complaints alleging the security forces forcible expulsion of villagers from their homes including a claim that in the trauma and hardship resulting one of the applicants, a pregnant woman, gave birth prematurely to twins who died. Her complaints were later rejected as unsubstantiated when she failed to give evidence before Commission Delegates, Comm. Rep., March 7, 1996 to be published in R.J.D. 1997.
[8] 8416/78, See n.2.
[9] *Brüggeman and Scheuten*, see n.6.

Commission is tentative about its competence to strike down any particular legal regime on abortion, the possibility is still there.[10]

7. Information about abortion

The only case before the Court concerned the complaint by two women's counselling organisations, two individual counsellors and two women of childbearing age that they were affected by an Irish Supreme Court injunction which restrained the two organisations from providing certain information to pregnant women concerning abortion facilities outside Ireland.[11] In Ireland there was at that time a statutory prohibition of abortion with no apparent exceptions.

The Court held that the State did not have an unfettered or unreviewable discretion in the field of morals. It concluded that the restriction was unnecessary, giving weight to the sweeping nature of the injunction regardless of the age, health or circumstances of the woman concerned, the fact that it was not against the law for a woman to travel abroad and that it prevented the provision of information about abortion facilities which were available lawfully in other Contracting States. It also noted that the counselling was non-directive which lessened any alleged link between the counselling and the destruction of unborn life and that in any case the information was available in other forms (via magazines and telephone directories). It found that the ban appeared to penalise women who were less resourceful or educated and created a risk that women, in the absence of proper counselling, might seek abortion at later stages and fail to take advantage of medical supervision after an abortion.

Even where abortion is not lawful, women may therefore claim the right to access to information from others relating to abortions performed lawfully in another Contracting State, at least, where another person or body is willing to give the information. It is arguable whether the State or public authority could be obliged to make available such information themselves.

8. Expression of views in respect of abortion

The Commission has found it justifiable under Article 10 for individuals to be penalised where they express their views on abortion in certain circumstances to which others may object. It has found that it was an acceptable restriction on freedom of expression where a doctor employed by a Catholic hospital was sacked following expression of views favourable to abortion, in a letter to a newspaper.[12] It emphasised the contractual link freely undertaken by the doctor with an organisation whose convictions on abortion were well-known. On the other hand the Commission also found it justified for the protection of the reputation of others under the second paragraph of Article 10 where a doctor was fined for expressing the opinion that abortion advice centres were embryo-killer syndicates and the trade union organisation advocating them was "Nazi".[13] The Commission gave weight to the light penalty. It might perhaps find restrictions disproportionate if they went

[10] *The Att.-Gen. v. X and others* in Ireland in 1992 was an example of how a blanket prohibition could affect a young teenage girl, pregnant from an alleged rape who had been prevented by injunction from leaving Ireland to seek an abortion in the United Kingdom. The Irish Supreme Court on March 5, 1992 accepted that termination of pregnancy could be permissible under the Irish Constitution where it was established as a matter of probability that there was a real and substantial risk to the life of the mother if the termination was not effected, with the result that the case did not come to Strasbourg. There would conversely be the other end of the spectrum where for example in the case of mentally ill woman, steps were taken to carry out an abortion dispensing with her consent.

[11] *Open Door Counselling* and *Dublin Well Woman v. Ireland.*

[12] *Germany,* 12242/86, (Dec.) September 6, 1989, 62 D.R. 151.

[13] *Germany,* 12230/86, (Dec.) December 12, 1987, unpublished.

beyond relatively small fines or sanctioned persons for the expression of more moderate or considered views outside the context of special contractual relationships.

9. Position of medical staff

There has only been one case indirectly raising issues as to the participation of medical staff in abortion procedures. In a Swedish case, three trainee midwives objected to being required in their training to insert contraceptive coils which they considered to have an abortive effect.[14] The case was struck off when the midwives were allowed to qualify with their certificate indicating that they had not conducted such procedures.

10. Freedom to demonstrate

Where in an Austrian case an association against abortion carried out a public demonstration which was disrupted by others in favour of abortion, the Commission found that it had a right to be protected by the State in the exercise of its freedom of assembly though in the circumstances the State had not failed in its obligations (*i.e.* it accepted the argument, *inter alia*, that more intrusive police intervention would have escalated the violence that occurred).[15]

States may restrain the activities of protesters for or against abortion, in the interests of preventing crime or disorder and protecting the rights of others. Thus it was a legitimate restriction to impose an injunction on a Dutch applicant preventing him maintaining a presence outside an abortion clinic, handing out leaflets and seeking to dissuade women entering. Under Article 9, the activities which primarily aimed at persuading women not to have an abortion did not constitute the expression of a belief.[16]

---

[14] *Sweden*, 12375/86, (Dec.) October 7, 1987, unpublished.
[15] *Plattform Ärzte v. Austria*, 10126/82, (Dec.) October 17, 1985; 44 D.R. 65.
[16] *Netherlands*, 22838/93, (Dec.) February 22, 1995, 80–A D.R. 147.

AIDS

Key provisions:

Articles 3 (prohibition of inhuman treatment); 5 (liberty and security of person); 6 (fair trial within a reasonable time); 8 (respect for private life); 14 (prohibition of discrimination).

Key case law:

X v. France, March 31, 1992, Series A, No. 234–C; 14 E.H.R.R. 483; *Vallée v. France*, April 26, 1994, Series A, No. 289; 18 E.H.R.R. 549; *Karakaya v. France*, August 26, 1994, Series A, No. 289–B; *A and others v. Denmark*, February 8, 1996, R.J.D., 1996–I, No. 2; *Z v. Finland*, February 25, 1997, R.J.D., 1997–I, No. 31; *D v. U.K.*, May 2, 1997, R.J.D., 1997–III, No. 37.

1. General considerations

No case has ever been brought alleging that a State has failed to protect an individual's right to respect for life or security of person through inadequate regulation of public blood bank facilities. It would appear that where State liability for contamination of blood transfusions may have arisen, Contracting States have taken the responsibility of providing a monetary fund to which there has been a possibility of applying for compensation. It has been in the context of such proceedings for compensation that many applications have arisen, involving allegations of delay in the outcome.

The stigma and social difficulties facing AIDS sufferers have not been subject to much exposure in applications, presumably since these are matters of pervasive effect rather than express Governmental policy. Issues have arisen concerning the disclosure of medical details of AIDS sufferers; the risk of inhuman treatment resulting from expulsion to a country where no drugs treatment or support care is available[1] and sentencing and release procedures applicable to convicted prisoners suffering from AIDS.[2]

2. Delay in compensation proceedings

A number of applicants who developed HIV as a result of contaminated blood supplies have had a judgment in their favour by the Court to the effect that the proceedings for compensation have taken an unreasonable length of time. Such proceedings have been found to concern the determination of civil rights within the meaning of Article 6, paragraph 1 as the outcome would be decisive for private rights to damages for injuries.[3]

The Convention organs have emphasised the particular need for expedition in proceedings where the applicant is suffering from a disease such as HIV or full-blown AIDS where deterioration and death may ensue very rapidly. In *X v. France*, the applicant, a haemophiliac who had received blood transfusions in a state hospital, discovered that he was HIV positive and filed a claim for compensation to the relevant Government authority. When he died just over two years later, his appeal was still pending at the Administrative Court of Appeal. The Court found that the period of over two years was

---

[1] *D v. U.K.*

[2] *Grice v. U.K.*, 22564/93, (Dec.) April 14, 1994, 77–A D.R. 90; *R.M. v. U.K.*, 22761/93, (Dec.) April 14, 1994, 77–A D.R. 98.

[3] In *X v. France*, the Court dismissed the Government's argument that the proceedings raised public law issues of the State's exercise of its regulatory authority rather than civil rights.

unreasonable. Though the matter of establishing the State's liability was complex, the Government should have been aware that proceedings were imminent and ought to have commissioned an objective report on liability immediately after the commencement of the cases against them. While two years might not have been dilatory for the average administrative court proceedings, the Court considered that given the incurable nature of the infection and the applicant's reduced life expectancy, exceptional diligence was called for on the part of the domestic authorities, notwithstanding the number of similar pending cases.

The crucial importance of what was at stake was emphasised in other cases.[4] Even where the applicants had themselves contributed not inconsiderably to the delay, the Court found this did not dispense the courts from ensuring compliance with the requirement of reasonable time which in these cases involved the need for exceptional diligence. Furthermore, although in *Karakaya v. France* and *Vallée v. France* the applicants had received compensation from a State fund during the administrative proceedings, the Court found that what was at stake in the proceedings continued to be of great importance, in both pecuniary and non-pecuniary terms. The requirement of exceptional diligence did not apply to proceedings brought by relatives of a deceased AIDS victim, which had commenced after the death had occurred.[5]

3. Discriminatory treatment

(a) *Sentencing and release procedures*

The only cases before the Commission raising allegations of prejudical treatment of HIV or AIDS sufferers have related to the approach taken by the courts in sentencing, and the policy adopted by the prison authorities in early release, of convicted applicants with the disease.[6] While the Commission noted that questions of length of sentence generally fell outside the scope of Article 5 and that there was no right as such to early release, it did find that where procedures relating to the release or sentencing of prisoners appeared to operate in a discriminatory manner, an issue could arise under Article 14 in conjunction with Article 5. It rejected the cases on their facts, however, for perhaps less than convincing reasons.

In *Grice v. United Kingdom*, where the applicant, suffering full-blown AIDS and sentenced to four years, was refused early release from prison on compassionate grounds, he argued that the Home Office was discriminating against HIV/AIDS sufferers, none of whom had ever been released early on compassionate grounds, whereas prisoners suffering from other non-life threatening illnesses, such as senile dementia or treatable illnesses like cancer, were being released. The Commission noted that the applicant's life expectancy had been given by his doctor at trial as two years and then later as 6–12 months but while in prison he had not suffered any sudden deterioration in his condition, he had not been incapacitated in any way or threatened by the development of the opportunistic infections to which AIDS sufferers are prone. The Commission concluded that there was no indication that the applicant had been treated differently by the Home Secretary in the exercise of his discretion as to early release on compassionate grounds.[7]

[4] See *Vallée v. France*, where proceedings for compensation had lasted four years by the date of the Court judgment; *Karakaya v. France*, where proceedings had taken four years three months; *A and other v. Denmark*, periods of five years ten months; six years and two months disclosed violations.

[5] *A and others v. Denmark.*

[6] *Grice and R.M.*, n.2 above.

[7] It is to be noted that the Commission did not comment on the applicant's arguments disputing the Government's contention that death had to be imminent for a person to obtain early release, *i.e.* the sufferers of senile dementia or treatable cancer. It is difficult to assess, if it was correct that persons threatened with less urgent conditions were benefitting from early release, what objective or reasonable justification there could be for treating those with AIDS differently.

In *R.M. v. United Kingdom* in sentencing the applicant who had AIDS, the Court of Appeal expressly refused to take into account his medical condition. It took the approach that on appeals on sentence by AIDS sufferers it was not for the court to alter an otherwise proper sentence to achieve a desirable end, which was rather for the royal prerogative of mercy. Before the Commission, the applicant argued that there was a general practice by the courts of accepting as a substantial mitigating factor in sentence an illness which would definitely shorten the offender's life and that the Court of Appeal had singled out HIV/AIDS sufferers for less favourable treatment. The Commission noted the medical monitoring which even a year into the applicant's sentence still gave him a life expectancy of months and possibly up to two years and found that he had not suffered any serious deterioration or failed to receive proper care in prison. In these circumstances the Commission found that it was not unreasonable or disproportionate for the Court of Appeal not to take his illness into account in mitigating the sentence to be imposed. There was also a reference to the margin of appreciation. The Commission did not address the applicant's arguments that reasonable or not, other sufferers of illnesses which limited life expectancy in a less or as equally drastic way were benefitting from mitigation of sentence.[8] While there may indeed have been nothing wrong or unreasonable in the way the applicant was treated in prison where fortunately he did not become very ill, the Commission's approach ignored the point that Article 14 complaints are about the risk of particular vulnerable groups being singled out for different treatment and that such differences are not compatible under Convention principles if not objectively and reasonably justified.

(b) *Other areas*

There has as yet been no case where it has been alleged that information relating to a person's HIV status has been used to their detriment, for example, as a basis for dismissal from employment or as the basis for depriving them of some service or benefit. Whether that would raise a problem would depend very much on the facts of the case. There is no right to employment as such under the Convention and acts by private persons or bodies would not necessarily engage the responsibility of the State. The circumstances of the case would have to support the contention that the act or deprivation interfered with an aspect of private life, for example, and that the State owed an obligation to provide protection against such interference even by private bodies.

4. Disclosure of medical condition to others

Disclosure of medical details of an HIV/AIDS sufferer to particular persons or to a court may be accepted as justified under Article 8 where there are legitimate interests in doing so and there are adequate safeguards. However, where general public disclosure is concerned there is less likely to be a convincing justification. The Court has emphasised that the interest of the individual in confidentiality of medical records will weigh very heavily in the balance and measures compelling disclosure attract the most careful scrutiny.[9] Respect for confidentiality of health data is identified as being a vital principle in the legal systems of all the Contracting Parties, crucial not only to respect the privacy of the patient but also to maintain confidence in the medical profession and health services.[10]

---

[8] There was the example of Ernest Saunders who had his sentence reduced by the Court of Appeal in the light of medical evidence of pre-senile dementia (May 16, 1991).

[9] *Z v. Finland*, para. 96.

[10] *ibid.*, the Court cited a recommendation of the Committee of Ministers (Council of Europe), which pointed out that lack of confidence might lead persons to avoid seeking assistance, which would endanger their own health and general community where transmissible diseases were involved — R(89) 14 on the ethical issues of HIV infection in the health care and social settings adopted October 24, 1989, explanatory memorandum paras 166–168.

In *TV v Finland*,[11] in respect of allegations concerning disclosure of a prisoner's HIV conditions to persons within the prison, the Commission found that access by prison and medical staff to information concerning his status prima facie constituted an interference with his right to respect for his private life within the meaning of Article 8 of the Convention. However, this disclosure was not unlawful, pursued the aim of protecting the rights of others with whom he came in contact and there was no evidence that the information was passed beyond the staff who dealt with him and who could justifiably expect to receive information relating to a disease which he carried. Impliedly, the case might have been decided differently if in fact it had appeared that the personal information relating to his condition had been circulated more widely than those immediately dealing with him or that the information had been stored in such a way as to make it accessible to others unconnected with him.

In *Z v. Finland*, disclosure of the applicant's HIV status was made during a criminal trial where her ex-husband was facing charges of attempted manslaughter on the basis that he had forced sexual intercourse with women when he knew that he was HIV positive. Four principal points were at issue: the court orders requiring the applicant's doctors to give evidence at the trial; the seizure of her medical records; the decision to make the material in the file accessible to the public from 2002; and the disclosure of her name and medical condition in the Court of Appeal's judgment. All four were undisputed as constituting interferences with private and family life and the principal argument concerned the justification of the measures. The Court found that the first three pursued legitimate aims — the prevention of crime in relation to the measures of investigation and protection of the rights of others in maintaining the transparency of court proceedings through public access to files. However, the Court doubted that the publication of the applicant's full names as well as her medical condition following their disclosure in the Court of Appeal's judgment could be justified for any aim, including the prevention of crime.[12]

As to whether the four measures could be justified as recovery under the second paragraph of Article 8, the questioning of the applicant's doctors was acceptable since it was carried out in camera and the proceedings bound by confidentiality enforceable under civil and criminal law: this furnished adequate and effective safeguards against abuse. The seizure of her medical records and inclusion in the file was also proportionate. The Court was uninterested in allegations that not all the material was relevant to the investigation and not prepared to question the domestic court assessment in that respect, referring to the domestic court's primary role in assessing the relevance of evidence and the margin of appreciation. However the order which would make the material public by 2002 was disproportionate in its effects on the applicant, which outweighed any general interest in making the files public. It also found that the publication of her identity and condition in the Court of Appeal judgment was disproportionate, in particular, since the lower court had felt able to issue an abridged version of its judgment excluding the name and part of the reasoning.

5. Inhuman and degrading treatment

Access to medical treatment or standards of medical care have not arisen directly but in connection with expulsion of persons from Contracting States to countries where the standards of care and treatment are deficient. The United Kingdom Government

---

[11] 21780/93, (Dec.) March 2, 1994.
[12] The Government argued that the Court of Appeal had to publish these details since her evidence as to when she informed her husband of her status was crucial to the finding that he knew his own HIV status at the times of the offences. Otherwise Art. 6, para. 1 with regard to the conviction would not have been satisfied, in their view.

strenuously resisted the claims in *D v. United Kingdom*, where an applicant suffering AIDS alleged that on expulsion to St Kitts his life-expectancy would be shortened and his final days subject to lack of medical care and support. The Government argued that finding a violation would open the floodgates to claims from AIDS sufferers who were refused entry to European States where inevitably higher standards of medical and support care were available. The Commission dismissed this on the basis that United Kingdom responsibility was engaged in this particular case since, rather than expelling the applicant on arrival, they prosecuted him for drugs possession and held him in jail, where he became dependent on the drugs treatment provided. The argument that he would suffer the natural consequences of a disease contracted outside the U.K. did not divert responsibility either, since the Commission considered that the lack of treatment and adequate support would lead in all probability to painful and degrading circumstances prior to his death. The Court held that Government responsibility could arise in respect of treatment stemming from factors relating to the applicant's personal situation on return to St Kitts. On the basis of the severe deterioration of health of D by the time of the Court hearing, it found that it would disclose a violation of Article 3 to expel him. It dealt with the case on the basis of its exceptional facts, implying that less extreme cases might not lead to the same conclusions.

Armed forces

Key provisions:

Articles 5 (liberty); 6 (fair trial); 8 (private life); 10 (freedom of expression).

Key case law:

Engel v. Netherlands, June 8, 1976, Series A, No. 22; 1 E.H.R.R. 647; *Hadjianastassiou v. Greece.* December 16, 1992, Series A, No. 252–A; 16 E.H.R.R. 219; *Vereinigung Demokratischer Soldaten Osterreichs v. Austria*, December 19, 1994, Series A, No. 302; 20 E.H.R.R. 55; *Mitap and Mûftüğlu v. Turkey*, 15530–1/89, (Rep.), December 8, 1994 annexed to the judgment of the Court March 25, 1996, R.J.D., 1996–II, No. 6 concerning the length of proceedings only; *Findlay v. U.K.*, February 25, 1997, R.J.D., 1997–I, No. 30; *Kalaç v. Turkey*, July 1, 1997, R.J.D., 1997–IV, No. 41; *Grigoriades v. Greece*, November 25, 1997, R.J.D. 199–VII, No. 57; *Larissis and others v. Greece*, February 24, 1998, to be published in R.J.D. 1998.

1. General considerations

Armed forces personnel continue to enjoy the rights guaranteed under the Convention although the special disciplinary context may allow certain limitations on their exercise which could not be imposed on civilians.[1] Obvious and inevitable restrictions of military service will not raise issues, *e.g.* rules on uniform and haircuts[2] but joining up does not waive fundamental rights, *inter alia*, to liberty and fair trial.

2. Military discipline

Matters purely of internal discipline are unlikely to raise issues where the sanctions do not involve deprivation of liberty or other punishments serious enough to fall within the concept of a criminal penalty.[3] Any detention which involves a deprivation of liberty within the meaning of Article 5 will attract its procedural guarantees. Whether a restriction for a soldier, as opposed to a civilian, constitutes a deprivation of liberty depends on the extent to which it deviates from the normal conditions of life in the armed forces of Contracting States. The case law indicates that light arrest, involving restriction to quarters in off-duty hours, was not sufficient but that strict arrest, involving being locked in a cell day and night and exclusion from normal duties was.[4] The procedural guarantees will include the right to be brought promptly before an officer exercising judicial functions who has the power to order release and the right to bring proceedings challenging the lawfulness of the detention.[5]

3. Military justice

Where a criminal charge is involved, Article 6 rights play a full role. A prisoner is entitled, *inter alia*, to fair hearing, an independent and impartial tribunal, and within a reasonable time trial. Potentially, this may mean legal representation and legal aid if he cannot afford it.

---

[1] *Engel*, para. 57.
[2] 8209/78 *Switzerland*, (Dec.) March 1, 1979, 16 D.R. 166.
[3] See Part IIA: Fair trial guarantees, General principles: Criminal charge.
[4] *Engel*, paras. 59–63.
[5] Article 5, para. 3, *e.g. De Jong, Baljet and Van den Brink v. Netherlands*, May 22, 1984, Series A, No. 77; 8 E.H.R.R. 20; Article 5 para. 4, *e.g. Engel*.

The system of military court martial came under challenge in a number of old cases, but on examination the Commission was satisfied that the military tribunals conformed with requirements of Article 6, having regard to, *inter alia*, the presence of irremovable civilian judges, the irremovability of military members during their mandate and the finding that the military members were not answerable to any authority.[6] The first serious case to illustrate the dangerous hierarachical dependence of a military system was *Mitap and Müftüğlu v. Turkey*. The Commission disliked in principle the situation that civilians were subject to the jurisdiction of military courts, commenting that this *per se* raised doubts as to independence and impartiality. It found the presence on the court martial of an army officer and two military judges (who were linked with the military hierarchy for the purposes of their career and subordinate to the commander of the state of martial law whose security forces were carrying out the arrests) was not cured by the presence of two civilian judges and gave objective reason to doubt the independence and impartiality of the tribunal. Since a body lacking independence and objectively could not guarantee a fair hearing, there was a violation of Article 6, paragraph 1 on that basis without it being necessary to examine any individual allegation of unfairness of procedure.

The system in the United Kingdom was also found to disclose serious structural problems in *Findlay v. United Kingdom*. The applicant in the case attacked a broad range of features of the court martial system: the connection between the officers on the court martials with the convening officer who was their direct or ultimate superior; the multifarious role of the convening officer as prosecutor and confirmer of sentence; the lack of reasons for the decision given; the secretive appeal structure; and the role of the judge advocate-general. The Commission and Court found the district court martial lacked independence and impartiality. The Court emphasised the hierarchical links between the court martial members and the convening officer, who was central to the prosecution and the fact that the decision of the court martial was not effective until confirmed by him. This was contrary to the well-established principle that the power to give a binding decision which may not be altered by a non-judicial authority is inherent in the notion of "tribunal" and can be seen as a component of the "independence" criterion. The role of the judge advocate-general was certainly not seen as remedying these defects since the advice which he gave was not made public. The inadequacies of the review proceedings were not examined in detail by the Court which noted that where criminal charges were concerned, an applicant was entitled to a first instance tribunal which fully met the requirements of Article 6. In light of these findings, no further points were settled in the case.

4. Restrictions on private life

A prohibition on homosexual acts in private between soldiers could, the Commission decided in an old case, be considered as necessary for the protection of morals and the prevention of disorder given the special conditions of army life. It appeared to accept the reasons for the prohibition given by the Ministry of Defence to Parliament as legitimate (*e.g.* the communal life, need for absolute trust and confidence, risk of blackmail or coercion of younger or more junior men).[7] The case however involved an offence in respect of some-one under the age of 21. Cases are now pending with the Commission concerning the disciplinary steps taken against members of the armed forces who are discovered to be homosexual, involving allegations of invasion of privacy as a result of the investigative process, lack of respect for private life and discrimination on grounds of sexual

---

[6] *e.g.* 12717/87 *Belgium*, (Dec.) September 8, 1988, 57 D.R. 196; 8209/78 *Switzerland*, (Dec.) March 1, 1979, 16 D.R. 166.
[7] 9237/81 *U.K.*, (Dec.) October 12, 1983, 34 D.R. 68.

orientation.[8] Issues appear likely to arise as to the extent to which Article 8 will apply where applicants knew the prohibition on homosexuals in the army but nonetheless took the risk of joining up in the knowledge that if they were discovered proceedings were likely. Assuming however that this consideration is inextricable from the central issues of respect for private life and discrimination, much would appear to turn on whether the Commission and Court accept the argument that considerations of morale (*e.g.* the attitude of other enlisted men to homosexuals and its allegedly crucial role in maintaining effective defence forces) can justify investigation of private sexual life and the serious penalty of discharge.

5. Restrictions on freedom of expression and freedom to receive information

Interferences with soldiers' access to outside sources of information have been treated with some robustness by the Commission and Court which are not overly sympathetic to the protective attitude of State authorities, although acknowledging that the proper functioning of an army presupposes rules preventing the undermining of military discipline.[9] Soldiers still enjoy freedom of expression and to receive and impart information. An assertion by the Austrian authorities that a magazine was a threat to discipline and to service efficiency had to be substantiated by specific examples, of which none were given.[10] The magazine in question was not found by the Court to overstep what was permissible in the context of a mere discussion of ideas, including army reform, which must be tolerated in the army of a democratic state. There was thus a violation in respect of both the magazine producers, whose publication was not allowed to be distributed internally and in respect of the soldier who was fined for distributing it. Where an applicant was prosecuted for distributing leaflets to British soldiers, there was a distinction to be drawn, the Commission found, between publications aimed at inciting disaffection and those expressing opinions as to the policy of using the army in Northern Ireland. Since the applicant was expressly encouraging soldiers to go absent without leave as a means of protest and had not been dissuaded by other means from giving up her activities, the Commission found that her conviction and sentence to 8–9 months imprisonment was not disproportionate to the aim pursued.[11]

Security considerations are given full weight where measures are applied in respect of the disclosure of information by army personnel. In *Hadjianasstiou v. Greece*, where an officer was sentenced to five months for revealing military data in a study submitted to a private company, the Court referred to the special responsibilities incumbent on military life. Since the officer was involved in an experimental missile programme and bound by a duty of discretion, the Court agreed with the Government that the disclosure was capable of revealing the State's progress in weapons development and thus damage security interests.

Where a soldier expresses criticism of the armed forces, domestic authorities' reaction must be proportionate. In relation to an admiral who made critical statements on television, the Commission accepted that suspension was proportionate reaction given the nature of his comments which were found by the domestic courts to discredit the Government information policy and, by condemning modern warfare and matters of defence policy, gave rise to doubts that he would fulfill his obligations to the State.[12] Where however the criticism was conducted internally, by means of the applicant's letter to a senior officer, in terms which did not name any other officer critically but raised

---

[8] *e.g.* 31417/96 *Lustig Prean v. U.K.*
[9] *Vereinigung demokratischer soldaten case* para. 36; *Grigoriades v. Greece,* para. 45.
[10] *Vereinigung demokratischer soldaten,* case, *ibid.*
[11] *Arrowsmith v. U.K.,* 7050/75, (Rep.) October 12, 1978, 19 D.R. 5.
[12] 23576/94 *Germany,* (Dec.) November 29, 1995.

matters of general public concern about the army as an institution, the Court found disciplinary sanction of three months' imprisonment disproportionate.[13]

6. Freedom of religion

Where members of the armed services have been penalised or subject to measures resulting from religious affiliations or activities, issues have arisen under Article 9. These cases primarily relate to steps taken in the Greek army against proselytisers and in the Turkish army against Islamic fundamentalists.[14] The importance of respecting the inner spiritual convictions of a person is such that it is arguable that adherence to a particular religion should in itself justify sanctions of dismissal, without at least there being overt expressions of belief or acts with demonstrable outside effects on other military personnel or the functioning of the service.

The Convention organs have however taken a restrictive approach. In *Kalaç v. Turkey*, where a military judge was forced into early retirement allegedly as a result of his fundamentalist beliefs, the Court found that in choosing to pursue a military career he had accepted the restrictions implied by a system of military discipline, including regulations forbidding, *inter alia*, an attitude inimical to the established order reflecting the requirements of military service. Since the applicant was able to fulfill the normal forms through which a Muslim practiced his religion and the reasoning for the order was based not on his religious opinions but his conduct and attitude,[15] it found that the compulsory retirement had not interfered with any right guaranteed under Article 9.[16]

A distinction was drawn by the Convention organs in a Greek case where air force officers who were members of the Pentecostal church were tried for proselytism.[17] The interference with their rights to manifest their beliefs was found to be justified where the proselytism related to servicemen in the applicants' unit having regard to the special character of the relationship between a superior and subordinate in the army which rendered the subordinate more susceptible to influence. Conversely, where the offences related to proselytism of civilians, outside this special relationship, the interferences were not found to be justified.

Cross-reference

Part IIA: General considerations: Criminal charge
Part IIB: Freedom of expression
Part IIB: Freedom of religion (conscientious objectors)

---

[13] *Grigoriades v. Greece.*

[14] See, *e.g. Kalaç;* 18673/91 *Hamarattürk v. Turkey,* (adm.) January 10, 1995 struck off March 5, 1996 where the applicant alleged that he had been arrested, questioned, ill-treated and dismissed from the airforce on the basis of his fundamentalist Islamic beliefs; No. 23372/94 etc. *Larissis and others v. Greece.*

[15] A fine distinction: the conduct included the adoption of unlawful fundamentalist opinions. The Court has effectively accepted that disciplinary action based on military objection to particular alleged opinions does not interfere with rights under Art. 9.

[16] See also 14524/89, *Turkey,* (Dec.) January 6, 1993, 74 D.R. 14 where a military cadet was dismissed from an academy in Turkey, no interference with religious belief was found as the Commission accepted that the dismissal was for disciplinary reasons. Since these nonetheless included grounds that he had participated in fundamentalist activities, the Commission commented that the military disciplinary regime may by its nature impose certain restrictions, which may include a duty to refrain from participating in the fundamentalist movement, whose aim and programme was to ensure the pre-eminence of religious rules.

[17] *Larissis.*

Arrest

Key provisions:

Article 5, paragraph 1(c) (right to liberty exception of lawful arrest for the purpose of bringing before the competent legal authority on reasonable suspicion of committing an offence, or where reasonably necessary to prevent the commission of an offence or fleeing after commission of an offence.

Key cases:

Brogan and others v. U.K., November 29, 1988, Series A, No. 145–B; 11 E.H.R.R. 117; *Fox, Campbell and Hartley v. U.K.*, August 30, 1990, Series A, No. 182; 13 E.H.R.R. 157; *Murray v. U.K.*, October 28, 1994, Series A, No. 300–A; 19 E.H.R.R. 193; *Lukanov v. Bulgaria*, March 20, 1997, R.J.D., 1997–II, No. 34; *Erdagöz v. Turkey*, October 22, 1997, R.J.D., 1997–VI, No. 54; *K.-F. v. Germany*, November 27, 1997, R.J.D., 1997–VII, No. 58.

1. General considerations

Arrest in this section refers to the use of power to detain in order to investigate or prevent crime. The key issues have arisen from the standard of suspicion justifying arrest and only to a lesser extent, the conditions and procedural safeguards surrounding the arrest. Requirements of lawfulness impose conformity with domestic procedural safeguards and generally the Convention organs have not been overly rigorous in their scrutiny, assuming the bona fides of the police and requiring only the minimum indications of grounds for the arrest, sufficient to exclude clear arbitrariness or oppression.

2. Existence of arrest or detention

In the ordinary course of events, there is no doubt as to whether a person has been held or detained by means of the exercise of a power of arrest. Occasionally, there is a question mark as to the nature and degree of the loss of liberty.[1]

3. Grounds of arrest

Three heads of arrest are included in Article 5, paragraph 1(c). Most cases have concerned arrest on reasonable suspicion of having committed an offence, while the heads of reasonably necessary to prevent an offence or "to prevent a person fleeing after an offence" have been seldom invoked.[2]

"Offence" in this context appears to enjoy a wide definition. In *Brogan and others v. United Kingdom*, the applicants argued that arrest under prevention of terrorism legislation on suspicion that a person is or has been involved in acts of terrorism was not on suspicion of having committed a specific offence but of involvement in unspecified acts of terrorism which could not be regarded as an "offence" for the purpose of Article 5, paragraph 1(c). The Court found that the definition of terrorism as the use of violence for political ends was well in keeping with the idea of an offence.[3]

[1] See Part IIB, Deprivation of liberty.

[2] See, however, *Lukanov*, the Commission found that where there is no reasonable suspicion of an offence having been committed the applicant's detention cannot be justified by an alleged danger of fleeing having committed an offence. The Court found it unnecessary to decide. Also *Eriksen v. Norway*, May 27, 1997 R.J.D. 1997–III, No. 37, para. 86 concerning detention pending decision whether to impose a further period of security detention of a person convicted of an offence and subject to a special preventative sentence.

[3] The Court cited its findings in *Ireland v. U.K.* judgment January 18, 1978, Series A, No. 25, paras. 196–197.

4. Reasonable suspicion of having committed an offence

The standard is simply one of a reasonable suspicion. Old Commission cases establish that it is not required that the existence and nature of the offence be definitely proved since that is the purpose of the investigation.[4]

The fact that domestic law does not set the same standard of suspicion will not necessarily disclose a violation on arrest, since the Convention organs will examine whether on the facts of the individual cases there nonetheless existed a reasonable suspicion.[5]

The Court found that "reasonable suspicion" presupposed the existence of facts or information which would satisfy an objective observer that the person concerned may have committed the offence. However, what is to be regarded as reasonable will depend on the facts.[6] Terrorist crime, it held, fell into a special category due to considerations of urgency and reliance on information which might be reliable but could not be revealed without risk to the source. Therefore the same standards could not always apply, subject to the rider that the criterion is not stretched to the point that the essence of the safeguard is impaired.[7]

A failure by the Government to provide facts or information supporting the existence of a reasonable suspicion may disclose a violation, particularly where there are countervailing official indications that the suspicion is ill-founded. In *Erdagöz v. Turkey*, the applicant alleged that his arrest for producing false evidence (*i.e.* that an attack had been committed on his shop) to the police was motivated by police resentment against him for complaints which he had made. No fact was apparently adverted to by the Government as justifying the arrest and detention of the applicant for 24 hours and the Commission noted that a suspect was prosecuted for the attack on the shop which he had reported to the police.[8] However, the Court considered that suspicion was based on specific facts (*e.g.* the applicant's conduct) and that the purpose of the deprivation of liberty was to confirm or dispel the suspicion that he had falsely reported a criminal offence. It saw no reason to disagree with the public prosecutor's finding that the 24 hours detention was for that purpose. The Court accordingly appears to require convincing evidence before it will find bad faith on the part of the police.

In *Fox, Campbell and Hartley v. United Kingdom*, where the applicants had been arrested on suspicion of being terrorists in Northern Ireland under a prevention of terrorism provision, the Court found that, in the absence of any information by the Government as to the basis of the suspicion, it was not possible for the Court to find the arrest justified, even with reference to the fact that it could not expect highly sensitive information to be divulged. The Government had to furnish as least some information capable of satisfying the Court that the applicants were reasonably suspected, particularly since domestic law itself set a lower threshold of merely honest suspicion. The fact that two suspects had had previous convictions for acts of terrorism connected with the IRA was not sufficient for an arrest some seven years later.

---

[4] *e.g.* 8083/77 (Dec.) March 13, 1980, 19 D.R. 223 where an applicant solicitor who failed to appear before the court when a case was relisted was arrested for contempt of court, the fact that the court of appeal found that there had been no contempt did not mean that a reasonable suspicion had not existed at the time; 9627/81, (Dec.) March 14, 1984, 37 D.R. 15.

[5] *Fox, Campbell and Hartley*, para. 31.

[6] *ibid.*, para. 32; *Italy* 27143/95 (Dec.) January 14, 1997, 88–A D.R. 94, where the Commission noted the risks attached to basing reasonable suspicion on statements of Mafia "pentiti" and had regard to whether the domestic courts had assessed their credibility.

[7] *ibid.*, paras. 31–32; also No. 8098/77, (Dec.) December 13, 1978, 16 D.R. 11: headnote reference to arrest on espionage (ordered by a judge) where suspicions were based on a small number of elements may nevertheless be qualified as reasonable, the decision giving weight to the judge's knowledge and experience to conclude the basis of suspicion, *i.e.* visits to East Germany, the reasons for which did not satisfy the judge.

[8] 21890/93 (Rep.) May 23, 1996.

Where the Government is able to point to indirect facts supporting their suspicion, as in the *Margaret Murray and family* case where the applicant was arrested under a similar provision as in *Fox, Campbell and Hartley*, there may be no violation.[9] In that case, the Court recognised the need for use of confidential sources in fighting terrorism and was also influenced by findings of domestic courts in the applicant's false imprisonment action where the judge had found the arresting officer transparently honest and that the applicant was genuinely suspected of having beeen involved in collecting funds for the purchase of arms for the IRA, the Court commenting that honesty and bona fides were indispensable elements of reasonableness. It added a new factor, the short period that the arrest lasted, *i.e.* four hours (which strangely suggests the strength of the suspicion required alters with duration of the arrest). Emphasising the special exigencies of investigating terrorism, it concluded that there was sufficient facts or information which could provide a plausible and objective basis for a suspicion that she might have been involved in the collection of funds for the IRA.

However where the allegations in proceedings against a suspect rely on matters which do not disclose an offence, the arrest and detention may fall outside the permitted exception, since the existence of reasonable suspicion requires that the facts relied on can be reasonably invoked as falling under prescribed criminal behaviour. Thus, in *Lukanov v. Bulgaria*, where the applicant, a minister of the previous regime, was arrested and detained allegedly for misappropriation of funds, the Commission found that the grounds of the accusations referred solely to his transfer of monies in aid to the Third World which was not an offence. Thus the facts invoked against the applicant at the time of his arrest and during his continued detention could not in the eyes of an objective observer be construed as amounting to the criminal offence of misappropriation of funds and there was no reasonable suspicion of his having committed an offence to justify the detention.[10]

5. Purpose to bring before a competent legal authority

This is the purpose underlying Article 5, paragraph 1(c) read in conjunction with Article 5, paragraph 3. Applicants arrested under all three heads must all be brought before a judge.[11]

It has sometimes been argued that the apparent purpose of an arrest was not to bring before a competent legal authority but to gather information without necessarily intending to charge the person. In *Brogan and others*, where the applicants argued that they were neither charged nor brought before a court, the Court agreed with the Commission that the existence of the purpose (to bring before a court if sufficient and usable evidence had been obtained during the police investigation) had to be considered independently of the achievement of that purpose. Arrest under Article 5, paragraph 1(c) did not presuppose that charges have to be brought but that the criminal investigation be furthered by way of confirming or dispelling the concrete suspicion. Evidence may prove unobtainable or impossible to produce in court. In that case, there was no indication that the police investigation was not in good faith and it could be assumed that, if they had been able, the police would have laid charges and brought the applicants before the competent legal

---

[9] The Commission had found a violation seeing no real distinction with *Fox, Campbell and Hartley* the elements relied on by the Government being insufficient to found reasonable suspicion (*e.g.* her brother's conviction in the U.S.A. on arms buying charges).

[10] The Court found a violation on the basis that the detention was not "lawful" but for similar reasons, paras. 42–45.

[11] *Lawless v. Ireland,* July 1, 1961, Series A, No. 3, pp. 51–52, para. 14 where the Government unsuccessfully argued a construction excluding the second and third heads, *i.e.* suspicion that a person would commit an offence or flee having committed one. The arrest of persons suspected of IRA membership for the purposes of internment, without the prospect of bringing them before a judicial authority was found by the court to be contrary to Art. 5, para. 1(c) and 5 para. 3, though covered by Ireland's derogation under Art. 15.

authority. The fact that they were questioned about specific offences showed that their arrest was grounded in concrete suspicions.[12]

5. Lawfulness and procedural safeguards

It is not required that arrest be ordered by a judge[13] but the individual must be brought promptly before a judge for the purposes of Article 5, paragraph 3.[14] The arrest must be carried out in accordance with a procedure prescribed by law according to the second sentence of Article 5, paragraph 1 and must also be "lawful" in terms of the various sub-paragraphs (see Part IIB: Deprivation of Liberty, Lawfulness).[15] Reasons for the arrest must also be given promptly under Article 5, paragraph 2 (see Part IIB: Reasons for arrest and detention).

Cross-reference

Part IIB: Deprivation of liberty
Part IIB: Pre-trial detention
Part IIB: Review of detention

---

[12] See, *e.g. K-F v. Germany*, paras. 57–62.
[13] 7755/77 (Dec.) May 18, 1977, D.R. 9, p. 210.
[14] See Part IIB: Pre-trial detention.
[15] *e.g.* the Court's finding in *Lukanov v. Bulgaria*.

Childcare cases

Key provisions:

Articles 6 (fair hearing); 8 (respect for family life); 14 (prohibiting discrimination).

Key case law:

W, B and *R v. U.K.*, July 8, 1987, Series A, No. 121; 10 E.H.R.R. 29, 74 and 87; *O* and *H v. U.K.*, July 8, 1987, Series A, No. 120; 10 E.H.R.R. 82 and 95; *Olsson v. Sweden*, March 24, 1988, Series A, No. 130; 11 E.H.R.R. 259; *Eriksson v. Sweden*, June 22, 1989, Series A, No. 156; 12 E.H.R.R. 183; *Margareta and Roger Andersson v. Sweden*, February 25, 1992, Series A, No. 226; 14 E.H.R.R. 615; *Rieme v. Sweden*, April 22, 1992, Series A, No. 226–B; 16 E.H.R.R. 155; *Hoffman v. Austria*, June 23, 1993, Series A, No. 255–C; *Keegan v. Ireland*, May 26, 1994, Series A, No. 290; 18 E.H.R.R. 342; *Hokkanen v. Finland*, September 23, 1994, Series A, No. 299–A; 19 E.H.R.R. 139; *Kroon v. Netherlands*, October 27, 1994, Series A, No. 297–C; 19 E.H.R.R. 263; *McMichael v. U.K.*, February 24, 1995, Series A, No. 307–B; 20 E.H.R.R. 205; *Johansen v. Norway*, August 7, 1996, R.J.D., 1996–III, No. 13; *X, Y and Z v. U.K.*, April 22, 1997, R.J.D., 1997–II, No. 35.

1. General considerations

This section concerns three situations where care, custody and contact with children may raise issues under the Convention. The first category involves the most common cause of complaint, namely, intervention by State authorities to remove children from their families and subsequent decisions taken as to contact, custody and adoption. The second category concerning regulation by the courts of custody and contact disputes following divorce or separation of the parents has produced fewer significant cases. Thirdly, there is a small group of cases dealing with issues of parental rights arising in non-conventional family groupings.

Given the seriousness of the interferences in the first category, the Convention organs give complaints careful scrutiny. They generally confine their role in line with the Court's pronouncements on the nature of European supervision, in particular, that it is not their function to substitute their view on the merits for that of the domestic authorities. In this area, the domestic courts are particularly well placed to assess the requirements of the welfare of the children and under the "margin of appreciation" doctrine, a significant measure of discretion is accorded to domestic authorities in the performance of their functions and in their evaluation of the factors which may appear to them to be critical for the protection of the health or morals of a child. Consequently, if, after judicial proceedings in which the parent's interests are fairly protected, a judgment is issued removing custody or contact on the basis that the measure is necessary for the welfare of the children, it is unlikely that an application would succeed on the basis of a complaint that the decision was wrong. The cases have concentrated on procedural aspects: access to court, delay, etc. The merits of a decision may however be challenged indirectly through the requirement, outlined below, that decisions must be supported by relevant and sufficient reasons.

2. Interferences by domestic authorities

Steps taken *vis-à-vis* parents regulating contact with their children, removing custody or parental responsibility prima facie constitute interferences with family life which require justification under Article 8, paragraph 2. Parents include natural fathers, where there has been cohabitation or other factors showing a relationship of sufficient constancy as to create *de facto* family ties.[1]

The extent to which interferences may occur in respect of other family members or concerned persons depends on the nature of the relationship with the child. In grandparent cases,[2] the Commission has taken the view that links between grandparents and grandchildren will vary from family to family and each case must be examined on its facts to determine whether there were sufficient links to constitute "family life" and thereby bring the relationship within the protection of Article 8. In determining whether the decisions taken by the social services interfere with the rights guaranteed under this provision, the Commission considered that different standards would normally apply than where a parent was involved. For example, a grandparent's access to a child is normally at the discretion of the child's parents in any case and regulation of access by a local authority *per se* would not constitute an interference. There might however be an interference where a local authority diminished the access necessary to preserve a normal grandparent-grandchild relationship.

The Commission has accepted that an uncle may have a relationship with a child of such a nature as to attract the protection of Article 8, where he had acted as a "father figure" and lived in close contact with the child, such that refusal of access by the social services when the child was taken into care disclosed an interference.[3] An older case also indicates that a fosterparent may have sufficient links with a child to attract the protection of Article 8 of the Convention.[4]

Children in care may themselves, through an appropriate representative, complain that their rights under the Convention have been infringed by measures taken by social services. The Court found a violation under Articles 6 and 8 in the *Eriksson v. Sweden* case for both mother and child due to severe and lasting restrictions on access and lack of any court remedy for this denial. In *Eriksson*, however, there was no issue of the mother's standing to make complaints on behalf of the child. In other cases, the Commission has had regard to whether the parent had any legal right to represent the child. In *Hokkanen v. Finland*, since in the domestic proceedings the father had been deprived of legal custody and had no right in domestic terms to represent the child, the Commission found that he could not complain on behalf of the child in its proceedings. It showed more flexibility in a case introduced on behalf of three children by the solicitor who had represented them in the domestic care proceedings and who complained of the unjustifiable delay as prejudicing the welfare of the children. Although at the time of the application he was no longer representing them or had standing in domestic terms, the Commission noted the importance that children's rights be practically and effectively protected and that in the absence of any conflict of interest or the existence of more appropriate representation,

---

[1] *See Keegan*, para. 44: a child born out of a relationship of two persons cohabiting outside marriage *ipso iure* is part of the "family unit" for the purposes of Art. 8 and a family bond exists even if at the time of birth the parents are no longer co-habiting or if the relationship has ended. Also *Kroon v. Netherlands*, para. 56 where the natural father did not cohabit but there was a longstanding relationship from which four children were born. However in *MB v. U.K.* 22920/93 (Dec.), April 6, 1994, 77–A D.R. 108, the Commission was not prepared to find family life existed where the applicant claimed to be the father of a child born to a married woman and a right to prove the link through a blood test — the Commission distinguished *Keegan* on the basis the mother disputed his claims, there was no element of planning or cohabitation and thus insufficient links in fact or law to bring the case within Art. 8.

[2] *Branton v. U.K.*, 12399/85, (Dec.) March 9, 1988, unpublished; *Price v. U.K.*, 12402/86, July 14, 1988, 55 D.R. 224; *Lawlor v. U.K.*, (Dec.) 12763/87, July 14, 1988, 57 D.R. 216.

[3] *Boyle v. U.K.*, (Rep.), February 9, 1993, Series A, 282–B (settled before the Court); see n.7.

[4] 8257/78, (Dec.) July 10, 1978, 13 D.R. 248.

the solicitor had sufficient links with the children and the subject-matter of the claim to represent them before the Commission.[5]

The case law has established a number of key areas where violations may arise.

(a) *Procedural protection of rights*

The first United Kingdom cases before the Court established the important principle that the decision-making process in childcare matters must afford sufficient procedural protection of parents' interests.[6] Where in *W v. United Kingdom*, for example, the local authority passed a parental rights resolution in respect of the applicant's child S and proceeded to take a series of decisions — placement in long-term foster-care with a view to adoption, restriction and termination of access — without advance consultation or discussion with the applicant, the Court noted that it was crucial in an area where decisions may prove irreversible (*i.e.* a child may form new bonds with his alternative carers) that there is adequate protection for parents against arbitrary interferences. In the circumstances of this case, the Court found that the applicant was not informed or consulted in advance in respect of a number of decisions which affected his relationship with S and that he was as a result insufficiently involved in critical stages of the decision-making. The Court accordingly held that the applicant had not been afforded the requisite consideration of his views or protection of his interests and that in this respect there had been a violation of Article 8 of the Convention.

Since these decisions, particular attention had been paid to the procedural fairness of the decision-making process regarding parents and other members of the family, whose relationship with a child has been subject to interference. Relevant factors include the opportunity to make submissions, in person or in writing, before decisions are reached[7]; access to the reports and documents relied on in the decision-making[8] and the provision of legal representation to parents.[9]

The level of consultation or involvement in the decision-making process required may differ in respect of non-parental relatives.[10]

(b) *Access to court*

A parent's rights to access to and custody of a child constitute "civil rights" the determination of which requires a fair hearing before an independent and impartial

---

[5] *SP, DP and AT v. U.K.*, 23715/94, (Rep.) April 11, 1997, 89–A D.R. 31 case settled (decision on admissibility May 20, 1996).

[6] This does not automatically require access to court, lack of which would tend to raise issues under Article 6 where civil rights were concerned, but refers rather the process of intervention by the social services, which may be crucial for the development of events, notwithstanding the possibility of court proceedings at later stages. See *W, B, R, O* and *H v. U.K.*

[7] *e.g. Boyle v. U.K.*, where the uncle was a *de facto* father to the child taken into care, the Commission found a violation in that there was no meaningful consultation with him by the social services, which took the decision to end access at a conference to which he was not invited and without prior invitation of his views; *U.K.*, 17071/90, (Dec.) February 13, 1990 where a mother complained that her child's name had been put on a child abuse register, her position had been adequately safeguarded by the opportunity to submit her views on the alleged non-accidental injury to her son in writing to the case conference which made the decision.

[8] *e.g. McMichael*, where the Children's Hearing only summarised orally the reports concerning the applicants' and their child.

[9] *e.g.* 14114/88, (Dec.) December 12, 1988; 15993/90, (Dec.) January 15, 1990; 16184/90, (Dec.) May 7, 1990. The Court also relies on this factor in *Johansen.*

[10] *Price,* see n.2. while the decision to end all access of the applicants to their grandchild constituted an interference with their right to respect for family life, the Commission did not expect that grandparents should be involved in the procedures to the same extent as parents but found it sufficient that the local authority consulted the grandparents regularly, allowed them to make representations at case conferences and provided a procedure whereby they could obtain a review of the case.

tribunal pursuant to Article 6. In less technical terms, where an important aspect of parent's relationship with a child is at stake, a parent should be able to challenge the decision in a court. A violation was found, for example, in *R v. United Kingdom*, where the mother of a child in care under a parental rights resolution and to whom access had been refused by the local authority was unable to go to a court to challenge that refusal.[11] Where a natural father had no standing in care proceedings concerning a child taken into care and no prospect of applying for contact or access, the case was settled after being declared admissible.[12] Inability of a natural father to challenge before a court the adoption of a child disclosed a violation in *Keegan v. Ireland*.

Access to court for other relatives would not appear to be regarded an automatic requirement, having regard to the basic principle that Article 6, paragraph 1 only applies to procedures concerning the recognition of a right which has a legal basis in domestic law. Thus, the Commission has found that Article 6, paragraph 1 could not be invoked by grandparents, since it did not consider that under English law grandparents enjoyed a right of custody of or access to their grandchildren.[13]

(c) *Delay in proceedings*

Childcare proceedings must be managed with particular expedition, having regard to the importance of what is at stake and since the nature of the issues is such that the lapse of time may influence their outcome.[14] In *H v. United Kingdom*,[15] where an application for access was not decided for almost two years, the judge had refused access but criticised the delay as "quite deplorable" and commented that it had seriously prejudiced the position of the applicant, who by that point had not seen the child for three and a half years during which time she had been settled for 19 months with prospective adopters. Under Article 6, the Court found a violation since the applicant had not received a fair hearing within a reasonable time having regard to the importance of what was at stake for her. Under Article 8, there was also a violation since the delay had led to a *de facto* determination of the issue whereas an effective respect for the applicant's family life required that the question be determined solely in light of all the relevant considerations and not by the mere effluxion of time.

Whether the length of proceedings will disclose a violation under Article 8 will depend largely on the prejudicial effect on the outcome of the proceedings. Under Article 6, it will be influenced by the general considerations applicable to length complaints, such as the

---

[11] 11468/85, (Dec.) October 15, 1986, 50 D.R. 199; (Rep.) April 15, 1988, 56 D.R. 138; also *Campbell v. U.K.;* 11240/84 (Rep.) May 13, 1988, 56 D.R. 108, concerning lack of access to court to challenge reduction in natural father's access to his son in care — the case was settled after admissibility on an undertaking by the Government to introduce legislation allowing parents to apply to court on matters of access generally. The Children Act 1989 followed.

[12] 11468/85, (Dec.) October 15, 1986, 50 D.R. 199. The case settled on the basis of proposed legislative reforms, *i.e.* the Family Law Reform Act 1987 which was to allow natural fathers to apply for parental rights orders which would place them in the same position as other parents. Pursuant to the Children Act 1989, a natural father is now a "parent" for all purposes and has a right to be a party to care proceedings relating to his child as well as the possibility of obtaining parental responsibility through an agreement or court order.

[13] *Lawlor*, above n.2.

[14] Proceedings concerning a parent's access to his or her child, who has been placed in public care, require by their very nature to be dealt with urgently —*Johansen*, para. 88.

[15] Also 16817/90 *Paulsen-Medalen and Svensson v. Sweden*, February 19, 1998, to be published in R.J.D., 1998, where two years and five months delay in hearing of an appeal in access application.

complexity of the case and whether the applicant contributed to the delay.[16] (See Part IIA: Fair Trial, Length of proceedings.)

(d) *Relevant and sufficient reasons*

As stated above, the Commission and Court do not consider themselves as courts of appeal from domestic courts and shy away from substituting their opinion on the merits. However they do not as result limit their review of a case solely to procedural matters. This was established in the *Olsson v. Sweden* case, where the applicants' three children were taken into care, the social authorities considering that their development was in danger due, *inter alia*, to their parents' inability to satisfy their need for stimulation and supervision. In care, the children were separated and placed in foster-homes up to 600 km from their parents' home. In assessing whether this interference with the parents' rights was justified under the second paragraph of Article 8 as "necessary" in the children's interests, the Court repeated the principle that a margin of appreciation was left to the State in assessing the necessity of measures but held that it exercised a supervisory jurisdiction which was not confined to ascertaining whether the State had exercised its discretion reasonably, carefully and in good faith. It had also to consider whether the reasons adduced to justify an interference were "relevant and sufficient". On the facts of the case, it found that the decision to take the children into care initially was supported by such reasons (*e.g.* evidence that the children were retarded in their development, the fact that other measures had been tried without success). Regarding the implementation of the care order however, the Court found that, particularly since the measure was seen as temporary, the placing of the children in separate homes at such long distances was not supported by relevant or sufficient reasons. In this respect, there was a violation of Article 8.

The Convention organs will therefore review the decisions of domestic courts to determine whether they are supported by reasons which are both relevant and sufficient.[17] Where a court does not go into detail in its judgment, for example, expressly refraining from repeating evidence out of sympathy for the mother, the Commission has taken into account the evidence (medical and other reports) before the court in assessing whether the decision is adequately supported.[18] It is questionable whether, if a court failed to give any reasons at all for its decision, although there was material before it which might have furnished "relevant and sufficient reasons", the Commission could or should embark on a reconstruction of what the court might have been thinking. It might be arguable that the failure to give reasons could in itself constitute a violation of Article 8 of the Convention.

(e) *Rehabilitation*

The taking into care of a child should normally be regarded as a temporary measure to be discontinued as soon as circumstances permit and any measures of implementation should

---

[16] See *e.g. M v. U.K.* 13228/87, (Dec.) February 13, 1990, where the wardship proceeding took 20 months and the judge commented that there was no sensible explanation for the delay. The Commission found that the time taken had not been unreasonable under Art. 6 and that the case had not been determined solely by the effluxion of time contrary to Art. 8. The Commission referred to the complexity of the case, which involved four children, and the failure of the applicant to take steps to expedite the matter — she agreed to the procedural steps which led to the longest periods of delay. The case can also be distinguished from *H v. U.K.* as the applicant had enjoyed access to the children during the proceedings and she had been partially successful, two of the children being returned to her. See Part IIA: Fair trial, Length of proceedings.

[17] *e.g. Johansen*, where there were relevant reasons to support the permanent placement in the mother's conduct and the need for stability but these were not sufficient, *i.e.* the mother's lifestyle was improving and access was going well; also *Andersson*, where there were relevant reasons in the apparent difficulties and stress to the child but that these were not sufficient to justify the almost complete deprivation of contact, by even letter and telephone, over a period of one and a half years.

[18] *e.g. M v. U.K.*, see n.16.

be consistent with the ultimate aim of reuniting natural parent and child.[19] In *Hokkanen v. Finland*, it was said that Article 8 confers a right for parents to have measures taken with a view to being reunited and that there is an obligation on the authorities to take such measures.[20] However, while there is a presumption of rehabiliation in favour of the parent, particular importance is attached to the best interests of the child, which may override those of the parent. A parent cannot claim a right to measure which would harm the child's health and development.

Thus, measures taken with the aim of permanently depriving a parent of contact or custody, for example permanent placement with a view to adoption, must only be applied in exceptional circumstances and can only be justified if motivated by an overriding requirement pertaining to the child's best interests. Where a mother's access to her daughter in care was going well and there were signs of improvement in her life, the difficulties experienced by the social authorities in respect of measures concerning her son and the risk of disrupting the daughter's placement if access was given, did not disclose such overriding requirement.[21]

The obligation to take measures to reunite parent and child is not absolute, however. The Court has acknowledged the need for preparatory steps and the requirement to balance the interests and rights and freedoms of all concerned. Nonetheless, there would appear to be an obligation that the authorities take all necessary steps to facilitate reunion as can reasonably be demanded in the special circumstances of each case. Failure to give proper or any consideration to rehabilitation may therefore raise issues.[22]

(f) *Other issues*

The above passages illustrate the main areas under Articles 6 and 8 with which the Commission and Court have so far been concerned. It is not excluded however that issues could arise under other provisions of the Convention, given the controversial situations that can develop.

It is not inconceivable that admissible complaints could arise under Article 3 concerning the alleged inhuman or degrading treatment of children subject to the perhaps over-zealous attentions of a local authority. The circumstances surrounding the removal of a child from its home by a local authority and the subsequent medical examination and interviews could arguably inflict a level of distress and suffering on the child that brought the treatment within the scope of Article 3. In the context of compulsory medical treatment, the Court has found that as a general rule treatment which was a therapeutic necessity would not violate Article 3[23]; action by a local authority which had the bona fide intention of protecting that child might however still fall foul of Article 3 if it had departed from perceived ideas about desirable practices.

Unjustified removal of a child from its home could also raise problems under Article 5 concerning arbitrary detention. A failure to respect the religious affiliations of a child in

---

[19] *Johansen* para. 78; in *Rieme*, the Court found that the gradual re-introduction of access between the applicant and his daughter did not disclose any hindrance of their reunion, having regard to the length of time she had lived in the foster home.

[20] *e.g. Eriksson*, where the care order had been lifted but the social authorities continued to limit access under a prohibition of removal from the foster home: the Court noted that while difficulties might arise for children on the termination of public care where they have spent long periods away from their natural parents, the unsatisfactory situation ensued in this case from a failure to ensure any meaningful access between mother and child with a view to reuniting them. See also *Olsson*, para. 81; *Andersson*, para. 91.

[21] *Johansen.*

[22] *e.g. U.K.* 18546/91, (Dec.) August 31, 1992, where the social services took an immediate decision to have a baby adopted where the mother after birth was admitted to a psychiatric unit — case was struck off after a settlement was reached.

[23] *Herczegfalvy v. Austria*, September 24, 1992, Series A, No. 242–B; 15 E.H.R.R. 437.

care could fall within the scope of Article 9 (freedom of religion) and a failure to ensure the proper education of a child in care could raise a problem under Article 2 of the First Protocol (right to education).

Since it is arguable that the Convention provisions impose a positive obligation on the State to protect the rights of children, issues may arise where a local authority has failed to take steps to protect them from an abuser or has acted negligently in removing a child where insufficient grounds exist. In light of the House of Lords decision in X *and others v. Bedfordshire County Council*,[24] that actions for negligence against the social services will not lie in respect of their duties to protect children, the question arises whether this would disclose a failure to provide procedural protection, denial of access to court or lack of effective remedy.[25]

3. Regulation of disputes by the courts

Increasingly, the State is not directly involved in taking children into care but is called on to regulate the custody of children between different claimants, generally, in divorce and separation cases. Mostly these cases are dismissed by the Commission since the decisions taken by the courts, having regard to the margin of appreciation, could be justified as being in the interests of the child. Two cases reached the Court.

The case of *Hoffman v. Austria* indicated that reliance by the courts on discriminatory factors, not related to the welfare of the children, would disclose a violation of Article 8 in conjunction with Article 14. But the narrow margin in the Court (5–4) indicated that disapproval of a domestic court approach to the facts of a case may resemble an overruling of its assessment of the welfare of the children.[26]

The case of *Hokkanen* raised issues as to the responsibility of the State to enforce custody and access orders in respect of one party. A violation of Article 8 was found due to the inaction over several years of the authorities in enforcing the court orders for access where the grandparents refused to return a child to the applicant father. While the Government argued that there were limited options open to the authorities in face of wilful intransigence of the persons with custody, the Court, without specifying what else they could have done and noting that coercion was undesirable, found that the only steps taken by the social authorities had been to hold three meetings and that it could not be said that reasonable efforts to facilitate reunion had been made. In many divorce cases, the custodial parent obstructs the access rights of the absent parent and by his/her attitude makes access unworkable, with the result that the courts finally terminate access. It is perhaps arguable that the intransigence of one parent should furnish "relevant and sufficient" reasons for terminating the access of the other. Where however the effect on the children is established as being damaging, the Convention organs may find it difficult to interfere with the assessment of the domestic courts.

[24] (1995) 3 All E.R. 353.
[25] Cases have been introduced before the Commission by, *inter alia,* the children in the Bedfordshire case and other parents and individuals unable to pursue damages claims for alleged negligence of the social services.
[26] The applicant mother, a Jehovahs witness, while awarded custody by the two lower courts, lost to the father in the Supreme Court which relied heavily on her religious affiliation, finding her in breach of the law in bringing up the children as Jehovah's witnesses, and disagreeing with the lower court's assessment of the childrens welfare, considering that the mother's refusal of blood transfusions posed a risk and that the children if left with her would become social outcasts. The majority of the Court found that the Supreme Court was clearly influenced, as shown by its tone and phrasing, by its considerations regarding the applicant's religion. This difference in treatment was based solely on the applicant's religion and conflicted with the findings of the lower courts which had been supported by expert psychological evidence concerning the children. The minority considered that it was legitimate for the Supreme Court to look at the effect of the mother's religious affiliation on the children's welfare and that the decision could not be said to be based only on the mother's religion. They found that it was not for the Convention organs to substitute their opinion concerning the children's welfare.

4. Parental rights in non-conventional families

Presumptions of paternity in favour of the married father have been found to pursue the legitimate aims of certainty and security in family relationships. However, there may be circumstances where the presumption clearly flies in the face of reality and social and biological reality should prevail. In *Kroon and others v. Netherlands*, an irrebuttable presumption of paternity in favour of the husband of the mother of the child was found to disclose a lack of respect, where the husband had long disappeared from the scene and the biological father was unable to have his paternity recognised.[27]

Homosexual relationships do not fall within the scope of "family life" for the purposes of Article 8. In a case where two women lived together in a long-term lesbian relationship, sharing parental roles in respect of a child born to one of them by artificial insemination by donor (AID), the partner of the mother could not rely on Article 8 to claim a right to obtain parental authority over the child.[28] The Commission found that, despite the evolution of attitudes towards homosexuality, Article 8 did not import a positive obligation on a State to grant parental rights to a woman who was living with the mother of a child. While homosexual relationships could raise issues under the concept of "private life", the restriction complained of in this case did not reveal any curtailment of the enjoyment of their private life. Furthermore, homosexual couples could not, in the Commission's view, be equated with heterosexual couples for the purposes of comparison under Article 14 in relation to rights of parental authority.

Where domestic systems do not provide for the recognition of the change of gender of a transsexual, the Court having regard to the controversial nature of the transsexual phenomenon and the use of AID, has not found that Article 8 imposed a positive obligation to recognise in law the parental role of the transsexual father.[29] It did accept that the relationships of a transsexual, his partner and the partner's child fell within the scope of Article 8 as *de facto* family life but did not consider that they suffered any practical prejudice from the lack of formal legal recognition as would impose an obligation on the State to take any steps. The Commission had given weight to the emotional or psychological needs of the family against which it found no overriding factor militating against recognition. It remains to be seen whether with time and further evolution in attitudes the Court's view on this point will change.

Cross-reference

Part IIA: Length of proceedings
Part IIA: Access to court
Part IIB: Homosexuality
Part IIB: Transsexuals

---

[27] Contrast *MB v. U.K.*, above n.1, where the applicant claimed to be the biological father of a child born in wedlock who was living with the mother and her husband. The Commission found no issues arising under Arts. 6, 8 and 14, in respect of the domestic courts' refusal to order a bloodtest on the child to allow the applicant to prove his claim, in particular, since this would disrupt the stability and security of the home where the child was going to be brought up. Issues could also arise where a married father separated from the mother of a child was unable to rebut the presumption of paternity.

[28] 15666/89 *Kerkhoven and others v. Netherlands*, May 19, 1992, unpublished.

[29] *X, Y and Z v. U.K.*, April 22, 1997, R.J.D., 1997–II, No. 35.

Compensation for detention

Key provision:

Article 5, paragraph 5 (enforceable right to compensation for arrest or detention contrary to the provisions of Article 5).

Key case law:

Wassink v. Netherlands, September 27, 1990, Series A, No. 185–A; *Brogan and others v. U.K.*, November 29, 1988, Series A, No. 145–B; 11 E.H.R.R. 117; *Fox, Campbell and Hartley v. U.K.*, August 30, 1990, Series A, No. 182; 13 E.H.R.R. 157; *Thynne, Gunnell and Wilson v. U.K.*, October 25, 1990, Series A, No. 190; 13 E.H.R.R. 666; *Sakik and others v. Turkey*, November 26, 1997 to be published in R.J.D., 1997.

1. General considerations

The right to compensation for arrest or detention is conditioned on the existence of a breach of one of the other four paragraphs of Article 5.[1] Such a breach must have been established directly or in substance. Where the Court or Committee of Ministers has given a decision as to breach in a previous application or where a domestic court had found a breach of one of the paragraphs but rejected the claim for compensation, the Commission can proceed directly to consider Article 5, paragraph 5. If there is no finding by domestic courts, the Convention organs must examine whether the applicant is a victim of arrest or detention in contravention of the provisions of Article 5 before proceeding to paragraph 5.[2]

2. Availability of compensation

The right to compensation must be enforceable. An opportunity to apply for *ex gratia* payment would not be adequate. It presumably extends only to financial compensation. However, in *Bozano v. France*, the Commission stated that the right to compensation might be of broader scope than mere financial compensation but could not confer a right to secure release since that was covered by Article 5, paragraph 4.[3]

The existence of the right in domestic law to obtain compensation for the breech must be established with a sufficient degree of certainty. In *Sakik and others v. Turkey*, where the Government argued that the applicants could have made various applications for compensation, the Court noted that there was no example of any person obtaining compensation by these methods and that the constitutional provisions relied on appeared to cover only detention which was unlawful in domestic terms. It accordingly found a violation.

3. Existence of damage

The Commission and Court disagreed as to whether the existence of the right could at domestic law be made dependent on the existence of damage. In *Wassink v. Netherlands*, there was a failure to comply with procedure prescribed by law[4] under Article 5, paragraph

---

[1] In *Thynne, Gunnell* and *Wilson*, the Commission rejected the argument of the Government that the provision did not apply to violations of Art. 5, para. 4 (lack of review of lawfulness of detention) but only to where there was "unlawful" arrest and detention.

[2] *e.g.* 6821/74 *Austria*, (Dec.) July 5, 1976, 6 D.R. 69 and 7950/77 March 4, 1980, 19 D.R. 213.

[3] 9990/82 *France*, May 15, 1984, 39 D.R. 119.

[4] No registrar was present at the hearing.

1 but the applicant could only apply for compensation under Dutch law if he could show damage. The Commission took the view, based on its earlier case law,[5] that the Article 5, paragraph 5 right to compensation was not conditional on damage. The Court found Article 5, paragraph 5 was complied with, if it was possible to apply for compensation in respect of a deprivation of liberty effected in conditions contrary to the other paragraphs 1–4, but that States were not prohibited from making the award dependent on the ability of the person to show damage resulting from the breach. It distinguished victim status which can exist even if there was no damage but held that there could be no question of compensation if there was no pecuniary or non-pecuniary damage to compensate. This was stated to be without prejudice to its Article 50 considerations.

4. Domestic lawfulness

Where there is no possibility of applying for compensation for a breach of Articles 5, paragraphs 1–4, there will be a violation. The Convention organs have rejected arguments by the United Kingdom Government that the right should only accrue where the arrest or detention was unlawful in domestic terms or arbitrary. Since the Convention is not incorporated in domestic law and it is only possible to challenge domestic unlawfulness in the courts in the United Kingdom, this leads to automatic breaches of Article 5, paragraph 5 where arrest or detention under the other provisions is lawful in domestic terms but fails to comply with Convention standards.

Violations of Article 5, paragraph 5 were accordingly found in *Brogan and others v. United Kingdom* (breach of Article 5, paragraph 3 for delay in being brought before a judicial officer); in *Fox, Campbell and Hartley v. United Kingdom* (a lack of conformity with Article 5, paragraph 1(c) standard of reasonable suspicion on arrest) and in *Thynne, Gunnell and Wilson v. United Kingdom* (breach of Article 5, paragraph 4) for lack of review of the lawfulness of the continued detention of discretionary lifers).

4. Adequacy of compensation under domestic law

Issues may arise if the amount of compensation is derisory. An applicant awarded £350 for four and a half hours unlawful detention by the police argued that it did not reflect the seriousness of the breach, would not discourage other infringements, was out of proportion to the costs of an action and would lead to the refusal of legal aid in future cases. The Commission agreed that, since the Convention guaranteed rights that were practical and effective, a right of compensation which set levels too low might no longer be "enforceable" in practical terms. However, it considered that the amount awarded for the short detention period could not be said to be so low as to be negligible for the purposes of Article 5, paragraph 5.[6]

---

[5] *e.g.* 10313/83, (Dec.) July 12, 1984, 39 D.R. 225, where the Commission relied on *Artico v. Italy,* May 13, 1980, Series A, No. 37, para. 35 in which the Court stated that for Art. 6, para. 3(c) an applicant need not show that lack of legal representation caused actual prejudice and the existence of a violation was conceivable even in the absence of prejudice and that prejudice was only relevant in the context of Art. 50.
[6] 28779/95 *U.K.*, (Dec.) November 27, 1996.

Corporal punishment

Key Articles:

Article 3 (prohibition of inhuman and degrading treatment); Article 8 (respect for family and private life); Article 2 of the First Protocol (right to education and respect for the right of parents to ensure education of children in conformity with their religious and philosophical convictions).

Key case law:

Campbell and Cosans v. U.K., February 25, 1982, Series A, No. 48; 4 E.H.R.R. 293; *Tyrer v. U.K.*, April 25, 1978, Series A, No. 26; 2 E.H.R.R. 1; *Costello-Roberts v. U.K.*, March 25, 1993, Series A, No. 247–C; 19 E.H.R.R. 112.

1. General considerations

The Convention organs take a critical view of corporal punishment. This reflects the position that almost alone in Contracting States the United Kingdom considers that there may be legitimate physical punishment of children.

2. Judicial corporal punishment

There is only one case. It concerned the use of the birch in the Isle of Man as a punishment, in the case of the 15-year-old applicant Tyrer, for assault on another pupil in his school and to which he had pleaded guilty in the juvenile court. The punishment, three strokes was inflicted in circumstances where he was required to take down his clothing and bend over a table, held by two policemen while a third administered the strokes. The skin was raised but not cut by the birch and the applicant was sore for a week and a half afterwards.

In finding this treatment was degrading punishment contrary to Article 3, the Court gave particular significance to the institutionalised nature of the violence, referring to the deliberate treatment of an individual as an object in the power of the authorities which inflicted a punishment constituting an assault on personal dignity and physical integrity. It also had regard to the psychological effect — mental anguish — resulting from the delay of three weeks from sentencing and the way the applicant was kept waiting in the police station before the punishment. The fact that the applicant had to strip aggravated the degrading aspect but was not a determining factor.

It is clear that in finding the punishment degrading and rejecting the argument that local conditions justified it,[1] the Court was heavily influenced by the fact that judicial corporal punishment was not found in the great majority of Contracting States.

3. As a means of discipline in school

The United Kingdom has produced single-handedly the leading cases in this area. The use of corporal punishment in its State schools has been held to be incompatible with parental convictions and, where suspension results, may disclose a denial of education.[2] Whether or

---

[1] The Government argued under Art. 63, para. 3, that Art. 3 had to be applied with due regard to local requirements in territories. However, the Court found that public opinion in favour of the punishment was not sufficient — there would have to be positive and conclusive proof of a requirement for the punishment imposed by the conditions in the island and there was no indication that criminal justice would falter without it.

[2] *Campbell and Cosans.*

not it will constitute punishment contrary to Article 3 depends on the circumstances of each personal case.[3]

(a) *Interference with education and parental convictions*

Concerning State schools, the Court found that there was a breach of the right of parents to ensure their children's education in accordance with their religious and philosophical convictions where parents objected to the potential use of the belt ("tawse") in the schools in Scotland attended by their children. The rejection of physical punishment was of the necessary cogency and seriousness to constitute a "philosophical conviction" and a view worthy of respect in a democratic society. Where one child was suspended since the parents refused to accept his return to school subject to the condition of accepting physical punishment as a disciplinary sanction, there was an additional violation of the child's right to education.[4]

(b) *Inhuman and degrading treatment*

In privately run schools, the Court has found that the State is responsible for regulating the conduct of those schools and it can examine whether disciplinary measures infringe the provisions of the Convention. However, in *Costello-Robberts v. United Kingdom*, it found that the punishment complained of — the boy was slippered three times on the buttocks through his shorts with a rubbersoled gym shoe — was not of the level of severity required to fall within the scope of "degrading punishment". There was in particular no evidence of any severe, longlasting effects. It merely expressed reservations about the automatic imposition of this kind of punishment (after reaching a certain number of demerit marks) and the way in which the boy had to wait for three days for the punishment to be inflicted.

However, in *Y v. United Kingdom*,[5] the Commission found a violation of Article 3. The circumstances were more severe, since the boy was caned four times through his trousers by the headmaster who took several steps back and ran before striking. The boy had complained of severe pain afterwards and had four weals across his buttocks with heavy bruising and swelling. The Commission found this disclosed degrading treatment and punishment having regard to the significant physical injury and humiliation which he suffered. The case was settled before the Court.

The Commission found that the humiliation aspect of corporal punishment was of particular significance in the *Warwick v. United Kingdom* case,[6] concluding that there was a violation of Article 3 by way of degrading punishment where a 16-year-old girl, a female of marriageable age, was caned on her hand by a male headmaster in the presence of another male teacher.

(c) *Invasion of physical and moral integrity*

The argument that the infliction of minor corporal punishment discloses a violation of Article 8, respect for private life, as an invasion of moral and physical integrity is unlikely to be successful in light of the Court's judgment in *Costello-Roberts*. The Commission,

---

[3] In *Y v. U.K.*, October 8, 1991, Series A, No. 247–A; 17 E.H.R.R. 233 and *Warwick v. U.K.* 9471/81 (Rep.), July 18, 1986, 60 D.R. 5, the Commission observed that, as a general rule, moderate corporal punishment in schools would constitute institutionalised violence of the kind observed in the *Tyrer* case. It emphasised that cases depend on the individual circumstances.

[4] See section Part IIA: Education.

[5] *Y v. U.K.*, see n.3.

[6] See n.3, (Dec.).

rejecting a violation of Article 3, nonetheless had considered that the scope of Article 8 was wider and that a separate issue arose which disclosed a violation. Corporal punishment was in its view an invasion of physical and moral integrity, respect for which had not been consented to by reason of enrolment in a private school and there was no justification advanced for its necessity. The Court did not exclude the possibility that Article 8 might afford protection in the disciplinary field wider than Article 3. However, it considered that sending a child to school inevitably involved some degree of interference with private life and the treatment in this case did not entail such adverse effects on physical or moral integrity sufficient to bring it within the scope of the prohibition of Article 8.

Parental chastisement

Conversely, there have been parents who have claimed the right to chastise their children. There were cases introduced by Swedish parents who objected to the Code of Parenthood which imposed a complete prohibition on the physical punishment of children by their parents.[7] The Commission held that the Swedish law, which imposed a normal measure for the control of violence extending to the chastisement of children by their parents, was intended to protect the potentially weak and vulnerable and did not interfere with the parents' right to respect for private and family life. The claim that philosophical views of parents should enable them to birch their children met with no sympathy.

Where the law permits physical chastisement, issues may arise where this level is set too high, or is too vague to apply effectively and allows inhuman and degrading treatment to be inflicted on a child. A Contracting State is arguably under a positive obligation to ensure the children are effectively protected from treatment contrary to Article 3 through its laws. Thus where a step-father was prosecuted for assault on a boy with a cane but acquitted, it was argued on the boy's behalf that the provision in English law for the defence of reasonable chastisement as applied in practice deprived children of effective protection. The Commission found a violation of Article 3.[8]

Cross-reference

Part IIB: Education
Part IIB: Torture and ill-treatment

---

[7] 8811/79, (Dec.) May 13, 1982, 29 D.R. 104 and 12154/86, (Dec.) October 23, 1987.

[8] *A. v. U.K.,* (Rep.) September 18, 1997, pending before the Court. The commission found that domestic law, which provided for a defence of reasonable and moderate chastisement, failed to provide the child applicant with effective protection against corporal punishment which was degrading within the meaning of Art. 3.

Defamation and the right to reputation

Key provisions:

Article 6 (access to court); Article 8 (respect for private life); Article 10 (freedom of expression).

Key case law:

Lingens v. Austria, July 8, 1986, Series A, No. 103; 8 E.H.R.R. 103; *Oberschlick v. Austria*, May 23, 1991, Series A, No. 204; 19 E.H.R.R. 389; *Castells v. Spain*, April 23, 1992, Series A, No. 236; 14 E.H.R.R. 445; *Tolstoy v. U.K.*, July 13, 1995, Series A, No. 323; 20 E.H.R.R. 442; *Prager and Oberschlick v. Austria*, April 26, 1995, Series A, No. 313; 21 E.H.R.R. 1; *De Haes and Gijsels v. Belgium*, February 24, 1997, R.J.D., 1997–I No. 30; *Oberschlick No. 2 v. Austria*, July 1, 1997, R.J.D., 1997–IV No. 42.

1. General considerations

The right to honour and good reputation as such is not guaranteed by Article 8, although matters relating to private life will fall within the scope of that provision.[1] Most complaints arise in the context of proceedings for defamation, or procedural problems connected with obtaining redress through the courts for slights to reputation. There are two categories of claimant — those claiming protection of private life and those who have an interest in publishing information — whose interests conflict. However, where a question arises of interference with private life by publication in the mass media the State has to find a proper balance between the Convention rights involved, the right to respect for private life and freedom of expression.[2]

2. Access to court

The right to enjoy a good reputation is a civil right under Article 6, paragraph 1 and applicants may generally claim the right of access to court to pursue defamation proceedings.[3] The general principle is that while access to court is not absolute, it may only be restricted for legitimate aims pursued in a proportionate manner and a restriction must not impair the essence of the right.[4] The procedural and substantive limitations on defamation actions must be assessed in light of those considerations.

(a) *Lack of legal aid*

Since in the United Kingdom there is an exclusion of legal aid for defamation actions, a number of cases have arisen alleging that this deprives applicants of effective access to court. While a blanket ban, allowing no discretion or regard to prospects of success, might appear *per se* disproportionate, the Commission has concentrated on the individual

---

[1] 10733/84 (Dec.) March 11, 1985, 41 D.R. 211 where Spanish officers complained about a punishment imposed on them in relation to the civil war period as infringing their right to honour and reputation (*i.e.* loss of rank and privileges).

[2] 11366/85, (Dec.) October 16, 1986, 50 D.R. 173 where the fact the applicant was not successful in his defamation action did not show that the State had failed to protect, there being no indication that the courts gave inadequate consideration to the applicant's interests in striking the balance.

[3] *Helmers v. Sweden*, October 29, 1991, Series A, No. 212; 15 E.H.R.R. 285 referring to *Golder v. U.K.*, February 21, 1975, Series A, No. 18; 1 E.H.R.R. 524.

[4] *Ashingdane v. U.K.*, May 28, 1985, Series A, No. 93; 7 E.H.R.R. 528.

circumstances in each case, the merits of the claims and to what extent each applicant has managed to take proceedings relating to the substance of his case without legal aid. It has found that legal aid could legitimately be restricted with regard to financial criteria and certain categories of cases, referring to the inherent riskiness of such cases, and has found no arbitrariness arising from the lack of legal aid.[5]

Where domestic law limits defamation actions to persons and excludes actions for group defamation, there is no right in issue in domestic law in respect of the latter to attract the guarantee of Article 6.[6]

(b) Privilege and immunities from actions for defamation

Where certain categories of persons are protected from actions for defamation, issues arise as to whether this constitutes restriction on access to court. So far, the privilege attaching to members of Parliament and to particular officials with public functions has been found to pursue legitimate aims in a proportionate manner.

In *Fayed v. United Kingdom*, where privilege attached to the report of Department of Trade Inspectors which allegedly defamed the applicants, the Court recognised as a legitimate aim that the Inspectors be free to report in the public interest in regulating public companies and found that the principle of proportionality was respected since, *inter alia*, the Inspectors and Secretary of State were bound by rules of rationality, legality and procedural propriety. It also found that the limits of acceptable criticism were wider where businessmen in large public companies were concerned, particularly, where they have knowingly laid themselves open to close scrutiny of their acts in their active campaign in public relations to clear their bids for the House of Fraser.

Parliamentary privilege is generally recognised as compatible with the Convention, pursuing the legitimate aim of free Parliamentary debate in the public interest.[7] The Commission found privilege of Irish parliamentarians for statements in the *Dáil* (lower house of the legislature) which were alleged to suggest medical negligence by a senior medical figure and financial misdealings by a former minister was not disproportionate since the nature of the comments was restrained and concerned matters of public debate, the doctor and former minister were only implicated indirectly and not named and the complaints were reviewed by the Committee of Privileges.[8] Whether it would be different if there had been a gratuitous, malicious or named attack would perhaps depend on whether the internal parliamentary body responded adequately to complaints.

3. Interference with freedom of expression

Convictions or damage awards imposed in respect of defamatory statements constitute interferences with the freedom of expression and the cases turn on issues of necessity and proportionality. Where the media is involved, journalist applicants tend to win. Great emphasis is laid on freedom of expression as one of the essential foundations of a democratic society and on the importance of the freedom of the press to impart ideas and

---

[5] *e.g. Winer v. U.K.,* 10871/84, (Dec.) July 10, 1986, 48 D.R. 154, where the applicant pursued proceedings himself and obtained a settlement; *Munro v. U.K.,* 10594/83, (Dec.) July 14, 1987, 52 D.R. 158, where the applicant claimed that he was unable to take action for defamation against a malicious employer, the Commission considered that he did bring the issues before the Industrial Tribunal in proceedings for unfair dismissal, where the reasonableness of the employer's belief in his dishonesty was considered.

[6] *U.K.* 11862/85, (Dec.) July 18, 1986, where the applicant could not sue as member of the class of gypsies in regard to disparaging posters in local shops.

[7] 3374/67 Collection of Decisions 29, p.29; *Golder v. U.K.,* 4451/70 (Rep.), June 1, 1973, p.44, para. 93; though conversely a Parliamentarian cannot claim a right to privilege where the legislature waives it — 19890/92 *Switzerland*, (Dec.) May 3, 1993, 74 D.R. 134.

[8] *Ireland,* 25646/94, (Dec.) January 17, 1996, 84–A D.R. 122; *Ireland* 29099/95, (Dec.) January 17, 1996.

information and act as a public watchdog.[9] In that role, journalists are allowed a certain leeway to exaggerate, and even to be provocative, as long as there is an issue of public interest and an underlying basis of fact.[10]

Where critical comment by journalists is made on matters of public interest and relating to the conduct of politicians, the importance of the freedom of political debate and the consideration that limits of critical comment are wider for politicians, who inevitably and knowingly open themselves to public scrutiny, are key factors. In *Lingens v. Austria*, where a journalist was convicted in a private prosecution for criticising the Chancellor of Austria for supporting an individual allegedly involved in war crimes and accusing him of immoral, undignified conduct, the Court found the articles relevant to current debate and that the position in domestic law, which required a journalist to prove not only facts but value judgments, imposed an impossible requirement. In *Oberschlick v. Austria*, where a journalist was fined for quoting a formal complaint lodged against a politician in criminal proceedings which accused him of making discriminatory statements concerning immigrant women's rights to family allowances, the Court found the article contributed to a debate of public importance on the treatment of foreigners and that it was undisputed that the publication was factually correct in reproducing the complaint. In these circumstances, the interference could not be justified as necessary, even if the applicant had been provocative and misleading in his form of presentation.[11]

The important role played by politicians themselves in contributing to public debate and a free democratic process has also been recognized. Elected representatives represent their constituents, defending their concerns and interference in that role calls for the closest scrutiny. In *Castells v. Spain*, a violation of Article 10 was found where a member of Parliament was convicted for an article attributing acts of violence to the Government, receiving a suspended sentence of one year and barred from public functions for one year. It was accepted that the purpose of the conviction was to protect order but the matter concerned issues of public interest and he had not been allowed to prove truth or good faith. The Court stated that limits of permissible criticism were wider in relation to governments than to private individuals or even politicians and that the dominant position of governments made it necessary for them to respond with restraint.

On the other hand, where attacks are made on the judiciary, special regard is had to the need of the judiciary to enjoy public confidence and the limits of permissible criticism may be narrower. In *Prager and Oberschlick v. Austria*, the Court by a narrow margin found the conviction of a journalist for alleging serious misconduct by certain judges justified for maintaining the authority of the judiciary and protecting judges' reputations. Referring to the "special role of the judiciary" as the guarantor of justice, it considered that the classification by the domestic courts of the impugned passages as unjustifiably defamatory fell within the margin of appreciation and that the applicant could not invoke good faith or compliance with professional ethics since the research which he had undertaken did not appear adequate to substantiate such serious allegations and he had not given any judge an opportunity to comment on the accusations against him.[12]

---

[9] e.g. *Lingens*.

[10] e.g. *Prager and Oberschlick*, para. 38; see *Oberschlick No. 2*, below.

[11] The Commission had commented that where a politician's own statements had been provocative, others had a right to be provocative back! See also *Oberschlick No. 2* where the journalist was fined for calling a politician a *Trottel* (an idiot) — the Court found a violation noting that in context the article responded to deliberately provocative statements by the politician and had a factual basis.

[12] Narrow majorities: Courts 5–4, Commission 15–12. The minority put less weight on need to protect judges who also had to act under public scrutiny. See, however, *De Haes* and *Gijsels*, where journalists were found to have defamed judges in critical articles about a controversial child custody case — the Court noted that though the journalists might have been polemical and aggressive, their comments had a basis of fact (unlike *Prager and Oberschlick*) and were proportionate to the ongoing public debate.

4. Injunctions and size of awards

Outside the sphere of journalistic and political debate, restraints on defamatory publications have been found more justifiable. An injunction imposed on Count Tolstoy, sued by Lord Aldington for passages on a book alleging involvement in sending prisoners of war and refugees to the Soviet Union, was found to be proportionate, not exceeding the purpose of preventing repetition of allegations found to be defamatory.

The size of the damages award imposed on Tolstoy by a jury, which exceeded one million pounds, was however disproportionate and in breach of Article 10. There was a lack of adequate safeguards in the procedure, since national law allowed the jury great latitude and awards could only be set aside on appeal on limited grounds.

5. Right of reply

While it would be doubtful that a right of reply to defamatory comments would be implied under the Convention, the Commission has found that where it exists in domestic law this does not impringe on the freedom of expression of the other party obliged to publish.[13]

Cross-reference

Part IIA: Access to court
Part IIB: Private life
Part IIB: Freedom of expression

---

[13] *Spain*, 13010/87, (Dec.) July 12, 1989, 62 D.R. 247: it was not necessary for courts to verify the content of the reply as it had to be prompt to be effective.

Deprivation of liberty

Key provisions:

Article 5, paragraph 1 (right to liberty and security of person, subject to exceptions sub. paras. a–f).

Key case law:

Lawless v. Ireland, July 1, 1961, Series A, No. 3; 1 E.H.R.R. 15; *De Wilde Ooms and Versyp v. Belgium,* June 18, 1971, Series A, No. 12; 1 E.H.R.R. 373; *Engel v. Netherlands,* June 8, 1976, Series A, No. 22; 1 E.H.R.R. 706; *Ireland v. U.K.,* January 18, 1978, Series A, No. 25; 2 E.H.R.R. 25; *Van Droogenbroeck v. Belgium,* June 24, 1982, Series A, No. 50; 4 E.H.R.R. 443; *Guzzardi v. Italy,* November 6, 1980, Series A, No. 39; 3 E.H.R.R. 333; *Bozano v. France,* November 18, 1986, Series A, No. 111; 9 E.H.R.R. 297; *Weeks v. U.K.,* March 2, 1987, Series A, No. 114; 10 E.H.R.R. 293; *Nielsen v. Denmark,* November 28, 1988, Series A, No. 144; 11 E.H.R.R. 175; *Ciulla v. Italy,* February 22, 1988, Series A, No. 148; 13 E.H.R.R. 346; *Drozd and Janousek v. France,* June 26, 1992, Series A, No. 240; 14 E.H.R.R. 745; *Kemmache No. 3 v. France,* November 24, 1994, Series A, No. 296–C; 19 E.H.R.R. 349; *Quinn v. France,* March 22, 1995, Series A, No. 311; 21 E.H.R.R. 529; *Benham v. U.K.,* June 25, 1996, R.J.D., 1996–III, No. 11; *Amuur v. France,* June 10, 1996, R.J.D., 1996–III, No. 10; *Bizzotto v. Greece,* November 11, 1996, R.J.D., 1996–V, No. 21; *Lukanov v. Bulgaria,* March 20, 1997, R.J.D., 1997–II, No. 34; *Tsirlis and Kouloumpas v. Greece,* July 1, 1997, R.J.D., 1997–IV, No. 4; *Guilia Manzoni v. Italy,* July 1, 1997, R.J.D., 1997–IV, No. 41; *K.-F. v. Germany,* November 27, 1997 to be published in R.J.D., 1997; *Raninen v. Finland,* December 16, 1997 to be published in R.J.D., 1997.

1. General considerations

The case law indicates the importance of physical freedom and emphasises that exceptions are exhaustively limited to those set out in the sub-paragraphs of Article 5, paragraph 1 (see sections below) and which are to be interpreted narrowly.[1] If the detention does not fall within any of these categories then it cannot be justified under Article 5, paragraph 1 however "useful" the aim might be.[2]

The principal aim is to prevent arbitrary deprivation of liberty. The emphasis is on procedural rights, with little scope for challenging the merits of decisions of deprivation of liberty.

2. Existence of deprivation of liberty

Whether someone is deprived of their liberty depends on examination of the concrete situation, account being taken of a whole range of criteria, such as the type, duration, effects and manner of the implementation of the measure in question.[3] In ordinary

---

[1] *Winterwerp,* para. 37.

[2] *e.g. Ciulla,* para. 41: arrest and detention before the issuing of a compulsory residence order on a mafia suspect as a preventive measure based on suspicion could not be regarded as following conviction within sub-para. 1(a) or as for the purpose of bringing him before a court within sub-para. 1(c) despite the acknowledged importance of the fight against the mafia. Also the *Engel* case para. 57, where the claim of special exclusion for military discipline not accepted.

[3] *Guzzardi,* para. 92; 8334/78 (Dec.), May 7, 1981, 24 D.R. 103, where though a threat to detain in accordance with the law could not constitute a violation of Article 5 para. 1, it was implied that threatening with arbitrary or unjustified detention could infringe the right to security of person.

circumstances, any element of compulsion restricting a person to custody or to attend a particular location falls within the scope of Article 5, paragraph 1.[4] Even where a person has submitted voluntarily to a particular regime of detention, this does not exclude the operation of Article 5 with regard to challenging the lawfulness or seeking to obtain discharge. In *De Wilde, Ooms and Versyp v. Belgium*, where the Government argued that the applicants had given themselves up to the police voluntarily, the Court considered that liberty was too important for a person to lose the benefit of protection under Article 5 merely because he might have surrendered himself. Scrupulous supervision was still required that measures were necessary for the purposes of Article 5, paragraph 1.

The apparent ability of a person to leave the place of detention may not be decisive, regard being had to the reality of the situation. In respect of asylum claimants restricted on arrival in airports to zones or holding areas, the Commission found that since they were able to leave the airport, by taking a plane elsewhere, they were not in fact deprived of their liberty.[5] The Court in *Amuur v. France* however found that the mere fact that an asylum seeker may leave the country does not exclude the deprivation of liberty, since this may be a theoretical possibility if no other country is offering the protection which they seek or is prepared to take them in. Thus an asylum seeker held in restricted conditions for an extended period of time may claim to be deprived of liberty.[6]

In certain contexts however, restrictions which might constitute deprivation of liberty if imposed on an adult civilian, will not for other categories of person. In *Engel v. Netherlands*, it was found that military life imposed a special disciplinary regime on persons stricter than in civilian life and it was necessary to examine whether a restriction clearly deviated from normal conditions of life in the armed forces in Contracting States, having regard to the nature, duration, effects and manner of execution of the penalty in question. Light arrest which meant confinement in off-duty hours to military premises, without being locked up, was not covered. Nor was aggravated arrest, where for 12 days an applicant was confined in off-duty hours to a specially designated place and barred recreation. However, strict arrest even for short periods where a person was locked in a cell by day and night and no longer fulfilled duties was a deprivation of liberty, as was committal to a disciplinary unit, where persons were held in an establishment which they could not leave for periods of months and were locked in cells at night.

Special considerations also apply to children, since they are inevitably subject to restrictions in the home and school context. The taking of a girl from school for questioning by the police in relation to enquiries about pilfering was not found to be a deprivation of liberty, apparently since it was not intended to be and there were no irregularities.[7] In *Nielsen v. Denmark*, measures taken by the parental rights holder involving admittance of a boy of 11–12 years to a hospital psychiatric ward against his will, were not found by the Court to disclose a deprivation of liberty. It emphasised family and parental rights under Article 8 and the inevitable restrictions imposed on children who

[4] Order to be taken by force to undergo bloodtest (paternity suit) found justified under Art. 5, para. 1(b): *Austria* 8278/78, (Dec.) December 13, 1979, 18 D.R. 154; *Switzerland*, 24722/94 April 10, 1995, 81–A D.R. 130 where an applicant, suffering from a nervous disorder acting bizarrely was taken by the police to the police station, the Commission found no deprivation of liberty, since he agreed to go, the police acted out of humanitarian reasons and in the police station he was free to move around; conditional release or release on licence has not yet been found to affect liberty *e.g. Sweden*, 12778/87, (Dec.) December 9, 1988, 59 D.R. 158.

[5] 19066/91, *Austria*, April 5, 1993, 74 D.R. 179, where lebanese applicants refused entry to Austria and placed in special transit area but offered a plane to Cyprus and free to leave Austria. The Commission applied the same reasoning in *Amuur*, where Somali nationals were kept in a holding area in Orly airport while refugee claims being decided.

[6] The Court appears to imply that short periods while practical matters are arranged with regard to the person's repatriation or granting of asylum would only constitute a restriction on movement. Twenty days in *Amuur* was beyond this.

[7] 8819/79, (Dec.) March 19, 1981, 24 D.R. 158.

in school and elsewhere have to abide by certain rules, and who may have to be hospitalised for medical treatment. Since the decision to place the child was taken, on the basis of medical advice, with the view of protecting the child's health and the conditions in the ward and the treatment which he received were not inappropriate (though the door was locked — this was to protect the children and avoid disturbance to other patients), the nature of the restrictions was not such as to be similar to the cases of deprivation specified in Article 5, paragraph 1. The Court gave little weight to the view of the child, since at age 12 it must still be possible for him to be admitted to hospital at the request of the holder of parental rights. The Commission had found a deprivation of liberty which was not justified, since he was not mentally ill in any real sense[8] and having regard to his understanding and views, it could not be regarded as a voluntary placement.

It would therefore appear that as long as there is some medical or educational justification for placements agreed by parental rights holders, confinement of children to particular establishments will not constitute a deprivation of liberty.

Not surprisingly perhaps, prisoners who are already under detention cannot claim a deprivation of liberty where they are subject to a more restrictive form of confinement. This is regarded instead as a modification of the conditions of lawful imprisonment.[9] Thus prisoners cannot invoke Article 5 in relation to the type of regime to which they are subjected, or in relation to the location of their prison.[10] Where there was a "deplorable delay" in transferring a prisoner from one regime to one far more suitable, he was still subject to the same lawful deprivation of liberty, although the difference in quality of life was of immense significance for him.[11] Issues could only arise if there was some failure to conform to lawful requirements with regard to the type of detention.[12]

3. Relationship with freedom of movement

The borderline between a deprivation of liberty and a restriction on freedom of movement, subject to separate protection under Article 2 of Protocol 4 is a difference of degree and intensity and not nature or substance.[13] In the United Kingdom context, exclusion orders which may restrict persons suspected of terrorism from entering mainland United Kingdom from Northern Ireland have not been found to impose restrictions of such a nature or degree as to constitute a deprivation of liberty (see Part IIB: Freedom of movement).

4. Relationship with "security of person"

While Article 5, paragraph 1 guarantees not only the right to liberty but "security of person" this latter aspect has proved to have no real independent existence. It cannot be used to cover ideas of physical integrity which fall, where appropriate, within the scope of Article 8 and in more extreme cases, Article 3.[14] In *East African Asians v. United Kingdom*, the Commission found the use of the concept of "security of person" in juxtaposition to the right to liberty referred to the aspect of arbitrary interference with liberty.[15] The

---

[8] There were difficulties, since though the mother had won custody after divorce, the boy repeatedly ran away to live with his father.
[9] 7754/77, (Dec.) May 9, 1977, 11 D.R. 216.
[10] 11703/85 *U.K.*, (Dec.) December 9, 1987, 54 D.R. 116; 11208/85 *U.K.*, (Dec.) March 4, 1986, 46 D.R. 182.
[11] *Ashingdane v. U.K.*, May 28, 1985, Series A, No. 93; 7 E.H.R.R. 528.
[12] See below: "In accordance with law and lawfulness."
[13] *Guzzardi*, para. 93.
[14] *e.g.* 5573/72, (Dec.) July 16, 1976, 7 D.R. 8; *U.K.*, 7050/75, (Dec.) October 12, 1978, 19 D.R. 5; *U.K.*, 11208/84, (Dec.) March 4, 1986, 46 D.R. 182, where it did not apply to an integration policy of republican and unionist prisoners alleged to place them at physical risk; nor in *Akdivar v. Turkey*, (Rep.), para. 229 R.J.D. 1996–IV No. 15 destruction of home, livelihood and personal security in village destruction by security forces.
[15] 4403/70 etc. *U.K.* (Rep.) December 14, 1973, 78–A D.R. 5.

application of entry regulations did not constitute an interference with this right notwithstanding the threat to the applicants' personal existence posed by the measures excluding them from the United Kingdom.

The Court in *Bozano v. France* also appeared to equate the notion to the arbitrary aspect of interference with liberty. Where an applicant was removed from France by the police by way of a "disguised extradition", it stated that what was at stake was not only the right to liberty but the right to security of person and concluded that the measures taken to circumvent a court decision against extradition were neither "lawful" nor compatible with the right to security of person.

In the case of disappearances in custody, where arbitrariness and lack of safeguards are acutely in issue, the Commission has found violation of the aspect of "security of person" together with the right of liberty. It noted that compliance with procedures and the existence of safeguards were essential to prevent the risk of extra-judicial execution and torture.[16] Indeed disappearances disclose a particularly grave violation of Article 5.[17]

5. "In accordance with a procedure prescribed by law" and lawfulness

Article 5, paragraph 1 imposes two lawfulness critieria: firstly, in the first paragraph that a deprivation of liberty must be in accordance with a procedure prescribed by law; and secondly, in each sub-paragraph listing the exceptions, a requirement that the detention, arrest or order be lawful. These overlap, since the Court considers that "lawful" covers procedural as well as substantive rules, and are regarded as underlining the importance of the aim of Article 5, paragraph 1 to prevent arbitrary detention.[18]

Most cases appear to consider both requirements of "lawfulness" together.[19] It is regarded as referring essentially to domestic lawfulness, both substantive and procedural, which is for national authorities to interpret.[20] The Court has also stated that it is not its role to assess the facts which led a national court to adopt one decision rather than another, otherwise it would be acting as a court of third or fourth instance.[21] Nonetheless since compliance with domestic law is an integral part of the obligations of Contracting States, the Court is competent to satisfy itself of such compliance where relevant, subject to its inherent limits in the European system of protection.[22] The Convention organs have a certain jurisdiction to review whether domestic law has been complied with and the manner in which this is done, in particular to ensure that domestic law is not interpreted or applied in an arbitrary manner, since no arbitrary detention can ever be regarded as "lawful".[23] As in other aspects of lawfulness under other provisions of the Convention, it

---

[16] *Kurt v. Turkey,* 24276/94 (Rep.) December 5, 1996 pending before the Court.

[17] *ibid., Cyprus v. Turkey,* 8007/77, (Rep.) October 4, 1983, 72 D.R. 5.

[18] *Winterwerp v. Netherlands,* October 24, 1979, Series A, No. 33, para. 4; 2 E.H.R.R. 387.

[19] *e.g. Ranineu v. Finland* (unlawful arrest of conscientious objector).

[20] It can include measures based on custom, as in *Drozd and Janousek,* where applicants sentenced in Andorra but held in France alleged there was no statutory or legal basis for their detention there but the Court found that the practice was based on well-established custom and while not expressly provided for, there were references in Andorran law and French regulations applied to the situation.

[21] *Kemmache No. 3,* para. 44; *France,* 10689/83, (Dec.) July 4, 1984, 37 D.R. 225, where Barbie claimed that that his arrest was not lawful (*i.e.* disguised extradition), the Commission found that the decision of the Court of Cassation upholding the execution of the arrest warrant as lawful was not arbitrary.

[22] *Lukanov,* para. 41, where on examination of the provisions of Criminal Code relied on the Court was not persuaded that the applicant's participation in a collective decision to send aid to the Third World constituted a criminal offence under Bulgarian law at the time.

[23] *Winterwerp,* paras. 40 and 45; *Tsirlis and Kouloumpas,* where the applicants, Jehovah's witness ministers were convicted and detained by military courts for refusal to take up national service, although under domestic law ministers of known religions including Jehovah's witnesses were exempt from national service — the Court found that their detention had no basis under domestic law and was arbitrary; *P.L. v. France* 21503/93, (Rep.) April 11, 1996, pending before the Court, where a convicted prisoner had a right to have deducted the period of pre-trial detention, the Commission found the refusal to take into account a period of detention on remand which the courts had annulled as unlawful (and which thus ceased to have legal existence) was arbitrary.

has been interpreted as referring in addition to the "quality of law", *i.e.* compatibility with the rule of law, that the rules be sufficiently accessible and precise.[24]

In practice, this gives much leeway to domestic systems but might also help to avoid breaches which are technical and lacking, essentially, in merit.[25] The fact that a conviction is quashed on appeal does not render it unlawful[26] nor the fact that detention is found to be justified by the courts on an interpretation which is novel, although reasonably foreseeable.[27]

Where an order for detention is later quashed by a superior court it does not automatically affect the validity of the detention retrospectively.[28] In *Benham v. United Kingdom*, where the applicant was committed for failure to pay his poll tax by magistrates who failed to comply properly with the requirement to verify if his failure was due to culpable neglect, the Court had regard to the position at domestic law concerning the review by higher courts of magistrates' decisions. Since it found that the Divisional Court's decision could not be said to indicate with any certainty that the magistrates' decision was in excess of jurisdiction as opposed to an error made within its jurisdiction it was not established that the order was invalid *ab initio* and the detention unlawful. Nor did it find any element of arbitrariness in the magistrates' decision to commit, referring to no apparent bad faith or failure to attempt to apply the legislation.[29] This appears, unsatisfactorily, to indicate that if a superior domestic court, when quashing an order of detention, refrains from clearly specifying the nature of the irregularity in the decision to detain, the Court may refrain from deciding for itself whether the detention was unlawful in domestic terms.

Where the way in which a prisoner is detained appears to contravene a requirement of domestic law, there may be scope for an issue to arise. There must be some relationship between the ground of permitted deprivation of liberty relied on and the place and conditions of detention.[30] In *Bizzotto v. Greece*, where a judge convicted a drug addict and indicated that he should be detained in an appropriate clinic for treatment, the Commission found that his detention in an ordinary jail did not comply with the measures ordered against him in domestic law. The Court took the view that since the applicant had been convicted and sentenced for the purposes of punishment, the decision of the court at the same time to order his detention in a prison with medical facilities did not affect the main ground for his detention, which lay under Article 5, paragraph 1(a). It considered that provisions laying down the arrangements for implementing sentences could not in principle have any bearing on the "lawfulness" of a deprivation of liberty. If the failure to comply could concern something more fundamental than a manner of implementation of a sentence, for example, detention of a mental health patient in a prison, the result might

[24] *Amuur,* where the legal rules applying to the holding of asylum seekers in international airport zones did not have the quality of law, since the relevant instructions contained no guarantees against arbitrary interferences, *inter alia,* by way of court review, access to legal, humanitarian or social assistance, time-limits or procedures.

[25] *e.g.* 9997/82 *Germany,* (Dec.) December 7, 1982, 31 D.R. 145: where the applicant complained that procedure did not provide for an extra duty judge appointed to cope with urgent situation of many arrests, the Commission referring to the Constitutional Court's finding that the appointment was legally based found that there was no reason to interfere with the appreciation of domestic law by the national authorities, there being nothing arbitrary about the circumstances in which the decision was taken to appoint the judge; *U.K.* 28574/95, (Dec.) November 25, 1996, 87–A D.R. 118, where there was a failure to abide by immigration rules in considering all the applicant's submissions concerning the deportation but the Court of Appeal did not find the procedural irregularities affected the lawfulness of his detention, the Commission rejected the complaints under Art. 5, finding the defect sufficiently remote from the procedural and substantive requirements for detention.

[26] 7629/76 *Germany,* (Rep.) March 9, 1978, 13 D.R. 57.

[27] *Zamir v. U.K.* 9174/80, (Rep.) October 11, 1983, 40 D.R. 42.

[28] *e.g. Bozano,* para. 55.

[29] The Commission had differed. See also the detailed separate opinion from Mr N. Bratza and the dissenting opinions in the Court.

[30] *Ashingdane,* para. 44.

perhaps be different. However, it is unlikely that a person convicted of offences in respect of whom a judge had made comments or recommendations on the need for treatment could claim successfully under Article 5 if the authorities failed to respond.

6. The permitted exceptions

These are not exclusive of each other. Detention may fall within more than one category.[31]

Article 5, paragraph 1(a): conviction by a competent court

This sub-paragraph refers to lawful detention after conviction. It does not require the conviction itself to be lawful in the sense that it is maintained on appeal. The fact that the first instance court's ruling is overturned as disclosing an error does not take the detention pending the appeal outside the exception.[32]

"Court" for the purposes of this exception has been described as an organ which is judicial in that it is independent of the executive and the parties to the case and offers adequate guarantees.[33] There has been little case law on the point.

Detention after conviction by a competent court requires not only that the detention follow the conviction in point of time but must result from, follow and depend upon or occur by virtue of the conviction.[34] The passage of time may break the causal link between a conviction and period of detention or continued detention, where the prolongation has no longer any connection with the objectives of the initial decision or was based on an assessment that was arbitrary or unreasonable in terms of those objectives.[35] Sufficient causal connection between the conviction and the detention has been found where a discretionary life prisoner was recalled to prison on revocation of his licence[36]; where the Court of Appeal has ordered that time spent in custody pending the appeal not be counted towards sentence[37]; when orders for the preventive detention of convicted recidivists have been renewed.[38]

Enforcement by a Contracting State of a custodial sentence passed by the courts of another State falls within this exception, although the enforcing State should not provide assistance if the conviction is the result of a flagrant denial of justice.[39]

Article 5, paragraph 1(b): obligation imposed by law or non-compliance with order of the court

This head of detention requires that a measure is taken to secure the execution of specific and concrete obligations. The obligation does not have to arise from a court order but may

---

[31] *e.g. Silva Rocha v. Portugal,* November 15, 1996, R.J.D., 1996–V, No. 23, where a prisoner was detained by a court after committing acts constituting an offence but without criminal responsibility due to his mental state: Articles 5, para. 1(a) and (e) applied; *Eriksen v. Norway* May 27, 1997 R.J.D. 1997–III, No. 37 where an applicant's detention on special security grounds was based on Art. 5, para. 1(a) and (c).

[32] *e.g.* 7629/76, *Germany,* (Rep.) March 9, 1978, 13 D.R. 57; 9132/80, *Germany,* December 16, 1982, 31 D.R. 154: Art. 5, para. 1(a) applies where by domestic law detention after the first instance is nonetheless classed as detention on remand pending the appeal.

[33] *e.g. Switzerland,* 7341/76, (Rep.) March 4, 1978, 15 D.R. 35: the chief military prosecutor did not qualify; *Switzerland,* 17571/90, (Dec.) September 2, 1993, 75 D.R. 139, the Military Court of Appeal did.

[34] *Weeks,* para. 42.

[35] *Van Droogenbroeck* para. 40. See *Weeks,* para. 51: recall to prison of a discretionary lifer, on ground of his aggressive, unstable behaviour, was not arbitrary or unreasonable in terms of the objectives of the sentence imposed on the applicant.

[36] *Weeks.*

[37] *Monnell and Morris v. U.K.,* March 2, 1987, Series A, No. 115; 10 E.H.R.R. 205.

[38] *e.g.* 9167/80, October 15, 1981, 26 D.R. 248; *Eriksen v. Norway.*

[39] *Drozd and Janousek;* 16462/90 *France,* January 19, 1994, 76 D.R. 18: where the applicants were convicted in Andorra but sent to serve their sentences in France. No indications of such flagrant denial of injustice in either case.

also derive from the law *per se*, although it must be sufficiently specific and concrete.[40] This has included short term internment for psychiatric observation ordered by a court[41]; four-day detention on order of a court for non-payment of a fine[42]; judicial order to undergo a blood test[43]; arrest for non-compliance with a compulsory residence order[44]; obligation to submit to a security check on entry to Great Britain[45]; committal by magistrates for failure to pay the community charge[46]; and, detention following refusal to agree to be bound over.[47]

The aim of the detention must be to secure the fulfillment of the obligation, not to punish.[48] In *McVeigh v. United Kingdom*,[49] the Commission noted that as soon as the obligation has been fulfilled the basis for the detention under this ground ceases. It was also of the view that while there was no express requirement to that effect, the provision was primarily intended to cover the situation where a person has wilfully or negligently failed to perform an obligation. Therefore while detention in the absence of a prior breach of duty was not excluded, it considered that in order to exclude arbitrary deprivation of liberty the circumstances must warrant the use of detention to secure the obligation and generally it will be required to show that the person was given an opportunity to fulfil the obligation and failed.[50]

Article 5, paragraph 1(c); suspicion of committing a criminal offence, etc.

See Part IIB: Arrest.

Article 5, paragraph 1(d): detention of minors

The purpose of the deprivation of liberty of a minor must be either for "educational supervision" or for the purpose of bringing the minor before the competent legal authority. Where in *Bouamar v. Belgium*, a 16-year-old juvenile was held in a remand prison without any purpose of bringing proceedings, the Court rejected the Government's claim that the measure was part of an educative programme in a general sense. The only reason for the placement was that no proper place was available and there were no staff or facilities available in the prison to carry our any educational aim.[51]

---

[40] *Guzzardi*, para. 101: where the warning of a police chief to a mafiosi suspect was not sufficient; *Lawless* (Rep.) December 19, 1959: measures to secure public order and State security were not concerned with the execution of specific obligations.

[41] 6659/74 *Germany*, (Dec.) December 10, 1975, 3 D.R. 92.

[42] 6289/73 *Ireland*, (Dec.) July 7, 1977, 8 D.R. 142.

[43] 8278/78 *Austria*, December 13, 1979, 18 D.R. 154.

[44] 8916/80 *Italy*, (Dec.) October 7, 1980, 21 D.R. 250; see, however, *Ciulla*, where the arrest and detention predated the compulsory residence order and so fell outside Art. 5, para. 1(b).

[45] *McVeigh and others v. U.K.*, 8022/77, etc. (Rep.), March 18, 1981, 25 D.R. 15.

[46] *Benham*.

[47] *Steel and others v. U.K.*, 24838/94, (Rep.), April 9, 1997 pending before the Court, where the applicants (a "hunt" and a "motorway" protester) refused the magistrates' order to agree to be bound over to keep the peace. The Commission rejected complaints that the order was too general or unspecific or that there was any arbitrariness in the procedure since the applicants were given the opportunity to agree and avoid detention.

[48] 7341/76, *Switzerland*, (Rep.), March 4, 1978, 15 D.R. 35 (punishment for breach of military discipline); 10600/83, *Norway*, October 14, 1985, 44 D.R. 155 (detention of conscientious objector to secure acceptance of military service).

[49] *McVeigh*, see n.63.

[50] *ibid.*: despite any prior, voluntary failure on the applicants' part, their arrest and detention on entry to Great Britain was justified exceptionally due to the exigencies of fighting terrorism and the relatively short duration of the measures. The Commission talked of striking a balance between the need to ensure fulfillment of the obligation and the right to liberty. Also 10179/82, *France*, (Dec.) May 13, 1987, 52 D.R. 111 where the balance was struck in holding a person for several hours at a police station for an identity check.

[51] February 29, 1988, Series A, No. 129.

Detention of a minor held for observation in specialist centre was found to be for the purpose of bringing him before the competent legal authority, since he was suspected of committing offences and was to be brought before the Juvenile Commission in due course. The length of time (eight months) was not so excessive or unjustifiable as to cast doubt on the genuine purpose of the detention *i.e.* to obtain medical reports.[52]

Article 5, paragraph 1(e): mental health patients, vagrants, etc.

See Part IIB: Mental health.

In respect of vagrants, the Court in *De Wilde* accepted the Belgian definition of persons without fixed abode or means of subsistence and no regular trade or profession. The detention applied to the applicants in the case was found to fall within that definition and disclosed no arbitrariness in the decision or procedure whereby they were placed at the disposal of the Government.[53]

Article 5, paragraph 1(f): pending expulsion or extradition

See Part IIB: Detention pending extradition.

6. Types of detention not covered by the exceptions

Where a court has ordered release, some delay in carrying out the decision may be inevitable although the authorities should keep this to a minimum. Where an applicant remained in custody for a further seven hours while certain formalities were being carried out, the Court found no violation.[54] Where applicants have been deliberately retained in custody pending the authorities' intention to apply other measures, the detention has been found to fall outside the exceptions allowed by Article 5.[55] Detention on arrest which exceeded the statutory maximum of 12 hours by 45 minutes,[56] was also found to disclose a violation by the Court in *K.F. v. Germany*.[57] It distinguished the cases in which some delay in release had been accepted, since in those cases the period of detention was not laid down in advance by a statute but ended as a result of a court order. Whereas in *K.F. v. Germany*, the maximum period was laid down in law as obligatory and the authorities were under a duty to comply with it.

Internment or detention without trial is excluded.[58] In *Lawless v. Ireland* the ministerial power to detain persons suspected of being engaged in activities prejudicial to public order or State security could not be considered as detention for failure to comply with an order of court or to secure the fulfilment of an obligation prescribed by law nor for the purpose of bringing the person before a court under Article 5, paragraph 1(c). In *Ireland v. U.K*, the internment power in Northern Ireland fell outside Article 5, paragraph 1(c) since whether or not persons were in fact suspected on reasonable grounds of involvement in terrorist offences, their detention was not for the purpose of bringing them before a judicial authority which was the other essential element of paragraph 1(c).

---

[52] *Switzerland*, 8500/79, (Dec.) December 14, 1979, 18 D.R. 238.

[53] In *Guzzardi*, the Government failed in their argument that mafia suspects were subject to restrictions as a type of vagrant.

[54] *Manzoni*.

[55] *Quinn; Doran v. Netherlands* 15268/89, (Rep.) July 8, 1993. See section, Detention pending expulsion and extradition.

[56] The Commission found that a delay of 45 minutes was not such as to deprive the applicant of his liberty in an arbitrary manner contrary to the subject and purpose of Art. 5, para. 1 (Rep.) September 10, 1996.

[57] Though in *Lawless v. Ireland v. U.K.*, valid derogations (Art. 15) were found to be in place.

[58] 7397/76, *Switzerland*, (Dec.) December 13, 1977, 11 D.R. 58 settled after (Rep.) March 8, 1979, 15 D.R. 105.

Other examples of detention not permitted by Article 5, paragraph 1 include deprivation of liberty of a person confined and placed under guardianship for extravagance and idleness[59]; possibly, collusion by State agents with private individuals to bring within State territory against his will a person living abroad; preventive measures, including compulsory residence, based on a policy of general prevention against individuals such as the mafiosi, who are a danger on account of their continuing propensity to crime (without reference to the commission of any specific offence).[60]

Cross-reference

Part IIB: Arrest
Part IIB: Extradition
Part IIB: Mental Health
Part IIB: Pre-trial detention
Part IIB: Review of detention

---

[59] *Stocké v. Germany*, March 19, 1991 Series A, No. 199 (Rep.): the Commission considered this, if proved, might render arrest and subsequent detention unlawful within the meaning of Art. 5, para. 1; however *Reinette v. France*, 14009/88, (Dec.) October 2, 1989, 63 D.R. 189: where suspected terrorist on St. Vincent was dragged onto runway near French military plane where officers executed letters rogatory, the Commission found no reason why co-operation between St Vincent and French authorities could raise problems under Art. 5.
[60] *Guzzardi*, para. 102; see also *Ciulla*, where the arrest and detention predated the court order of compulsory residence and thus fell outside Art. 5, para. 1(b).

Derogation: states of emergency

Key provision:

Article 15.

Key case law:

Lawless v. Ireland, July 1, 1961, Series A, No. 3; 1 E.H.R.R. 15; *Ireland v. U.K.*, January 18, 1978, Series A, No. 25; 2 E.H.R.R. 25; *Brannigan and McBride v. U.K.*, May 26, 1993, Series A, No. 258–B; 17 E.H.R.R. 539; *Aksoy v. Turkey*, December 18, 1996, R.J.D. 1996–VI, No. 26.

1. General considerations

Article 15 permits a Contracting State to derogate from its obligations under the Convention, excepting Article 2 (save in respect of deaths resulting from lawful acts of war), 3, 4 and 7, in time of war or other public emergency threatening the life of the nation and to the extent strictly required by the exigencies of the situation.

In examining derogation cases, the Convention organs examine the substantive complaint first and then, if they find a violation, they proceed to examine whether it is covered by the derogation in question.[1] This leaves no uncertainty as to what measures are in breach of the Convention. While there is a requirement of strict limitation of derogations to the exigencies of the crisis, in practice the Convention organs have given States considerable leeway.

Currently, there are derogations in force in respect of United Kingdom (concerning the situation in Northern Ireland) and in respect of Turkey (state of emergency in the South-East).

2. Obligation to inform the Secretary General of the Council of Europe

The Secretary-General should be informed without undue delay of the reasons for the derogation and the measures being taken. This appears to require identification of the laws concerned, and possibly also the provision of the texts.[2]

In *Aksoy v. Turkey*, where compliance was not adverted to in Commission proceedings, the Court stated that it could raise the point of its own motion, although it did not do so in view of its finding that the measure was not strictly required. This strongly hints that the Turkish notification was inadequate. The judgment reveals that no specific measures relating to Article 5 had been detailed in the notification beyond a reference to a power of the State of Emergency Governor irrelevant to the case.[3]

---

[1] Thus violations of various provisions of Art. 5 were found in respect of internment without trial in *Lawless* (Art. 5, para. 1(c) and 3); in the *Ireland v. U.K.* case, extra judicial detention imposed on terrorist suspects was not in compliance with Art. 5, para. 1(c), 2, 3 or 4; in *Brannigan and McBride*, there was a failure to comply with the requirement of promptness in Art. 5, para. 3, in respect of the power to hold persons for up to seven days without being brought before a judge; and in *Aksoy*, detention for 14 days without being brought before a judicial officer was clearly outside the requirements of Art. 5, para. 3. In all but *Aksoy*, the derogation conformed with the requirements of Art. 15.

[2] In *Lawless*, the Irish Government had provided a copy of the relevant Proclamation and Act and the reasons were given as being "to prevent the commission of offences against the public peace and order and to prevent the maintaining of military or armed forces other than those authorised by the Constitution." No issue arose in respect of the U.K. derogation in the *Ireland v. U.K.* and *Brannigan and McBride*, the Court referring without comment to the notifications which had been made by the U.K. Government.

[3] *Aksoy*, paras. 31–32.

There is no requirement for the Contracting State to promulgate in its territory the notice of derogation.[4]

3. Time of war

No derogation concerning a state of war has yet been in issue.

4. State of emergency threatening the life of the nation

This refers to an exceptional situation of crisis or emergency which affects the whole population and constitutes a threat to the organised life of the community.[5] The Court allows a wide margin of appreciation. By reason of their direct and continuous contact with the pressing needs of the moment, the national authorities are in a better position than international judges to decide both on the presence of such an emergency and the nature and extent of the derogations necessary to avert it. The margin of appreciation is not altogether unlimited, the Convention organs being empowered to rule on whether States have gone beyond the extent strictly required by the exigencies of the crisis.[6]

In *Brannigan and McBride v. United Kingdom*, the Court rejected the submission of the applicants and intervenors arguing against a wide margin of appreciation particularly where the crisis was of a quasi-permanent nature as in Northern Ireland and the rights essential for the protection of detainees. It merely stated that in excercising its supervision it would give appropriate weight to relevant factors such as the nature of the rights affected, the circumstances leading to and the duration of the emergency situation.[7]

The existence of an emergency claimed by a Government has not yet been rejected. In *Lawless v. Ireland*, the Court found that the existence of such an emergency was reasonably deduced by Irish Government having regard, *inter alia*, to the existence on their territory of a secret army engaged in violent, unconstitutional activities, the operation of this army outside its territory seriously jeopardising relations with its neighbour and the steady, alarming increase in terrorist activities. The existence of such an emergency was not in issue in the *Ireland v. United Kingdom* case, nor contested in the *Aksoy* case, in relation to PKK activity in south-east Turkey.

5. "Strictly required by the exigencies of the situation"

The Court has accepted measures as justified by this high standard even where there was, arguably, considerable doubt as to their efficacy or necessity. It has paid considerable attention to the existence of safeguards mitigating against abuse and given weight to the willingness of the authorities to introduce additional safeguards as the situation evolves. Notably, in the only case *Aksoy*, where the derogation fell foul of this requirement, the Government failed to provide a convincing reason for the length of time of incommunicado detention and there was a manifest lack of safeguards against abuse.

In *Lawless* and *Ireland v. United Kingdom*, the Court accepted the arguments that the ordinary law had proved it was unable to check terrorism and steps were necessary to counter the difficulties of obtaining evidence to convict persons involved with the IRA on account of the secret and terrorist nature of the groups and the fear inspired by them. In *Ireland v. United Kingdom*, the Court found that a power to detain someone unsuspected of a crime or offence but for the purposes of obtaining information could only be justified in very exceptionable circumstances but that these existed in Northern Ireland at this time

---

[4] *Lawless,* para. 47.
[5] *ibid.,* para. 28.
[6] *Ireland v. U.K.,* para. 207; *Lawless,* para. 28.
[7] *Brannigan and McBridge,* paras. 41–43.

(*e.g.* the alleged need to question persons who were too scared to give evidence freely). The Court did not accept the argument that the use of extra-judicial detention was proven to be ineffectual. The Court stated that it was not its role to judge in the place of the U.K. Government what was the most prudent or most expedient policy to combat terrorism and it had to exercise its power of supervision, not in light of retrospective considerations but only having regard to the conditions and circumstances reigning at the time.

In contrast in *Aksoy*, which concerned the power to detain for up to 30 days,[8] the Court acknowledged the difficulties of investigating terrorist crimes but found the period unacceptable, as being exceptionally long and leaving the applicant vulnerable to arbitrary interference with the right to liberty and to torture. It noted a lack of detailed reasons as to why judicial intervention was not practicable. The Government had referred solely to difficulties of investigations in a vast geographical area, where a terrorist organisation was receiving outside support.

The factor of abuse of power may be relevant. In *Lawless v. Ireland*, the Court included in its reasoning that it had found no indication that the powers were used against the applicant for any other purpose than that for which they were granted (*e.g.* involvement with the IRA).

In *Brannigan and McBride v. United Kingdom*, it was argued that the derogations were not a genuine response to an emergency situation but to counter the Court's decision in *Brogan v. United Kingdom*, where the power of detention of terrorist suspects for up to seven days was found in breach of Article 5, paragraph 3. The Court found that the power had been considered necessary under terrorism measures since 1974 and that the derogation was clearly linked to the persistence of the emergency situation. As for the apparent interim nature of the derogation, it noted that this was expressed to be subject to review of the possibilities of introducing judicial control and found that this disclosed a process of continued reflection entirely in keeping with the spirit of Article 15. It found that absence of judicial control could be considered necessary having regard to the various reports on terrorism concerning the difficulties of investigating and prosecuting terrorist crime. It noted, without rejecting, the Government's view that it was essential to prevent disclosure to the detainee and his legal advisers of the information on which the extension of detention was required and that the independence of the judiciary would be compromised if judges were involved in the granting of extensions. It observed that in Northern Ireland the judiciary was small and vulnerable to attack and the Government understandably attached great importance to public confidence in the independence of the judiciary.[9]

On the issue of safeguards, recourse to formal courts has not been required, but weight has been given to any participation by courts or the judiciary in a reviewing procedure of the measures as applied.[10] Reference has also been made to the constant supervision by Parliament or other independent bodies, although the practical effectiveness of this is not apparent. In *Ireland v. United Kingdom*, where the safeguards were less apparent or effective than in *Lawless*, the Court placed emphasis on the fact that the authorities responded to the situation by evolving towards protecting individual liberties in the measures as amended, and commented that while the provision of satisfactory judicial, or at least administrative, remedies was desirable from the outset, it would be unrealistic not to distinguish the phases. It could not be expected of a State struggling against a public emergency to render itself defenceless by being required to provide complete safeguards

---

[8] Fourteen days detention in the case of the applicant.

[9] It did not question whether it was justifiable to take the view that the judiciary could be compromised by participating in decisions on detention or would be rendered any more vulnerable than they were already.

[10] In *Lawless*, reference is made to a detention commission of which two of the three members were judges and in *Ireland v. U.K.* to a valuable but limited recourse to courts at common law alongside a certain measure of protection from the advisory committee, commissioners and appeal tribunal.

from the outset. On this view, Article 15 allows, pragmatically, for progressive adaptations in providing human rights protection, without the apparent need to establish that the initial draconian response was in fact necessary.

In *Brannigan and McBride*, where the applicant and the intervenors argued the safeguards were negligible, the Court noted that safeguards did exist and did provide an important measure of protection against arbitrary detention, *e.g.* habeus corpus, the right to see a solicitor after 48 hours and to inform a relative or friend. The operation of the legislation was also subject to regular independent review.

In *Aksoy*, the Court found insufficient safeguards compared to those available in *Brannigan and McBride v. United Kingdom*. There was a denial of access to lawyers, doctors, relatives and friends which left the applicant completely at the mercy of those holding him. The Government's reliance on the supervision by public prosecutor and the prohibition of torture in Turkish law was not enough.

4. Consistency with other obligations under international law

The only case where other international obligations were identified was *Brannigan and McBride*, where the applicants referred to the U.K.'s obligations under the International Covenant on Civil and Political Rights and claimed that it was essential for valid derogation from Article 4 of the Covenant that the derogation had been officially proclaimed. The Court noted that the Secretary of State had made a statement to the House of Commons detailing the reasons for the derogation, which was sufficiently formal and public in its view.

Cross-reference

Part IIB: Deprivation of liberty
Part IIB: Pre-trial detention

Detention pending extradition and expulsion

Relevant provisions:

Article 5, paragraph 1 and paragraph 1(f) (lawful detention pending extradition or expulsion); Article 5, paragraph 4 (review of lawfulness of detention).

Key case law:

Bozano v. France, December 18, 1986, Series A, No. 111; 9 E.H.R.R. 297; *Soering v. U.K.*, July 7, 1989, Series A, No. 161; 11 E.H.R.R. 439; *Kolompar v. Belgium*, September 24, 1992, Series A, No. 235; 16 E.H.R.R. 197; *Quinn v. France*, March 22, 1995, Series A, No. 311; 21 E.H.R.R. 529; *Chahal v. U.K.*, November 15, 1996, R.J.D., 1996–II, No. 22.

1. General considerations

A person may be detained pending extradition or expulsion subject to the general safeguard of lawfulness imposed by Article 5, paragraph 1 and the specific context of Article 5, paragraph 1(f) which provides the exception to the right to liberty of "lawful arrest or detention" which is "with a view" to extradition or expulsion. Undue length of detention may render it incompatible with this provision.

2. Lawfulness

The detention must be "in accordance with a procedure prescribed by law" and also be "lawful".[1] The dominant theme is the prevention of arbitrariness. (See Part IIB: Deprivation of liberty.)

In *Chinoy v. United Kingdom*, where the applicant complained that in the extradition proceedings in the United Kingdom the magistrate had considered tapes allegedly obtained in breach of French law, the Commission found no breach of the lawfulness criteria of the detention since the use was not in breach of English law and not arbitrary.[2] Where steps are taken by the authorities by way of "disguised extradition", issues may arise as to the lawfulness. In *Bozano v. France*, the French courts had refused an extradition request. The procedure whereby the police proceeded to enforce a deportation order, which had the effect of delivering the applicant to the requesting State, was found by the Court to disclose arbitrariness, in particular in the way in which it was executed, suddenly and forcibly, preventing the applicant from making use of any remedies theoretically available to him and not giving him the choice of destination.

3. With a view to extradition or expulsion

Only the existence of extradition proceedings justifies the detention. In *Quinn v. France*, the failure to release the applicant for 11 hours pending the French authorities' instigation of extradition proceedings by the Swiss constituted detention outside the scope of the exceptions in Article 5, paragraph 1.

---

[1] *e.g.* 15268/89 *Doran v. Netherlands,* (Rep.) July 8, 1993 where the release of the applicant had been ordered but the public prosecutor telephoned the prison to retain him in pending the intention to have him apprehended for the purposes of extradition, the Commission found that it was not in accordance with a procedure prescribed by law as required by Art. 5, para. 1.

[2] 15199/89, (Dec.) September 4, 1991: reference was made, *inter alia,* to the domestic assessment of the relevance of the tape and the purpose of the proceedings.

In *Chahal v. United Kingdom*, in the context of expulsion, the Court has said that all that is required is that action be taken with a view to deportation and that it is immaterial for the purposes of Article 5, paragraph 1(f) whether the underlying decision to expel can be justified. Nonetheless if it is apparent that the detention is for some other purpose resulting from some misuse of power it ceases to be justifiable.[3]

Where for a legal, practical or administrative reason, a person held for the purposes of extradition or expulsion cannot in fact be removed, issues may arise that the detention can in those circumstances be considered as justified as being "with a view to extradition". In the *Ali v. Switzerland* case, the Commission noted that the Swiss wanted to extradite the applicant to Somalia but were unable to do so since he had no travel document. Since the execution of the extradition was impossible, the detention could no longer be considered "with a view to extradition" within the exception of Article 5, paragraph 1(f) and disclosed a violation of Article 5, paragraph 1.[4]

4. Effect of length

If insufficient diligence by the authorities is shown in the extradition or expulsion proceedings, the detention may cease to be justifiable for the purpose of Article 5, paragraph 1(f).[5] Although in *Quinn v. France* a period of almost two years detention pending extradition was found to exceed a reasonable time,[6] the Convention organs will accept considerable delays, taking into consideration, *inter alia*, the conduct of the applicant, the complexity of the case and the lack of arbitrariness.[7]

Two years and eight months was found by the Court in *Kolompar v. Belgium* to be not unreasonable since the extradition proceedings proper were completed less than one month after the decision to release in respect of other criminal charges and the detention was continued due to the applicant's successive applications for release, in which the courts gave their decisions within a normal time and in which he delayed in making submissions and made applications for adjournment. He could not, the Court said, complain of a situation which he had largely created.[8]

In *Chahal v. United Kingdom*, a period of over three years and five months was acceptable to the Court due to the seriousness and difficulties of the issues (allegations of risk on return to India and national security issues) and the procedural safeguards in place against arbitrary detention. This overruled the Commission which noted delays between procedural steps in the domestic proceedings and gave weight to the need for utmost expedition where the person was unconvicted and without charge.

---

[3] 7317/75, (Dec.) October 6, 1976, 6 D.R. 141.

[4] 24881/94, (Rep.) February 26, 1997 pending before the Court.

[5] *e.g.* 8081/77, (Dec.) December 12, 1977, 12 D.R. 207; 7317/75 above n.8.

[6] Where three months were taken for the first decision, then ten months to issue the extradition order, in which context the remedies utilised by the applicant did not significantly delay the proceedings.

[7] *Chahal*, paras. 117 and 123; 15933/89, *Osman v. U.K.*, (Dec.) October 14, 1991, the longest detained person without trial in the U.K., (almost six years at date of his second application) facing extradition to Hong Kong — as regarded the length of proceedings, the Commission noted that there were no specific time requirements in the Convention and an assessment of diligence depended on all the circumstances. It looked at the complexity of the case (several countries involved, voluminous documentation) the conduct of the applicant (his failure to ask for expedition and his repeated habeas corpus applications) and, since the applicant appeared to be drawing out the proceedings deliberately, found that he could not complain of delay. There was also no lack of diligence on the part of the authorities.

[8] The Commission considered that there must be a responsibility on the State to prevent the undue prolongation of extradition proceedings in finding the correct balance between the restrictions on the right to liberty and international obligations. Belgium could not simply adopt a passive attitude and was required to take positive steps to expedite the proceedings.

5. Remedies

Where there is a breach of Article 5, paragraph 1(f), the applicable provisions concerning effective redress are Article 5, paragraph 4 which requires access to a review of the lawfulness of the detention and Article 5, paragraph 5 which requires an enforceable right to compensation in domestic law.

The Commission has found that habeas corpus complies with Article 5, paragraph 4 in providing the means to challenge the lawfulness of the detention for the purposes of the extradition.[9] A delay of two and a half months in habeas corpus proceedings challenging lawfulness in a deportation case was found to comply with the requirement of promptness in Article 5, paragraph 4 — this is longer than has been found compatible in review of other types of detention but was with regard to the complexity of the issues and the significance the case had for all asylum-seekers at that time.[10]

Cross-reference

Part IIB: Deprivation of liberty
Part IIB: Reasons for detention
Part IIB: Review of detention

---

[9] 19319/91 *U.K.,* (Dec.) September 2, 1992.
[10] 28021/95 *U.K.,* (Dec.) November 27, 1996.

Discrimination

Key provision:

Article 14 (prohibition against discrimination).

Key case law:

Belgian Linguistic case, July 23, 1968, Series A, No. 6; 1 E.H.R.R. 252; ; *Kjeldsen, Busk Madsen and Pedersen v. Denmark,* December 7, 1976, Series A, No. 23; 1 E.H.R.R. 711; *Marckx v. Belgium,* June 13, 1979, Series A, No. 31; 2 E.H.R.R. 330; *Van der Mussele v. Belgium,* November 23, 1983, Series A, No. 70; 6 E.H.R.R. 163; *Abdulaziz, Cabales and Balkandali v. U.K.,* May 28, 1985, Series A, No. 94; 7 E.H.R.R. 471; *Lithgow and others v. U.K.,* July 8, 1986, Series A, No. 102; 8 E.H.R.R. 329; *Johnston v. Ireland,* December 18, 1986, Series A, No. 112, 9 E.H.R.R. 203; *Darby v. Sweden,* October 23, 1990, Series A, No. 187; 13 E.H.R.R. 774; *Inze v. Austria,* October 28, 1987, Series A, No. 126; *Hoffman v. Austria,* November 29, 1992, Series A, No. 222; *Pine Valley Developments Ltd and others v. Ireland,* November 29, 1991, Series A, No. 222; 14 E.H.R.R. 319; *Schüler-Zgraggen v. Switzerland,* June 24, 1993, Series A, No. 263; 16 E.H.R.R. 405; *Burghartz v. Switzerland,* February 22, 1994, Series A, No. 280–B; 18 E.H.R.R. 101; *McMichael v. U.K.,* July 18, 1994, Series A, No. 291–B; *Karlheinz Schmidt v. Germany,* February 24, 1995, Series A, No. 308; 20 E.H.R.R. 205; *Gaygusuz v. Austria,* September 16, 1996, R.J.D., 1996–IV, No. 14; *Stubbings and others v. U.K.,* October 22, 1996, R.J.D., 1996–IV, No. 18; *Van Raalte v. Netherlands,* February 21, 1997, R.J.D., 1997–I, No. 29; *Canea Catholic Church v. Greece,* December 16, 1997 to be published in R.J.D. 1997.

1. General considerations

Article 14 encapsulates a crucial human right. Discrimination, in its many insidious forms, could be described as one of the fundamental evils afflicting society and is at the heart of many tangible atrocities. However, its role in the Convention system is limited both by its drafters and the approach adopted by the Commission and Court.

According to the case law, an applicant must establish that he is subject to a difference in treatment from others in a comparable position in the enjoyment of one of the rights guaranteed under the Convention, which difference cannot be objectively and reasonably justified having regard to the applicable margin of appreciation.

2. Protection only of enjoyment of guaranteed rights and freedoms

By its formulation, the provision has been tied to the other substantive rights in the Convention. An applicant complaining of discrimination must allege it in respect of, for example, freedom of religion or fair trial. It is useless to invoke it the area of employment rights, housing provision, political office, pay, access to private leisure facilities, and media.

In the *Belgian Linguistics* case,[1] the Court noted that the provision had "no independent existence" and it was as though it was an integral part of each of the substantive articles. Further, extreme discrimination has been held by the Commission as constituting degrading treatment contrary to Article 3.[2]

---

[1] p. 34, para. 9.
[2] See below *East African Asians v. U.K.* (Rep.) December 14, 1973, 78–A D.R. 5 in relation to race discrimination. The same argument was run in *Abdulaziz* concerning sex discrimination. While the Commission found a degrading treatment finding inherent in a violation of Art. 14, the Court found no separate issue under Art. 3.

Where the alleged discrimination relates to a matter which falls within the scope of one of the substantive articles, the provision may become operable. Thus special treatment of taxation under Article 1 of the First Protocol bestows on it an exclusion from the normal guarantee of protection for property but where taxation legislation appears to single out persons for unfavourable treatment, issues may arise under that provision in conjunction with Article 14.[3] Sentencing matters generally fall outside the scope of Article 5 but issues have been held as possibly arising if sentencing policy appears to effect individuals in a discriminatory manner.[4] In *Inze v. Austria*, concerning a difference in land inheritance between children born in and out of wedlock, the Court emphasised that under Article 1 of the First Protocol it was not for the Court to say who should inherit. However, Article 14 came into play where by operation of law a distinction operated based on birth as regarded the chances of inheritance.

3. Difference in treatment

Not all differences in treatment are relevant for the purposes of Article 14. The examination for discrimination is only meaningful if the applicant is seeking to compare himself to others in a comparable or analogous position or is in a "relevantly similar" situation to those others.[5]

For example, married couples are not in analogous situations with unmarried couples since they have chosen a particular legal regime to govern their relations, marriage having a special status which continues to be characterised by a distinct corpus of rights and obligations[6]; IRA Category A prisoners cannot seek to compare themselves with prisoners of no security risk[7]; advocates are not in analogous positions to other professions, even others connected with the law like the judiciary or bailiffs, the professions in question being characterised by a corpus of rights and obligations of which it would be artificial to isolate one element[8]; companies subject to nationalisation are not in an analogous situation to property owners subject to compulsory purchase.[9]

This may appear at times to overlap with the objective and reasonable justification concept (see 5. below, Justification for difference in treatment) since a finding that two situations are not comparable will generally rely on factors, akin to objective and reasonable justification, disclosing material difference.[10]

4. On grounds of personal status

The Court has stated that Article 14 is only concerned with discriminatory treatment having as its basis a personal characteristic or "status" by which persons or groups of persons are distinguishable from each other.[11] It thus aims to strike down the offensive singling out of an individual or members of a particular group on their personal attributes. Article 14 lists the obvious ones: sex, race, colour, language, religion, political or other

---

[3] *Lindsay v. U.K.*, 11089/84, (Dec.) November 11, 1986, 49 D.R. 181.
[4] *Nelson v. U.K.*, 11077/84, (Dec.) October 13, 1986, 49 D.R. 170; *R.M. v. U.K.*, 22761/93, (Dec.), April 14, 1994, 77–A D.R. 98.
[5] *Markx*, para. 32; *Van der Mussele*, para. 46.
[6] *Lindsay*, above n.3.
[7] *U.K.*, 19085/91, (Dec.) December 9, 1992.
[8] *Van der Mussele*.
[9] *Lithgow*.
[10] See *e.g., Stubbings and others*, where, in effect, the Court held that victims of deliberate and negligently inflicted injury were not in analogous positions since the prescription rules applicable to the two categories had developed separately and different considerations applied to them and even if they were in analogous positions, there was reasonable and objective justification since they had different characteristics.
[11] *Kjeldsen*, para. 56.

opinion, national or social origin, etc. The list is not exhaustive, Article 14 referring to "any ground" and concluding with "or other status".

The limits of the concept of personal status have not been much discussed. It does not extend to differences in treatment deriving from differing rules applicable between regional jurisdictions within a State, where, in other words, the difference results from the geographical location where the person finds himself, rather than any personal characteristic. Thus it is not a difference in treatment on grounds of personal status for people in Scotland to be subject to the poll tax before people living in England[12] or where a juvenile offender in Scotland did not enjoy an entitlement to remission accorded to such offenders sentenced in England and Wales.[13] The Commission has noted that many Contracting States have regional jurisdictions, with differing rules and procedures and takes the view that Article 14 cannot require universally identical laws throughout their jurisdiction. Geographical difference presumably could base a claim for discrimination where there was an abusive or oppressive element or where it was apparent that a particular area was subject to a law because its citizens were individuals sharing a common personal element, beyond their residence in the location.

5. Justification for difference in treatment

While Article 14 is not expressly subject to exceptions, it has been interpreted as incorporating the practical recognition that not every difference in treatment in the enjoyment of the protected rights and freedoms can be prohibited. The Court in the *Belgian Linguistics* case noted that a literal application of the French version *"sans aucune distinction"* would lead to "absurd results" and referred to the inherent differences existing in legal situations and problems which call for differing legal solutions. The test applied to assess which differences in treatment are objectionable or not is whether they are based on objective and reasonable justification. The existence of the justification has to be assessed in relation to the aims and effects of the measure under consideration, regard being had to the principles which normally prevail in democratic societies. It must not only pursue a legitimate aim but there must be reasonable relationship of proportionality between the means employed and the aim sought to be realised. Therefore, the concepts of legitimate aim, proportionality, are brought in and also, inevitably, the margin of appreciation.[14]

Whether there is objective and reasonable justification will depend on the circumstances of each situation. Administrative difficulties generally should not suffice, as in the *Darby v. Sweden* case where this was the sole basis for barring non-residents who worked in Sweden from an exemption to church tax available to residents in Sweden.

6. Relationship with substantive complaints

In many cases, an applicant subject to a particular measure will argue that it infringes a substantive right, without necessary justification and that he is, by the implementation of that measure, subject also to unjustifiable discrimination. Where a violation is found of the substantive article, it is often the case that the Convention organs will find no separate issue to arise under Article 14. It is a practice which may not be based on unavoidable logic but rather gives proof of a certain judicial economy. For example, in *Moustaquim v. Belgium*,[15] the Court found the proposed measure of expelling the applicant, a second

---

[12] *U.K.*, 13473/87, (Dec.) July 11, 1988.
[13] *Nelson*, see n.4; see also the dissenting opinion of Mr Bratza in *John Murray v. U.K.*, (Ref.) where a person detained in police custody in Northern Ireland was not allowed a solicitor present in interview whereas a different policy was adopted in England and Wales.
[14] *Belgian Linguistics* case p. 35, para. 10.
[15] February 18, 1991, Series A, No. 193.

generation immigrant, to a country in which he had no family, disclosed a violation of Article 8, but found it unnecessary to examine the complaint under Article 14. However, the applicant's claim that this measure constituted discrimination since it was imposed on him due to his nationality was arguably a separate legal issue, the fact that the complaint concerned the same measure not logically precluding the existence of two separate grounds of violation.

Conversely, a finding of no violation of a substantive article does not preclude the examination of the discrimination complaint, as in *Abdulaziz v. United Kingdom* where the claims under Article 8 were rejected.[16] This is the type of case where the essence of the complaint is the discriminatory application of the measures, which otherwise disclose no fundamental incompatibility with the provisions of the Convention.

There are some cases where it is more difficult to analyse whether the case is essentially about the substantive provision or discrimination. There have been decisions, where the Convention organs have chosen to examine the complaints under Article 14 alone. In *Hoffman v. Austria,* the applicant, who lost custody of her children to her divorced spouse in a decision which gave considerable weight to her beliefs as a Jehovah's witness, invoked Articles 8 and 14. Since the deprivation of her family rights was based on apparent discrimination on religious grounds, the Court found a violation of Article 14 and considered that it was not necessary in its view to look at Article 8 alone since it would involve the same arguments.[17]

To succeed in establishing a violation of a substantive provision and discrimination under Article 14 would require showing that separate arguments and considerations of some significance arose.

7. Particular discrimination areas

(a) Sex

The Court has emphasised that, advancement of equality of the sexes being a major goal in Contracting States, it would require very weighty reasons for a difference in treatment on grounds of sex to be compatible with the Convention. Such reasons have been lacking in a number of cases, which, interestingly, tend more to concern discrimination against men than against women.

A court decision refusing a woman a disability pension which had as its only basis the assumption that women gave up work on having children was a difference of treatment based on sex, for which there was no objective and reasonable justification.[18] An inability of a man to add his surname before that of his wife's, while the law allowed a woman to add hers to her husband's name was a difference of treatment based on sex without convincing justification, the Court rejecting the Swiss Government's arguments that family unity required a single joint surname nor finding any genuine tradition at stake.[19] An obligation on a man to pay a fire service levy in lieu of actual service based on a local tradition of male participation in the fire brigade was discrimination in conjunction with Article 1 of the First Protocol and Article 4, paragraph 3(d) since women, who did not

---

[16] *Abdulaziz:* there was no interference with family life since the applicants and their spouses had no expectation of a grant of residence and could live together elsewhere; whereas the rules were applied differently depending on whether the British citizen spouse was male or female.

[17] See also the Commission's approach in *Stubbings.* While the applicants also complained of a prescription rule which barred their access to court contrary to Art. 6, their main argument was analysed by the Commission as alleging that this hindrance on access to court was unreasonable and disproportionate since it did not apply to other categories of litigant suffering from injuries — essentially discrimination and to be treated under Article 14.

[18] *Schuler-Zgraggen.*

[19] *Burghartz.*

serve, did not have to pay either. Even assuming that it might have been justified in imposing an obligation of service on men alone, this obligation no longer operated and there was no justification in treating men and women differently for the imposition of financial contributions.[20] Rules allowing the entry of foreign wives of citizens but not foreign husbands might pursue the legitimate aim of protecting the labour market but that aim could not be justified by differentiating between men and women for impact on employment.[21] Where childless women over 45 were exempted from paying social security contributions towards child benefit, it was found that there were equally men who were unable to procreate and that whether or not it was a legitimate aim to spare the feelings of childless women, it did not provide justification for the difference in treatment.[22]

The Commission to some extent accepted positive discrimination in favour of women as objective and reasonable justification for difference in treatment in the context of tax.[23] This was where rules had developed with the aim, the Commission accepted, of encouraging women to work and advance the equality of the sexes, which resulted in a situation that where the wife was the major breadwinner of a married couple the tax allowance proved more favourable than where the major breadwinner was the man. The Commission accepted the aim as legitimate, noting that the difference only applied in 3 per cent of cases. It considered the margin of appreciation must be wider in the realm of taxes and pragmatically accepted that systems of taxation inevitably differentiate between groups of taxpayers and marginal situations might arise. The discrepancy in treatment was not particularly large or widespread and it is possible that the case would have proceeded differently if there had been a significant financial disparity.

Some limited differences between men and women have been found acceptable concerning procedural rights relating to children.[24]

(b) *Marital status*

Marriage consisting of a special legal regime, differences of treatment between non-married couples or parents and married couples have been found not to disclose discrimination. Differences in the rights enjoyed by natural fathers and married fathers over their children were accepted in particular due to the differences in the nature of relationships of fathers with children born out of wedlock.[25] Since the importance of marriage is perhaps diminishing in practice and domestic law, it is less certain that all differences in treatment between married and unmarried men in respect of their children will be found justified.[26]

(c) *Race*

In the *East African Asians*[27] case, the Commission analysed discrimination based on race as forming a special form of affront to human dignity. In aggravating circumstances, it could

---

[20] *Karlheinz Schmidt.*

[21] *Abdulaziz.*

[22] *Van Raalte*, paras. 42–43. Also *AP v. Austria* 20458/92 (Rep.) October 15, 1996 pending before the Court, where the Commission found discrimination in the inability of a father to claim parental leave payments when staying at home to look after a child.

[23] *Lindsay*, see n.3.

[24] *MB v. U.K.*, April 6, 1994, 77–A D.R. 108: finding objective and reasonable justification in treating natural fathers differently from the natural mother as regards the automatic grant of parental responsibility, flowing from the different links with the child based on biological considerations; *Rasmussen op. cit.*, para. 33: where the husband faced a stricter time bar in parternity matters than his wife. The Court found that this inequality had objective and reasonable justification given that the child's interests were often closely linked to the mother's.

[25] *McMichael*, para. 98.

[26] *e.g.* the fact that allegedly parental responsibility can be removed by the court from natural fathers who break up with the mother of children but not that of a divorced or separated father.

[27] Above, n.2.

constitute degrading treatment. This was found in respect of the exclusion from the United Kingdom of Asians from East Africa who were British citizens of varying categories, but who had nowhere else to go since their residence was rendered difficult or illegal in their African state of origin and who were at risk of being "shuttlecocked" from one place to another. This disclosed a difference of treatment based on racial grounds, since the legislation targeted a particular racial group in permitting unrestricted entry of people with a grandparental connection in the United Kingdom which operated in favour of "white" expatriate citizens. There was also the element of publicly being singled out for a difference in treatment, with reference to the debates in Parliament which showed the legislation was aimed at Asians from East Africa.

Where the discrimination alleged is more indirect, it is likely to be harder to substantiate or bring under Article 14. In *Abdulaziz*, where rules rendered it more difficult for spouses of arranged marriages from India and Pakistan to enter,[28] the Court found that these rules applied without differentiation between persons on grounds of race or ethnic origin and that it was legitimate for immigration purposes to favour persons having close links with the United Kingdom. Similarly, different treatment as to entry and residence applying to non-citizen aliens from inside and outside the European Union has been found to be objectively and reasonably justified on the basis of the special legal regime concerned.[29]

In other immigration cases, concerning expulsion of non-British parents with British citizen children, it was found by the Commission that even assuming these children were in a comparable position with children with British parents, any difference in treatment was objectively and reasonably justified in relation to the fact that under Article 8 the expulsion had been found to be a legitimate immigration measure.[30]

(d) *Religion*

Reliance on a parent's membership of a religious community (Jehovahs' Witnesses) in a court decision on the custody of the children constituted a difference in treatment in *Hoffman v. Austria*.[31] While it pursued a legitimate aim (protection of health and rights of the children) it was not reasonably proportionate to base the decision essentially on a difference in religion.[32] This was by a majority of 5–4, the minority agreeing with the Austrian Supreme Court that account could be taken of blood transfusions and risks of social isolation concerning the children's welfare. The majority were in effect relying on the tenor of the Supreme Court's judgment, that its tone and attitude were negative on the religious aspect without taking into account the evidence accepted in the lower courts of the emotional need of the children for their mother and the fact that courts could order blood transfusions if necessary for them. Also the Supreme Court gave weight to the legislation on religious education and to its view that the mother had been wrong to bring the children up as Jehovahs Witnesses since this was not the religion of the parties at the time of their marriage, an objection based purely on disapproval of the mother unrelated to the children's welfare.

The Court found no objective and reasonable justification in *Canea Catholic Church v. Greece* for the situation whereby the applicant church could not take legal proceedings to protect its property rights due to a denial of its legal personality, where as the Orthodox Church and the Jewish Community could do so, without any formality or required procedure.

[28] Concerning ancestry links with the United Kingdom and that the parties to a marriage must have met.
[29] *Moustaquim* para. 49, see n.15.
[30] *U.K.* 23938/94, (Dec.) October 23, 1995.
[31] *Hoffman*.
[32] *ibid*.

(e) *Birth*

While it may be legitimate to protect and nurture traditional family relationships, the Court considers, having regard to the importance of social integration, that there is no justification for subjecting children out of wedlock to different rules in relation to the possibility of inheriting property from parents. In *Marckx v. Belgium*,[33] the Court found no objective or reasonable justification under Article 14 in conjunction with Article 8 in that a child born out of wedlock was subject to rules whereby the mother had to take special steps for the family link to obtain legal recognition and in limiting the unmarried mother's ability to leave property to a child born out of wedlock. It was not enough, as the Government argued, that the mother could take steps to protect the child.[34] The Court also rejected the notion that unmarried mothers were less likely to wish to take the responsibility for caring for a child as unproved by the figures and that the risk of upsetting "legitimate" families by allowing "illegitimate" members to share family property was a legitimate motive for depriving a child of fundamental rights.

An Austrian variant in *Inze v. Austria* concerned the precedence taken by a legitimate child over one born out of wedlock as regarded designation as the principal heir to take over a farm in case of intestacy. Examining the case under Article 14 in conjunction with Article 1 of the First Protocol, the Court found the justifications general and abstract. It rejected the Government's reference to the "convictions" of the local rural population.

(f) *National origin and minorities*

Exclusion from emergency unemployment assistance of the applicant due to his national origin was not justified where he had satisfied all the other material critieria of eligibility applicable to Austrian claimants.[35]

Arguments have been attempted that discrimination is revealed where, statistically, members of a particular national minority are subject to a disproportionate risk of death or ill-treatment. However, regarding allegations in applications from South-east Turkey that forcible evacuation of villages, torture and death in custody discloses discrimination against people of kurdish origin, the Court, relying on the Commission's findings, has found them unsubstantiated.[36]

---

[33] See also *Johnston*, similar situation in Ireland, but having found a violation of Art. 8, no separate issue was found under Art. 14.

[34] Referring to the recognition by Committee of Ministers that the single mothers and children were a form of family no less than others (resolution of social protection) (*Marckx*, p. 14).

[35] *Gaygusuz:* he had worked and paid contributions, the sole reason for exclusion being his non-national status.

[36] *Akdivar v. Turkey*, September 16, 1996, 1996–IV, No. 15, para. 99. Similar allegations are made in Northern Ireland that a disproportionate number of persons killed by the security forces are from the Catholic community.

Education

Key Articles:

Article 2 of Protocol No. 1 (right to education); Article 14 (prohibition of discrimination).

Key case law:

Belgian Linguistics case, July 23, 1968, Series A, No. 6; 1 E.H.R.R. 252; *Kjeldsen, Busk Madsen and Pedersen v. Denmark*, December 7, 1976, Series A, No. 23; 1 E.H.R.R. 711; *Campbell and Cosans v. U.K.*, February 25, 1982, Series A, No. 48; 4 E.H.R.R. 293; *Costello-Roberts v. U.K.*, March 25, 1993, Series A, No. 247–C; 19 E.H.R.R. 112; *Valsamis v. Greece*, December 18, 1996, R.J.D., 1996–VI, No. 4.

1. General considerations

There have been few cases exploring the substance of the guarantee that "no person shall be denied the right to education". This possibly reflects the fact that in general the Contracting States cater adequately for perceived educational needs.

The Court in an early case held that the provision enshrines the right of everyone to education.[1] But education is a wide concept. There is a whole range of academic, technical, vocational and professional training which may be pursued until the grave. It would be an expensive exercise for a State to guarantee such further studies and training on an unlimited scale.[2]

There is Commission case law to the effect that the right to education is concerned primarily with elementary education and not necessarily advanced studies such as technology. This is derived from two cases, where the Commission rejected summarily the complaint of a 27-year-old applicant that he was unable to continue specialist technological studies in prison[3] and where the Commission found that foreign students, who were claiming to follow various studies but were being expelled from the United Kingdom, could not rely on Article 2 as granting them a right to stay in the country.[4]

2. Access to education

Access to education cannot, practically, be without limitations, notwithstanding the absence of any express restrictions in Article 2 of the First Protocol.

Suspension of a 16-year-old for bad behaviour was not found to be a denial of education where his return to school was conditional on his undertaking to be of good behaviour.[5] Where, however, in *Campbell and Cosans v. United Kingdom*, a boy was suspended as a result of a refusal by himself and his parents to accept the disciplinary use of the "tawse" in a Scottish school which conflicted with the parents' right to ensure the teaching of their children in line with their philosophical convictions, there was also a finding by the Court of a denial of education to the boy.

No case has been brought questioning selection procedures or eligibility for places in

---

[1] *Kjeldsen*, para. 50.
[2] The only reservation made by the United Kingdom under the Convention relates to Art. 2 of the First Protocol, stating that the principle in the second sentence of Art. 2 is accepted only so far as it is compatible with the provision of efficient instruction and training, and the avoidance of unreasonable public expenditure. The validity of the reservation is untested.
[3] *U.K.*, 5662/72, (Dec.) March 13, 1975, 2 D.R. 50.
[4] *U.K.*, 7671/76, (Dec.) May 19, 1977, 9 D.R. 185.
[5] *U.K.*, 13477/87, (Dec.) October 4, 1989, unpublished.

universities or similar institutions. Where a State makes available advanced educational institutions, it is likely that the Commission would, notwithstanding its old precedents, consider itself competent to examine whether an applicant was being denied access to it on unreasonable and arbitrary grounds. It has rejected complaints of expulsions on disciplinary grounds on the basis that this has not been shown to injure the substance of the right under Article 2 of Protocol No. 1.[6]

However while there may be a right to education for a child, there is no right of access to a particular State school of choice. Parents who complained of the closure of a local school had their application rejected on the basis that the children were able to attend another school a mile further away.[7]

There is no obligation on the State to provide any specific educational system. The provision does however guarantee that persons subject to the jurisdiction of a State should have the right to avail themselves of the educational institutions existing at a given time. At the same time the Court recognises that the right to education calls for regulation by the State "regulation which may vary in time and place according to the needs and resources of the community and individuals".[8]

While there is a right to start and run a private school, this must be subject to conditions, namely, regulation by the State to ensure fulfillment of its responsibility to provide a proper educational system, even in the private sector. The Commission found in *Ingrid Jordebo v. Sweden*[9] that the State's refusal to allow a private school to run senior classes (above 16 years) was not incompatible, having particular regard to the reasons given *i.e.* an absence of teachers with the requisite qualifications.

3. State schools and private schools

The Commission and Court have found that the State is responsible for both State schools and privately run schools.[10] The State cannot absolve itself from its responsibility of securing the right of education to everyone by delegating its obligations to private bodies.

On the other hand, States are not obliged to grant subsidies to private education, for the establishment or running of private education.[11] A right cannot be derived to obtain from the authorities the creation of a particular kind of establishment.[12] Problems may however arise where they hand out money to some educational institutions but not others or permit discrimination in the entrance requirements (see below).

4. Education in accordance with philosophical convictions

There is in effect no absolute right for parents to have their children educated in accordance with their philosophical convictions, only a right to have such convictions respected.[13] Setting and planning of school curricula fall in principle within the competence of the State, with questions of expediency which may legitimately vary from country to country. It is not forbidden from imparting through education information or knowledge of a directly or indirectly religious or philosophical kind. Nor can parents object to the integration of such teaching into the school curriculum or otherwise all

---

[6] *Turkey*, 24515/94, (Dec.) January 17, 1996, 84–A D.R. 98.

[7] *U.K.*, 11644/85 (Dec.) December 1, 1986, unpublished.

[8] *Belgian linguistics* case: pp. 31–32 where it was not incompatible for the State to refuse to subsidise in the Dutch unilingual region primary school education in French (p. 42).

[9] 11533/85, (Dec.), March 6, 1987, 51 D.R. 125.

[10] *e.g. Keldjsen; Costello-Roberts.*

[11] 6853/74 (Dec.), March 9, 1977, 9 D.R. 27; 23419/94 *Austria*, September 6, 1995, 82 D.R. 41.

[12] *i.e.* in the context of language teaching in the *Belgian Linguistics* case p. 33, para. 9.

[13] *Family H. v. U.K.*, 10233/83, (Dec.), March 6, 1984, 37 D.R. 105.

institutionalised teaching would risk becoming impracticable. Many subjects cannot avoid having some philosophical complexion or even religious elements, bearing in mind that some religions have a very broad dogmatic base and offer answers to every question of a philosophical, cosmological or moral nature.[14]

The concept of "convictions" has been defined by the Court as denoting views that attain a certain level of cogency, seriousness, cohesion and importance. It had more difficulty with notion of "philosophical" which has varying meanings and connotations from the serious to the trivial but held that it denoted in this context such convictions as are "worthy of respect in a democratic society" and which do not conflict with the fundamental right of the child to education. In *Campbell and Cosans*, the Court found that the applicants' views as to the use of the "tawse" in the Scottish school attended by their sons related to a weighty and substantial aspect of human life and behaviour, namely, the integrity of the person and the propriety or otherwise of corporal punishment. It found that the provision of education subject to this disciplinary condition failed to respect the applicants' philosophical convictions.

On the issue of the substance of what is taught, the State in fulfilling its duties must take care that information is conveyed in an objective, critical and pluralistic manner and must not pursue aims of indoctrination that might be considered as not respecting parents' philosophical convictions. What that might mean will vary on one's own views. In the *Kjeldsen and others v. Denmark* case, the parents objected to sex education. The Court, having examined the material in question, found that Denmark had not overstepped the limit in the conveying of necessary factual information to enable the children "to take care of themselves and show consideration for others in that respect" without in any way attempting to exalt sex or incite them in such practices. The Court also gave weight to the fact that those parents who nonetheless objected were free to send their children to private schools or to educate them at home.

In *Valsamis v. Greece*, the child applicant was suspended for one day for failing to participate in Greek National Day celebrations as a Jehovah's Witness and her parents complained that this conflicted with their convictions since the event was nationalistic and commemorated a war. The Government countered that it was a communal celebration of an idealistic and pacifist character. The Court considered that as Jehovah's Witnesses, members of a known religion, they were entitled to rely on respect for their religious convictions in the context of Article 2, which required States to respect their convictions throughout the entire State education programme. Respect also meant more than acknowledgement or taking into account and implied some positive obligation in addition to a primarily negative undertaking. However, in this case, it found that the child was exempted from religious studies, that there was nothing in the purpose of the parade or its arrangements which could offend the applicants' pacifist convictions to an extent prohibited by Article 2 nor were they deprived of their right to guide their children in line with their convictions.[15] It did however express surprise at the obligation on children to take part in activities outside school on holidays. Basically, the Court appears to have considered that the disciplinary step was mild and the nature of the participation outside the prohibited area of indoctrination.[16]

---

[14] *Valsamis,* (Rep.), para. 38; *Kjeldsen,* para. 53.

[15] The Court's majority come close to assessing whether the applicants' objections were in fact justified in terms of their own beliefs, a dangerous approach risking an appearance of insensitivity and intolerance.

[16] A minority of the Commission and Court found that compelling children to participate on a school holiday could be seen as an indirect attempt to indoctrinate them with a patriotic value system difficult to reconcile with parents' right freely to choose the manner in which their children are educated. There was no plausible reason why it was necessary for her education to attend, particularly where she was already excused religious education classes.

5. State education and home education

The State may provide for a compulsory system of education. This is not without controversy, since, not infrequently, parents objecting to the State system prefer to educate their children at home. The Commission has found that State regulation of home education is part of its responsibilities to enforce educational standards and where refusal of permission for home education has been based on its inadequacy, the Commission has effectively found that the State's assessment of the children's right to education prevailed over the parents' particular convictions.[17]

6. Special educational needs cases

A series of United Kingdom cases raised the issue of conflict between parents and education authorities as to the educational needs of children with perceived problems. The Commission in practice gives leeway to the educational authorities in assessing what a child might require, and as to the efficient use of educational resources, with only the weak rider that parental views be taken into account as far as might be consistent with the needs of the child. In *Graeme v. United Kingdom*,[18] where the child was epileptic, with other associated problems, the parents considered that he should not be taken out of mainstream schooling, advocating that handicapped children not be marginalised. The education authority made the child a ward of court and placed him in a special school. The Commission found the child's right to effective education prevailed over the parents' view, to the extent that could be regarded as a philosophical conviction. While it examined the complaints concerning the standard of the education, including complaints of abuse and lack of access to Christian teaching, it found them ill-founded. Impliedly, the Commission stills retains a supervisory role and in a grossly unreasonable or arbitrary case might find the education authority were not in fact pursuing the effective education of the child.

7. Discrimination

Where unequal treatment is apparent as regards access to education, violation may arise under Article 14. In the *Belgian Linguistics* case, a violation was found where French-speaking children resident in a particular Flemish area were denied access to French-speaking schools outside that area but compelled to attend local Dutch-speaking schools.[19]

While a State is not obliged to fund particular educational schemes, Article 14 requires that authorities do not discriminate in the provision of available financial subsidies. However differences of treatment have been found justified where the State makes lesser

---

[17] In *Family H. v. U.K.*, see n.13, the applicants had insisted on educating their dyslexic children at home and been convicted for failing to comply with orders requiring the attendance of the children at a State school. The Commission found that it was not its task to decide whether the parents' or the State's views as to education were better for the children. The Commission considered that as part of their responsibility the State had to verify and enforce educational standards. Thus obliging parents to co-operate in the assessment of their childrens' educational standards by an education authority to ensure a certain level of literacy and numeracy while nevertheless allowing children to be educated at home could not be said to disclose a lack of respect. In a Swedish case, 17678/91, (Dec.) June 30, 1993, the parents, misssionaries, obtained permission to educate their children until a certain age, when permission was withdrawn on grounds that their education required an increasing specialisation which the parents were not qualified to give and an increasing emphasis on social contact — the Commission found that the State had acted within its margin of appreciation in assessing the parents' capabilities in providing a viable alternative to state schooling.

[18] *U.K.*, 13387/88, (Dec.) February 2, 1990, unpublished; *Netherlands*, 25212/94, July 4, 1995, 82 D.R. 129.

[19] Though other complaints of unequal treatment were dismissed as not having been made out, the Court accepting the aim of promoting linguistic unity within regions and knowledge of the normal language of a region as in the public interest and not disclosing any discrimination.

grants available to private educational institutions than to public ones[20] or gives preference to particular organisations providing a particular need.[21]

Cross-reference

Part IIB: Corporal punishment

[20] *U.K.*, 7782/77, (Dec.) May 2, 1978, 14 D.R. 179 where it was legitimate and not unreasonable for the State to require the private body to foot 15 per cent of capital costs as opposed to public ones.
[21] 23419/94 see n.11: state subsidies were provided to church schools which were a widespread feature of the education system.

Electoral rights

Key provisions:

Article 10 (freedom of expression and to receive and impart information); Article 3 of Protocol No. 1 (free elections ensuring the free expression of the people in the choice of the legislature).

Key case law:

Mathieu-Mohin and Clerfayt v. Belgium, March 2, 1987, Series A, No. 113; 10 E.H.R.R. 1; *Gitonas v. Greece*, July 1, 1997, R.J.D., 1997–IV, No. 42; *Pierre-Bloch v. France*, October 21, 1997, R.J.D., 1997–VI, No. 53; *Bowman v. U.K.*, February 19, 1998, to be published in R.J.D. 1998.

1. General considerations

The Convention ascribes much importance to the values of democratic society. The human rights guaranteed in it are seen as being best guaranteed by "an effective political democracy" (preamble). The proper and fair functioning of the mechanism of electing democratic and representative law-making bodies could therefore be expected to assume key importance.

The sparse case law is perhaps an indication of healthy democratic systems. Perhaps more significant is the fact that Article 3 of the First Protocol is the only provision which is phrased in collective and general terms, rather than as a specific individual right. The provision does confer rights. In *Mathieu-Mothin and Clerfayt v. Belgium*, the Court explained that the impersonal phrasing is in fact intended to give greater solemnity to the commitment and reflect the fact that it was not concerned with abstention or non-interference but with a positive obligation to hold democratic elections. There are, however, implied limitations and a wide margin of appreciation. Such limitations must not impair the essence of the rights such as to deprive them of their effectiveness and should pursue a legitimate aim in a proportionate manner.[1] Nonetheless, as applied in practice, the individual has some difficulty in establishing that personal restrictions in fact thwart the "free expression of the people" as a whole.

2. Legislature

(a) *National legislatures*

The legislature is not necessarily restricted to the national parliament or assembly. Considering the federal or cantonal structure of some Contracting States, regard must also be had to the constitutional system of the Contracting State. For example, the diets of the German Länder are legislatures for the purpose of Article 3.[2]

However, local authorities with purely delegated powers will not qualify. While the regional councils of Belgium may submit bills, they do not become law until passed by Parliament and the Commission found that the councils had no legislative power, such power being concentrated exclusively in the national legislature.[3] The abolition of the GLC in London was not found to disclose a problem, since it was a creature of statute, its

---

[1] *Mathieu-Mohin*, para. 52; *Gitonas*, para. 39.
[2] *Germany*, 27311/95, (Dec.) September 11, 1995, 82–A D.R. 158.
[3] 6745 and 6746/74, (Dec.) May 30, 1995, 2 D.R. 110.

powers purely derivative, subordinate and subsidiary to Parliament which held absolute constitutional authority. While the GLC had considerable power, it was of an administrative nature, subject often to approval from executive authority. In particular, it did not exercise any inherent rule-making power and those powers delegated to it by Parliament were subject to its ultimate control.[4]

Referenda, however significant in national politics, do not generally form part of an election for the legislature.[5]

(b) *European Parliament*

The Commission was initially doubtful that the drafters intended to cover anything but national legislatures. In 1979, it considered that the European Parliament was an advisory body with certain supervisory and budgetary powers but noted that developments in the structure of the EEC might make it necessary for the Contracting States to guarantee Article 3 rights in respect of new representatives bodies which might assume at least in part the powers and functions of the national legislative bodies.[6] Eight years later, when a "Green" challenged the French apportionment of seats in the European Parliament,[7] the Commission noted that the European Parliament's role had increased following the Single European Act but it still did not constitute a legislature within the ordinary meaning of the term.[8]

3. Right to vote

Article 3 does not expressly guarantee the individual right to vote but refers generally to "conditions" to ensure free expression of the "people". While an old case stated that the principle of universal suffrage was to be implied,[9] the cases refer to limitations as being generally recognised. Exclusions of groups must however not be arbitrary or affect the expression of the free opinion of the people. There has been no challenge as yet to the age limit for voting, or by excluded groups such as prisoners, although limitations on voting rights of persons convicted of collaboration during the war were found acceptable.[10]

Limitations on the vote arising from residence requirements have been found acceptable.[11] Though the Commission has regretted the absence of a uniform electoral procedure

---

[4] 11391/85, (Dec.) July 5, 1985, 43 D.R. 236; 5155/71, (Dec.) July 12, 1976, 6 D.R. 13 where local authorities in Northern Ireland were not "legislatures".

[5] *e.g.* a prisoner unable to vote in the referendum for entry of U.K. to EEC 7096/75, (Dec.) October 3, 1975, 3 D.R. 165.

[6] 8612/79, (Dec.) May 10, 1979, 15 D.R. 259, where a Belgian resident in France was unable to vote in European Parliament elections.

[7] *Tête v. France*, 11123/84 (Dec.) December 9, 1987, 54 D.R. 52.

[8] Further developments post-Maastricht are in issue in a case *Matthews v. U.K.*, 24833/94 (Rep.) October 29, 1997 pending before court where the applicant, resident in Gibraltar, is unable to vote in the European Parliament elections. The majority of the Commission maintained its view while six dissenters took the view the European Parliament did now qualify as a legislature.

[9] 2728/66 Coll 25 p. 38.

[10] 6573/74, (Dec.) (1974) 1 D.R. 87: concerning discrimination, the Commission found objective and reasonable justification in preventing persons who had grossly misused in wartime their right to participate in public life from misusing their political rights in the future; also 8701/79 *Belgium,* (Dec.) December 3, 1979, 18 D.R. 250 where permanent deprivation of the vote for a person convicted of colloboration was not found arbitrary or calculated to prejudice the free expression of the opinion of the people. In respect of prisoners there is less readiness to accept that additional punishments by way of loss of civil rights beyond the deprivation of liberty are necessary.

[11] 7566/76, December 11, 1976, 9 D.R. 124, where a British citizen living abroad could not vote in elections for Parliament; nor was it discrimination that diplomats and servicemen abroad could vote since they were not in a comparable position, being posted abroad because of their duties and remaining closely linked with their country and under Government control — impliedly accepting as a valid consideration an alleged risk of electoral fraud in postal votes by other persons.

in all member States concerning voting for expatriates in the EEC.[12] Exclusion of geographical areas from voting for the legislature may be justified by historical considerations, as in the case where a citizen of Jersey could not claim the right to vote for the United Kingdom Parliament although it had legislative power over the Channel Islands. The Commission noted that Channel Islanders were not resident in the United Kingdom and that they had their own elected legislature, making reference to the exceptional and particular historical relationship between the two areas.[13]

4. Right to stand for election

While an individual right to stand for election is implied by Article 3, it is not without limitation. States are allowed considerable latitude in their constitutional regulation of parliamentarians' qualifying status.[14] Examination of complaints seem to focus on two criteria: whether there has been arbitrariness and whether the restriction interferes with the expression of the opinion of the people.

Age-limits on candidates in Belgium (25 for House of Representatives and 40 for the Senate) were not arbitrary or unreasonable.[15]

Systems of subsidies to political parties according to the number of votes gained (which may penalise smaller parties) was not found by the Commission to be a condition which blocks the free expression of the people.[16] Nor was objection taken to the conditions imposed on any group putting itself forward in an election to obtain 100 or 500 signatures of support. This was considered to be justified as preventing the electorate from being confused by groups which could not assume political responsibility.[17] A requirement of 200 signatures or three members of the regional parliament on a list was compatible in an Austrian case, in light of the Constitutional Court's reasoning, namely, that the conditions were easily satisfied by a party with a reasonable chance of success and pursued a legitimate aim of preventing undue splitting of the vote of a proportional representation system.[18]

Obligations to pay deposits have been found acceptable, where the amount did not impose an unbearable burden and it was seen as pursuing a legitimate aim of promoting the emergence of sufficiently representative currents of thought.[19]

Authorities are apparently not under an obligation to assist candidates, even where such assistance may be indispensable. Where a German prisoner complained that the authorities refused to circulate in prisons his publications and official forms to collect the 500 signatures necessary for a candidate to stand for election, the Commission recalled that the right to stand was not absolute, noting that prisoners were not prohibited from standing or voting, that the circulation of materials might have an effect on internal order and security and that other parties were also not afforded the possibility of circulating material in prison or collecting signatures.[20]

Disqualifications may legitimately be imposed where an elected member is already a member of another legislature. This was challenged by a member elected for the Northern Ireland Assembly in 1982, who was disqualified since he was a member of the legislature of the Republic of Ireland. The Commission agreed that Article 3 must also include the right to take up a seat if elected. But it found the restrictions not irreconcilable with

---

[12] 8612/79 see n.6.
[13] *X v. U.K.*, 8873/80, (Dec.) May 13, 1982, 28 D.R. 99.
[14] *Gitonas*, para. 39.
[15] 6745 and 6746/74, see n.3.
[16] 6850/74, (Dec.) May 18, 1976, 5 D.R. 90.
[17] 6850/74, *ibid.*
[18] 7008/75, (Dec.) July 12, 1976, 6 D.R. 120.
[19] *France*, 12897/87, (Dec.) December 3, 1990, 67 D.R. 166) where the "Greens" complained that the deposit was only reimbursed if 5% of the votes was attained.
[20] 11728/85, (Dec.) March 2, 1987, unpublished.

Article 3. Under Article 14, where a complaint was made that this condition was not applied to Commonwealth countries, the Commission considered it sufficient to rely on the special historical tradition and special ties existing with those countries as objective and reasonable justification.[21]

Whether persons should be disqualified because of service for local authorities was challenged in the context of Greece and United Kingdom. In *Gitonas v. Greece*, the rule disqualifying persons who had held particular public offices in the constituency over the previous three years was found to pursue the legitimate aim of preventing undue influence on the electorate or unfair advantage over other candidates and not to be arbitrary or disproportionate in application. It was not found disproportionate in the United Kingdom that local authority officers were required to resign if standing in elections, the rules reflecting a legitimate concern to maintain the political impartiality of local government officers.[22]

5. Conditions ensuring the free expression of the opinion of the people

Elections should not be under any form of pressure as to the choice of candidates and an elector must not be induced unduly to vote for any party.[23] No constraint must be exercised in respect of parties or candidates, particularly where there are minorities involved, in which context particular aspects may take on significance. Thus there was careful scrutiny of allegations concerning the way language groupings were "juggled" in various Belgian regional and legislative bodies.[24]

Article 3 does not as such require any type of electoral system *e.g.* proportional, or majority vote with one or two ballots (all of which are part of the common heritage of political traditions in Contracting States).[25] There is reference to a "wide margin of appreciation" and the necessity to assess any electoral system in light of the political evolution of the country concerned.[26]

However, whatever the chosen system, a general principle of equality of treatment of all citizens has been identified.[27] This does not mean that all votes must have the same weight regarding the outcome of the election or that all candidates have equal chances of success. There is an acceptance that wasted votes are inevitable in all systems. There is reference also by the Court to the conflicting objectives sought by electoral systems which are both to reflect fairly faithfully the opinion of the people and to channel currents of thought to promote the emergence of a sufficiently clear and coherent political will.[28] Systems which aim to restrict the number of candidates or parties have been acceptable in light of the latter factor.[29]

A proportional representation system which was favourable to minority groups was accepted as enabling the people to express their opinion freely and as such was clearly in line with the requirements of Article 3 of the First Protocol. To the extent that this

---

[21] *M v. U.K.* 10316/83, (Dec.) March 7, 1984, 37 D.R. 129.
[22] *Ahmed and others* 22954/93, (Rep.) May 29, 1997 pending Court. Under Art. 10 however, there was a violation; see below.
[23] *Moureaux v. others*, 9267/81 July 12, 1983, 33 D.R. 97 at p. 131.
[24] *Mathieu-Mohin*.
[25] 7140/75, (Dec.), October 6, 1975, 7 D.R. 95.
[26] *Mathieu-Mohin* para. 54: features existing in one State might be unacceptable in another but could be justified by the context.
[27] *Mathieu-Mohin*, para. 54.
[28] *Mathieu-Mohin*, para. 54.
[29] *Tete v. France*: see n.7; the discounting of parties/lists with less than 5% of the vote in a proportional representation system was legitimate to foster the emergence of sufficiently representative currents of thought and the forfeiture of deposits and no repayment of publicity expenses incurred by such lists was compatible in pursuit of this aim.

disclosed discrimination, it was justified in pursuing the aim of protecting the minority.[30] In respect of the Liberal Party's complaints about the majority vote system in the United Kingdom, the mere fact that not all votes would have the same weight was not sufficient to disclose a problem. It was left open whether there would be a problem if the system used resulted in a pattern whereby particular religious or ethnic groups or communities could never be represented.[31]

Access of candidates to media coverage is an important aspect of campaigning. In a French case, the Commission appeared to accept that issues could arise from the way time was distributed on radio and television between different groupings but given the wide margin of appreciation the regulations in question were not unjustified or disproportionate.[32]

Rules in Belgium concerning the eligibility of candidates who took the parliamentary oath in either French or Flemish to sit in particular groupings in the legislature and with different powers was not incompatible with Article 3 given the intention to achieve an equilibrium between the country's various regions and communities and to defuse language disputes in the country. Regard was also had to the wide margin of appreciation, a margin which was even greater given the system was incomplete and provisional pending installation of a permanent system.[33]

6. Free elections at reasonable intervals

An increase from four- to five-year intervals for elections to the diet of a German Länder was accepted. The Commission commented that the purpose of Article 3 was to ensure that fundamental changes in public opinion were reflected in the opinions of the representatives of the people. That aim however had to be balanced by the consideration that a Parliament must be able to develop and execute legislative programmes and that too short an interval would act as an impediment to planning and lead to petrification of the political groupings in Parliament which might then cease to bear any resemblance to the will of the electorate.[34]

7. Article 10: freedom of expression

This provision cannot be interpreted as bestowing the right to vote on an individual.[35] However, freedom of expression and to receive and impart information may be relevant where restrictions are placed on candidates or others' ability to participate in electoral debate or express their views.

A concern to prevent political groups which espouse violence from achieving public exposure generated controversial cases in Ireland and the United Kingdom.[36] However, restrictions imposed on the broadcasting of interviews with Sinn Fein members were

---

[30] 8364/78, (Dec.) March 8, 1978, 15 D.R. 247, where Northern Ireland unionists challenged the proportional representation system with the single transferable vote in operation in Northern Ireland whereas a simple majority vote applied elsewhere in the United Kingdom for elections to the European Parliament. It was argued that this discriminated against Protestants and was motivated by appeasement of the republican community.
[31] 8765/79, (Dec.) December 18, 1980, 21 D.R. 211.
[32] *Tete v. France,* see n.7: 30 minutes to big parties, five minutes to small parties. See also: *Huggett v. U.K.* 24744/94, (Dec.) June 28, 1995, 82–A D.R. 98: independent candidate at EP elections complained of not being allotted air time, which was confined to main political parties (at least 12.5% vote). No problem with this under Art. 10 since air time was inevitably limited.
[33] *Mathieu-Mohin.*
[34] 27311/95, see n.2.
[35] *e.g.* 7096/75, October 3, 1975, 3 D.R. 65.
[36] *Purcell v. Ireland,* 15404/89, April 16, 1991, 70 D.R. 262; *Brind and others v. U.K.,* 18714/91, May 9, 1994, 77 D.R. 42.

accepted, even though Sinn Fein was a lawful political party and could present candidates who could take office locally and in the legislature. It was argued, *inter alia*, that terrorists drew sustenance and support from the media coverage. The Commission gave particular weight to the aims pursued by both Governments in fighting terrorism and assessed the measures as proportionate, since the information itself could be broadcast in the United Kingdom[37] and other means existed in the media in Ireland.

Restrictions on the activities of individuals publicising single issues during campaigns and on the ability of local authority officials to participate in local campaigns were however found disproportionate by the Commission. In *Bowman v. United Kingdom*, where the applicant had been prosecuted for distributing leaflets publicising the views and voting record of the candidates on abortion, the Commission found that the prohibition of the expression of factual information, of potential relevance to voters on issues of public interest, was not convincingly justified by the aim of the legislation which was to prevent corrupt electoral practices.[38] In *Ahmed v. United Kingdom*,[39] restrictions on local authority officials' activities such as canvassing for their wives in local elections or participation in local political party activities were disproportionate and did not reflect any clear necessity.

8. Article 6: access to court

In general, electoral and political rights of a candidate, voter or elected representative fall outside the scope of Article 6 as not concerning "civil rights". Its guarantees have been held not to apply to proceedings reviewing the legality of an election[40] or to proceedings whereby an elected candidate was removed from office for expenses irregularities and barred from standing again for a year. So far the penalties imposed, such as disqualification, have not by their nature or severity rendered Article 6 applicable in its criminal aspect.[41]

However, the progressive interpretation of the concept of "civil rights" brought the issue before the Court in *Pierre-Bloch v. France*,[42] where the Commission by nine votes to eight held that there was no violation of Article 6, paragraph 1 in relation to the proceedings involving the disqualification of the applicant, elected to the National Assembly, for one year for expenses irregularities, and the imposition of a payment order. The Court, by a wider margin of seven votes to two, confirmed that civil rights and allegations did not cover political ones, such as the right to stand for election or the obligation to limit campaign expenditure. The fact that there was an economic aspect to the disqualification proceedings did not render them civil. The minority considered, *inter alia*, that pecuniary obligations to pay the overspent amount of expenses were civil obligations, not relating purely to electoral law issues. The Court also found that the two penalties imposed were not of such a nature of severity as to bring the proceedings within the criminal sphere.[43]

Cross-reference

Part IIA: Fair trial guarantees, Access to Court
Part IIB: Freedom of expression

---

[37] Through the use of actor voice overs.
[38] 24839/94, (Rep.) September 12, 1996. The Court disapproved rather of the total barrier to the publication of information posed in practice by the limit of £5 placed on expenditure for that purpose (1983 Representation of the People Act, s.75).
[39] n.22.
[40] 11068/84, (Dec.) May 6, 1985, 43 D.R. 195.
[41] 24359/94 *France*, (Dec.) June 30, 1995, 82–B D.R. 56.
[42] 24194/94 *France*, (Rep.) July 1, 1996.
[43] While the applicant was liable to prosecution with heavy fines and the possibility of imprisonment, this, if it occurred, would be separate from the disqualification proceedings.

Environment

Key Articles:

Articles 8 (private life and home); 13 (right to an effective remedy); Article 1 of the First Protocol (peaceful enjoyment of possessions).

Key case law:

Powell and Rayner v. U.K., February 21, 1990, Series A, No. 172; 12 E.H.R.R. 355; *Lopez Ostra v. Spain*, December 9, 1994, Series A, No. 303–C; 20 E.H.R.R. 277; *Guerra and others v. Italy*, February 19, 1998, to be published in R.J.D. 1998.

1. General considerations

There is no provision specifically geared for protection of any "environmental" rights. It is perhaps difficult to fit the traditional notion of individual human rights with the collective interest of protection of ecosystems, the atmosphere, or other environmental concerns. An early unpromising case by the Commission stated unreservedly: "no right to nature preservation is as such included among the rights and freedoms guaranteed by the Convention" with the result that an organisation set up to protest military use of marshland was unable to claim infringement of any protected right.[1] No right existed in another case to an environment of any particular quality.[2]

But it is a reflection of the growing recognition of the importance of environmental issues that matters of environmental protection, quality of the environment and assertions of the need for protection against, or information concerning, environmental threats are increasingly appearing in cases.

2. Indirect environmental interests

In numerous cases concerning complaints by persons of restriction on use of their land, the Commission has held that measures of town planning, building restrictions and sometimes even confiscation have been justified, protection of the environment being necessary in the "general interest" or for the protection of the rights of others. Preservation of rural areas thus obtains recognition under the Convention where it comes to State action in controlling their citizens' use of property. For example, when an applicant was prosecuted for inhabiting an old bunker on land she had bought in Jersey, the Commission recognised that planning controls are necessary and desirable to preserve areas of natural beauty.[3] Positive obligations placed on landowners, for example, to plant particular types of tree in their forest land have also been found in the general interest for the protection of the environment.[4]

3. State responsibility for infringing environmental concerns

Where an individual complains that the State is responsible for harming the environment, the Convention organs have been less ready to find infringement of Convention rights. Since there is no general environmental right guaranteed, an application will generally

---

[1] 7407/76, (Dec.) May 13, 1976, 5 D.R. 161.
[2] *Rayner v. U.K.*, 9310/81, (Dec.) July 16, 1986, 47 D.R. 5.
[3] *U.K.*, 11185/84, (Dec.) March 11, 1985, 42 D.R. 275.
[4] *Sweden*, 12570/86, (Dec.) January 1, 1989, 59 D.R. 127.

only be feasible where there is an individual interest at stake which can be brought under expressly guaranteed rights, for example, the right to respect for home, and private life, or peaceful enjoyment of property. The individual has to point to direct and strongly prejudicial effect[5] and even then for a violation to be found, there must be no important public interest to outweigh his. Proportionality is likely to be the key consideration.

In a Norwegian case, while accepting that the building of a dam which would flood large areas of land traditionally used for reindeer herding could constitute an interference with the private life or lifestyle of two Lapps, the Commission found the measure justified in view of the relatively small area concerned in the vast northern region and that the actual impact on the individual was outweighed by the general and economic interest.[6]

In three United Kingdom cases, house owners complained of the serious interference with their lives caused by aircraft noise. Two of them, which were settled after admissibility, involved very serious noise interference from extensions and increased flights to Heathrow airport and a lack of any redress, including an inability to sell the property with change of use to obtain a reasonable price.[7] Although the issues were never settled on the merits, the cases seem to imply that where State developments occur which seriously impinge on occupation of private homes, without counterbalancing compensation to enable sale and removal elsewhere, there may be violations of Articles 8 of the Convention and Article 1 of the First Protocol, as well as potential issues of access to court or lack of remedies under Articles 6 and 13.[8]

In the third case,[9] where the first applicant lived several miles from the airport in an area of low aircraft noise and the second applicant lived over one mile away, the Commission found State responsibility for noise nuisance caused by airports, since the State regulates air traffic and constructs airports. It considered that considerable noise nuisance could undoubtedly affect a person's physical well-being and interfere with his private life and enjoyment of home. It had regard however to the fact that the second applicant came later to the property and must have been aware that it was not a peaceful environment and that air traffic could increase. Also the noise was not at the intolerable levels of previous cases and his property had not been shown to be unsaleable. Accordingly, the Commission concluded that the interference complained of was not disproportionate to the

[5] *e.g.* 12816/87, (Dec.) January 18, 1989, 59 D.R. 186: a complaint about noise from a military shooting range was rejected where it was not used in such a way as to cause important noise nuisance and the applicants had not been exposed to an intolerable and exceptional noise nuisance of such a level or frequence as to amount to a possible interference with private life or their right to peaceful enjoyment of their possessions (while on some days the noise was alleged to be unbearable, no firing was carried out on weekends or public holidays and a limit was in place of firing during other days up to 22.00 at the most four days a month). Also 28204/95 *Tauira and others v. France*, (Dec.) December 4, 1995, 83–B D.R. 112, where applicants in the Pacific areas under French jurisdiction complained unsuccessfully that the nuclear tests at Muratoa placed their lives and health at risk from the radiation and contamination of the water and sealife. However, since they lived at considerable distances, the Commission found that the complaints referred only to potential consequences which were too remote to be considered as directly affecting their personal situation (no sufficiently established degree of probability that damage would occur to their health where they were or that tests would, for example, fracture the atoll).

[6] 9278/81 and 9415/81 *Norway*, (Dec.) October 3, 1983, 35 D.R. 30.

[7] *Arrondelle v. U.K.*, 7889/77, (Dec.) July 15, 1980, 19 D.R. 186, (Rep.) May 13, 1982, 26 D.R. 5: admissible under Arts. 6, 8, 13 and 14 and Art. 1 of the First Protocol — settled on payment of £7,500 by the Government; *Baggs v. U.K.*, 9310/81, (Dec.) October 16, 1985, 44 D.R. 13, (Rep.) July 8, 1987, 52 D.R. 59 where the house, quarter of a mile from a runway, was overflown by day and night, resulting in "intolerable conditions". Admissible under Arts. 8 and 13 and Art. 1 of the First Protocol — settled on payment of £24,000.

[8] The Commission found violation in *Powell and Rayner* under Art. 13 since there was no possibility of action in nuisance for the increase in noise since entry of the property, no possibility of compensation and official noise control measures were ineffective. The Court finding no arguable claim on the substantive provisions did not consider the matter further (see Part IIB, Remedies). The procedural aspect was therefore never resolved and awaits a case which proceeds on the merits on substantive and procedural grounds together.

[9] *Powell and Rayner*, decisions on admissibility, see n.2, and (Dec.) October 16, 1985, unpublished.

legitimate aim of running an airport.[10] The Commission adopted similar reasoning for the first applicant with the rider that the interference was so low that it was left open whether it reached a level that interfered with his private life and home.

The case of *Lopez Ostra v. Spain* showed the Convention organs were prepared to find a violation where there was a combination of a clear and significant risk to health and serious impingement on private life and home and the lack of timely and effective steps to deal with the situation. It also confirmed that States bear responsibility for the activities of private companies where such are subject to regulation from local authorities.[11] The applicant complained of pollution from a plant treating waste which began to operate without a licence and was situated 12 metres from her home. The Court noted that she had had to live with the plant for a number of years and considered the domestic findings of significant health effects were convincing.[12] The Court seemed to accept that actual damage to health was not required for Article 8, since "unnaturally severe environmental pollution may affect individuals' well-being and prevent them from enjoying their homes in such a way as to affect their private and family health adversely without however seriously endangering their health".[13] There was a violation of Article 8, but the conditions were not severe enough for Article 3 to bite.

4. Access to information about environmental risks

Where there are risks to health from severe environmental pollution, it now appears that persons who may claim to be affected may derive a right to obtain information about those risks from the relevant authorities under Article 8 of the Convention. While Article 10 contains a freedom to receive information, the Court has maintained its view that this relates basically to information which others wish to impart. In *Guerra and others v. Italy*, the applicants, who lived near to a chemical factory which had experienced a serious explosion in the past and had been found to fall short of standards, claimed that they had not been given information about the risks produced by the factory or the measures to be adopted in case of an accident. The Commission, finding a violation of Article 10, emphasised the importance of access to information in the field of health and welfare and was prepared to impose a positive obligation under Article 10. The Court however, holding that Article 10 could not in the circumstances of this case impose an obligation on the State to collect and disseminate information, nonetheless found a violation of Article 8, considering that state had not fulfilled its obligation to secure the applicants' right to respect for private and family life through its failure to provide the applicants with essential information about the risks posed to them by severe environmental pollution.

Cross-reference

Part IIB: Freedom of expression
Part IIB: Private life

---

[10] The decision contained the statistics as to the key importance of the airport as a U.K. port and income earner.
[11] Even though the plant was run by a private company, the State was responsible since permission was given for building by the planning authorities and the State gave a subsidy. It was noted that the local authority did little to resolve the lawfulness of the plant's activities and indeed appealed against the closure.
[12] *e.g.* the applicant's child suffered from acute bronchopulmonary infections.
[13] para. 51.

Expropriation and confiscation

Key provisions:

Article 1 of Protocol No. 1 (peaceful enjoyment of possession); Article 6 (access to court/ fair hearing).

Key cases:

Sporrong and Llonroth v. Sweden, September 23, 1982, Series A, No. 52; 5 E.H.R.R. 35; *James v. U.K.*, February 21, 1986, Series A, No. 98; 8 E.H.R.R. 123; *Lithgow and others v. U.K.*, July 8, 1986, Series A, No. 102; 8 E.H.R.R. 329; *Agosi v. U.K.*, October 24, 1985, Series A, No. 108; 9 E.H.R.R. 1; *Erkner and Hofauer v. Austria*, April 28, 1987, Series A, No. 117; 9 E.H.R.R. 464; *Håkansson and Sturesson v. Sweden*, February 21, 1990, Series A, No. 171; 13 E.H.R.R. 1; *Papamichalopoulos and others v. Greece*, June 24, 1993, Series A, No. 260–B; 16 E.H.R.R. 440; *Hentrich v. France*, September 22, 1994, Series A, No. 296– A; 18 E.H.R.R. 440; *Holy Monasteries v. Greece*, December 9, 1994, Series A, No. 301–A; 20 E.H.R.R. 1; *Air Canada v. U.K.*, May 5, 1995, Series A, No. 316; 20 E.H.R.R. 150; *Matos e Silva v. Portugal*, September 16, 1996, R.J.D., 1996–IV, No. 14; *Katikaridis v. Greece*, November 15, 1996, R.J.D., 1996–V, No. 20; *Akkuş v. Turkey*, July 9, 1997, R.J.D., 1997–IV, No. 43.

1. General considerations

Considerable room for manoeuvre is accorded in respect of expropriations and confiscations. A wide margin of appreciation applies to planning, nationalisation or other legislative interventions due to the complex or policy nature of the measures.[1] Examination of these cases tends to focus on whether a fair balance has been struck between the public and private interest and whether the applicant has been left with a disproportionate burden.[2]

Since property rights fall within the scope of Article 6, paragraph 1 as civil rights, procedural safeguards generally apply regarding access to court for determination of claims and regarding requirements, *inter alia*, of fairness, reasonable length of proceedings, independent and impartial tribunals. (See Part IIA: Fair Trial, Fairness.)

2. Expropriation

(a) *De facto deprivation*

Generally, where ownership of the property remains or some form of exploitation, by way of sale or receipt of rents for example, the measure will not be regarded as a *de facto* expropriation or deprivation of property within the meaning of the second sentence of the first paragraph of Article 1 of Protocol No. 1 but an interference with peaceful enjoyment of possessions within the meaning of the first sentence.[3] However in *Papamichalopoulos and others v. Greece*, where the navy constructed a naval base and officers' resort on the applicants' land, the Court found that although there had been no formal expropriation, their land was occupied, and being unable to sell, mortgage or even gain entry, they had

---

[1] *Sporrong*, para. 26; *James*, para. 46: the margin of appreciation is applied both to the assessment of the existence of a problem of public concern and the remedial action necessary.

[2] *e.g. Lithgow*, para. 120.

[3] *e.g. Sporrong*, para. 65; *Matos e Silva*, para. 85.

lost all ability to dispose or make use of it. This, combined with the failure of attempts to remedy the situation, entailed sufficiently serious consequences to disclose a *de facto* expropriation incompatible with their right to the peaceful enjoyment of their possessions, the general guarantee set out in the first sentence of Article 1.

Whatever the classification of the measure under Article 1 of Protocol No. 1, the balancing exercise underlies the Convention organ's examination.[4]

(b) *Public interest*

The Court has stated that it will respect the legislature's judgment as to what is in the public interest unless it "manifestly without reasonable foundation"[5] and that the notion of "public interest" was necessarily extensive.[6]

Public interest has been accepted as the aim in all cases so far. It has included *de facto* expropriation for national defence policy in building a base and officers' resort,[7] transfer of monastery land for the purpose of ending illegal sales, encroachments and abandonment of property and in controlling development[8]; price control systems for land purchase and rights of preemption for the prevention of tax evasion.[9]

(c) *Proportionality — striking a fair balance*

In assessment of whether a fair balance has been struck, or the applicant required to bear an excessive and disproportionate burden, the Convention organs look at the circumstances as a whole, considering issues of lawfulness, the length of time involved, procedural safeguards and the effect on the applicant, in particular, whether compensation is available.[10]

Arbitrariness and lack of procedural safeguards were found to render the preemption measure in *Hentrich v. France* disproportionate. The use of the power was selective, unforeseeable and punitive, no reasons were given and the applicants were not afforded an adversarial procedure in which to counter the allegations of tax evasion. In *Håkansson and Sturesson v. Sweden*, however, there was no lack of proportionality where the applicants were aware of the risk of not obtaining a permit to retain the estate bought at auction and although they had paid more, they received as compensation a sum reasonably related to the market price plus the auction costs.[11]

The manner and effects of the *de facto* expropriation were incompatible in *Papamichalopoulos*, namely, the seizure of the land, the length of deprivation and lack of any remedial action by the State subsequently.

---

[4] *Sporrong*, para. 69.

[5] *James*, para. 46; *Lithgow*, para. 122.

[6] *Hentrich*, para. 39.

[7] *Papamichalopoulos*.

[8] *Holy Monasteries*: while the Court acknowledged that there were doubts as to the reasons where the property was not given to needy farmers but to agricultural co-operatives and public bodies, this nonetheless did not deprive the measure of its overall objectives as being in the public interest.

[9] *Hakansson and Sturesson; Hentrich;* also *U.K.*, 12736/87, (Dec.) May 5, 1988, 56 D.R. 254 (compulsory purchase for motorway construction), *U.K.*, 13135/87, (Dec.) July 4, 1988, 56 D.R. 268 (compulsory purchase to enforce habitable standards of housing).

[10] *e.g.* 12736/87, see n.9, (where compulsory purchase by a local authority of leased premises below habitable standards was proportionate since warnings given, the applicant was given extra time for implementation of repairs and the property was in substantial state of disrepair) and 13135/87, see n.9 (expropriation of parts of Highland estate for road widening was reasonably proportionate, having regard to the compensation fixed by a Land tribunal after a hearing with representation for the applicants).

[11] In *Hentrich*, however, the risk of pre-emption was also known and the applicants received the purchase price plus 10 per cent and costs. The Court found that this was not sufficient to compensate for the loss of a property acquired without fraudulent intent. The arbitrary, punitive nature of the measure seems to be the main distinguishing feature.

The length of the proceedings concerning the expropriation measures may disclose a violation under Article 6, paragraph 1, where there is an unreasonable delay. It may also form a decisive or significant part in the finding of violation under Article 1 of Protocol No. 1. Thus in *Erkner and Hofauer v. Austria*, where land consolidation proceedings took more than 16 years, the Court held that the complaints of the unreasonableness of length of proceedings under Article 6 could be distinguished from the question as to whether the disputed transfer was compatible with right of property, in which context length is one element. On the latter, the Court found a violation referring to the disproportionate burden imposed on the applicants resulting from the uncertainty and also the lack of flexibility of the system (*e.g.* no compensation for loss on the forced exchange where worse land was allotted and there were no means of altering the position of owners during that time).[12] In other cases, where the essence of the complaint has been the delay in proceedings, with no separate effect on property rights, the Court has found it unnecessary to decide whether the delay in the proceedings also disclosed a violation of Article 1 of Protocol No. 1. Any effect on value of property or pecuniary damage is in that context to be taken into account in assessing just satisfaction for the breach of Article 6.[13]

The right to compensation is not express. The reference to deprivation being subject to the conditions provided by principles of international law was found to be relevant only to the position regarding non-nationals and it does not therefore incorporate international law principles for nationals as regards compensation.[14] However, the existence and extent of compensation is a material factor in the balance of the general interest and private rights, otherwise the protection of Article 1 of Protocol No. 1 against confiscations would be illusory and ineffective.[15]

On the issue of the standard of compensation, deprivation without compensation in an amount reasonably related to the value of the property would normally be disproportionate, exceptional circumstances being required to justify a lack of compensation.[16] However, full compensation is not necessarily required since measures of economic or social reform may call for less than full market value.[17] In *Lithgow and others v. United Kingdom*, concerning nationalisation, to which other considerations might apply than to ordinary expropriation, the Court stated that it would respect the legislature's judgment unless manifestly without reasonable foundation, the test generally applied since.

Lack of any compensation is therefore a significant feature. In *Erkner and Hofauer v. Austria*, the lack of compensation for forced transfer of good land for worse, combined with delay and the inflexibility of the procedure, rendered the measures in violation of Article 1 of Protocol No. 1. In the Holy Monasteries, where there was no compensation for the transfer of ownership of large areas of monastery land, the Court found a violation, rejecting the Government's arguments as to the exceptional circumstances in which the property was acquired and used.[18]

Methods of calculation have been unsuccessfully attacked and indeed, having regard to the standard of "manifestly without reasonable foundation" an assessment procedure

---

[12] Also *Matos e Silva*, where there was a violation of Art. 6 for 13 year expropriation proceedings and a violation of Art. 1 of Protocol No. 1 since the long period of uncertainty as to what would become of their property and as to compensation aggravated the detrimental effects of the measures.

[13] See *e.g. Brigandi v. Italy*, February 19, 1991, Series A, No. 194–B.

[14] *Lithgow*, paras 111–119.

[15] *e.g.* 7987/77 *Austria*, (Dec.) December 13, 1979, 18 D.R. 31 (expropriation of property for road construction: complaint about level of compensation): the Commission took the view that there was no right to any particular amount of compensation but there would be a problem if there was a substantial reduction of compensation such as to be regarded as affecting the very substance of the right to compensation.

[16] *e.g. Holy Monasteries*, para. 71.

[17] *Lithgow*, para. 121.

[18] The Commission, finding no violation, had found exceptional circumstances arising from the historical background of the monasteries which had acquired their property at a time when they served important educational and social functions, which the State had now assumed.

would have to be grossly unfair or arbitrary to offend. In *Lithgow and others v. United Kingdom*, where the applicant companies made numerous criticisms of the unfairness of the calculation process, the Court, *inter alia*, found the fact that there was an international practice in some areas did not indicate that this was the only way, referring to the thorough Parliamentary process during which valuation issues had been thrashed out.

In other cases, failure to make payments inflation proof or to discount certain heads of damage has not been enough to render the compensation unreasonable.[19] An assessment method therefore that is geared at least ostensibly to compensating for the property will pass muster even if the method used or figure reached differs greatly from that preferred by the aggrieved owner. The approach that the valuation is "reasonably related" to the property in question is sometimes used.[20]

Delay by the State in paying compensation due on expropriation, which due to 70 per cent inflation, caused the applicant substantial loss, was however found by the Court to render the compensation inadequate.[21] An inflexible presumption that adjoining owners of expropriated land used for roads benefitted from the development and could not claim compensation for damage was "manifestly without reasonable foundation", leaving the applicants to bear an individual and excessive burden.[22]

3. Forfeiture and confiscation measures

Draconian powers for the seizure of goods in the customs or criminal context which pursue lawful and legitimate purposes have proved acceptable, subject to minimum requirements of procedural safeguards.[23]

The approach of the Court has been to regard confiscation as a control of use of property rather than deprivation. This places an emphasis on the general purpose of the measure rather than the effect on the applicant's property rights. In *Agosi v. United Kingdom*, smuggled kruggerrands obtained from the applicants by fraud had been seized by Customs which refused to exercise its discretion to return them to the applicant. The Court considered that, while in one sense the seizure disclosed a deprivation, it formed a constituent part of the procedure for the control of use of gold in the United Kingdom. Similarly, in *Air Canada v. United Kingdom*, where an airliner was seized on discovery of a large cannabis resin shipment on board but released on payment of £50,000, the Court did not accept, as argued by the applicant, that they had been deprived of both airplane and money but held that the measures were part of the system for the control of use of an aircraft used to carry drugs.

It is accepted that smuggled goods will generally be the object of confiscation, a practice existing in many Contracting States. While the Commission in *Agosi v. United Kingdom* considered that there had to be a link between the behaviour of the owner of smuggled goods and the breach of the law, such that the innocent owner should be entitled to

---

[19] *e.g.* 13135/87, see n.9, where the Land Tribunal granted about a sixth of the claimed loss of amenity and future costs of upkeep of fencing etc. in relation to land expropriated for road widening, the Commission found the method of assessment reasonable and that the lack of inflation proofing did not bring it outside margin of appreciation. Also 7987/77 *Austria*, (Dec.) December 13, 1979, 18 D.R. 31 where assessment of agricultural value without account being given to future mineral potential was not unreasonable; *U.K.* 14265/88, (Dec.) January 19, 1989, 59 D.R. 281, where the applicant who had never lived in the inherited property only received site value on expropriation, though he would have got more if it had been occupied.

[20] *e.g. Håkansson and Sturesson*, para. 54.

[21] *Akkuş*.

[22] *Katikaridis*, paras 49–50, where the applicants had strong arguments that the flyover constructed deprived their remaining land of value.

[23] See, *e.g. Handyside v. U.K.*, December 7, 1976, Series A, No. 24, para. 62, where there was seizure and destruction of copies of "The Little Red Schoolbook", the Court commented that the second paragraph on control of use set up the State as sole judges of the necessity of an interference. Later cases mitigated this extreme approach.

recovery, the Court observed that this was not a common practice in Member States, where the fault of owner might be only one element in the balancing exercise.

The Court did hold in *Agosi v. United Kingdom* however that there were procedural requirements implicit in the protection of property rights, namely that there should be procedures which enabled reasonable account to be taken of the link between the conduct of owner and breach of law and allow the owner to put his case to the responsible authorities. In both *Agosi* and *Air Canada*, the possibility of judicial review of the Customs Commissioners' decisions were found to furnish sufficient procedural protection, although the decisions were essentially unreasoned limiting the ability to challenge them.[24]

---

[24] In *Agosi*, the Commission had found a violation in that the domestic courts could not give the necessary weight to the owner's innocence and judicial review was not realistically available in the absence of reasons to challenge. In *Air Canada*, although no reasons were given at the time of confiscation beyond the presence of drugs, the Court considered that against the history of previous warnings of security laxness by Customs, the company could not realistically claim to be unaware of the reasons. Taken with the important aim of combatting drug trafficking the measures of seizure and return of the aircraft on payment of money were not disproportionate.

Extradition

Relevant provisions:

Article 3 (prohibition on torture, inhuman and degrading treatment), Article 13 (right to effective remedy).

Key case law:

Soering v. U.K., July 7, 1989, Series A, No. 161; 11 E.H.R.R. 439; *Chahal v. U.K.*, November 15, 1996, R.J.D., 1996–II, No. 22.

1. General considerations

Extradition is accepted by the Convention organs as a legitimate and desirable means of enforcing criminal justice between States.[1] There is no right not to be extradited.[2] Principally issues arise under the Convention regarding allegations of breaches of human rights which will occur in the receiving State if the extradition is carried out.

2. Risk of violations in receiving country

(a) *Ill-treatment*

Where on proposed extradition an applicant faces a real risk of treatment contrary to Article 3 in the receiving State, the responsibility of the expelling State is engaged and a violation arises. This principle was established in *Soering v. United Kingdom*, where conditions on death-row in Virginia were found such as to expose the applicant facing two charges of capital murder to the real risk of inhuman and degrading treatment.

The risk alleged must relate to a treatment which attains a certain minimum level of severity, taking into account all the circumstances, including the physical and mental effects, and where relevant the age, sex and health of the victim.[3] The way in which an extradition is enforced, even if involving the use of force or tranquillizers, has not yet been found by the Commission to go beyond the inevitable trauma involved in the legitimate enforcement of an extradition decision.[4]

The Court has emphasised that the prohibition contained in Article 3 is absolute.[5] Therefore, if there is a real risk of Article 3 treatment in the receiving State, no principle of international enforcement of justice would appear to justify implementing the extradition.

The risk of the ill-treatment alleged must be real and account will be taken of the assurances given by the authorities of the State requesting extradition to those of the State

---

[1] *Soering*, paras. 86 and 89, noting the legitimate interests of the international community in facilitating the bringing to justice of offenders who move easily about the globe and the dangers facing States which were obliged to become safe havens for alleged criminals.

[2] *Soering*, para. 85.

[3] In *Soering*, the death row disclosed inhuman treatment having regard to average length of detention waiting execution (6-8 years) with the ever present and mounting anguish of awaiting a execution, the stringency of the custodial regime in the Mecklenburg correctional centre compounded by the length of time involved, the applicant's personal circumstances, in particular his youth, and some indications that he was suffering from an abnormality of mind which had substantially impaired his mental responsibility for his acts. In *Kirkwood v. U.K., 10479/83, (Dec.) U.K.,* March 12, 1984, 37 D.R. 158 the Commission had not found the death row would involve Art. 3 treatment having regard to the fact that the element of delay derived from procedural safeguards used by prisoners.

[4] 25342/94, (Dec.) September 4, 1995, 82–A D.R. 134, where applicant had to be given sedatives in view of her resistance at the departure and was extradited in circumstances where she had attempted to commit suicide due to the strain of the imminent extradition.

[5] *Chahal*, paras. 80–81.

requested. The fact that the requesting State has ratified the Convention may also be relevant. Where IRA prisoners were to be extradited from the Netherlands to the United Kingdom and were alleging that they would be ill-treated in the Maze prison, the Commission, in dismissing the complaints as manifestly ill-founded, had regard to assurances given to the Dutch authorities by the Deputy Director of the Maze prison and the fact that the United Kingdom had recognised the right of individual petition.[6] Where an applicant faced extradition to face murder charges in Texas, the Commission found that the undertaking given by the prosecution authorities to the State Department that the death penalty would not be applied was sufficient. While the applicant argued that such undertaking was not binding on the executive and judicial authorities, the Commission considered that it was the attitude of the prosecution authorities which was decisive in that case.[7]

(b) *Death penalty*

Extradition to face the death penalty, if imposed judicially after a fair trial, would not appear to infringe the requirements of Article 3. In *Soering*, the Court rejected the argument of Amnesty International that while Article 2 allowed judicial execution it was nonetheless contrary to Article 3 to impose it. The two provisions had to be read in harmony with each other and Article 3 could not have been intended to include a general prohibition of the death penalty. The Court did not exclude however that in certain circumstances an issue might arise under Article 3 concerning, for example, the disproportionality of the sentence to the crime committed and personal circumstances of the accused, as well as the conditions of detention awaiting executions such as the death row phenomenon.

Where a country has ratified Protocol No. 6 which in Article 1 abolishes the death penalty, it would however appear to be in potential violation of this provision and Article 3 of the Convention to extradite or expel someone to face a real risk of the death penalty being imposed.[8] Where the applicant faced extradition from Macao to China for repeated vehicle thefts in respect of which the death penalty was an option, the Commission applied Rule 36[9] to Portugal. The case was struck off when following the Constitutional Court's decision the Macao High Court revoked an order that extradition should proceed.

(c) *Other violations in receiving State*

There is no general principle that a State cannot surrender an individual unless satisfied that the conditions awaiting him in the receiving country are in full accord with each of the safeguards of the Convention.[10] Where the applicant in *Soering* invoked Article 6, claiming that if he was extradited he would face a breach of Article 6, paragraph 3(c) because of lack of legal aid for certain appeal applications, the Court did not exclude that an issue might be raised under Article 6 where the fugitive to be extradited had suffered or

---

[6] 12543/86, *Netherlands*, (Dec.) December 2, 1986, 51 D.R. 272 See Part IIB: Immigration and Expulsion, on theCommission's increasing readiness to find problems within Contracting States which are not cured by their acceptance of the right of individual petition.

[7] 22742/93 *France*, (Dec.) January 20, 1994, 76–A D.R. 164. However in *Soering* the undertaking to inform the trial court of the wish of the United Kingdom that the death penalty should not be applied was not enough to diminish the risk in view of the prosecution's intention to seek the death penalty as merited.

[8] 22742/93 *France*.

[9] Commission's Rules of Procedure — by which the Commission requested a suspension of the extradition as an interim measure. Matter was considered resolved under Art. 30, para. 1(b) although the applicant did not agree to withdraw: 25862/94 *Portugal*, (Dec.) November 27, 1995, 83–A D.R. 88.

[10] *Soering*, para. 112.

risked suffering a "flagrant denial" of a fair trial in a requesting country.[11] That was however not the case in *Soering* where flattering remarks were made as to the democratic character of the legal system which respected the rule of law and afforded not inconsiderable procedural safeguards.

The meaning in practice of a "flagrant denial" of a fair trial has not been explored. Where an applicant complained of extradition to Hong Kong, the Commission did not find his allegations that at his trial he would face contested evidence taken in his absence in Malaysia or that a co-accused might be offered immunity to testify against him disclosed such a risk.[12] Nor was the trial facing a Russian facing extradition from Finland to Russia found to disclose the exceptional circumstances adverted to by the Court.[13]

3. Extradition proceedings: fairness

Extradition proceedings in the sending State do not themselves fall within the scope of Article 6, paragraph 1 since they do not involve the determination of the criminal charge. Even where a limited examination of the merits is undertaken in committal proceedings by the magistrates this cannot be considered part of the determination of the charges on which the extradition is sought.[14]

4. Remedies

Where it is alleged there is a risk of Article 3 treatment on return, the Court held in *Soering*, disagreeing with the Commission, that judicial review furnished an effective remedy against extradition. The Court found that the approach of the courts, giving the "most anxious scrutiny" to claims of risk of ill-treatment was sufficient, notwithstanding the formally limited scope of the examination in judicial review. While the Court in *Chahal v. United Kingdom*, concerning expulsion, found judicial review inadequate, this was due at least in part to the inability of the courts to undertake any independent scrutiny of the national security considerations which were at the basis of the decision to expel. Although there is reference to the inability of the courts to decide the question solely with the question of risk without reference to security considerations, the Court did not appear to overrule its previous case law and it remains to be seen whether it would maintain its general view of the effectiveness of judicial review in an extradition case, where risk was not the sole question but other elements irrelevant to Article 3 played a decisive role in the decision to uphold the extradition.

---

[11] Also *Germany*, 10383/83, (Dec.) May 3, 1983, 36 D.R. 209 where the Commission stated that, where there was a real risk that a person extradited for common law offences would be tried for political offences, a violation could not be ruled out if the prosecution for political reasons could lead to an unjustified or disproportionate sentence being passed.

[12] 15933/89 *Osman v. U.K.*, (Dec.) October 14, 1991 unpublished. In an earlier application, predating *Soering*, the applicant's complaint under Article 7 that he would face retrospective penalties when the Chinese took over Hong Kong was dismissed on the basis that the United Kingdom could not be held directly responsible for any measures which might be imposed (14037/89, *U.K.*, (Dec.) March 13, 1989). A third application (19319/91, *Osman v. U.K.*, (Dec.) September 2, 1992) claiming that although Hong Kong has given assurances that it would respect the speciality rule (prohibition of prosecuting offences other than those in respect of which the return was ordered etc.) that this would not protect him when China took over, was rejected on the basis that the complaints were largely hypothetical and the lack of responsibility of the United Kingdom for the future acts of China.

[13] 16832/90, (Dec.) May 28, 1991, 69 D.R. 321 where the applicant alleged that KGB cases were decided by the Supreme Court as the first and only instance, with less publicity than usual proceedings; 22742/93, see n.7: risk to fairness of trial from alleged media publicity too hypothetical.

[14] *Kirkwood*, see n.3; more recently 24501/94 *Luxembourg*, (Dec.) May 20, 1994, 77–A D.R. 144.

Cross-reference

Freedom of assembly

Key provision:

Article 11 (freedom of peaceful assembly).

Key case law:

Plattform "Ärzte für das leben" v. Austria, June 21, 1988, Series A, No. 139; 13 E.H.R.R. 204; *Ezelin v. France*, April 26, 1991, Series A, No. 202; 14 E.H.R.R. 362.

1. General considerations

Exercise of this freedom is often closely connected with freedom of expression (Article 10) and thought, conscience and religion (Article 9). Article 11 is the *lex specialis* where an assembly is concerned but the other two rights may be taken into account in examining the effect and proportionality of the interference.[1] As with freedom of expression, freedom of peaceful assembly is one of the foundations of a democratic society.[2] It covers not only public meetings but private meetings,[3] and static gatherings as well as public processions. It is capable of being exercised by not only individuals but by those organising the assembly, such as associations.

The right does not extend to demonstrations where organisers and participants have violent intentions which result in public disorder.[4] Where a Government argued that an assembly was unlikely to be peaceful due to reactions of other groups, the Commission considered that it was the intention to hold a peaceful assembly which was significant and the possibility of violent counter-demonstrations could not as such remove the right from the scope of first paragraph.

Article 11 is not to be interpreted restrictively. The fact that an assembly is illegal will not necessarily remove it from the scope of the right, at least where it is peaceful in nature. Thus where an applicant was convicted for participation in an organised sit-in in a road, the Commission found that although it was illegal it was not actively violent and that the interference required to be justified in terms of the second paragraph.[5]

2. Regulation of assemblies

The requirement to obtain authorisation for an assembly does not as such constitute an interference.[6]

Whether a ban on processions is justified will depend generally on whether there is an identifiable public order basis and whether the duration and extent of the ban are proportionate to that aim. In *"Christians Against Fascism v. United Kingdom"*, where there was a one month ban on processions in London imposed by the police, the Commission considered that a general ban could only be justified if there was a real danger of disorder which could not be avoided by less stringent measures. On the facts of the case, the Commission accepted the ban since there was a tense atmosphere; the police presence at other processions had not stopped damage to persons and property and 2,400 officers had been necessary to police a National Front march. It also noted as regarded proportionality that the meetings could still be held in London, as well as processions outside London.

---

[1] *Milan Rai v. U.K.*, 25522/94, April 6, 1995, 81–A D.R. 146; see also *Ezelin* para. 35.
[2] *e.g. Switzerland* 8191/78, (Dec.) October 10, 1979, 17 D.R. 93.
[3] 8191/78 case *ibid.*
[4] *U.K.*, 8440/78, July 16, 1980, 21 D.R. 138.
[5] *G. v. FRG*, 13079/87, (Dec.) March 6, 1989, 60 D.R. 256.
[6] 8191/78, see n.2.

Once there is some connection with public order, the Commission tends to afford a broad margin of appreciation as to authorities' measures.[7] Where a ban on a public rally in Trafalgar Square was applied to "Peace Now", a non-partisan group advocating negotiations in Northern Ireland, the Commission accepted the necessity to prohibit the meeting even though there was no real expectation of violence. The policy, based on politically sensitive considerations, to ban all rallies relating to Northern Ireland in that central location, was perceived as following the aim of prevention of disorder in a general sense. Nor was it disproportionate since it appeared that in the past where consent had been given to a meeting for a Ulster group it had turned into a political rally and it was reasonable for the authorities to seek to avoid a recurrence. It again was noted that it was open to hold the rally in other locations.[8]

3. Penalties for participation in public demonstrations

Minor criminal sanctions following protests which breach public order or obstruct the highway have been not found disproportionate.[9]

Where a penalty is imposed on a person for participation in a lawful assembly where there is no indication that they behaved in an unlawful or unruly manner, issues of proportionality are likely to arise. In *Ezelin v. France*, the applicant lawyer participated in a demonstration, during which some participants shouted insults and painted graffitti. Disciplinary proceedings were brought against him and he received a reprimand for breach of professional discretion. The argument that the applicant had been free to participate but sanctioned only afterwards was not successful. There was an interference resulting from the sanction imposed on him for failing to disassociate himself from the demonstrators' insulting acts by leaving the procession. While the Court accepted that it pursued the prevention of disorder and that the penalty was light, the importance of the right was such that no sanction was compatible with Article 11 where a participant was not guilty of any reprehensible act in taking part in a demonstration that had been lawful and not prohibited.

4. Protection of "peaceful assemblies"

Freedom of peaceful assembly, if it is to be effective, cannot be limited merely to an obligation on the State not to interfere. The Court has found that positive measures may be required to regulate conduct between individuals. Participants must be able to hold a demonstration without fear of physical violence from those who oppose their ideas otherwise they will be deterred from openly expressing their opinions. In a democracy the right to counter demonstrate cannot extend to inhibiting the exercise of the right to demonstrate.[10]

Positive measures appear to impose a duty to take reasonable and appropriate measures to enable lawful demonstrations to proceed peacefully. It does not involve an absolute guarantee and there is a wide discretion accorded to the authorities as to the means to be used. No violation was found in *Platform Arzte v. Austria*, where counter-demonstrators

---

[7] *e.g.* 8191/78, see n.2, where there was a ban on all political meetings following a controversy over cantonal reorganisation and local feeling ran high; 9905/82, (Dec.) March 15, 1984, 36 D.R. 187, where there was a ban on a meeting of a pro-German unification group in Austria, justified by Austria's constitutional and international obligations to safeguard Austrian statehood.

[8] *Milan Rai*, see n.1.

[9] 9278 and 9415/81 *G and E v. Norway*, (Dec.) October 3, 1983, 35 D.R. 30, where Lapps arrested for participation in public protest outside Parliament after staying for 4 days in a tent in area open to public traffic; *G v. FRG*, see n.5: conviction for sit-in in road which was a non-violent obstruction of traffic.

[10] *Plattform "ärzte"*, para. 32.

disrupted the applicant association's open air service, interrupting with loudspeakers and throwing eggs. Although the applicant association claimed the authorities had failed to protect its freedom of peaceful assembly, the Commission found, and the Court agreed, that the authorities had not failed in their duty since the police had been present in large numbers and had interposed themselves between the opposing groups and no damage or serious clash had occurred.

Cross-reference

Part IIB: Freedom of association
Part IIB: Freedom of expression
Part IIB: Religion, thought and conscience

Freedom of association

Key provision:

Article 11 (freedom of association).

Key case law:

National Union of Belgian Police v. Belgium, October 27, 1975, Series A, No. 19; 1 E.H.R.R. 518; *Swedish Engine Drivers' Union v. Sweden,* February 6, 1976, Series A, No. 20; 1 E.H.R.R. 617; *Schmidt and Dahlstrom v. Sweden,* February 6, 1976, Series A, No. 21; 1 E.H.R.R. 632; *Le Compte, Van Leuven and De Meyere v. Belgium,* June 23, 1981, Series A, No. 43; 4 E.H.R.R. 1; *Young, James and Webster v. U.K.,* June 26, 1981, Series A, No. 44; 4 E.H.R.R. 38; *Sibson v. U.K.,* April 20, 1993, Series A, No. 258–A; 17 E.H.R.R. 193; *Sigurjónsson v. Iceland,* June 30, 1993, Series A, No. 264; 16 E.H.R.R. 462; *Gustafsson v. Sweden,* April 25, 1996, R.J.D., 1996–II, No. 9; *United Communist Party and others v. Turkey,* January 30, 1998 to be published in R.J.D., 1998.

1. General considerations

The freedom of association is a general capacity for all persons to join with others without interference by the State to attain a particular end.[1] It does not imply a right to attain the end sought.[2] It implies a negative right, not to be compelled to join an association, an aspect which has relevance in the area of trade unions, which has furnished much of the case law. Freedom of assembly is an associated right which is dealt with separately.

2. Formation and dissolution of associations

The Commission has expressed doubt as to whether the refusal to give legal status to an association constituted an interference within the scope of Article 11, pargraph 1, where it considered that registration could not be considered an obstacle to the association pursuing its objectives.[3] However, in more recent decisions, the refusal to register has been found to be an interference without discussion.[4]

Where decisions by the authorities relating to the formation and dissolution of associations are found to interfere with the rights under Article 11, assuming such measures are prescribed by law, a considerable margin of appreciation is left to the authorities as to the necessity of the regulation. In a French case, concerning refusal of registration of the applicant's association promoting surrogate motherhood as contrary to the criminal code (incitement of child abandonment), the Commission found the interference was justified having regard in particular to the margin of appreciation applying to the controversial subject of surrogacy and considering that that the applicant could still carry out activities. Similar leeway was given where a Portuguese association supporting the old royal house of Braganza was dissolved, the Commission finding that such a decision could be considered as necessary to promote public order.[5]

---

[1] It does not guarantee a general social ability to mix with others, *e.g.* a prisoner cannot derive a right to associate with other prisoners — where applicants were in isolation punishment the Commission took view that the complaints were incompatible *ratione materiae* as Art. 11 concerned freedom to form or be affiliated to groups or organisations pursuing particular aims. Despite the Government's argument in *United Communist Party v. Turkey,* it applies to political parties.

[2] 6094/73 *Association X v. Sweden,* (Dec.) July 6, 1977, 9 D.R. 5.

[3] *FRG* 14223/88 (Dec.), June 5, 1991, 70 D.R. 218.

[4] *Sidiropulos and others v. Greece,* 26695/95, (Rep.) April 11, 1997, pending before the Court.

[5] *Portugal,* 23892/94, (Dec.) October 16, 1995, 83–A D.R. 57 though the activities of the association hardly seemed a real threat to undermine the State; *Austria,* 8652/79, (Dec.) October 15, 1981, 26 D.R. 89: banning of Moon sect associations; *Italy,* 6741/74, (Dec.) May 21, 1976, 5 D.R. 83: ban on fascist party.

Nonetheless in recent cases involving measures against associations alleged to pursue objectives contrary to the State, the Commission and Court have emphasised that democratic societies have to tolerate the discussion of a wide range of opinions, including those opposed to officially-sanctioned positions and that interferences have to be convincingly justified. The refusal of Greek authorities to register a Macedonian cultural association was an undisputed interference with its members' freedom of association which was not justified by relevant and sufficient reasons or proportionate. It found that it was not established that the association harboured separatist intentions or violent intention, and the fact that it promoted the idea of a "Macedonian" minority did not justify the measure.[6]

3. Public law institutions

Article 11 does not cover public law institutions. An obligation on a person to join a professional or occupational institution which is of a public law nature, pursuing aims of public regulation of the profession, will not offend, although it is relevant whether the applicant is able to join other professional associations to protect his interests.[7]

The fact that an association fulfills some statutory functions will not be decisive where the principal object is to protect the professional interests of its members. In *Sigurjonsson v. Iceland*, the Government argued that FRAMI (taxi association) was a professional organisation of public law character, carrying out a role in price-fixing of services under approval of the administration. The Court found notwithstanding these aspects it was primarily a private law association which protected the professional interests of its members and promoted solidarity, for example, by negotiation and presenting demands relating to working hours.

4. Trade union aspects

Trade union freedom is a special aspect of the freedom of association. But it does not guarantee any particular treatment of trade unions or their members by the State. The phrase "for the protection of his interests" indicates that the provision is intended to cover the protection of the occupational interests of members by trade union action. This will include the right for the trade union to be heard although the State is left with a free choice in the means to be used towards this end. Under national law, trade unions should be enabled in conditions not at variance with Article 11 to strive for the protection of their members' interests.[8]

(a) *State responsibility*

Even if a Government is not directly responsible for the actions of or agreements reached by unions and employers, where the domestic law in force renders lawful such measures, State responsibility under Article 1 is engaged. Contracting States must therefore maintain supervisory control over trade unions and the way they wield their powers.[9]

---

[6] *Sidiropulos,* see n.4; see also *United Communist Party v. Turkey,* where the Court found that references in the Communist Party's constitution to the Kurdish problem, perceived by the Turkish Government as posing a threat to the State's territorial integrity, did not justify the dissolution of the party. Its constitution was geared to the democratic process and it had not engaged in activities at a variance with its Constitution (it had in fact been dissolved immediately after its formation).

[7] *Le Compte;* 14331–2/88, (Dec.) September 8, 1989, 62 D.R. 309 (obligation to join the *ordre des architectes;* 13570/88, (Dec.) July 2, 1990, 66 D.R. 188 (bar associations in Spain); 14596/89, (Dec.) July 10, 1991, 71 D.R. 58 (Austrian chambers of trade).

[8] *National Union of Belgian Police,* p. 18, para. 39.

[9] *Young, James and Webster.*

(b) *Right of consultation*

The right to be consulted by the executive before measures are adopted is not implied. In *National Union of Belgian Police v. Belgium*, where only a restricted number of trade unions were officially consulted, the National Union was able to present claims and make representations nonetheless, and while its lack of formal consultative status may have made it less attractive to prospective members, this did not disclose an interference under Article 11.

(c) *Collective bargaining*

Article 11 does not secure any particular treatment of unions or their members by the State such as the right that the State enter into any collective agreement with them. It has been found that this is not indispensable for the effective enjoyment of trade union freedom and in no way constitutes an element necessarily inherent in the right, even where this may damage the union through reducing its membership.[10]

(d) *Preferential treatment/discrimination*

As implied above, the practice by State authorities in conferring special recognition on particular unions has been found to be compatible with the Convention. The Belgian system of conferring consultation status on three unions of state officials and not on the applicant police union, was found to pursue a legitimate aim of ensuring a coherent and balanced staff policy, avoiding "trade union anarchy". Nor were the means used disproportionate as the disadvantage to the applicant was not deemed to be excessive.[11] A similar policy in Sweden did not offend proportionality, where the State preferred to sign collective agreements only with widely represente unions, to avoid excessive numbers of negotiating parties. The Court found no ill-intentioned designs in that policy.[12]

(e) *Right NOT to join a trade union*

In the leading case of *Young, James and Webster v. United Kingdom*, the Court found that a notion of a "freedom" implied some choice in its exercise. Thus a negative right could not be excluded from the ambit of Article 11.[13] The test it applied was to examine whether in the particular case before it the form of compulsion struck at the very substance of the right guaranteed. Since the three applicants has received notices terminating their employment for failure to join a union, this was found to be the case. The Court noted that even had the applicants joined another union, they would still have been dismissed and it considered that their freedom of action had been rendered non-existent or of no

---

[10] *Schmidt and Dahlstrom*, para. 34: *Swedish engine drivers union* case where the State had entered into a collective agreement with three large federations but refused to do so with the smaller union, the Court noted that it was not mentioned specifically as a right, nor accepted in all Contracting States. Since individuals were free to join any trade union and the applicant union was able to engage in various kinds of activity, the fact that the executive had refused to enter into a collective agreement did not disclose a breach even if the union membership was suffering as a result; 18881/91 *Denmark*, (Dec.) January 13, 1992, 72 D.R. 278.

[11] *National Union of Belgian Police*.

[12] Also *Association X*, see n.2, where one student association was chosen as the official body with compulsory membership and the applicant association complained of discrimination, the Commission found nothing unreasonable in the authorities choosing one union in order to concentrate students together to facilitate the proper administration of the university.

[13] See also *Sigurjonsson*, where the Court's views on the negative right were stronger, noting that few Contracting States imposed such compulsory membership, that most contained protections in domestic law; and referring to the growing recognition on international level, *i.e.* ILO, EU, Council of Europe.

practical value. This individual right outweighed the alleged general desirability of closed shops in the public interest. The Court was not persuaded that unions could not pursue their interests without compulsory memberships.[14]

While in *Young, James and Webster*, the Court emphasised the element of exertion of pressure to compel someone to join an association contrary to his conviction, referring to Articles 9 and 10, it is not necessary for an applicant to object to trade union membership on any particular point of principle.[15] In *Sigurjonsson v. Iceland*, the Government argued that the taxi association was non-political and that membership was not a question of the applicant's beliefs since he had previously joined the association. The Court considered that Articles 9 and 10 could still be affected since the applicant held a belief in freedom of occupation. Since he now wished to leave and was subject to compulsion striking at the heart of the right, there was a violation. The nature and strength of the objection may however be of relevance in the balancing exercise in assessing the proportionality of any interference.[16]

The Court's approach is to consider whether a proper balance is struck between the interests of the individual and any general interest in maintaining the compulsory membership, but has stated its objections to what may be construed as abuse of a dominent position.[17]

Compulsion which falls short of dismissal or removal of livelihood[18] may not strike at the heart of the right. In *Sibson v. United Kingdom* (a closed shop case), where an employee was faced with being sacked or moved to another depot, on roughly equivalent terms and pursuant to the terms of his contract, there was no violation.

(f) *Trade union relationships with members*

The right to join a trade union does not include the right to join a union of one's choice regardless of the rules. Trade unions must remain free to decide in accordance with union rules questions relating to admission to and expulsion from the union. Protection is primarily against interference by the State, although the State has to protect the individual against abuse of a dominant position. Expulsion from a union which was in breach of union rules, pursuant to arbitrary rules or entailing exceptional hardship, could constitute such abuse.[19]

Other objections of members to internal union rules have not disclosed abuse, *e.g.* where a union subscribed to compulsory collective home insurance on behalf of members.[20]

(g) *Trade union pressure on employers*

The position of the employer who may be the subject of intense union pressure is perhaps less protected by the Convention. While Article 11 applies to an employer forced to sign a collective agreement by a trade union, it does not extend to granting a right not to join a collective agreement.[21] The Court has referred to a wide margin of appreciation noting the sensitive character of the social and political issues involved and the wide divergence of practice in Member States. It also gives weight to the interests of trade unions in

---

[14] Also *Sigurjonsson*, para. 41.
[15] Two applicants had objected to trade union policies and one to its political affiliations.
[16] *e.g. Sibson*, para. 29.
[17] *Young, James and Webster*, para. 63.
[18] *Sigurjonsson*: removal of taxi licence.
[19] *U.K.*, (Dec.) May 13, 1985, 10550/83, 42 D.R. 178: where the applicant was expelled from APEX due to TUC pressure. The Commission found that the expulsion was the act of a private body not engaging State responsibility since the applicant did not lose job and the measure was not in breach of union rules.
[20] *Sweden* 13537/88, (Dec.) May 7, 1990, 65 D.R. 202.
[21] para. 52.

undertaking industrial action, noting that the individual right to join trade unions for the "protection of his interests" implies action can be taken to protect occupational interests of trade unions.[22]

Thus, in *Gustafsson v. Sweden*, where a restaurant owner was placed under considerable pressure by lawful industrial action aimed at securing his participation in a collective bargaining agreement, the Court found no violation having regard in particular to the margin of appreciation, the special character of collective bargaining in Sweden[23] and the consideration that the applicant could have avoided membership of an employer's association by an alternative, substitute agreement.[24] The view of the Court majority seemed to discount the relevance of the applicant's political objection to joining a collective agreement and imply that the infliction of economic damage is not enough to strike at the heart of the right where an employer is concerned.

(h) *Prohibition on trade union membership*

A special exception is contained in the second paragraph of Article 11, namely, the lawful imposition of restrictions on the exercise of rights by police, armed forces and administration of the State, which is not qualified by reference to the necessity of the measures. When GCHQ staff were not permitted to be members of any existing trade union, the Commission found that their functions were similar to that of police and vital to national security and therefore could be considered as part of the administration of the State. While the applicants argued that "restrictions" could not mean extinction of the right, the Commission found that, having regard to the wide margin of appreciation accorded to States in the protection of national security and the background of previous disruption by industrial action, the measure was not arbitrary and thus disclosed no violation.[25]

(i) *Right to strike*

The right to strike is not expressly guaranteed and it has not been regarded as indispensable to the exercise of Article 11 rights.[26] Where a German teacher, a civil servant, was fined for voting to go on strike, the Commission noted that Germany generally accepted the right to strike but that due to the special character of civil servants, the right was not given to them. Since there were no other elements restricting rights under Article 11, paragraph 1, the Commission considered the ban acceptable.[27]

---

[22] *Gustafsson*, para. 45.
[23] The Government emphasised that the applicant was challenging an important element in the "Swedish model" of industrial relations which was important to the Swedish welfare state, *i.e.* control by collective agreements rather than legislation.
[24] See also the Commission's opinion that the harsh measures (which led the applicant to sell his restaurant) were not counterbalanced by strong legitimate interests in forcing the applicant to sign a collective agreement; and two dissenting judges who considered that compulsion to enter a collective bargaining system was equally an infringement on negative freedom of association since it was incompatible with an element inherent in that freedom, *i.e.* freedom for the the applicant to neotiate his own labour agreements.
[25] *U.K.*, 11603/85, (Dec.) January 20, 1987, 50 D.R. 228.
[26] *Schmidt and Dahlstrom*, para. 36.
[27] *Germany*, (Dec.) 10365/83, July 5, 1984, 39 D.R. 237.

Freedom of expression

Key provision:

Article 10 (freedom of expression and to impart and receive information).

Key case law:

The Sunday Times (No. 1) v. U.K., April 26, 1979, Series A, No. 30; E.H.R.R. 245; *Barfod v. Denmark*, February 22, 1989, Series A, No. 149; 13 E.H.R.R. 493; *Oberschlick (No. 1) v. Austria*, May 23, 1991, Series A, No. 204; *The Observer and The Guardian v. U.K.*, November 26, 1991, Series A, No. 216; 14 E.H.R.R. 153; *The Sunday Times (No. 2) v. U.K.*, November 26, 1991, Series A, No. 217; 14 E.H.R.R. 229; *Thorgeirson v. Iceland*, June 25, 1992, Series A, No. 239; 14 E.H.R.R. 843; *Chorherr v. Austria*, August 25, 1993, Series A, No. 266–B; 17 E.H.R.R. 352; *Jersild v. Denmark*, September 23, 1994, Series A, No. 298; *Vereniging Weekblad "Bluf!" v. Netherlands*, February 9, 1995, Series A, No. 306–A; 20 E.H.R.R. 189; *Piermont v. France*, April 27, 1995, Series A, No. 314; *Prager and Obserschlick v. Austria*, April 26, 1996, Series A, No. 313; 21 E.H.R.R. 1; *Goodwin v. U.K.*, March 27, 1996, R.J.D., 1996–II, No. 7; *De Haes and Gijsels v. Belgium*, February 24, 1997, R.J.D., 1997–I, No. 30; *Oberschlick v. Austria (No. 2)*, July 1, 1997, R.J.D., 1997–IV, No. 42; *Worm v. Austria*, August 29, 1997, R.J.D., 1997–V, No. 45.

1. General principles

Freedom of expression has provoked some of the most concentrated and emphatic case law from the Convention organs. It involves the cleaner cases (fewer terrorists or other undesirables) and raises neat issues of principle for practitioner, politician, academic and civil right activitists alike.

Freedom of expression is, the Court has underlined, one of the key pillars on which an effectively functioning democracy rests. This fundamental importance underlies the cases. Since the media are the most public and identifiable manifestation of the passage of ideas, information and opinions and the most likely to feel the effect of any official restrictions, a large percentage of cases involve journalists. The Court has recognised the role of the media in the free flow of information and ideas in a democratic society. They are the "watchdog" of democracy and there is a very strong presumption in practice in favour of the media being able to operate unhindered.

The restrictions allowed under the second paragraph of Article 10 must be narrowly interpreted and the necessity for the restrictions convincingly established, in addition to being lawful and pursuing legitimate aims.

However, the above must be read subject to the Court's view of the role of the Convention organs. The adjective "necessary" implies a "pressing social need" in respect of interferences. Contracting States have a certain margin of appreciation in assessing whether such a need exists although this is subject to a "European supervision" of both the law and decisions applying it. This involves examining whether in light of the case of the whole the measure was proportionate to the legitimate aim pursued and whether the reasons adduced by the national authorities were relevant and sufficient.[1] Factors of significance in balancing the interest in freedom of expression against other claimed interests include the nature and severity of the restriction, its duration,[2] the public interest for and against

---

[1] *e.g. Sunday Times No. 2*, para. 47.
[2] *Sunday Times No. 1*: it was relevant that Thalidomide case had been dormant pending settlement for some years, in a "legal cocoon" from public enquiry.

exercise of the right,[3] whether the reasons for the restriction continue to be valid in light of changing circumstances and the nature of the publication/expression in issue, in particular its tone and balance, its factual accuracy and the relevance to public debate of any comment or opinion.

2. Scope of the right

The freedom covers not only information and ideas of a popular, uncontroversial nature but also those which might offend, shock or disturb. It protects the substance of the ideas and information expressed and the form in which they are conveyed.[4] It covers artistic expression and commercial speech band (see sections 6 and 7 below).

3. Who can invoke the right?

Legal persons who are editors and publishers of magazines may claim to be victims as well as individuals such as journalists.[5] Trade unions, such as the NUJ, cannot claim to be victim of restrictions affecting their members.[6] In *Purcell v. Ireland*, though the measure was aimed at the broadcasting company, the journalists and producers of programmes were also victims, since as employees they were bound to comply with the guidelines which it issued.

4. Media

The Convention organs scrutinise closely measures banning publication by the press. While they may accept that measures pursue legitimate aims, they have required convincing justification. Journalistic freedom is accepted as covering possible recourse to a degree of exaggeration, even provocation.[7] A defence of fair comment should also be available.[8]

(a) *Injunctions and preventive measures*

Where the matter to be reported is of public interest or importance, it is hard for a State to find justification for preventive injunctions in the absence of established damage to an interest of at least equal importance. Prior restraints are not inherently incompatible with Article 10 but call for careful scrutiny. The Court has noted that delay in publication in the press leads to staleness quickly depriving news of interest and value.[9]

An injunction was not found to be "necessary" in *Sunday Times (No. 1) v. United Kingdom*, where articles on the Thalidomide drug scandal raised matters of undisputed public concern and were moderate and balanced in nature. Notwithstanding the domestic courts' concern to prevent "trial by newspaper" in pending civil proceedings, the Court commented that courts could not operate in a vaccum and the media had a role in reporting matters that came before the courts, the public having a right to receive such information.

---

[3] Where measures are taken to protect public order against disturbance, as in *Chorherr* (a protester arrested at a military parade) or in *Benn and Adams v. U.K.*, 28979/95 and 30343/96, January 13, 1997, 88–A, D.R. 137 (terrorist aspect — see below) the balance is more readily found to have been respected. See, however *Piermont v. France*, where measures against a MEP were not regarded justified by public order.

[4] *e.g. Oberschlick (No. 1)*, para. 57, *Jersild*, para. 31.

[5] 9615/81, (Dec.) May 5, 1983, 32 D.R. 231.

[6] *e.g.* 11553/85 and 11658/85 *Hodgson and others v. U.K.*, (Dec.) March 9, 1987, 51 D.R. 136; *Purcell v. Ireland*, 15404/89, (Dec.) April 16, 1991, 70 D.R. 262.

[7] *e.g. Prager and Oberschlick*, para. 38, *De Haes and Gijsels*, para. 46.

[8] *e.g. Lingens; Oberschlick (No. 1)*.

[9] *Sunday Times (No. 2) v. U.K.*, para. 51.

Measures to prevent publication or distribution on the basis of the confidential nature of the subject-matter generally cease to be justifiable or proportionate once the material has been made public. Seizure of a weekly periodical publishing classified material from the Dutch security service was found to be disproportionate since 2,500 copies had already been sold at night and the continued ban no longer served any purpose, notwithstanding the Court's acknowledgment that the security services could claim a high level of protection.[10] Similarly, although initially an interlocutory injunction on the *Observer* and *Guardian* preventing publication of material from the book by an ex-MI5 official could be justified as necessary to maintain the authority of the judiciary[11] and also to protect national security, once the book was published in the United States with no ban on importation into the United Kingdom, the Court found that the interest of the plaintiff litigant in maintaining confidentiality had ceased to exist for the purposes of the Convention.[12] The interest identified at that later stage of maintaining confidence in MI5 and preventing their agents publishing in an unauthorised fashion did not justify the injunctions against the newspapers (as opposed to steps against the author himself and accounts for profits for use of confidential material).[13]

(b) *Penal sanctions for publication*

Where an article has been published and the journalist, editor or publisher is pursued by way of criminal sanction, the sanction constitutes an interference that requires convincing justification under the second paragraph. Where an article is based on fact and addresses matters of public interest, the balance is in favour of freedom of expression, notwithstanding polemical, aggressive or even provocative aspects.[14]

In this area, a certain weight is given to the need to protect judges from criticism. The "special role of the judiciary", which as the guarantor of justice must enjoy public confidence to function, successfully outweighed other considerations in *Barfod v. Denmark*, where a journalist was convicted for defamation in respect of an article criticising lay judges[15] and in *Prager and Oberschlick v. Austria*, where the applicants published a strongly-worded critique of the Vienna criminal judges, stepping over the limit of permissible exaggeration.[16] Where however in civil proceedings journalists were found to have defamed judges in *De Haes and Gijsels v. Belgium*, there was a violation despite certain provocative elements as the articles had an undisputed factual basis.[17] Where an article

---

[10] *Vereniging Weekblad "Bluf!" v. Netherlands;* also *Harman v. U.K.* case, where a solicitor, who allowed a journalist to read the documents produced by the Government and read out in open court, was found in contempt of court — 10038/82, (Dec.) May 11, 1984, 38 D.R. 53, (Rep.) May 15, 1986, 46 D.R. 57 settled after admissibility.

[11] Namely to safeguard the position of a litigant until trial of the substantive issues.

[12] The measure was initially proportionate and supported by relevant and sufficient reasons since the book was only in manuscript form at that time, it was unclear what damaging disclosures might be made and the substantive action would be prejudiced by the publication.

[13] There was a large minority in the Commission and Court, with a stricter view on the acceptability of prior restraints, finding a violation from the outset, having regard to the fact that many allegations had been aired in previous publications, that prior restraint was doomed to failure with multinational publishing and to the public interest in receiving information. Reference was also made to the strict U.S. position against prior restraints.

[14] *e.g. Oberschlick No. 2,* where the journalist in calling a politician an idiot (*trottel*) was commenting, albeitly provocatively, on the politician's statements which were themselves provocative.

[15] The journalist criticising the court's composition implied that judges voted in favour of their local government employer in Greenland in relation to a controversial tax measure.

[16] Narrow majorities: Court 5:4, Commission 15:12. The majority were influenced by serious nature of the allegations (including breach of law and professional obligations) and that the applicant journalist could not invoke good faith or compliance with professional ethics since his research did not appear adequate to substantiate such serious allegations and he had not given any judge an opportunity to comment. The minority put less weight on need to protect judges. In the Commission, the minority considered that judges had to act under public scrutiny and should tolerate even exaggerated forms of criticism if based on irrefutable fact.

[17] The articles referred to a controversial child custody case, including allegations of child abuse and criticising the decision of the court in favour of the father, making imputations of cowardice and bias. See also section Part IIB: Defamation.

could reasonably be assessed as prejudicing the outcome of a trial by stating an opinion of guilt, the interests in maintaining the authority and impartiality of the judiciary rendered the imposition of a relatively light penalty by way of fine a not disproportionate interference.[18]

Criticism of police officers and politicians has been subject to a more robust approach and more concern to avoid the stifling of open debate.[19] In *Thorgeirson v. Iceland*, the conviction of a journalist for defamation of the police ("beasts in uniform") was not found to be justified to protect the rights of police officers. The Court noted that the article was based on objective fact — a known case of ill-treatment — and though expressed in strong terms it concerned a matter of public interest, its main thrust being to urge the setting up of an impartial enquiry.

Criminal sanction of individuals who make racist or anti-Semitic statements has been found generally justifiable by the Commission.[20] However, there is a fine line between legitimate reporting of nasty social phenomenon and the unacceptable repetition of racist propaganda. In *Jersild v. Denmark*, a television programmer was convicted in relation to a documentary on "greenjackets" during which they expressed racist views. The case turned on the weight given to the freedom of the press to report versus the offensive nature of the views transmitted and the possible risk to encouraging those views by exposure. For the majority of the Court[21] finding a violation, the key factors were that the applicant did not express the racist views himself but was participating in the current public discussion on racism in the country, intending to portray the mentality and background of racist individuals. It was relevant that the film was part of a serious news programme aimed at an informed audience and that its presentation clearly showed that its aim was not racism. "Interviewing" was also noted to be an important means of TV journalism and punishment of a journalist for views of the person interviewed would seriously hamper the contribution of the press to discussion of matters of public interest and should not be envisaged without particularly strong reasons.

(c) *Other restrictions on reporting*

The Commission has found that the administration of justice may require the exclusion of the press from court[22] or that secrecy of jury deliberations be maintained.[23] It is also compatible to impose conditions of accreditation on journalists who attend courts in a

---

[18] *Worm*, paras 52–58.

[19] See *e.g. Worm* para. 50. See also section Part IIB: Defamation; *Lingens v. Austria; Oberschlick v. Austria; Castells v. Spain.*

[20] *e.g.* 9777/82 *Belgium,* (Dec.) July 14, 1977, 34 D.R. 158, concerning a criminal conviction for publishing a pamphlet denying the extermination of the Jews; while the Commission acknowledged the freedom included material tending to shock or offend, this was subject to para. 2 and a State was able to confiscate, injunct or punish in respect of particularly odious ideas likely to offend a large number of people.

[21] 12:7 : the minority of the Court put greater emphasis on the huge importance of fighting racism which endangers the rights of others, in particular those targeted and this outweighed the "good intentions" of journalists who could be required to make more active criticism of racial discrimination (the applicant had not directly criticised the views expressed). For them, the idea of provoking a healthy reaction displayed an optimism belied by experience.

[22] 13366/87 *U.K.* (Dec.), December 3, 1990, 67 D.R. 244: exclusion of press during sentencing part of a trial. The Commission assumed that there was an interference, given the important role played by media in reporting on the administration of justice, but Art. 6 was of particular weight in a trial context, and it allowed for proceedings to be in camera, the exclusion was at the request of the defendant and the journalists' interests were outweighed.

[23] 24770/94, *U.K.*, (Dec.) November 30, 1994, concerning heavy fines for newspaper and editors for contempt of court for publication of jurors' opinions on a controversial trial. The Commission found the prohibition justifiable, even though absolute, *e.g.* protection for jurors to speak freely in jury room, though it left open whether this would still apply in connection with a serious research project or where interests of justice of a particular trial required disclosure.

privileged capacity.[24] Prohibitions on publishing certain details may raise issues if shown unnecessary. In one case, settled before admissibility, the name of a witness was subject to prohibition even though she was named in open court to avoid prejudicing the defence.[25]

The unfettered and unpredictable power of juries to award damages in defamation was the subject of a complaint by *The Times*, which considered that this disclosed an unjustifiable restriction on their journalistic activities. The Commission found that a newspaper could claim to be a victim even where no defamation proceedings had been bought if the state of the law was too vague to allow the risk of proceedings to be safely predicted. However the newspaper had not established such vagueness by reference to any award or any specific article in which it had in any way been inhibited from imparting information.[26]

Regarding restrictions imposed in respect of publications alleged to prejudice pending proceedings, the Commission found it legitimate to impose a postponement of a TV programme on the Birmingham Six. It had been scheduled for immediately after the close of the case before the Court of Appeal with portrayal of judges, counsel and witnesses by actors but the domestic court objected since this was inviting the public to make their own judgments as to the evidence and witnesses and might undermine confidence in the Court of Appeal when it issued its judgment. The Commission found the restriction proportionate, agreeing that this method differed from reporting the proceedings in the press which was unaffected and having regard to its duration of eight weeks until the judgment was given. Although objectively judges would not be influenced, the appellants had a right to be assured that they would not be affected by external matters.[27] Similarly, the banning of a Channel Four "Court Report" intending to report a controversial Official Secrets trial, by way of dramatic reconstruction with actors reading edited highlights of the proceedings, was found to be justified having regard to the real risk of prejudice if watched by the jury and since the programme could be issued with the same information read by news readers.[28]

As indicated by the Birmingham Six and Channel Four examples above, television journalism has an impact and immediacy which sometimes attracts interference from State authorities anxious to protect from nefarious influences. The Commission has accepted the necessity felt by both the Irish and U.K. Governments to prevent any television exposure of members of the Sinn Fein (and other groups) which might serve the ends of the violent terrorists with whom they are asserted to be linked. In *Purcell v. Ireland*,[29] the measure prevented coverage of, *inter alia*, Sinn Fein members by way of interviews or recordings on any subject. In finding the restriction proportionate, the Commission stated that the defeat of terrorism was a public interest of the utmost importance and referred to the difficulty of striking a fair balance where advocates of violence seek access to the media for publicity purposes. It was noted that TV and radio were media of considerable power and influence and that their opportunity to correct, qualify or comment was more limited compared to the press. It was also relevant that the ban, although inconvenient, did not in fact prevent news items being produced on any subject. Regarding a similar ban in the United Kingdom which allowed coverage of live interviews on TV but with use of actors' voice-overs, the Commission observed that there was no restriction as to the words or images

---

[24] 23869/94 *Switzerland*, (Dec.) December 24, 1995, 80–B D.R. 162): accredited journalists were given prior information and copies of judgments automatically. The refusal of this status did not amount to infringement of the right to seek, receive or impair information and it was not shown that the applicant was denied access to hearings or to judgements.

[25] *Crook and NUJ v. U.K.* 11552/85, (Dec.) July 15, 1988, 56 D.R. 148.

[26] *Times Newspapers* 14631/89, (Dec.) March 5, 1990, 65 D.R. 307.

[27] 14132/88, (Dec.) April 13, 1989, 61 D.R. 285.

[28] *Hodgson*, see n.6.

[29] *Purcell*, see n.6.

transmitted and while the logic of the voice-over might be open to dispute, it could be regarded as one aspect of a very important area of domestic policy, namely, combatting terrorism.[30]

Outside the area of publication, journalists may claim some protection in their role as public watchdogs. This does not extend to an immunity from providing information or film when ordered to do so by a court which considers the material relevant in criminal proceedings.[31] However, in the *Goodwin v. United Kingdom* case, where a journalist was fined for contempt of court for refusing to identify the source of his information about a private company's confidential financial report, the Court found that the £5,000 fine for contempt of court was a disproportionate restriction on his freedom of expression and that the coercion exerted on a journalist risked having a chilling effect on future work and the willingness of sources to give information. Safeguards to the press were seen as of particular importance in maintaining freedom of expression in the interests of democratic society. Thus, limitations on the confidentiality of journalistic sources called for the most careful scrutiny. Since an injunction had effectively stopped the leak through the press, the alleged need to uncover the source to obtain the missing plan and prevent other possible leaks was not sufficient in the balance against the vital public interest in the protection of journalistic sources. It would seem therefore that only an overriding requirement in the public interest, perhaps to prevent a serious crime or unmask the perpetrator of a serious crime, would justify the compulsory identification of journalistic sources.[32]

Where journalists deliberately breach confidentiality, sanctions may be found justified. Where a parliamentary journalist was convicted and fined for publishing a confidential parliamentary document, the Commission found the measure could be justified for preventing disclosure of material received in confidence and was not disproportionate since the applicant was an accredited journalist who had known the document was confidential and use of penalties was aimed at maintaining the credibility of the system.[33] Accounting for profits on publication of confidential material was also held justifiable, where *The Times* complained of being accountable for profits from the "Spycatcher" publications.[34] While the applicants alleged a vital public interest in the information about Government misdoings, the Commission found that the interference with the newspaper's freedom of expression was minor, since there was no prior restraint, few profits to account for and the information was obtained from an employee bound by confidentiality, which *The Times* had knowingly published.

5. Broadcast licensing

Key case law:

Groppera Radio and others v. Switzerland, March 20, 1990, Series A, No. 173; 12 E.H.R.R. 321; *Autronic AG v. Switzerland*, May 22, 1990, Series A, No. 178; 12 E.H.R.R. 485; *Informatsverein Lentia and others v. Austria*, November 24, 1993, Series A, No. 276; 17 E.H.R.R. 93.

Article 10 contains specific reference in the third sentence of the first paragraph to the provision not preventing States from requiring the licensing of broadcasting, television or

---

[30] *Brind v. U.K.*, 18714/91, (Dec.) May 9, 1994, 77 D.R. 42.

[31] Where the BBC were summoned to produce film of a riot: the Commission found that it was a normal civic duty to give evidence and it was not satisfied that this would result in greater risk to camera crews beyond that already incurred in filming such episodes — 25978/94, (Dec.) January 18, 1996, 84-A D.R. 129.

[32] A large minority (11:7) was satisfied with the balancing exercise conducted by the House of Lords which was in the best position to assess the damage and interests in question. Walsh J. also found it objectionable to confer on journalists a special legal privilege not enjoyed by other persons.

[33] 10343/83, (Dec.) October 6, 1983, 35 D.R. 224.

[34] 14644/89, (Rep.) October 8, 1991, 73 D.R. 41.

cinema enterprises. Briefly, national licensing systems are accepted as necessary for the orderly regulation of broadcasting enterprises and to give effect to international rules. Licensing is for the purpose of organising the technical aspects primarily. However, even where the licencing fulfills that function, it must still satisfy the requirements of paragraph 2. According to the Commission, the third sentence only applies to broadcasting, not to receipt of broadcasts whereas the Court found no need to decide since even if it was applicable there still had to be compliance with the requirements of the second paragraph.[35]

There is a recognition that restrictions should be minimal, with a presumption in favour of free access to transmissions.[36] Where a monopoly is imposed, even if it can be said to contribute to the quality and balance of programmes and be consistent with the third sentence, it may not prove to be justified in terms of the second paragraph, particularly since it requires a pressing need to justify such a severe restriction. In Austria, a violation was found in circumstances where it was impossible to set up a private radio or TV station. The argument that this would prevent private monopolies was not in the Court's view borne out by other European countries of comparable size. Quality and variety could be maintained by other means (licencing conditions, etc.); there was no technical need for restrictions as frequencies were available and the *raison d'être* of rigid monopoly no longer held since transmissions entered from other countries.

Some preferential treatment may be acceptable. The Dutch system of offering regional frequencies on a priority basis to public TV broadcasting organisations was compatible with the third sentence, and pursued the legitimate aim of maintaining pluralism, diversity and non-commercialism for audiences in the area.[37]

6. Commercial advertising

Key case law:

Barthold v. Germany, March 23, 1985, Series A, No. 90; 7 E.H.R.R. 383; *Markt Intern Verlag GmbH v. Germany*, November 20, 1989, Series A, No. 164; 12 E.H.R.R. 161; *Casado Coca v. Spain*, February 24, 1994, Series A, No. 285; 18 E.H.R.R. 1; *Jacubowski v. Germany*, June 23, 1994, Series A, No. 291; 19 E.H.R.R. 64.

Commercial speech is covered. Matters relating to professional practice are not removed from the sphere of Article 10 because of the financial element.[38] In *Markt Intern Verlag GmbH v. Germany*,[39] the Commission stated that democratic society was based on the articulation of economic interests. It rejected the Government view that Article 10 only covered artistic, religious, political and scientific matters and excluded purely competition-related promotional statements.[40]

Regarding professional rules against advertising, these are justifiable where the penalties are slight and pure advertising involved. The Court noting the wide variety of rules in

---

[35] In *Groppera*, a ban on cable re-transmission of radio programmes in Switzerland from an unlicensed station in Italy fell within the third sentence and pursued the legitimate aim of protecting the international telecommunications order (the station failed to comply with basic telecommunications principles) and the rights of others (those stations given licences).

[36] In *Autronic*, the Court noted developments in international telecommunications, *e.g.* the European Convention on Transfrontier Television and the less restrictive attitude adopted in various countries. It found no necessity to refuse a company authorisation to receive by dish aerial uncoded Russian television programmes, where no confidential information was concerned and the programmes aimed at the general public.

[37] 25987/94, (Dec.) November 29, 1995, 84-A D.R. 149.

[38] *Barthold*, (Rep.), para. 61: the Court did not find it necessary to decide since the article concerned included information and opinions on matters of public concern.

[39] (Rep.), paras 202–3.

[40] See also *Casada Coca*, para. 35: no distinction between profit-making forms.

States has commented that the domestic authorities are in the best place to assess where to strike the balance.[41] In *Barthold v. Germany*, the injunction on a vet for making statements in the press disclosed a violation. The Court held that the prohibition was disproportionately wide since it covered his expression of views about the problems of emergency night service and might discourage vets from giving their views in public debate and hamper the press in its role as public watchdog. A ban on pure commercial advertising by a lawyer who sent circulars to collection agencies was found justified in the interests of clients and the profession and was not disproportionate given the lightness of the penalty.[42] A disciplinary warning given to a lawyer for breaching an advertising ban was not disproportionate in *Casado Coca v. Spain*.[43]

Restrictions on publications found by domestic courts to damage commercial interests of others have not been found objectionable. In *Markt Intern*, where an injunction was issued against a magazine to prevent publication of critical information about trading practices of particular enterprises, the Commission found a breach,[44] but the Court did not. The Court found that while large undertakings opened themselves to public scrutiny and specialised press served a legitimate purpose, there were limits on criticism. It gave weight to the fact that the domestic courts had assessed the issues, and the fact that different views were possible did not permit substituting its opinion for that of the domestic courts.[45]

7. Artistic and cinematic

Key case law:

Muller v. Switzerland, May 24, 1988, Series A, No. 133; 13 E.H.R.R. 212; *Otto Preminger Institute v. Austria*, September 20, 1994, Series A, No. 295–A; 19 E.H.R.R. 34; *Wingrove v. U.K.*, November 25, 1996, R.J.D., 1996–V, No. 23.

There have been few cases, authorities perhaps feeling their interests less challenged by works of art. Controversy tends to arise where the "work" provokes religious or moral outrage. Freedom to receive and impart information and ideas includes the opportunity to take part in the public exchange of cultural, political and social information and ideas of all kinds, including artistic expression.[46] Artists cannot claim a wide right however but are subject to duties and responsibilities under the second paragraph of Article 10. In *Otto Preminger Institute v. Austria*, the Court stated that these included an obligation to avoid gratuitously offending others and infringing their rights, since this could not contribute to any public debate capable of furthering progress in human affairs. This approach would appear to place a strict burden on artists to avoid offending, since what is or is not gratuitous may be rather subjective, as shown in the *Otto Preminger* case, where the Court appeared to agree with the authorities that the provocativeness of the film outweighed the artistic merits, while the Commission took the view that the satirical elements predominated.

A wide margin of appreciation is generally afforded by the Court to Contracting States when regulating freedom of expression in relation to matters liable to offend intimate personal convictions within the sphere of morals or, especially, religion.[47] The Court

---

[41] *Casada Coca, ibid*, paras. 54–55.
[42] *Germany* 14622/89, (Dec.) March 7, 1991, 69 D.R. 272.
[43] Also *Colman v. U.K.* settled before the Court 16632/90, October 19, 1992, Series A No. 258–D, where the Commission found no violation where a doctor was prevented from newspaper advertising for patients.
[44] The Commission gave more weight to the press role of the publication and to the factual basis of the article.
[45] See also *Jacubowski*, where prohibition of a circular on grounds of unfair competition was not disproportionate.
[46] *Muller*, para. 27.
[47] *Wingrove*, para. 58.

considers that there is no uniform concept of morals, or of the requirements of the protection of religious beliefs, which differ from place to place and time to time. Local State authorities which are in direct and continuous contact with the vital forces of their country are thus, in principle, in a better position to give an opinion on the exact contents of these requirements as well as the necessity of the measures designed to meet them.[48] It found in *Muller v. Switzerland*, where a painter and exhibitors were convicted for displaying paintings depicting sexual acts, that the domestic court's view that the emphasis on sexuality in some of its cruder forms was "liable grossly to offend the sense of sexual propriety of persons of ordinary sensitivity" was not unreasonable. It was not persuaded by the applicant's arguments that there had been no public outcry[49] and that he had been able to exhibit abroad and other areas of Switzerland without trouble. The Court was also influenced by the factor that the paintings were open to the public at large without restriction.

There was more public outrage in the *Otto Preminger* case,[50] where the Salzburg authorities, at the prompting of the Catholic diocese, ordered the seizure and forfeiture of a film protraying God, Christ and the Virgin in a satirical manner which was about to be shown in Salzburg. The Court emphasised the protection of religious beliefs and the responsibility of the State to ensure the peaceful enjoyment of those rights under Article 9. It accordingly found that the measure pursued the legitimate aim in protecting others from being insulted in their religious feelings. The seizure was necessary since there was a high proportion of Catholics in Tyrol (87 per cent), and although the film was only open to adults, there had been sufficient publicity about the film to render the proposed screening "public" enough to cause offence. The Court considered that the authorities had weighed up the artistic elements against offensiveness and it could not disagree with their view of provocativeness of the film. Consequently, the measures taken to ensure religious peace in the region and protect persons who might feel under attack were within the margin of appreciation of the authorities.

The element of risk of public outrage and disturbing religious peace appeared absent from *Wingrove v. United Kingdom*, where a short video did not pass the British Board of Film Classification on grounds that it was blasphemous in its portrayal of Christ in a sexual context. The Court however found that the decision pursued the legitimate aim of protecting the rights of others not to be offended in their religious beliefs. Having regard to the wide margin of appreciation and the particular contents of the film, the decision was not arbitrary or unreasonable. It did not accept the argument that such a video could be restricted in its distribution, since once videos were marketed they were commonly lent, copied and otherwise escaped any regulation.[51]

---

[48] *Muller*, para. 35, *Wingrove*, para. 58. Also *U.K.* 17634/91 (Dec.) September 2, 1991: conviction for outraging public decency of artist and gallery owner for the public display of freeze-dried foetus earrings as a sculpture was justified — given the wide margin of appreciation in the area of morals and the public element of the display. No issue arose from the lack of defence of artistic merit.

[49] There were some complaints — one man had thrown a painting on the floor and stamped on it.

[50] The Court found no violation by 6:3, while the Commission was 9:5 violation for the seizure and 13:1 violation for the forfeiture. The Commission noted that the film was based on a play freely available in shops and was only open to an interested and limited feepaying adult audience. It did not find the film gratuitously offensive.

[51] The Commission distinguished *Otto Preminger* and *Gay News* (below), where the findings were reached by courts rather than an administrative institution, and detected no risk, in view of the video's classification and distribution, that an unsuspecting person might be exposed to it. In the *Gay News* case 8710/79, (Dec.) May 7 1982, 28 D.R. 77, where there was a conviction for blasphemy for a poem detailing homosexual acts by Christ, the Commission found it compatible for a State to prohibit attacks of a particular severity on others beliefs, noting that in this case the material was available to the general public and that the judicial authorities found it blasphemous after a thorough investigation.

8. Pornography

Key case law:

Scherer v. Switzerland, March 25, 1994, Series A, No. 287; 18 E.H.R.R. 276.

Criminal measures taken in respect of sale, distribution or trade in pornographic materials have generally been found by the Commission to conform with the requirements of Article 10 as being necessary for the prevention of crime or the protection of morals.[52]

Regarding the view that the protection of morals cannot extend to persons who wish to use such materials, this may have some relevance in the context of whether the pornographic material was on display to the general public or restricted. In *Scherer v. Switzerland,*[53] the Commission found a violation in relation to the conviction of a porn shop owner for showing obscene homosexual films in part of his premises on the basis that it was not open to the public and there was no question of the protection of morals of adults generally as none were confronted unintentionally with the material. There were no particularly compelling reasons for the prosecution given. This case distinguished an early application rejected as inadmissible where the measures related to a chain of video shops open to the general public.[54]

9. Parliamentary and electoral context

Key case law:

Castells v. Spain, April 23, 1992, Series A, No. 236; 14 E.H.R.R. 445; *Piermont v. France,* April 27, 1995, Series A, No. 314; 20 E.H.R.R. 301; *Sadik Ahmet v. Greece,* November 15, 1996, R.J.D., 1996–V, No. 15; *Bowman v. U.K.,* February 19, 1998, to be published in R.J.D. 1998.

The importance of freedom of expression for those participating in the democratic process has been acknowledged in a number of cases. Special privileges by way of immunity from suit in defamation have been found to be compatible with the Convention.[55] The requirement for elected respresentatives to be able to participate freely in political debate received recognition in *Castells v. Spain,* where a conviction of a senator for an article on the Basque situation which "insulted" the Government disclosed a violation. The Court found that freedom of expression was "especially important" for an elected representative who represents his electorate and defends their interests. This applied to political debate inside and outside the legislature and any interferences called for the closest scrutiny. The Court further considered that it was permissible to criticise governments more widely than in relation to private citizens and that governments should show restraint in resorting to criminal proceedings. While it might be compatible to take action against defamatory accusations devoid of factual basis or formulated in bad faith, in the case itself, the senator had not been afforded the chance to prove the factual basis of the article was true.

The protection of Article 10 extends to visiting European Union Parliamentarians. Measures to expel and prohibit the entry in French Polynesia of a German MEP invited by a local political party were not found justifiable, notwithstanding factors of the political

---

[52] 9615/81 (Dec.) March 5, 1983, 32 D.R. 231; seizure of magazines destined for overseas markets justified for protection of morals, not insofar as safeguarding morals of those outside its jurisdiction, but legitimate concern of legislator to stop U.K. becoming centre of flourishing export trade.

[53] Case struck off before Court when applicant died.

[54] 16564/90, (Dec.) April 8, 1991.

[55] See section Part IIB: Defamation.

atmosphere of the time, since the meeting had been peaceful, no disorder had arisen from the visit and her views had been a contribution to the existing local democratic debate in Polynesia.[56]

Where it is considered that an elected MP is expressing views that are dangerously provocative, States must still react in a suitable and adequate manner, using the means usually available in a democratic State. While the Commission in *Sadik v. Greece*[57] noted that moderation in political debate may be desirable to avoid, for example, exacerbating ethnic tensions, in the absence of clear elements of incitement to violence, the imposition of a prison sentence on a MP for words used in an election campaign could not be regarded as proportionate.[58]

In the context of election campaigns, the rules limiting expenditure for candidates should not operate as a blanket ban on single issue campaigners wishing to convey information to electors. This was the Commission's view in *Bowman v. U.K.*,[59] where an anti-abortion campaigner was regularly prosecuted for distributing leaflets about electoral candidates' views on abortion and related issues. The Commission was not convinced that the expenditure rules aimed at preventing corrupt practices justified prosecution of persons for factual, relevant information in which electors might have interest and where there was no indication of unfair distortion of the electoral process.

10. Statements threatening national security and public safety

Key case law:

Zana v. Turkey, November 25, 1997, to be published in R.J.D. 1997.

The Court has accepted, in the context of South East Turkey, that steps taken to prosecute and convict a person for statements in support of the PKK, an illegal terrorist organisation, could be said to pursue the legitimate aims of maintaining national security and public safety.[60] Whether the measures could be justified as necessary and proportionate under the second paragraph of Article 10 appear to turn on a consideration of the perceived impact of the statements concerned. In finding the conviction justified, in the *Zana v. Turkey* case, the Court noted that there had been serious disturbances in the region at the time and gave weight to the fact that the applicant was a former mayor of Diyarbakir (the principal city of the region) and that his statement gave express support to the PKK as a "national liberation movement" and referred in ambiguous, contradictory terms to PKK massacres as "mistakes". While the applicant did not express approval as such of violence, his words were, in the Court's view, open to several interpretations, and in light of the tensions existing at the time, they could be viewed as likely to exacerbate an already explosive situation.

There are other similar cases pending the Commission and Court, in which prosecutions and convictions for statements, articles and books are in issue. These raise difficult and sensitive issues as to the extent to which the State should be able to punish and seek to prevent the communication of ideas and information concerning a bitter and violent conflict, which might appear directly or indirectly to assist or support terrorist groups. The

---

[56] *cf. Benn and Adams v. U.K.*, 28979/95 and 30343/96, see n.3 — the exclusion order preventing Gerry Adams from attending a political meeting in London at the invitation of Tony Benn, M.P. was however justified in the context of the fight against terrorism and sensitive considerations relating to the peace process.

[57] The Court upheld the Government's preliminary objection on exhaustion.

[58] He had used the words "Turks" or "Turkish" to identify Moslems of Western Thrace.

[59] *U.K.*, 24839/94, (Rep.) September 12, 1996. The Court found the £5 limit on expenditure imposed by section 75 of the 1983 Representation of the People Act was a disproportionate restriction.

[60] *Zana v. Turkey*, para. 50.

laws in issue prohibit, for example, the reporting of statements or announcements by terrorist leaders; the naming or identifying of security or public officials which might render them a target for attack; and statements which promote the idea of "Kurdistan" as a separate entity from the Turkish State. The Commission has adopted the approach of assessing whether the impugned statements or publications could be reasonably regarded as inciting or encouraging violence, the use of words denying the territorial integrity of the State not being sufficient in itself.[61]

11. Obligations and restrictions in employment sphere

Key case law:

Glasenapp v. Germany, August 28, 1986, Series A, No. 104; 9 E.H.R.R. 25; *Kosiek v. Germany*, August 28, 1986, Series A, No. 105; 9 E.H.R.R. 328; *Vogt v. Germany*, September 26, 1995, Series A, No. 323; 21 E.H.R.R. 205.

Where contractually a person is bound by reasonable terms of confidentiality or loyalty, measures to suspend or dismiss for breach have generally been compatible, for example, where a doctor expressed views on abortion objectionable to his Catholic hospital employer[62] or civil servants have been penalised for revealing official secrets.

In *Vogt v. Germany*, however, where the applicant was an appointed civil servant, a teacher, the Court narrowly found a violation where she was suspended from a post for Communist party activities.[63] While it was open to a State to impose a duty of discretion on civil servants, freedom of expression still applied to them. Since she was a member of a lawful party, and there was no criticism of her work (as regarded any alleged risk of indoctrinating children), the majority found the interference disproportionate.[64]

12. Freedom to receive information

Key case law:

Gaskin v. U.K., July 7, 1989, Series A, No. 160; 12 E.H.R.R. 36; *Open Door and Dublin Well Woman v. Ireland*, October 29, 1992, Series A, No. 246; 15 E.H.R.R. 244.

There is no clear approach in the case law as to the extent of this element of Article 10. There is a hint in *Gaskin v. United Kingdom*[65] that this freedom only relates to information which others wish to pass on. The Commission stated that the applicant had no right to obtain the information against the will of the local authority which retained it. The Court refrained from expressly supporting that assertion, merely indicating that the provision basically prohibited a Government from restricting a person from receiving information that others wish or may be willing to impart. There was however no obligation on the authority in that case to provide the information.

---

[61] *e.g. Sürek v. Turkey*, Nos. 24122/94, 24735/94 and 24762/94 and *Sürek and Ozdemir v. Turkey*, No. 23927/94, (Reps.) January 13, 1998, pending before the Court. See also *Castells v. Spain, Sadik v. Greece* (for Parliamentary and electoral context, above); *Purcell v. Ireland*, see n.6 and *Brind v. U.K.* see n.30 (concerning acceptable restrictions on TV and radio reporting about Sinn Fein members).

[62] *Germany*, 12242/86, (Dec.) September 6, 1996, 62 D.R. 151.

[63] In *Glasenapp and Kosiek*, where the applicants, probationary civil servants, were dismissed for expression of particular political views, the Court found no violation on the special consideration that there was no right of entry to the civil service.

[64] 10 votes to 9: the minority gave greater weight to German history, the State's commitment to democratic order and considered that since the civil service was vital to the proper functioning of the State it was within its margin of appreciation to insist on conformity to strict rules.

[65] July 7, 1989, Series A, No. 160; 12 E.H.R.R. 36.

In *Open Door and Dublin Well Woman v. Ireland*, there was a violation where a court injunction prevented the provision of information services concerning abortion by the applicant counsellors. The Court found the ban disproportionate in the circumstances, since it was absolute, the counselling given was neutral and the information lawfully available elsewhere in Ireland or by contact outside in a less supervised manner, which posed a risk to those women who sought abortion at a later stage and who did not receive counselling or proper after-care.

At the moment, the provision cannot be used to derive a general right of access to information.[66]

Cross-reference

Part IIB: Army (section, freedom of expression)
Part IIB: Defamation and right to reputation
Part IIB: Prisoners' rights
Part IIB: Private life

---

[66] See, however, *Guerra and others v. Italy*, February 19, 1998, to be published in R.J.D. 1998, where the Court found a violation of Art. 8 in respect of the authorities' failure to provide the local inhabitants with information about risks to health from a chemical factory. Part IIB: Environment.

Freedom of movement

Key provision:

Article 2 of Protocol No. 4 (liberty of movement within a State and freedom to leave) — the United Kingdom has not ratified.

Key case law:

Guzzardi v. Italy, November 6, 1980, Series A, No. 39; 3 E.H.R.R. 333; *Raimondo v. Italy*, February 22, 1994, Series A, No. 281–A; 18 E.H.R.R. 237; *Piermont v. France*, April 27, 1995, Series A, No. 314; 20 E.H.R.R. 301.

1. General considerations

Where restrictions on movement are concerned, Article 2 of Protocol No. 4 is regarded as the *lex specialis*. Article 5 which concerns deprivation of liberty has not been extended by the Convention organs beyond the context of physical detention.

2. Restriction on movement

Whether there has been a deprivation of liberty rather than a restriction on movement depends on examination of the concrete situation, but is a distinction of degree and intensity, not one of nature or substance. Account is taken of a whole range of criteria: the type, duration, effects and manner of implementation of the measures restricting the individual's liberty. In *Guzzardi v. Italy*, the confinement of an applicant to an island was found to be cumulatively a deprivation of liberty within the meaning of Article 5. While the area to which he was confined was much larger than a cell, it covered a tiny fraction of the island, nine-tenths of which consisted of a prison. He had to remain in his dwelling between 22.00 and 07.00 hours, report twice daily to the authorities and could only leave the island under strict supervision — a state of affairs which lasted 16 months. Conversely, in *Raimondo v. Italy*, special police supervision, where the applicant could not leave home without informing the police and was under an obligation to report on certain days and to remain at home between 21.00 and 07.00 hours, was considered only a restriction on movement. Also, exclusion orders restricting persons in Northern Ireland from entering Great Britain have not been considered to constitute a deprivation of liberty.[1]

Refusal of a passport which did not prevent the application in Sweden from moving to other Nordic countries was still an interference with freedom of movement since freedom to leave a country implies freedom to leave for any country to which he may be admitted.[2]

Minor impediments or conditions imposed on the freedom of movement will not be seen as interfering, *e.g.* the obligation to carry an identity card and present it on request of the police.[3]

3. "Lawfully" within the territory

Freedom of movement applies only to persons lawfully within the territory. This refers to domestic law, which may lay down the conditions to be fulfilled. Thus aliens provisionally

---

[1] *e.g.* 13709/88 and 13944/88, (Decs.) October 11, 1989, unpublished.
[2] 19583/92 *Finland*, (Dec.) February 20, 1995, 80 D.R. 38.
[3] 21609/92 *Belgium*, (Dec.) September 9, 1992, 73 D.R. 136.

allowed to stay in a certain district can only be regarded as lawfully in the territory as long as they comply with the conditions of their admission.[4] Nor is the provision applicable to an alien whose residence permit has been revoked.[5]

An alien who has passed immigration control cannot claim necessarily to be "lawfully" in the territory, a claim made by the applicant MEP in *Piermont v. France* who was stopped after her passport had been checked at New Caledonia airport. The Court considered that at such an airport passengers remained liable to checks as long as they were within its perimeter. Since the applicant was served with the order preventing her entry while still in the airport she could not be considered as having been lawfully within the territory.

4. Legitimate restrictions

Where citizens are concerned, the restrictions imposed have generally been found compatible with Article 2 of Protocol No. 4. Considerations of lawfulness, necessity, legitimate aim and proportionality apply.

Refusal by Finland to issue a passport to a Finnish citizen resident in Sweden was an interference with freedom of movement but justified as necessary in the interests of national security and the maintenance of the *ordre public* since the applicant had failed to report for his military service. The Commission noted that the applicant had not invoked any ground warranting a departure from the usual rule, *e.g.* special need for travel and that he was able to re-apply at any time. It considered also that Contracting States were entitled to a wide margin of appreciation in the organisation of their national defence.[6] An injunction prohibiting an anti-abortionist campaigner from entering within 250 metres of an abortion clinic for six months was justified for the protection of the rights of others having regard to limited area and duration of the measure.[7]

Where the authorities exceed the justification of the measure in domestic terms, issues may arise. In *Raimondo v. Italy*, special supervision measures imposed on the applicant, suspected of mafia crimes, were considered as necessary and proportionate until revoked by the courts. The measures ceased to be necessary or lawful from the filing of the revocation decision by the court in the registry or at the latest when applicant was informed a week later.

5. Overlap with other provisions

While in *Piermont v. France*, the applicant MEP, as an alien subject to lawful measures, did not succeed in claims based on freedom of movement in respect of expulsion measures preventing her attendance of meetings in French Polynesia and New Caledonia, breaches of Article 10 were found since the measures disclosed unjustifiable interferences with her freedom of expression.[8] There was no point taken that Article 2 of Protocol No. 4 was the *lex specialis* or that no separate issues could arise where an alien was lawfully restricted in her movement. When in a United Kingdom case, Gerry Adams, Sinn Fein President, was stopped from attending a meeting in the House of Commons, by an exclusion order allegedly imposed for that purpose, the Commission noted that Article 2 of Protocol No. 4 had not been ratified by the United Kingdom. While it examined the case on the basis

[4] 14102/88 *Sweden*, (Dec.) October 9, 1989, 63 D.R. 195; 12068/86 *Germany*, December 1, 1986, 51 D.R. 237.
[5] 21069/92 *S. Mar.*, (Dec.) July 9, 1993, 75 D.R. 245.
[6] See 19583/92, n.2 above.
[7] 22838/93 *Netherlands*, (Dec.) February 22, 1995, 80–A D.R. 147.
[8] See Part IIB: Freedom of expression.

that there had been an interference with freedom of expression, it found the measure justified as necessary to protect national security and prevent disorder and crime.[9]

Cross-reference

Part IIB: Deprivation of liberty
Part IIB: Freedom of expression

---

[9] 28979/95 and 30343/96 *Adams and Benn v. U.K.,* (Dec.) January 13, 1997, 88–A D.R. 137.

Gypsies and minorities

Relevant Articles:

Article 8 (private life, family life and home); Article 14 (discrimination); Article 1 of the First Protocol (peaceful enjoyment of property); Article 2 of the First Protocol (right to education).

Relevant case law:

Bryan v. U.K., November 22, 1995, Series A, No. 335–A; 21 E.H.R.R. 342; *Buckley v. U.K.*, September 25, 1996, R.J.D., 1996–IV, No. 16.

1. General considerations

The Convention guarantees rights in respect, primarily, of the individual. The Convention organs emphasise this in an insistence that an applicant must be able to claim to be a victim, with direct effect on his enjoyment of a protected right. Complaints by a person that he is prejudiced in a general, indirect way due to his membership of a group conflict with this approach.

Complaints tended until recently to slip between the provisions.[1] The cases have derived principally from the United Kingdom, relating to the siting of gypsy caravans. These have highlighted the difficulties facing gypsies, whose ability to lead nomadic lives has been seriously hindered, *inter alia*, by the legislative provisions rendering unauthorised stationing of caravans on the highway or other land a criminal offence; the shortfall of official sites throughout the country and difficulties of obtaining local authority planning permission for their own sites. This is a global situation that could be described as undermining the viability of the gypsy way of life but which is difficult for the Commission to examine as a whole, confined as it is to the individual circumstances of each case and being reluctant to embark on abstract investigations.

It remains to be seen whether cases will emerge from the Central and Eastern Contracting States which have large *Roma* populations, with perhaps different and more extreme types of problems.

2. Right to respect for private life, family life and home

Planning controls on the use of land, a common feature in Contracting States, have generally been found by the Commission to be justified in the public interest, for example prohibiting development in green belt or areas of rural amenity[2] or for the rights of others, for example, the contractual rights of a site owner.[3] An individual who has been refused

---

[1] *e.g. Frankham v. U.K.*, 11862/85, (Dec.) July 18, 1986, where posters in local shops opposed gypsy sites implying that gypsies were dirty, smelly and attracted vermin, the applicant gypsy could not take action for defamation since English law did not recognise group defamation and consent was not forthcoming for prosecution for incitement to racial hatred. The Commission found no violation of Art. 6, which could not grant substantive rights of defamation where none existed or of Art. 8; *Ruby Smith v. U.K.*, 18401/91, (Dec.) May 6, 1993 where a gypsy living on an official site was threatened with summary eviction, it was argued that she was in an impossible situation, having regard to the shortfall of sites and to the existence of the designation system in the area making it a criminal offence for gypsies to station their caravans on public or private land without consent. However, when during the proceedings the applicant was granted permission by the local council to remain, the Commission avoided looking at the effect of the situation as a whole since, it found, that there was real indication that she wanted to travel elsewhere and so she was no longer a victim.

[2] *Chater v. U.K.*, 11723/85, (Dec.) May 7, 1987, 52 D.R. 250; *Herrick v. U.K.*, 11185/84, (Dec.) March 11, 1985, 42 D.R. 75.

[3] *P. v. U.K.*, 14751/89, (Dec.) December 12, 1990, 67 D.R. 264.

permission to occupy land is not in a strong position under the approach adopted by the Commission, which takes the view that Article 8 does not contain an express right to take up living accommodation. The Court has also stated that individual preferences cannot outweigh the general interest.[4] The fact that planning and site provision is an area of policy and discretion has also resulted in a wide margin of appreciation being accorded to the authorities and a reluctance to impose positive obligations on the State to provide accommodation in a particular place.[5]

Where however a gypsy family is established on a particular site and faced with expulsion, the Commission found that issues may arise. The lack of reasonable alternatives for the Buckley family, who had been refused planning permission for the caravan on their own land and faced with enforcement measures, was the basis for the Commission's finding of a violation. Both the Court and Commission accepted that the family's settlement on their land, even though never authorised, nonetheless fell within the scope of "home" under Article 8. The Commission also relied on a Norwegian case[6] concerning Lapps which held a minority could claim the right to respect for its particular lifestyle as being "private life", "family life" and "home". In its view a gypsy could therefore claim that his way of life which involved living in a caravan attracted protection under Article 8.

Regarding the compliance with the requirements of Article 8, the Court took a stricter line than the Commission. The Commission approached the balancing exercise from the point of view that gypsies from their lifestyle had more limited options open to them and that they had special requirements. It found that the applicant's interest in security for herself and her children and the continuation of their lifestyle outweighed the slender public interest in planning controls in that case. The Court emphasised however that in the area of planning controls the authorities enjoyed a wide margin of appreciation under Article 8. Although it noted the importance of respect for home, in effect this was given little weight. It was unimpressed by allegations of the unsuitability of the alternative official site nearby, commenting only that it was not as satisfactory as her own land and discounting matters of individual preference. The Court considered that it was not its role to enter into the merits of planning decisions, and it was sufficient to verify, as in this case before the planning inspectors, that the competing claims were given due consideration in a fair procedure.

In light of the Court's decision, where there is some form of alternative site, a finding of violation is unlikely where a gypsy family is refused planning permission for their land.[7] Issues might still arise perhaps where eviction measures are imposed arbitrarily or in circumstances of extreme hardship. It will however be difficult for any gypsy to establish that there is no alternative at all to remaining on their own land.[8]

---

[4] *Buckley,* para. 81.
[5] *Buckley,* para. 75; *U.K.,* 14455/88, (Dec.) September 4, 1991, where the applicant gypsies had sought unsuccessfully in the courts to enforce the statutory obligation on local authorities to provide sufficient sites to prevent being continually moved on from place to place. The Commission, though noting the lack of adequate provision, saw the applicants' claims as directed against the policy areas of legislation and enforcement mechanisms and was not prepared to go so far in that case to find that the respect for family and private life extended to obliging the authorities to build sites. Art. 8 was, impliedly, about respect for homes already in existence.
[6] *G. and E. v. Norway,* 9278/81, and 9415/81, (Dec.) October 3, 1983, 35 D.R. 30.
[7] *e.g. Webb v. U.K.,* 31006/96, (Dec.) July 2, 1997, where an alternative local authority site had been proposed, although criticised by the applicants as unsuitable.
[8] This will be particularly hard where a gypsy has given up a nomadic way of life, perhaps through force of circumstance, and adopted conventional housing for some period of time, as in the *Burton v. U.K.* case 31600/96, (Dec.) September 10, 1996, where the applicant had given up a nomadic life for 17 years and only when dying or cancer tried to resume life in a caravan but found no official site available in the area or any land available with planning permission. The Commission found that the local authority had made not unnegligible attempts to find sites and other accommodation but in the circumstances they could not be held in breach of Art. 8 in failing to provide such a site.

3. Discrimination

A gypsy must be able to claim a difference in treatment in respect of a right guaranteed under the Convention — which will tend to exclude cultural and social rights — and that he is a direct victim of the measure. Even where a difference in treatment is found to exist, the question remains whether it may be found to have a reasonable and objective justification.

In *P v. United Kingdom*,[9], the Commission considered that the difference in regimes between private mobile home sites and official gypsy sites as regarded legal protection was justified as they were run for different purposes. Private sites were not for nomads whereas official sites were meant to cater flexibly for the short stays of nomads and did not have to offer security of tenure.

A glaring difference in treatment in the enjoyment of private, family life and home was the designation system which rendered it a criminal offence for a gypsy to station his caravan on public land or on private land without authority.[10] However, while the issue was raised in *Ruby Smith v. United Kingdom*,[11] she was found not to be a victim and the designation system in *Buckley* was only examined, indirectly, in the context of Article 8, as indicating that the applicant had few options open to her. Since the Criminal Justice and Public Order Act 1994 is now in force, this difference has been eradicated to allow all persons to be prosecuted in such circumstances.

Allegations are not uncommonly made that gypsies are treated more unfavourably than others who make applications for planning permission. Difficulties however of establishing that a refusal to a gypsy was based on grounds of his ethnic origin or that permission was granted to an non-gypsy in comparable circumstances render success before the Commission unlikely. It would be required for blatant reliance on irrelevant planning factors, or a planning policy based on a clearly discriminatory element for serious issues to arise.[12]

4. Education

Several pending cases before the Commission expressly refer to the problem faced by gypsy children, unable to attend school regularly when their family is forced to move on from place to place. However in light of *Buckley v. United Kingdom*, it would seem that as long as there was alternative permanent accommodation elsewhere, gypsies would be unable to rely on their children's need for constant school attendance as the reason for remaining on their own land.

5. Access to court

Regarding the adequacy of court review of planning decisions, the Court's judgment in *Bryan v. United Kingdom* indicates that special considerations apply in the planning sphere. Bryan, facing enforcement measures in respect of his barn conversion, had argued that the procedures were inadequate, since the inspector in planning enquiries was not sufficiently independent of the Executive and the High Court's scope of review, on points of law insufficient to address his complaints. The Court found that while the planning inspector did not present guarantees of independence, the procedures were basically fair and the possibility of appeal in points of law to the High Court was sufficient review in a special

---

[9] See n.3.
[10] Caravan Sites Act 1968 (ss.10–12).
[11] See n.1.
[12] In *Webb*, where the applicant gypsies claimed that special allowance was required in the application of planning laws, the Commission found that there had not been such disregard of their position as gypsies as to disclose discrimination.

area of administrative discretion. As a result, it would appear that gypsies who generally have problems on the merits of cases (for example, whether planning considerations outweigh personal circumstances) will effectively be deprived of any independent scrutiny of their cases and the planning authorities given an almost exclusive decision-making power if they keep within domestic law.

Cross-reference

Part IIA: Access to court
Part IIB: Discrimination

Hindrance in the exercise of the right of individual petition

Key provision:

Article 25, paragraph 1 in fine (undertaking not to hinder the effective exercise of the right of individual petition).

Key case law:

Cruz Varas v. Sweden, March 20, 1991, Series A, No. 201; 14 E.H.R.R. 1; *Akdivar v. Turkey*, September 16, 1996, R.J.D., 1996–IV, No. 15; *Aksoy v. Turkey*, December 18, 1996, R.J.D., 1996–IV, No. 26; *Aydin v. Turkey*, September 25, 1997, R.J.D.–VI, No. 50.

1. General considerations

The right of individual petition is the keystone of the supervision process, since it is individuals and private organisations who provide the vast bulk of the cases under Article 25. The final sentence of the Article intends to safeguard the open and unimpeded access of the individual to the Convention organs by imposing the obligation on Contracting States not to hinder the exercise of the right of individual petition to the Commission.[1] In examining issues arising under Article 25, the Commission and Court have regard to the fundamental principle of interpretation of the Convention, that it must be seen as guaranteeing rights which are practical and effective as opposed to theoretical and illusory.[2] As an indication of its importance, the Commission will also raise hindrance under Article 25 *ex officio*, such being a matter pertinent to its own functioning.[3]

Express obligations are imposed on States which sign the European Agreement relating to persons participating in the proceedings before the Commission and Court of Human Rights. This covers, for example, co-operation in allowing applicants to enter or leave territory for the purpose of attending hearings (Article 4).

It is a healthy sign that relatively few complaints are made that a Contracting State has either failed to co-operate with the Commission in the examination process or that it has interfered with the applicant in some way. Where allegations do arise of deliberate interference by a Government with an applicant, which the Government denies, the Commission is in a difficult position and may be faced by factual problems which it is ill-equipped to resolve.[4]

2. Procedural right

Article 25 was described in *Cruz Varas v. Sweden* as a procedural right which could be invoked by individuals. The Commission followed a practice of making findings as to whether a Government had failed to comply with its obligations, until in *Akdivar v.*

[1] Art. 25 does not apply, strangely, to proceedings before the Court nor to inter-State cases.
[2] *e.g. Cruz Varas*, para. 99; *Aydin v. Turkey*, (Rep.) March 7, 1996, para. 212.
[3] *Campbell v. U.K.*, 13590/88 (Rep.), July 12, 1990, Series A, No. 233–A, p. 33.
[4] See, *e.g. Kurt v. Turkey*, (Rep.) December 6, 1996, paras 241–248, pending before the Court, where the applicant produced numerous contradictory statements about her intentions and her representatives alleged Government pressure while the Government alleged PKK pressure on her for the purposes of anti-State propaganda. Some allegations may prove impossible to clarify, as in *Aksoy*, where the applicant was tortured by Palestinian hanging while in police custody and then killed by unknown gunmen shortly after his case was communicated to the Government. His lawyer claimed that two days before the shooting, the applicant had stated that he was being followed and that his life was in danger. The Commission was "deeply concerned" by the death of the applicant but unable to resolve the matter one way or the other. It therefore did not find any failure to comply with the obligation under Art. 25, a conclusion shared by the Court.

Turkey, the Court made a finding of violation of Article 25, although stating that it was of a procedural nature distinguishable from the substantive rights.

Having regard to the procedural character of the right, the admissibility criteria appear to have no role, as regards at least the exhaustion of domestic remedies. Whether the Commission or Court would consider it appropriate to apply the six month time-limit to prevent stale issues is unlikely but an allegation dating back a considerable period without any convincing reason for failure to raise it earlier would presumably be a factor against the matter being taken up.

3. Hindrance

Hindrance in its normal meaning is not synonymous with complete obstruction but would appear to cover any step which renders the application process more difficult. Indeed, though it was initially questioned whether there could be hindrance where an applicant pursued his petition, it would have meant that few successful allegations of interference could be made since the applicants who were most effectively intimated would have ceased to pursue their cases at all.[5] The Court made this position clear in *Akdivar* where indeed one applicant had withdrawn his application entirely before the Delegates and the remaining applicants had continued notwithstanding the alleged intimidation.

4. Types of hindrance

(a) *Prisoners' correspondence and solitary confinement*

The occasional stopping of a letter to the Commission was not considered sufficient to raise an issue[6] and in *Campbell v. United Kingdom*,[7] the opening of letters to the Commission, without tampering or delaying, was insufficient to disclose any prejudice in the presentation of the applicant's application to the Commission.

The same *Campbell* alleged in an earlier application that he was being punished for his applications to the Commission by being put in solitary confinement. The Commission took the complaint seriously enough to pursue the matter with the Government. The facts however indicated that he was held in segregation because he wanted to spend time on his various litigations and refused to go on normal routine which would have involved working instead of spending time in his cell with his books and papers. Thus, there was no clear punitive intent and no indication that it in fact hampered his right of petition.[8]

(b) *Intimidation of applicants*

Contact by State authorities with applicants concerning their application to the Commission is likely, save in exceptional and convincingly innocuous circumstances, to raise serious issues. The Court's approach in *Aydin v. Turkey* however indicates that applicants must provide some concrete and independent proof of any harassment alleged.[9]

---

[5] In *Kapan v. Turkey*, (Dec.) January 13, 1997 88–A D.R. 17: the applicant failed to appear at a Commission hearing in Strasbourg or before delegates in Turkey, his lawyers claiming that he was in fear of his life. However, in view of his continued silence to all approaches, including a request for written confirmation of his intention to continue the application, the Commission struck the case off. To give up these cases is perhaps unsatisfactory. But it underlines the reality that the system relies on applicants with the courage to complain and to maintain their complaints by physically appearing to clarify any disputes of fact.

[6] *Hosein v. U.K.*, 18264/93, (Dec.) September 8, 1993.

[7] The Commission did find a violation of the Art. 8 correspondence right, as did the Court, which found it unnecessary to examine Art. 25 since this aspect was not pursued during its proceedings.

[8] 12323/86, (Dec.) July 13, 1988, 57 D.R. 148.

[9] Paras. 116–117: it disagreed with the Commission's approach, see n.12.

Questioning of applicants about their applications amounts to an illicit and unacceptable form of pressure on applicants to withdraw their applications.[10] Even if contact by the authorities with applicants with a view to investigation of their complaints on a domestic level was compatible, the Commission considered that applicants' lawyers should be present and that it was never legitimate to question them about the circumstances in which they decided to make their application, their motivation or what they intended to say in the application with a view to testing the accuracy of submissions made on their behalf.[11]

Governments are expected by the Commission to make a proper and serious response to allegations of intimidatory interferences with the right of individual petition which the Commission are examining. A failure to do so may support a finding of hindrance.[12]

(c) *Intimidation of lawyers*

Attempts to institute criminal and even disciplinary proceedings against the lawyers of applicants relating to their participation in the submission of applications to the Commission will also disclose a violation of Article 25, since this may have the effect of dissuading an applicant or his or her lawyer from pursuing a case, placing obstacles in the path of pursuing an application and deter future applications.[13] A violation was found in *Kurt v. Turkey* where a Government representative after a Commission oral hearing took the initiative in contacting the prosecution authorities with a view to taking action against the applicant's lawyer in relation to allegations made by him which the applicant had not maintained in her oral evidence.

5. Failure of the Government to comply with procedural request

(a) *Failure to comply with interim measures*

The refusal of a Government to comply with a Commission request for suspensive measures under Rule 36 of its Rules of Procedure is not *per se* a failure to comply with Article 25. In *Cruz Varas v. Sweden*, where the Swedish authorities expelled the applicant to Chile despite the Commission's request to suspend the measure pending its examination of allegations that he risked torture and ill-treatment on return, the Court found that no power to make binding interim measures could be derived from Article 25 or Rule 36. However it did accept that an individual could complain if steps were taken which

---

[10] *Akdivar*: violation of Art. 25 found where an applicant, and a villager with the same name as another applicant, had been videotaped in interviews denying their applications and stereotyped statements signed by several applicants denying their allegations were produced by the Government.

[11] See also *Kurt*, para. 247, see n.4, where the Commission found that contacts with an applicant to verify whether the application was genuine were inacceptable, since where such doubts existed, it was for the Commission to verify the existence of a valid application; *Ergi v. Turkey* 23818/94, (Rep.) May 20, 1997, para. 180 pending before the Court, the Commission found that there was no justification for the authorities, particularly the anti-terror police, to question an applicant about his application, even in the context of verifying his legal aid application to the Commission.

[12] *Aydin*: see n.2, the Commission found a violation of Art. 25, where the applicant, alleging rape by gendarmes, complained, *inter alia*, that she and her husband were picked up and questioned by police and her husband assaulted. Its finding was based on its consideration that the allegations were genuine, supported by some evidence and that the Government's response to the Commission's requests for clarifications were unsatisfactory, even spurious in themselves. However, the Court found that there was insufficient factual basis for it to find that the applicant had been intimidated or harassed in circumstances disclosing an interference with the right of individual petition.

[13] It noted in that context that Art. 2 of the European Agreement (General considerations, above) conferred immunity from legal process in respect of oral or written statements made by lawyers assisting applicants before the Commission (though Turkey had not ratified this agreement).

interfered with the right effectively to pursue an application. On the facts of this case, having found no substantiated risk of ill-treatment, the Court noted that while compliance with the request would have facilitated the applicant's presentation of his case, in fact he remained at liberty in Chile and his counsel was able fully to present his views in his absence, without any indication of being hindered to any significant degree. However the Court commented that failure to comply with a Rule 36 request where a violation of Article 3 was later found would aggravate the breach.

In future, whether or not there is a violation of Article 25 resulting from failure to comply with such a request appears to depend on the events which follow, in particular, the effect of the refusal on the applicant's ability to pursue his case, and probably, on whether there is a substantive breach of the Convention.

(b) *Documents and other facilities*

A failure by a Government to provide documents or information, or to facilitate the taking of evidence before delegates might also potentially raise issues where this substantially hindered the Commission's task in examining a case.[14] Alternatively, the Commission may draw inferences from the failure of the Government to respond to questions or requests and proceed to find substantive violations.[15] The Commission has referred in a number of cases involving the taking of evidence to the Court's statement in the *Ireland v. United Kingdom* case that the conduct of the parties when evidence is being taken may be taken into account in the assessment of evidence.[16]

---

[14] This also could lead to a finding that a State had failed in its obligation under Art. 28, para. 1(a) to furnish all necessary facilities to the Commission in its examination of a case (Art. 38 after November 11, 1998).
[15] *e.g. Ergi,* see n.11, where failure to provide gendarme witnesses requested by the Commission Delegates was taken into account in assessing the evidence.
[16] January 18, 1978, Series A, No. 25, para. 161; *Ergi,* see n.11.

Home

Key provision:

Article 8 (respect for home).

Key case law:

Gillow v. U.K., November 24, 1986, Series A, No. 109; 11 E.H.R.R. 335; *Chappell v. U.K.*, March 30, 1989, Series A, No. 152; 12 E.H.R.R. 1; *Niemietz v. Germany*, December 16, 1992, Series A, No. 251–B; 16 E.H.R.R. 97; *Funke v. France*, February 25, 1993, Series A, No. 256–A; 16 E.H.R.R. 287; *Murray v. U.K.*, October 28, 1994, Series A, No. 300–A; 19 E.H.R.R. 193; *Buckley v. U.K.*, September 25, 1996, R.J.D., 1996–IV, No. 16; *Mentes v. Turkey*, November 28, 1997, to be published in R.J.D. 1997; *Camenzind v. Switzerland*, December 16, 1997, to be published in R.J.D. 1997.

1. General considerations

Home has been given a wide definition by the Convention organs. It is not necessary that a home be lawfully established, significance attaching rather to the nature of the occupation.[1] Further, since "home" and "private life" may overlap with business and professional activities, the scope of Article 8 has been found to extend to offices. This is seen as consonant with the essential purpose of Article 8 to protect the individual against arbitrary interferences by public authorities.[2] As in other aspects of Article 8, while it is primarily interferences by public authorities which are concerned, there may in certain circumstances be positive obligations imposed on a State to protect the right to respect for home from others.[3]

2. Regulation of occupation

Any interferences with "home" must comply with the requirements of the second paragraph of Article 8. The Court has stated that the importance of the right to respect for home, which is pertinent to personal security and well-being, must be taken into account in determining the scope of the margin of appreciation allowed to Governments.[4] However, in the balancing exercise of private against the general interest, certain features such as the perceived nature of planning controls have taken on significance.

In *Gillow v. United Kingdom*, where the applicants were refused permission to reside in their house in Guernsey, the Court's emphasis was on the lack of any pressing social need

---

[1] *Buckley*, paras. 52–54, where the applicant gypsy established her home on land without planning permission — see also *Buckley*, Comm. Rep. para. 63 where the Commission found that "home" is an autonomous concept which does not depend on classification under domestic law, but on the factual circumstances, namely, the existence of sufficient and continuous links, citing *U.K.*, 7456/76, (Dec.) February 8, 1978, 13 D.R. 40; *Gillow*, para. 46 where though absent from their house for almost 19 years, due to professional reasons, the applicants intended it to be their home, keeping their furniture there and with no other home elsewhere.

[2] *Niemietz*, para. 30–31, where a search of a lawyer's office and seizure of documents by the police interfered with private life, home and correspondence; *Chappell*: search of premises used for residential and business purposes. However not all business activities will qualify — 23953/94, *Austria*, (Dec.) September 6, 1995, 82 D.R. 51, where a bar open to the public which had been showing pornographic videos was searched, the Commission found that nature of the premises and the business activities had to be taken into account. No interference with home or private life was found.

[3] *Whiteside v. U.K.*, 20357/92, (Dec.) March 7, 1994, 76–A D.R. 80 see "Private life, 3. State obligations". Positive obligations are only likely to arise in respect of serious infringements in the personal sphere. Unsolicited mail is not sufficient: 24967/94, *Netherlands*, (Dec.) February 20, 1995, 80 D.R. 175.

[4] *Gillow*, para. 56.

for the restriction, with a failure on the part of the authorities to give sufficient weight to the applicants' personal circumstances notwithstanding the legitimate interest in controlling population on the island. In contrast, in *Buckley v. United Kingdom*, the applicant gypsy's right to respect for the home established on her land was not of manifest weight against the Court's consideration that in the area of planning controls national authorities are in principle better placed to evaluate local needs and conditions and in the exercise of discretion involving a multitude of factors the authorities enjoy a wide margin of appreciation. In *Buckley*, the emphasis was on whether there was a procedure whereby the authorities assessed the competing interests and since the planning inspectors reached their decisions on the basis of relevant and sufficient reasons, the refusal of planning permission did not exceed the margin of appreciation. Although the applicant had argued that she had no practical alternative open to her and that her personal circumstances were pressing, the Court, with less sympathy than in *Gillow*, stated that Article 8 did not allow individual's preferences as to their place of residence to override the general interest.

3. Searches of property

Where the authorities enter property to search, the interference may well cross the boundaries of most, or all, the separate protected interests under Article 8.[5] Requirements of customs control, investigation of terrorism or other crime, protection of the rights of others in the area of copyright have been accepted as legitimate aims for searches.[6]

The case law has concentrated on the requirements that searches be "lawful" and attended by adequate procedural safeguards against arbitrariness and abuse.[7] Where orders are issued by courts, with an element of judicial supervision built in, there is likely to be sufficient safeguard, as in *Chappell v. United Kingdom* where the applicant attacked unsuccessfully the draconian nature of *Anton Pillar* orders.[8] However, even where a court makes the order, it is necessary for its scope to be contained within identifiable limits. In *Niemietz v. Germany*, the Court found the order for search and seizure of documents without any limitation to be disproportionate, particularly in the context of its interference in that case in the confidentiality attaching to correspondence and documents of a lawyer.[9] The minor nature of the offence which led to the search was also of relevance in that case.[10]

[5] *e.g. Niemietz* (search of lawyer's office); *Funke* (customs search of house); *Mentes v. Turkey*, where soldiers searched and burned houses, there was grave interference with private and family life and home.

[6] *Funke, Murray, Chappell;* also *Camenzind v. Switzerland*, aim of maintaining telecom regulations.

[7] *Funke*, paras. 54–57, where the customs authorities had exclusive competence to assess the expediency, number, length, and scale of investigations and the procedural safeguards were too lax and full of loopholes — the Court was not impressed by the allegedly strict supervision of a senior customs official and the presence of a police officer; *Camenzind v. Switzerland*; search of house by PTT official verifying conformity of telephones with regulations found by the Court to have adequate safeguards (including attendance of local public official on request), given the limited nature of the search.

[8] It was sufficient that the plaintiff's solicitor rather than a court official carried out the order, since he was subject to heavy sanctions in breach of the undertakings to the court; also the order was only granted *ex parte* if certain conditions fulfilled and was subject to limitations; *Funke*, where Court commented on lack of judicial supervision of wide Customs powers; *Vella v. Malta*, 18420/91, January 20, 1994 (Rep.) February 17, 1993, 76 D.R. 29: complaint of search of home by police without requirement for judicial warrant, settled after admissibility.

[9] The possibility of an independent observer was mentioned as a procedural safeguard that might be required in that context. See 15882/89 *Austria*, (Dec.) March 29, 1993, 74 D.R. 48 where search of a lawyer's office was attended by necessary safeguards, including attendance by a representative from a lawyers' association.

[10] See also *Funke*, para. 58, where the Court found that the lack of any criminal complaint against the applicant whose home was searched was relevant. *McLeod v. U.K.*, 24755/94, (Rep.), April 9, 1997 pending before the Court: entry of the police of the applicant's home due to an alleged risk of breach of the peace — the majority of the Commission found that the limited and restrained measure was not disproportionate, while the minority considered that the measure was disproportionate in the absence of risk to life and limb or risk of serious damage to property.

The manner in which the search is conducted must also be compatible with the requirements of Article 8. However, the circumstances existing in Northern Ireland have been found to necessitate the precautions used by the army on entering houses.[11]

---

[11] *e.g. Murray v. U.K.:* included briefly confining the occupants in one room.

Homosexuality

Relevant Articles:

Articles 8 (private and family life) and 14 (discrimination).

Leading cases:

Dudgeon v. U.K., October 22, 1981, Series A, No. 45; 4 E.H.R.R. 149; *Norris v. Ireland*, October 26, 1988, Series A, No. 142; 13 E.H.R.R. 186; *Modinos v. Cyprus*, April 22, 1993, Series A, No. 269; 16 E.H.R.R. 485; *Laskey, Jaggard and Brown v. U.K.*, February 19, 1997, R.J.D. 1997–I, No. 29.

1. General considerations

The Convention organs have made a limited contribution to resolving the problems of stigmatisation and discrimination facing persons who are homosexual. While they made the important step of rejecting the criminalisation of adult homosexual acts, there have been conservative responses to claims in the realm of family life, differing ages of consent and discrimination generally. There are however cases currently pending before the Commission which may indicate that the time is appropriate for further developments.[1]

2. Right to private life

Dudgeon v. United Kingdom established the important principle that private sexual conduct, which is a vital element of an individual's personal sphere, cannot be prohibited merely because it may shock or offend others. In such an intimate aspect of private life, there must exist particularly serious reasons before interferences can be justified. The Court underlined in this context two of the hallmarks of a democratic society: tolerance and broadmindedness. In *Norris v. Ireland* it rejected the claim that in the area of morals States should enjoy extensive leeway as to what morals should require. The prohibition by criminal law of consensual sexual activities between adult homosexuals in private constitutes therefore an unjustified interference with the right to respect for private life. A homosexual applicant can claim to be a victim of a measure through the mere existence of the criminal offence since this has a direct and continuous effect on his life. The Convention organs have not been persuaded by arguments that an individual applicant had not been prosecuted or threatened with prosecution, that there was no real incidence of prosecutions[2] or that there was a claimed policy of no prosecutions.[3]

As to what activities fall within the scope of "private life", the Commission has yet to directly consider the effect of the United Kingdom definition of "private" as restricted to acts in the presence of not more than two adults. In *Johnson v. United Kingdom* where the police raided a homosexual party,[4] it noted that the raid had been motivated by a tip off as to the possible involvement of minors and found that the applicant, who was not subject to any charge, had not established that the existence of this aspect of sexual offences legislation continuously or directly affected his private life. An applicant who was prosecuted for involvement in group adult activitives could possibly claim to be a victim of

---

[1] *Sutherland v. U.K.*, 25186/94, (Rep.) July 1, 1997, pending before the Court, concerning differing age of consent 18 and 16 for homosexual and heterosexual acts.

[2] *Dudgeon*, and *Norris*. It was noted in Dudgeon that private prosecutions were possible.

[3] *Modinos*, where the Att.-Gen. could not bind his successors.

[4] *U.K.*, 10389/83, (Dec.) July 17, 1986, 47 D.R. 72.

interference. It would have to be determined in those circumstances whether the State sanction of group sexual activities could be considered as necessary for one of the legitimate aims allowed, such as the protection of morals, prevention of corruption of the young or prevention of disorder. In *Laskey, Jaggard and Brown v. United Kingdom*, however, involving group sado-masochistic activities, the Court expressed doubts whether these could in the circumstances of the case be considered an aspect of "private life".[5] In any event it found that the prosecution of such acts as assault and wounding, notwithstanding the consent of the adult victims, was justified for the aim of the protection of health, having regard to the extreme nature of the acts concerned.

3. Age of consent

Measures prohibiting acts with minors under 21 was found justified in *Dudgeon v. United Kingdom*, the Court finding that a margin of appreciation was left to Contracting States as to appropriate safeguards, including the age of consent, required for the protection of the young.

Complaints about the age of consent of 21, which was considerably higher than in many other Contracting States, were rejected until 1994. In *X v. United Kingdom*[6] the Commission though acknowledging that 21 could be seen as high and that it might seem inconsistent to allow 18 years olds to vote and enter legal transactions, nonetheless felt that the Government could rely on the Wolfenden Committee report, which had investigated comprehensively sexual offence legislation and recommended the age of 21 as necessary to protect young men from influences of an undesirable kind.[7]

Fifteen years later in 1993, in *Wilde, Greenhalgh and Parry v. United Kingdom*, where two of the applicants were 20, the difference in age of consent was challenged as too high, in current times, for the legitimate exercise of the State's margin of appreciation.[8] The case was overtaken by the entry into force of the Criminal Justice and Public Order Act 1994 which lowered the age to 18 and the Commission struck the case from its list as having been resolved. In *Sutherland v. United Kingdom*, introduced by an applicant under 18, now pending before the Court, the Commission has found a violation of Article 14 in conjunction with Article 8 concluding that there is no objective and reasonable justification for the difference in age of consent of 18 for male homosexuals and 16 for heterosexuals.[9]

4. Right to family life

Despite the modern evolution of attitudes, the relationship of gays and lesbians do not, according to the Commission, fall within the scope of the right to family life. Consequently, where the United Kingdom refused the homosexual partner of a British citizen leave to enter the United Kingdom to live with his partner, the Commission found the refusal could not interfere with any family right. While it could raise issues regarding private life, the Commission found that it had not been shown that the applicants were not

---

[5] *e.g.* the group was large, organised and circulated videos.

[6] 7215/75, (Rep.) October 12, 1978, 19 D.R. 66.

[7] It referred to an earlier German case where the Commission noted studies indicating a specific social danger in the case of masculine homosexuality, resulting from the fact that male homosexuals often constituted a distinct socio-cultural group with clear proselytising tendency towards adolescents and a resulting social isolation; 5935/72, (Dec.) September 30, 1975, 3 D.R. 46.

[8] *U.K.*, 22382/93, (Dec.) January 19, 1995, 80–A D.R. 132.

[9] *Sutherland*, see n.1, paras. 64–65: referring to contemporary medical opinion to the effect that sexual orientation is fixed in both sexes by the age of 16 and that men aged 16–21 are not in need of special protection because of any risk of their being "recruited" into homosexuality; and rejecting the argument that society was entitled by this means to express disapproval of homosexuality and its preference for the heterosexual lifestyle.

able to live somewhere else or that their link to the United Kingdom was an essential element of their relationship.[10]

This approach maintains an emphasis on the traditional heterosexual couple as the core of the notion of family, which is becoming increasingly less the norm. The Convention organs have been slowly extending family life to situations where there is *de facto* family life between heterosexuals outside marriage. However, this has not extended to gays and lesbians with longstanding stable relationships, even where there have been children in the household. In *Kerkhoven v. The Netherlands*,[11] where two lesbians lived in a long-term relationship and shared parenting roles in respect of the child born by AID (artificial insemination by donor), the Dutch courts refused an application by the partner of the child's mother for parental authority. The Commission found that Article 8 did not import a positive obligation on a State to grant parental rights to a woman who was living with the mother of a child. While homosexual relationships could fall within the scope of private life, the Commission found that the refusal of parental authority did not infringe on the private lives of the applicants. This approach seems to overlook or discount the problems which might arise on the death of the child's mother, where in the absence of any legal recognition of a parenting role of the partner, the partner may be at a disadvantage in upholding claims for continued custody of the child.

5. Right to marry

In view of the express wording of Article 12 "Men and women" and the reference to applicable national laws, the Commission is currently unlikely to find that a right to marry could exist for homosexuals where the Contracting State forbids it. However in those countries where gay marriages are allowed, it may be that the Convention organs would have to accept that "family" relationships could be formed and any inequalities there would be harder to justify.

6. Discrimination

Where differences of treatment are concerned, it will depend very much on the area of right concerned whether the Commission will accept that the homosexual can claim to be in an analogous position for the purposes of comparison. Even if he could, there will still remain the obstacle of establishing that the difference concerns a substantive right guaranteed under the Convention and that there is no objective or reasonable justification for the difference.

In the context of family life, the Commission found in *Kerkhoven* that a lesbian couple could not claim to be in a relevantly similar position as a heterosexual one as regarded parental authority.

Regarding justifications for differences, the alleged need to protect young men has become less sustainable in light of *Sutherland*, which refers to studies indicating that sexual proclivities are fixed by early adolescence and young males are not in any special need of protection from being "perverted" away from heterosexuality. Other prejudices as to homosexuality may also be open to successful challenge in the near future. In particular, there are cases pending before the Commission questioning the basis for dismissing

---

[10] 9369/81, (Dec.), May 3, 1983, 32 D.R. 220: U.K. 11716/85, (Dec.) May 14, 1986, 47 D.R. 274, when the partner of a lesbian died, the lesbian's eviction from the partner's home (the partner was secure tenant of local authority housing) did not disclose any violation. Spouses, cohabitees or other relatives would have enjoyed a legal right to continue the tenancy. The Commission found no family life at stake. Under private life and home, it noted that the partner had not been the tenant, had no legal right to remain and any interference was justified in light of the contractual rights of the landlord.
[11] 15666/89, (Dec.) May 19, 1992, unpublished.

gays and lesbians from the armed forces, despite an earlier case which accepted the alleged need in the special context of the armed forces to protect from coercion and blackmail and maintain trust and confidence.[12]

Cross-reference

Part IIB: Armed Forces
Part IIB: Discrimination
Part IIB: Private life

---

[12] 9237/81, (Dec.) October 12, 1983, 34 D.R. 68; see Part IIB: Armed Forces.

Housing and tenancy

Key provisions:

Article 1 of Protocol No. 1 (peaceful enjoyment of possession); Article 6 (access to court/fair hearing).

Key case law:

Sporrong and Llonroth v. Sweden, September 9, 1982, Series A, No. 52; *James v. U.K.*, February 21, 1986, Series A, No. 98; 8 E.H.R.R. 123; *Gillow v. U.K.*, November 24, 1986, Series A, No. 109; 13 E.H.R.R. 593; *Mellacher v. Austria*, December 19, 1989, Series A, No. 169; 12 E.H.R.R. 391; *Spadea and Scalabrino v. Italy*, September 28, 1995, Series A, No. 315–B; *Scollo v. Italy*, September 28, 1995, Series A, No. 315–C; *Velosa Barreto v. Portugal*, November 21, 1995, Series A, No. 334.

1. General considerations

There is no right to housing or accommodation in the Convention. Generally, for issues to arise, an applicant must have an already existing property right. The cases have related principally to Government regulation of leases and rents. Such measures generally constitutes a control of use and, if severe enough, *de facto* expropriation or outright deprivation as in *James v. United Kingdom* where statute conferred a right to long leaseholders to acquire the freehold of the Duke of Westminister's property in London. Where a person enjoys a property right to the housing, an interference will raise issues under Article 1 of Protocol No. 1[1] while Article 8 may become applicable, if the circumstances are such that occupation of property renders it his home (see Part IIB: Home). Once property or contractual rights are in issue, an applicant may generally also claim access to court and the procedural safeguards of Article 6.

In these cases, the Convention organs carry out a balancing exercise in which effect on the applicant's rights is weighed against the wider interests.[2] Measures pursuing social or economic policies tend to attract a wide margin of appreciation.[3]

2. Regulation of ownership

The transfer of property from one private person to another is not *per se* contrary to the Convention.[4] Transfers may pursue legitimate social and economic policies and implement social justice, as in *James*, where the transfer of long leases could be reasonably considered to remedy a social injustice.[5] The margin of appreciation, where expropriation is concerned, is wide due to the nature of the political, economic and social issues involved. The Court in this area has stated that it will respect the legislature's judgment as to what is in the public interest unless it is "manifestly without reasonable foundation".[6]

---

[1] See, however, 19217/91, (Dec.) January 21, 1994, 76–A D.R., where the Commission held that the right to live in a property of which one is not the owner was not a possession right (dispute inheritance rights over a chateau).

[2] *Sporrong*, para. 69: whether under Art. 1 of Protocol No. 1 or Art. 8 the Convention organs conduct a balancing exercise.

[3] *James*, para. 46.

[4] *ibid.*

[5] Where the building or premium lease leaseholder either had carried out the building work or paid an intial capital sum with long term repair responsibility with the landlord making no contribution to maintenance.

[6] *James*, para. 46: the Court is not keen to enter into assessments of policy and the margin is applied both to the assessment of the existence of a problem of public concern and the remedial action necessary.

3. Rent and tenancy control

A wide margin of appeciation applies also to rent control measures. Measures intervening in existing contracts may be acceptable, where there are legitimate social and economic aims to make accommodation more accessible to the less affluent. Thus in *Mellacher v. Austria*, the striking reductions, up to 79 per cent in some cases, did not disclose a violation. The Court did not consider that it violated the principle of freedom of contract in that parties had entered into the agreement as to rents on freely determined market principles. The burden on the landlords was not found to be disproportionate and it was not for the Court to decide whether this was the best solution.[7]

In Italy, where there was a shortage of rented accommodation, owners of rented flats were obtaining eviction orders but were unable to have them enforced, due to a law suspending the enforcement of evictions. Since the owners in *Spadea and Scalabrino v. Italy* and *Scollo v. Italy* could still sell the property and receive rents this was a control of use not a deprivation of property. The Court found that the suspension was a legitimate measure aimed at managing the effects of expiry of many leases, and the resulting hardship and social tensions. As regarded proportionality, while the applicants attacked the government policy which led to the situation of many leases expiring together without taking steps to make sure other accommodation was available, the Court noted that the shortage of housing was a universal problem in modern society and that the law provided exceptions for landlords who urgently required their property. Where in *Spadea*, the tenants were very old and infirm and the period involved was not overly excessive apparently, the measure was not disproportionate. However in *Scollo*, where the applicant claimed priority, since he was disabled and the tenant had stopped paying rent, there was a violation since the authorities failed to implement their own provisions to give him priority. A fair balance was found to be struck in *Velosa Barretto v. Portugal*, where the applicant was prevented from taking possession of the house inherited from his parents to live in himself. The measure aimed at the social protection of tenants and the domestic courts had found that he had no urgent need for the property, as he lived with other members of his family.

4. Housing restrictions

The Channel Islands' strict residential housing control was found in *Gillow v. United Kingdom* to pursue the legitimate aim of regulating population to prevent overdevelopment and maintaining of the economy. However, refusal of both temporary and permanent licenses to the applicants, who returned to live in a house on Guernsey which they had built 20 years before was found disproportionate. In the balancing exercise, the Court emphasised the importance of "home" as pertinent to personal security and well-being and that special circumstances weighed in favour of the applicant, namely, that they had been in lawful occupation, had rented out the house as part of the available housing stock on the island which now needed repairs and no one else could have lived there in the meantime. In contrast, in *Wiggins v. United Kingdom*,[8] the applicant, who on divorce from a local Guernsey resident, lost his exempt status and was refused a licence, was not subject to a disproportionate interference since he was offered the possibility of applying for a licence to occupy part of the property (which consisted of three flats) and if he carried out certain alterations.

---

[7] See, also, *e.g. U.K.* 15434/89, (Dec.) February 15, 1990, 64 D.R. 232, where the applicant who let property by way of licenses to prevent application of Rent Acts was affected by a House of Lords judgment requiring courts to look at the true legal nature of transactions and not give effect to sham devices to avoid rent acts. The Commission referred to the wide margin of appreciation enjoyed by States in determining and remedying social problems and found that it was not a disporportionate effect to reduce rent by some £45.

[8] *U.K.* 7456/76, (Dec.) February 8, 1978, 13 D.R. 40.

Cross-reference

Part IIB: Expropriation and confiscation
Part IIB: Home
Part IIB: Planning and control of use of propery
Part IIB: Property rights

Immigration and expulsion

Key provisions:

Article 3 (inhuman and degrading treatment); Article 8 (respect for private and family life); Article 13 (effective remedy before national authority); Article 14 (prohibition against discrimination) and Article 2 of the First Protocol (right to education). Article 3 of Protocol No. 4 (specific prohibition of expulsion of nationals) has not been ratified by the United Kingdom.

Key case law:

Abdulaziz, Cabales and Balkandali v. U.K., May 28, 1985, Series A, No. 94; 7 E.H.R.R. 471; *Moustaquim v. Belgium*, February 18, 1991, Series A, No. 193; 13 E.H.R.R. 802; *Soering v. U.K.*, July 7, 1989, Series A, No. 161; 11 E.H.R.R. 439; *Berrehab v. Netherlands*, June 21, 1988, Series A, No. 138; 11 E.H.R.R. 322; *Cruz Varas v. Sweden*, March 20, 1991, Series A, No. 201; 14 E.H.R.R. 1; *Vilvarajah v. U.K.*, October 30, 1991, Series A, No. 215; 14 E.H.R.R. 248; *Beldjoudi v. France*, March 26, 1992, Series A, No. 234–A; 14 E.H.R.R. 801; *Nasri v. France*, July 13, 1995, Series A, No. 324; 21 E.H.R.R. 458; *Gul v. Switzerland*, February 19, 1996, R.J.D. 1996–I No. 3; *Boughanemi v. France*, April 24, 1996, R.J.D. 1996–II, No. 8; *C v. Belgium*, August 7, 1996, R.J.D., 1996–III, No. 12; *Chahal v. U.K.*, November 15, 1996, R.J.D., 1996–V, No. 22; *Nsona v. Netherlands*, November 28, 1996, R.J.D., 1996–V, No. 23; *Ahmut v. Netherlands*, November 28, 1996, R.J.D., 1996–VI, No. 24; *Ahmed v. Austria*, December 17, 1997, R.J.D., 1996–VI, No. 26; *Bouchelkia v. France*, January 29, 1997, R.J.D., 1997–I, No. 28; *H.L.R. v. France*, April 29, 1997, R.J.D., 1997–III, No. 36; *D v. U.K.*, May 2, 1997, R.J.D., 1997–III, No. 37; *Mehemi v. France*, September 26, 1997, R.J.D., 1997–VI, No. 51; *El Boujaïdi*, September 26, 1997, R.J.D., 1997–VI, No. 51; *Boujlifa v. France*, October 21, 1997, R.J.D., 1997–VI, No. 54.

A. Introduction

1. General considerations

Immigration, and the arrival of people seeking asylum, if once tolerated or encouraged by Western European States for economic reasons or by virtue of political and philosophical conviction, are now subject to increasing restrictions. This has an effect not only on those outsiders seeking entry but also on people belonging to long-established communities in Contracting States, who do not enjoy full citizenship status and find the host authorities depressingly keen to resort to deportation as a measure of control. A not insignificant number of countries have changed their laws of nationality and citizenship placing the possibility of obtaining security of residence for non-nationals and their families even further out of reach.

The Convention organs are not immune to the general atmosphere of "Fortress Europe". They recognise the legitimate concerns of immigration control, without questioning too deeply the motivation behind it.[1] It is an area where, given the current political sensitivity of the issues, the Convention organs are unlikely to give vent to much

---

[1] See, *e.g. Moustaquim*, para. 43: "The Court does not in anyway underestimate the Contracting States' concern to maintain law and order, in particular in exercising their right, as a matter of well-established international law and subject to their treaty obligations, to control the entry, residence and expulsion of aliens." Also, *Abdulaziz*, para. 67: "the Court cannot ignore that this present case is concerned not only with family life, but also with immigration . . .".

creative interpretation. Their record may, to some, be disappointing. Immigrant communities and refugees are particularly vulnerable and, it might be thought, in special need of protection. The Commission has been responsive to the hardship disclosed in some cases and there have been a number of settlements which have left the issues on the merits unresolved. Both Commission and Court have found violations where the exercise of the power to expel has exceeded what they find acceptable. However, overall, the case law is negative, discloses disagreement between the Commission and Court, and can be criticised as logically inconsistent.

There are two important groups of cases. The first concerns situations where applicants claim that the expulsion will expose them to torture or ill-treatment — this will often be a refugee case, where the applicant has applied unsuccessfully for asylum under the Geneva Convention[2] or where refugee status has been revoked. The second concerns decisions by immigration authorities to expel, or refuse entry to, persons seeking to remain with or join other family members. There are also associated issues of private life, denial of education where children are obliged to accompany a parent who is being expelled; and the effectiveness of remedies for applicants claiming to be at risk of torture and ill-treatment or interference with their family lives.

Before dealing with the substantive issues, the problem of exhaustion of domestic remedies deserves individual mention.

2. Exhaustion of domestic remedies

The requirement for exhaustion of domestic remedies applies in the normal way. Special considerations arise as to the "effectiveness" of remedies as regards the scope of the review of immigration decisions offered by domestic authorities and having regard to the potential irreversibility of expulsions where individuals may face death or torture on their return.

The Commission's case law establishes that a remedy without suspensive effect is not effective for expulsion complaints for the purposes of Article 26 where there is a risk of persecution.[3] Where a person, if successful in the application, could later return from the country to which they had been sent and where there were no allegations of ill-treatment, lack of suspensive effect did not render an available remedy ineffective.[4]

Where a person alleges risk of death or ill-treatment if expelled, the Court, differing from the Commission (see below: Access to Court and Remedies) has found in the context of Article 13 that judicial review furnishes an effective remedy for the decision refusing asylum or entry. Consequently, judicial review must be considered in light of current case law as potentially an effective remedy which must be exhausted if the case is to be declared admissible.

An application can be rejected as premature as in a French case concerning Tamils, where the request for asylum had been refused but no expulsion order had been made and it was still possible once the order issued to appeal to the administrative courts which would have suspensive effect. This avenue of appeal was rigorous since it required a written application to be made within 24 hours of service of the expulsion order (although an applicant had the right to ask for an interpreter and legal counsel). The applicants' arguments that this rendered the appeal nugatory as a safeguard in practice were unsuccessful before the Commission, and ultimately the Court, indicating a somewhat strict approach.[5]

---

[2] United Nations 1951 Convention on the Status of Refugees.

[3] See, e.g. 7465/76, (Dec.) September 29, 1976, 7 D.R. 153; 14312/88 Germany, (Dec.) March 8, 1989, 60 D.R. 284.

[4] See, e.g. 12097/86, (Dec.) July 13, 1987, 53 D.R. 210 where a Swiss, Austrian and Algerian, complaining under, inter alia, Arts. 8 and 9 were to be expelled from Denmark.

[5] Vijayanathan and Pusparajah v. France, August 27, 1992, Series A, No. 241–B, there was no decision yet to expel and the risk of an irreversible step being taken was mitigated by the possibility of an appeal — the Court upheld the Government's preliminary objection that the applicants could not yet claim to be victims.

However, in special circumstances, the Commission has found that a failure to pursue domestic remedies through non-compliance with procedural formalities may not disclose a basis for rejecting an application for non-exhaustion. The Commission has considered that, where there is a serious allegation that an applicant will be ill-treated if he is expelled, the domestic authorities should examine the case on the merits. This was the approach adopted in *Bahaddar v. Netherlands*.[6] The case concerned a Bangladeshi, with an apparent history of involvement in an armed separatist movement, whose asylum appeal was rejected as inadmissible when his lawyer failed to submit grounds within the time-limit. There had been a dispute as to the authenticity of the documents submitted by the applicant to substantiate his claims and it had taken the applicant time to obtain further information from Bangladesh. This conflict of facts had not been the basis of any examination of the merits. There was also reference to a judge's finding on an interim measure that on the new evidence the existence of well-grounded fear of persecution could not be excluded.

B. Expulsion: risk of ill-treatment

1. Responsibility of the expelling Government

While there is no right to asylum as such guaranteed under the Convention, where an applicant faces a real risk of torture or ill-treatment, including extra-judicial or arbitrary execution[7] on expulsion to a particular country, issues arise under Article 3 of the Convention. This is also where the Commission may apply Rule 36 of its Rules of Procedure to request interim measures suspending the measure pending the Strasbourg proceedings (see Part IA3: Interim Relief — Rule 36). Where there is a real risk of a "flagrant denial" of Articles 5 and 6 rights on return to a country, issues may arise engaging the responsibility of the expelling State.[8] However, these issues have not been explored in any substantive way in the cases so far.

Under Article 3, the obligation of the State extends in respect of everyone within their jurisdiction to a duty not to expose them to an irremediable situation of objective danger even outside their jurisdiction.[9] The argument of the United Kingdom Government in *Soering v. United Kingdom* that a State should not be held accountable for acts committed outside its jurisdiction was rejected by the Court which found that Article 3 enshrined one of the fundamental values of the democratic societies making up the Council of Europe and considered that the provision should be interpreted so as to make its safeguards practical and effective. A State cannot therefore deport any persons with callous and convenient disregard for their likely fate once they have left its soil.

Responsibility arises whether the source of the risk is the Government or authorities in the receiving State or other groups, such as rival warring or political factions[10] or organised

---

[6] *Bahaddar v. Netherlands*, 25894/94, (Dec.) May 22, 1995, (Rep.) September 13, 1996. The Court however, in its judgment of February 19, 1998, upheld the Government's non-exhaustion objection, finding it was still possible for the applicant to lodge a fresh application in the Dutch courts.

[7] Since judicial execution is provided for in Art. 2 of the Convention, the mere fact of the possibility of execution following judicial process may not be sufficient: elements of the treatment received during the process (*e.g.* death row phenomenon), lack of judicial safeguards, disproportionate nature of the sentence would however be relevant.

[8] See, *Soering*, para. 113 and *Drozd and Janousek v. France and Spain*, June 26, 1992, para. 110; *M.A.R. v. U.K.*, 28038/95 (Dec.), January 16, 1997, admissible, where the applicant, a convicted drugs offender, to be expelled to Iran to an alleged islamic justice system without the least procedural safeguard under Arts 5 and 6, as well as risk of treatment contrary to Art. 3.

[9] *Kirkwood v. U.K.*, 19479/83, (Dec.) March 12, 1984, 37 D.R. 158: an extradition to the United States where the applicant complained of the risk of facing the death penalty.

[10] 23985–87–88/94, (Dec.) November 28, 1994: concerning deportation of Lebanese applicants who alleged that the Hezbollah would target them as Israeli collaborators, where the Commission cited an Amnesty report which described the Hezbollah as an important political force with semi-governmental services and the largest faction in the Parliament.

crime groups,[11] where there is no indication of the authorities being able to provide protection.[12] The Commission seemed also prepared to accept risk to a Lebanese woman from her husband's family of being confined to a rigorous form of "house arrest" for refusal to comply with her husband's wishes in conformity with a local tradition.[13]

Threat to life may also arise from impact of an expulsion on a person's health apart from deliberately inflicted injury by others. For example, Rule 36 was applied by the Commission where the removal of a pregnant woman with a history of premature labour posed a significant risk to the life of the unborn child, although the application was later rejected under Article 3 when after the birth there was no apparent risk to health to mother or child from an expulsion at that time.[14] The psychological impact of the threatened expulsion to Algeria of the applicant Nasri, born deaf and dumb, was found by the Commission to constitute treatment of such severity as to violate Article 3. It had regard to his upbringing since the age of four in France where all his family lived and to the fact that his communication and perception skills were those of a 7–8 year old. The expulsion threatened him with prolonged sensory deprivation in an unfamiliar environment and to inflict on him such fear and anguish might humiliate him and crush his personality.[15]

The proposed expulsion of the applicant suffering from AIDS from the United Kingdom to St Kitts where he would no longer receive drugs treatment and had no family to care for him, was found in breach of Article 3, although the Court referred to exceptional circumstances and compelling humanitarian considerations. By the time of the Court hearing the applicant was in extreme ill-health and it seems implied that in less drastic cases, a different result might be reached.

2. Type of ill-treatment alleged

The type of ill-treatment to be established is, in line with Article 3 case law,[16] severe. Generally, a significant risk to health, physical or psychological, from deliberate ill-treatment or conditions has to be alleged. However, even alleged risk to life is generally still considered in the context of Article 3. The Commission has stated that Article 2 would only be in issue where the loss of life was a "near certainty" as a consequence of the expulsion.[17]

The following are generally not covered: risk of criminal trial and imprisonment following a criminal conviction or for desertion[18]; economic hardship; risk of difficulties in travelling through military checkpoints from lack of identity cards[19]; refusal of a passport

---

[11] *H.L.R. v. France,* where the applicant alleged that on return to Colombia he would be at risk from the drug trafficking circles regarding whom he had given information to the French authorities. The Court, unlike the Commission, found that the risk was not substantiated.

[12] *e.g. Ahmed v. Austria,* where a violation was found in respect of the proposed expulsion of the applicant to Somalia in a state of civil war where he risked treatment contrary to Art. 3 with no indication of any public authority being able to protect him.

[13] 25849/94 Sweden, (Dec.) November 16, 1994. Rule 36 was applied, though the case was later rejected as the applicant had not substantiated that she was at any real risk of such treatment.

[14] *Poku and others v. U.K.,* 26985/95, (Dec.) May 15, 1996, unpublished; also *Choudry v. U.K.,* 27949/95, (Dec.) May 13, 1996, unpublished: where a woman had a history of psychiatric illness, with medical evidence indicating that the stress of removal to an environment where little treatment was available would lead to a risk of suicide, the case was communicated by the Commission but declared inadmissible when she moved to Ireland and the risk of expulsion disappeared.

[15] *Nasri v. France.* The Court, finding a breach of the right to respect for family life under Art. 8, strangely found it unnecessary to look at the Art. 3 allegations in respect of the same removal.

[16] See Part IIB: Torture. Inhuman and degrading treatment.

[17] *Bahaddar,* see n.6.

[18] *Popescu and Cucu v. France,* 28152–3/95, (Dec.) September 11, 1995: existence of criminal proceedings in Romania not enough to raise issues on expulsion from France of Romanian applicants; 7334/76, (Dec.) March 8, 1976, 5 D.R. 154: deserter from Jordanian army in 1967 war; see also cases of persons evading military service in the Serbian army, *e.g.* 22508/93 *R.B. family v. Sweden and Finland,* (Dec.) October 21, 1993 and *Tahiri v. Sweden,* 25129/94, (Dec.) January 11, 1995 (concerning a Muslim Kosovo Albanian being returned to Serbia).

[19] *Vilvarajah.*

on return[20]; threat of prosecution and heavy sentence (*e.g.* ten years) for conscientious objection to service in the army.[21]

However, threat of prosecution for political offences may constitute Article 3 treatment, although the Commission considered that there must be a definite and serious risk of being prosecuted on such a basis and of receiving a long and severe sentence if convicted.[22]

3. Absolute right

The right under Article 3 is absolute. Once a risk of Article 3 treatment is established, the threat posed by the applicant cannot reduce the level of protection afforded by the Convention. Thus in *Chahal v. United Kingdom*, the Court rejected the Government argument that the risk to the Sikh applicant, an alleged terrorist, on return to India had to be weighed against the threat to United Kingdom security if he remained. The Convention guarantee is thus wider than the Geneva Convention pursuant to which a refugee can forfeit his status. A Contracting State has to make do (not unreasonably perhaps) with using its criminal law to deal with any threat posed by a person on its territory.[23]

Similarly, where refugee status has been granted, a State will be required to have proper reasons for revoking that status and expelling the individual. In *Ahmet v. Austria*, a conviction of an applicant for robbery did not justify the revocation of his refugee status and proposed expulsion, in the absence of any circumstances rebutting the risk of persecution.

4. Existence and assessment of risk

An applicant has to substantiate that he faces a real risk of torture or ill-treatment.[24]

(a) *Imminence and safeguards*

Expulsion must be imminent and not subject to safeguards diminishing the risk.[25]

Where the applicant to be expelled suffers from problems of health or disability, assurances by the expelling State that steps will be taken to ensure appropriate treatment have proved relevant.[26] Adverse comment was made by the Commission in finding violations in *Nasri v. France*, and *D v. United Kingdom* of the absence of any steps taken by the expelling Government as regards verifying the available facilities or treatment.[27]

---

[20] *Beldjoudi*, (Rep.) para. 74.

[21] See, *e.g.* 11017/84, (Dec.) March 13, 1986, 46 D.R. 176: applicant was to be expelled from Germany to the former Yugoslavia pre-outbreak of conflict.

[22] 11933/86 *Switzerland*, (Dec.) April 14, 1986, 46 D.R. 257, where Turkish applicant alleged that on his return he would be prosecuted for political activities conducted abroad against the regime in Turkey or receive a long sentence. The case cites an extradition case which refers to unjustified or disproportionate sentence but complaints rejected as not made out on the facts.

[23] *Chahal*, judgment paras 79–81, (Rep.) para. 104.

[24] See, *e.g. Vilvarajah* judgment paras 103 and 111.

[25] See, *e.g. Vijayanathan*, (Rep.) September 5, 1995, paras 118–121; 27249/95 *Sweden*, (Dec.) September 15, 1995, 83–A D.R. 91, where two 16–17 year old Ugandan brothers were held in Sweden in psychiatric care *inter alia*, for suicidal tendencies, their complaints under Art. 3 regarding an outstanding expulsion order were rejected since the Commission found that no enforcement of the order would be possible while compulsory medical care was necessary and, further, the police were under instructions only to enforce the order if the applicants would be met in Uganda by a representative of the Ugandan child welfare authority and a representative of the Swedish consulate.

[26] *Kebe v. France*, 29244/95, April 18, 1996, the applicant's complaints of expulsion to Senegal on the basis of his mental illness were rejected under Arts. 3 and 8 since, *inter alia*, the French Government had ensured that appropriate care would be available on his return; 31362/96, (Dec.) January 23, 1997 where French Government stated the expulsion of the applicant to Morocco would only occur on the basis that his treatment in appropriate establishment for his mental conditions would be guaranteed which Commission found sufficient even if level of care would differ from that available in France.

[27] *Nasri*, (Rep.) para. 61; *D v. U.K.*, (Rep.) para. 59.

Available safeguards have also been of crucial relevance where the expulsion is of children, with the ill-treatment alleged deriving from the circumstances of their removal. Safeguards such as ensuring reception by welfare authorities and the existence of a care structure in the receiving State can be identified as reducing any alleged risk of psychological or physical harm. The failure of the Netherlands Government to investigate the personal situation of a nine-year-old girl who was being returned to Zaire or to take adequate steps themselves to ensure that she was properly met on her return received critical comment in *Nsona v. Netherlands* but since Swissair had taken their own initiatives the Government escaped a finding of violation.

Assurances made by the Governments of receiving States may be relevant but are scrutinised carefully. In *Chahal*,[28] an assurance of the Indian Government given to the United Kingdom authorities that the applicant, a Sikh militant, would receive the same legal protection as any other Indian citizen on his return did not satisfy the Convention organs as providing an effective guarantee.[29] It is perhaps conceivable that in a particular case a Government could provide sufficient guarantees to offset an alleged risk of ill-treatment but the quality of the guarantees would presumably have to increase in persuasiveness where the evidence of risk was strong or the nature of the risk particularly grave.

Where a person claims ill-treatment if expelled to a Contracting State, the Commission has previously given weight to the possibility of an applicant exercising the right of individual petition, presumably on the basis that a State's adherence to the Convention renders risk of ill-treatment less likely to materialise, taking into account the mechanisms which should be in place to safeguard the guaranteed fundamental rights.[30] That problems may however arise in Contracting States is illustrated by CPT (Committee for the Prevention of Torture) reports and statements on conditions in places of detention which have recently revealed serious problems. While a violation based on a proposed expulsion from one Contracting State has yet to be found, the Commission has applied Rule 36 to an expulsion from France to Spain of an ETA member, possibly motivated by severe criticisms of the methods of the *guardia civil* by the CPT and to an expulsion of a Kurd from the Netherlands to Turkey.[31]

(b) *Substantiating the level of the risk*

The Court holds that, given the absolute character of the provision and the fact it enshrines one of the fundamental values of the democratic societies making up the Council of Europe, its examination of the existence of a risk of ill-treatment in breach of Article 3 must be rigorous. It will if necessary, assess the risk in light of material obtained *proprio motu*.[32]

The mere possibility of ill-treatment is not enough.[33] Thus it may not be sufficient for an applicant to point to general unsettled situation in a country or his membership in a group that occasionally faces problems.[34] It seems that the applicant has to establish that

---

[28] *Chahal*, judgment, para. 105 and (Rep.) para. 113.

[29] In light of the consideration that there was insufficient judicial control of police activities targeting Sikhs.

[30] *e.g.* 12543/86, (Dec.) December 2, 1986, 51 D.R. 272; 28152–3/95, *Popescu and Cucu v. France* see n.36, where applicants could invoke the ECHR in Roumania.

[31] 31113/96, *France*, (Dec.) December 5, 1996. France did not comply and returned the applicant but did apparently take the precaution of handing him to the ordinary police not the *guardia civil*. Since he did not receive any ill-treatment, the Commission rejected the complaints under Art. 3 as manifestly ill-founded; *Netherlands*, 33124/96, (Dec.) February 25, 1997 partly admissible, where the applicant claims he would be subject to ill-treatment, as member of a family involved in illegal separatist activities.

[32] *Vilvarajah*, paras 107–108.

[33] *ibid.*, para. 111.

[34] *e.g. Tahiri v. Sweden*, 25129/94, (Dec.) January 11, 1995 where the Commission found no problem under Art. 3 to send back to Serbia a Muslim Kosovo Albanian and also 22508/93, (Dec.) October 21, 1993, where a Muslim family complained of being sent back to Serbia to an area where Muslims were subject to harassment.

he faces a specific, personal risk of treatment contrary to Article 3. In *Vilvarajah v. United Kingdom* concerning the expulsion of five Tamil applicants to Sri Lanka, the Court did not consider that it was enough that the situation was unsettled or that some Tamils might possibly be detained or ill-treated. This threat was apparently not specific enough to these five applicants, even in light of the fact that during the Convention proceedings three of the applicants were subjected to ill-treatment in Sir Lanka. The Court found that there was no special feature which would have enabled the Secretary of State to foresee that they would be treated in this way.

Presumably however where there are indications of a high level of risk attaching to membership of a particular group it should be possible to establish the requisite substantiation of risk to the particular person, where at least the person is known to be implicated or wanted in connection with that group's activities. The difficulties of reaching an assessment of risk to a particular person are demonstrated in *Paez v. Sweden*[35] where the Commission by 15 votes to 14 found no violation if the applicant was returned to Peru. He was a supporter of the Sendero Luminoso, a terrorist group, and members of his family had been arrested and one had disappeared. However, the majority noted that he was not a leading member, had not participated in any terrorist atrocities and in particular he could not point to any warrant of arrest or similar evidence which would show that he would be of particular interest to the authorities. The minority members noted, *inter alia*, that his mother and sisters had been granted asylum; that the refusal to the applicant seemed to rely on his terrorist affiliations, a ground not relevant under Article 3; and that the interest shown by the Peruvian press in the ayslum seekers in Sweden was a significant factor increasing the risk.[36]

Risk must exist at the time when the person is expelled, or is to be expelled. There was evidence supporting the allegations of the applicant *Cruz Varaz* that he had suffered torture at some time in the past but his complaints concerning his expulsion to Chile failed since at the time when he was returned democratic developments had begun in the country and the voluntary return of refugees had commenced. Conversely in *Chahal* (para. 80)[37] the Commission and Court found that, despite apparent improvements in the human rights record of India with respect to Sikhs, including the creation of a National Human Rights Commission, they were still not satisfied that the police in the Punjab in particular and security forces elsewhere in the country were under effective democratic control. Thus, there was a real risk that the applicant, a high profile and leading Sikh militant, would be a target of special interest on his return and there were substantial grounds for believing that he would be exposed to a real risk of ill-treatment.

Where a person is not yet expelled but subject to an expulsion order, the time which is relevant for assessing risk is not the time when the order was made but the time when he may be deported.[38] Previous conditions only remain relevant to the extent that they cast light on the present situation.

(c) *Factors and materials taken into account*

Existence of a real risk may be supported by previous incidences of ill-treatment on arrest and detention, in respect of which medical and psychiatric reports are very useful, if not

---

[35] *Paez v. Sweden* 29482/95, (Rep.) December 6, 1996; settled before the Court, October 30, 1997, R.J.D. 1997–VII, No. 56.

[36] *Bahaddar*, see n.27, the necessary level of risk was found where applicant involved in minor way in the Shanti Bahini a group using violent means to achieve autonomy of Chittagong Hill Tracts in Bangladesh and though not able to prove arrest warrant against him, he had been named as obtaining funds for them in a court case introduced by a private person.

[37] *Chahal*, judgment paras 99–107, (Rep.) paras 108–114.

[38] At the time the Commission or Court considers the case if the person has not been expelled, *e.g. Chahal*, para. 97.

essential. Also relevant are considerations whether an applicant's involvement in opposition has been publicised and likely to be known to the authorities or other groups in the receiving State. The Commission and Court will refer to Amnesty Reports and the UNHCR as well as reports by the UN Committee against Torture and country reports of the U.S. State Department, and these sources may be regarded as highly relevant but are at most persuasive.[39] The reports of the CPT promise to be particularly relevant as concerns Contracting States.[40]

Factors which cast doubt on an applicant's case include inconsistencies in accounts to national authorities and the existence of serious doubts as to the authenticity of the documents.[41] Weight, often decisive, is given to domestic authorities' experience in dealing with applications.[42] Applicants must therefore be able to point to flaws or shortcomings in any assessment by the domestic authorities of the merits of their case.

(d) *Shuttlecocking*

State immigration policies sometimes give rise to the risk of asylum seekers or stateless persons being shunted from country to country. "Shuttlecocking" was an element in the Commission's finding of a violation of Article 3 in the *East African Asians* case,[43] where applicants holding British citizenship were refused entry to the United Kingdom and in some cases, forced to and fro unable to obtain entry to the United Kingdom or elsewhere.

The Commission has also stated that the repeated expulsion of an individual, whose identity it is impossible to establish, to a country where his admission is not guaranteed, may raise an issue, particularly where an alien is deported over a long period of time repeatedly from one country to another without any country taking measures to regularise his position.[44] Deliberate steps to render oneself stateless are however likely to prejudice a case.[45]

---

[39] *e.g.* UNHCR figures and reports referred to in *Vilvarajah* dealing with situation in Sri Lanka and mention of Amnesty International's position on return without detail given; *Ahmed v. Austria*, (Rep.), the Commission requested the United Nations High Commissioner for Refugees (UNHCR) for recent information on the situation in Somalia and cited its opinion as to the risk posed by inter tribe rivalry, *Paez* see n.35, cites CAT (UN Committee Against Torture), Peru's report to ECOSOC, U.S. State Department Report and the HRC report on Peru as well as Human Rights Watch and Amnesty International.

[40] *e.g.* its First Public Statement on Turkey was cited in *Aydin v. Turkey*, 23178/94, (Rep.), March 7, 1996, para. 159.

[41] *e.g. Nsangu v. Austria*, 25661/94, (Rep.), May 22, 1995 where Commission noted inconsistencies in story (*i.e.* it was not claimed that her husband was an active member of opposition party until second renewed asylum proceedings, and there were doubts about the documents, *e.g.* how her husband obtained particular documents allegedly showing he was wanted by the Zairean authorities). Also 31026/96, *Netherlands*, (Dec.) October 24, 1996 where the Commission noted the alleged arrest warrant was undated and contained outdated wording in a form not used since 1990 and thus found no substantiation of any real risk of ill-treatment of woman who claimed that she had been raped because she had refused to marry a general in Zaire. See also the strong weight given by the Court in *Nsona* to the fact that the aunt lied trying to bring her niece in, presenting a forged entry in a document naming her as being her own daughter. In those circumstances Dutch authorities could not be blamed for refusing, once this was discovered, to accept allegations unsupported by evidence and no interference with respect to family life could be imputed to the Government.

[42] *Cruz Varas*, para. 81 and also many cases before the Commission where references are made quoting the findings of the domestic authorities.

[43] 4403/70 and others, (Rep.), December 14, 1973, 78–A D.R. 5.

[44] 7729/76, (Rep.) July 17, 1980, 21 D.R. 73: the applicant was of African origin with no identity papers, subject to a series of arrests in Belgium, moving to and fro from one country to another. The case was settled when he left for Senegal, in agreement with the Belgian Government who gave him a travel document. See also 10978/84 (Dec.), March 5, 1986, 46 D.R. 112: the applicant of Algerian origin claiming to be stateless was repeatedly expelled from the Netherlands over 20 times. The Commission found that he was primarily responsible for his plight; for example, he had not taken steps to seek Algerian citizenship, nor shown why he could not do so nor substantiated that he was ever expelled to the Netherlands from Belgium rather than going back of his own free will.

[45] *Popescu and Cucu*, see n.18, where the applicants renounced their Romanian citizenship in an apparent effort to render themselves stateless and avoid expulsion from France.

(e) *Expulsion of children*

Issues have arisen as to whether the manner of implementation of expulsion or its effects are so traumatic for children as to constitute treatment contrary to Article 3.

Proposed expulsions of children where it has been alleged that there is no one to care for them on arrival in the receiving State have been declared admissible under Article 3. Two such cases settled, *Taspinar v. Netherlands*[46] where the applicant, resident in the Netherlands, brought his son to the Netherlands but was refused a residence permit for him with the result that the seven/eight year old boy was to be sent back to Turkey where allegedly no one remained to take care of him and *Bulus v. Sweden*, where a Syrian boy who had lived on the run for two years avoiding expulsion was threatened with return to Syria, where he would allegedly have had to fend for himself.[47] However, in *Nsona*, where a nine-year-old girl was sent back to Zaire, while there was critical comment made of the failure of the Dutch authorities properly to investigate her personal situation and to take adequate measures in respect of her arrival, the circumstances did not reach the minimum level of severity prohibited by Article 3, in particular since the girl was not left unattended at the airport due to the initiative of the airline and she was brought back to the people previously taking care of her.

In exceptional circumstances, the conditions facing children on expulsion to another country may disclose treatment of such a severe nature as to inflict on them inhuman and degrading treatment contrary to Article 3. A high threshold is set for treatment from mere change of environment and living standards to fall within the scope of Article 3 and allegations require specific and concrete substantiation.

In *Fadele v. United Kingdom*, children, with British citizenship, living in the United Kingdom lost their mother in an accident and the Nigerian father was refused leave to join the children in the United Kingdom, with the consequence that the children were forced to join him in Nigeria. The case was declared admissible, reflecting the extreme hardship which the children faced, but not resolved on the merits, since the case settled when the father was granted residence and the family returned.[48] However, in *Sorabjee v. United Kingdom*,[49] where the three-year-old British child was threatened with removal to Kenya with her mother who was being expelled, the Commission found that difficulties in obtaining treatment for problems with her hands and the risk of isolation from the Asian and African communities did not expose her to risk of treatment within the scope of Article 3. In *P.P. v. United Kingdom*,[49a] where children, British citizens, were obliged to accompany their mother to Jamaica, the alleged risk to their psychological health and physical well-being from the change in environment was found to be unsubstantiated: there was only mention of one child having suffered rashes. Similarly, in *Jaramillo v. United Kingdom*, the Commission found the alleged risk to a four-year-old child if sent to Colombia where his father was involved in drug trafficking circles did not disclose any substantiated or immediate risk.[50]

The situation where a child has the right to stay in a Contracting State but the custodial parent is being expelled also does not in the Commission's view constitute Article 3 treatment, even though it places the parent in the dilemma of taking the child, who will

[46] 11026/84, (Rep.) October 9, 1985, 44 D.R. 262: leave to remain given.
[47] *Bulus v. Sweden*, 9330/81, 35 D.R. 57, (Dec.) January 19, 1984 and 39 D.R. 75 (Rep.): limited leave to remain and compensation given.
[48] The family lived in a compound which was filthy, with open sewers. The children attended no school and spoke no Nigerian language. The youngest suffered bouts of malaria including convulsions requiring blood transfusions and hospitalisation and all three suffered from typhoid, respiratory infections and gastro-entiritis — 13078/87, (Rep.) July 4, 1991, 70 D.R. 159.
[49] 23938/93, (Dec.) October 23, 1995, unpublished.
[49a] 25297/94, (Dec.) January 16, 1996.
[50] 24865/94, (Dec.) October 23, 1995, unpublished.

then lose educational and other advantages, or of leaving it in the United Kingdom in care. The Commission appears to find it compatible with the requirements of Article 3 that the parent has the opportunity to bring the child and they are not forced to be separated.[51] The mere loss of benefits to which the children are entitled by their citizenship is not enough.[52]

C. Effect on family life

Apart from Article 3 ill-treatment issues, the principal ground on which expulsion measures have been contested has been Article 8 in respect of its disruption of "family life".

Approach to the cases is a balancing exercise whether viewed as interference where a decision is taken to expel a person previously lawfully resident or an allegation of failure to comply with a positive obligation to respect family life by granting entry. In weighing the individual's interest against the general policy concerns, a restrictive approach is taken to almost every factor: from the weight given to the nature of family life concerned, the importance of immigration concerns and public order, the high threshold of acceptable hardships to individuals and the wide margin of appreciation afforded to the State.

1. Existence of family links

(a) "Family life"

For the Court, where a child is born of a marriage, there is *ipso iure* family life between the parent and child, which only exceptional circumstances can break. This has been extended to parent-child relationships where there has been no cohabitation or marriage.[53] The fact in *C v. Belgium* that the father was imprisoned, then deported or that his son went to live with an aunt did not constitute exceptional circumstances. The Court did not comment on the aunt-niece relationship in *Nsona*.

The Commission in older cases excluded the mere existence of blood ties as being sufficient save between married parents and their minor children.[54] It has held that adult children and their parents and the other categories of relatives must show ties of dependency going beyond normal emotional ties, *e.g.* monetary and practical, evidence of regular contact.[55] This does not make allowance for the extended families found in some cultures,[56] or where families are poor, unable to contribute to each others support financially and are separated over time with no opportunity to make contact and develop demonstrable relationships. It is perhaps doubtful that this approach still applies to adult children-parent relationships in view of the Court's approach above.

---

[51] See, *e.g. Singh v. U.K.* 22471/93, (Dec.) September 6, 1994, unpublished, mother was expelled while children remained in the United Kingdom as wards of court. However there was evidence that the mother consented to wardship and the family took that step on behalf of the children, since they did not want them to leave with her, *i.e.* there was no forcible separation.

[52] See *Sorabjee v. U.K.*, see n.49; *Jaramillo v. U.K.*, 24865/94, see n.50 and *P.P. v. U.K.*, see n.49a.

[53] *Gul*, para. 32; *Boughanemi*, para. 35.

[54] In *Berrehab*, the Commission stated that cohabitation was not an essential factor in the context of parents and minor children 10370/84, (Dec.) March 8, 1985 41 D.R. 196.

[55] *e.g.* 9492/81, (Dec.) July 14, 1982, 30 D.R. 232 no "family" life was found by the Commission between the applicant Cypriot family and the parents' adult sisters who lived in the United Kingdom where there was an absence of any special links of dependency.

[56] The Commission left open in *Askar v. U.K.* 26373/95, (Dec.) October 16, 1995 whether the applicant's mother, two sisters, seven brothers and three of his children qualified as "family" in refugee family reunification case where the applicant had become head of the family in Somali terms.

(b) *Verification procedures*

Applicants seeking leave to enter often find themselves required to prove the claimed relationship with persons resident in the country. This has not been found to raise problems as long as fair opportunity has been given to present family claims.

Where an applicant complained about the procedures whereby his purported wife and son were refused entry, the Commission found that a country was entitled to set up domestic verification procedures for family claims and that it could not intervene as a supervisory body to decide if a decision was wrong but only whether the authorities acted outside what might reasonably be required of them under Article 8 in ensuring the right to respect for family life.[57] In *Miah v. United Kingdom*,[58] entry was refused to a child when the immigration authorities were not satisfied that he was the son of the putative father settled in the United Kingdom. Even though a DNA test later revealed that there was a probable relationship but entry was still refused since the son was no longer a minor, the Commission found that there was no bad faith on the part of the immigration authorities at the time of the initial refusal and there had been a fair opportunity to present the claims.

2. Spouses

The principles governing the extent of the State's obligation to admit spouses were laid down by the Court in *Abdulaziz, Cabales and Balkandali v. United Kingdom*:

- there is no general obligation on a Contracting State to respect the choice by married couples of the country of matrimonial residence;
- States enjoy a wide margin of discretion;
- it is relevant whether there are obstacles to establishing the marital home elsewhere, in the country of the spouse or applicant's own origin or whether there are any special reasons why they should not be expected to do so:
- it is relevant whether when married they were aware of the problems of entry and limited leave situation.

Since in *Abdulaziz*, there were no obstacles or special reasons and the couples were aware of their problematic immigration status at the time of marriage, no violation of Article 8 was found. It remains to be seen what relevance would or should be given to a situation where an applicant married in circumstances where neither spouse knew the problems of immigration status. Arguably, they would have to give a convincing explanation for ignorance of a potential problem. It is not obvious however that expectations at the time of marriage could ever play a significant role in finding a violation.

Many cases were, and are rejected using the above criteria, with reference to the lack of obstacles to the spoused living elsewhere and their knowledge of the precarious immigration status beforehand. Occasionally, reasons have been put forward that an applicant cannot be expected to join a spouse elsewhere — for example, health, or the fact that the spouse would leave a business or employment[59] — but the Commission so far has not accepted any as constituting a sufficient obstacle or special reasons. The fact that an applicant suffered illness on a previous visit to Pakistan was not enough[60]; where a wife submitted that she was unable to live in Bangladesh as she was constantly ill there, the Commission found "no serious obstacles" existed and noted that she had lived there herself

---

[57] 8378/78, (Dec.) May 14, 1980, 20 D.R. 168.
[58] 19546/92, *U.K.,* (Dec.) March 13, 1992, unpublished.
[59] 25073/94, *U.K.,* (Dec.) February 28, 1996, unpublished.
[60] *Akhtar v. U.K.,* 17229/90, (Dec.) February 12, 1992, unpublished.

for 12 years previously.[61] A successful claim would require strong substantiation and a high level of danger to health. However even in *Kamara v. United Kingdom*[62] where it was argued that no appropriate treatment was available in Sierra Leone for a particular intestinal disorder and epilepsy, supported by report from consultant who was the only qualified neurologist in Sierra Leone, this argument was outweighed by the fact the illness was long standing and known before the spouses married, and that the deportation order on the husband was issued before the marriage.

It may be noted that in most of these unsuccessful cases the spouse with residence rights or citizenship is nonetheless of a similar background to the spouse to be expelled, for example, having originated from the same part of the world, which will render, for the Commission's purposes, the possibility of the couple being able to set up the family unit elsewhere a practical option. Where the spouse has no such prior or family connections elsewhere, the hardship involved in setting up married life in an African or Asian country is conceivably more significant: this would appear to be the unstated reason for declaring admissible an Austrian case *Adegbie v. Austria*,[63] where the Nigerian spouse was subject to proceedings for illegal residence and threatened with deportation, which would have required his civil servant Austrian wife to accompany him to Africa. In *Beldjoudi v. France*, part of the reasoning for finding a violation in expelling the applicant to Algeria, was that his wife was French, with French parents, had always lived there and to be uprooted to go to Algeria, where she did not speak the language, would cause her real practical or even legal obstacles and the interference might therefore imperil the unity or even existence of the marriage.[64] This appears to put an unfortunate emphasis on the ethnic or racial origins of the spouse but would still appear to be only one factor in the balancing exercise against legitimate immigration interests.

The Commission has accepted that a country may exclude as a matter of policy more than one wife entering to live with a man settled in the United Kingdom. In *Bibi v. United Kingdom*,[65] the Commission found that excluding surplus wives was a legitimate aim under the second paragraph of Article 8 for the preservation of a Christian-based monogamous culture dominant in that society (as pursuing the protection of morals and of rights and freedoms of others). It also recalled its findings in an unpublished Dutch case that a Contracting State cannot be required to give full recognition to polygamous marriages in conflict with their own legal order, referring to bigamy laws.

The primary purpose rule was applied in numerous cases in the United Kingdom to refuse entry to or expel foreign spouses where the immigration authorities found that the primary purpose of the marriage was to gain entry to the United Kingdom. The Commission stopped short of ever appearing to agree with a finding of primary purpose, refraining from holding that Article 8 did not apply at all to a relationship or that there was no real marriage, rejecting cases having regard to lack of obstacles to family life being pursued elsewhere or knowledge of precarious immigration status.[66] In cases however, where a spouse had been refused, and continued to be refused, entry on the primary purpose rule but nonetheless the marriage continued for years, the partners travelling for visits and founding a family, the Commission communicated the applications to the United Kingdom. These were mostly settled or otherwise resolved. In *Goraniya v. United Kingdom*[67] (concerning a marriage of seven years and two children born) the U.K. gave leave to enter

---

[61] 18713/91, *U.K.*, (Dec.) April 1, 1992, unpublished.
[62] 24831/94 *U.K.*, (Dec.) August 31, 1994, unpublished.
[63] *Adegbie v. Austria* 26998/95, (Dec.) April 9, 1996, subsequently settled 90–A D.R. 31 (Rep.), September 15, 1997.
[64] *Beldjoudi*, para. 78.
[65] 19628/92, *U.K.*, (Dec.) June 29, 1992, unpublished.
[66] *e.g.* 14742/89, *U.K.*, (Dec.) April 4, 1990; 16382/90, *U.K.*, (Dec.) September 7, 1990.
[67] 16243/90, (Dec.) October 21, 1992.

and the applicant was found to have ceased to be a victim. In another *M v. United Kingdom*[68] (a nine-year marriage and two children) the application was struck off after the husband was given leave to enter.

3. Children

(a) *Entry to join family*

Where a child previously living apart from a parent outside a Contracting State is refused entry to join the family, violation may conceivably arise where the child has no practical alternative. However, there must be shown to be substantial existing family ties, which may be difficult where the child has lived at some distance for some time, and real obstacles to returning to the country of origin. For example in *Ahmut v. Netherlands*, the 15-year-old son left Morocco where he had been brought up by other relatives to join his father in the Netherlands. The Court noted that the boy had lived most of his life in Morocco with which he had strong linguistic and cultural links, there were other family members in Morocco, the separation was the result of the conscious decision of the father to move to the Netherlands and there was nothing to stop them continuing the degree of family life they had before. While the father might prefer to intensify his family links with his son in the Netherlands, Article 8, the Court said, did not guarantee a right to choose the most suitable place to develop family life. Since the father had arranged for the son to go to boarding school it was not necessary to examine whether the other relatives in Morocco were willing to look after him.[69]

The fact that the family is able to return to join the child may also be a decisive consideration. In *Gul v. Switzerland*, where the Turkish father lived in Switzerland and had applied unsuccessfully for his 12-year-old son to join him, the Court observed that the parents had caused the separation by moving to Switzerland and while it was admittedly difficult from a humanitarian point of view, there were no obstacles preventing them from living in Turkey, in particular since they could continue to receive their invalidity pension and benefits if they returned to Turkey and it was not proved that the mother's state of health was still such that she could not receive appropriate treatment in Turkey.

The situation would conceivably change if, in such a case as *Gul*, the parent had succeeded in obtaining refugee status, in which case the argument that the family could return would be far weaker.[70]

(b) *Expulsion of custodial parent(s)*

Whether removal or exclusion of a parent or parents from a Contracting State is incompatible with the requirements of Article 8 as regards a child with residence rights will depend on a number of factors: the extent to which family life is effectively ruptured, whether there are insurmountable obstacles in the way of the family living in the country of origin of one or more of them, whether there are factors of immigration control (*e.g.* history of breaches of immigration law) or considerations of public order (*e.g.* serious or persistent offences) weighing in favour of exclusion.[71] The age and "adaptability" of the children are regarded as particularly significant.[72]

---

[68] 13519/88, (Dec.) September 7, 1989.
[69] The Commission majority found that the correct balance had not been struck, having regard to the fact that he was a minor, the expulsion threatened his ties with his father, that his previous carer (his grandmother) was old and unlikely to care for him as she did before and that father and son had lived together for four years.
[70] The father in *Gul* had been refused refugee status though granted a residence permit.
[71] See, *e.g.* 9285/81, (Dec.) July 6, 1982, 29 D.R. 205 and 11970/86, (Dec.) July 13, 1987.
[72] See, *e.g. Sorabjee, P.P.* and *Jaramillo*, see nn.49, 49a, 50.

While the applicants have argued that weight should be given to the British citizenship of children, the Commission has found no material weight, whether obtained *ius sanguine* though a parent or through the citizenship of accident of *ius soli*.[73] The Commission was also unpersuaded by arguments as to "constructive expulsion" where a child British citizen forced by circumstances to accompany a non-national parent would be deprived of the benefits of the country of nationality and face long years of "exile" until able to return as an adult and face the difficulties adapting to life there again. Although this might constitute hardship, it would nonetheless not appear to disclose any effective bars to enjoying family life elsewhere.

Save for the case of *Fadele v. United Kingdom*,[74] no case concerning the expulsion of a custodial parent has yet been declared admissible, indicating that where young children are concerned, there are generally no obstacles to them accompanying the parent abroad.

(c) *Expulsion of divorced or separated parent*

Where a non-national parent is being expelled and the children are in the custody of the other parent (with citizenship or residence rights), after separation or divorce, family links may arguably be ruptured between parent and child since there is no possibility of the child accompanying the parent.[75]

Whether the expulsion will in this situation disclose a violation will depend on a number of factors, in particular, the nature and strength of the parent's links with the child.[76] In *Berrehab v. Netherlands*, the application was brought by father, ex-wife and child in respect of the proposed expulsion of the father, after divorce, which threatened to break the ties between father and child. The fact the parents no longer cohabited was not decisive for the existence or otherwise of family life where the relationships arose out of a lawful and genuine marriage and the father saw the child four times a week, regular and frequent contact, providing the strength of his ties. The Court also had regard to the fact the father had been lawfully resident in the Netherlands for many years, had a home and job and that the Government had no real cause for complaint against him: therefore a balance was not achieved between the interest of immigration control and the applicants' mutual interests in continuing their family ties. The illegal nature of the parent's presence in the country has however been a decisive factor in rejecting other cases.[77]

---

[73] *e.g.* 11970/86 *U.K.*, (Dec.) July 13, 1987, unpublished, where the Commission found it compatible with Art. 8 to expect children of unlawful overstayers to follow their parents even if they had acquired theoretical rights of abode in the deporting country; *Sorabjee* and *Jaramillo*, see nn.49, 50 where the children had citizenship through their fathers.

[74] See n.48.

[75] Paradoxically, an applicant who has been divorced may therefore derive a right to stay in a country to enjoy access to a child whereas those who enjoy an ongoing married relationship are expected to uproot every family member and leave.

[76] Mere allegations of interest or links are clearly not enough: there must be strong indications of an ongoing relationship and commitment, *e.g. Poku*, see n.14, where the wife also had a son by a previous relationship and the links of the son with his father in the U.K. would be affected by removal to Ghana, the Commission noted the irregular nature of the contacts and the fact it had diminished to telephone contact such that the effect on "family life" would be minimal; *Dabhi v. U.K.* 28627/95, (Dec.) January 17, 1997 where the child's father had allegedly begun to show an interest after his lack of interest to the immigration authorities but no details had been given beyond a statement that he would like to see her.

[77] *McKenzie v. U.K.*, 26285/95, (Dec.) April 9, 1997, where the mother was expelled, the separation of the child from her father with whom she enjoyed frequent contact was not disproportionate since the mother had been unlawfully in the country and started the relationship, bearing the child when her immigration status was irregular. Whereas in *Berrehab*, the relationship had developed while the father was lawfully resident and the residence was not revoked for any misconduct or breach of condition but only because the marriage to a Dutch citizen had ended.

The effect of expulsion on extended family links is rarely of decisive weight. In *Poku and others v. United Kingdom*,[78] the partner of the Ghanian woman, who was to be expelled, had himself a child by a previous marriage. If he accompanied his wife to Ghana when she was expelled, his relationship with his daughter would be affected. This was not found to outweigh the legitimate concern to expel the wife who was an overstayer with a deportation order against her when she married. It was to be assumed that he must have been aware of her precarious status and the effect on other existing family relationships. While the child could hardly be said to be in that position, the Commission found that the situation resulted from the choice of her father rather than the interference of the State.

4. "Second-generation" immigrant expulsions

Where a State seeks to expel persons who have been legally settled in their territory but who have committed offences, the Convention organs look particularly at the extent of the links of the individual with the host State and receiving State: factors of the length of time spent, knowledge/ignorance of the language or culture, existence of family links or friends in the respective countries, dependency on the family which remains behind in the Contracting State, personal circumstances such as health or psychological state which may make the removal of potentially drastic effect on the individual. These have to be balanced against the reasons for the removal and the assessment made whether the interests of the prevention of crime or disorder are proportionate to the effect of the removal on the applicant. This case-by-case approach has been criticised as a "lottery" for national authorities, lacking legal certainty and the opposing view has been put forward that there should be at least a very strong presumption that aliens who have lived most, or all, of their lives in a country should no more be expelled than nationals.[79]

Disproportionate effects were found in a number of cases, where in effect an applicant had lived most of his life in the expelling state, his family lived there and he had no real links or knowledge with the receiving State.[80] However where applicants have some links with the country of origin, they have been less successful. In *Boughanemi v. France*, the Court found it probable that he retained links with Tunisia, noting that he did not claim that he could not speak Arabic, or that he had cut off all ties. It gave particular weight to his offences and none to the fact that he lived as man and wife with a Frenchwoman and had a child, since this had occurred after the deportation order.[81] In *C v. Belgium*, the

---

[78] See nn.14, 76.

[79] See *e.g.* Morenilla J. dissenting in *Nasri* considering that the expulsion of non-nationals for misconduct was discriminatory, cruel and inhuman; also Martens J. dissenting in *Boughanemi*, considering that expulsion might be exceptionally justified only where very serious crime (terrorism or leading position in drug trafficking) was involved.

[80] *Moustaquim* had arrived in Belgium aged two, all his close relatives were there and had acquired Belgian nationality, he had received all his schooling in French and visited Morocco only twice on holiday. *Beldjoudi* had been born in France, schooled there, knew no Arabic, had no links with Algeria apart from nationality and was married to a French woman who had always lived in France. *Nasri* had arrived in France with his family at age five, received some schooling and had lived throughout with his family, being particularly dependent on them as a deaf mute. Most of his family had become French nationals, he had no ties with Algeria and no knowledge of Arabic. In *Mehemi*, the only recent case to disclose a violation before the Court, the applicant had been born in France, schooled there and most of his family lived there, including his wife and three children (who had French nationality), who could not reasonably be expected to live anywhere but in France. See also *Lamguindaz v. U.K.*, 16152/90, (Rep.), October 13, 1992, Series A, No. 258–C, settled before the Court, where the Commission found a violation of Art. 8 for expelling the applicant who had lived in the United Kingdom with his family from age 7–8, was educatd there, his close relatives lived there and no real life links with Morocco; *cf. France*, 25439/94, (Dec.), April 5, 1995, 81–A D.R. 142.

[81] The fact that the applicant in *Bouchelkia* had had a child and married a French national, after the deportation order, was also discounted.

applicant had only moved to Belgium at the later age of 11 and still had links with Morocco.[82]

While in earlier cases, the Court found that the personal interests of the applicant outweighed quite significant criminal records,[83] there has been an apparent hardening in attitude and greater sympathy given to the public order policies of Contracting States. In *Boughanemi* (four convictions, *e.g.* theft and aggravated procurement) the Commission found a violation[84] but the Court did not. While the Court found the applicant's actual links to France weak, it "above all" attached importance to the fact the deportation was decided after he had been sentenced to almost four years imprisonment for, *inter alia*, living on the earnings of prostitution in aggravating circumstances.[85] Although the applicant in *Bouchelkia v. France* had lived in France since the age of two, the factor of his conviction for rape tipped the balance towards the interests of the State in expelling him. The Court has also referred negatively to applicants' lack of desire to acquire nationality of the expelled country.[85a]

D. Effect on private life

Expulsion of persons settled in a country may disclose an interference with private life as well as family life, but the Court has so far found interferences of both justified on the subsequent balancing of individual and general interest.[86] Applicants present in the country on a short-term or provisional basis may not be able to claim an interference with any established private life.[87]

Arguments by child applicants that their forced departure to accompany their foreign mothers would deprive them of growing and developing in their country of birth and nationality were rejected in the *Sorabjee* and *Jaramillo* cases.[87a] Presumably, if there are no effective obstacles to a small child living family life with its mother elsewhere there is no obstacle to private life either. "Private life" doubtfully applies to future benefits of living in a particular environment: there must be at least something specific to existing private life or elements relating to past private life.[88] Whereas "family" life has been held to extend to the development of potential relationships by the Commission in the case of natural fathers and their children,[89] it remains to be seen whether such an approach could be accommodated under Article 8 private life aspect.

---

[82] *e.g.* he had married a woman there (later divorced).

[83] *e.g. Moustaquim* (an alleged 147 offences, mainly petty theft, carried out as an adolescent) *Beldjoudi* (seven custodial sentences, the last eight years for aggravated theft) *Nasri* (over 10 convictions, one for gang rape).

[84] The Commission's approach, more liberally, is to examine where an applicant's social and family ties are, noting that legal ties of nationality may not reflect position in human terms (Rep.) para. 75.

[85] See also *C v. Belgium*, where the Court attached great importance to a drugs offence attracting five years sentence and referred to the scourge of drug trafficking in respect of which States not surprisingly showed "great firmness"; *Bouchelkia v. France*, where similar importance was attached to a conviction of rape, the fact that he was a minor (17) at the time not detracting from its seriousness; *Boujlifa v. France*, concerning armed robbery and other robbery offences.

[85a] *e.g. Boujlifa v. France*, para. 44.

[86] *e.g. C v. Belgium*, para. 25; *Boujlifa*, para. 41; *El Boujaïdi v. France*, paras 40–41; *Boujlifa v. France*, paras 44–45: where the applicants had lived most of their lives in the expelling State.

[87] *e.g.* 9478/81, (Dec.) December 8, 1981, 27 D.R. 243, where the applicant was to be deported from Germany to Indonesia, the Commission said that to the extent that the circle of acquaintances established during her stay in Germany disclosed relationships recognised as "private life" there could be no interference since the applicant knew at all time that her presence, and hence her ability to establish relationships, was temporary and subject to revocation.

[87a] See nn.49, 50.

[88] See *Gaskin v. U.K.*, July 7, 1989, Series A, No. 160 where information about past childhood was in issue.

[89] *Keegan v. Ireland*, (Rep.) February 17, 1993, Series A, No. 298.

E. Effect on education

Expulsion of a child of school age will inevitably entail disruption of education and claims have been made under Article 2 of the First Protocol in addition to Article 8 claims. The disruption to schooling does not itself interfere with family life.[90] Education will, arguably, be available at least at elementary level if not higher in most countries. It may be difficult to argue that deportation will deny "education" as such, although it may diminish the choice or quality of the education. Also, if a deportation measure is justifiable for the aim of legitimate immigration control where there is interference with family life it would be strange if Article 2 of the First Protocol granted residence rights for the purpose of education. The Commission has on that basis dismissed in very brief terms Article 2 of the First Protocol complaints where the expulsion has been found compatible with Article 8.[91] In *Ebibomi v. U.K.*,[92] the two sons (aged 21 and 20) in full-time education claimed that they were supported by their mother financially and emotionally and if she was expelled their education would be prevented. The Commission found that the practical difficulties which might arise from the removal of their mother, which was compatible with Article 8 as a legitimate measure of immigration control, could not be construed as a deprivation of their right to education.

F. Access to Court and Remedies

The Commission considers that there is no "civil right" to nationality or to a right of residence. Article 6 has no application to asylum, expulsion or deportation proceedings or the like.[93] An applicant expelled or refused entry cannot claim a right to a court procedure to challenge the merits or lawfulness of the decision.

This is a restrictive approach, apparently based on the view that questions of entry or residence of the aliens involve discretionary acts of public authorities or are governed by public law.[94] An alien may therefore reside lawfully in a country with his family for decades and be expelled, with drastic effects on family life, private life, livelihood and health, without recourse to a court, with full procedural guarantees, to challenge the decision. In other areas (see *e.g.* social security, pensions, tax) the Commission and Court have seen less clear distinction between public and private law areas and have had regard to effect on private life with analogies to matters such as contract.[95]

Lack of access to court aside, applicants may invoke Article 13 of the Convention, a right to an effective remedy. This is subject to the precondition of Article 13 — that there is an "arguable claim" of a violation of another provision of the Convention (see Part IIB: "Remedies") and in practice will generally only become operative once a substantive complaint has been declared admissible.

The limited scope of judicial review is unlikely to be regarded as furnishing an effective remedy in cases concerning family and private life issues, where matters of factual appreciation arise. Where however an applicant is alleging risk to life or ill-treatment

---

[90] 9492/81, *U.K.* (Dec.) July 14, 1982, 30 D.R. 232, where Turkish Cypriot family were deported and claimed that the eldest son was prevented from continuing his studies unjustifiably.

[91] *Sorabjee* and *Jaramillo.*

[92] 26922/95, *U.K.,* (Dec.) November 29, 1995.

[93] 8118/77, *Switzerland,* (Dec.) March 19, 1981, 25 D.R. 105, and 9990/82, *France,* (Dec.) May 15, 1984, 39 D.R. 119; *Askar v. U.K.* 26373/95, see n.74, where the applicant, granted refugee status, complained of the length of proceedings of the case which would determine the procedures for his family to apply to join him in the U.K.: complaint rejected as incompatible *ratione materiae* under Art. 6 and manifestly ill-founded under Art. 8 since the delay could not without other prejudice disclose a lack of respect under Art. 8.

[94] 7729/76, *U.K.,* (Dec.) December 17, 1976, 7 D.R. 164 — the expulsion of a U.S. citizen from the United Kingdom on security grounds was described as an act of state falling within the public sphere.

[95] Part IIA: Fair Trial Guarantees of General Principles: Civil rights and obligations.

falling within the scope of Article 3, the Court has accepted that the "reasonableness" test of judicial review would furnish the domestic courts with the possibility of reviewing an extradition or expulsion in light of allegations of serious risk of inhuman and degrading treatment and that where a decision put a life at risk, the courts, according to Lord Bridge, would give the case the "most anxious scrutiny". Judicial review therefore furnished an effective remedy in respect of an extradition in *Soering v. U.K.*, in respect of refusal of asylum to Tamils in *Vilvarajah* and an application to prevent expulsion after release from prison for an AIDS sufferer in *D v. United Kingdom*.[96] In *Chahal v. United Kingdom*, however, concerning a Sikh militant who was threatened with deportation to India for reasons of national security, domestic courts could not examine the evidence as to the threat to national security on which the Secretary of State claimed to rely. The Court found that the domestic courts were unable to review the decision of the Home Secretary with reference solely to the question of risk but could only satisfy themselves that the Home Secretary had balanced the risk against the danger to national security. This was ineffective in the circumstances.

Article 13 does not automatically require a court remedy. However, bodies which fail to provide sufficient procedural safeguards or who function by way of discretionary powers will be unlikely to qualify. In *Chahal*, the Court found that the hearing before an advisory panel gave a restricted review of the case and also insufficient procedural safeguards, namely, no entitlement to legal representation, provision of few details to the applicant and only a power of recommendation, not decision. The Court made positive note of the system in Canada adverted to by intervenors.[97]

The Secretary of State's ability to exercise his discretion in favour of an applicant on compassionate grounds or otherwise is unlikely to be regarded as an effective remedy. In *Youssef v. U.K.*, where the applicant was applying for entry to enjoy access to his son in the United Kingdom, such leave could only be granted on an exceptional basis as being outside immigration provisions, and it was within the discretion of the Adjudicator whether to make a recommendation for leave and then within the discretion of the Secretary of State as to whether he followed the recommendation. For the Commission, this provided insufficient guarantees of efficacy for the purposes of Article 13 of the Convention.[98]

Cross-reference

Part IIB: Deprivation of liberty
Part IIB: Discrimination
Part IIB: Extradition
Part IIB: Remedies
Part IIB: Torture and ill-treatment

---

[96] The Commission disagreed as to the effectiveness of judicial review in the earlier cases. In *Soering,* it noted the Government's acceptance that the courts could not review the exercise of the discretion of the Secretary of State on the basis that the applicant might be subjected to inhuman or degrading treatment on death row in violation of Art. 3. In *Vilvarajah,* where the Tamil applicants were to be expelled to Sri Lanka, complex evidential issues as to the existence of any risk arose which were not decided in the courts on judicial review, which the Commission noted had not even asked for disclosure of the material on which the Secretary of State had made his decision.

[97] The system provides a court review, with the confidentiality of national security material maintained by hearings in camera and the appointment of security cleared counsel to assist the court and to examine any witnesses in the absence of the applicant and his representative.

[98] 14830/89, (Rep.) June 30, 1992, Resolution DH(95) 246.

Interception of communications

Key provision:

Article 8 (respect for private life, home and correspondence).

Key case law:

Klass v. Germany, September 6, 1978, Series A, No. 28; 2 E.H.R.R. 214; *Malone v. U.K.*, August 2, 1984, Series A, No. 82; 7 E.H.R.R. 14; *Schenk v. Switzerland*, July 12, 1988, Series A, No. 140; 13 E.H.R.R. 242; *Huvig v. France*, April 24, 1990, Series A, No. 176–B; 12 E.H.R.R. 528; *Kruslin v. France*, April 24, 1990, Series A, No. 176–B; 12 E.H.R.R. 547; *A v. France*, November 23, 1993, Series A, No. 277–B; 17 E.H.R.R. 462; *Halford v. U.K.*, June 25, 1997, R.J.D., 1997–III, No. 39.

1. General considerations

Interception of communications, telephone tapping in its most well-known form, has generally been found, where it exists, to constitute an interference with one or more of the interests protected under Article 8, paragraph 1. In *Klaas and Klaas v. Germany*, the Court found that interception of communications (telephone and post) was an interference with private and family life, correspondence and, potentially, home.[1] Correspondence covers not just materials which cross by post but also telephone communications[2] and telexes.[3]

The bulk of the Convention organ's examination of interceptions has concentrated on the lawfulness of the measures in the broad sense of conformity with the rule of law — that the powers are grounded in accessible and foreseeable legal rules and verifying the existence of safeguards against abuse. There have been not inconsiderable findings of violations on the former ground. It might therefore be claimed that the Convention has been a useful tool in subjecting the use of covert technological techniques by the State to proper regulation.

2. Telephone tapping

(a) *Content of communication*

Article 8 applies regardless of the content of the telephone conversation. In *A v. France*, the Government argued that conversations taped relating to the commission of murder did not relate to private life. The Commission held that the mere fact that a conversation concerned the public interest did not deprive it of its private character, while the Court did not specify why it did not accept this argument. In *Halford v. United Kingdom*, conversations by telephone were covered, whether business or private, as was use of an office telephone.

However, where an applicant utilised an open air channel, the interception did not constitute interference with "private life" since the conversation was on a wavelength accessible to other users and could hardly be classified as "private" communications.[4]

(b) *Establishing an interference*

As intended, many of the subjects of telephone tapping are oblivious to the interference. Others may suspect without any concrete proof. It may be only during a trial that the telephone tapping is disclosed in the interests of the prosecution.

---

[1] Para. 41.

[2] *A v. France*, para. 37.

[3] *Campbell Christie v. U.K.*, 21482/93, (Dec.) June 27, 1994, 78–A D.R. 119.

[4] *i.e.* by using a radio channel for civil aircraft, he exposed himself to the risk: *B.C. v. Switzerland*, 21353/93, (Dec.) February 27, 1995 80–A D.R. 101. The Commission also noted that the contents were not revealed in the proceedings for breach of communications regulations.

In *Klaas and Klaas*, however, the applicants attacked the legislation on the basis, *inter alia*, that while the State had the right to use interception measures, there should be provision for informing the subject after the measures had been lifted and for court control of the imposition and execution of such measures. They had no proof or indication that they were subject to any measures in fact. The Court stated in very broad terms that "under certain conditions", an applicant may claim to be the victim of a violation occasioned by the mere existence of secret measures or of legislation permitting secret measures.[5]

This was repeated as a basis for finding interferences in *Malone v. United Kingdom* "apart from any measures actually taken against him".[6] However, the existence of victim status and interference was admitted by the U.K. Government who without furnishing any details, accepted that as a suspected receiver of stolen goods he was member of a class of persons against whom interceptions were liable to be employed. Regarding metering, although the Government stated that it had not been employed in his case, the Court still found that he was in a class of persons potentially liable to be directly affected by the practice and could on the basis of the *Klaas and Klaas* case claim to be a victim quite apart from any concrete measure taken against him.

However, although the Commission appeared to apply the *Klass* principles in a number of cases,[7] it has developed a more restrictive approach. It deals at the admissibility level with many unsubstantiated, often delusional complaints. It has adopted a filter approach, unwilling to embark on a detailed examination of the state of domestic law and practice every time a complainant alleges that the CIA or the freemasons are tapping his telephone. A reasonable likelihood test was taken from *Hilton v. United Kingdom*,[8] which dealt with secret files.

The case of *Hilton*, while paying lipservice to the *Klass* statement, relied on another general passage which held that the relevant conditions (giving rise to victim status from the mere state of law) were to be determined in each case according to the Convention right alleged to have been infringed, the secret character of the measures objected to and the connection between the applicant and those measures.[9] The Commission considered that *Klaas and Klaas* could not be interpreted so broadly as to cover every person in the United Kingdom who thought the Security Service might have compiled information about them: it considered that the category of persons likely to be affected was significantly smaller. It could not be necessary to require actual proof of a file but that there must at least be a reasonable likelihood that the Security Service had compiled a file and retained it.

The reasonable likelihood test was used in *Campbell Christie v. United Kingdom*,[10] where the applicant trade union leader discovered from a television documentary that the telexes addressed to him from overseas were being routinely intercepted and in *L.C.B.* and *McGinley*, where the complaints of telephone tapping were rejected on the basis that the applicants had not adduced sufficient evidence to demonstrate a reasonable likelihood that the nuclear test veterans or their children would be subject to interception measures as a result of their campaigning.[11] A fine distinction was drawn in *Halford* where the Government accepted that there was a reasonable likelihood that calls on the applicant's

[5] Para. 34.
[6] Para. 64.
[7] *e.g. Mersch and others v. Luxembourg*, (Dec.) 10439/83, 43 D.R. 34, where there was a general challenge to new legislation which authorised interceptions; *L v. Norway*, 13564/88, (Dec.) June 8, 1990 the Commission found it unnecessary on the basis of Klass to establish whether or not a tapping of the applicant's phone was established; *Spillman v. Switzerland*, 11811/85, (Dec.) March 8, 1988, 55 D.R. 182.
[8] *U.K.* 12015/86, (Dec.) July 6, 1988, 57 D.R. 108.
[9] *Klass*, para. 34.
[10] See n.3. The Government accepted that there was a reasonable likelihood of interception.
[11] 23413/94, (Dec.) November 28, 1995, 83–A D.R. 31; *McGinley v. U.K.*, (Dec.) November 11, 1995, unpublished.

office phone were intercepted, which was not unlawful in domestic law. In respect of allegations of bugging her home telephone on the public lines however, the Court, adopting the Commission's approach, found no reasonable likelihood on the evidence presented, namely, the applicant had no specific information that her home telephones were bugged and it would have been unlawful for the police to have taken this step.

3. "In accordance with law"[12]

The notion refers, firstly, to the interference having some basis in domestic law and, secondly, to the quality of law, *i.e.* those aspects which render it compatible with the notion of the rule of law, including accessibility, foreseeability as to the circumstances in which and conditions under which authorities are empowered to interfere, which should be such as to provide protection against arbitrary interferences.

Insufficient basis in domestic law was the basis for violations in *Malone*, where the powers relating to the interception of post and telephone communications, including metering, were not clearly incorporated in legal rules as to the scope and manner of their exercise. An absence of a prohibition against measures was not sufficient. Similarly, the Court found in *Halford*, that there was no basis in domestic law for interception of "private" telecommunications systems, since the Interception of Communications Act 1985 did not apply to it nor was there any general law of privacy.

When applicants allege that the authorities fail to comply with the domestic law provisions, the Commission accords domestic authorities a wide margin of appreciation in their assessment. Where, in an Italian case, the Court of Cassation found that the regulations were followed and conditions fulfilled regarding the existence of adequate suspicion, the Commission did not find that the lawfulness criterion was breached.[13]

As to the quality of law, interceptions are regarded as serious interferences which render it essential to have clear detailed rules particularly since technology continually becomes more sophisticated.[14] Relevant factors are the existence of a definition of the categories of persons or offences which may attract measures, limits on duration, regulation of the circumstances in which records are destroyed, and whether the originals are available for inspection by the judiciary.[15] The Commission has recognised that flexibility is required by the subject-matter and that the concept of foreseeability does not require definition of terms like "national security" or "economic well-being" when used as pre-conditions for the application of measures. In *Campbell Christie*, the Commission rejected the argument that the discretion afforded by these terms was too wide and undefined and that it should be subject to judicial input through adversarial argument in courts to establish full meaning of the terms. It considered that it was acceptable for the terms to be elaborated by administrative and executive statements and instructions.

4. Necessity

Interception is acknowledged as potentially pursuing the aim of preventing crime and disorder in the police investigation context[16] and as being in the interests of national security, in which latter context the Court has acknowledged a wide margin of appreciation.[17] There has been no real scrutiny of the purposes of the systems as such in

---

[12] See Part I: "Convention approach".

[13] It noted that "its power to review national authorities' compliance with domestic law is limited": 13274/87 *Italy*, (Dec.) September 6, 1990, 66 D.R. 164; also *Kruslin*, para. 29 where the Court would not contradict settled case-law of French courts as to the basis of investigating judge powers.

[14] *Kruslin*, para. 33.

[15] *ibid.* para. 35.

[16] *Malone*,

[17] *Klass*, para. 49; *Leander*, para. 59.

the absence of obvious abuses. The key point has been whether there exist adequate and effective guarantees against abuse.[18] This provides some overlap with "in accordance with law" but where the latter looks at whether the way the law is formulated provides sufficient safeguards by way of accessibility and foreseeability, the former rather concerns concrete procedural checks.

Relevant features include the existence of any independent scrutiny in the implementation process, significance attaching to judicial input or parliamentary supervision of the executive.[19] Although it has been commented that judicial control would ensure the most effective supervision offering the best guarantees of independence, impartiality and procedure, the lack of it is not necessarily fatal where other independent bodies exist with sufficient powers and competence to exercise continuous and effective control.[20] In *Campbell Christie*, the applicant argued that there was no court and parliamentary control in the U.K. but the Commission found that an independent tribunal with limited review powers and an independent commissioner of high judicial rank, whose thorough and critical approach to his functions was disclosed in his reports, were acceptable.

Limitations as to duration of warrants and requirement for prior authorisation have also been considered as safeguards.[21]

There is no requirement that a person subject to measures be informed afterwards, the Convention organs allowing that the secrecy and efficacy of the system would be undermined by such notifications.[22] Nor is it necessary that a tribunal ruling on complaint by an applicant give reasons for a negative ruling, instead of confirming merely whether or not there has been a contravention of the statutory provisions.[23]

The Commission and Court have shown a pragmatic attitude in assessing the efficacy of procedural safeguards. No system, it is said, can rule out abuse by over-zealous officials but where a procedure is in place designed to reduce measures to the necessary minimum and ensure their conformity with the necessary provisions, unless there is evidence to the contrary the Court will assume that the authorities are properly applying the legislation.[24] In the area of security checks, the Commission has taken a stance of setting a minimum necessary standard, rejecting arguments based on the existence of better protection systems elsewhere. Since the aim is to balance the needs of the State against the protection of individual rights a system of effective, not foolproof, checks against abuses is required. For an issue to arise where there is a system of checks in place, it requires a fundamental inadequacy, evidence of abuse or failure to control or a clear gap in the protection, as in *Halford*, where the legislation omitted private telecommunication systems.

5. Postal interferences

The above considerations apply equally to interception of mail, although there are fewer cases dealing expressly with such allegations. While numerous complaints are made by persons suspicious of receiving envelopes or parcels which are torn and taped back together

---

[18] *Klass*, para. 50.
[19] *e.g. ibid.* where an officer qualified for judicial office carried out scrutiny and there was supervision by parliamentary body of the executive minister. Also *Mersch* case, see n.7, where senior judge involved in review and *Spillman v. Switzerland*, see n.7, where safeguards were in conformity with *Klass*, in particular, the feature of judicial control within 24 hours.
[20] *Klass*, paras 55–56.
[21] *Mersch*; *L v. Norway*, see n.7.
[22] *Klass*, para. 68; *Campbell Christie*, see n.3; *L. v. Norway*, see n.7; *Spillman*, see n.7.
[23] *Campbell Christie*, see n.3.
[24] *Klass*, para. 59: the Commission in *Campbell Christie*, see n.3, found this evidence was not furnished by the fact the Interception of Communications Tribunal had never made a determination in favour of an applicant nor was it impressed by unsubstantiated rumours in the media that there was routine interception of British businessmens' communications.

by the postal authorities, the Commission has tended to apply a robust approach, requiring some form of substantiation of "interference" and has applied the "reasonable likelihood" test to reject them.[25] Regarding mishandling by the Post, an old Commission case states that Article 8 does not guarantee the perfect functioning of the postal service.[26]

There are some contexts where interference with mail is in fact routine or not unexpected e.g. prisons. There are also criminal law provisions regulating what may be sent by post, in particular, pornography.[27] Interferences based on enforcement of criminal law provisions are likely to be found justifiable, where in compliance with domestic law.

6. Use of material in court proceedings

The use in evidence at trial of material obtained by the police using interceptions has been examined under Article 6 "fairness" considerations. It seems to be an accepted source of evidence in domestic courts where lawfully obtained, subject to a warrant and procedural safeguards. Issues are most likely to arise under Article 8 if material is obtained without regard to domestic lawfulness or made public in circumstances which infringe private life without any corresponding relevance to the interests of preventing crime.[28]

However, the lawfulness is not decisive to fairness as shown in *Schenk v. Switzerland*, where the taping by a hired assassin of a telephone call with the applicant handed over to the police was unlawful, as it was not ordered by the investigating judge. The Court considered its use did not render the applicant's trial automatically unfair or disclose a ground of violation *per se*. It had regard to the circumstances, namely, the applicant had knowledge of the tape and how it was taken and was able to challenge its use and contents by calling the assassin or police inspector as witnesses. The Court found that the rights of defence were not disregarded. It also attached weight to the fact that it was not the only evidence on which the conviction was based and that there was an investigation carried out into the conduct of the hired assassin.[29]

Cross-reference

Part IIA: Evidence
Part IIB: Surveillance and secret files
Part IIB: Prisoners

[25] *Firsoff v. U.K.* 20591/92, (Dec.) December 2, 1992 applicant (involved with groups which attempt to visit Stonehenge at the summer solstice) alleged illicit opening of his parcels; the Commission found that there was insufficient evidence that he was a person or belonged to a category of persons in respect of whom the police would consider clandestine surveillance measures were necessary. No reasonable likelihood that his mail was interfered with by the police rather than merely damaged in transit (the opinion of the parcel service).

[26] 8383/78, October 3, 1979, 17 D.R. 227: reference to the volume of mail, statistical likelihood of some miscarriage which are generally known and special means provided to ensure safe delivery of particular letters on demand.

[27] *e.g.* 7308/75, (Dec.) October 12, 1978, 16 D.R. 32: stoppage of packages containing obscene materials.

[28] *Mutatis mutandis, Z v. Finland,* where medical material concerning a witness was made public.

[29] See also *Chonoy v. U.K.* 15199/89, (Dec.) September 4, 1991, where the applicant was held pending extradition in London and during magistrates committal proceedings taped conversations obtained by U.S. agents in Paris were used, complaints under Arts. 5 and 8 were rejected. There was no indication that the U.K. authorities had been involved in taking the recording, even assuming that it had been unlawful in France and it was subject to limited use in court (no indication that it was read out or made known to public). Given the purpose of fulfilling extradition obligations and fighting drug trafficking, there was no lack of respect under Art. 8 and as regarded detention under Art. 5, para. 1(f) this was not arbitrary, or procedurally or substantively unlawful.

Marriage and founding a family

Relevant provisions:

Article 12 (right to marry and found a family); Article 14 (prohibition against discrimination).

Relevant case law:

Airey v. Ireland, October 9, 1979, Series A, No. 32; 2 E.H.R.R. 305; *Rees v. U.K.*, October 17, 1986, Series A, No. 106; 9 E.H.R.R. 56; *Johnston v. Ireland*, December 18, 1986, Series A, No. 112; 9 E.H.R.R. 203; *F v. Switzerland*, December 18, 1987, Series A, No. 128; 10 E.H.R.R. 411; *Cossey v. U.K.*, September 27, 1990, Series A, No. 184; 13 E.H.R.R. 622.

1. General considerations

The traditional marriage enjoys a favoured position in the Convention singled out for separate treatment under Article 12 and resulting in special status, for example, where married relationships are considered in the context of family life and discrimination.[1] The Commission organs have intervened little in how States choose to regulate this area. For the Court the right to marry guaranteed by Article 12 refers to the traditional marriage between persons of opposite biological sex, which interpretation it found supported by the reference to founding of a family.[2]

2. The right to marry

Article 12 is dominated by the qualification "according to the national laws governing the exercise of this right". Persons are expected, for example, to comply with the procedural formalities imposed by the State. A German could not therefore claim a violation when the registrar refused to register his marriage which had not involved the completion of the necessary administrative forms but only a religious ceremony.[3]

The principle is that the national laws may govern the exercise of the right but not to injure its substance.[4] Generally recognised limitations such as capacity, consent, consanguinity or prevention of bigamy are likely to be compatible. For example, the Commission rejected a complaint from a muslim who could not marry a girl of 14 who lacked legal capacity despite his assertion that his religion permitted marriage to a girl over 12. The Commission commented that it would not be compatible to deprive a person or a category of persons of the full legal capacity to marry.[5]

The Court has found a bar on a transsexual marrying a person of his or her own original birth gender does not impair the essence of the right.[6] It took the view that a transsexual continues to enjoy the right to marry a person of the opposite birth gender and that it was not unreasonable for a State to take a biologically-based view of gender. However, it is

---

[1] *Lindsay v. U.K.*, 11089/84, (Dec.) November 11, 1986, 49 D.R. 181: married and unmarried couples are not in analogous positions for the purposes of tax, since marriage relates to a special regime of rights and obligations; *McMichael v. U.K.*, February 24, 1995, Series A, No. 307–B, para. 98 automatic parental rights for married fathers as opposed to unmarried fathers are objectively and reasonably justified.

[2] *Rees*; see however the Commission's opinions in *Rees* and *Cossey* and its view in *Hamer and Draper*, below, n.4.

[3] 6167/73, (Dec.) December 18, 1974, 1 D.R. 64.

[4] *Hamer v. U.K.*, 7114/75, (Rep.) December 13, 1979, 24 D.R. 5; *Draper v. U.K.* 8186/78, (Rep.), July 10, 1980, 24 D.R. 72; *Rees, Cossey.*

[5] *U.K.*, 11579/85, (Dec.) July 7, 1986, 48 D.R. 253.

[6] *Rees, Cossey.*

difficult to see that the "very essence of the right" is not impaired in such circumstances, since it becomes effectively a useless one. Marriage has thus been restricted where the State so wishes to a union between a man and woman both of biological origin as defined without reference to intervening phenomena.

However, practical prohibitions have disclosed problems in other contexts. The Commission held that prison authorities could not legitimately refuse a prisoner permission to get married while serving his sentence. *Hamer*, serving a five-year sentence, and *Draper* serving life, were not allowed to marry their girlfriends either inside the prison on a visit or by temporary leave for the purpose. It was irrelevant to the Commission that the couples would not have been able to consummate the marriage or cohabit. Marriage to the Commission was the formation of a legally-binding association between a man and a woman. The delay imposed on them before they could marry was found to injure the substance of their right to marry.

The imposition of time-limits has also been found incompatible, in *F. v. Switzerland* where the Swiss attempted to regulate the frequency of divorces. A three-year prohibition on re-marriage was imposed on an applicant after having been granted his third divorce. The Government argued that such temporary prohibitions were not arbitrary or disproportionate, pursuing the aim of preserving the stability of marriage, the protection of the rights of the future spouse and compelling proper reflection (impliedly no bad thing in this applicant's case). The Court disagreed, finding the restriction unreasonable, disproportionate and affecting the very essence of the right. A paternalistic attitude to regulate the marriage of legally capable adults was therefore rejected as constituting an acceptable public policy interest.

3. Divorce

The Convention organs consider that the ordinary meaning of Article 12 relates to the formation of marital relationships and not their dissolution. The Court held that a restriction on divorce in a country adhering to the principle of monogamy cannot be regarded as injuring the substance of the right guaranteed by Article 12.[7] Developments in society with regard to the availability of divorce were irrelevant given the clear meaning of the text and the intent of the drafters, as shown from the *travaux préparatoires*, who deliberately omitted reference to dissolution of marriage. In *Johnston v. Ireland* therefore, the applicant's inability to obtain the dissolution of the marriage with his first wife to allow him to marry the woman with whom he had lived for over eight years and with whom he had founded a family, did not disclose a violation of Article 12.

Conversely, where divorce is permitted in domestic law, the Commission has not found that this infringes the right to marry.

4. Founding a family

This may include the founding of a family by adoption, such adoption being governed under Article 12 by national laws. In a Dutch case the applicant and her husband who wished to adopt a Polish boy were refused permission as the proposed adoption did not fulfil the conditions set down in domestic law with regard, *inter alia*, to the difference in ages between themselves and the child. Their complaint was rejected as the measure was in accordance with national laws.[8] In the absence of arbitrariness, it would be unlikely that matters of eligibility or procedural requirements for adoption under domestic law would raise issues under Article 12.

---

[7] *Johnston*, para. 52.
[8] 8896/80, (Dec.) March 10, 1981, 24 D.R. 177, which is more positive than an earlier case which stated that there was no right to adopt a child not a natural child of the couple concerned — 7229/75, (Dec.) December 15, 1977, 12 D.R. 32.

Regarding practical obstacles, prisoners have unsuccessfully claimed the right to conjugal visits, the Commission finding that no such right could be derived from Article 12.[9] With increasing concessions being made in prison regimes particularly in the Nordic countries, the Commission hinted however that the situation might be reviewable in the future.[10] The issue was subject to two communications to the United Kingdom Government in combination with a complaint about a refusal to allow artificial insemination by donor treatment (AID) of prisoners' wives, who due to age or health could not await their husbands' release. Where it was a matter of allowing a brief procedure for a prisoner to provide the necessary sample for his wife's doctor, there appeared to be little justification to put in the balance against the enjoyment of the right under Article 12. However, the cases were struck off when permission was granted.[11]

Where a couple is infertile the extent to which they could derive a right of access to new medical technologies is unexplored. There are aspects of resource allocation and costs which would make it unlikely that a couple could require a State to furnish treatment but where treatment is available, the procedures might perhaps be amenable to challenge on grounds of arbitrariness or discrimination.

---

[9] *Switzerland*, 8166/78, (Dec.) October 3, 1978, 13 D.R. 241: where husband and wife were detained in same prison, lack of conjugal visits were justifiable in the interests of security and good order under Art. 8, with no separate issue under Art. 12; 6564/74, *U.K.*, (Dec.) May 21, 1975, 2 D.R. 105 no infringement by locking some-one up as no right to be given the actual possibility at all times to procreate!
[10] 8166/78, above.
[11] 10822/84, (Dec.) May 7, 1987, and 17142/90, (Dec.) July 10, 1991; 20004/92, (Dec.) May 7, 1993 struck off when applicants failed to pursue it.

Mental health

Key provisions:

Article 5, paragraph 1(e) (lawful detention of persons of unsound mind); Article 5, paragraph 4 (review of detention); Article 8 (private life); Article 3 (prohibition of ill-treatment).

Key case law:

Winterwerp v. Netherlands, October 24, 1979, Series A, No. 33; 2 E.H.R.R. 387; *X v. U.K.,* October 24, 1981, Series A, No. 46; 4 E.H.R.R. 188; *Luberti v. Italy,* February 23, 1984, Series A, No. 75; 6 E.H.R.R. 440; *Van der Leer v. Netherlands,* September 27, 1990, Series A, No. 170; 12 E.H.R.R. 267; *Wassink v. Netherlands,* February 21, 1990, Series A, No. 185–A; *Koendjbiharie v. Netherlands,* September 28, 1990, Series A, No. 185–B; 13 E.H.R.R. 820; *Keus v. Netherlands,* October 25, 1990, Series A, No. 185–C; 13 E.H.R.R. 700; *Megyeri v. Germany,* May 12, 1992, Series A, No. 237–A; 15 E.H.R.R. 584; *Herczegfalvy v. Austria,* September 24, 1992, Series A, No. 242–B; 15 E.H.R.R. 437; *Johnson v. United Kingdom,* October 24, 1997, R.J.D., 1997—VII, No. 55.

1. General considerations

The principal cases concern the procedures and safeguards relating to detention of persons on grounds of mental illness. Surprisingly few cases relate to the other disabilities imposed on mentally ill persons in the enjoyment of basic rights and freedom, or to any allegations of ill-treatment within institutions. This presumably is a sad reflection that this vulnerable group of people face grave problems in putting forward claims.

2. Admissibility points

The admissibility criteria apply in the ordinary way. A mental health patient is generally required to exhaust effective domestic remedies and to comply with the six-month period. (See Part IB — Admissibility Checklist.)

3. Grounds for detention

Article 5, paragraph 1(e) refers to person of "unsound mind". The Court in *Winterwerp v. Netherlands* noted that this was not a term which leant itself to precise definition since psychiatry was a progressing field, both medically and in social attitudes. It is not sufficient that a person's views or behaviour deviates from the established norms. The concept is to be narrowly interpreted given the importance of the right to liberty.

The Convention organs will examine whether domestic law is compatible with the Convention.[1]

There are three basic requirements to establish that detention of a person of "unsound mind" falls within sub-paragraph 1(e)[2]:

- "a true mental disorder" has to be established by objective medical expertise before the competent domestic authority except where it is an emergency procedure;

[1] e.g. *Winterwerp v. Netherlands:* the law which applied to persons with a mental disorder of such a kind as to render them a danger to themselves or others was found to be compatible.
[2] *Winterwerp,* para. 39.

- it has to be of a kind or degree to warrant compulsory confinement; and
- the validity of the continued detention depends on the persistence of the disorder.

In the assessment of whether the person should be detained as of "unsound mind", the authorities have a certain discretion or margin of appreciation with regard to the evaluation of the evidence subject to Convention supervision. This will usually involve an examination of whether there was psychiatric evidence to support the view. There has as yet been no case where the official medical view of the existence of mental illness has been put into doubt. Regarding the moment when the person should be released, the Court has found that the authorities may legitimately proceed with caution and a certain time may lapse while his condition is considered.[3] The authorities also enjoy a certain discretion as to the timing and the conditions under which a person is released. Thus, in *Johnson v. U.K.*, the Court did not consider that it automatically followed from a diagnosis that an applicant's mental disorder no longer persisted that he should be immediately or unconditionally released. However, any deferral of release had to be compatible with the purpose of Article 5, paragraph 1 and not be unduly delayed.

Concerning emergency procedures, the Court will examine the facts leading to the emergency detention and the available medical reports or evidence at the time.[4] In *Winterwerp*, it considered the applicant's bizarre behaviour justified the steps taken (he was stealing, stripped off his clothes, etc.).[5] The Commission in *O'Reilly v. Ireland* found admissible issues arising as to the justification of the extreme step of emergency detention, based on the complaint of the applicant's spouse and a visual examination by a general practitioner from the end of a garden.[6] In *Kay v. United Kingdom*, where the Secretary of State ordered the recall to hospital of a prisoner whose prison sentence expired without first obtaining an up-to-date medical report of his state of mental health, the Commission found a violation since there was no emergency to justify this omission.[7] The time which should elapse before a full evaluation of the applicant's state occurs should be brief on any view of matters. The Court in *Winterwerp* found that a six-week delay was rather long but not so excessive as to render the detention unlawful.[8]

4. Procedure prescribed by law

The authorities must conform to requirements imposed by domestic law in the proceedings concerning detention. Violations may result even from technical breaches, as in *Wassink v. Netherlands*, where the registrar of the court was not present at the hearing as required by law. In *Van der Leer v. Netherlands*, the applicant was confined without being heard although pursuant to the relevant law the judge should have heard her in the absence of

---

[3] *Luberti v. Italy*, para. 29 where the applicant's detention continued pending court examination of the file and reports fell within this margin; *Johnson*, where the Court found over three years elapsing from a tribunal finding that the applicant was not mentally ill until his release did not fall within the authorities' discretion in managing his release into society. It commented critically that the Mental Health Review Tribunal and the authorities did not have the necessary powers to ensure that the conditions attached to his release (namely placement in a supervised hostel) could be implemented within a reasonable time.

[4] In *Wassink*, the judge had four medical reports in front of him, (two doctors had appeared and he had spoken to the others on the telephone); he also had statements from applicant's wife and a police report (the applicant had attacked a neighbour and made threats): there was thus no grounds for questioning the weight of the evidence on which the judge relied to extend the emergency confinement by three weeks.

[5] Also *X v. U.K.*, on recall of a person under conditional release, complaints by his wife of threats and fears for safety supported by her doctor, were sufficient.

[6] *Ireland*, 24196/94, (Dec.) January 22, 1996, 84–A D.R. 72; settled (Rep.), December 3, 1996 (IR £14,000, plus legal costs).

[7] *U.K.* 17821/91, (Rep.) March 1, 1994.

[8] Para. 42.

any objection from the psychiatrist to a hearing. The Court commented that at the very least the judge should have given reasons for not doing so and there was a violation since an essential procedural requirement was not satisfied. The latter seemed to hint that a non-essential infringement of domestic procedure might not fall foul of the Convention.

5. Review of the lawfulness of the detention

Since the validity of detention under Article 5, paragraph 1(e) depends on the persistence of the disorder, the review required by Article 5, paragraph 4 includes verification of the applicant's mental state as necessitating detention.

Habeas corpus was not adequate in *X v. United Kingdom*, where the applicant was recalled after conditional release, since the court did not examine whether in fact the applicant's disorder persisted or that the continuation of the compulsory confinement was necessary in the interests of public safety.

However, there is no right to obtain a review of the location or conditions of detention, as found in *Ashingdane v. United Kingdom*,[8a] where the applicant disputed the justification of his continued detention at Broadmoor. Judicial control was not guaranteed of the legality of all aspects or details of the detention. The question of entitlement to a more appropriate regime did not concern "lawfulness" for the purpose of Article 5, paragraph 4.

(a) "Court"

The review must be conducted by "court". To satisfy this concept, the body must have a power to decide. In *X v. United Kingdom*, the Mental Health Review Tribunal only had advisory powers and no binding power to order release. A specialised body of this kind may be a "court" provided that it enjoys the necessary independence and offers sufficient procedural safeguards. A public prosecutor did not qualify in *Winterwerp v. Netherlands*.

(b) *Procedural requirements*

The review must conform with procedural safeguards. Having regard to the factor of mental illness, special safeguards may be required to protect persons who are not fully capable of acting for themselves. While mental illness may justify restricting or modifying the exercise of their right of review, it cannot however justify impairing the very essence of that right.

There was a violation in *Winterwerp*, where neither the applicant nor his representative were present in the proceedings before the courts which issued the orders of detention. The Court considered that the applicant must be heard either in person or through a representative. Further, answering the Government's point that the applicant had failed to instruct a lawyer, it was not for the person with unsound mind to take the initiative to obtain legal representation before applying to a court. The necessity for legal assistance was underlined in *Megyeri v. Germany*, where the applicant challenged his detention in psychiatric hospital but was not represented before the court conducting the review. The Court found that where a person was confined in psychiatric institution on the basis of commission of acts which would have constituted criminal offences but for which he could not be held responsible on the grounds of mental illness, he should, unless there are special circumstances, receive legal assistance in subsequent proceedings concerning the continuation, suspension or termination of his detention. It was doubtful that the applicant could address the medical and legal points arising and had regard to the importance of what was at stake for him.

[8a] May 28, 1985, Series A, No. 93 — para. 52. The applicant had been recommended as fit for transfer to an ordinary hospital.

294

What is required by way of procedure at the hearing may be minimal where emergency considerations apply. In *Wassink*, the Court found it compatible with Article 5, paragraph 4 that the President of the court consulted experts and witnesses by telephone, although failing to read his notes to the applicant or his counsellor and in the absence of the registrar who was required by law.[9] The Court was influenced by the fact that the power exercised was an emergency one limited in duration to three weeks and considered that it nonetheless had established the medical basis for continued detention.[10]

Having regard to Article 5, paragraph 4 cases dealing with other forms of detention, it is likely that access to documents and reports may be required, tempered however by the consideration whether an applicant should on health grounds be allowed to see particular documents.[11]

(c) *Timing of reviews*

A person detained as being of unsound mind is entitled both to a speedy decision and to take proceedings at reasonable intervals.[12] The latter applies where there is no automatic periodic judicial review, the Court commenting in *X v. United Kingdom* that it is not for it to specify which system of judicial review is appropriate.

However, no initial review is required where detention is ordered by a court at the end of judicial proceedings. In these circumstances, the review of lawfulness is regarded as incorporated. An initial review by a court is only required under Article 5, paragraph 4 where the decision to detain is taken by an administrative authority.[13]

A distinction may be made between the speed at which an applicant taken into detention or recalled should obtain a review and the time which should be taken in reaching decisions on release or continuance at later stages.

The first review should take place very rapidly. In *Wassink*, the Commission found that the applicant's discharge after three-weeks emergency confinement could not be considered to have followed so speedily that it made a review of detention superfluous. A five-month delay on a hearing after recall was not surprisingly found excessive in the *Kay v. United Kingdom* case.

Four months for a court to issue a decision on an application for release was not speedy in *Koendjbiharie v. Netherlands*. Where in another case it took almost three months to decide on application for release, the Commission, rejecting the case as inadmissible, commented that while on first sight this seemed excessive and required factors to justify it, it was not excessive in light of the applicant's conduct in challenging the impartiality of the expert and the conducting of thorough medical examinations.[14]

Where an applicant's conduct contributes to the length of proceedings rendering it impossible to obtain an examination, this will be a relevant factor in assessing whether the court has acted reasonably.[15] However, the fact that an applicant applies for adjournments or shows disinterest does not absolve the court from acting speedily. In *Kay v. United Kingdom*,[15a] the Commission found the system of review inherently slow, since it frequently

---

[9] There was however a violation in the latter respect under the stricter requirements of Art. 5, para. 1 as to a "procedure prescribed by law".

[10] The Commission found the nature of the proceedings by telephone unsatisfactory and that there were considerable risks of arbitrariness in the procedure which was not sufficiently judicial.

[11] See Part IIB: "Review of detention".

[12] A court must decide speedily and at reasonable intervals *Herczegfalvy*, para. 75.

[13] *Luberti*, para. 31.

[14] *Boucheras v. France*, 14438/88, (Dec.) April 11, 1991, 69 D.R. 236.

[15] e.g. *Keus*; *Luberti*. However in *Van der Leer* para. 35, the fact that the applicant absconded while the application for release was pending did not absolve the court from reaching a speedy decision since she could have been brought back against her will at any moment.

[15a] See n.7.

took six months for cases to come before the Mental Health Review Tribunal. In his case there was a two-year delay, the applicant's own requests for adjournments and disinterest not being relevant, since anyway the first hearing had been set for five months after recall.

Regarding reviews at reasonable intervals, an automatic review once per year was considered reasonable in *Megyeri*. In *Herczegfalvy v. Austria*, the Court found intervals of 15 months and two years were not speedy but in not remarking on the period of nine months seemed to find that was compatible. It noted that the Austrian system recommended a yearly interval.

6. Access to court

The factor of mental illness may justify restrictions on access to court. In *Ashingdane* where leave was required to bring actions in relation to acts done in pursuant of the Mental Health Act 1959, the Court found that this pursued the legitimate aim of preventing those responsible for the care of mental patients being unfairly harassed by litigation and that the essence of the right was not impaired, since it was only a partial exclusion of liability.[16]

However, the proceedings to detain a person *per se* do not involve the determination of a person's civil rights and obligations under Article 6, paragraph 1, the *lex specialis* being the court control imposed by the special provisions of Article 5.[17]

7. Ill-treatment

In the context of force feeding, constraints and compulsory administation of drugs, the Commission has found that compulsory medical treatment does not violate Article 3 if necessary from the medical point of view and carried out in conformity with standards accepted by medical science. While in *Herczegfalvy*, the Commission accepted that the treatment was necessary and that use of physical force may be necessary if treatment appears imperative, it was not convinced that the manner of application was compatible with Article 3. It doubted that it was necessary to insist on immediate administration and to apply massive force when it was clear that it was causing a worsening of the applicant's condition. It found that the fettering to bed for several weeks when he was in a very bad physical state, combined with isolation, was excessive and disclosed inhuman and degrading treatment. The Court restricted itself to the medical necessity, holding that a measure which was a therapeutic necessity cannot be inhuman or degrading. While the duration of the period of handcuffing and restriction in a security bed was "worrying", there was nothing to disprove the Government's argument that according to the psychiatric principles accepted at the time, medical necessity required it.

For an Article 3 case to have any success, it would appear necessary to show that the authorities applied treatment clearly injustifiable by any established medical norm.[18]

---

[16] See n.8a, *i.e.* if there was bad faith or negligence the case could proceed with leave of the court.

[17] *Neumeister v. Austria*, June 27, 1968, Series A, No. 8, para. 23.

[18] *Buckley v. U.K.*, 28323/95, (Dec.) February 26, 1997 where the administration of drugs in circumstances which lead to the patient's death did not disclose grounds for negligence in domestic law, there was no basis for the Commission to find a violation.

8. Right to treatment

No right to treatment appropriate to the applicant's condition has been derived from Article 5, paragraph 1(e).[19] So far there has been no significant case challenging, for example, the holding of mentally-ill prisoners in ordinary prisons or in a regime where no treatment is available, although it might be considered that failure to provide the appropriate regime for a mentally ill prisoner would disclose the kind of arbitrariness to which Article 5 is usually opposed. Article 3 issues might arise if conditions were such as to impose inhuman and degrading treatment on the applicant, but the threshold for Article 3 has been set very high in the context of prison detention.

9. Limitation of capacity to act

The loss of capacity to administer property concerns "civil rights and obligation" under Article 6, paragraph 1. In this context, a lack of proper access to a court with requisite guarantees may constitute a breach.[20]

Where other measures of control are applied to persons under mental health supervision, issues will arise if these do not, *inter alia*, comply with lawfulness criteria,[21] pursue legitimate aims or are disproportionate.[22]

Cross-reference

Part IIA: Fair trial guarantees, Access to Court
Part IIB: Compensation for arrest or detention
Part IIB: Deprivation of liberty
Part IIB: Review of detention
Part IIB: Torture, inhuman and degrading treatment

---

[19] See n.8a, *Ashingdane*, where the applicant was kept up to 19 months longer in the strict Broadmoor regime despite being scheduled for transfer to a more open hospital (union problems), the Court found this did not render the detention unlawful or outside the scope of Art. 5, para. 1(e); also *Winterwerp*, where the applicant unsuccessfully claimed the right to have treatment to enable detention to be as short as possible and that his meetings with psychiatrists were too short, too many tranquillisers, etc.

[20] See *Winterwerp*, where the applicant automatically lost capacity by law when committed to hospital in a process not affording the requisite guarantees.

[21] *Finland*, 18969/91, (Rep.) June 30, 1993: complaints by person under guardianship of mail censorship: violation of Art. 8 due to total absence of detail in law as to the permissibility of an interference with a ward's correspondence, the purpose and duration of such an interference etc.

[22] *U.K.* 26494/95, (Dec.) February 27, 1997 admissible under Art. 8, concerning complaints from an involuntary patient that medical and other reports automatically went to a specific relative, without the possibility to apply for another person to exercise the role of nearest relative.

Pensions

Key provisions:

Article 6, paragraph 1 (fair hearing guarantees); Article 1 to Protocol No. 1 (right to property); Article 14 (prohibition of discrimination).

Key case law:

Schuler-Zgraggen v. Switzerland, June 24, 1993, Series A, No. 263; 16 E.H.R.R. 405; *Massa v. Italy*, August 24, 1993, Series A, No. 265–B; 18 E.H.R.R. 266; *Gaygusuz v. Austria*, September 16, 1996, R.J.D., 1996–IV, No. 14; *Süssman v. Germany*, September 16, 1996, R.J.D., 1996–IV, No. 15; *Stamoulakatos (No. 2) v. Greece*, November 26, 1997, R.J.D., 1997–VII, No. 58.

1. General considerations

Where a pension is based on private contract with private institutions, it will be considered as both a "civil right" for the purposes of attracting the right to a court with the requisite procedural guarantees to determine disputes in proceedings and the right to a court and as a pecuniary right classifying as property within the meaning of Article 1 of Protocol No. 1. Where the pension concerned is derived from a public or State context, the issues overlap to some extent with those arising in the area of social security or welfare benefits and it is less automatic that these two provisions apply.

The Commission has stated that there is no right to receive a pension guaranteed in the Convention.[1] Where no basis for entitlement exists it is unlikely that the Convention provisions can offer any ground of complaint.

2. Civil Rights: applicability of Article 6, paragraph 1

Where a pension is linked to contract or akin to a private contractual relationship or private insurance, Article 6, paragraph 1 in its civil context is likely to apply. Even where the pension may be derived from the State or other public institutions pursuant to statute the Court assesses whether public or private law elements predominate.[2]

Where a pension is awarded following industrial accident on the basis of contributions or insurance premiums paid by the employer on behalf of his employees, such insurance can be considered grafted onto the employment contract, itself governed by private law and similar to private insurance. In those circumstances, an entitlement to a pension may be regarded as a civil right within the meaning of Article 6, paragraph 1.[3]

Following the approach of the Court in *Schuler-Zgraggen v. Switzerland*, where Article 6 applied to refusal of a benefits claim since it concerned an interference with the applicant's means of subsistence and was an individual economic right, it would appear that pension claims of a similar character would attract the same treatment. Where civil servant pensions disputes have arisen, Article 6 has been held to apply notwithstanding the public law context, on the basis of similarity with private law employment contract or the

---

[1] *U.K.*, 9776/82, October 3, 1983, 34 D.R. 153.
[2] See Part IIB: Welfare Benefits.
[3] *Minniti v. Italy*, 9630/81, (Dec.) October 13, 1986, 49 D.R. 59, declared admissible on length issues (proceedings over nine years). Cited in *Italy*, 10659/83, (Rep.) July 3, 1989, 69 D.R. 7 where violation of length found for over nine years. Also *Feldbrugge v. Netherlands*, May 29, 1986, Series A, No. 99 concerning health insurance allowances.

pecuniary nature of the pension entitlement.[4] In recent cases, the Court has stated, without qualification, that it has found no reason to depart from its case law that the right to a pension is a civil right.[5]

3. Property rights

Where a person has contributed to a pension fund, this may, according to the Commission, in certain circumstances create a property right in a portion of such a fund and a modification of the pension rights under such a system could in principle raise an issue under Article 1 of Protocol No. 1. Where the payments are to a social security system, even assuming that this gives rise to a right to derive a benefit from the system, it cannot be interpreted as entitling that person to a pension of a particular amount.[6] A right to a pension based on employment can in certain circumstances be assimilated to a property right, where special contributions were paid or the employer has given a more general undertaking to pay a pension on conditions which can be considered part of the employment contract.[7]

An applicant must however satisfy domestic legal requirements governing the right before Article 1 of the First Protocol can apply. Thus where by moving to Australia, the applicants ceased to qualify for future pension increases this did not amount to a deprivation of possessions.[8] The requirement to pay contributions for a minimum period to accrue a right must also be satisfied, where applicable.[9] Rules providing for the co-ordination of a pension with other state benefits have also been found compatible with Article 1 of Protocol No. 1.[10]

Since the operation of a social security system is essentially different from the management of a private life insurance company, having to take account of political considerations, particularly those of financial policy, it is conceivable that, due to a deflationary trend, a State may be obliged to reduce the amount of pension payable, as in the case of German reunification. This kind of fluctuation is not seen by the Commission as having anything to do with the guarantee of ownership as a human right.[11] Thus the fact that an applicant's pension was less than he could have received under the former East German system was not a problem. But the Commission did add that his level of pension was sufficient and did not deprive him of basic means of existence.[12] The Commission may therefore consider proportionality issues (*i.e.* effect and hardship) where a substantial reduction which might be regarded as affecting the substance of the right is concerned.[13]

4. Discrimination

To disclose discrimination, differences in eligibility or quantification have to be in respect of persons in relevantly similar situations and without reasonable and objective justification

---

[4] *Massa; Sussman*

[5] *e.g. Stamoulakatos (No. 2) v. Greece,* para. 31.

[6] *e.g. Muller v. Austria,* (Rep.) October 1, 1975, para. 30, 3 D.R. 25; 10671/83, (Dec.) March 4, 1985, 42 D.R. 229; 25044/94, May 15, 1996, *Austria* where Commission held the applicant was entitled to benefit from the social insurance system to which he had contributed but not entitled to pension of a particular amount.

[7] 10671/83, see n.6; 12264/86, July 13, 1988, 57 D.R. 131.

[8] 9776/82, see n.1.

[9] *Italy,* 7459/76 October 5, 1977, 11 D.R. 114 where the applicant dismissed from job on criminal conviction also lost his pension as he had not by that time secured the necessary seniority.

[10] 10671/83, March 4, 1985, 42 D.R. 229.

[11] 5849/72, *Austria,* (Rep.) October 1, 1975.

[12] 24077/94, *Germany,* May 21, 1996, 3 D.R. 25.

[13] 25044/94, *Austria,* see n.6, where the Commission found that calculation could not be said to have been carried out in an arbitrary manner in the applicant's case.

for difference in treatment.[14] It must also concern a complaint falling within the scope of another substantive provision. In *Vos v. Netherlands*,[15] where a woman lost her invalidity benefits on becoming entitled to a pension on the death of her husband (which did not happen to men on the deaths of their wives), the Commission found that her complaints fell outside the scope of Article 1 of the First Protocol and thus outside Article 14. In light of *Schuler-Zgraggen v. Switzerland*, *Gaygusuz v. Austria* and *Van Raalte v. Netherlands*,[16] however, issues could arise from differences based on sex or race where the pension was sufficiently linked to employment or established pecuniary rights (see Part IIB: Welfare Benefits).

Cross-reference

Part IIA: General Principles, Civil rights
Part IIA: Discrimination
Part IIB: Welfare benefits

---

[14] 9776/82, see n.1: when, by moving to Australia, the applicants ceased to be eligible for future pension increases, there was reasonable and objective justification since they had left the U.K. and there was a relevant social security scheme in Australia. It was inevitable that in such circumstances a person might find that he will be worse off than if he had stayed in the U.K. or moved to other EEC countries; 24077/94, *Germany*, see n.12: even assuming that Art. 14 applied, an applicant in East Germany was not in a comparable position to persons living in the West or to those in East Germany who paid supplementary contributions, and anyway it was objective and reasonable to make pension rights conditional on the payment of contributions.

[15] 10971/84, *Netherlands*, (Dec.) July 10, 1985, 43 D.R. 190.

[16] *Van Raalte v. Netherlands*, February 21, 1997, R.J.D., 1997–I, No. 39, where differences in social security contributions paid by men and women fell within the scope of Article 1 of the First Protocol and disclosed discrimination contrary to Art. 14.

300

Planning and use of property

Key provision:

Article 1 of Protocol No. 1 (peaceful enjoyment of possessions); Article 6 (access to court/fair hearing).

Key case law:

Sporrong and Llonroth v. Sweden, September 23, 1982, Series A, No. 52; 5 E.H.R.R. 35; *Allan Jacobsson v. Sweden*, October 25, 1989, Series A, No. 163, 12 E.H.R.R. 56; *Tre Traktorer v. Sweden*, July 7, 1989, Series A, No. 159; 13 E.H.R.R. 309; *Fredin v. Sweden*, February 18, 1990, Series A, No. 192; *Pine Valley Developments v. Ireland*, November 29, 1991, Series A, No. 222; 14 E.H.R.R. 319; *Raimondo v. Italy*, February 22, 1994, Series A, No. 281–A; 18 E.H.R.R. 237; *Bryan v. U.K.*, November 22, 1995, Series A, No. 335–A; 21 E.H.R.R. 342; *Buckley v. U.K.*, September 25, 1996, R.J.D., 1996–IV, No. 16.

1. General considerations

Control of use of property, the "third rule" of Article 1 of Protocol No. 1, is compatible where necessary in accordance with general interest. A wide margin of appreciation is accorded to the authorities. Where in particular planning considerations are involved, the Court has emphasised the complex issues[1] and that this is an area where the authorities exercise discretionary powers. As with use of expropriation powers, weight is given to the exercise by the legislature of its role to implement measures in the general interest.[2]

In older cases, the approach was taken that States were the sole judges of the necessity of a control of use and that the Convention organs were restricted to supervising the lawfulness and purpose (if legitimate) of the restriction.[3] More recently, in line with the general development of case law, there is examination of the proportionality of the measures applied. Whether a planning restriction is regarded as an interference with peaceful enjoyment of possessions or a control of use appears to depend on the intended primary purpose of the measure but the same considerations appear to apply in this area whichever classification is used.[4] Even where property is seized and ownership is lost in the area of confiscation this is regarded not as a deprivation of property but as a control of use due to the purpose of the measure in, for example, controlling the importation of gold or fighting drug-trafficking (see Part IIB: Expropriation and confiscation). This section deals with planning type restrictions and preventive measures.

2. Planning restrictions

(a) *General interest*

The Convention organs accept without particular scrutiny planning restrictions which affect building and development on property or occupation rights. Environmental concerns provide grounds of justification in the most general terms.[5]

---

[1] *Allan Jacobsson.*

[2] *e.g. Sweden*, 11763/85, (Dec.) March 9, 1989, 60 D.R. 128: legislation extending fishing rights to all in private water (end of exclusive fishing rights for landowners). Weight given to decision of democratic institutions and legislators in passing the measure as necessary in the general interest.

[3] *e.g. Handyside v. U.K.*, December 7, 1976, Series A, No. 24; 10378/83, (Dec.) December 7, 1983, 35 D.R. 235.

[4] See *Sporrong*, para. 69, where striking a balance is seen as underlying each part of Art. 1 of Protocol No. 1.

[5] See *e.g. Pine Valley*, development refused in green belt; *Fredin*, refusal of exploitation of a gravel pit; *U.K.*, (Dec.) 11185/84 March 11, 1985, where the applicant converted bunker on land in Jersey for residential purposes and was subject to enforcement proceedings including threat of criminal prosecution — the Commission considered planning controls in an area of outstanding natural beauty were *prima facie* in the general interest; 20490/92, (Dec.) March 8, 1994, 76–A D.R. 90: enforcement procedures against intensified use of house as Buddhist pilgrimage centre, where Commission found planning controls are necessary and desirable to preserve and improve landscapes in town and country.

(b) *Proportionality*

Consideration is given to whether the applicant knew or was subject to the restriction when he took over the property,[6] the existence of legitimate expectations or acceptance of the risk on purchase,[7] the extent to which the restriction prevents use of the land[8] and the availability of procedures importing flexibility and fairness.[9] So far, there have been no situations where control of use has been found disproportionate to the general interest being pursued.[10]

For example, where in *Tre Traktorer v. Sweden*, a restaurant lost its licence to sell alcohol, there was a control of use of the business and premises but no violation. There had been a progression of measures having regard to the company's discrepancies in its bookkeeping on alcoholic beverages and although there was a heavy burden on the company to justify itself (it alleged the shortfall was from thefts) there was a wide margin of appreciation and the measure not disproportionate. In *Phocas v. France*, where the restriction of the applicant's ability to develop his property by an urban development plan was treated as an interference with enjoyment of possessions,[11] the measure was found not disproportionate since there were procedures by which the applicant could require the State within a set period to buy his property.

3. Article 6 rights and planning cases

Proceedings relating to property rights, including disputes as to permitted use of the land, concern civil rights and obligations. However, following *Bryan v. United Kingdom* it appears that limited court review of points of law in planning cases may suffice insofar as access to court is concerned. In *Bryan*, where the applicant alleged that the procedures before planning inspectors from which limited appeal lay to the High Court were insufficient to comply with the requirements of Article 6, paragraph 1 the Court commented that limited review was a frequent feature of systems of judicial control of administrative decisions throughout Member States and this case illustrated the typical exercise of discretionary judgment in the regulation of citizen's conduct in the sphere of town and country planning. It found that the limited review by the High Court of factual questions was reasonably to be expected in specialised areas of law where the facts were already established in a quasi-judicial procedure conforming with many of the safeguards of Article 6, paragraph 1. Thus the Court found that the planning inspector was bound to decide fairly and impartially and gave a fair hearing, notwithstanding a lack of independence or decision-making power, and that the High Court's review powers were sufficient.

4. Preventive measures

Measures aimed at preventing persons suspected of involvement in organised crime from using their property constitute a control of use and have generally been found to pursue

---

[6] *Allan Jacobsson; U.K.* 11723/85, (Dec.) May 7, 1987, 52 D.R. 250, where enforcement proceedings against applicant for use of property for vehicle repair and haulage but the use had at all times been unlawful; 20490/92 *op. cit.*: no right for extension of permitted use of building beyond what in existence at time of acquisition.

[7] *e.g.* in *Fredin*, the Court found no legitimate expectation to continue the exploitation of the gravel pit which was winding down and in *Pine Valley*, where the applicants were involved in commercial development which entailed risk.

[8] *Allan Jacobsson*, where he had one house on the property in which he could live but could not build a second.

[9] *ibid.*, where the prohibitions were reviewed every couple of years and applications for exceptions allowed interests to be weighed.

[10] Interference with enjoyment of possessions under the first sentence of the first paragraph has been found more frequently where measures have been severe in their effects, *e.g. Sporrong* (long term restrictions imposed by expropriation permits).

[11] April 2, 1996 R.J.D. 1996–II, No. 7: It was a measure preliminary to possible expropriation.

the general interest and to be proportionate, in which context adequate procedural safeguards against arbitrariness are required.[12] In *Raimondo v. Italy*, where the seizure was a temporary measure, the Court found that it aimed at preventing the use of property in organised crime, which purpose appeared to be decisive in light of the Court's emphasis on the importance of fighting Mafia crime, in which context confiscation of this kind was a real and effective weapon. While the initial measures were not disproportionate however, the Court did find a violation when, after the domestic court ordered the property restored, there was a delay in removing the entries of the measures from the public register.[13] Since the court had ordered rectification, the continuation of the measure was neither provided for by law or necessary in the public interest.

Cross-reference

Part IIB: Expropriation and confiscation
Part IIB: Gypsies
Part IIB: Home
Part IIB: Housing and tenancy
Part IIB: Property

---

[12] *Italy*, 12386/86, (Dec.) April 15, 1991, 70 D.R. 59, where there was confiscation of property from a person suspected of membership of mafia type organisation, the Commission found it was clearly in the general interest as designed to prevent the illicit use of possessions the lawful origin of which not established, the State enjoying wide scope in measures for crime prevention in face of a disturbing level of organised crimes. The Commission gave attention to whether there was an effective judicial guarantee in the procedure allowing the applicant a reasonable opportunity to put his case. Since the courts established the facts in adversarial proceedings and there was no indication of arbitrary assessment of evidence (it could and did order restitution if the applicant proved property was bought with his own money), the measures were not disproportionate.
[13] Seven months for a lorry and four years for some real property, which had the effect of restricting enjoyment of property and would form a blot on the title, causing practical difficulties.

Pre-trial detention

Key provision:

Article 5, paragraph 3.

Key case law:

Neumeister v. Austria, June 27, 1968, Series A, No. 8; 1 E.H.R.R. 91; *Matznetter v. Austria*, November 10, 1969, Series A, No. 10; 1 E.H.R.R. 198; *De Jong, Baljet and Van Den Brink v. Netherlands*, May 22, 1984, Series A, No. 77; 13 E.H.R.R. 433; *Schiesser v. Switzerland*, December 4, 1979, Series A, No. 34; *Vallon v. Italy*, May 22, 1984, Series A, No. 77; 8 E.H.R.R. 20; *Brogan and Others v. U.K.*, November 29, 1988, Series A, No. 145–B; 11 E.H.R.R. 117; *B v. Austria*, March 28, 1990, Series A, No. 175; 13 E.H.R.R. 20; *Huber v. Switzerland*, October 23, 1990, Series A, No. 188; *Letellier v. France*, June 26, 1991, Series A, No. 207; 14 E.H.R.R. 83; *Kemmache No. 1 v. France*, November 27, 1991, Series A, No. 218; 14 E.H.R.R. 520; *Toth v. Austria*, December 12, 1991, Series A, No. 224; 14 E.H.R.R. 551; *Clooth v. Austria*, December 12, 1991, Series A, No. 225; 14 E.H.R.R. 717; *Tomasi v. France*, August 27, 1992, Series A, No. 241–A; 15 E.H.R.R. 1; *W. v. Switzerland*, January 26, 1993, Series A, No. 254–A; 16 E.H.R.R. 591; *Brincat v. Italy*, January 26, 1993, Series A, No. 254; 17 E.H.R.R. 60; *Kemmache No. 3 v. France*, November 24, 1994, Series A, No. 296–C; 19 E.H.R.R. 349; *Yağci and Sargin v. Turkey*, June 8, 1995, Series A, No. 319; 20 E.H.R.R. 505; *Mansur v. Turkey*, June 8, 1995, Series A, No. 321; 20 E.H.R.R. 535; *Van der Tang v. Spain*, July 13, 1995, Series A, No. 321; *Aksoy v. Turkey*, December 18, 1996, R.J.D., 1996–IV, No. 26; *Scott v. Spain*, December 18, 1996, R.J.D., 1996–VI, No. 27; *Muller v. France*, March 17, 1997, R.J.D., 1997–II, No. 32; *Sakik and others v. Turkey*, November 26, 1997, R.J.D., 1997–VII, No. 58.

1. General considerations

There are two principal aspects under Article 5, paragraph 3 — first, concerning the time permissible for a person arrested on reasonable suspicion of committing an offence (or the other two grounds under Article 5, paragraph 1(c)) to be held before being brought before a judicial officer; secondly, limiting the time during which such a person should be detained pending trial.

There is no right to bail as such, the release pending trial expressed only as an alternative to trial within a reasonable time. A suspect does however have the right to appear before a judicial authority with the power to release.

2. Initial arrest period

It is a fundamental safeguard against abuse of power by the police or any equivalent officer with the power of arrest that the person is brought "promptly" before a judicial authority. It prevents oppression, coercion, arbitrary arrest and ill-treatment, giving less opportunity for marks to fade or for a person's will to be broken by pressure and isolation.[1] The Convention organs have emphasised the importance of judicial control against arbitrary deprivation of liberty as a fundamental ingredient of the rule of law.[2]

Two principal issues have arisen in the case law: what qualifies as "promptly" and as a judicial officer.

---

[1] *e.g. Aksoy*, para. 78.
[2] *Brogan*, para. 58.

(a) *Promptly*

The Court has held that the degree of flexibility attaching to the notion is very limited. While individual circumstances must be taken into account in assessing promptness, their significance can never be taken to the point of impairing the very essence of the right.[3]

Brogan and Others v. United Kingdom indicates that four days may in exceptional circumstances, such as the difficulties attaching to terrorist investigations, be acceptable but beyond four days was unacceptable, exceeding the plain meaning of the word "promptly" and allowing a serious weakening of the guarantee to the extent of impairing its essence.[4] For ordinary crimes, it would seem that the Court would set a shorter maximum but the point is not expressly decided. Practical excuses are unlikely to be successful. Delay of five days for an applicant to be brought before a military court was not found to be justified by an intervening weekend and the absence of personnel on manoeuvres, since this eventuality was foreseeable and steps could have been taken, such as sitting over the weekend.[5]

Extension of the period to seven days for terrorist suspects was found to be compatible with the power to derogate under Article 15, where this was required by the exigencies of a state of emergency and attended by safeguards against abuse.[6] A period of 14 days in Turkey was considered prima facie to be too long, impliedly with or without attendant safeguards.[7] (See Part IIB: Derogation.)

The review of police or administrative detention should be automatic. It is insufficient that an applicant can apply for review.[7a]

(b) *Judge or other officer authorised by law to exercise judicial power*

The judicial officer does not have to hold the status of a judge but he must have some of a judge's guarantees. This includes independence of the executive and of the parties; the procedural requirement of hearing the individual himself; the substantive requirement of reviewing the continuation of the detention by reference to legal criteria; and the power to order release.[8]

Appearance before a court is not by itself a sufficient guarantee, where the question of justification for the continued detention is not to be dealt with until later.[9] Where the officer or tribunal has no power to release, they lack the requisite judicial power and there will also be a breach.[10] Issues also are likely to arise where the judicial officer has no power to release by operation of law, *e.g.* where statute acts in certain categories of cases to remove the discretion to release.[11]

An officer who combines functions of investigation and prosecution is likely to be lacking the necessary independence and impartiality. There was a breach where the *auditeur militaire* (judge advocate), although independent from the military authorities,

---

[3] *ibid.*, para. 59.

[4] Violations — four days six hours, four days 11 hours; five days 11 hours, six days 16^1/$_2$ hours.

[5] *Koster v. Netherlands*, November 28, 1991, Series A, No. 221. The rules also imposed a maximum of four days.

[6] *Brannigan and McBride.*

[7] *Aksoy*, paras 82–84.

[7a] *e.g. Van der Sluijs and others v. Netherlands*, May 22, 1984, Series A, No. 78, para. 46; 9017/80 (Dec.) *Sweden*, October 13, 1982, 31 D.R. 72.

[8] *Schiesser*, para. 31.

[9] *Van der Sluijs and others v. Netherlands*, para. 46.

[10] *e.g. De Jong*, where the *auditeur militaire* had made recommendations subject to non-binding practice of acceptance; *Aquilina v. Malta*, 25642/94, (Dec.) January 17, 1997 where a magistrate had no power to release until the Att.-Gen. had been consulted.

[11] 30307/96 and 32819/96 *U.K.* (Dec.) December 1, 1997 pending before the Commission concerning s.25 of the Criminal Justice and Public Order Act 1994.

could be called upon to perform prosecution functions once a case was referred to the military court and was therefore not independent of the parties to the potential criminal proceedings.[12] Similarly, in *Huber v. Switzerland*,[13] where a Swiss district-attorney took decisions relating to pre-trial detention and also conducted the investigation and drew up the indictment, there was a violation. Although the district attorney did not in fact act as prosecutor in the final proceedings as was possible under the applicable procedure, he could not be regarded as independent of the parties and his impartiality was capable of appearing open to doubt. Although the Court has not ruled out that a judicial officer may carry out other functions, he must do so without calling his impartiality and independence into doubt. It is the objective appearances at the time of decision of detention on remand which are material.[14]

(c) *Other procedural safeguards*

Representation by a lawyer has not been found to be required for the purposes of Article 5, paragraph 3[15] although issues may arise under Article 6, paragraph 3(c) (see Part IIA: Legal Representation in criminal proceedings).

(d) *Relationship with Article 5, paragraph 4: review of lawfulness of detention*

Article 5, paragraph 4 is a guarantee of a different order to, and additional to, that provided by Article 5, paragraph 3. They can be applied concurrently, although obviously the procedure for bringing a person before a judge may have a certain incidence on compliance with paragraph 4.[16]

3. Length of detention on remand

As concerns the continuation of detention on remand, the role of the domestic authorities is seen as ensuring that the pre-trial detention of an accused person does not exceed a reasonable period. They must examine all the circumstances arguing for or against the existence of a genuine public interest justifying, with a due regard to the presumption of innocence, a departure from the rule of respect for individual liberty and must set them out in decisions on the applications for release. It is essentially on the basis of the reasons given in these domestic decisions and of the true facts mentioned by the applicant in his appeals that the Court considers it is called upon to decide whether or not there has been a violation of Article 5, paragraph 3.[17]

Continuation of a reasonable suspicion that the applicant has committed an offence (the principal ground under Article 5, paragraph 1(c)) is a *sine qua non* for the validity of the detention but with the lapse of time this no longer suffices and the Court must then establish whether the other grounds given by the judicial authorities continued to justify the deprivation of liberty. Such grounds must be relevant and sufficient and the competent national authorities must display "special diligence" in the conduct of the proceedings.[18] It is not apparent up to what moment, or lapse of time, that suspicion alone will continue to

---

[12] *De Jong*, para. 49.

[13] *Huber*, paras 42–43, reversing *Scheisser* which appeared to indicate that it was the effective concurrent exercise of dual functions which was problematic (para. 34).

[14] *Brincat*, para. 21.

[15] *Schiesser*, para. 36.

[16] e.g. *De Jong*, where there was a breach of Art. 5, para. 3 for a delay of seven, eleven and six days before applicants brought before a court and of Art. 5, para. 4 for an inability to obtain review of the lawfulness of the detention over the same period.

[17] e.g. *Letellier*, para. 35; *Mansur*, para. 52.

[18] e.g. *Yaği and Sargin*, para. 50; *Letellier*, para. 35.

justify detention but it is likely to be a matter of months, since the Commission has found a violation in the period of 14 months in *Can v. Austria*.[19] A period of detention may not be justified on the basis of the alleged shortness of time alone.[20] In the absence of reasons, or where an uninformative stereotyped form of decision is given by the courts, it would be unnecessary to consider whether they acted with particular diligence since there would be no sufficient grounds for the continued detention.[21]

The period of detention is calculated from the date of arrest/commencement of detention on Article 5, paragraph 1(c) grounds until the judgment/conviction at first instance.[22]

Assessment of reasonableness can take into account a period of detention which is itself outside the Convention organs competence *ratione temporis*, since whether continued detention in the later period is justified may depend on the time already spent in custody.[23]

(a) *Relevant and sufficient grounds*

(I) SERIOUSNESS OF THE SUSPICION

Existence and persistence of serious indications of guilt are relevant but cannot alone justify a long period of pre-trial detention and cannot be used to anticipate a custodial sentence.[24] After a certain period of time, persistence of reasonable suspicion no longer suffices and the Court examines whether the other grounds relied on by the judicial authorities justify the deprivation of liberty.[24a]

(II) PROTECTION OF PUBLIC ORDER

Some offences by their gravity and the public reaction to them may give rise to public disquiet capable of justifying pre-trial detention at least for a time. However, the Court had rejected Government claims on this ground in a number of cases, considering that this can only be justified in exceptional circumstances and must be based on sufficient evidence of facts indicating that the accused's release would actually disturb public order. There was insufficient evidence in *Letellier v. France* where the Government referred to the "profound and lasting" disturbance to public order resulting from a premeditated murder.[25] While in *Tomasi v. France*, where an officer was involved in an armed terrorist attack which resulted in death and serious injuries, some risk of disorder might have existed at the beginning but it must have disappeared after a certain time.

(III) RISK OF PRESSURE ON WITNESSES OR COLLUSION WITH CO-ACCUSED

This is a relevant and unexceptional ground but as soon as the risk diminishes the ground will no longer be valid. With the passage of time, risk to the gathering of evidence has

---

[19] *Can v. Austria*, 300/81. (Rep.) July 12, 1984, Series A, No. 96 (settled before the Court).

[20] *Yağci and Sargin*, para. 54.

[21] *e.g. Mansur*, where court gave stereotyped identical form of orders renewing detention and on three occasions no reasons were given; *Yağci and Sargin*, where the courts looked at the case four times in a three month period, but gave stereotyped refusals, with no explanation of why there was a danger of absconding.

[22] *B v. Austria*, para. 39: even where domestic law classifies detention pending appeal as detention on remand.

[23] *e.g. Mansur*, where there was a period of one year 28 days after recognition of the Court's compulsory jurisdiction but five years three months before.

[24] *e.g.* a period of five years seven months, in *Tomasi*, para. 89.

[24a] *Letellier*, para. 35.

[25] *Kemmache*, para. 52: counterfeiting did not qualify either.

often been found to disappear, as in *Kemmache No. 1 v. France* where the risk ended once the witnesses were questioned, the file closed and sent to court. Where, as in *W v. Switzerland*, findings of risk of collusion and interference are maintained on the basis of scrupulous examination of the evolving circumstances, the Court is unlikely to disagree but where, as in *Clooth v. Austria*, decisions continuing detention are stereotyped and refer to the needs of investigation in a general and abstract fashion, it may be found that the detention ceases to be justified on this basis.

(iv) Risk of repetition of offences

The Court and Commission have accepted the view of domestic courts that the applicant's previous convictions for similar offences meant they could reasonably fear he might commit new offences.[26] But where domestic authorities relied on an alleged precarious psychological state of the suspect from previous offences of different kind, this would only furnish a ground for extending confinement if accompanied by therapeutic measures.[27] A mere reference to the person's antecedents is not sufficient to justify refusing release.[28]

(v) Danger of absconding

The risk of absconding has to be assessed in light of the factors relating to the person's character, his morals, home, occupation, assets, family ties and other links with the country in which he is prosecuted. The expectation of heavy sentence and the weight of evidence may be relevant but not as such decisive and the possibility of obtaining guarantees (*e.g.* payment of security, other forms of judicial supervision) may have to be used to offset any risk.[29]

The Convention organs have criticised domestic courts who rely on this ground without indicating any factual basis, repeat stereotyped decisions or fail to consider the possibility of obtaining guarantees from applicants to ensure their appearance, *e.g.* financial conditions. In *Tomasi v. France*, the Court considered that the domestic courts gave no proper considerations to this aspect, their decisions unreasoned as to why the risk of absconding was decisive despite the applicant's clean record and status as shopkeeper. The fact that an applicant faced a serious prison sentence if convicted could not be the sole basis for finding such a risk.[30] Where the likely sentence can be anticipated and the period in detention is deductable, the lessening incentive to abscond is one of the relevant factors that should be taken into account.[31]

There must be continued grounds for believing the risk to subsist. In *Kemmache No. 1 v. France*, there was some basis for suspicions since he had previously failed to appear before the court on spurious grounds of car "mechanical" failure. Since however the courts did not rely on this ground after a particular date and had no fresh grounds, this could not be used to justify further detention. However, findings of links with foreign countries, including funds or family, have provided sufficient grounds.[32]

Regarding the type or level of guarantees that may be legitimately required by domestic authorities, these are not limited to money but can include residence and movement restrictions.[33] The level of bail set should not be set too high and should not be aimed at

---

[26] *Toth*, para. 70.
[27] *Clooth*, para. 40.
[28] *Muller*, para. 44.
[29] *e.g. Letellier, Matzenetter; Hauschildt,* below, n.67.
[30] *e.g. Letellier,* para. 43, concerning a mother of two children who ran her own business.
[31] *Can v. Austria,* 9300/81, (Rep.) July 12, 1984, Series A, No. 96.
[32] *e.g. W v. Switzerland,* January 26, 1993, Series A, No. 254–A; *Van der Tang.*
[33] *e.g. Schmid v. Austria,* 10670/83, (Dec.) July 9, 1985, 44 D.R. 195.

reparation of loss but to ensure the presence of the accused.[34] But where the applicant is implicated in large scale financial dealings of a fraudulent nature larger sums may not be unreasonable.[35]

(b) Conduct of the proceedings: special diligence

Courts must show "special diligence" in bringing cases of detained persons to trial, notwithstanding the existence of strong suspicion or other relevant grounds for the detention.[36] However, the right to special diligence had been held not to prevail over the proper administration of justice and there is an obligation on judges to clarify the facts and collect evidence prior to trial.[37] Even where one case was not particularly complex but was delayed when it was joined to another, the Court found that the decision was taken to join in the interests of the proper administration of justice and the inevitable slowing down of the case was not incompatible with the speed requirement.[38]

Consideration is had to the complexity of the investigation, the number of defendants, the nature of the legal issues, and the international elements by way of letters rogatory.[39] A substantial gap in proceedings may be fatal as in *Vallon v. Italy*[40] where, although the Commission refused to question the merits of the decision to issue letters rogatory, an eight-month delay between the reply and the setting down for trial founded a violation.[41] Also relevant are errors made by the authorities[42]; unnecessary, cumbersome procedures[43]; the complexity of the case[44] and the conduct of the applicant. In respect of the latter, applicants are not required to co-operate actively with the judicial authorities and cannot be blamed for taking full advantage of the resources afforded by national law in their defence. Where conduct of an applicant goes beyond this, revealing an obstructive attitude, or contributing substantially to delaying proceedings, is perhaps a fine line.[45]

---

[34] *e.g. Can v. Austria*, see n.31, where the Commission criticised the sum as being set at the value of property subject to the arson attack rather than assessed in relation to the applicant, his assets and his relation to the persons to provide the security; *Neumeister*, paras 13–14.

[35] *e.g. W v. Switzerland*, January 26, 1993, Series A, No. 254–A, where the Court found the rejection of the applicant's offer of financial guarantee of CHF 30,000 not unreasonable since the provenance of money was unknown and the sum derisory in light of the size of the case (large scale fraud involving 60 companies).

[36] *e.g. Letellier*, para. 35.

[37] *e.g. Matzenetter*, para. 12; *B v. Austria*, para. 45.

[38] *Van der Tang, Can v. Austria*, see n.31. See also 9627/81 *Ferrari-Bravo v. Italy*, (Dec.) March 14, 1984, 37 D.R. 15: 4 years 11 months was found to be justified by the complexity of the affair and the exceptional difficulties posed by the nature of the case (subversive terrorist aspects) and the fact the case was joined to other accused was reasonable for the administration of justice, and it was not required for the cases to be severed.

[39] *e.g. Matzenetter*, para. 12; *B v. Austria*, para. 45.

[40] Settled before the Court.

[41] *Woukam Moudefo v. France*, October 11, 1988, Series A, 141–B (Rep.) where there was four and half months delay before he was interrogated and a delay of one year in taking action on failure of certain witnesses to appear for a "confrontation" though their statements had already been taken beforehand.

[42] In *Tomasi*, there were numerous errors and omissions on part of the judicial authorities, *e.g.* proceedings instituted in court without jurisdiction.

[43] *Toth*, where on each new application either for release or for extension in detention, the file itself was transferred (rather than copies) causing suspension of investigation, which was not reconcilable with the importance of the right to liberty.

[44] *W v. Switzerland*: exceptional complexity of case (largest economic crime dealt with) was a significant factor in finding no violation (by a narrow majority of 5:4) in a rather long period of over 4 years. On the other hand, in *Scott v. Spain*, after four years 16 days of investigation there were only two statements from the Finnish rape victim and four medical certificates in the file. The alleged difficulties in serving letter rogatory to Finland would not justify the delay and the duty of "special diligence" was not observed.

[45] *Yagci and Sargin*, where the Government attacked the applicants' tactics, filing of evidence and walking out of court room in protest at security arrangements but the Court found no indication that they were obstructive in their attitude and even if some elements slowed things down this did not account for the length of time in issue.

Table of lengths of detention

Matznetter v. Austria	—2 years, almost 2 months: no violation
Letellier v. France	—2 years, 9 months: violation
Kemmache v. France	—2 years, 10 months: violation
Toth v. Austria	—2 years, 1 months, 2 days: violation
Tomasi v. France	—5 years, 7 months: violation
Clooth v. Austria	—3 years, 2 months, 4 days: violation
B v. Austria	—2 years, 4 months, 15 days: no violation
Woukam Moudefo	—3 years, 2 months, 25 days — Commission violation (settled before Court)
Can v. Austria	—14 months, 26 days — Commission violation (settled before Court)
Van der Tang v. Spain	—3 years, 1 month, 27 days: no violation
W. v. Switzerland	—4 years, 3 days: no violation (narrow decision 5:4)
Quinn	—1 year: no violation
Scott v. Spain	—4 years, 16 days: violation
Muller v. France	—almost 4 years: violation
Ferrari-Bravo v. Italy[46]	—4 years, 11 months: Manifestly ill-founded
Hauschildt v. Denmark[47]	—2 years, 9 months: Manifestly ill-founded[48]
Di Stefano v. U.K.[48a]	—19 months: Manifestly ill-founded[49]
Deschamps v. Belgium[50]	—23 months: Manifestly ill-founded[51]

---

[46] 9627/81, *Italy,* March 14, 1984, 37 D.R. 15.

[47] 10486/83, (Dec.) October 9, 1986, 49 D.R. 86.

[48] Not excessive, having regard, *inter alia*, to the substantial activity of the courts (136 court sessions in 18 months).

[48a] 12391/86, (Dec.) April 13, 1989, 60 D.R. 182.

[49] See p.324. Complex fraud with 100 witnesses and 3,000 pages of documents and though applicant claimed strong ties with U.K. for 20 years, he was still an Italian citizen and also had alleged links with organised crime abroad.

[50] 13370/87, *Belgium,* (Dec.) July 4, 1991, 70 D.R. 177.

[51] Dangerous personality, death threats to witness, not unduly prolonged.

Prisoners' rights

Key provisions:

Article 3 (prohibition of inhuman and degrading treatment); Article 5, paragraph 4 (review of lawfulness of detention); Article 8 (respect for family life, private life and correspondence); Article 13 (effective remedy for Convention breaches); Article 14 (discrimination).

Key case law:

Golder v. U.K., February 21, 1975, Series A, No. 13; 1 E.H.R.R. 524; *Silver v. U.K.*, March 25, 1983, Series A, No. 61; 5 E.H.R.R. 347; *Campbell and Fell v. U.K.*, June 28, 1984, Series A, No. 80; 7 E.H.R.R. 165; *Schonenberger and Durmaz v. Switzerland*, June 20, 1988, Series A, No. 137; 11 E.H.R.R. 202; *McCallum v. U.K.*, August 30, 1990, Series A, No. 183; 13 E.H.R.R. 596; *Campbell v. U.K.*, March 25, 1992, Series A, No. 233–A; 15 E.H.R.R. 137; *Herczegfalvy v. Austria*, September 24, 1992, Series A, No. 242–B; 15 E.H.R.R. 437.

1. General considerations

A convicted prisoner's deprivation of liberty does not mean that he loses the protection of the other fundamental rights in the Convention. The enjoyment of these must however inevitably be tempered by the reasonable exigencies of his situation and the requirements of security will weigh significantly in any balancing exercise of justification. A large proportion of the cases before the Commission and Court are introduced by prisoners, who are perhaps in a particularly vulnerable position, almost all, if not all, aspects of their lives being subject to regulation by authority. The potential for interference and restriction in fundamental rights and freedoms is considerable and reflected by the wide number of issues raised in prisoner cases. These are examined below, following brief comment on non-exhaustion of domestic remedies.

2. Exhaustion and remedies issues

A prisoner, notwithstanding the difficulties of his position, financial and practical, is generally required to exhaust domestic remedies available in the United Kingdom. If a remedy is available, he is expected to find a lawyer, apply for legal aid and pursue proceedings in courts, including available appeals.

The principle that only effective remedies need to be exhausted applies. The Board of Visitors, which cannot enforce its conclusions, is not effective nor the Parliamentary Commissioner for Administration who has no power of rendering a binding judgment. The Secretary of State has been found to constitute an effective remedy where a prisoner is complaining about the misapplication of one of the prison rules in his case but not where the prisoner challenges the rule itself.[1] The Commission has hinted a doubt at the former assumption in a case where the applicant prisoner's complaint about interference with correspondence was summarily discounted as groundless by the Home Office but proved correct before the Commission.[2] Notwithstanding suspicion that the prison authorities do not always give detailed consideration to prisoners' grievances, the basic approach is that the prison authorities must be given an opportunity to remedy mistakes before the

---

[1] *Silver.*
[2] *W v. U.K.*, 16244/90, (Rep.) May 4, 1993, unpublished.

Strasbourg organs embark on examining State responsibility for alleged violations. The Commission accordingly in this case, in the context of Article 13 gave the authorities the benefit of the doubt "in the absence of any indication or evidence that as a matter of practice petitions to the Secretary of State are not properly or adequately examined".

Whether the courts may furnish an effective remedy will depend on the subject-matter of the complaint. Mere doubt about prospects of success does not exempt from exhaustion.[3] Civil claims for assault, negligence, trespass to goods would be required by Article 26 in appropriate cases.[4] Where an applicant challenged the content of a prison rule e.g. concerning censorship of correspondence, the position in Silver v. United Kingdom was that judicial review, limited to examining whether the measure was arbitrary, in bad faith, for an improper motive or ultra vires was not sufficient. However, the possibility that judicial review may permit challenge of prison rules was illustrated in Leech v. United Kingdom, where the Court of Appeal in a judicial review application challenging the opening and reading of legally privileged correspondence, found that the prison rule was ultra vires in that it allowed reading and stopping of confidential letters with a solicitor on wider grounds than merely to ascertain if they were in truth bona fides communications. As a result, complaints to the Commission by the same prisoner Leech about interference with his legal correspondence when he was held in Scottish prisons failed for non-exhaustion since he did not pursue the case to the final court, i.e. the House of Lords, which could have decided whether to uphold the Court of Sessions rejection or to follow the view of the Court of Appeal in English cases.[5]

Complaints under Article 9 by orthodox Jewish prisoners of the Secretary of State's refusal to allow a Jewish welfare association to provide them with kosher food was rejected for non-exhaustion, the Commission considering that this was a decision which should have been challenged by judicial review since there was a prison rule which required prisoners to be provided with food of a particular standard and it could be argued that the Secretary of State should take into account special dietary requirements in providing sufficient food of the necessary quality. This was notwithstanding the applicants pointing to a similar application which had been unsuccessful.[6]

Where, in McCallum v. United Kingdom, complaints were made that conditions of confinement in a special detention unit (the Inverness cages) were contrary to Article 3,[7] the Government drew attention under Article 13 to judicial review precedents dealing with prison conditions, arguing that where conditions are so severe as to be inhuman or degrading, they would fall within the scope of review of the proper exercise of power. The point was ceded by applicant's counsel before the Court, which did not pursue it further.

3. Conditions of confinement

Minor unpleasantnesses, however unnecessary, petty or deliberately provoking will not raise any issues under Article 3. More extreme treatment may receive examination by the Commission but the case law indicates that the threshold is very high and in fact, no prisoners held in prison after conviction have secured a finding of a violation before the Court. To succeed it seems that a prisoner must prove a degree of isolation reaching levels of sensory or social deprivation, with medical evidence of significant impairment of health

[3] See Part I 6 — Admissibility Checklist.
[4] U.K., 14462/88, (Dec.) April 12, 1991, prisoner alleging medical negligence in treatment of an injured hand — non-exhaustion since he had not instituted a claim for damages.
[5] 20075/92, (Dec.) August 31, 1994, unpublished; Veenstra v. U.K. 20946/92, August 8, 1994, unpublished, non-exhaustion where there was no application by way of judicial review in respect of opening in a Scottish prison of letters from his lawyers.
[6] U.K. 13669/88, (Dec.) March 7, 1990, 65 D.R. 245.
[7] McCallum v. U.K., 9511/81, (Rep.) May 4, 1989.

resulting from that confinement. Anything less would appear to need gross abuse by the authorities, such as a lack of any security or other justification for severely punitive restrictions.

(a) *Solitary confinement*

Segregation *per se* is not inhuman or degrading. While the Commission acknowledges that prolonged removal from association is undesirable and that complete sensory deprivation coupled with complete social isolation can ultimately undermine the personality and could in certain circumstances amount to inhuman treatment which could not be justified by the requirements of security, in practice the threshold for inacceptable circumstances is set very high.[8] The Commission, pursuant to the general Article 3 approach, examines the particular circumstances, for example, the duration, stringency, objective of the measures and, most importantly, the effects on the person.[9]

However, even in *Ensslin and others v. Germany*, where there were reports of marked physical and mental deterioration in prisoners in segregation, the Commission found that there was no sensory deprivation, having regard, *inter alia*, to the provision of radio, TV and exercise and no complete social isolation, since they had contacts with their lawyers and each other, save for limited periods. It was also satisfied that there was no deliberate attempt to punish or break resistence. In *Windsor v. United Kingdom*, there was evidence that after 14 months' lockdown the applicant was suffering from lack of sleep, was highly agitated and anxious, having developed an obsessive compulsion to cope with the lockdown, but the Commission found that conditions did not constitute such complete sensory deprivation as would undermine his personality. In particular, he received visits and was not deprived of association or exercise for excessively long periods. It accepted the Government assertion that prisoners were fed throughout.[10]

In *McFeeley and others v. United Kingdom*,[10a] where Republican prisoners on a "dirty protest" complained of severe disciplinary sanctions and conditions of confinement,[11] the Commission, having regard to the self-imposition and security aspects, found that the circumstances were not severe enough to disclose treatment prohibited under Article 3, notwithstanding its criticism of the inflexible attitude of the authorities, who were more concerned to punish the offenders than to resolve the deadlock. Dealing separately with the complaint about the restricted diet imposed in combination with cellular confinement, for which there was no security or other justification, the Commission considered that this was a stringent and wholly undesirable form of punishment, but although harsh, it was still not severe enough to infringe Article 3.

Even where a prisoner may have brought harsh restrictions on himself by revolt or fundamental non-co-operation, the Government is not excused from its obligations thereby and must constantly monitor conditions with a view to ensuring the health and well-being of all prisoners.[12]

---

[8] *Ensslin and others v. Germany*, 7572/76, 7586/76 and 7587/76, (Dec.) July 8, 1978, 14 D.R. 64.

[9] 10263/83, *R. v. Denmark*, (Dec.) March 11, 1985, 41 D.R. 149.

[10] *Windsor v. U.K.*, 18942/91, (Dec.) April 6, 1991; the applicant had alleged that prisoners had gone for periods of days without food. In this kind of case, the Government's ability to provide convincing records of conditions is significant.

[10a] 8317/78, (Dec.) May 15, 1980 20 D.R. 44.

[11] *e.g.* loss of remission, cellular confinement, loss of privileges (*i.e.* visits, letters, tuck shop, exercise), no clothing cold temperatures due to smashed windows; alleged denial of access to toilet facilities for long periods, hosing down of cells and inmates with cold water, slopping out procedure, strip searches, restricted diet.

[12] *X v. U.K.*, 8231/78, 28 D.R. 5, (Dec.) March 6, 1982; *McCallum; Ensslin* cases; *Windsor v. U.K.*, where the entire prison was locked down, in an extreme situation, but Commission found that there was a progressive relaxation as prisoners were eased back into a normal routine; *McFeeley*, see n.11; *McCallum v. U.K.*, 9511/81 (Dec.) July 9, 1984, where confinement in "cages" was kept under constant review; *Ensslin*, see n.8; *Windsor v. U.K.*, see n.10.

On the matter of duration, 15 months in a cell of six square metres was not contrary to Article 3, even though there was a comment that the length was undesirable.[13] 23 months cellular confinement for refusal to wear prison uniform was "severe" isolation but mitigated by daily visits from various persons and thus not sufficiently serious.[14] Where an IRA prisoner complained of 760 days of solitary confinement, the Commission found that he did not suffer from either sensory or social deprivation, with no physical symptoms besides loss of weight and although this length of time was "undesirable", it fell short of treatment contrary to Article 3.[15]

(b) *Prison uniform and work*

There is nothing inherently degrading about the requirement to wear a prison uniform or to work.[16]

(c) *Cell conditions*

Overcrowding combined with slopping out, were features criticised as inhuman and degrading by the Committee for the Prevention of Torture.[17] However, these conditions have not been raised before the Commission.

The use of solitary confinement cells consisting of cage-like areas attracted criticism by the Commission in *McCallum*[18] as being harsh but it noted the relatively short periods of detention involved *i.e.* 3–4 months, the provision of regular exercise, and continued enjoyment of correspondence and visiting rights. Since there was also no indication of ill-effects on the prisoner, the complaints were rejected as manifestly ill-founded.

(d) *Nature of place of detention*

It has occasionally been argued that a prisoner, by the nature of his health or sentence, requires a particular regime of detention. However, in *Ashingdane* (mental health) and *Bizzotto* (drug addict), the Court dismissed the contention that location of detention impinged on the lawfulness of the detention for the purposes of Article 5, paragraph 1.[18a] No issues would appear likely to arise under Article 3 in the absence of severe inhuman and degrading circumstances resulting from the inappropriate regime.

4. Medical treatment

Complaints about the adequacy of medical treatment offered and received are not uncommon from prisoners. However, the nature of the failure likely to meet Article 3's

---

[13] *R v. Denmark*, see n.9, where the applicant had two half hour periods of exercise and contact with prison staff, visits, medical examinations. The reason for the confinement — the complexity and seriousness of the ongoing investigation — was taken into account.

[14] *X v. U.K.*, see n.12.

[15] 8158/78 (Dec.) July 10, 1980, *X v. U.K.*, 21 D.R. 95: he received visits and exercise, and regard was had to his security classification, attempts to escape and influence on other prisoners.

[16] *McFeeley*, see n.11; *X v. U.K.*, see n.12, where prison uniform was a justified interference with private life, pursuing the aim of preventing escape.

[17] Report of visit 1990–1994 CPT/inf(91)15.

[18] 9511/81, see n.12.

[18a] *Ashingdane v. U.K.*, May 28, 1985, Series A, No. 93; *Bizzotto v. Greece*, November 15, 1996, R.J.D., 1996–V, No. 21. See Part IIB — "Deprivation of Liberty" (5. In accordance with law and lawfulness) and Mental Health (8. Right to Treatment).

high threshold has yet to be determined.[19] Where in *Lockwood v. United Kingdom*[20] a prisoner had been reporting sick for months without receiving, in his view, serious consideration and only after a collapse and admittance to his hospital was discovered to have a tumour in his chest, the Commission found that the alleged suffering resulting from the months of delay before he received proper medical treatment did not disclose sufficiently severe treatment. It noted that, from the materials submitted, proper diagnosis would not have altered significantly the course of his illness or the treatment finally received. Since the prison doctor did begin treatment and testing, the factor of delay while not "negligible" in its psychological effect, was not sufficient to disclose inhuman and degrading treatment.

Complaints that ill-health or age render an applicant unfit for detention have so far failed. While the Commission has considered that a problem might arise if no or insufficient treatment was given, it requires convincing medical evidence that the prisoner is unfit for detention or that the facilities provided place health in danger.[21] Even where prisoners were suffering from potentially fatal illnesses such a HIV with limited life expectancy, it was adequate that they were found to be receiving proper monitoring and care and that serious complications had not yet developed.[22] It remains to be seen whether the Commission would react differently where a prisoner was clearly in the final stages of a terminal illness. It might be argued that to require a person to die in confinement subject to the continual restrictions is inhuman and degrading.[23]

Conversely, where allegations are made of prisoners being forcibly drugged to render them compliant, problems arise of exhaustion of domestic remedies and sufficient substantiation of the prisoner's version of events. In *Freeman v. United Kingdom*,[24] a prisoner alleged that he was physically held down by prison staff and injected with drugs against his consent. He pursued an action for assault unsuccessfully up to the House of Lords but since the domestic courts found his complaints as to lack of consent unsubstantiated and the Commission did not have any basis to reject the courts' findings as arbitrary or unreasonable, the complaint was rejected.

Where treatment is based on therapeutic necessity, complaints under Article 3 are unlikely to succeed. In *Herczegfalvy v. Austria*, which concerned a person detained as mentally ill, the Commission found that compulsory sedation, being fettered to a bed for several weeks and forced artificial feeding reached levels of inhuman and degrading, having regard to the disproportionate manner of application. The Court, less emotive, conceded that the duration of the coercive measures was "worrying" but accepted that there was a therapeutic necessity according to the psychiatric principles accepted at the time. For the Court, established medical principles were decisive and a measure which was therapeutic cannot at the same time be inhuman and degrading. This appears to imply that forced feeding of a person on hunger strike might not fall within the scope of Article

---

[19] See, *e.g. Hurtado v. Switzerland*, January 28, 1994, Series A, No. 280–A, where the Commission found a delay in examining the applicant after a violent arrest (he had cracked ribs) disclosed a violation of Art. 3 but the case settled before the Court.

[20] *U.K.*, 18824/91, (Dec.) October 14, 1992.

[21] *B v. Germany*, 13047/87, (Dec.) March 10, 1988, 55 D.R. 271 where a concentration camp survivor's claims that he was unfit for detention were not substantiated by his own doctors, thus despite the special hardship that detention might cause him, manifestly ill-founded; 8224/78, *Switzerland*, (Rep.) December 5, 1979, 18 D.R. 148, where the applicant, 74, suffering from diabetes and other disorders claimed unsuitability for confinement, the Commission did not exclude the possibility that detention of a man of such age and ill-health could raise a problem under Art. 3 but not in this case where the prison had a medical service with staff of considerable expertise; 7994/77, *Netherlands*, (Dec.) May 6, 1978, 14 D.R. 238; 9044/80 *Italy*, (Rep.) December 8, 1982, 33 D.R. 41.

[22] *U.K.* 22564/93, (Dec.) April 14, 1994, 77–A D.R. 90; *U.K.* 22761/93, (Dec.) April 14, 1994, 77–A D.R. 98.

[23] The case of Guiseppe Conlon who died in prison in the United Kingdom, compassionate release having been refused and then granted too late, is a case which comes to mind.

[24] *U.K.* 12016/86, (Dec.) October 13, 1986.

3 and to deny the possibility that a person could choose from motives of his own dignity or self-determination to refuse painful or humiliating, albeit life-saving, treatment. The Commission's view that treatment had to be not only to be medically necessary but carried out in conformity with humane standards is perhaps preferable.

5. Strip searches

Strip searches, including rectal examinations, have not been found a problem under Articles 3 or 8, where carried out for security reasons. Where a Dutch prisoner was required to urinate in front of a prison officer to provide a sample for testing for use of illegal drugs,[25] the Commission found that the circumstances were not severe enough for Article 3. Although it disclosed an interference with his private life, regard was had to the reasonable and ordinary requirements of imprisonment in which wider measures of interference might be justified than for persons at liberty. The measure was accordingly necessary for the prevention of crime and disorder. In *M'Feeley v. United Kingdom*, frequent strip searches were found to be necessitated by the exceptional security requirements of the Maze prison, where experience showed dangerous objects had been smuggled in. The Commission found that while the circumstances were personally humiliating they were not deliberately degrading, referring to the lack of physical contact and the presence of a senior officer to prevent abuse.[25a]

6. Visiting rights and access to family

The Commission considers that continued contact by a prisoner with his family and friends takes on added importance in the context of Article 8 since normal means of continuing relationships have been removed. It has noted the European Prison Rules which emphasise the need to encourage links. Consequently, the Commission finds that Article 8 requires the State to assist prisoners as far as possible to create and sustain ties with people outside prison in order to facilitate their social rehabilitation. That said the Commission has not been generous in its application of the principle.[26]

There is no right to unlimited visiting.[27] In theory however there should be good reasons for obstacles placed in the way of contacts. Obstructiveness deriving from a policy of moving a prisoner around at short notice for "cooling off" with the result that relatives arrived at a prison only to find he had been moved was the basis of *Seale v. United Kingdom*,[28] declared admissible under Article 8 and then settled.[29]

Prisoners held in special security categories are unable to derive from Article 8 the right to unsupervised visits or to visits unencumbered by partitions or screens, in particular where IRA prisoners and their families are concerned. The Commission has found that although such restrictions were prima facie an interference, they were justified in the interests of public safety and the prevention of crime and disorder.[30] In *Boyle v. United Kingdom*,[31] the Commission commented on the insensitivity of the prison authorities in not permitting the applicant greater contact with his wife which inevitably gave rise to considerable resentment over long years of imprisonment but found on the whole that the

[25] 21132/93 (Dec.) April 6, 1994, 77–A D.R. 75.
[25a] See n.11.
[26] e.g. where non-family contacts did not require protection X v. U.K. 9054/80, October 8, 1982, 30 D.R. 113 — refusal of permission for visit by campaign group to a prisoner not disclose interference under Art. 8.
[27] X v. U.K., 9054/80, see n.26.
[28] 9466/81, (Rep.) May 15, 1986, 36 D.R. 41.
[29] £800 for wasted travel costs, an apology and agreement to issue an instruction that relatives holding an outstanding visitors order should be informed promptly after a transfer had been made.
[30] 8065/77, (Dec.) May 3, 1978, 14 D.R. 246.
[31] 9659/82, (Dec.) May 5, 1983, annexed to (Rep.), May 7, 1986.

balance struck between the applicant and his wife and administrative and security considerations was not so unreasonable as to interfere with the right to respect for family life.

Visits by families are often rendered difficult where a prisoner is held in a prison far from his close relatives. The Commission holds however that a prisoner cannot derive from Article 8 a right to choose the place of confinement and that separation from family and the hardship that it causes inevitably flows from imprisonment. It will only be in exceptional circumstances that the location of a prison a long way from a prisoner's home or family might infringe the requirements of Article 8.[32]

In *Campbell and Fell v. United Kingdom*[33] the Commission considered the difficulties arising from overcrowding in prisons in Northern Ireland in finding no problem in the refusal to transfer prisoners from England. However, in a later series of Republican prisoner cases, the availability of prison space in Northern Ireland did not swing the balance in favour of transfer. It found no exceptional circumstances arising from the separation of IRA prisoners in England from their families in Northern Ireland or the Republic of Ireland.[34] In some cases, parents were elderly, in ill-health and unable to make the long journey, or other relatives not in receipt of State assistance could not afford the trip with the result that some prisoners received very few visits at all over long periods. The Commission commented on the fact that their place of imprisonment resulted from the prisoners' arrest and trial for serious offences committed in England and noted the serious security considerations attaching to this category of prisoner. Where it was argued that the security classifications did not reflect any real security risk on transfer[35] or the prisoner was not by health or classification a security threat, the Commission still did not consider this sufficient to bring the cases into the "exceptional" category. Even if there was a difference in treatment in that non-republican prisoners of high security classification had been transferred, such difference was justified by the special and sensitive considerations arising out of the disposal of IRA prisoners within the prison system against the background of the political situation which remained subject to complex pressures.[36]

It would appear that where transfers are concerned, the Commission is reluctant to impose positive obligations on Contracting States and an applicant would have to establish circumstances of extreme hardship and arbitrariness by the authorities.

7. Correspondence

Article 8 expressly guarantees the right to respect for correspondence and the Commission has emphasised that this applies to prisoners, subject to the ordinary and reasonable requirements of imprisonment. There should in principle be a free flow of correspondence and any stopping of a letter to a prisoner requires justification in rules which are accessible and public. In *Silver v. United Kingdom*, the stopping of letters to outside bodies or letters complaining about prisoners' convictions or treatment in prison was not "in accordance

---

[32] 5229/71, (Dec.) October 5, 1972, Coll. 42, p. 14 and 5712/72, (Dec.) July 15, 1974 Coll. 46: reference to thousands of miles over the sea; 15817/89, October 1, 1990, 66 D.R. 251, while there was an interference from a refusal to transfer a Scot from a prison in England to one in Scotland to enable him to see his fiancée, it was a proportionate interference, provision being made for temporary visits under strict security conditions.

[33] *U.K.*, 7819/77, (Dec.) May 6, 1978, paras. 30–33 14 D.R. 186.

[34] *McCotter v. U.K.*, 18632/91, December 9, 1992; *P.K. and others* 19085/91, December 9, 1992; *McDowd and McKenna v. U.K.*, 21596/93, (Dec.) September 1, 1993.

[35] When prisons wanted to, they could provide the security necessary for moving prisoners.

[36] 23956/94 (Dec.) November 28, 1994, *McKenny v. U.K.; Vella v. U.K.*, 23958/94, (Dec.) November 28, 1994.

with law" as the measures were unforeseeable, the relevant orders not having been published.[37]

Regarding justifiable restrictions, the Commission referred in *Silver* to the perhaps understandable desire to support prison staff by preventing floods of outside criticism but it gave much greater weight to the need of prisoners to make outside contacts and express feelings to those outside contacts. It saw no necessity and indeed great dangers in a system which prevented prisoners obtaining access by letter to lawyers for advice and which might prevent steps being taken to preserve vital evidence supporting a prisoner's claims.

In *Silver*, many restrictions were found unnecessary, *e.g.* the restrictions on letters to family and friends, complaints about public authorities and the requirement of prior ventilation of complaints before letters could be sent to legal advisers or members of Parliament. Later cases found that it was unnecessary to stop letters to the press[38]; letters of complaint to lawyers which have not been put to prison authorities; letters from lawyers to a prisoner instructed by his wife on his behalf[39]; matters intended for publication; letters to persons unknown to prisoners before their imprisonment[40]; letters seeking penfriends[41]; complaints to the police about ill-treatment to others[42]; letters concerning the institution of private criminal prosecutions; and letters to unofficial organisations.[43]

The following measures may be necessary, *e.g.* restrictions on correspondence of a business nature (which may involve the proceeds of crime)[44]; the naming of other prisoners in the prison, which may raise security considerations[45]; the naming of prison officers in a context which raises a threat[46]; threats of violence[47]; letter naming a prison officer with imputations made against him intended for publication.[48]

Mere delay in sending a letter may be a violation although this is subject to the acceptance that where instructions are required as to whether a letter should be stopped, some time will elapse. Three weeks for a letter, not urgent in nature, was found to be acceptable.[49]

Regarding other restrictions on correspondence, the imposition of letter quotas may be justifiable, having regard to the vast quantity of mail the authorities have to deal with, at least where the level set is not unduly restrictive and the effect minimal.[50] There is no interference from the obligation to use prison notepaper assuming it is readily available.[51] A denial of notepaper altogether may disclose a violation.[52] As for the cost of correspondence, the State is not obliged as a general principle to pay postage for prisoners

---

[37] *e.g. W v. U.K.*, 16244/90, (Rep.) May 4, 1993 where an unofficial agreement with police whereby letters of complaint were held back while the governor investigated was not "in accordance with law"; *Calogero Diana v. Italy*, November 15, 1996, R.J.D., 1996–V, No. 21 where the power to censor mail was undefined and unrestricted.

[38] *McCallum*, see n.7.

[39] *Schonenberger and Durmaz.*

[40] *X v. U.K.*, 8575/79, (Rep.), July 2, 1985.

[41] *Grace v. U.K.*, 11523/85, (Rep.), December 15, 1985.

[42] *McCallum*, see n.7.

[43] *Farrant v. U.K.*, 7291/75, 50 D.R. 5.

[44] *Silver.*

[45] *ibid.*

[46] *W v. U.K.*, (Dec.) December 12, 1991.

[47] *Silver*, (Rep.), paras 413–415; *Grace*, see n.41.

[48] *W v. U.K.*

[49] *Silver; McCallum*, see n.7, a delay of almost a month was found compatible while the authorities contacted the addressee with a query.

[50] *Chester v. U.K.*, 12395/86, (Rep.) May 17, 1990 applicant had sent 600 letters, eight-thirty per week and it was not unreasonable to limit him to 24 Christmas cards.

[51] *Farrant*, see n.43.

[52] *T v. U.K.*, 8231/78, (Rep.) October 12, 1983, 49 D.R. 5.

but depending on particular circumstances a failure to do so might severely restrict their ability to communicate by post. The provision of one paid letter a week was sufficient in *Boyle v. United Kingdom*[53] to respect the applicant's right to correspondence.

Errors and mistakes are no justification for a failure to send a letter or for not notifying that the Post Office has returned a letter as the address was incomplete.[54] On the other hand, accidental opening due to an administrative oversight (*e.g.* novice censor, failure to notice a marking) when accompanied by an apology, may not disclose a problem where there is no indication of a deliberate flouting or disregard of the applicable rules.[55] A Government is expected to maintain proper records relating to the handling of mail and where a dispute arises as to whether letters have been received, it cannot discharge its obligations by merely supplying a record of incoming mail.[56]

Although prison regimes are showing increasing flexibility regarding access to telephone facilities, the Commission's approach has been to hold that there is no right to communications by telephone where adequate provision by way of mail is made.[57] Where telephone use is allowed, restrictions on the number of calls or authorised recipients are unlikely to raise problems in the current climate.[58]

8. Access to lawyers and to court

A prisoner cannot be barred from taking action in the courts or be required to obtain prior consent by the Home Secretary to contact a lawyer for the purpose of taking possible action. Such a restriction is a breach of the principle of access to court, access for everyone being a crucial guarantee of the respect of the rule of law on a domestic level.[59]

Further, even a Category A prisoner is entitled under Article 6 to out of hearing visits with his legal adviser, as he can claim a legitimate and vital interest in keeping the subject-matter of such consultations confidential.[60] Other conditions imposed on access of a solicitor, including search and continual close presence of prison officers may be justified by security considerations.[61] Refusal of consultation with a doctor for an independent medical examination concerning alleged injuries may raise an issue under Article 6, paragraph 1 where it concerns possible litigation for assault by prison officers, though there is as such no automatic right to such facilities.[62]

Regarding letters, imposing a delay on consultation by letter with a solicitor regarding possible claims pending internal enquiries — "prior ventilation rule" — was found to disclose violations of both Article 6 (access to court) and Article 8 (respect for correspondence).[63] *Campbell v. United Kingdom* settled that it was unjustified to open any correspondence with a lawyer outside the presence of the applicant and in the absence of good reason. A blanket opening rule was incompatible and where there was reason to suspect abuse or illicit enclosures, opening might be justified if guarantees against abuse

---

[53] *Boyle, v. U.K.*, 9659/82, (Dec.) May 5, 1983.
[54] *Grace*, see n.41.
[55] *Ryder v. U.K.*, 14176/88, (Dec.) January 19, 1989; *Hosein v. U.K.*, 18264/91, struck off September 8, 1993 when the Government admitted two letters, to the Commission and to an M.P. were found to have been wrongly stopped after an investigation and no further hindrance followed.
[56] *Messina v. Italy*, February 26, 1993, Series A, No. 257–H: the list contained the letters received at the prison and sent to the investigating judge to be censored, without trace of what happened afterwards.
[57] *Boyle*, (Dec.) 9658–9/82, see n.53.
[58] *Chester v. U.K.*, 32783/96, September 11, 1997; *Bamber v. U.K.*, 33742/96, (Dec.) 1997.
[59] *Golder*, paras 35–36.
[60] *Campbell and Fell*.
[61] *Campbell v. U.K.*, 12323/86, (Dec.) July 13, 1988, 57 D.R. 48.
[62] *Campbell and Fell*, (Rep.) paras 153–156.
[63] *Ibid.*, paras. 105–111; *U.K.*, 10621/83, (Dec.) March 11, 1985: screening of legal correspondence concerning pending court proceedings disclosed an admissible issue of interference with access to court. Settled.

were offered by allowing the prisoner to be present. The same considerations were found to apply to the opening of letters to the Commission, which were likely to contain complaints about the prison and lead to risk of reprisals by staff.

A prisoner without funds is in a difficult position as regards pursuing his civil rights in a court. The Commission has found that refusal of legal aid on the basis that there are no prospects of success is not incompatible with requirements of access to court, given that there is no specific right to legal aid in respect of civil matters in the Convention. There is the rider that the refusal may be shown to be arbitrary. However, the Commission has accepted the refusal of legal aid even where counsel had stated there was a prima facie case supported by medical evidence.[64]

9. Practice of religion and beliefs

Occasional complaints have been made concerning interference with religious beliefs or matters of conscience by prison regimes. No serious issues have yet been found to arise. Claims by Orthodox prisoners that prison food failed to respect dietary requirements was contested strongly by the Government and failed for non-exhaustion.[65] The failure to be able to eat a particular item or lack of provision of a preferred item is insufficient. Short of compulsion to breach a strict religious dietary requirement or failure to provide sufficient food compatible with that diet, complaints are likely to fail.[66]

What constitutes a religious commitment is perhaps a sensitive area. There has been no success as yet in claiming that working is against a religious belief.[67] Where a prisoner claimed that it infringed his vegan beliefs to work in a prison workshop which entailed contact with dyes, the Commission which considered that vegan convictions in relation to animal products could fall within the scope of Article 9, appeared sceptical noting the Government's point that the applicant first refused to work on the basis that he preferred work outdoors and rejected the case, referring to the dubious substantiation of any link between the dyes and animals and the minor nature of the penalties which he suffered for refusing to work.[68] Where a life prisoner, converted to Islam after conviction complained that while he had changed his name by deed poll, the prison refused to use this name for some internal prison purposes, the question of whether this interfered with any religious belief was left undecided when the case settled.[69]

A personal belief that one is a political prisoner does not give rise to a right to wear personal clothing.[70]

The provision of facilities or the opportunity to worship or contact with religious ministers is probably required by Article 9. In *Chester v. United Kingdom*,[71] a prisoner complained that he had been deprived of the possibility of attending religious services in the chapel which the Government stated had been closed down as being insecure. The case was communicated but later struck off, after it appeared that the applicant had received

---

[64] 8158/78, *U.K.*, (Dec.) July 10, 1980, 21 D.R. 95: The Commission commented that it was open to the prisoner to initiate proceedings by other means and referred to the fact that he had been able to find a lawyer to bring the case to Strasbourg. There is no explanation for the difference of opinion between the legal aid authority and counsel and it seems unsatisfactory to state a prisoner can rely on obtaining charitable assistance from outsiders for pursuing legal rights.

[65] 13669/88, see n.6.

[66] *e.g.* a claim that coffee or tea is prohibited and the alternative of hot chocolate unavailable.

[67] 8231/78, (Dec.) March 6, 1982, 28 D.R. 5.

[68] *U.K.*, 18187/91, (Dec.) February 10, 1993.

[69] *Islam v. U.K.*, 26651/91 (Dec.) May 13, 1996. In *Lant v. U.K.*, 11046/84, December 10, 1985, 45 D.R. 236: the Commission dismissed a complaint by a murderer who wished to lose his infamous name. It was compatible with Art. 8 in the interests of prison administration to retain the name for internal purposes.

[70] 8231/78, see n.67.

[71] *U.K.*, 14747/89, (Dec.) October 1, 1990.

visits from the chaplain in his cell, services were conducted in the segregation unit and the applicant lost interest in pursuing the complaint.

10. Education, leisure facilities and expression

Limitation on educational or leisure activities may be justified by security or associated considerations as in the case of *Boyle v. United Kingdom* where a complaint concerning prohibition of pursuit of sculpting activities in his cell was found justified by the risk posed by the sculpting tools. The refusal to Boyle, a prolific writer, of a typewriter was also rejected on the basis that there was no indication that the lack of one hindered his freedom to communicate or impart ideas in manuscript.[72] Where in *M'Feeley*[73] there were drastic restrictions on access to library, TV and radio facilities, the Commission had regard to the prisoners' own responsibility for the protest campaign being waged. Similarly, restriction on access to the library to a prisoner who refused clothes was acceptable in light of his own difficult behaviour and the fact that he received books via the education officer.[74]

Violation of freedom of expression was found however where there was a restriction on access to newspapers and periodicals by a difficult prisoner, which reduced his contact with the outside world and was not, unlike other restrictions, justified by considerations of security or order.[75] In the same case a general prohibition on sending out academic or scientific writings fell foul of Article 10.

Access to outside publications may be legitimately restricted to prevent crime and disorder or the protection of the rights of others, as in a case of a prisoner who complained that the authorities confiscated the anti-semitic "Gothic Ripples" literature.[76]

11. Internal prison discipline

Whether internal prison disciplinary proceedings attract the procedural guarantees of Article 6, paragraph 1 depends on whether they fall within the *Engel* criteria (see Part IIA: Criminal Charge). Loss of remission was found to constitute a penalty akin to a deprivation of liberty in *Campbell and Fell*. Where significant punishment is imposed for offences which are criminal in nature, rather than an internal breach of discipline, Article 6 may apply with its procedural guarantees.

Regarding the Board of Visitors' compliance with Article 6 requirements, it was found in *Campbell and Fell* to be impartial and independent of the executive. While there may have been good reasons to exclude the public from the proceedings, there was nonetheless a violation in that no steps were taken to make the decision public. Lack of legal assistance of the applicant's own choosing for consultation before or at the hearing also disclosed a violation of Article 6, paragraph 3(b) and (c). It was however compatible with Article 6, paragraph 3(b) that the prisoner was only informed of charges five days before the hearing and that he received notices relevant to the proceedings only the day before, it being noted that he did not make a request for an adjournment. It is perhaps unlikely in the context of prison detention that liberal facilities will be considered necessary for the purposes of Article 6. The requirement for free legal representation under Article 6, paragraph 3(c) is also conditional in the interests of justice. Whether a prisoner could claim legal

---

[72] (Dec.) see n.53.
[73] 8317/80, May 15, 1980, 20 D.R. 44.
[74] *T v. U.K.*, see n.52.
[75] *ibid.*, see n.52.
[76] 13214/87, (Dec.) December 9, 1988, 59 D.R. 244.

representation is likely to depend on the nature and complexity of the issues and the importance of what is at stake for the applicant.

Cross-reference

Part IIA: General Principles, Criminal charge
Part IIB: Education
Part IIB: Private life
Part IIB: Marriage and founding a family
Part IIB: Review of detention

Private life

Key provision:

Article 8 (respect for private life).

Key case law:

Klass v. Germany, September 6, 1978, Series A, No. 28; 2 E.H.R.R. 214; *Dudgeon v. U.K.*, October 22, 1981, Series A, No. 45; 4 E.H.R.R. 149; *Rasmussen v. Denmark*, November 28, 1984, Series A, No. 87; 7 E.H.R.R. 371; *X and Y v. Netherlands*, March 26, 1985, Series A, No. 91; 8 E.H.R.R. 235; *Gaskin v. U.K.*, July 7, 1989, Series A, No. 160; 12 E.H.R.R. 36; *B v. France*, March 25, 1992, Series A, No. 232–C; *Niemietz v. Germany*, December 16, 1992, Series A, No. 251–B; 16 E.H.R.R. 97; *Funke v. France*, February 25, 1993, Series A, No. 256–A; 16 E.H.R.R. 297; *Costello-Roberts v. U.K.*, March 25, 1993, Series A, No. 247–C; 19 E.H.R.R. 112; *Klaas v. Germany*, September 22, 1993, Series A, No. 269; 18 E.H.R.R. 305; *Burghartz v. Switzerland*, February 22, 1994, Series A, No. 280–B; 18 E.H.R.R. 101; *Fayed v. U.K.*, September 21, 1994, Series A, No. 294–B; 18 E.H.R.R. 393; *Murray v. U.K.*, October 28, 1994, Series A, No. 300–A; 19 E.H.R.R. 193; *Stjerna v. Finland*, November 25, 1994, Series A, No. 299–B; *Guillot v. France*, October 24, 1996, R.J.D., 1996–V, No. 19; *Laskey, Jaggard and Brown v. U.K.*, February 19, 1997, R.J.D., 1997–I, No. 29; *Z v. Finland*, February 25, 1997, R.J.D., 1997–I, No. 31; *M.S. v. Sweden*, August 27, 1997, R.J.D., 1997–IV, No. 44.

1. General considerations

Private life is not a concept which has received exhaustive definition by the Convention organs, who have generally preferred as in most areas to restrict themselves to the particular problem in hand. Considering the potential width of the term, the number of cases which deal with "private life" has been relatively few. It is a notion which also tends to overlap with the other interests protected under Article 8 — family life, home and correspondence, as in *Klass v. Germany*[1] where interception of communications (mail and phone) was potentially an interference with family and private life, correspondence and home while in *Mentes and others v. Turkey*,[2] the Commission found that the deliberate destruction of the applicants' homes and possessions by the State security forces cut across the entire personal sphere protected by Article 8, family life, private life and home and it was not necessary to distinguish them.

The concept stands for the sphere of immediate personal autonomy. This covers aspects of physical and moral integrity.[3] It is wider than the right to privacy. As the Commission has put it, it ensures a sphere within which everyone can freely pursue the development and fulfillment of his personality.[4] This necessarily comprises the right to an identity[5] and includes the right to develop relationships with other persons, in particular in the emotional field and including sexual ones with other persons.[6] Thus for the Commission the notion of private life is not limited to "an inner circle" in which the individual may live his own personal life as he chooses and exclude therefrom the outside world not encompassed within this circle, but extends further, comprising to a certain degree the

[1] Para. 41.
[2] 23186/94, (Rep.) March 7, 1996, para. 185 to be published in R.J.D. 1997 (judgment November 28, 1997).
[3] *X and Y v. Netherlands,* para. 22.
[4] 6825/75, (Dec.) March 4, 1976, 5 D.R. 86.
[5] *Burghartz,* (Rep.) para. 47.
[6] *Brüggeman and Scheuten v. FRG,* 6959/75, (Rep.) July 12, 1977, 10 D.R. 100.

right to establish and develop relationship with other human beings and the outside world.[7] The Court has been more hesitant in making such broad statements[8] but was clear in its inclusion of intimate aspects of sexual life in the adult homosexual cases.[9]

2. Extent of the "private" sphere

There are limits on the personal sphere or inner circle. While many measures by the State will affect an individual's possibility of developing his personality by doing what he wants, not all can be considered to constitute an interference with private life under Article 8. The Commission has found that the claim to respect for private life is automatically reduced to the extent that an individual brings his private life into contact with public life or other protected interests.[10] Thus it found no interference with private life where photographs were taken of a person participating in a public incident[11] nor in respect of communication of statements made in the course of public proceedings.[12] In *Friedl v. Austria*, the Commission considered it highly relevant, as regarded the taking of photographs by the police and their retention in files, to what extent the taking of the photographs amounted to an intrusion in the individual's privacy, whether it related to private matters or public incidents.

In the *Icelandic dog* case,[13] the Commission stated that protection of Article 8 did not extend to relationships of the individual with his entire immediate surroundings insofar as they did not involve human relationships (see below: Pets). In the context of abortion, the Commission took the view that pregnancy could not be said to pertain uniquely to the sphere of private life.[14] The life of the pregnant woman was seen as closely connected with the developing foetus and not every regulation of the termination of unwanted pregnancies would constitute an interference with the right to respect for private life.

3. State obligations: non-interference and positive protection

A Contracting State must not only restrict its own interferences to what is compatible with Article 8, which provides a primarily negative undertaking, but may also be required to protect the enjoyment of those rights and secure the respect for those rights in its domestic law.[15] The extent to which a State may be under a positive obligation to take particular measures will vary with the differing situations obtaining in Contracting States which enjoy in this respect a wide margin of appreciation in determining the steps to be taken to ensure compliance with the Convention having regard to the needs and resources of the community and individuals.[16]

Insofar as positive obligations are concerned, the Court has helpfully indicated that the notion of "respect" is not clear cut. It has stated that a fair balance must be struck between the interests of the individual and those of the community and in striking that

---

[7] *Friedl v. Austria*, (Rep.) May 19, 1994, Series A, No. 305–B, p. 20, para. 45.

[8] See *Stjerna*, para. 37 and *Burghartz*, para. 24.

[9] *Dudgeon*, para. 41 (see Part IIB: Homosexuality).

[10] See also *Ludi v. Switzerland*, June 15, 1992, Series A, No. 238, para. 40 where the Court excluded criminal activities from "private life"; Mr Geus in his dissenting opinion in *Burghartz* (Rep.) who applied the principle that private life ends where public life begins and thus since in his view an individual's surname was the most manifestly public feature as it was that by which everyone else and the authorities identified him, it could not form part of private life.

[11] 5877/72, 45 Coll. 90.

[12] 3868, 34 Coll. 10.

[13] 6825/75, see n.4.

[14] *Brüggeman*, see n.6; see Part IIB: Abortion.

[15] *Costello-Roberts*, para. 26.

[16] e.g. *Abdulaziz and others v. U.K.*, May 28, 1985, Series A, No. 94, para. 67.

324

balance, the aims referred to in the second paragraph may be relevant.[17] The cases indicate that the impact on the applicant's rights must be serious and significant as in *X and Y v. Netherlands* (which concerned a serious infringement of physical and moral integrity, *i.e.* rape), *Gaskin v. United Kingdom* (where fundamental values and essential aspects of private life or identity were concerned) or *B v. France* (where the interference was daily and acute).[18] No positive obligation was found in *Costello-Roberts v. United Kingdom* (where the chastisement was minor)[19] and *Rees* and *Cossey* (where the rights claimed by transsexuals were "controversial"). Whether an important State interest is involved may also be significant, as in *Abdulaziz and others v. United Kingdom* (where vital State interests in immigration were concerned) and *Rees* and *Cossey* (claimed State interest in maintaining a historical birth record).

4. Privacy

The lack of a right to privacy in the United Kingdom, in particular, against press intrusions (for example, the taking of photographs) or the disclosure in the media of highly intimate, non-defamatory details of private life, has not yet been subject to significant challenge.

The question was raised in the *Winer v. U.K.*[19a] case, where the applicant complained not only of difficulties in suing for defamation but of the lack of redress in respect of factual revelations in a book of various love affairs. The Commission noted the need for domestic law to balance the conflicting rights of freedom of expression and right to private life, which appeared weighted more on the side of the former but on the facts of that case (he was relatively successful in his defamation action and settled the case) it was not established that the balance was unfairly struck. Other cases have been introduced, concerning the taking of photographs[20] and a campaign of harassment by an ex-boyfriend which stopped short of actionable torts or crimes,[21] but were rejected for non-exhaustion, indicating that problems of exhaustion may arise where the domestic law situation leaves a doubt as to the existence of a remedy or appears to be subject to progressive interpretation.

The extent to which issues might arise under private life for press intrusion might be influenced by the extent to which the person concerned courted attention, the nature and degree of the intrusion into the private sphere and the ability of diverse domestic remedies to provide effective and adequate redress.[22]

---

[17] *e.g. Rees v. U.K.,* October 17, 1986, Series A, No. 106, para. 37.

[18] See also *Whiteside v. U.K.,* 20357/92, (Dec.) March 7, 1994, 76–A D.R. 80 where the harassment was extreme and frequent.

[19] See also *Netherlands,* 24967/94, (Dec.) 80–A D.R. 175, February 20, 1995: no positive obligation to protect from unsolicited mail, having regard to the interests of freedom of expression, link of mail concerned with funding costs of student facilities and that commercial information at issue could be easily ignored.

[19a] 10871/84, (Dec.) July 10, 1986, 48 D.R. 154.

[20] In *E.N. v. Ireland,* 18760/91, (Dec.) December 1, 1993 in proceedings for personal injuries, the defendant's insurance company had taken photographs of the applicant plaintiff when outside her house and several of her through a window in order to verify her state of health. The applicant complained that the taking of the photographs was an infringement of her private life (and family life and home) but was unsuccessful since the Commission found that she had not pursued an action which would test the extent of her constitutional protection, *i.e.* non-exhaustion.

[21] *Whiteside,* see n.18, where it was claimed that the piecemeal protection by domestic law was inadequate to provide protection. There were however recent developments in domestic case-law hinting at an extension of injunctive relief to general "harassment" type situations which threatened physical harm or ill-health so the applicant was again expected to test the matter further in the courts, *i.e.* non-exhaustion.

[22] 28851/95 and 28852/95 (Dec.) January 16, 1998 introduced by Earl and Countess Spencer concerning press coverage of their private lives. Cases declared inadmissible for non-exhaustion, since, on the facts of their case, an action for breach of confidence was available to them.

5. Personal information

Protection of personal data falls within the scope of private life.

(a) Content of "personal data"

The Commission has not provided any detailed analysis as to what personal data consists of, although a whole realm of data exists in the public domain or may relate to a person's public life. It is arguable that the fact of recording and using any personal data is an interference. While in an old case the obligation to carry identity cards and show them to police was considered not to constitute an interference as the cards did not disclose information relating to private life (the card did include name, address, sex, date and place of birth and could exclude mention of personal identification number on request)[23] more recently, in *Friedl v. Austria*,[23a] the personal data relating to establishing of identity by the police was enough to fall within Article 8.

(b) Access to personal data

Where information is stored by public bodies which relates to the private life of a person, issues may arise from a refusal to grant access. The principal case so far is *Gaskin v. United Kingdom*, which falls short of conferring any general right of access to data. The applicant, in local authority care almost all his childhood, was refused access to his files, which were described as forming a substitute record for the memories and experience of the parents of a child not in care, or the only coherent record of the applicant's early childhood and formative years. A person's entitlement to information of that kind was derived from its relation to his basic identity — it had formative implications for his personality because the information related to a period in which reliable memories did not exist. The Commission held that in principle persons should not be obstructed by the authorities from obtaining such very basic information without specific justification.[24] The Court commented that the finding of violation in the case was without prejudice as to whether general rights of access to personal data and information could be derived from Article 8. Notwithstanding the fact that confidentiality of the records protected the children and rights of the contributors and was important for the receiving of objective and reliable information, it concluded that the applicant had a vital interest in receiving the information and that there was a failure to strike the appropriate balance as there was no independent procedure whereby access could be allowed where a contributor gave an improper reason for refusing, failed to reply, gave consent or could not be traced.

Where an applicant's access to personal information held by social services is made subject to certain conditions, the Commission has examined the reasonableness of the conditions. It was not arbitrary or unreasonable, in respect of a person with a history of mental illness and where the records related to a brief period, to provide for access to be given to the applicant's doctor who was to judge whether or not the applicant should receive them.[25] On the matter of security files, the Convention organs have not found any requirement of access or disclosure. Interferences, assessed against a wider margin of appreciation, may be justified, where there are sufficient safeguards against abuse or arbitrary use of powers.[26]

---

[23] 16810/90, (Dec.) September 9, 1992, 73 D.R. 136.
[23a] See n.7.
[24] Para. 89.
[25] 27533/95, *U.K.*, (Dec.) February 28, 1996, 84–A D.R. 169.
[26] *Martin v. Switzerland*, 25099/94, (Dec.) April 5, 1995, 81–A D.R. 136, where the applicant at least had partial access. Applicants in other surveillance cases have had no possibility of access but the Commission has not picked up any issues. See Part IIB: Surveillance.

(c) *Collection and retention*

The recording of personal information for purposes of criminal investigation generally concerns private life but may be justified. This includes records of past offences, but also information obtained by the police in investigations where no criminal proceedings are brought and even where there is no reasonable suspicion in relation to a specific offence, where special considerations such as fighting terrorism can justify retention. In *McVeigh v. United Kingdom*[27] questioning, searching, fingerprints and photographing of the applicants and subsequent retention of the relevant records constituted an interference but was justified in the interests of public safety and prevention of crime. This was where the applicants were arrested and detained under prevention of terrorism legislation when they arrived in England from Ireland. Even though no criminal charge was brought against them, the Commission accepted that the information was relevant for intelligence purposes and found that there was a pressing social need to fight terrorism which outweighed what it considered as minor infringements of the applicants' rights. Similarly in *Murray v. United Kingdom*, on the arrest of the applicant, the recording of personal details and photographing were considered to be within the legitimate bounds of the process of investigation of terrorist crime. None of the details were found to be irrelevant to the arrest and interrogation procedures, which seems to imply that the Convention organs will at least impose a check on the nature and extent of the information which the police and security forces take it upon themselves to record, albeit subject to a wide margin of appreciation.

The mere taking and storing of photographs by the police of a public demonstration was not even an interference in the *Friedl v. Austria*[27a] case. There was no identification of the persons on the photographs apparently and the photographs remained in a general administrative file and were not put in a data processing system. The Commission emphasised that the photographs were not taken in any operation invading the applicant's home. The taking of personal data establishing identity and recording that data was an interference but justified since taken for the purpose of pursuing a prosecution even though that did not ensue due to the trivial nature of the offences. Also the data was kept only for a general administrative file about the event and not entered into any data-processing system. This was only a "relatively slight interference" with the applicant's right to respect for his private life. In *Martin v. Switzerland*, the retention of files destined purely for archivage for a period of 50 years did not constitute an interference since there was no effect on private life.[28]

Another major area of personal records is the medical. The taking and storing of such records associated with treatment will generally be justified under the second paragraph of Article 8, unless there is some failure or shortcomings as regards its use or disclosure to others.[29]

The compulsory requirement to provide information to a census (including sex, marital status, place of birth) was found to be an interference with private and family life but the Commission was satisfied that the interests of the individual were sufficiently safeguarded (replies were strictly confidential, names not used in the computer analysis and original forms not to be released in the Public Records Office for 100 years) and that the aim of economic well-being of the country was pursued.[30]

---

[27] *U.K.*, 8022/77, (Rep.) March 18, 1981, 25 D.R. 15.
[27a] See n.7.
[28] See n.26.
[29] 14461/88, (Dec.) July 9, 1991, 71 D.R. 141: the retention of information in hospital records about psychiatric confinement after the applicant's release constituted an interference but was justified *e.g.* where a strict confidentiality rule was observed, with no access of the public and where the system of storing records served legitimate interests in running the hospital and safeguarding patients' own rights. This was notwithstanding the fact that the applicant's detention had been found illegal in domestic proceedings.
[30] 9702/82, (Dec.) October 6, 1982, 30 D.R. 239.

Compulsion by tax authorities to reveal details of personal expenditure (and thus intimate details of private life) was an interference but justified where the applicant had recently sold properties and the issue arose as to how he had disposed of large sums. It was accepted as necessary in the interests of the economic well-being of the country that he establish these matters and there was perhaps a hint that such powers wielded more indiscriminately would be disproportionate.[31]

(d) *Disclosure of personal records*

Disclosure to the public or third parties of personal information constitutes interference less easily justified having regard to the recognition that the protection of personal data is of fundamental importance to a person's enjoyment of his private and family life.[32] The public interest in disclosure must outweight the individual's right to privacy, having regard to the aim pursued and the safeguards surrounding its use.

The showing of a photograph of an applicant from police files to third persons constituted an interference but was justified for prevention of crime and proportionate since the photograph was used solely for investigation, was not generally available to the public and had not been taken in a way which intruded on his privacy, *i.e.* lawfully by police during earlier arrest.[33] Use by a court of an old police report in order to assess the criminal responsibility of the accused was found to be necessary for the prevention of crime.[34] Disclosure of details of arrest by the police to the press was found, assuming this to be an interference, to be justified as being factual, summary and pursuing the legitimate aim of informing the public on matters of general interest.[35] While in *Z v. Finland*, it was found necessary to order the disclosure of a witness's medical records for the purposes of a trial, the publication of the witness's name and HIV status in the appeal court judgment was not justified as necessary for any legitimate aim.[36] The vital principle of confidentiality of medical data was emphasised in *Z v. Finland* and in *M.S. v. Sweden*. However in the latter, the Court found that it was legitimate for State medical institutions to pass onto social insurance authorities details of the medical history of a claimant for benefit. The measure was proportionate since the details disclosed were relevant to the claim, there was a duty of confidentiality and staff incurred civil and/or criminal liability for abuse.

Provisions for general disclosure of categories of records to the public in the future may disclose issues where containing highly personal information. In *Z v. Finland*, a further breach was disclosed from the fact that criminal files containing details of the applicant's medical records (HIV status) would be made public within 10 years, while she might still be alive.[37]

A system of personal identity numbers (*e.g.* used in civic registration and covering many administrative matters: tax, health, social services, etc.) may not interfere as such but use of the system will be covered if it effects private life. Thus the Commission found an

---

[31] 9804/82, (Dec.) December 7, 1982, 31 D.R. 231.

[32] *Z v. Finland*, para. 95; *M.S. v. Sweden*, para. 41.

[33] *Doorson v. Netherlands*, 20524/92, (Dec.) November 29, 1993, 75 D.R. 231.

[34] 8344/78, (Dec.) May 7, 1981, 24 D.R. 103; 7940/77, (Dec.) May 9, 1978, 14 D.R. 228 which hinted at the possibility that the disclosure to the public of a criminal record would constitute an interference in the context of defamation proceedings — rejected on facts as proceedings were still pending and the applicant could apply for a hearing in camera.

[35] *Netherlands*, 24774/94, (Dec.) April 6, 1995 where details appeared in the press following the applicant's arrest on suspicion of indecent assault on a boy, referring to police confiscation at his home of large quantities of child pornography. He alleged that the police had given incorrect details to the press and details which would enable persons in his neighbourhood to recognise him.

[36] See Part IIB: AIDS.

[37] There was provision for a longer period in other cases. The collection and use of the details in the criminal case against her husband was justified for the prevention of crime. *cf. Martin* case, see n.26 (50 year period).

interference where the applicant's name appeared in a register of defaulting tax debtors to which the public had access, including credit companies.[38] However, the interference, of a minor nature, was accepted as necessary in the interests of the economic well-being of the country. The applicant had not shown that he was in fact refused credit because of the register and regard was had to the fundamental Swedish principle of public access to official documents. There the Commission appeared to lend weight to the general desirability of public access to official data registers.

6. Reputation and defamation

The right to honour and good reputation as such is not guaranteed by Article 8, where there is no interference with private life involved.[39] The right to enjoy a good reputation is however a civil right for the purposes of Article 6, which guarantees access to court and fair determination of the issues. See Part IIB: Defamation and the right to reputation.

7. Names

Names are not only a form of personal identification but also constitute a link to family and involve to a certain degree the right to establish relationships with others.[40] Since there is little common ground in Contracting States, the Court affords a wide margin of appreciation as to the restrictions on permissible changes of name. There are accepted public interest considerations such as the importance given to the stability of family names, accurate population registration, safeguards to the means of personal identification and of linking the bearers of a particular name to given family.

Restrictions have, ultimately, been found compatible with respect for private life.[41] In *Stjerna v. Finland*, where the Finnish applicant claimed his surname caused problems since it was Swedish and was liable to be mispronounced by Finnish speakers, caused delays in mail and gave rise to the prejorative nickname "churn", the Court was not persuaded that there was any particular inconvenience or singularity in his name, noting that many names gave rise to nicknames and distortions.[42]

In France, where strict rules apply to the giving of first or Christian names, the Court found that it was also compatible with Article 8 to prohibit the registration of a baby with the name of "Fleur de Marie". The Court, noting that the child could use the name in daily life, if not for official documents, found the "certain complications" which might arise were insufficient to raise issues of interference with family or private life. The Commission, noting that the naming of a child at birth was undeniably an intimate part of the emotional life of its parents had found no violation by a narrower margin of 13:11.[43]

Other restrictions accepted by the Commission include the refusal of the prison authorities for administrative purposes to use the name obtained by deed poll after an

---

[38] 10473/83, (Dec.) December 11, 1985, 45 D.R. 121.

[39] 10733/84, (Dec.) March 11, 1985, 41 D.R. 211.

[40] *Stjerna*, para. 37 citing *Burghartz*, para. 24.

[41] Though discriminatory differences applied to men and women on marriage disclose a violation of Art. 14 in conjunction with Art. 8: *Burghartz*.

[42] The majority of the Commission found that there could in principle be no right to change one's surname under Art. 8 but did not exclude exceptional cases where carrying a name caused suffering or such practical difficulties that the right under Art. 8 was affected. This did not exist in this case. The minority found no necessity for the restriction in change.

[43] *Guillot v. France*: The large minority of the Commission, with whom two judges agreed, found that first names were well inside the sphere of private life and that there should be rigorous control of interference in their choice. They considered the name unusual, and not any more ridiculous than the anachronistic saints names (*e.g.* *Scholastique, Poppon, Polycarpe*) which were allowed. There was no necessity for the restriction and the fact that there was no real prejudice caused by the lack of official registration was not an argument against interference in this sphere.

applicant's sentence began[44]; inability of a woman to use her maiden name at elections (as candidate or voter)[45]; inability of a woman to take a name used by her ancestors 200 years before.[46]

8. Sexuality and gender matters

The Commission established very early that a person's sexual life was undoubtedly part of his private life of which it constitutes an important aspect, private life guaranteeing a sphere within which a person can establish relations of different kinds including sexual ones. Thus the choice of affirming and assuming one's sexual identity comes within protection of Article 8.[47] The Court has, in the context of consensual sado-masochistic acts, commented that it is not however every sexual activity carried on behind closed doors which will necessarily fall within the scope of Article 8. It doubted in that case, where the activities were organised, involving a large number of persons and the making and distribution of video-tapes, whether the conduct fell entirely within the notion of private life, although in the absence of dispute by the Government or Commission, it assumed an interference with private life for the purposes of the case.[48]

Matters relating to individual sexual life are of a particularly intimate nature within the scope of private life and require particularly sound reasons to justify interference. The hallmarks of a democratic society, tolerance and broadmindedness, have to be borne in mind and it is not enough that a particular activity might shock, disturb or offend.[49] Criminal law prohibition of consensual adult homosexual activity in private has accordingly found to be unjustified. (see Part IIB: Homosexuality.)

Some aspects may be subject to state interference if in accordance with paragraph 2, particularly where the protection of children is concerned.[50] Article 8 does not protect sex for remuneration professionally or activities amounting to prostitution.[51] While the disciplinary sanction of a police officer for cohabiting with a homosexual engaged in prostitution was an interference, it did not go beyond what was necessary for the purpose of prevention of disorder (*i.e.* to protect the good reputation of the police force).[52]

In *Laskey, Jaggard and Brown v. United Kingdom*, the Court found criminal sanctions on sado-masochistic behaviour, even conducted between consenting adults in private for sexual gratification, to be justified for the protection of health, taking the view that the State was entitled to regulate conduct involving physical harm which was not of a trifling or transient nature but in fact extreme. This infliction of injury was sufficient to distinguish the case from the homosexual cases. It also commented, rather censoriously,

---

[44] *Lant v. U.K.* 11046/84, (Dec.) December 10, 1985, 45 D.R. 236: since it only concerned some, not all, of internal prison documents and official prison contexts, incompatible *ratione materiae* as not concerning the right to respect for private life but relating to the public administration of prisons.

[45] *Hagmann-Hüsler v. Switzerland*, 8042/77, (Dec.) December 15, 1977 12 D.R. 202 the Commission noted that she could add it to her other married name.

[46] *Boij v. Sweden*, 16878/90, June 29, 1992: where no particular inconvenience, only a wish by the applicant to manifest a closer link with ancestors.

[47] *e.g.* 9369/81, (Dec.) May 3, 1983, 32 D.R. 220; *Brüggeman and Scheuten v. Germany*, 6959/75, May 19, 1976, 5 D.R. 103.

[48] As to whether non-sado-masochistic sexual activities between more than two persons would qualify as "private life" is unexamined as yet — see Part IIB: Homosexuality.

[49] *Dudgeon*, para. 60.

[50] 5935/72, September 30, 1975, 3 D.R. 46: justified to convict homosexual of acts with children under 16.

[51] 11680/85, March 10, 1988, 55 D.R. 178: conviction for unnatural debauchery — paid homosexual relations — 10 days' imprisonment.

[52] Also he was only dismissed but did not lose pension rights; 12545/86, (Dec.) December 12, 1988, 58 D.R. 126.

that its finding on the grounds of health should not be interpreted as negativing the right of the State to deter acts of this kind on moral grounds.[53]

The daily aggravation of a humiliating nature facing a transsexual who was unable to obtain a change of name and official papers to reflect gender re-assignment was sufficient to disclose a breach of Article 8.[54] Inability to obtain legal recognition, where this aggravation was not present, and which involved changing the historical birth certificate system in the United Kingdom did not qualify in the cases of *Rees* and *Cossey*. (See Part IIB: Transsexuals.)

9. Other personal relationships

The determination of an applicant's legal relations with a putative child concerns private life, even where what is at issue is a father's attempt to disprove paternity.[55] However, where an applicant claimed that respect for private life in the sense of establishing relationships was infringed by the refusal of a court to order a blood test to prove whether he, rather than the husband, was the biological father of a child of a married woman, the Commission found that the decision was justified in the interests of the child, who was remaining with the mother and her husband and required the stability and security of that home.[56]

Close relationships short of family life will generally fall within the scope of private life, for example the links between a foster mother and child she has looked after[57]; relationships between persons engaged to be married[58]; relationships between homosexuals and their partners[59]; and the links formed by a person who has lived for years in a particular country.[60]

The means by which a person pursues relationships may also attract the protection of Article 8. Penalties for use of a citizen's radio was an interference although justified by the need to regulate such use.[61] In two transsexual cases, *Sheffield v. United Kingdom* and *Horsham v. United Kingdom*, the Commission considered that the constraints placed on transsexuals due to the lack of legal recognition of their change of gender impinged on their ability to form relationships.[62]

10. Pets

Many would argue that the nature and strength of links between an owner and his pet bring the relationship within the scope of "private life". However, in the *Icelandic dog* case[63]

---

[53] The argument before the Commission that the law prohibited commonly practised types of masochism, heterosexual or otherwise, was rejected in *V, W, X, Y and Z*, 22170/93, January 18, 1995 as the applicants had not shown themselves to be victims by any direct or continuous effect on their private lives: *i.e.*, no prosecution or threat of prosecution or investigation; the conduct alleged was of a different nature and degree than the extremes in the *Laskey* case and the Commission was not satisfied that the *Laskey* case set a precedent for a spate of prosecutions, there being no indication that any other cases had been sought.

[54] *B v. France.*

[55] *Rasmussen*, para. 33. The Commission took a stronger line, considering that effective respect for private and family life required a State to make available for the alleged father of a child an effective and accessible remedy by which he could have established whether he is the biological father. It found a violation in the procedural discrimination between the spouses as only the father faced a time bar in paternity matters. The Court found that this inequality had objective and reasonable justification.

[56] *M.B. v. U.K.*, 22920/93, (Dec.) April 6, 1994, 77–A D.R. 108.

[57] 8257/78, (Dec.) July 10, 1978, 13 D.R. 248.

[58] 15817/89, (Dec.) October 1, 1990, 66 D.R. 251.

[59] *e.g.* 9369/81, (Dec.) May 3, 1983, 32 D.R. 220 see Part IIB: Homosexuality.

[60] *e.g. Bouchelkia v. France*, January 29, 1997, R.J.D. 1997–I, No. 28, para. 41.

[61] 8962/80, (Dec.) May 13, 1982, 28 D.R. 112.

[62] *Sheffield v. U.K.*, 22985/93 and *Horsham v. U.K.*, 23390/94, (Reps.) January 21, 1997 pending before the Court.

[63] 6825/75, see n.4.

where the applicant was refused permission to have a dog in the city of Reykjavik, the Commission did not consider that private life extended to relationships with dogs. It considered that the keeping of dogs overlapped into the public sphere, necessarily involving interferences with the life of others.

In *Artingstoll v. United Kingdom*,[63a] an elderly man enlisted arguments that it was good for his health to have a dog, medical evidence strongly supporting this, to persuade that the refusal to allow a dog in his council communal sheltered housing was an unjustified interference with his private life. The Commission avoided categorically rejecting the idea of private life as encompassing the companionship of pets. In rejecting the case, it relied on the fact that when the applicant took up the lease it should have been known by him that dogs were not allowed. Therefore the State was not responsible for the alleged interference. Later cases, more drastically, had owners of allegedly dangerous breed dogs complaining that the destruction of their pets was in violation of their right to private life. The Commission returned to its view in the *Icelandic dog* case.[64]

11. Compulsory measures of safety and health

The Commission has found that the numerous measures which States decide to take to protect the public against various dangers cannot be considered as infringing private life, referring, *inter alia*, to safety appliances in industry, obligation to use pedestrian crossings or subways, and compulsory seatbelts.[65]

A compulsory medical intervention, even of a minor nature, interferes with private life. Although in practice physical interventions on the grounds of health have been found justified under the second paragraph of Article 8. Compulsory vaccination, TB tests or X-rays for children have been found to pursue the aim of protecting health, while the disadvantages adverted to were not comparable to the former ravages of disease.[66] Where severe damage and death occurred in some cases as the result of a State-provided vaccination scheme, the Commission found that there was no lack of proper consent, there being a general knowledge of potential risks and that the State had taken reasonable precautions.[67]

Compulsory testing has also been found justified in the context of prisons, where compulsory urine tests are imposed on prisoners to check for drugs. This is generally regarded as necessary to prevent crime and disorder in prisons although the Commission hinted that such measures would not be acceptable if applied to persons not detained.[68] Compulsory blood testing of a drunken driver was justified as necessary for the protection of the rights and freedoms of others[69] while compulsory psychiatric examination of a person facing criminal charges was justified for the prevention of crime even though the enquiries into private life were not relevant to the crime but criminal responsibility.[70] Court-ordered blood tests to resolve paternity have also been found justified for the protection of the rights and freedoms of others.[71]

[63a] 25517/97, (Dec.) April 3, 1995.

[64] *e.g. Bates v. U.K.*, 26280/95; *Foster v. U.K.*, 28846/95; *Brock v. U.K.*, 26279/95, (Decs.), January 16, 1996: in a number of cases the dogs had been found unmuzzled in public.

[65] 8707/79, (Dec.) December 13, 1979, 18 D.R. 255.

[66] 10435/83, (Dec.) December 10, 1984, 40 D.R. 251.

[67] 7154/75, (Dec.) July 12, 1978, 14 D.R. 31.

[68] *Netherlands*, 21132/93, (Dec.) April 6, 1994, 77–A D.R. 75.

[69] 8278/78, December 13, 1978, 18 D.R. 184.

[70] *Germany*, 8344/78, May 7, 1981, 24 D.R. 103.

[71] 8278/78, (Dec.) December 13, 1979, 18 D.R. 154.

12. Measures of administrative control

Appointment of guardians in respect of mentally ill persons has been found justified for the prevention of crime and disorder where, for example, the guardian had the power to consent to treatment without which the applicant was a risk to his warders.[72]

Obligations to fill in census forms and tax details are interferences but may be justified for the economic well being of the country, although in the census cases weight has been given to the safeguards of confidentiality attached.[73]

13. Physical and moral integrity

Even where the State does not infringe itself on the private sphere of a person, it may be under a positive obligation to protect persons from incursions on their physical and moral integrity. The key case is *X and Y v. Netherlands*, where Y, mentally handicapped, was raped but had no legal capacity to appeal against the decision of the prosecution not to pursue criminal charges and her father had no standing to do so on her behalf. The Court found that positive obligations could arise requiring a State to adopt measures even in the sphere of the relations of individuals between themselves. It found civil law remedies offered insufficient protection in cases of wrongdoing of this kind and that the criminal law suffered from a deficiency regarding Y which disclosed a lack of respect for her private life.

Subsequently, the Commission has implied that a failure to provide adequate protection in criminal and civil law to persons suffering from harassment by another could disclose a breach of a positive obligation. In *Whiteside v. United Kingdom*, the woman applicant was allegedly being subjected to an intensely distressing campaign of harassment by a previous cohabitee. Government responsibility was engaged due to the persistent and distressing nature of the harassment and its effect on her and her way of life. However the case was rejected for non-exhaustion since recent case law development left a doubt as to whether an injunction for conduct calculated to impair health would be available to her.[74]

Positive obligations also arise in respect of children and the protection which they should receive from assaults. The Commission in *Costello-Roberts v. United Kingdom* considered that Article 8 might afford wider protection than Article 3. Although there was no violation of Article 3 (the slippering of the child applicant at school did not constitute degrading treatment), the same punishment could infringe the right to respect for private life.[75] However, the Court agreeing the slippering three times on the buttocks through shorts by a rubber-soled gym shoe was not sufficiently severe for Article 3, was not persuaded that Article 8 would provide wider protection in the area of physical integrity. While it did not rule out that disciplinary measures at school might in certain circumstances affect the right to respect for private life, not every act or measure which might affect adversely physical or moral integrity necessarily gave rise to interference. It had regard to the fact that the sending a child to school necessarily involved some degree of interference with private life. More relevantly perhaps, the Court reasoned that the treatment in this case did not have sufficiently adverse affects for his physical or moral integrity to bring it within the scope of the prohibition contained in Article 8.

The Commission also had taken the view that moral integrity may be infringed by use of violence on others. In *Klass v. Germany*, the Commission was of the opinion that the sight by a child of its mother being violently arrested amounted to a negative experience with considerable repercussions on the child's state of mind, causing her considerable

---

[72] 8518/79, (Dec.) March 14, 1980, 20 D.R. 193.
[73] *e.g.* 9702/82, (Dec.) October 6, 1982, 30 D.R. 239 and 9804/82, (Dec.) December 7, 1982, 31 D.R. 231.
[74] 20357/92, (Dec.) March 7, 1994, 76–A D.R. 80.
[75] It considered that the sending of a child to a school did not amount to consent by the parents to corporal punishment and there was no necessity for such punishment in a democratic society.

distress and amounting to an interference with her private life. Since the use of force was disproportionate, the interference was not justified. The Court differed, finding no violation since the facts on which the child relied were not established and leaving the principles undiscussed.

14. Environment

Considerable noise or other nuisance and pollution can undoubtedly affect physical well-being and interfere with private life and the amenities of home. This may also give rise to pressing personal interest in having access to information relating to the extent and risk involved. (See Part IIB: Environment.)

Cross-reference

Part IIB: Defamation
Part IIB: Discrimination
Part IIB: Environment
Part IIB: Homosexuality
Part IIB: Transsexuals

Property

Key provisions:

Article 1 of Protocol No. 1 (peaceful enjoyment of possession); Article 6 (access to court/fair hearing).

Key case law:

Marckx v. Belgium, June 13, 1979, Series A, No. 31; 2 E.H.R.R. 330; *Sporrong and Lönnroth v. Sweden*, September 23, 1982, Series A, No. 52; 5 E.H.R.R. 35; *James v. U.K.*, February 21, 1986, Series A, No. 98; 8 E.H.R.R. 123; *Van Marle v. Netherlands*, June 26, 1986, Series A, No. 101; 8 E.H.R.R. 483; *Erkner and Hofauer v. Austria*, April 28, 1987, Series A, No. 117; 9 E.H.R.R. 464; *Inze v. Austria*, October 28, 1987, Series A, No. 126; 10 E.H.R.R. 394; *Tre Traktorer v. Sweden*, July 7, 1989, Series A, No. 159; 13 E.H.R.R. 309; *Mats Jacobsson v. Sweden*, June 28, 1990, Series A, No. 180–A; 13 E.H.R.R. 79; *Fredin v. Sweden*, February 18, 1990, Series A, No. 192; 13 E.H.R.R. 784; *The Holy Monasteries v. Greece*, December 9, 1994, Series A, No. 301–A; *Stran Greek Refineries v. Greece*, December 9, 1994, Series A, No. 301–B; 19 E.H.R.R. 293; *Gasus Dosier v. Netherlands*, February 23, 1995, Series A, No. 306–B; 20 E.H.R.R. 360; *Pressos Compania Naviera and others v. Belgium*, November 20, 1995, Series A, No. 30; 21 E.H.R.R. 301; *Agrotexim and others v. Greece*, October 24, 1995, Series A, No. 330; 21 E.H.R.R. 250; *Phocas v. France*, April 2, 1996, R.J.D., 1996–II, No. 7; *Matos e Silva v. Portugal*, September 16, 1996, R.J.D., 1996–IV, No. 14; *National & Provincial Building Society and others v. United Kingdom*, October 23, 1997, R.J.D., 1997–VII, No. 55.

1. General principles

Three limbs or distinct rules to the protection of property rights are contained in Article 1 of Protocol 1 — in the first sentence of the first paragraph which generally sets out the principle of non-interference with property; in the second sentence of the first paragraph relating to deprivation of property subject to conditions; and, in the second paragraph relating to control of use, also subject to specific conditions.[1] Before determining whether the first general rule had been complied with, the Court determines whether the second two are applicable. The three rules are not however distinct or unconnected. The second and third are concerned with particular instances of interference with the general right and to be construed in light of the general principle of the first rule.[2]

Interference with property, whether expropriation or control of use, will generally be justified if it respects the requirement of lawfulness and can be regarded as pursuing the general or public interest. The Convention organs have imported a requirement of proportionality and the necessity to strike a fair balance between the demands of the community and the protection of the individual's interests.[3] The possibility of obtaining compensation is an element in assessing whether the individual bears an excessive burden.[4] General and public interest is given a wide meaning and where the legislature intervenes

[1] *Sporrong and Lönnroth, op. cit.,* para. 61.
[2] *James*, para. 37.
[3] *Sporrong*, para. 69.
[4] *e.g.* in *Sporrong*, where there was a violation in respect of long term expropriation permits on property which potentially affected ability to sell and was not counterbalanced by any opportunity to seek compensation or shorten the time limits. See section Expropriation, proportionality.

in an area of economic or social policy, the Court will respect the State's assessment unless manifestly without reasonable foundation.[5]

Where ownership remains and some ability to exploit the property, a finding of *de facto* expropriation in the sense of deprivation of property is unlikely. Such cases falling short of expropriation are rather dealt with as an interference in the peaceful enjoyment of possessions.[6] Where the purpose of the measure is not intended as such to control the use of property but to achieve other goals it will also tend to fall under the first sentence. For example, provisional land transfer in *Erkner and Hofauer v. Austria* was dealt with under the first sentence of the first paragraph as there was no actual deprivation of ownership until the consolidation plan issued and there was no aim to control use but to restructure and improve farming. Public interest declarations (pre-expropriation measures) in *Matos e Silva v. Portugal* were also dealt with under the first sentence of the first paragraph. There was no *de facto* deprivation since ownership remained and the applicants could still use the property in a restricted manner and were able to sell. In *Phocas v. France*, restriction on the right of property resulting from the urban development plan in Montpellier (which meant the applicant was unable to obtain planning permission to develop his property and left in uncertainty as to possible development/expropriation measures) was dealt with as an interference under first sentence first paragraph.[7]

2. Property

Property or possessions for the purposes of attracting the protection of Article 1 of Protocol No. 1 covers a wide range of interests. Possession has autonomous meaning not limited to ownership of physical goods: other rights and interests constituting assets can also be regarded as property rights.[8] Where in *Matos e Silva v. Portugal*, the Government disputed that the applicants owned part of the old royal lands that was subject to the expropriation measures, the Court agreed with the Commission that the applicants had occupied them undisputed for almost a century and the revenue which they derived from working them could qualify as possessions. In *Holy Monasteries v. Greece*, where the Government also disputed that the applicants owned the monastery land, the Commission considered that even if they held no registered title, they had "patrimony" rights *in personam*, which could be "possessions" without being property rights protected in Greek law. The Court held that the transfer of possession and control of the properties affected ownership and could not be regarded as a mere procedural exercise.

Article 1 of Protocol No. 1 only applies to existing possessions and does not confer a right to obtain property.[9] Driving licences are not items of property for purposes of Article 1 of Protocol No. 1.[10]

---

[5] *e.g. Lithgow* (nationalisation); *James* (sweeping leasehold reform); *Pressos Compania* (legislative intervention in pending tort claims).

[6] *e.g.* in *Sporrong* where the person still owned land and could dispose of it, and in *Fredin*, where though the license to exploit the gravel pit was removed the applicant did not thereby lose all meaningful use of the the the properties (*i.e.* it was only part of the land which included a farm).

[7] Despite a serious effect on his ownership rights however, the applicant was procedurally protected since he could apply for State to purchase his property which would occur within three years of his application and he had failed to use that procedure properly. See however *Pincock v. U.K.*, (Dec.) 14265/88, January 19, 1989, 59 D.R. 281, where informal expropriation plans which might discourage potential purchasers did not interfere with property (where a proposed motorway could take any number of possible routes).

[8] *Gasus Dosier*, where it was immaterial if the applicant's claim to the concrete mixer was a right of ownership or a security right *in rem* (ownership had passed to purchaser under contract subject to retention of title until full price paid which had not occurred at the time of seizure by tax authorities). Also, property rights by way of benefit of a restrictive covenant and receipt of annual rent are "possessions" U.K., 10741/84, (Dec.) December 13, 1984, 41 D.R. 226; and patents 12633/87, *Smith Kline v. Netherlands*, (Dec.) October 4, 1992, 66 D.R. 70.

[9] *Marckx*, para. 50; (Dec.) 11628/85, *Sweden*, (Dec.) May 9, 1986, 43 D.R. 270.

[10] 9177/80, *FRG*, (Dec.) October 6, 1981, 26 D.R. 255.

Where property rights cease or are altered pursuant to requirements or conditions fulfilled by law there is no interference with property.[11] There is some authority for the view that a trivial effect on property rights will not constitute an interference.[12]

(a) *Business and professional interests*

Possessions were concerned in the revocation of a licence to serve alcoholic beverages in a restaurant, since it formed part of the economic interests of the restaurant, one of the principal conditions for the carrying on of the business and loss of it affected good will and value of the restaurant.[13] Where accountants were refused registration as chartered accountants when the profession was regulated by new legislation, the Court found that they had built up a clientele over years, which had in many respects the nature of a private right and constituted an asset, and hence a possession.[14]

While the vested interests of a doctor in his private practice were "possessions", which could be interfered with by removal of a social security affiliation decisive to the running of his practice,[15] the withdrawal of a doctor's licence to dispense medicine was not an interference with property, where the conditions for its exercise no longer existed.[16] Goodwill of a professional practice was an element in its valuation but did not constitute a possession to the extent it was not necessarily linked to the profession in question. The Commission found that dispensing was not automatically connected with a doctor's practice. There could be no reasonable expectation as to the lasting nature of benefits which could be withdrawn in accordance with pre-existing lawful conditions, so there was no property right affected in the licence. Future income would only constitute a possession if the money was earned or an enforceable claim to it existed.

Mere expectations of notaries that existing rates of fees would not be reduced by law did not constitute a property right.[17] Customs officers' income affected by change of custom levying on the Greek entry to the E.U. did not fall within "possessions".[18] Their licences were not revoked, and it was not accepted that they had any vested economic interests or legitimate expectations of deriving future advantages. Nor had the income been earned or an enforceable claim to it come into existence.

(b) *Inheritance and succession rights*

Article 1 of Protocol No. 1 does not guarantee the right to obtain possessions by way of intestacy or involuntary dispositions, although differences in treatment in matters of

---

[11] *France*, 10443/83, (Dec.) July 15, 1988, 56 D.R. 20: disciplinary suspension of civil servant's pension did not constitute an interference with property rights where suspension fulfilled legal requirements; 10426/83 *Sweden* (Dec.) December 12, 1984 40 D.R. 234.

[12] *Langborger v. Sweden*, June 22, 1989, Series A, No. 155: requirement in lease to pay small 0.3 per cent of rent by way of commission to tenants association for negotiations in fixing rent not inconsistent with Art. 1. (The Commission said that the contribution was so small it was not interference.)

[13] *Tre Traktorer*.

[14] *Van Marle*: though the interference was not disproportionate, pursuing a legitimate aim in regulating a profession vital to the economic sector and provision for registration was made by way of proving competence by diploma or before a board.

[15] 11540/85, (Dec.) March 8, 1988, 55 D.R. 157: it was found to be a control of use in the general interest and not disproportionate, since the applicant did not meet the condition of being recommended by the appropriate authority, as part of comprehensive health care reform.

[16] *Batelaan and Huiges v. Netherlands*, 10438/83, (Dec.) October 3, 1984 41 D.R. 170: the applicants' licence was dependent on there being no chemist in the area and was withdrawn when a chemist began operating.

[17] 8410/78, *FRG*, December 13, 1979, 18 D.R. 216: where notaries were obliged to reduce fees for certain public bodies, *e.g.* universities, the claims for fees would only to be considered as possessions when they came into existence on grounds of services rendered and on basis of existing regulations.

[18] 24581/94, *Greece*, (Dec.) April, 6, 1995, 81–B D.R. 123.

inheritance may fall foul of Article 14 in conjunction with Article 1 of Protocol No. 1.[19] However, in *Inze v. Austria*, there was a property right in issue where the applicant, born out of wedlock, had acquired a right of inheritance with other heirs, but was precluded by his birth from being a principal heir.

(c) *Debts and claims*

Debts or claims have to be shown to be sufficiently established to be enforceable.[20] In *Stran Greek Refineries v. Greece*, an arbitration award in favour of a company pursuing damages against the State for breach of contract to build an oil refinery constituted "possessions", since it was immediately enforceable, final and with no right of appeal on the merits (although it was revocable on limited grounds on appeal). There was an interference when, due to a legislative measure, the award ceased to be enforceable. Although it might not have been in the State interest to pursue the contract, the State had intervened to alter the machinery set up under the agreement, after the judiciary had ruled on its validity and no provision for compensation had been made by way of counterbalance.

In *Pressos Compania Naviera and others v. Belgium*, the claims of applicants for negligence in pending proceedings against pilots alleged to have caused damage to their vessels were found to constitute assets, claims for compensation coming into existence under the rules of tort at the moment damage occurred. The Court noted that the applicants had a legitimate expectation that their claims would be dealt with in accordance with the law of torts and found that the 1988 Act which exempted the State and its pilots from negligent acts, deprived the applicants of their property rights. While the Court accepted the Government's arguments that the Act pursued the public interest (to protect the State's financial interests, harmonise laws with the Netherlands) it found the measure disproportionate since there was no measure of compensation. The Court also accepted the applicants' view that legal certainty did not require retrospective extinguishing of claims.[21]

In *National Provincial Building Society and others v. United Kingdom*,[22] where the applicants had pending claims for the recovery of tax paid under invalid regulations, the Court however expressed doubts these claims constituted possessions, since that they had not obtained an enforceable final judgment and it was questionable that they had a legitimate expectation that they would in light of the Government's clear intention to rectify the defects in the regulations. However, assuming that there was a control of use of possessions to secure payment of taxes, the Court found that the measure was remedial

---

[19] *Marckx*: limitation on an unmarried mother's ability to make gifts and legacies in respect of her child constituted discrimination contrary to Art. 14 in conjunction with Art. 1 of Protocol No. 1 but there was no violation under Art. 1 of Protocol No. 1 in relation to the daughter's inability to inherit.

[20] *Stran Greek*: the Commission's approach had been more hesitant; 7742/76, *FRG*, (Dec.), July 4, 1978, 14 D.R. 146 not excluded that debt can constitute a possession for Art. 1 of Protocol 1 — but applicants had to show entitled to the claim; *Belgium*, October 12, 1988, 12164/86, 58 D.R. 63 claim to debt may constitute a "possession" (applicant had found banknotes but only ever had a possibility of obtaining compensation — no evidence of having any claim to payment and a liability action could not be a possession).

[21] The Commission, though it found a violation of Art. 6, took a narrower view of possessions under Art. 1 of Protocol No. 1, finding that most applicants were not holders of established claims, only pending actions which opened possibility of securing payment of debts. In respect of one applicant who had obtained a judgment it was not an individual or excessive burden to bear as shipowners can cover losses by insurance, a limited action was possible against the pilot himself (max. limit on amount recoverable) and the accident took place before the 1983 court judgment which opened up possibility of recovery.

[22] *National & Provincial Building Society and others v. U.K.*, 21319/93, etc. (Rep.) June 25, 1996 as regarded "possessions" the Commission pointed out a divergence between the Court judgments in *Stran Greek* and *Pressos* — the Court having found that the domestic court judgment acknowledging *Stran*'s claim was not sufficiently established to be enforceable though the arbitration award was, while in *Pressos* tort claims qualified though no judgments had issued.

legislation to give effect to original intent of the legislators and there was an obvious and compelling public interest in achieving that intention. As to balance, it considered that the Government had always made it clear that the sums should be liable to tax noting that the invalidity worked by way of giving a windfall for building societies to exploit and accepting the Government view that liability imposed for the "gap period" when assessment periods changed was fair.[23]

(d) *Shareholders' interests*

A share in a company with an economic value is a possession, such that the loss of shares can constitute an interference with possession or deprivation of property.[24]

Shareholders in a company cannot claim that their property rights are affected by the expropriation of property of that company.[25] Despite the Commission's finding that in *Agrotexim v. Greece* the shareholders' rights were affected by the interference with the company's property and its capacity to enter into development projects, the Court upheld a preliminary objection of no victim status since in fact it was not the property of the shareholders which was affected by the expropriation but the company who could have acted through its liquidator. Thus the shareholders were not entitled to act on behalf of the company. It was not enough to allege a fall in the value of their shares. The corporate veil was maintained.

3. Domestic court regulation of private law disputes

Domestic court regulation of property disputes according to pre-existing law does not engage the responsibility of the State under Article 1 of Protocol No. 1. The fact that one party is inevitably unsuccessful is not sufficient, without some supervening act of administration or legislation affecting the applicant's position.[26] Whether or not the applicant's property rights were determined fairly would fall to be examined under Article 6, paragraph 1's procedural guarantees.

4. Property rights as civil rights

Rights of property have from early on been classified as falling "without doubt" within the scope of "civil rights" under Article 6, paragraph 1.[27] Where a measure affects business and economic interests, contractual relationships between applicants and others, Article 6 will apply, *e.g.* in *Tre Traktorer v. Sweden*, where there was the withdrawal of a alcoholic

---

[23] On Art. 6 see Part IIA, Fair trial guarantees, legislative interference in pending cases.

[24] *Bramelid and Malmstrom v. Sweden*, 8588–9/79, (Dec.) December 12, 1982, 29 D.R. 64.

[25] *Agrotexim v. Greece;* also 11189/86, *Sweden*, (Dec.) December 11, 1986, 50 D.R. 121: minority shareholder in a company could not claim to be victim of levying of tax or charges on the company but was a victim where a new shareholder was introduced free of charge which diminished relative value of his own rights as shareholder (left undecided if "power" aspect of shares to wield influence or control over company was "possessions").

[26] *e.g.* 10082/82, *U.K.*, (Dec.) July 4, 1983, 33 D.R. 247; order by House of Lords to pay B.P. £40 million following frustration of contract for exploitation of oil concession in Libya; *U.K.* 11949/86, (Dec.) December 1, 1986, 51 D.R. 195: eviction of tenant from leased property following annulment of lease by landlord; *Bramelid and Malmstrom v. Sweden*, see n.24, redistribution of company shares — where the State does intervene in legal relations of private individuals between themselves as regards property, the Commission stated that it must ensure the law does not create such inequality that a person is arbitrarily and unjustly deprived of property in favour of another; *Ruiz Mateos v. U.K.*, 13021/87, (Dec.) September 8, 1988, 57 D.R. 268: action for damages by Spanish companies in U.K. courts against the applicant.

[27] *Sporrong and Lönnroth*, para. 79, where the Court overruled the Commission's approach that there had been no determination since expropriation did not take place nor had there been any change in ownership.

licence for a restaurant which was a control of use of the premises. Rights to develop property in accordance with applicable laws and regulations are civil rights[28] as well as measures regulating the use of property to protect the environment.[29]

The normal requirements of Article 6 apply to property proceedings, save insofar as special consideration has been given to planning matters (see Part IIB: Planning and use of property).

Cross-reference

Part IIB: Expropriation and confiscation
Part IIB: Housing and tenancy
Part IIB: Planning and use of property

---

[28] *e.g. Fredin,* right to exploit gravel pit.
[29] *Oerlemans v. Netherlands,* November 27, 1991, Series A, No. 219: designation order protecting land in dyke reclamation area from particular uses likely to erode or damage soil or use of herbicides, which clearly affected the applicant farmer's use of his land in future.

340

Reasons for arrest and detention

Key provisions:

Article 5, paragraph 2 (right to be informed promptly in language understood of the reasons for the arrest or detention).

Key cases:

X v. U.K., October 24, 1981, Series A, No. 46; 4 E.H.R.R. 188; *Van der Leer v. Netherlands*, September 27, 1990, Series A, No. 170; 12 E.H.R.R. 267; *Fox, Campbell and Hartley v. United Kingdom*, August 30, 1992, Series A, No. 182; *Murray v. United Kingdom*, October 28, 1994, Series A, No. 300–A.

1. General considerations

This is a safeguard against arbitrary arrest, requiring the person to be informed of the grounds of arrest. It also provides an opportunity to challenge the reasonableness of the suspicion and to use the remedy provided by Article 5, paragraph 4 to challenge the lawfulness of the detention.[1]

2. Scope of the guarantee

Article 5, paragraph 2 applies not only to persons arrested under Article 5, paragraph 1(c) despite the apparent criminal law connotation of the words used although it may be subsumed as in the case of *X v. United Kingdom* by a finding of a violation of Article 5, paragraph 4.[2] In *Van der Leer v. Netherlands*, concerning the recall of a mental health patient, the Court held that the provision was to be interpreted autonomously as regards "arrested" and that it went beyond criminal law measures.[3] It was closely linked to Article 5, paragraph 4 which was not limited in scope to arrest. Thus a failure to inform the applicant of the measures against her disclosed a violation. It was not subsumed by a finding of a violation under Article 5, paragraph 4 for in this case the applicant, in voluntary residence at the hospital, was not informed at all that she had been deprived of her liberty by a compulsory measure and she should have been informed of this important change in her status, not merely to enable her to challenge the lawfulness.

3. Nature and form of information

The Court in particular has not been rigorous as to what form the information should take. The necessary information does not have to be given in writing or consist of a complete list of all the charges or disclose to the suspect all the information which might be available to the investigating judge.[4] It is not necessary for a person to be expressly informed since the Court has indicated that the surrounding circumstances of the arrest are

---

[1] 8098/77, (Dec.) December 13, 1978, 16 D.R. 11 and 9614/81 *Austria,* October 12, 1983, 34 D.R. 119. Art. 5 para. 2 is a weaker guarantee than Art. 6, para. 3(a) which applies to preparation of the criminal trial.
[2] The Court found it unnecessary to decide as in its view, it followed necessarily from its finding of a violation of Art. 5, para. 4 that to make effective use of right to challenge his recall the applicant had to be promptly and adequately informed of the facts which the authorities relied on and the issue was thus absorbed.
[3] Paras 27–28.
[4] *e.g.* 8098/77, (Dec.) December 13, 1978, 16 D.R. 111.

sufficient for the person to deduce the reasons.[5] As to how indirect the notification can be, the Commission and Court have differed.

In *Fox, Campbell and Hartley v. United Kingdom*, the Commission found a violation, since the applicants were not directly informed at the time of arrest that they were suspected, *inter alia*, of information gathering and courier work for the IRA, although they were questioned about particular activities and left to deduce why they were arrested. It considered that the elementary nature of the safeguard was such that it placed a direct burden on the arresting authorities to provide a detainee with adequate information as to the reasons for the arrest as soon as was practicable. The Court did comment that being told on arrest that they were held as terrorists was not enough but found no violation since all the applicants were interrogated and there was no ground to suppose that the reasons for their arrest were not brought to their attention during their interrogation within a matter of a few hours.

In *Murray v. United Kingdom*, the Commission found a violation where the applicant on arrest was asked questions about money and the U.S.A. which gave her only a very vague indication, not sufficiently precise to enable her to understand why she had been arrested. The Court again differed, noting that from the reference to her brother, it must have been apparent that she was being questioned about possible involvement in the purchase of arms in respect of which her brother had been convicted, and thus the reasons for arrest were sufficiently brought to her attention.

The degree of information will also depend on the kind of arrest or detention. In mere arrest for the security check purposes unrelated to the existence of particular suspicions (*i.e.* an obligation under Article 5, paragraph 1(b)) it was sufficient if information was provided promptly as to the legal basis of the arrest and the nature of the check, namely, that they were to be fingerprinted, photographed questioned and otherwise checked up on. Suspicion was not required under the relevant domestic order nor under Article 5, paragraph 1(b) so it was compatible with Article 5 that the applicants were not told what suspicions were being held against them during the 45–hour period of detention.[6]

A lesser standard also applies to arrest with a view to extradition where the information given need not be so complete as in the case of arrest for the purpose of bringing someone to trial.[7]

An applicant cannot claim any particular right to see the documents which initiated the investigation.[8] Nor does Article 5, paragraph 2 require the disclosure of the complete file, but sufficient information must be provided to facilitate the pursuit of the remedy envisaged under Article 5, paragraph 4.[9]

---

[5] *Fox, Campbell and Hartley;* See also the Commission's approach in 8916/80, *Italy,* (Dec.) October 7, 1980, 21 D.R. 250: warrant of arrest served on a person on arrival in Rome, after two days journey in police custody after his arrest in Costa Rica. In the circumstances, he must have known the basis since he had disobeyed a residence order by going abroad and it was for that failure he was arrested.

[6] *McVeigh and others v. U.K.,* 8022–25–27/77, (Rep.) March 18, 1981, 25 D.R. 15.

[7] 10819/84, (Dec.) July 5, 1984, 38 D.R. 230 concerning an applicant informed that he was suspected of fraud and arrested for purpose of extradition to U.S.; also 23916/94, *Greece,* (Dec.) April 6, 1995, where person was held for extradition, this did not involve the determination of a criminal charge so information given did not need to meet the requirements of Art. 5, paras. 2, 6 or 3(a) and information from the judge that extradition was sought by U.S. on charge of false billing was enough.

[8] *e.g. Lamy v. Belgium* March 30, 1989, Series A, No. 151, para. 32, *i.e.* the allegedly tendentious report which had sparked off the judicial investigation and which he had no knowledge of. He had seen the arrest warrant and had an interview with the investigation judge.

[9] 9614/81, (Dec.) October 12, 1983, 34 D.R. 119, where a judge had removed certain documents from casefile as it might hamper the investigation and the defence lawyers did not see them until returned to file a year later, the absence of the information did not hamper their exercise of Art. 5 para. 4 remedy.

4. Promptly

The person must be informed at or soon after the time of arrest or be able to deduce the reasons from the questioning or circumstances within a few hours of arrest. In *Murray*, where the applicant was arrested at 7.00 and questioned from 8.20–9.35, this was sufficiently prompt. In *Clinton and others v. United Kingdom*, the Commission stated that no more than a few hours should elapse save in exceptional circumstances such as the serious incapacity of the arrested person to comprehend the reasons that might have been given. Thus, where an applicant was merely told that he was arrested under a particular provision and not questioned until next day, the Commission found that the alleged practical problems in assembling an interview team so late at night were not sufficient where the fundamental importance of the right to liberty was at stake.[10]

5. Access to legal representation or to contact family

Article 5, paragraph 2 does not guarantee the right to call a lawyer.[11] Access to a lawyer is generally dealt with under Article 6, paragraph 3(c) (see Part IIA: Fair trial guarantees, Legal Representation in criminal proceedings) but as yet there is no automatic right to a solicitor from the first moment of arrest. Access to doctors and relatives were mentioned amongst safeguards justifying derogation under Article 15 by the United Kingdom in respect of Article 5, paragraph 3 concerning provisions allowing the detention of suspects for up to seven days without being brought before a judicial officer.[12] Inability of detained suspects to contact their wives in the *McVeigh and others v. United Kingdom* case lead to a finding of violation by the Commission of Article 8.[13]

---

[10] 12690/78, (Rep.) October 14, 1991, C.M. Resolution DH(95)4 January 11, 1995: violation.
[11] 8828/79, (Dec.) October 5, 1982, 30 D.R. 93.
[12] *Brannigan and McBride v. U.K.*, May 26, 1993, Series A, No. 258–B, para. 64.
[13] 8022–25–27/77, *U.K.*, (Rep.) March 18, 1981, 25 D.R. 15.

Religion, thought and conscience

Key provision:

Article 9 (freedom of thought, conscience and religion).

Key case law:

Darby v. Sweden, October 23, 1990, Series A, No. 187; 13 E.H.R.R. 774; *Hoffmann v. Austria*, June 23, 1993, Series A, No. 255–C; 17 E.H.R.R. 293; *Kokkinakis v. Greece*, May 25, 1993, Series A, No. 260–A; 17 E.H.R.R. 397; *Manoussakis v. Greece*, September 26, 1996, R.J.D., 1996–IV, No. 17; *Valsamis v. Greece*, December 18, 1996, R.J.D., 1996–VI, No. 4; *Kalaç v. Turkey*, July 1, 1997, R.J.D., 1997–IV, No. 41.

1. General considerations

The relationship of churches and State has a troubled history in Europe. Where a State has a bias to a particular religion (for example, constitutional protection) there is potential for issues arising as regards the effect of this preference on other religious groups. It is questionable to what extent in multi-ethnic Europe one group can justifiably be given preferential treatment over another and what weight should be given to the history and traditions of the particular country. The arrival on the scene of other "religions" with differing cultural and social dimensions, poses special problems where practices conflict with expected ways of doing things.

Issues arise as to what may genuinely claim protection as a "religion" or matter of conscience; what may be considered manifestations of those beliefs which require protection; and, what justifications exist for interfering with those beliefs and practices. There are also questions as to what extent the State is under a positive obligation to protect religious beliefs from offence by others.

2. Religion, thought and conscience

There has been little detailed discussion about the nature of the beliefs which fall within the scope of these concepts. It is a sensitive area, what one person holds as sacred appearing absurd or anathema to another. The Commission has perhaps shown a tendency to rely on other methods of rejecting cases concerning the more controversial beliefs, using the justified exceptions under Article 9, paragraph 2 and the possibility of finding that a claimed interference or restriction does not in reality prevent the manifestation of a particular religion, thought or belief.

For the Commission, Article 9 covers "the sphere of private, personal beliefs", religious creeds or the "forum internum".[1] The Court more generally emphasises its importance as a foundation of democratic society and as part of the identity of believers and that their conception of belief is also a precious asset to atheists, agnostics and the unconcerned.[2]

More concretely, the Commission was prepared to assume that veganism was a belief falling within Article 9[3]; pacifism was accepted as a philosophy involving the commitment in theory and practice to the securing of political and other objectives without the resort to the threat or use of force[4]; Scientology[5] was accepted without discussion; Druidism was left

---

[1] *e.g.* 10358/83, (Dec.) December 15, 1983, 37 D.R. 142; "primarily" added in 11308/84, *Netherlands*, March 13, 1986, 46 D.R. 200.

[2] *Kokkinakis*, para. 31.

[3] *U.K.*, 18187/91, (Dec.) February 10, 1993, unpublished.

[4] 7050/75, *Arrowsmith v. U.K.*, (Rep.) October 12, 1978, 19 D.R. 5.

[5] 7805/77, *Sweden*, (Dec.) May 5, 1979, 16 D.R. 68.

open[6]; the Krishna consciousness movement was accepted without argument.[7] In the cases before the Court, Jehovah's Witnesses qualified.[8]

Article 9 does not cover mere "idealistic activities", for example, the activities of a German legal association which gave advice to prisoners.[9] It also did not cover the stance taken by IRA prisoners with regard to "special category status".[10] The Commission has added that there is no right as such under Article 9 to "conscientious objection".[11]

3. Victim status

Individuals, churches and associations with religious and philosophical objects are capable of exercising Article 9 rights.[12] However a legal person cannot exercise freedom of conscience[13] and a corporate profitmaking body cannot rely on Article 9 rights.[14]

4. Manifestation and practice

Religion and beliefs pertaining especially to the inner sphere, the Commission has emphasised that the term "practice" as employed by Article 9, paragraph 1 does not cover each act which is motivated or influenced by a religion or belief. There is a distinction between "manifestation" and motivation. There is also the idea that the act must directly express the belief. Article 9 protects acts intimately linked to beliefs or creeds such as acts of worship and devotion which are the aspects of the practice of a religion or belief in a generally recognised form.[15]

For example, in *Arrowsmith v. United Kingdom*, the leaflets distributed to soldiers may have been motivated by the applicant's pacifist ideals but were not in the Commission's view expressing pacifist ideals but specifically urging soldiers not to go to Northern Ireland. This was not a manifestation of her beliefs in the sense recognised by the Commission.[16] Marriage, although considered desirable for muslims, cannot be regarded as a form of expression, thought or religion.[17] Non-payment of taxes by Quakers to prevent

---

[6] *Chappell v. U.K.*, (Dec.) July 14, 1987, 53 D.R. 241: assuming Druidism to be a religion the closing of Stonehenge was an interference.

[7] *Iskcon v. U.K.*, 20490/92, (Dec.) March 8, 1994, 76–A D.R. 90, though the Commission referred to assuming that the limitation on the use of the building owned by the organisation constituted an interference with their right to manifest their religion.

[8] *e.g. Kokkinakis.*

[9] 11308/83, *Netherlands*, above, n.1.

[10] Nor was the wearing of non-prison uniform the manifestation of a belief under Art. 9 — 8318/78, May 15, 1980, 20 D.R. 44.

[11] *e.g.* 7705/76, (Dec.) July 5, 1977, 9 D.R. 196. This is a problem which arises in the many countries which impose military service. The Commission has taken a rather unsympathetic view having regard to the necessity for the heavy burden of military service to be shared by citizens in an equitable manner. It is therefore legitimate for States to be restrictive of granting total exemption from service, both military or substituted and acceptable under Art. 14 in conjunction with Art. 9 for total exemption to be applied only to members affiliated to a religious community whose position is well known and governed by strict informal controls *e.g.* Jehovah's witnesses. Other persons without such membership must suffer to avoid the possibility of allowing shirkers! — 10410/83, (Dec.) October 11, 1984, 40 D.R. 203.

[12] 7805/77, (Dec.) May 5, 1979, 16 D.R. 68; 8118/77, (Dec.) March 19, 1981, 25 D.R. 105; 12587/86, (Dec.) July 14, 1987, 53 D.R. 241.

[13] 11921/86, (Dec.) October 12, 1988, 57 D.R. 81.

[14] 7865/77, (Dec.) February 27, 1979, 16 D.R. 85.

[15] *e.g.* 10358/83, and 10600/83, see n.1.

[16] 7050/75, (Rep.) October 12, 1978, 19 D.R. 5: also 11567–8/85, (Dec.) July 6, 1987, 53 D.R. 150 where distribution of leaflets was seen purely as an incitement to indiscipline, not a manifestation of a religious belief.

[17] *e.g.* 11579/85, (Dec.) July 7, 1986, 48 D.R. 253 where a muslim claimed an interference with his right to religion since the law of the United Kingdom prevented him marrying a 14-year-old girl. Marriage is to be governed by the specific provisions of Art. 12, which allows traditional European notions of marriage to prevail as provided in national laws.

contribution to arms is not covered,[18] nor the wish to have one's ashes scattered on one's own land.[19]

Freedom to manifest one's religion has been found to include the right to try and convince one's neighbour[20]; kosher diet[21]; and it was accepted that a high caste Sikh would have transgressed his belief if he undertook such work as cleaning floors.[22]

5. Interferences with Article 9 rights

Measures preventing a person from manifesting his belief in a manner recognised under Article 9 or penalising him for doing so will generally constitute a limitation requiring justification under the second paragraph, as for example, criminal sanctions imposed on the use of premises as a place of worship[23] or, as in *Kokkinakis*, where the Jehovah's Witness applicant was convicted for proselytising.

However, where an applicant's belief conflict with contractual and employment conditions, the Convention organs have adopted an approach of finding that the resulting dismissal does not necessarily interfere with the manifestation of religion. In *Stedman v. United Kingdom*, the alleged lack of protection of the applicant's beliefs, since she could be required to work on Sundays by her employer, did not disclose an interference with her beliefs, since she was not dismissed for her beliefs but for failing to agree to work certain hours.[24] While in *Kalaç v. Turkey*, compulsory retirement of a military judge for his fundamentalist beliefs was not an interference with his freedom of religion but a disciplinary matter, the Court noting that he had joined the army knowing of the restrictions imposed on its members.

Requirements to act in a particular way will also not necessarily constitute an interference with Article 9 rights notwithstanding the person's objection to them on grounds of principle.

In *Valsamis v. Greece*, where a child Jehovah's Witness was suspended from school for failure to participate with her school in a procession on a Greek national day, the Court found that she had been exempted from religious education and the Orthodox mass, and that the obligation to take part in the school parade was not such as to either offend her parents' religious convictions under Article 2 of Protocol No. 1 or amount to an interference with her right to freedom of religion. Although the applicants objected to participation on the grounds of their pacifist beliefs, the Court considered that there was nothing in the purpose or arrangements of the parade to offend them to an extent forbidden by the Convention provisions. Its own view was that the national day, which the Government stated commemorated Greece's attachment to democracy, liberty and human rights, served both pacifist objectives and the public interest and a military presence at

---

[18] 10358/83, (Dec.) December 15, 1983, 37 D.R. 132.

[19] 8741/79, (Dec.) March 10, 1981, 24 D.R. 137.

[20] *Kokkinakis,* where the applicant Jehovah's witness, had been convicted for proselytism in respect in particular of gaining entry to an orthodox christian's house and seeking to persuade her to change her beliefs. The Court acknowledged that where several religions co-existed it may be necessary to place restrictions on this freedom to reconcile the interests of the various groups.

[21] *D.S. and E.S. v. U.K.,* 13669/88, (Dec.) March 7, 1990, 65 D.R. 245.

[22] *U.K.,* (Dec.) 8231/78, March 6, 1982, 28 D.R. 5.

[23] *Manoussakis.*

[24] *Stedman v. U.K.* 29107/95, (Dec.) April 9, 1997 89–D.R. 104 referring to 24949/94, *Finhard,* (Dec.) December 3, 1996 where an employee of the Finnish State Railways was dismissed for failing to respect his working hours on the basis that to work after sunset on a Friday was forbidden by the Seventh-Day Adventist Church, of which he was a member. The Commission held that the applicant was not dismissed because of his religious convictions but for having refused to respect his working hours. Thus although the refusal was motivated by religious convictions, such a situation did not give rise to protection under Art. 9, para. 1. Also the applicant had failed to show that he was pressured to change his religious views or prevented from manifesting his religion or belief (*inter alia* he was free to resign).

some of the parades did not alter their nature.[25] This case seems to show that the offensiveness of particular measures to religious beliefs must meet a certain threshold of seriousness.

6. Justified limitations

Restrictions on manifestations of belief or practice, where in conformity with requirements of lawfulness,[26] may be justified, *inter alia*, on grounds of health and public safety (*e.g.* motorcycle helmets), security (access to certain publications where the applicant is in prison) or where there is a clearly perceived harm or threat to others.[27] The factors of necessity, pressing social need and proportionality apply. Where religious beliefs come into conflict with other interests, it has not been apparent that they are given any particular weight as such in the balancing exercise. In *Iskcon v. United Kingdom*,[28] where the applicant Krishna society was subject to enforcement notices relating to the increased influx of pilgrims to the manor used as a religious centre, the Commission found the factor of their religious freedom was sufficiently taken into account by the planning authorities despite an unfortunate letter from the planning authorities referring to the religious factor not being "relevant" to the decision. However, the Commission interpreted this in the positive sense that the decision was taken on proper planning grounds and not on the basis of objection to the religious activities. Druids who are barred access to sites in or around Stonehenge have also found their complaints have been rejected as justified in the interests of protection of a historical site as well for public safety and the prevention of crime and disorder.

Where a Jehovah's Witness was convicted for proselytism, the Court considered that a distinction had to be drawn between bearing witness and proselytism by improper means (force, offering of material or social advantages by inducement, and improper pressure on persons in distress or need). Since the liability of the applicant was established without any reference to whether he used improper means, but on the basis of a general prohibition and there was no indication of improper means on the facts,[29] the conviction was not justified by a pressing social need. The imposition of criminal sanctions on Jehovah's Witnesses for using premises as a place of worship without authorisation was also found disproportionate, having regard to the framework of law and practice which placed prohibitive conditions on the practice of religious non-orthodox movements.[30] The Court found that the relative leniency of the penalty immaterial.[31]

---

[25] Majority of 7:2 while the Commission found no violation by 17:12. The dissenting views considered that the applicants' own perception of the significance of the parade to their own beliefs should be accepted unless obviously ill-founded and unreasonable which they were not in the present case and that there was certainly no necessity for the child to participate in a public event of this kind.

[26] "Prescribed by law": see *e.g.* the Commission's finding in *Kalaç* that the measure dismissing the fundamentalist judge was not based on rules with the quality of law, in the sense of being adequately defined and foreseeable. See Part IA: "Convention Principles and Approach".

[27] *Manoussakis*, para. 40; States are entitled to take steps to verify whether a movement, ostensibly for religious aims, carries on activities which are harmful to the population. This did not apply to Jehovah's witnesses, a "known religion".

[28] *op. cit.*, n.7.

[29] *Kokkinakis*; the Court appears to have accepted the applicant's arguments that the woman concerned was an experienced adult with intellectual abilities who was not unduly influenced by the applicant's actions in calling at her door.

[30] *e.g.* authorisation from the Minister not subject to any requirement to give a decision in a particular time (the applicants' request was still pending without any explanation for the delay) and wide grounds of refusal; also role of the Orthodox church in consenting to authorisation being given.

[31] 20,000 drachma fines and three month prison terms convertible into a pecuniary penalty of 400 drachmas per day.

7. State obligation to protect religion from others

Positive obligations may arguably arise requiring the State to take steps to protect the exercise of religious freedom from others. However, it would appear that this will only arise where the threat is of a particular severity. While in the *Lemon v. United Kingdom*[32] case, the Commission found the law of blasphemy an acceptable means of protecting the religious feelings of offended Christians in the context of Article 10, it rejected complaints of an applicant muslim that the inability to prosecute blasphemous attacks on the Islamic faith was contrary to Article 9 and that it disclosed discrimination contrary to Article 14 in that such protection was only available to Christians.[33] The Commission, in very brief reasoning, considered that the Government could not be said to have interfered in the applicant's right to manifest his beliefs and that Article 9 did not guarantee a right to bring proceedings against publishers of works that offended the sensitivities of any individual or group. Since this was found to render the complaint outside the scope of Article 9 (incompatible *ratione materiae*), the discrimination complaint was rejected on the same basis. The reasoning is not convincing since if the law did adequately protect muslims it should have been rejected as manifestly ill-founded, and issues would still have arisen under Article 14, where the objective and reasonable justification in favouring the religious feelings of one group, albeit the historically dominant one, might have been difficult to find.

Cross-reference

Part IIB: Army
Part IIB: Discrimination
Part IIB: Marriage and the right to found a family
Part IIB: Prisoner's rights

---

[32] U.K. 8710/79, May 7, 1982, 28 D.R. 77 where the applicants were convicted in a private prosecution of the criminal offence of blasphemy for publication of a poem ascribing to Christ promiscuous homosexual practices, the Commission found the conviction pursued the legitimate aim of protecting the rights of others, namely the private prosecutor, not to be offended in religious feelings by publications. It did not consider the offence of blasphemy was *per se* anachronistic and though in rather guarded terms it accepted that attacks on the religious feelings of citizens which attain a certain level of severity may constitute a criminal offence, the measure was not disproportionate in the circumstances of this case, referring to the fact that the prosecutor was deeply offended and none of the courts had any doubt as to the blasphemous nature of the publication.

[33] *Choudhury v. U.K.*, 17439/90 (Dec.) March 5, 1991: concerning Salman Rushdie's "Satanic Verses".

Remedies

Key provision:

Article 13 (effective remedy before a national authority).

Key case law:

Delcourt v. Belgium, January 17, 1970, Series A, No. 11; 1 E.H.R.R. 355; *Handyside v. U.K.,* December 7, 1976, Series A, No. 24; 1 E.H.R.R. 737; *Klass v. Germany,* September 6, 1978, Series A, No. 28; 2 E.H.R.R. 214; *Silver v. U.K.,* March 25, 1983, Series A, No. 61; 5 E.H.R.R. 347; *Abdulaziz and others v. U.K.,* May 28, 1985, Series A, No. 94; 7 E.H.R.R. 471; *James v. U.K.,* February 21, 1986, Series A, No. 98; 8 E.H.R.R. 123; *Lithgow v. U.K.,* July 8, 1986, Series A, No. 102; 8 E.H.R.R. 329; *Leander v. Sweden,* March 26, 1987, Series A, No. 116; 9 E.H.R.R. 433; *Boyle and Rice v. U.K.,* April 27, 1988, Series A, No. 131; 10 E.H.R.R. 425; *Plattform "Arzte für das Leben" v. Austria,* June 21, 1988, Series A, No. 139; 13 E.H.R.R. 204; *Kamasinski v. Austria,* December 19, 1989, Series A, No. 168; 13 E.H.R.R. 36; *Powell and Rayner v. U.K.,* February 21, 1990, Series A, No. 172; 12 E.H.R.R. 355; *Vereinigung Demokratischer Soldaten Österreichs v. Austria,* December 19, 1994, Series A, No. 302; *Akdivar v. Turkey,* September 16, 1996, R.J.D., 1996–IV, No. 15; *Chahal v. United Kingdom,* November 15, 1996, R.J.D., 1996–V, No. 22; *Aksoy v. Turkey,* December 18, 1996, R.J.D., 1996–IV, No. 26; *Valsamis v. Greece,* December 18, 1996, R.J.D., 1996–VI, No. 27; *D v. U.K.,* May 2, 1997, R.J.D., 1997–III, No 37; *Halford v. U.K.,* June 25, 1997, R.J.D., 1997–III, No. 39; *Aydin v. Turkey,* September 25, 1997, to be published in R.J.D., 1997–VI, No. 50; *Mentes v. Turkey,* November 28, 1997, to be published in R.J.D. 1997; *Camenind v. Switzerland,* December 16, 1997, to be published in R.J.D. 1997; *Kaya v. Turkey,* February 19, 1998, to be published in R.J.D. 1998.

1. General considerations

Taking the principal consideration that it is the obligation first and foremost of Contracting States to secure to every individual their rights and freedoms,[1] Article 13 is the countervailing requirement that an individual has the opportunity to obtain redress for violations in the domestic system.[2] If a Contracting State fulfills this requirement, the Convention organs role will diminish. It may be said that observance of this provision is the most crucial to the effective protection of rights in Contracting States. It is however a technical and procedural provision. Its role has been whittled away by interpretation and arguably not given its proper prominence.[3] Applicants are also sometimes reticent in raising Article 13 complaints, perhaps preferring to concentrate on what they see as the core substantives issues.[4]

---

[1] Art. 1 of the Convention.

[2] See, *e.g. Boyle and Rice,* (Rep.) para. 73 citing *Handyside,* para. 48.

[3] There is perhaps a suspicion that the Convention organs are seduced by the more interesting questions arising under the substantive provisions (possibly trespassing on the role of domestic authorities when involving themselves in rather detailed factual assessments) whereas they should be encouraging domestic bodies to carry out this function.

[4] *e.g.* in *McCann and others v. U.K.,* September 27, 1995, Series A, No. 324, where there was an Art. 2 violation but no complaint raised under either Arts. 6 or 13 by the relatives of the dead terrorists, who had been unable to pursue civil proceedings due to the nature of the case.

2. Limitation to "arguable claims" of violations

Article 13 requires a remedy for everyone whose rights under the Convention have been violated. Thus the provision is linked to breaches of substantive rights. No breach of Article 13 is possible in isolation.

The words of the provision appear to require that a person must establish an actual breach of a substantive provision. The Court thought that this was unduly restrictive. Until a court or other body has investigated a claim, it will not necessarily be apparent whether there has been an unjustifiable interference with a right. Accordingly, it held that a remedy must be guaranteed to anyone who "claims" that his rights have been violated.[5] This was translated by the Court in *Silver v. United Kingdom* into the notion that a person with an "arguable claim" of being a victim of a violation of the rights in the Convention should be able to seek a remedy.[6]

The Commission, which was setting a high standard for the manifestly ill-founded inadmissibility criterion, applied the approach that Article 13 could be breached even if the substantive complaint was inadmissible, as there could still in the appropriate circumstances be said to be an arguable claim.[7] The Court in *Boyle and Rice v. United Kingdom* noted the Commission delegate's explanation that to be arguable a claim "only needs raise a Convention issue that merits further examination" and that a conclusion that a claim was manifestly ill-founded could be reached after considerable oral and written argument. It preferred its own view in *Airey v. Ireland* that a finding of manifestly ill-founded meant that there was not even a prima facie case against the respondent State.[8] It held, bluntly, that on the ordinary meaning of the words it was difficult to conceive that a claim that was manifestly ill-founded could nevertheless be arguable. It declined to give an abstract definition of arguability, each case to be determined in the light of the particular facts and issues. It added that it would not however necessarily regard itself bound by the Commission's view that a substantive complaint was manifestly ill-founded when determining the arguability of the claim for the purposes of Article 13.

In *Powell and Rayner v. United Kingdom*, the Commission's continued adherence to its view was rejected by the Court,[9] maintaining its preference for the ordinary meaning of the words and finding that different standards between Article 27, paragraph 2 (manifestly ill-founded) and Article 13 would undermine the coherence of this dual system of enforcement at national level, since a State could not be required to make available a remedy for a grievance which was so weak as not to warrant examination on its merits at international level. The Court firmly rejected the Commission's practice which took the merits into account in assessing the manifestly ill-founded criterion.[10] Since then, it is

---

[5] *Klass*, para. 64.

[6] Para. 113.

[7] See *e.g. Boyle and Rice*, (Rep.) where the Commission had rejected as manifestly ill-founded Art. 8 complaints regarding the applicant's imprisonment but declared admissible the complaints with respect to the alleged lack of effective remedies for these complaints. It defined an arguable claim as one concerning a right guaranteed in the Convention, not wholly unsubstantiated on the facts and giving rise to a *prima facie* issue under the Convention. It examined the substantive complaints finding some had not been substantiated therefore not arguable and that others, substantiated, were arguable.

[8] October 9, 1979, Series A, No. 32, para. 18.

[9] See also *Plattform Ärzte* case, where the Commission declared inadmissible the Art. 11 complaints linked to failure to protect a demonstration (as it was not shown that the authorities failed to take adequate steps) but declared admissible the complaint under Art. 13, holding that a claim could be arguable, irrespective of whether or not it is well-founded — 10126/82 October 17, 1985, 44 D.R. 65.

[10] This mixing of admissibility and merits perhaps derives from the very early days of the Commission before the Court was fully operational and the Commission had a more decisive role. It also had a more economic attitude in later years with the increasing backlog, with a reluctance to waste time in prolonged examinations where the case was likely to be rejected. It still holds hearings however on the admissibility and merits in serious cases, and issues provisional opinions on the merits at the same time as declaring complaints admissible.

possible to detect an increased tendency in the Commission to declare cases admissible, having adjusted the threshold of admissibility and a greater number of Commission reports on the merits finding no violation.

As a result, it is very rare to find a violation of Article 13 without the presence of a violation of a substantive provision, and not at all without an admissible complaint. However, conversely, the fact that a complaint was declared admissible by the Commission does not require a finding of an arguable claim for Article 13. This occurs where a number of complaints under different provisions are declared admissible together, the Commission's practice not to split issues based on the same facts, even if some complaints are clearly more substantial than others.[11]

3. Remedies for non-conformity of statute or law

The Commission has taken the view that Article 13 cannot be interpreted as requiring a means by which the conformity of statute with the Convention can be examined in domestic law.[12] The Court endorsed this approach in *James v. United Kingdom*.[13] To hold otherwise would be tantamount to requiring incorporation of the Convention in domestic law and this could not in the Court's view be imposed *de facto* by the Convention organs. In any event, it considered that if the substantive laws were found, as in *James*, to conform with Article 1 of Protocol No. 1, it would be sufficient for the purposes of Article 13 that the aggrieved property owner could go the courts to secure compliance with the relevant laws.[14]

In relation to secondary legislation, the Commission found that the immigration rules in issue in *Abdulaziz and others v. United Kingdom* did not attract the immunity of legislation; and in *Boyle and Rice* that the immunity did not apply to the prison rules, standing orders and administrative circulars, basing itself on the application of Article 13 in the *Silver* case to prison norms.[15] The Court agreed in *Abdulaziz*, finding that the applicants were victims of norms that were incompatible with the Convention and that there was be no effective remedy as required by Article 13.

The approach has been extended by the Commission in *Johnston v. Ireland* where it held that Article 13 does not guarantee an effective remedy in respect of a constitutional provision.[16]

4. Relationship with access to court

Where the more specific guarantees of Article 6 apply, Article 13 as the more general provision does not apply, its requirements being less strict and accordingly absorbed by

---

[11] *e.g. Valsamis,* where a girl Jehovah's Witness was suspended from school, the application principally concerned complaints under Arts. 9 and 2 of the First Protocol of the Convention but the Art. 3 complaint was also declared admissible. On the merits, arguable claims were found under Arts. 9 and 2 of the First Protocol but none for allegations under Art. 3; *Halford v. U.K.,* where complaints under Art. 8 were admissible for claims of tapping of office and home phones but there was an arguable claim and breach of Art. 13 in respect of the former alone, since on the merits there was no reasonable likelihood that the latter were bugged.

[12] See *Young, James and Webster v. U.K.,* (Rep.) December 14, 1979, referring in support to the wording of Art. 13 "notwithstanding that the violation has been committed by persons acting in an official capacity" which it interpreted as indicating that it was not meant to cover legislation. The Court found it unnecessary to decide: June 26, 1981, Series A, No. 44.

[13] Referring to a dictum in *Swedish Engine Drivers' Union* case; February 6, 1976, Series A, No. 20, para. 50 and *Ireland v. U.K.* January 18, 1978, Series A, No. 25. Also later *Lithgow,* para. 206.

[14] See also concurring opinions in *James* which add that this restrictive interpretation is supported by the existing legislation of Contracting States since it was improbable that the drafters intended to cover statute as few states had provision for constitutional challenge by individuals of legislation and the dissenters, who saw no reason to exempt acts of the legislature from Art. 13 and that the approach of the Court in *Silver* and *Abdulaziz* should be maintained.

[15] *Boyle and Rice,* (Rep.) para. 78; *Silver* judgment paras. 124–127.

[16] Series A, No. 112, (Rep.) para. 151: the complaint was dropped by the applicants before the Court.

Article 6 which is the *lex specialis*.[17] Thus where proceedings falling within the scope of Article 6 are involved, there is no possibility of issues arising under Article 13, whether or not there is a violation of Article 6.[18]

Where a violation is alleged in respect of a court's decision, Article 13 does not require appeal to a higher court, having regard to the approach that Article 6 does not require courts of appeal to be set up.[19] Where the highest national court is alleged to have breached the Convention, the application of Article 13 is subject to a similar implied limitation.[20] Presumably, where the court proceedings are themselves in compliance with the requirements of Article 6, this is sufficient for the purposes of the Convention.

The difficulties of relating the guarantees of Articles 6 and 13 have been highlighted in the recent series of Turkish cases, where it is alleged in effect that the criminal and civil justice systems are ineffective, and for a combination of reasons such as intimidation of applicants and their lawyers, the conditions prevailing in the state of emergency regions, applicants have been exempted from exhausting the theoretically available remedies. In *Akdivar v. Turkey*, the Commission was divided as to whether the situation in which the applicant villagers had no effective avenue of address for the destruction of their village by security forces disclosed a violation of Article 6 or 13 or, as the majority found, both.[21] The Court did not resolve the theoretical approach, since it found that in light of its rejection of the Government's preliminary objection, upholding the Commission's view that the applicants were exempted under Article 26 from pursuing theoretical remedies, it was unnecessary to decide whether there was a violation of Articles 6 and 13. In subsequent cases, where there has been a failure to provide any redress in the system for village destruction, torture, killings and disappearances there has been a preference to rely on Article 13[22] on the basis that the applicants' complaints related essentially to a lack of proper investigation.

Article 5, paragraph 4 (review of the lawfulness of detention) is also *lex specialis* in the area covered by it.[23]

5. No separate issue: procedural rights contained in substantive provisions

Not infrequently, where the violation under a substantive provision involves findings of lack of procedural safeguards, the Convention organs find that no separate issues arise

---

[17] *e.g.* in *Kamasinki,* para. 110; *W v. U.K.,* July 8, 1987, Series A, No. 121, para. 86.
[18] *e.g.* only where there is a criminal charge or civil right is Art. 13 superceded by Art. 6 which is more stringent — 8588/79 etc. (Dec.) December 12, 1983, 38 D.R. 18.
[19] *Delcourt,* para. 25; also 13135/87, *U.K.,* (Dec.) July 4, 1988, 56 D.R. 268: where applicants could not require appeal to a higher court from the Land Tribunal's allegedly derisory compensation assessment.
[20] See *e.g.* 8603/79, (Dec.) December 18, 1980, 22 D.R. 220; *Leander v. Sweden* (Rep.) May 17, 1985 (Art. 13 not normally grant a further remedy against the acts and decisions by the highest national court); *Observer and Guardian v. U.K.,* para. 76, the Court referred to the *James* principle that there was no obligation to incorporate, so no remedy guaranteed allowing a Contracting State's laws to be challenged on the ground of being contrary to the Convention; *Callaghan v. U.K.* 14739/89, (Dec.) May 9, 1989, 60 D.R. 296 no right to review by a higher court in criminal matters *i.e.* not cover miscarriage of justice where trial nonetheless fair; and *Pizzetti v. Italy,* Series A, No. 257–C, (Rep.) December 10, 1991, para. 41, the Convention not guarantee the right to a second level of jurisdiction and provisions of the Convention cannot be held to oblige States to set up bodies to exercise supervision over judicial bodies — Art. 13 not applicable when alleged violation is embodied by judicial decision.
[21] See minority (*M. Norgaard, Schermers* and *Bratza*) which found the problem was at heart one of effectiveness of remedies — Article 6 it was recalled did not require criminal proceedings to be brought against others (the basis of the investigation system which was being criticised) and there were a whole host of theoretical remedies, which in the special circumstances in the south-east had had their effectiveness undermined. It was not only court remedies at stake but other types of remedies would have been possible *e.g.* rehousing.
[22] *e.g. Aksoy v. Turkey; Mentes v. Turkey; Aydin v. Turkey.*
[23] *e.g. Brannigan and McBride v. U.K.,* May 25, 1993, Series A, No. 258–B, para. 76.

under Article 13. For example, in *Hokkanen v. Finland*,[24] no separate issue was found under Article 13 since the complaints amounted in substance to those already dealt with under Articles 6 and 8 in regard to length of custody and child access proceedings and the non-enforcement of custody rights.[25] However, in *Kaya v. Turkey*, the Court held that its findings under Article 2 as regarded the procedural deficiencies of the forensic examination and investigation into a death did not exclude a further finding of a breach of Article 13, the requirements of which were broader.

6. Effectiveness

Where an individual has an arguable claim that he is the victim of a violation of the rights set forth in the Convention he should have a remedy before a national authority which had the power both to decide his claim and if appropriate to give redress.[26]

An absence of any possibility to seek relief at national level will disclose a violation.[27] However, the fact that an application to a court fails is not sufficient to indicate that the remedy was ineffective.[28] Where settled case-law indicates that a person has no standing to lodge a complaint, the possibility to seek a review by the courts will not constitute an effective remedy.[29]

It does not necessarily have to be a judicial remedy, although the powers and procedural guarantees are relevant in determining whether the remedy is effective.[30] A non-judicial body may for example have difficulties satisfying notions of independence which in some spheres may undermine any real efficacy of a remedy.[31]

Effectiveness as a standard may vary depending on the subject matter. Where secret surveillance was in issue, the Court took the approach in *Klass v. Germany* that remedies only had to be as effective as they could be given the restricted scope for recourse inherent in such

[24] *Finland*, September 23, 1989, Series A, No. 299–A.
[25] See also *Ergi v. Turkey*, 23818/94, (Rep.) May 20, 1997 pending before the Court, violation of Art. 2 including lack of procedural safeguards by way of effective investigation, no separate issue under Art. 13.
[26] *Silver*, para. 113, *Klass*, para. 64. See also the Commission in *Leander* which gave the view that the "authority" must be sufficiently independent and have the power to examine fully the issues arising under the Convention or under corresponding domestic provisions and have power to render a binding decision affording redress where appropriate (para. 90).
[27] *e.g. Halford* (no remedy against telephone tapping of office phones); *Valsamis* (no remedy to challenge the requirement of Jehovah's Witness pupils to participate in parades).
[28] *Camenind v. Switzerland*, where the applicant could not complain of a house search since under domestic law he had ceased to be effected by it.
[29] See, *e.g. Purcell v. Ireland*, 15404/89, (Dec.) April 16, 1991, 70 D.R. 262: aggrieved producers and journalists could challenge under constitutional provisions the conformity with freedom of speech of Sinn Fein reporting restrictions and it was irrelevant that a previous challenge to an almost identical order had failed in the courts; also Court in *Sunday Times (No. 2)*, November 26, 1991, Series A, No. 217, para. 61 citing *Soering*, para. 122; *Murray family v. U.K.*, October 28, 1994, Series A, No. 300–A; D.R. 100, where the applicant alleged domestic law provided an excuse for such actions, an action for trespass to property was still considered to furnish an effective remedy in respect of the entry and search by soldiers of the applicant's home, the feeble prospects of success in the circumstances not detracting from the "effectiveness"; *Costello-Roberts*, the Court found that the possibility of suit for assault was effective in regard to corporal punishment at school, even though case-law indicated it would fall within the scope of the reasonable and moderate chastisement exception, since effectiveness did not depend on the certainty of a favourable outcome. The Commission had found the remedy ineffective, with no prospects of success, referring to two previous cases where assault cases had failed on worse facts (*Warwick v. U.K.* 9471/81, (Rep.) July 18, 1986, 60 D.R. 5 and *Y v. U.K.*, October 29, 1992, Series A, No. 247–A) where it has also found violations of Art. 3).
[30] *e.g. Klass*, para. 67. Also the Commission in *Powell and Rayner* (Rep.) para. 54 rejected a submission that there was a general right to a court in all circumstances; 12573/86, (Dec.) March 6, 1987, 51 D.R. 283, effective remedy may be provided by non-judicial authority: thus it was sufficient that the Federal Department, the higher administrative authority to the Federal Office of Police, could set aside the disputed measure (refusal of asylum), it was not established that it merely endorsed decisions from below.
[31] *Chahal, op. cit.*, paras. 153–154.

a system and referred to the possibility of an aggregate of remedies as satisfying the requirements of Article 13 (see below).[32] In *Chahal*, where the applicant alleged that he would face torture and death on expulsion to India, the Court found that due to the irreversible damage which would be caused, the scope of review by the courts was deficient, since it did not carry out a scrutiny independent from considerations of national security and the possibility of review by the advisers who only had a power to recommend was insufficient.[33] In the context of allegations of torture, the Court had held that given the nature of the right safeguarded under Article 3, Article 13 imposes, without prejudice to other remedies which might be available, an obligation on States to carry out a thorough and effective investigation of such incidents. Thus in *Aksoy v. Turkey*, a violation was found in respect of the complete lack of reaction of the public prosecutor to the physical condition of the applicant who appeared before him after a long period in custody. In *Aydin v. Turkey*, the lack of prompt reaction by the public prosecutor to an allegation of rape of a girl in gendarme custody, failing to obtain the necessary expert medical examination or to seek any factual corroboration, and the deferential attitude disclosed towards the gendarmes, also disclosed a violation, having regard to the centrality of the public prosecutor's role in Turkey to the system of remedies as a whole. In the area of other substantive rights, it is perhaps less likely that such stringent requirement would be imposed.

As in the area of non-exhaustion of domestic remedies, there is a certain burden on the Government to show that the available remedies are effective. In *Vereinigung Demokratischer Soldaten Österreichs v. Austria* the Government alleged a number of remedies were available in the courts whereby the association could have had its journal distributed but the Court found that the Government had not put forward any example showing the application of the alleged remedies in a case similar to the present one and had therefore failed to show that the remedies would have been effective.

7. Aggregate theory

The Court applied for a while a theory that where no single remedy may itself entirely satisfy the requirements of Article 13, the aggregate of remedies provided for under domestic law may do so. Thus, in *Leander v. Sweden*, in respect of allegations of invasion of privacy through secret files, the Court found overall that the safeguards of the Chancellor of Justice, ombudsman, and presence of parliamentarians on the national police board sufficed.[34] This may be logical where in the context of secret surveillance, the thrust of the Convention organs' concern has been to ensure an adequate framework to guard against abuse of power. It is not a satisfactory approach where an applicant is in a situation where he requires a remedy with a more tangible and individual result. The Court has not relied on this theory for many years.

Cross-reference

Part IIB: Prisoners' Rights
Part IIB: Admissibility, exhaustion of domestic remedies
Part IIB: Compensation for detention
Part IIB: Immigration and Expulsion
Part IIB: Review of detention

---

[32] Para. 70.
[33] Paras 151–155: it was also noted that the procedures before the advisers were lacking *i.e.* no legal representation and no information given as to the grounds for the expulsion.
[34] See however the dissent of President Ryssdal, who noted no binding power of decision, and lack of any specific responsibility for enquiry into particular complaints.

Review of detention

Key provision:

Article 5, paragraph 4 (right to speedy review of lawfulness of detention by a court).

Key case law:

De Wilde, Ooms and Versyp v. Belgium, (Art. 50) June 18, 1971, Series A, No. 12; 1 E.H.R.R. 435; *Van Droogenbroeck v. Belgium*, June 24, 1982, Series A, No. 50; 4 E.H.R.R. 443; *Sanchez-Reisse v. Switzerland*, October 21, 1986, Series A, No. 107; 9 E.H.R.R. 71; *Weeks v. U.K.*, March 2, 1987, Series A, No. 114; 10 E.H.R.R. 293; *Bouamar v. Belgium*, February 29, 1988, Series A, No. 129; 11 E.H.R.R. 1; *Lamy v. Belgium*, March 30, 1989, Series A, No. 151; 11 E.H.R.R. 529; *E v. Norway*, August 29, 1990, Series A, No. 181–A; 17 E.H.R.R. 30; *Thynne, Wilson and Gunnell v. U.K.*, October 25, 1990, Series A, No. 190; 13 E.H.R.R. 666; *Toth v. Austria*, December 12, 1991, Series A, No. 224; 14 E.H.R.R. 551; *Megyeri v. Germany*, May 12, 1992, Series A, No. 237–A; 15 E.H.R.R. 584; *Herczegfalvy v. Austria*, September 24, 1992, Series A, No. 242–B; 15 E.H.R.R. 437; *Wynne v. U.K.*, July 18, 1994, Series A, No. 294–A; *Kampanis v. Greece*, July 13, 1995, Series A, No. 318–B; 21 E.H.R.R. 43; *Hussain v. U.K.*, February 21, 1996, R.J.D., 1996–I, No. 4; *Prem Singh v. U.K.*, February 21, 1996, R.J.D., 1996–I, No. 4; *R.M.D. v. Switzerland*, September 26, 1997, R.J.D., 1997–VI, No. 51; *Sakik and others v. Turkey*, November 26, 1997, to be published in R.J.D., 1997–VII, No. 58.

1. General considerations

There is a right of review of the lawfulness of all the categories of detention provided for in Article 5, paragraph 1. However, the scope of the obligation under Article 5, paragraph 4 is not identical and its requirements will vary according to the kind of deprivation of liberty in question. It no longer applies once a person is released.[1]

2. Review of detention imposed by a court

Where sentences of detention are imposed by competent courts, the decision of supervision is incorporated in the decision made by the court at the close of the judicial proceedings. Thus in respect of sentences imposed by competent courts within the meaning of Article 5, paragraph 1(a), the review of lawfulness is inbuilt in the conviction and appeal procedures.[2] Only where the decision of detention is taken by other authorities, administrative or executive, is there a right of recourse to a court pursuant to Article 5, paragraph 4. No right to parole or release on licence for convicted persons can therefore be derived from Article 5, paragraph 4.

This principle has been applied to mandatory life sentences, which are imposed by courts as fixed sentences reflecting the gravity of the offence, without the special considerations attaching to other types of detention (see below). There is no right to review of continued detention or release at later stages notwithstanding the apparent practice to examine risk and dangerousness as the major factors governing continued

---

[1] *e.g. W v. Sweden*, 12778/87, (Dec.) December 9, 1988, 59 D.R. 158 conditional release; persons in hiding or on the run *R. v. U.K.*, 25527/94, (Dec.) November 29, 1995.

[2] *De Wilde*, para. 76.

detention after the so-called tariff or punitive period.[3] Where, in *Wynne v. United Kingdom* the applicant imprisoned for murder, committed a crime while released on licence and was recalled following conviction and sentence to a discretionary life sentence, the Court found that he continued to be detained subject to the initial mandatory sentence and the fact that he was also subject to a discretionary life sentence did not entitle him to a review of the lawfulness of that detention.[4]

3. Special types of sentences

Where sentences are passed with the aim of social protection and rehabilitation of offenders, since the grounds relied upon by the courts in sentencing (risk and dangerousness) are by their very nature susceptible of change with the passage of time, new issues may arise which affect the lawfulness of the detention. These types of sentence attract the right to review under Article 5, paragraph 4. The principle was first applied in respect of sentences of detention imposed on recidivists in *Van Droogenbroeck v. Belgium*[5] and then extended to the imposition of discretionary life sentences in the United Kingdom, which were found also to be based not only on the gravity of the offences but also on considerations of risk and dangerousness which were by their nature susceptible to change with the passage of time.

In *Weeks v. United Kingdom*, the applicant's recall after release on licence was compatible with Article 5, paragraph 1(a) as derived from his original conviction when he was sentenced to a term of discretionary life imprisonment for robbery.[6] Nonetheless, Article 5, paragraph 4 came into play as the court found that new issues of lawfulness in light of the principles of the Convention might arise if the decision not to release or to redetain were not based on grounds consistent with the objectives of the sentencing court. The right to review had to be wide enough to bear on those conditions which were essential for the lawful detention of a person subject to the special kind of deprivation of liberty both on recall to prison and at reasonable intervals during the course of his imprisonment. Thus Weeks whose sentence was imposed by the judge on grounds of the risk which his unstable personality presented, had the right to review on recall to prison after release. Similarly, in the case of *Thynne, Wilson and Gunnell v. United Kingdom*, three discretionary lifers, whose tariff had expired, could claim a review of their continuing detention.

The Court has not directly addressed the question whether there was any right to a review during the tariff period since in any case the tariffs had expired in *Thynne, Wilson and Gunnell*. While the case was before the Commission, the policy (subsequently changed) was that the tariff was not disclosed to prisoners and the Commission took the view that the right to review existed throughout the period of imprisonment. Since this case, the Commission relying on the implications of the Court's judgments has nonetheless dismissed cases from discretionary lifers as premature where their tariff has yet to expire.

Where minors convicted of murder or other serious offences are sentenced to detention at Her Majesty's Pleasure, the Commission and Court rejected the Government's argument that this is a fixed sentence imposed due to the gravity of the offence, finding

---

[3] A tariff period is set for the period of deterrence and retribution to be served before the possibility of release in the cases of mandatory life, discretionary life, custody for life and detention of children at Her Majesty's Pleasure. A major consideration concerning release in all categories after the expiry of tariff is risk or dangerousness.

[4] Even long periods of release on licence do not break the chain of causation with the original conviction, *e.g.* *Vincent King v. U.K.*, 23812/94, (Dec.) October 10, 1994, where the applicant was recalled 17 years after release.

[5] 11082/84, *Belgium*, March 4, 1988, 69 D.R. 27, where in respect of an offender placed at the disposal of the Government as a recidivist, an additional penalty of 10 years was left to the discretion of the executive after the expiry of a four year sentence, the judicial review required was not incorporated in the initial decision whereby the executive was empowered to order or not a deprivation of liberty.

[6] At age 17, he had stolen 35 pence using a starter pistol with blank cartridges.

that it was an indeterminate sentence based on a special factor subject to change with the passage of time. Indeed both adopted the argument of the applicants' counsel that if the sentence was indeed a life sentence by which the child forfeited its liberty for the rest of its days, there might be problems under Article 3. The Court had regard in particular to the nature and purpose of the sentence, noting that the sentence was imposed because of the youth of the offender and held that an indeterminate sentence on a young person could only be justified by considerations based on the need to protect the public which must of necessity take into account any developments in personality or attitude as he grew older. There was accordingly a violation of Article 5, paragraph 4 in the lack of any judicial review of continued detention for two applicants, *Prem Singh v. United Kingdom* and *Abed Hussain v. United Kingdom*, who had both served their tariffs.[7]

4. Scope of review

The "court" must be able to decide on the issue of "lawfulness". It is not required to cover every question and it does not guarantee a right to judicial control of such scope as to empower the "court" on all aspects of the case to substantiate its own discretion for that of the decision-making authority.[8]

Judicial review in the United Kingdom was not wide enough for review of continued detention of the discretionary lifer, as it was unable to verify whether his detention was consistent with and justified by the objectives of the indeterminate sentence imposed on him, namely, whether he continued to pose a risk necessitating detention.[9]

5. Procedural requirements of review

The review must be of a judicial character and give the individual the guarantees appropriate to the kind of deprivation of liberty in question.[10] The mere fact the review is conducted by a court or judge is not decisive. For example, in *De Wilde, Ooms and Versyp v. Belgium*, magistrates ordered the detention on vagrancy but in a summary procedure without the requisite guarantees necessary to the seriousness of what was at stake, which gave it the character of an administrative decision.

Direct access to court is not always required. In *Sanchez-Reisse v. Switzerland*, where the applicant argued that he could not apply directly to court without his request going via the police office, the Court found it was legitimate and necessary for the executive to have the power to comment, access not thereby being impeded or the power of the court hindered.[11] However Article 5, paragraph 4 presupposes the existence of a procedure in conformity with its requirements without the necessity of instituting separate legal proceedings in order to bring it about. Thus the Court rejected the argument of the Government in *Prem Singh v. United Kingdom* that the applicant could apply for judicial review of the Parole Board decision in order to obtain an oral hearing.

---

[7] Whether or not the tariff fixing procedure itself is compatible with the requirements of the Convention (Art. 5, paras 1 and 4 or Art. 6) is itself under challenger in a number of cases *e.g. Watson v. U.K.*, 21387/93 (Dec.) October 21, 1996 (discretionary lifer; *T.V. v. U.K.*, 24724/94 and *V. v. U.K.* 24888/94 (children detained at Her Majesty's Pleasure) pending before the Commission.

[8] *Weeks*, para. 59, *Van Droogenbroeck*, para. 49; *Toth*, para. 87.

[9] *Weeks*.

[10] *De Wilde*, para. 76; also, in *Weeks* para. 66 where there was no full disclosure of adverse material when a prisoner was recalled, the procedure was therefore not judicial in character.

[11] Para. 45.

(a) *Power to release*

A power to release is necessary. In *Weeks*, the ability of the Parole Board to recommend release, which did not bind the Secretary of State, was not sufficient.[12] In *E v. Norway*, the general power of the courts to review and rule invalid administrative decisions was found sufficient notwithstanding no precedent in a similar case of a court overruling an administrative decision. However, lack of precedents in successfully invoking an alleged remedy may indicate that the existence of the remedy is insufficiently certain, and that it is accordingly lacking the accessibility and effectiveness required for Article 5.[13]

(b) *Adversarial procedure*

The procedure should be adversarial, providing the applicant with the opportunity to present his case effectively. While the Court has in some cases tended to acknowledge the need for a hearing before a judicial authority, the procedure required in each case is not identical.[14] Where in *Sanchez-Reisse* the applicant was challenging his detention with a view to extradition, the Court found that he should have been provided in some way or other with an adversarial procedure. This could have included the possibility of submitting written comments on the objectives of the Federal Police Office which went before the Federal Court with his request for release. It did not find that his personal presence was relevant or necessary to the court's decision.

Failure to provide access to relevant documents and reports which deprives the applicant of the ability to properly participate in the proceedings has been found to render the review defective.[15] Where counsel was unable to inspect documents in the file before the court ruled on whether to hold the applicant on remand, whereas Crown counsel was familiar with file, there was a failure to ensure equality of arms and the proceedings were not truly adversarial as required by Article 5, paragraph 4.[16] Where prosecution counsel was present before the Court of Appeal whereas the applicant and his lawyer were not, the procedure did not ensure equal treatment and was not truly adversarial.[17]

(c) *Legal representation*

Legal representation may be required depending on the nature of the proceedings and the capabilities of the applicant. It was found to be essential in *Bouamar v. Belgium* concerning a juvenile, that a lawyer be present at the hearings where he was remanded in custody in prison, otherwise an essential safeguard would be denied, and in *Megyeri v. Germany*, concerning a person detained on ground of mental illness. Where the detainees are foreigners and unfamiliar with the legal system, legal representation also affords an important guarantee.[18] In *Woukam Moudefo v. France*[19] where the appeal concerned questions of law, the Commission found that the applicant was unable, without a lawyer, to present his case properly and satisfactorily. It was not enough that the court addressed questions of public order of its own motion and it was the fundamental role of defence counsel to stress the crucial problems which may be raised by an appeal and which may otherwise not be examined by the court and to clarify the applicant's submissions.

---

[12] Also *Prem Singh* and *Abed Hussain*.

[13] *e.g. Sakik and others v. Turkey*, where there was no example of any person in police custody having successfully invoked the constitution, or Convention when applying to a judge for release.

[14] *De Wilde*, para. 78.

[15] *Weeks*, paras 60–69, *Abed Hussain*, para. 58.

[16] *Lamy v. Belgium*, March 30, 1989, Series A, No. 151.

[17] *Toth*.

[18] *Sanchez-Reisse* para. 47.

[19] 10868/84, (Rep.) July 8, 1987 settled before the Court October 7, 1988, Series A, No. 141–B.

(d) *Presence at oral hearing*

Equality of arms may require that the applicant be able to appear at a hearing, in addition to submitting written submissions, in particular where the prosecution is present.[20]

In *Abed Hussain v. United Kingdom* and *Prem Singh v. United Kingdom*, having regard to what was at stake (a substantial term of imprisonment) and that questions of the applicants' personality and level of maturity were important to deciding on their dangerousness, Article 5, paragraph 4 required an oral hearing in the context of an adversarial procedure involving legal representation and the possibility of calling and questioning witnesses.[21] Similarly, hearings, at which the applicant and/or his legal representative are present have been found necessary in cases dealing with review of detention on grounds of mental health.[22]

(e) *Effective access*

Where a time-limit or procedural requirements renders an apparent review procedure theoretical, the Commission has found that it did not comply with the requirements of Article 5, paragraph 4. In *Farmakopoulos v. Belgium*,[23] where the applicant was held in detention pending extradition to the United Kingdom pursuant to an arrest warrant issued in his absence, he had, according to practice, 24 hours from the service of the enforcement order to appeal although no mention of this possibility of appeal was included in the order. The Commission held that the shortness of time and lack of information made available did not afford the applicant a real opportunity to have the lawfulness of his detention reviewed, in particularly noting the ignorance of aliens of language or procedures in this context.

Similarly, in *R.M.D. v. Switzerland*, there was a violation of Article 5, paragraph 4, since, notwithstanding the availability of court review procedures in each canton, the applicant was unable to have practical and effective access to them, since he was repeatedly transferred from one cantonal jurisdiction to another.

6. Speedily

A person taken into detention is entitled to a decision as to the lawfulness of that detention being taken with some expedition. In appropriate cases, Article 5, paragraph 4 also requires the opportunity for review of continued detention at reasonable intervals, where such is not provided automatically.[24]

Different considerations will apply depending on the nature and circumstances of the detention. Release within three weeks was not sufficient to render a review unnecessary in relation to a person taken into detention on mental health grounds.[25] Regarding detention under Article 5, paragraph 1(c), gaps of seven, 11 and six days before applicants were brought before the military court was not speedy.[26] Thirty-one days and forty-one days was not sufficiently speedy for review of lawfulness of detention for extradition in *Sanchez-Reisse v. Switzerland* where the case was not complicated, did not require detailed

---

[20] The Commission in *Prem Singh* had particular regard to the fact that the applicant had been released and the reasons for his recall were based on disputed issues of fact relating to his conduct on which witnesses could have been heard who were relevant to the allegations against him.

[21] See also *Kampanis:* applicant held on remand unable to attend the court hearing which decided on continuation though prosecutor present.

[22] See Part IIB: Mental Health (5b. Procedural requirements).

[23] (Rep.) December 4, 1990, struck off before the Court March 27, 1992, Series A, No. 235.

[24] *X v. U.K.*, para. 52.

[25] *Wassink v. Netherlands*, September 27, 1990, Series A, No. 185–A.

[26] *De Jong, Baljet* and *Van den Brink v. Netherlands*, May 22, 1984, Series A, No. 77.

investigation, and the case file and information about the applicant's health were to hand. Almost eight weeks was too long in *E v. Norway* where the Court rejected the excuse of a court vacation period, since it was for the state to organise necessary administrative arrangements to deal with urgent matters. Similarly in *A.T. v. United Kingdom*,[27] a gap of almost 14 months between the expiry of the applicant's tariff and the first review by the new system of Parole Board hearings was not justified by the difficulties in introducing a new procedure and the need to establish priorities amongst the prisoners. In such cases, there was indeed a particular need for expedition in holding the first review.

Regarding the intervals at which reviews of continued detention should be made available, in *A.T.*, a gap of almost two years between the first and second review was not justified, particularly in view of the Board's recommendation that he should be reviewed in a year and a deferral took place for no apparent reason. Periods of nine months to one year have been accepted by the Court in mental health cases.[28]

The dilatoriness of the applicant in pursuing proceedings may be a relevant factor, as in *Kolompar v. Belgium*, where the Court noted the unusually long period but considered that the State could not be held responsible for the delays to which the applicant's conduct gave rise and that he could not complain validly of a situation which he had created.[29]

7. Relationship with Article 13

Together with Article 5, paragraph 5 which provides for compensation, Article 5, paragraph 4 is the *lex specialis* for remedies in respect of detention. Article 5, paragraph 4 requirements are stated as being stricter than those of Article 13.[30]

Cross-reference

Part IIB: Compensation for detention
Part IIB: Extradition
Part IIB: Immigrants and expulsion
Part IIB: Mental health
Part IIB: Pre-trial detention
Part IIB: Reasons for arrest and detention

---

[27] *U.K.*, 20488/92, (Rep.) November 29, 1995.

[28] *Herczegfalvy Megyeri* (see Part IIB: Mental Health).

[29] *Kolompar v. Belgium*, September 24, 1992, Series A, No. 235–C: applicant held for extradition for two years and eight months but had applied for postponements, successive applications for a stay of execution or for release. The Commission had found not sufficiently speedy since despite the applicant's own conduct there was still an obligation on the State to take positive steps to expedite the proceedings.

[30] *De Jong*, para. 60; *De Wilde*, para. 95.

Right to life

Key provision:

Article 2 (right to life).

Key case:

McCann, Farrell and Savage v. U.K., September 27, 1995, Series A, No. 324; 21 E.H.R.R. 97; *Andronicou and Constantinou v. Cyprus*, October 9, 1997, R.J.D., 1997–VI, No. 52; *Kaya v. Turkey*, February 19, 1998, to be published in R.J.D. 1998.

1. General considerations

This section concerns, principally, the use of force by State agents. This relates most obviously to the use of force by police, soldiers or other types of security forces which results in death or injury of an individual. Allied to this aspect there may be circumstances where the respect for life may arguably impose an obligation on the State to take steps to protect life.

The right to life guaranteed under Article 2 is one of the most important rights from which no derogation is possible. The situations where deprivation of life may be justified are exhaustive and must be narrowly interpreted.[1]

The situations listed in the second paragraph are therefore the only exceptions possible: defence of others, lawful arrest or prevention of the escape of a person lawfully obtained or in action lawfully taken for the purpose of quelling a riot or insurrection. The use of lethal force for these purposes must be no more "absolutely necessary". This necessity test indicates that a stricter and more compelling test must be applied than under other provisions of the Convention which refer to necessity alone. The use of force must be "strictly proportionate".[2] There should therefore be no, or at least less scope for the use of the device of "margin of appreciation". The Commission and Court have not yet made reference to the term expressly in this context.

However as always, the Convention organs will have regard to the particular circumstances of the use of force, in particular, the nature of the aim pursued, dangers to life and limb inherent in the situation and the degree of risk that the force employed might result in loss of life.[3]

Article 2 applies not only to situations where a person is killed but also in appropriate circumstances where a person is subject to a life-threatening attack but survives.[4]

2. Use of lethal force

(a) *Deliberate versus non-intentional infliction of loss of life*

Notwithstanding the use of the word "intentionally" in the first paragraph, Article 2 has been interpreted to cover the accidental deprivation of life by the use of lethal force. This question arose in the context of the death of a 13-year-old boy who was struck by a rubber bullet, fired by a soldier who was facing a barrage of missiles thrown by rioters. The

---

[1] *Stewart v. U.K.*, 10444/82, (Dec.) July 10, 1984, 39 D.R. 162.
[2] *ibid.*
[3] *ibid.*
[4] *e.g. Yaça v. Turkey*, 22495/93, (Rep.) April 8, 1997 pending before the Court; *Osman v. U.K.*, 23452/94, (Rep.) July 1, 1997 pending before the Court.

domestic courts had found that the soldier had not intended to injure the boy; that he had aimed at a rioter standing next to him, and his aim was deflected when a missile struck his shoulder. The Commission considered that Article 2 taken as whole must be intepreted as defining the situations where it is permissible to use force which may, whether intended or not, result in the deprivation of life. Any other interpretation would not, in the Commission's view, have been consistent with the object and purpose of the Convention or with a strict interpretation of the obligation to protect life.

(b) *Standard of domestic law*

In *McCann, Farrell and Savage v. United Kingdom*, the applicants argued that the applicable domestic law should protect the right to life. The Commission agreed to the extent that this required national law to regulate in a manner compatible with the rule of law the permissible use of force by its agents. Both Commission and Court did not accept that the fact that domestic law imposed a test of reasonable as opposed to absolute necessity indicated a failure to comply with the Convention standard.[5] A State was not bound to use the same formulation, which would be tantamount to requiring incorporation into domestic law of the Convention. The Court noted that the Convention test appeared stricter but did not consider that the difference between the two standards was sufficiently great to found a violation alone.

It was also argued in *McCann* that domestic law was too general. Specific, clear and detailed rules were required, reference being made, *inter alia*, to the UN Basic Principles on the Use of Firearms by Law Enforcement Officials. The Court however found that the rules of engagement for military and police personnel provided regulation of the use of force which reflected the domestic and Convention standard.

A case, however, where the criminal and/or civil courts rejected an applicant's claims on the basis of reasonable necessity in light of facts which the Convention organs found disclosed no justification under the Convention, would perhaps cast doubt on the adequacy of the domestic law standard.

(c) *Procedural requirements*

While it may be permissible for a State to use lethal force in certain limited circumstances, *McCann* establishes that there must be some form of effective official investigation, otherwise the protection offered by Article 2 would be rendered nugatory if there was no open and objective oversight into the circumstances of a killing.[6]

The form which such enquiries should take has not been defined. The Court found it unnecessary in *McCann*, where, notwithstanding the criticisms of the inquest into the killing of three IRA terrorists by the SAS on Gibraltar,[7] the inquest lasted 19 days, involving 79 witnesses including crucially the soldiers and police in the operation and served for the purposes of Article 2 to subject the killings to a thorough, impartial and

---

[5] The Government had argued that in practice the reasonable necessity test took into account all the factors required. The Commission, without agreeing, relied on a previous case to the effect that whether or not the application of the reasonable necessity standard permitted the use of force in contravention of Art. 2 could only be determined by an examination of the case before it. (*Kelly v. U.K.*, 17579/90, (Dec.) February 13, 1993, 74 D.R. 139).

[6] para. 161

[7] The relatives had alleged that they were hampered in their participation in the inquest, *inter alia*, by a lack of legal aid, no copies of documents or prior knowledge of witnesses' likely evidence and also the use of certificates of public immunity used by the Government to limit the scope of the enquiry. The Commission did not find however that an inquest had to furnish an exhaustive fact-finding enquiry — as long as the applicants could effectively participate (*i.e.* they were represented, could raise their various arguments as to premeditation of the killings and had access to the transcript) that was sufficient.

careful investigation.[8] The Commission had given more emphasis to aspects of independent and public scrutiny, which were also fulfilled in this case.[9] It had noted that the nature and degree of the scrutiny would depend on the circumstances, some cases being undisputed and requiring a minimum formality, whereas in others the facts might be unclear.

Procedural requirements have also been found to require the provision of an investigation into the circumstances of a shooting of a suspect during a clash, which includes adequate forensic examination.[10] In Turkey, where investigations into deaths are conducted by public prosecutors, these investigations have been found not to comply with the procedural obligations of Article 2 where no effective steps are taken to verify the factual events or the extent of responsibility of the security forces.[11]

(d) *Justifiable exceptions*

(1) DEFENCE OF OTHERS

In the case of *McCann*, SAS soldiers shot dead three IRA terrorists whom they said they believed where about to detonate a bomb in the centre of Gibraltar. In fact, there was no bomb in Gibraltar, nor were the terrorists carrying any arms or any object connected with any possible detonation of a bomb. Objectively therefore, three people were shot dead in circumstances where they posed no immediate risk and could have been taken into custody without difficulty. The case was surrounded by controversy. It was alleged that the security forces had deliberately executed the terrorists rather than bring them to trial.

The Commission commented in strong terms on the alleged shoot to kill policy, which would be in flagrant violation of the Convention. A terrorist's right to life is also protected under Article 2 and also his or her right to fair trial on any allegations of criminal actions. Both the Commission and Court however, looking at the soldiers' actions, found that they were under an honest belief, due to the information given to them, that it was necessary to shoot the IRA suspects to prevent them detonating a bomb. Such an honest belief which is perceived for good reasons to be valid at the time could still be justified under Article 2 even if it turned out to be mistaken. To hold otherwise would put an unrealistic burden on law enforcement officers.

A standard of honest and reasonable belief was also applied in *Andronicou and Constantinou v. Cyprus*, where a special security team shot both the hostage and the hostage-taker in an operation. The Court regretted the level of firepower used but giving allowance to "the heat of the moment", said the officers honestly and reasonably believed that they and the hostage were at risk from the hostage-taker and were entitled to open fire to eliminate that risk.

---

[8] However not all inquests are held with such promptness and thoroughness. Cases from Northern Ireland currently challenge the effectiveness of the inquest procedure, referring to the long delays before the inquests are held or conclude, the limited nature of the enquiry and the use of certificates to block access to information.

[9] *McCann*, (Rep.) para. 193. See also, *e.g. Aytekin v. Turkey*, 22880/93 (Rep.) September 18, 1997 pending before the Court, where the Commission found the enquiry conducted by a gendarme officer into a shooting by another gendarme officer lacked an appearance of objectivity and independence.

[10] In *Kaya*, where in particular the perfunctory nature of the autopsy on the alleged PKK suspect allegedly shot during a clash with the security forces, which gave no indication of the number of bulletholes and was imprecise, without testing for gunpowder traces, was found to be so inadequate as to amount to a failure to protect the right to life.

[11] In *Yaça*, see n.4, there was a failure to investigate the circumstances of the shooting of a newspaper seller as part of a series of attacks on an allegedly pro-PKK newspaper; in *Ergi v. Turkey* 23818/94, (Rep.) May 20, 1997 pending before the Court, where a girl was shot by a bullet fired during an alleged clash between the PKK and the security forces, the Commission found the lack of attempts to question the security forces or village witnesses at the scene and the unquestioning acceptance of a report put forward by the gendarmerie disclosed deficiencies.

(II) TO EFFECT A LAWFUL ARREST OR PREVENT THE ESCAPE OF SOMEONE LAWFULLY DETAINED

There has been no case concerning the second limb. Regarding the effecting of a lawful arrest, this was found in *Kelly v. U.K.*[12] to justify the use of lethal force by soldiers to stop a car of joyriders which drove through a checkpoint. The Commission accepted that given a reasonable belief that the occupants of the case were terrorists (in particular, their aggressive manner of driving which put the soldiers at risk) the shooting at the car could be justified as absolutely necessary to effect a lawful arrest. This finding flies in the face of the domestic court's findings in the civil proceedings that the soldiers could not rely on the defence of arrest since the occupants of the car had not committed any serious offence when the incident arose.[13] The Commission's decision does not explain this apparent contradiction. The level of force used to stop the car was also not found to be excessive or disproportionate, although the applicant had pointed out there was no attempt to fire at the tyres or take other steps to apprehend the vehicle and that no consideration was given to the known fact that cars going through checkpoints were as likely to be joyriders, drunken motorists or inadvertent drivers. The Commission gave special regard to the difficult situation in Belfast and to the extreme circumstances of this case, where the soldiers had only seconds to react to an apparently determined effort to evade the checkpoint which had caused one of their number minor injury.

Conversely in a Turkish case, where a soldier shot dead the driver of a car which passed through a checkpoint without stopping, the Commission distinguished it from *Kelly*, since the manner in which the driver, an ordinary civilian working for State authorities, behaved was not shown to be as suspicious.[14]

(III) ACTION LAWFULLY TAKEN FOR THE PURPOSE OF QUELLING A RIOT

Where in *Stewart v. U.K.*, a 13-year-old boy died from a plastic bullet striking his head, the applicant denied that there was a riot situation which might bring the death within the exception in the second paragraph of Article 2. The Commission considered that while definitions of what constituted a riot might differ between various jurisdictions, 150 people throwing missiles at a patrol of soldiers such that they risked serious injury did fall within the term. As to whether the firing of the bullet was "absolutely necessary" it considered the particular circumstances applying in Northern Ireland (the continuous public disturbances which had given rise to loss of life and that such events were often used as cover for sniper attacks). Notwithstanding the arguments raised by the applicant concerning the known risk to life from baton rounds, the Commission concluded in light of the threat facing the soldiers and the fact that the soldier's aim was disturbed when he fired, that death resulted from the use of force no more than absolutely necessary for the purpose of quelling a riot.

---

[12] See also *Farrell v. U.K.*, 9013/80, (Dec.) December 11, 1982, 30 D.R. 96, (Rep.) 38 D.R. 44 which had also raised the question of lawful arrest where the applicant's husband had been shot in the street by soldiers waiting to ambush a bank raid. The husband had been unarmed, carried no bomb but had failed apparently to respond to instructions to halt. The domestic court jury found that the use of force was reasonably necessary to effect a lawful arrest and to prevent crime. The case was declared admissible and settled, the issue not being resolved further.

[13] Carswell J. expressly found that the shooting would not be justified by the purpose of effecting a lawful arrest since the only arrestable offence known to be committed was theft of a car and reckless driving which did not justify use of lethal force. The exception he found to apply was use of reasonable force to prevent crime, namely, the escape of terrorists who would commit future offences, which general preventive justification does not exist under the Convention.

[14] *Aytekin.*

(e) Planning and control of the use of lethal force

The State has the responsibility in the planning and executing of operations to take steps to minimise the need for the use of lethal force. The Court has also referred to its role as evaluating whether the authorities were negligent in their choice of action.[15] Thus in *McCann*, although it was found that the soldiers' own actions did not contravene Article 2, the lack of care in evaluating and providing information to the soldiers and the failure to allow for other contingencies were identified, in the context of using soldiers trained to shoot to kill, as not conforming with this standard. In *Andronicou and Constantinou v. Cyprus*, the use of special teams, trained to kill, armed with sub-machine guns to intervene in a domestic dispute between a young couple was found by the Commission to increase the risk of injury and death. The Court, differing,[16] held that the decision to use the special teams was a considered one of last resort, and did not disclose any lack of care, given the circumstances in which Andronicou was known to be armed, and with a capacity for violence and Elsie Constantinou had been screaming repeatedly that he was going to kill her. The Court saw no problem in the fact that the teams carried machine guns, since *inter alia*, clear instructions had been issued as to their use and Andonicou was armed with a double shotgun. It did not find that the officers had been supplied with misleading information as in *McCann*.

Agents of the State are also expected to be trained to react with the degree of caution to be expected of law enforcement officers in a democratic society. Over-reaction was therefore a factor in finding a violation in *McCann*, where the suspects were shot repeatedly at close range and in the opinion of the Commission in *Andronicou and Constantinou v. Cyprus*[17] where officers reacted to two shots by a rate of firing which rendered almost inevitable the death of the hostage they were seeking to rescue.

Where operations take place in the vicinity of civilian populations, necessary steps must also be taken to avert the risk of inadvertent death or injury in any ensuing clash. In *Ergi v. Turkey*, where the security forces set up an ambush for the PKK at the entrance to a village, and a clash ensued with firing across the houses, the Commission, in the absence of any evidence to the contrary effect from relevant witnesses, concluded that these circumstances showed a lack of planning and control. In *Aytekin v. Turkey*, the Commission's finding of violation where a gendarme shot an unarmed man driving through a checkpoint relied, *inter alia*, on the inadequate manning levels at the barrier to cope with incidents and the lack of information from the Government to satisfy itself of the training and procedures for checkpoint controls.

3. The duty to protect life

(a) Protection from use of force or threat to life posed by others

Article 2 may give rise to positive obligations on the part of the State to protect life.[18] Several cases have been introduced by persons in Northern Ireland complaining that the State had failed to protect them from terrorists. In one case, where the applicant's husband and brother had been murdered, the applicant argued before the Commission that the United Kingdom had failed to provide an effective and commensurate response to the

---

[15] *Andronicou and Constantinou v. Cyprus,* para. 181.

[16] However, it found no violation by a narrow margin of five votes to four.

[17] 25052/94, (Rep.) May 23, 1996. Lefteris Andronicou, following a dispute with his fiancée Elsie Constantinou, held her in their flat while the authorities tried to negotiate her release and then sent in police special forces, who broke into the flat. Lefteris apparently fired his shotgun and the officers opened fire, as a result of which both he and Elsie died. He was hit by at least 25 bullets and Elsie by 2 bullets from the officers.

[18] 9438/81, (Dec.) February 28, 1983, 32 D.R. 190.

threat posed by terrorism. The Commission was not prepared to hold that a State is under an obligation to exclude all possible occurrence of violence, or to examine in detail whether the U.K. had adopted appropriate and efficient measures to combat terrorism. It was sufficient that there were 10,500 soldiers in the area, that hundreds of them had lost their lives in the conflict and it did not consider that the State had been obliged to take any further steps to protect her and her family. The same general overview was taken in *Yaşa v. Turkey*, where the applicant had been subject to a life-threatening attack as part of an alleged campaign on a pro-Kurdish newspaper. The Commission noted that the security forces were engaged in combatting terrorist groups.

Where however a person is subject to a known risk to life, the Commission has hinted that some obligation to take more specific measures may be necessary, although it is likely that the extent of the obligation is limited. In an early case,[19] where an applicant in Ireland who had for a while been given a bodyguard complained when the protection was removed, the Commission rejected the case, finding that the State was not under an obligation to provide a protection of this nature, at least not for an indefinite time. In *Osman v. United Kingdom* where the applicant's family was subject to a murderous attack by a school teacher whose behaviour had been increasingly bizarre and threatening, the Commission found that the United Kingdom was under an obligation to provide a framework of laws against such behaviour and a police structure to enforce them, but that the extent of their obligation to take specific steps of investigation or prevention would depend on the circumstances. In the absence of a clear and immediate risk to the family, the Commission was not prepared to find that defects in investigation or delay in taking preventive measures disclosed a breach of Article 2.[20]

(b) *Procedural requirements*

Insofar as procedural requirements might require investigation into instances of loss of life apart from the use of lethal force above,[21] the Commission has found, in the case of a series of murders by the nurse Beverly Allitt in a hospital, that the prosecution of the nurse, the possibility of civil proceedings, and an inquiry which had examined and made public its findings with regard to the procedures at fault in the hospital in question were sufficient mechanism for bringing the facts of the case to light. It did not consider it incompatible that the enquiry itself was not open to the public, its membership not wholly independent from the health authorities and its remit limited to the facts of the cases, taking the view that the wider issues of public health policy and funding were for public and political debate.[22]

As the approach of the Commission in *McCann* indicates, what may be required by way of investigation will vary with the circumstances of each case and it will not be in the case of every tragic occurrence that special steps by way of enquiry would be required.

---

[19] 6040/73, 44 Coll. 121.

[20] The Commission left open whether, as is the general principle in some continental jurisdictions that persons are under an obligation to go to the assistance of some-one in danger, it would disclose a breach of Art. 2 where the law of a State failed to provide such an obligation; *Hughes v. U.K.*, 11590/85, (Dec.) July 8, 1985, 48 D.R. 258 where the applicant's husband died of a heart attack, in circumstances when none of those at the school where he worked attempted resuscitation and delayed calling an ambulance: the Commission found that in any event there was no indication in this case that anyone there was qualified to do what was necessary or that it would have made any difference if they had called an ambulance earlier, since medical evidence established that he had died within 4–5 minutes of the attack.

[21] *McCann*, para. 161 refers to the provision of effective official investigation into killings *inter alios* by use of force by agents of the State.

[22] 23412/94, *Taylor family and others v. U.K.*, August 30, 1994, 79–A D.R. 127.

(c) *Medical services*

The question to what extent a State is under an obligation to protect a person's state of health is largely unexplored. It trespasses on an area of state health policy in which matters of finance are acute and controversial. In the case of *Association X v. United Kingdom*,[23] concerning complaints that the vaccination of children was causing severe brain damage and even death, the Commission held that States were under an obligation to take adequate measures to protect life and that this might raise issues in the area of medical care. However, in the case itself, it noted that there was no evidence that the vaccinations were administered poorly or that proper and adequate steps were not taken to avoid the risks of damage and death materialising. It appears to have given weight to the number of vaccinations which pursued the purpose of avoiding serious illness in comparison to the relatively few adverse reactions. It concluded that overall the system of supervision and control of those administering the vaccinations was sufficient to comply with the obligation.

In the case brought by the parents of children killed and injured by the attacks of the nurse Beverly Allitt,[24] the applicants sought to attack the system of national health as a whole. It was argued, *inter alia*, that the financial cutbacks and organisation of the local health services had led to the situation arising in which an untrained and dangerous individual could be allowed to care unsupervised for children. The Commission did not consider that Article 2 extended to an examination of the national health policy and practice in general. It noted that Allitt had been prosecuted by the criminal law, that the applicants could sue the health authorities for negligence and that an inquiry had been held which had examined and made public its findings with regard to the procedures at fault in the hospital in question.

In the absence of any immediate risk to life, it is unlikely that complaints about general standards or denial of medical care would be found to raise any issues.[25] In the case of *D v. United Kingdom*,[26] it was found, exceptionally, that the measure of expelling a person in the final stages of AIDS would breach Article 3. It had been argued, *inter alia*, that his life would be shortened and pain and suffering be caused by the withdrawal of medical treatment which would result from the expulsion to St Kitts which had minimal facilities. The Court's findings emphasised the severe state of the applicant's health and avoided any statement that the United Kingdom were under a responsibility not to remove life-maintaining medical care.

Cross-reference

Part IIB: Abortion
Part IIB: Extradition, Death penalty
Part IIB: Torture, inhuman and degrading treatment

---

[23] 7154/75, (Dec.) July 12, 1978, 14 D.R. 31.
[24] 23412/94.
[25] *X v. Ireland*, 6839/74, (Dec.) October 4, 1974, 7 D.R. 78, where a mother complained of the denial of a medical card to her severely disabled daughter which would have provided free medical care — the Commission found, whether Art. 2 would apply or not, on the facts it appeared that the daughter had been receiving medical assistance and her life had not been endangered.
[26] May 2, 1997, R.J.D., 1997–III, No. 37.

Surveillance and secret files

Key provision:

Article 8 (private life).

Key case law:

Klass v. Germany, September 6, 1978, Series A, No. 28; 2 E.H.R.R. 214; *Leander v. Sweden*, March 26, 1987, Series A, No. 116; 9 E.H.R.R. 433.

1. General considerations

Under this section, the clandestine process of information-gathering and storing by democratic states is considered. While surveillance techniques will frequently involve interception of communications, this has been treated separately due to the specific protection given to correspondence. Surveillance and intelligence gathering is a much wider and potentially unlimited field of activity. Many similar factors however come into play. The need for information gathering and storage is generally not questioned where it is in the context of police investigation or security, the legitimacy of the aims and the necessity of which is undoubted.[1] The concentration has been on lawfulness and procedural aspects to prevent arbitrariness or abuse.

2. Private life

Besides direct interception of telephone and mail, there are a myriad of methods, from the use of listening devices or bugs in privately-owned houses[2]; indirect information from intercepts in place on other persons[3]; collection of press reports; data from surveillance by Special Branch, photographs (usually from passport applications)[4]; long range cameras and drilling holes in wall.[5] Whether it may be arguable whether all methods involve an interference (for example, press cutting files gather publicly available information), the storing of information containing personal details is almost certainly likely to relate to "private life" within the meaning of Article 8, paragraph 1. The Commission's case law seems to indicate the barest details are sufficient (Part IIB: Private life, Personal information).

A security check *per se* is not objectionable for the Commission which held in *Hilton v. United Kingdom* that issues only arose where the check was based on information about a person's private affairs.[6]

3. Establishing an interference

While *Klass v. Germany* concerned interception of communications in particular, it also referred to "surveillance measures" in more general terms. The Court stated that it was

---

[1] *Leander*, para. 49: even where the subjects of the surveillance are perhaps surprising, as in the case of *Hewitt* and *Harman* who were civil rights lawyers and members of the Labour party, or *Campbell Christie* the trade union leader (21482/93, (Dec.) June 27, 1994, 78–A D.R. 119).

[2] *Redgrave v. U.K.*, 20271/92, (Dec.) September 1, 1993, unpublished.

[3] *Hewitt and Harman No. 1*, 12175/86, (Rep.) May 9, 1989, 67 D.R. 88.

[4] *Hewitt and Harman, ibid.*

[5] *Govell v. U.K.*, 27237/95 (Dec.) February 26, 1997.

[6] *Hilton v. U.K.*, 12015/86, (Dec.) 57 D.R. 108; *N v. U.K.*, 12327/86, (Rep.) May 9, 1989, 67 D.R. 123. For example, a security check might involve scrutiny only of the materials given by the person in the job application or cross reference in files where no entries exist.

enough for there to be in existence a system permitting the use of such measures for Article 8, paragraph 1 to be invoked by applicants as constituting an interference with private life. The Commission have added a gloss in *Hilton v. United Kingdom*,[7] adopted later by the Court,[8] to the effect that it cannot be open to anyone in the country to complain that they are subject to violations due to the activities of secret service activities but that an individual must show that there is a reasonable likelihood that he has been subject to such measures or is in a category of persons likely to be targeted. Once an applicant is in that category, it is not necessary to show that any information compiled and stored has been applied to his detriment.

In *Hilton*, the applicant did not establish a reasonable likelihood. It was only shown that the BBC had materials submitted in the context of her job application and that the Security Service objected to her due to her membership in a particular society. There was no indication that it had or continued to retain any information of a personal character about her. In *Hewitt and Harman No. 1 v. United Kingdom*, where an MI5 operative made revelations in an affidavit, a reasonable likelihood that secret surveillance occurred and files compiled was established. While in *N. v. United Kingdom* where the applicant was offered a post connected with Government defence projects subject to "enquiries" which he was later told were not satisfactory, the Commission found there was a reasonable inference that he was subject to security checks.[9]

The nature of an applicant's own activities may also render it reasonably probable that surveillance had been carried out and information gathered in secret files, as in the case of Vanessa Redgrave who found a bug on her premises which she alleged had been placed by the Government. The Commission noted that she was well-known for her involvement in a revolutionary party and controversial political causes, as well as evidence from documents showing United States security interest over a considerable period of time.

Once a file has been in existence, it is also likely that it will be presumed to exist at a later date, in the absence of rules of destruction.[10]

4. "in accordance with law"[11]

The basic principles have received significant examination in the area of interception of communications. It is established that the lawfulness criterion refers to the existence of a basis for the interference in domestic law, and the quality of the law, which is accessible and renders measures reasonably foreseeable, thus providing protection against arbitrariness. The requirement of foreseeability however is affected by the special context of secret controls concerning national security. Thus in *Leander v. Sweden* an individual could not claim to be able to foresee precisely what checks would be made by the Swedish special police service. Nevertheless in a system applicable to citizens generally the law has to be sufficiently clear in its terms to give an adequate indication as to the circumstances in

---

[7] See n.6.

[8] *Halford v. U.K.*, June 25, 1977, R.J.D., 1997–III, No. 39.

[9] *Esbester v. U.K.* 18601/91, (Dec.) April 2, 1993, D.E. and F, 18600–2 (Dec.) October 12, 1992, concerning applicants who applied unsuccessfully for civil service posts — the Commission accepted the Government's submissions that for two applicants their residence abroad rendered it impossible to carry out a satisfactory security clearance and their applications were not submitted for checking while for the third, offered a post at the Central Office of information subject to enquiries which were unsatisfactory, the Commission found it was a reasonable inference from the facts that a security check had been carried out which involved reference to recorded information concerning matters falling within the sphere of private life.

[10] *Hewitt and Harman v. U.K. (No. 2)*, 20317/92, (Dec.) September 1, 1993. The Government ceded an interference for these applicants, in respect of whom files had already been found to have been brought into existence years before.

[11] See also section Convention Approach, Lawfulness.

which and the conditions on which public authorities are empowered to resort to secret and potentially dangerous interference with private life.

Lack of a proper basis in domestic law for the activities of the security service disclosed a violation in *Hewitt and Harman No. 1 v. United Kingdom* and *N v. United Kingdom*, where there was only a 1952 Home Secretary directive, which though published did not have the force of law.

In assessing the quality of the law, the Court may take into account instructions and administrative practices without status of substantive law and whether powers are adequately defined. Thus in *Leander*, there was no problem since although there was only one administrative instruction, it was public. Although there was a wide discretion on what information could be entered, there were also significant limitations *e.g.* no entry in the register on the basis of expression of political opinion, detailed rules on how information on the register could be used and the system was subject to the necessity of measures for the purposes of national security. However, in *R v. Netherlands*,[12] this criterion was not met where the law defining the tasks of the Military Intelligence Services did not state the limits to be respected in carrying out their activities and there was no definition of categories of persons liable to be subject to measures of secret surveillance or the circumstances in which measures could be employed or the means to be employed.

Provisions do not have to be subject to comprehensive definition. In *Esbester v. United Kingdom* the Commission rejected the complaint that the phrase in the interests of national security was only partially defined since the subject-matter was inevitably couched in terms which had to be flexible and worked out in practice. It was enough that there were express limits, in particular, that the information could only be used where necessary to fulfil its specified functions. In *Hewitt and Harman No. 2*, the Commission was not impressed that other systems in other jurisdictions limited powers more narrowly, for example, to those who advocated the use of force, as opposed to a definition which potentially covered actions intended to overthrow parliamentary democracy by non-violent means.

5. Necessity and procedural safeguards

Regarding the necessity of measures, there is a wide margin of appreciation accorded to Contracting States in choosing the means of protecting national security.[13] The fact that a person finds themselves subject to security checks which bar them from employment or subject to secret surveillance is not enough to disclose a violation, whether justified on the facts or not.[14] The scrutiny of the Convention organs has concentrated rather on the existence of procedural safeguards, since the grant of such powers poses a risk of undermining, even destroying democracy on the ground of defending it. There must therefore be adequate and effective guarantees against abuse, and where these exist, there may be no violation. A pragmatic and not overly demanding approach, requiring an adequate framework of safeguards of a minimum level of protection, has been adopted.

In the context of procedural safeguards, the Court has referred to direct and regular control as constituting a major safeguard against abuse. It appears impressed by the involvement of judicial or parliamentarian bodies which can provide independent scrutiny of measures. In *Leander*, the safeguards which were found sufficient included the presence

---

[12] *Netherlands*, 14084/88, (Rep.) December 3, 1991, unpublished.

[13] *Leander*, para. 59.

[14] *Martin v. Switzerland*, 25099/94, (Dec.) April 5, 1995, 81–A D.R. 136, where the applicant born in Northern Ireland but living in Geneva was subject to secret police surveillance which he considered unjustified but was able to gain only limited access to the files held on him to refute their contents. Procedural safeguards were sufficient, manifestly ill-founded.

of parliamentarians on the National Police Board who participated in all decisions as to whether information should be released to a requesting authority and supervision by the Parliamentary Ombudsman and the Chancellor of Justice.

Following *Klass*, no problem arises from the failure to release information about past surveillance measures since it is the absence of communication which ensures at least partly the efficacy of the personal control procedure.

In *Esbester v. United Kingdom*, where the applicant attacked the procedures set up under Security Service Act 1989, the Commission found references to systems in other jurisdictions of limited relevance. While other arrangements might be more liberal, its role was to see if the system under examination in the concrete case passed the threshold imposed by Convention guarantees.[15] As a whole the 1989 Act provided adequate safeguards against abuse — the independent tribunal with lawyers of 10 years experience and a Commissioner of high judicial office who made annual reports to Parliament and recommendations to the Secretary of State. It did not therefore consider that inability of the Commissioner to render binding decisions, or the limited scope of the tribunal's review and its inability to verify or correct information recorded were decisive. In the absence of any indication that the system was not functioning as required by domestic law, it considered that the framework of safeguards achieved a compromise between the requirements of defending democratic society and the rights of the individual. When further complaint was made in *Hewitt and Harman No. 2 v. United Kingdom*, the Commission, in examining the Commissioner's reports, found that he was fulfilling his role actively and authoritatively, and therefore saw no reason to depart from its reasoning in *Esbester*, namely, the system functioned properly. The complaints, *inter alia*, that the tribunal did not hear witnesses on oath, its decisions were brief and that the Commissioner could not order the destruction of records where he found it unreasonable to retain them, were not given weight.

Regarding any right to consult the data held on files, with a view for example to correcting any erroneous entries, the cases do not indicate that this can be derived from Article 8 as yet. Although a right of consultation, even limited is commented on favourably in assessing the procedural safeguards available, no violation has yet been founded upon its absence.[16]

Cross-reference

Part IIB: Interception of communications
Part IIB: Private life

---

[15] *e.g. Hewitt* and *Harman (No. 2)* See n.10: comparison with other systems (Canadian and Australian) might indicate that the Government incorrectly assumed that other methods were not practicable but that did not assist in determining whether the concrete case passed the threshold.

[16] This point was raised unsuccessfully by *D. E.* and *F.* and the lack of any possibility to check and amend errors was referred to in *Hewitt* and *Harman No. 1*. See also *Leander,* para. 48, where the inability to check contents was part of the interference found to be justified, and *Martin,* n.14, where complete access was not found necessary.

Tax

Key provisions:

Article 5, paragraph 1 (right to liberty); Article 6 (access to court and fair trial); Article 1 of Protocol No. 1 (right to property).

Key case law:

Darby v. Sweden, October 23, 1990, Series A, No. 187; 13 E.H.R.R. 774; *Bendenoun v. France*, February 24, 1994, Series A, No. 284; 18 E.H.R.R. 54; *Gasus Dosier GmbH v. Netherlands*, February 23, 1995, Series A, No. 306–B; 20 E.H.R.R. 403; *Benham v. U.K.*, June 10, 1996, R.J.D., 1996–III, No. 10; *National & Provincial Building Society and others v. U.K.*, October 23, 1997, R.J.D., 1997–VII, No. 55.

1. General considerations

Tax receives special treatment under the Convention. Not surprisingly, in drafting the Convention, the Contracting States did not intend to undermine the basis on which their financing depends. An individual's right to freedom from interference in the enjoyment of his property is accordingly subject to the State's right to assess, levy and enforce contributions by way of tax under the second paragraph of Article 1 of the First Protocol. This provision is to be interpreted in light of the underlying principle in the first sentence of first paragraph of Protocol No. 1, namely, to achieve a fair balance between general interest of the community and the protection of the fundamental rights of the individual.[1]

There are few significant cases concerning the way in which States choose to tax or the levels of taxation. Where issues arise the ubiquitous margin of appreciation is present and wide. Arguable points arise more frequently in peripheral areas, as regards access to court and fairness of proceedings in tax-related matters or where there is apparent discrimination in tax matters.

2. Imposition of tax: assessment and levels

It is for national authorities to decide in the first place what kind of taxes or contributions are to be collected and the methods by which they are collected, such decisions commonly involving the appreciation of political, economic and societal questions which the Convention leaves within the competence of the Contracting States which enjoy a wide margin of appreciation.[2] The Commission has found no problems arising regarding the imposition on employers of the costly PAYE system,[3] the increase of contributions on certain categories of persons to benefit others[4] and the imposition of retrospective tax measures.[5]

---

[1] *Sporrong and Llonroth v. Sweden,* September 23, 1982, Series A, No. 52, para. 69.

[2] *Sweden,* 11036/84, (Dec.) December 2, 1985, 45 D.R. 211.

[3] *Austria,* 7427/76, (Dec.) September 27, 1976, 7 D.R. 148, where companies challenged the PAYE system which imposed the burden to deduct taxes, as increasing their costs and depriving them of property, the Commission found that this obligation fell within the second paragraph as being "necessary to secure the payment of taxes and contributions".

[4] *U.K.,* 7995/77, (Dec.) July 11, 1978, 15 D.R. 198, where the imposition of addtional class 4 national insurance contributions on certain self-employed without any alleged countervailing benefit from the system fell within the second part of second paragraph as justified as securing the payment of contributions which, in the general interest, were used for the financing of the social security system for lower earners.

[5] 8531/79, (Dec.) March 10, 1981, 23 D.R. 203, concerning the imposition of retrospective legislation to prevent deliberate trading losses in commodity futures to set off against tax — the Commission found the measure fell under the second paragraph of Art. 1 of Protocol 1 and examined whether it could reasonable be regarded as necessary for the aim or grossly disproportionate. The Commission found the measure not excessive: tax liabilities for the previous year had not yet been settled when measure came into force and the losses concerned were artificial.

But there may be limits. The Commission has stated that the imposition of tax would not generally be incompatible with Article 1 of Protocol No. 1 unless it amounted to a *de facto* confiscation of some part of the taxpayer's possessions.[6] A financial liability might conceivably effect adversely the guarantee of ownership if it placed an excessive burden on the person concerned or fundamentally interfered with his financial position.[7] Reference is also made in cases to whether the imposition of a tax is disproportionate or an abuse of the State's power to levy taxes.[8] The cases indicate that gross arbitrariness or misuse of powers would seem to be required for the Convention organs to find any violation.

3. Measures in enforcement of taxation and duties

Measures taken to ensure the payment of taxes or prevent defaulting have been generally found compatible with the second paragraph. Consideration is given to whether the measure is of such a kind that it can reasonably be considered as necessary for the purpose and whether its application is grossly disproportionate.[9] The imposition of a mortgage on a defaulter in favour of the authorities to ensure payments was not disproportionate[10] and the prevention of the removal of property (including money from a pension) from the country by a person with outstanding tax liabilities fell within the second paragraph.[11] The seizure by the tax authorities of a concrete mixer over which the vendor applicant had retained title was not a deprivation of property within the meaning of the first paragraph but a measure to secure the payment of taxes.[12] In the circumstances the applicant company was involved in a commercial venture, which by its very nature involved an element of risk. Proportionality was satisfied since it could have taken measures of protection, such as stipulating payment in advance which the tax authorities were not in a position to do in respect of defaulters, and the applicant was not without a measure of protection since it enjoyed priority over other creditors and an adequate review procedure before the courts.

4. Penalties and fines: failure to comply with tax authorities

Where a person is sanctioned for failure to comply with tax regulations, issues may arise where the sanction falls within the scope of "criminal charge" for the purposes of attracting the guarantees of Article 6 to the procedure.[13] In *Bendenoun v. France*, where a French taxpayer, accused of bad faith in relation to declared business receipts, was subject

---

[6] 9908/82, (Dec.) May 4, 1983, 32 D.R. 266: where in respect of income tax based on calculations related to items of personal expenditure, the tax authorities upped the applicant's tax to take into account large sums invested in companies on the basis that this expenditure was derived from his income unless shown to derive from capital or a gift.

[7] 11036/84 above n.2: where a profit-sharing tax was introduced but its level (0.2–0.5 per cent increase in social charges and 1 per cent of profits) not shown to be disproportionate or an abuse of the right to levy tax.

[8] 13013/87, (Dec.) December 14, 1988, 58 D.R. 163: concerning imposition of a once for all property tax on life assurance companies (7 per cent one off wealth tax on accumulated savings and benefits) where the applicants argued that they were singled out — the Commission noted the measure was introduced in light of national budget deficit considerations and to keep down inflation: referred to the "sovereign power" of the State and found no lack of proportionality or abuse.

[9] 7287/75, (Dec.) March 3, 1978, 13 D.R. 27 the duties, fines and forfeiture were not so disproportionate in this case since the judge could have regard to applicant's economic means and though very severe, were not excessive.

[10] 9889/82, (Dec.) October 6, 1982, 31 D.R. 237.

[11] *Sweden*, 10653/83, May 6, 1985, 42 D.R. 224.

[12] *Gasus Dosier GmbH v. Netherlands*.

[13] In *Max Von Sydow v. Sweden*, the actor was subject to a special supplement of 50 per cent of the extra tax assessed as due on income which he had not declared. He did not receive a public oral hearing in the proceedings before the tax and administrative courts. The case was declared admissible under Art. 6 — (Dec.) May 12, 1987, 53 D.R. 85 but settled (Rep.), 11464/85, October 8, 1985, 53 D.R. 121.

to tax surcharges (almost half a million francs), the Court agreed with the Commission that the tax surcharges concerned a "criminal charge" rendering the Article 6 applicable.[14] It noted the charges were imposed under the Tax Code which applied to everyone; were not intended as pecuniary compensation for damage but essentially as a punishment to deter reoffending; were posed under a general rule whose purpose was deterrent and punitive; and there was liability of committal to prison for non-payment.

Where a person is committed for failure to pay tax, this may constitute detention compatible with Article 5, paragraph 1(b) as lawful arrest or detention in order to secure the fulfilment of an obligation prescribed by law.[15] Issues have arisen in the context of poll tax, as to whether magistrates have complied with lawfulness criteria in exercising the power to commit defaulters.[16]

5. Civil rights

Article 6 does not apply to proceedings relating to the assessment or imposition of tax, including the consequences of a change in tax legislation.[17] In the *National & Provincial Building Society and others v. United Kingdom* where the applicants were claiming restitution of monies paid under invalid regulations however, the Commission found that Article 6 applied.[18]

6. Retrospectivity

There is no express prohibition on retrospective legislation outside the criminal sphere. However, in respect of a retrospective removal of tax relief which aimed to prevent tax avoidance, the Commission held that a retrospective measure imposing a liability or removing a relief must be regarded as more severe due to the uncertainty which it engenders, in particular since it prevents a taxpayer arranging his affairs to mitigate new liabilities. On the facts of that case however, the measure was not excessive.[19]

7. Discrimination

Differences in treatment of persons in relevantly similar positions may raise issues under Article 14 in conjunction with Article 1 of Protocol No. 1 since matters of taxation fall within the scope of that provision. The Commission has considered that a wider margin of appreciation will apply in this area than in others, since taxation systems inevitably differentiate between groups of taxpayers and the implementation of any system creates marginal situations. It noted that attitudes and goals to taxation will change and a government may need to strike a balance between the need to raise revenue and to reflect other social objectives, and the authorities are in the best position to assess those needs and

---

[14] However the Court found no violation of Art. 6 since the applicant had not established that the failure of the tax authorities to produce certain documents infringed defence rights.

[15] *Benham v. U.K.* See Part IIB: Deprivation of liberty. In accordance with a procedure prescribed by law.

[16] *e.g. Redfern and others v. U.K.*, No. 24842/94 etc. (Dec.) December 10, 1997, where magistrates committed persons under 21 for failure to pay poll tax, without stating their reasons for rejecting other alternatives to imprisonment as required by legislation.

[17] 11189/84, *Sweden*, (Dec.) December 11, 1986, 50 D.R. 121; companies complaining about increase in social contributions and a profit sharing tax resulting from new legislation; 8903/80, (Dec.) July 8, 1980, 21 D.R. 246 — demand by tax authorities for reimbursement of turnover tax from businessman; 9908/82, (Dec.) May 4, 1983, 32 D.R. 266 — imposition of revised tax assessments where obvious personal expenditure exceeded declared income; 13013/87, (Dec.) December 14, 1988, 58 D.R. 163 — imposition of once for all property tax on life assurance companies.

[18] The restitution proceedings were private law actions decisive for private law rights to quantifiable sums of money and the judicial review proceedings were closely interrelated with them.

[19] 8531/79, see n.5.

requirements. In *Lindsay v. U.K.*,[20] the margin of appreciation also applied to the moment when a Government thinks fit to amend the tax system. This was where the applicant was complaining of the unequal effect of taxation as to whether the husband or the wife was the principal earner and pointed to the pending proposal to render position of spouses identical. The Commission accepted that the tax position resulted from pursuing the aim of positive discrimination in favour of married women, encouraging them into the job market and was proportionate and within the margin of appreciation.

The Commission has also found that for the purposes of taxation married and unmarried couples could not claim to be in comparable positions, marriage constituting a regime which attracted specific rights and obligations. Different tax rates can be justified by the consideration of avoiding too high a burden on lower earners.[21] Differences applied to taxpayers who live abroad may be justified, as in the case where civil servants who worked abroad were liable to pay Austrian tax on part of their salary but were unable to claim a single breadwinner's allowance. The Commission having regard to the margin of appreciation found that the difference could be justified since it was difficult for the Austrian authorities to verify what happened outside their borders.[22] However in *Darby v. Sweden* where the applicant was liable to pay church tax in Sweden although he was not resident in the country but could not, unlike residents, apply for an exemption, the Court found no objective or reasonable justification in the alleged administrative difficulties that eligibility to non-residents would engender.

Cross-reference

Part IIA: General principles, Fairness
Part IIA: General principles, Civil rights and obligations
Part IIA: General principles, Criminal charge
Part IIB: Discrimination
Part IIB: Property

---

[20] *Lindsay v. U.K.*, 11089/84, (Dec.) November 11, 1986, 49 D.R. 181.
[21] 7995/77, see n.4.
[22] 12560/86, (Dec.) March 16, 1989, 60 D.R. 194.

Torture, inhuman and degrading treatment

Key provisions:

Article 3 (prohibition on torture, inhuman and degrading treatment or punishment).

Key case law:

Ireland v. U.K.. January 18, 1978, Series A, No. 25; 2 E.H.R.R. 25; *Tyrer v. U.K.*, April 25, 1978, Series A, No. 26; 2 E.H.R.R. 1; *Soering v. U.K.*, July 7, 1989, Series A, No. 161; 11 E.H.R.R. 439; *Tomasi v. France*, August 27, 1992, Series A, No. 241–A; 15 E.H.R.R. 1; *Herczegfalvy v. Austria*, September 24, 1992, Series A, No. 242–B; 15 E.H.R.R. 437; *Klass v. Germany*, September 22, 1993, Series A, No. 269; 8 E.H.R.R. 305; *Costello-Roberts v. U.K.*, March 25, 1993, Series A, No. 247–C; 19 E.H.R.R. 112; *Ribitsch v. Austria*, December 4, 1995, Series A, No. 336; *Akdivar v. Turkey*, September 16, 1996, R.J.D., 1996–IV, No. 15; *Chahal v. United Kingdom*, November 15, 1996, R.J.D., 1996–V, No. 22; *Aksoy v. Turkey*, December 18, 1996, R.J.D., 1996–VI, No. 26; *Aydin v. Turkey*, September 25, 1997, R.J.D., 1997–VI, No. 50; *Mentes v. Turkey*, November 28, 1997, to be published in R.J.D. 1997; *Ranineu v. Finland*, December 16, 1997, to be published in R.J.D. 1997.

1. General approach

Article 3 sets an absolute prohibition. There are no stated exceptions and no derogation is possible under Article 15. The Court has said that it enshrines one of the fundamental values of the democratic societies making up the Council of Europe[1] and calls for heightened vigilance.[2] It applies irrespective of the victim's conduct.[3]

That said, however, and perhaps as a result, the threshold for treatment falling within the scope of Article 3 has been set high by the Convention organs. The Commission in the *Greek Interstate* case distinguished acts prohibited by Article 3 from a "certain roughness of treatment", which might take the form of slaps or blows of the hand on the face or head.[4] The Court distinguished between the use of violence which is to be condemned on moral grounds and also in most cases under the domestic law of the Contracting States but which does not fall within Article 3.[5] The test established by the Court, and largely followed by the Commission, is that of attaining a certain minimum level of severity. There is perhaps a sentiment that to find a State in violation of this provision is particularly serious and not to be undertaken lightly. The basic approach is:

---

[1] *Soering*, para. 88.
[2] *Ribitsch*, para. 32.
[3] Governments have argued that in certain circumstances Art. 3 does not have full effect. The following justifications have been rejected: in *Chahal*, that the expulsion of the alleged Sikh terrorist applicant to India was justified due to the security considerations which he posed to the U.K. if he stayed; in *Tomasi*, that an applicant was a terrorist and involved in a crime of violence should be taken into account was smartly rejected by the Court which held that the fight against crime, and difficulties with regard to terrorism, could not justify limits being put on the protection to be afforded in respect of the physical integrity of individuals (para. 115).
[4] *The Greek case*, Nos. 3321–3/67 and 3344/67, 11 Ybk of the ECHR (Rep.) November 5, 1969 (1969), 501. More controversially, it commented that this was tolerated, even taken for granted by the detainees and that the point up to which people may accept physical violence as being neither cruel nor excessive depends on societies and different sections of them: see also the Commission in *Ireland v. U.K.*, in respect of detention conditions in holding centres, *i.e.* no bedding, compulsory physical "military drill" type exercises, even though some detainees were old and in poor condition — this was harsh, deliberate even illegal, a practice that was reprehensible and discreditable but not contrary to Art. 3.
[5] *Ireland v. U.K.*, para. 167.

". . . ill-treatment must attain a minimum level of severity if it is to fall within the scope of Article 3. The assessment of this minimum is, in the nature of things, relative; it depends on all the circumstances of the case, such as the duration of the treatment, its physical and mental effects and, in some cases, the sex, age and state of health of the victim."[6]

The Commission receives many complaints of distressing situations in which Article 3 is invoked. However, expulsion or extradition *per se* (without any risk to life being involved), the taking into care and adoption of a person's children, the imposition of long sentences of imprisonment, while they may all entail significant personal distress are not such as to fall within Article 3, particularly where the distress is a collateral effect of measures, primarily aimed at achieving other legitimate aims. There would have to be special elements bringing the case beyond the "usual" effect that the measure inevitably entails, such as discrimination based on racial grounds which degrade and stigmatise[7] or perhaps where the execution of the measure is unnecessarily and unjustifiably traumatic.[8]

The principal Article 3 treatment cases have risen in the context of physical ill-treatment inflicted by agents of the State — the archetypal police or prison officer brutality type case. This is gradually being extended to risk of severe physical or psychological harm where a State takes steps which may lead to a person being exposed to such harm, or even a positive obligation, to take steps to avoid such risk occurring. This is in the context of expulsion and extradition particularly but has been raised also in the context of punishment of children.[9]

Only individuals can invoke Article 3, not legal persons.[10]

2. Exhaustion of domestic remedies and administrative practice

Where an allegation is made of assault or ill-treatment in custody, a civil action for damages will generally be a remedy which should be exhausted for the purposes of Article 3.[11] However, States cannot in theory buy their way out of their obligations, torturing freely and paying up in the courts.[12] Thus a civil remedy may cease to be regarded as an effective remedy where there is an "administrative practice" of treatment contrary to Article 3.[13] This requires:

- a repetition of acts (a pattern such as the five techniques examined in *Ireland v. United Kingdom*, see below);
- official toleration, at a senior level. Mere tolerance at the lower and middle level of the hierarchy is not of itself conclusive. It is necessary to examine what measures have been taken by the authorities to prevent the repetition of such treatment.[14]

---

[6] *Ibid.*, para. 162.

[7] *East African Asians* case 4403/70, etc. (Rep.) December 14, 1973, 78–A D.R. 5; however, see also *Abdulaziz v. U.K.,* May 28, 1985, Series A, No. 94, para. 91, where the difference in treatment in immigration matters did not denote any contempt or lack of respect for the personality of the applicants but was intended solely to achieve the aims of protection of employment, economy and immigration control.

[8] *e.g.* Nos. 19579–82/92, April 4, 1993, the *Orkney* child care cases communicated under Art. 3 in relation, *inter alia*, to the circumstances of the dawn raid, the complete separation from families and familiar objects without any contact, intensive "interrogations" — the question would possibly have arisen whether these were accepted practices and without any therapeutic basis (applications later withdrawn).

[9] *e.g. Soering; Chahal; D v. U.K.,* May 2, 1997, R.J.D. 1997–III, No. 37 (expulsion cases); as regards corporal punishment of children in school (see Corporal punishment) *Costello-Roberts* and *A v. U.K.,* 25559/94, (Rep.), September 18, 1997 pending before the Court.

[10] 11921/86, (Dec.) October 12, 1988, 57 D.R. 81.

[11] *e.g.* 8462/79, (Dec.) July 8, 1980, 20 D.R. 184.

[12] *Donnelly et al, v. U.K.* 5577–5583/72, (Dec.) December 15, 1975, 4 D.R. 4.

[13] *op. cit,* n.4, 195–196.

[14] *Donnelly et al,* see, n.12.

It is not sufficient that the existence of an administrative practice be merely alleged, its existence must be shown by means of substantial evidence.[15]

While administrative practice has been alleged in applications from south-east Turkey, the Commission has not found it necessary to make any findings in light of its view that in each case declared admissible the applicants had either done all that could be expected of them by way of exhaustion or that there were no effective remedies available.[16]

The difficulties of establishing an administrative practice outside an interstate case are illustrated by the *Donelly and others v. United Kingdom*[17] case, which was rejected on, *inter alia*, grounds of non-exhaustion shortly before the Court found a practice of ill-treatment existing in *Ireland v. United Kingdom*.

3. Different categories of ill-treatment

Consideration is given to the particular circumstances of each case. Relevant factors include the manner and method of execution, the nature and context of the punishment[18]; premeditation and systematic organisation; age[19]; duration[20]; effect on health[21]; state of health[22]; public nature of the punishment[23]; and whether alternative courses were open to the authorities.[24]

(a) *Torture*

The Court in *Ireland v. United Kingdom* held that torture involves suffering of a particular intensity and cruelty, attaching a "special stigma to deliberate inhuman treatment causing very serious and cruel suffering". It saw support in a resolution of the UN General Assembly referring to torture as an "aggravated and deliberate form of cruel, inhuman or degrading treatment of punishment". It found, overruling the Commission, that the five interrogation techniques used in holding centres in Northern Ireland did not constitute torture but inhuman and degrading treatment. The techniques involved keeping detainees heads covered by a hood; submitting the detainees to continuous and monotonous noise of a volume calculated to isolate them from communication; deprivation of sleep; deprivation of food and water other than one round of bread and a pint of water every six hours; and

---

[15] Commission in *Ireland v. U.K.*, (Dec.) October 1, 1972, 41 Coll. 3/85.

[16] *e.g.* the Commission's decisions on admissibility in *Akdivar* and *Aksoy*.

[17] See, n.12, where individual applicants who claimed to have been ill-treated in custody in Northern Ireland, had either accepted settlements out of court or had civil claims pending.

[18] *e.g. Costello-Roberts*.

[19] Youth puts into question the compatibility of measures under Art. 3 as a general principle. This was an important element in *Soering* — judicial execution was not itself incompatible with the Convention; the length of detention on death row the result of the applications for stays and the judicial procedures available to protect against arbitrariness. The ICCPR and the American Convention on Human Rights prohibits the death penalty for those who commit the offence under 18; *Soering* was 18 at the time of the offence; see also *Hussain v. U.K.*, February 21, 1996, R.J.D., 1996–I, No. 4 para. 61 which indicates that mandatory life sentences are acceptable as punishment for adults, but not for children.

[20] The length of the wait on death row (six–eight years) "anguish and mounting tension" and long exposure to the stringent conditions on the death row was a significant factor in *Soering* (implying that shorter periods might not pose a problem.)

[21] Significant effect on health, whether physical or mental, is usually required for inhuman treatment and for practical purposes generally requires substantiation and medical evidence of some description.

[22] *Soering* was suffering abnormality of the mind when he committed the murders. This was found relevant to the acceptability of "death row phenomenon" for a given individual.

[23] See *Tyrer* below.

[24] In *Soering*, the Court took into account the possibility of achieving the purpose of obtaining the trial of the applicant for serious crimes by extraditing him instead to Germany. In *Chahal*, in response to the Government's allegations that he was a dangerous terrorist, it commented that it was open to the authorities to use the criminal justice system in the U.K. in respect of any offences committed.

making the detainees stand legs apart with their hands up against a wall for long periods. This was systematic but not sufficiently severe to be torture.

The Commission in its approach in cases has attached weight to the character of the pressure involved, whether it intended to break or eliminate the will and the premeditated, systematic nature of the treatment.[25] In *Ireland v. United Kingdom* case it found that the five techniques caused some physical pain which stopped when the treatment ceased, exhaustion and a number of acute psychiatric symptoms, which it could not be excluded continued to exist for some time afterwards (anxiety, disorientation, isolation etc.). While separately some of the techniques might not have fallen within Article 3, the techniques applied together were designed to impose severe mental and physical stress and suffering on a person in order to obtain information from him which constitutional torture.

There have been recent findings of torture in a series of Turkish cases, where the Commission has in particular given weight to the element of punishment or coercion.[26] In *Aksoy v. Turkey*, the infliction of palestinian hanging in interrogation which left the applicant partially paralysed was, without discussion, torture. In *Yagiz v. Turkey*, the beating of a nurse on the feet was torture. In *Aydin v. Turkey*, where an 17-year-old girl was raped in gendarme custody, rape was found to be ill-treatment of an especially severe kind, "inherently debasing" striking at the heart of physical and moral integrity, aggravated by the fact that it was committed by person in authority and involving acute physical and psychological suffering in a punitive and coercive context.[27]

The Commission also considers that there might be non-physical torture, namely the infliction of mental suffering, by creating a state of anguish and stress by other means.[28]

(b) *Inhuman treatment and punishment*

Inhuman treatment covers at least such treatment as deliberately causes severe mental and physical suffering.[29] The physical injuries referred to above in *Ireland v. United Kingdom* fell within this notion (where individual detainees were found to have been beaten and kicked by the security forces causing, for example, massive, substantial bruising, cuts to the head, a broken cheekbone, gross swelling) as did the injuries in *Tomasi v. France*, in which medical reports indicated a large number of blows of sufficient intensity (abrasions on face, chest and arms, haematoma on left ear).[30] In *Ribitsch v. Austria*, the applicant received bruises and haematomas on the inside and outside of the arm caused while in police custody and there was a medical report that he suffered cervical syndrome, vomiting, violent headache and a temperature, after treatment in which the applicant alleged that he was punched repeatedly, in the head, kidneys and right arm, kicked, and his head banged

---

[25] (Rep.) January 25, 1976, 402; *Greek case* 12/1 Ybk of the ECHR 461: where torture for the Commission implied inhuman treatment which had a purpose such as the obtaining of information or confessions or the infliction of punishment and that it was generally an aggravated form of inhuman treatment.

[26] *e.g.* in *Yagiz v. Turkey*, (Rep.) May 16, 1995, R.J.D. 1996–III, No. 13, it cites the UN Convention against Torture and other cruel, inhuman or degrading treatment which in Art. 1 includes elements of deliberateness for specific purposes of obtaining information or punishing or intimidating or coercing.

[27] (Rep.) para. 189. The Court agreed that it was an especially cruel act amounting to torture, and was prepared to find torture separately for the other aspects of ill-treatment *e.g.* blindfolding, being kept naked, beaten and pummelled with high pressure water — paras 82–86. See also *Sur v. Turkey*, 21592/93, (Rep.) September 3, 1996 settled before the Court (October 31, 1997 to be published in R.J.D. 1997), where the lesions inflicted during custody, from blows from sticks and electric shocks, disclosed torture.

[28] The *Greek case op. cit.*, n.4, p. 86 and 461.

[29] *e.g.* the Commission in the *Greek Interstate* case and *Ireland v. U.K.*; the Court in *Ireland v. U.K.* As regards mental suffering, see *e.g.* village destruction cases below; *Kurt v. Turkey*, 24276/94, (Rep.) December 6, 1996, pending before the Court, were the anguish of the mother whose son had "disappeared" in custody qualified.

[30] The Commission had commented that these were of apparently slight injury and felt it necessary to refer to the vulnerability of his position in custody, without outside contact with lawyer or family to justify classing the treatment as inhuman.

on the floor. The physical injuries and considerable psychological trauma constituted inhuman and degrading treatment. The Court added a very strong statement that in respect of a person deprived of liberty any recourse to physical force which has not been made strictly necessary by his own conduct diminishes human dignity and is in principle an infringement of the right in Article 3. This seems to deviate from the standard previously set in *Ireland v. United Kingdom*.

The use of force in the context of arrest although resulting in injury may fall outside Article 3, particularly if the circumstances disclose that it resulted from the conduct of the applicant. In *Klass v. Germany*, where police officers used force to affect an arrest on the applicant, a 48-year-old woman, who suffered a bruise to the temple, concussion, and contusion of the left shoulder joint, in circumstances where the police alleged that she had tried to run away, the Court found nothing to lead it to depart from findings of fact of the national courts who had found the use of force not excessive and not unlikely to have been caused in her struggles.[31] Similarly in *Hurtado v. Switzerland*,[32] where the applicant received cracked ribs from the officer kneeling on him, the Commission accepted that the force used in the circumstances of that arrest did not contravene Article 3.

Treatment was not sufficiently severe in consequences in *Tyrer v. United Kingdom*, where three strokes of the birch raised but did not break the skin; and in the context of school corporal punishment, three smacks from a shoe on the bottom through shorts causing no visible injury was not inhuman.[33] The Commission did find inhuman and degrading treatment in *Y v. United Kingdom*[34] where the punishment resulted in four weals on the bottom from cane, while in *A v. United Kingdom* the corporal punishment inflicted by the stepfather of repeated caning causing significant bruising reached this level.[35]

(c) *Degrading treatment or punishment*

This consists of treatment or punishment which grossly humiliates a person before others or drives him to act against his will or conscience.[36] The five techniques in the *Ireland v. United Kingdom* case were found by the Court to be degrading as well as inhuman since they were such as to arouse in their victims feelings of fear, anguish, and inferiority capable of humiliating and debasing them and possibly breaking their physical and moral resistance.[37] The purpose of the authority is particularly relevant, in the sense whether the measure denotes contempt or lack of respect for the personality of the person subjected to it and whether it is designed to humiliate or debase, instead of other aims.[38]

In *Tyrer v. United Kingdom*, to distinguish between punishment which is generally humiliating to adults and degrading punishment within Article 3, the Court held that the

---

[31] The Commission finding there was inhuman and degrading treatment gave weight to the minor nature of the traffic offence, the public nature of the incident in the presence of her daughter, the absence of convincing explanations for the injuries or that such a level of force was necessary on this applicant and found that the treatment aroused feelings of fear and inferiority capable of humiliating and went beyond inevitable elements associated with legitimate arrest.

[32] (Rep.) July 8, 1993, Series A, No. 280–A (settled before the Court): the arrest took place during a planned police operation breaking into a drug ring, when there was reason to believe the suspects were dangerous and nothing to support allegations that the police beat him in the flat and at the police station — the violent nature of the arrest was admitted by the Government.

[33] *Costello-Roberts*.

[34] (Rep.) October 8, 1991, Series A, No. 247–A settled before the Court.

[35] See n.9.

[36] *The Greek case*, n.4, p. 186.

[37] Para. 67.

[38] *Raninen v. Finland*, where the Commission found degrading treatment where the applicant, a conscientious objector was handcuffed publicly when unlawfully arrested by the military police. Notwithstanding the unjustified nature of the measure, the court noted a lack of mental or physical effects on the applicant and found that the treatment did not attain the required level of severity.

humiliation or debasement involved must attain a particular level, beyond that usual element. This will depend on the circumstances of the case, in particular, the nature and context of the punishment, the manner and method of execution. While the public nature of the punishment might be relevant, its absence is not fatal, since a person may be sufficiently humiliated in his own eyes even if not in the eyes of others.[39] For the Court in *Tyrer*, it was the "institutionalised violence" of the birching that was the crucial element, where the applicant was treated as an object in the power of the authorities and subjected to an assault on his personal dignity and physical integrity which is one of Article 3's main purposes to protect. There was the element of delay, leading to the mental anguish of anticipation; the official aura attending the procedure and inflicting of the punishment by strangers. The factor that the punishment entailed the stripping of clothes was only one aggravating element.

Where an applicant had defecated on arrest, attributed to the use of a stun grenade, and had been unable to change clothes until the next day at the earliest, the Commission found that the wearing of soiled clothes for one day, during a hearing before a judge and on various journeys resulting from the failure of the authorities to take the most elementary hygiene measures was humiliating and debasing and therefore degrading within the meaning of Article 3.[40]

Humiliating circumstances of a sexual nature rendered the infliction on a teenage girl of corporal punishment by a male teacher in the presence of another male teacher degrading treatment although the severity of the punishment was not such as to render it inhuman.[41]

4. Particular contexts

(a) *Punishment — type and length of sentence*

Matters of length of sentence are generally outside the scope of this provision.[42] However, elements of shocking disproportionality could raise an exception. In *Weeks v. United Kingdom*, where the applicant aged 17 received a life sentence for robbery of 35 pence, the Court commented, in finding that discretionary life sentences attracted the right to review of the lawfulness of continued detention, that otherwise a life sentence for such a minor crime by a young person would have been doubtfully compatible with Article 3.[43] The Commission has hinted that extradition where a person would be prosecuted for political offences or his political views or would receive an unjustified and disproportionate sentence would raise issues under Article 3.[44]

(b) *Compulsory medical treatment*

Where compulsory medical treatment, including force-feeding, being strapped down, compulsory administration of drugs, constitutes a therapeutic necessity in line with current medical practice, it cannot at the same time disclose inhuman or degrading treatment according to the Court in *Herczegfalvy v. Austria*. This was notwithstanding the "worrying" length of time that the applicant was handcuffed and held in a security bed. The

---

[39] e.g. *Tyrer*, para. 32.

[40] *Hurtado*, see n.32.

[41] *Warwick v. U.K.*, 9471/81, (Rep.) July 18, 1986, 60 D.R. 5: she was caned on the hand.

[42] e.g. 5871/72, (Dec.) September 30, 1974, 1 D.R. 54; also *Hogben v. U.K.*, 11653/85, (Dec.) March 3, 1986, 41 D.R. 231 where a drastic change in parole policy which dashed hopes of imminent release and increased effective length to be served was not covered.

[43] March 2, 1987, Series A, No. 114, para. 47.

[44] 10308/83, (Dec.) May 3, 1983, 36 D.R. 209; see however 11017/84, (Dec.) March 13, 1986, 46 D.R. 176 where the expulsion of person claiming conscientious objection to military service with a risk of long sentence for refusal did not constitute such treatment.

Commission had found a violation, imposing the additional requirement that the manner of application of the treatment must be compatible with Article 3. It found the timing and use of massive force and the long-term fettering involved was not so compatible.[45]

(c) Lack of or delay in medical treatment

The Commission has found that failure to provide necessary medical care to prisoners may disclose inhuman treatment. Where in *Hurtado*, the applicant suffering from ribs broken on arrest was not seen by a doctor for eight days, the Commission considered that there was an obligation on the authorities to adopt measures to safeguard the well-being of persons deprived of their liberty, particularly where in this case the applicant had been subject to an arrest procedure involving the use of force.[46]

In *D v. United Kingdom*, where expulsion meant a withdrawal of vital life-supporting medical and support care for an AIDS patient, the proposed measure was found to be a potential breach of Article 3.

(d) Prison conditions

The Convention organs have yet to find a violation of Article 3 arising solely from the conditions of imprisonment as opposed to physical ill-treatment. The standard of hardship accepted is high and presumably reflects an implicit acceptance that prison regimes require rigid discipline and severe restrictions on personal freedom. (See section Prisoners' rights.)

(e) Expulsion and extradition

The Convention organs, in *Soering v. United Kingdom*, established that it would not be compatible with the fundamental principles underlying the Convention if a Contracting State were knowingly to surrender a fugitive to another State where he would be at risk of torture however heinous a crime he might have committed. This has since been extended to measures of expulsion generally and a potential breach of Article 3 will be found where there are substantial grounds for believing that an applicant faces a real risk of being subjected to torture or to inhuman and degrading treatment or punishment if expelled (see Part IIB: Extradition and Immigration and expulsion).

(f) Village destruction in Turkey

The traumatic events alleged when Turkish security forces burnt houses in the south-east region, rendering villagers homeless and destitute has been found by the Commission to be sufficiently severe in their effects to constitute inhuman treatment. However, the Court in *Akdivar v. Turkey* found a lack of precise evidence about the circumstances of the burnings and did not pursue the examination. In subsequent cases, the Commission has found breaches of Article 3 where the applicant villagers were present and able to give details of the events, laying stress on the inherently violent nature of the experience and the anguish and distress caused in the process.[47] However, in *Mentes v. Turkey*, the Court finding a violation of Article 8 in respect of the burning of the applicants' homes, considered it unnecessary to examine the complaint under Article 3.

---

[45] Paras 82–83; (Rep.) paras 247–254: see Part IIB, Prisoners' rights, 5. Medical treatment.
[46] *op. cit.*, n.32. See also *U.K.*, 18824/91, (Dec.) October 14, 1992.
[47] *e.g. Mentes v. Turkey*, 23186/94, (Rep.) March 7, 1996, where children were present and left without clothing, threats of physical force were made; *Selcuk and Asker v. Turkey*, 23184–5/94, (Rep.) November 28, 1996, where an applicant and his wife were in danger from the fire as they sought to save their possessions. The Commission's delegates have heard the villagers give evidence. Both are pending before the Court.

5. Matters of proof and causation

(a) Standard of proof

The Court and Commission adopt an approach of the free assessment of evidence, without any formal burden of proof on either party. The Court in *Ireland v. United Kingdom* stated that it must examine all the material before it, and may obtain evidence *proprio motu*. To assess this evidence it adopts as the Commission did in *The Greek case*, the standard "beyond reasonable doubt".[48] Such proof may also follow from the coexistence of sufficiently strong clear and concordant inferences or of similar unrebutted presumptions of fact. In this context the conduct of the parties when evidence is being obtained has to be taken into account.[49]

In the *Ireland v. United Kingdom* case, following complaints by the Irish Government that the United Kingdom had not afforded on occasion the necessary facilities for the effective conduct of the investigation, the Court expressed regrets but this appeared to have no backlash on the assessment of the facts. However, a failure to produce relevant documents or witnesses has been taken into account by the Commission in drawing inferences and assessing facts in a number of Turkish cases.[50]

(b) Injuries in custody

Where a person held in custody suffers injury there is a strong inference as to causation. This was applied by the Commission in the *Ireland v. United Kingdom* case where there was medical evidence of injuries received by detainees while under the responsibility of the security forces, with no other credible explanation, beyond vague, unsubstantiated references to the possibilities of fights or riots. In *Tomasi v. France*, where the injuries clearly dated from the period in detention and the Government acknowledged that it could give no other explanation, the authorities were regarded as responsible.[51]

This presumption may be dislodged if there is some form of explanation by the authorities. In *Diaz Ruano v. Spain*,[52] concerning the shooting of the applicant's son while in police custody, the Commission accepted that the police officer shot when attacked and in self-defence. Although there were lesions and marks on the body supporting the applicant's allegations that his son was ill-treated, the Government submitted that the evidence was inconclusive, and the marks could have arisen after the shot was fired. Since there was no firm opinion as to timing from pathologists, the Commission did not find it established beyond reasonable doubt that the marks in question were caused while in police custody and as the result of treatment prohibited by Article 3.

(c) Relevance of domestic factfinding

While the Convention organs have always denied acting as a court of appeal or that they should substitute their opinion on the merits, they are not bound by domestic courts'

---

[48] A reasonable doubt means not a doubt based on a mere theoretical possibility but a doubt for which reasons can be drawn from the facts presented; *Ribitsch*, (Rep.) para. 104.

[49] *Ireland*, case para. 161.

[50] e.g. *Aydin v. Turkey*, (Rep.) (where failure to provide a full copy of a plan of a detention area was found significant); *Mentes v. Turkey*, (Rep.) (failure to provide investigation files lead to assumption no further steps taken); *Ergi v. Turkey*, 23818 (Rep.) May 20, 1997 pending before the court (failure to provide requested gendarme witnesses to an operation lead to assumption that no steps were taken by the authorities to protect the villagers).

[51] See also *Aksoy*, where the injuries were alleged to have been received while in custody, and must have occurred at about that time and the Government gave no convincing explanation for their cause or what might have happened in the brief delay between release and the receipt of medical treatment.

[52] *Diaz Ruano v. Spain*, (Rep.) August 31, 1993, Series A, No. 285–B settled before the Court.

findings in any formal sense. In *Ribitsch*, the Commission and Court both found a violation of Article 3 in respect of the injuries suffered by the applicant in police custody although in the domestic proceedings the police officer's conviction was quashed on appeal and this decision was upheld at third instance. The Court pointed out that it was not bound by domestic courts' findings of fact although it would undertake a thorough scrutiny where the Commission's findings were at a variance with the domestic courts. It proceeded to re-assess the evidence, giving significance to the existence of injuries, the fact that the injuries were not all explained by the policeman's story of a fall, the discrepancies in the police officer's versions of events, and the lack of any other witness to the fall. It relied on the findings of the first instance court as to credibility and impliedly criticised the second instance's inadequate reasoning, *inter alia*, its references to the applicant's lack of credibility due to his past criminal record and personal extravagance, which the Court found irrelevant to events while he was in police custody. The Commission majority reconciled their approach by pointing to the different purposes and scope of domestic criminal proceedings as compared to its own examination, which was not concerned with proving guilt but with responsibility of the State to comply with the requirements of the Convention in human rights protection.[53]

6. Relationship with Article 2

Since Article 2 provides for judicial execution, Article 3 cannot be interpreted as containing a general prohibition against the death penalty as inhuman punishment, although the case of *Soering* shows that the manner of an execution, the personal circumstances of the condemned person or the disproportionality to the offence committed as well as conditions of detention while awaiting execution may be capable of bringing the treatment within Article 3. The fact that all States have *de facto* abolished the death penalty and altered the scope of Article 2 does not indicate that this implied limitation on Article 3 is removed since they have chosen to implement a new protocol which allows each State to time its acceptance of this obligation.[54]

Where accidental harm is the consequence of a use of force which complies with the requirements of Article 2, paragraph 2, no issue arises under Article 3.[55]

Cross-reference

Part IIB: Corporal punishment
Part IIB: Extradition
Part IIB: Immigration and expulsion
Part IIB: Prisoner's rights

---

[53] The majority of the Commission also found no convincing explanation for the injuries provided by the Government. See Mr Bratza's separate concurring opinion, stating that while he did not question the decision of the appeal court to given the police officer the benefit of the doubt, the Government had not discharged the burden on them of providing a sufficiently convincing alternative explanation as to how the applicant came by his injuries. The minority in the Court and Commission observed that the State had conducted a close scrutiny of their own by independent courts at three levels and that it was not their task to substitute their own assessment of the facts for that conducted by the national courts unless these have proceeded improperly which was not the position. There was obviously reasonable doubt in this case.

[54] Protocol No. 6; see Extradition, Death penalty.

[55] *Stewart v. U.K.*, (Dec.) 10044/82, July 10, 1984, 39 D.R. 162.

Transsexuals

Relevant Articles:

Article 8 (respect for private and family life), Article 12 (right to marry); Article 14 (prohibition on discrimination).

Relevant cases:

Rees v. U.K., October 17, 1986, Series A, No. 106; 9 E.H.R.R. 56; *Cossey v. U.K.*, September 27, 1990, Series A, No. 184; 13 E.H.R.R. 622; *B v. France*, March 25, 1992, Series A, No. 232–C; 16 E.H.R.R. 1; *X, Y and Z v. U.K.*, April 22, 1997, R.J.D., 1997–II, No. 35.

1. General considerations

The problems facing transsexuals in obtaining recognition of their change of gender and the consequences on their enjoyment of the rights guaranteed under the Convention is an area disclosing a marked divergence between the Commission and Court. For the Court the matter raises legal, scientific, medical, social and ethical issues of a controversial nature, and in the absence of any clear consensus in Contracting States, it has accorded them a wide margin of appreciation.[1] Since complaints often require States to take steps to ensure rights rather than refrain from interference, questions of positive obligations arise, an area where the Court is generally more reluctant to impose stringent requirements. Indeed, in the balancing exercise between public and private interests it is apparent that there is a certain presumption in practice that, without significant tangible detriment to the individual, public interests will prevail, even of a presumed or general nature.[2] While the Court has stated that it is conscious of the seriousness of the problems facing transsexuals and stated that the position should be kept under review, only one case, *B v. France*, has been found to disclose a violation.

2. Change of birth certificate

The right to respect for private life does not require in the United Kingdom that the birth register amend birth certificates to record a transsexual's gender re-assignment, according to the Court in *Rees v. United Kingdom*, and *Cossey v. United Kingdom*. In balancing the general interest in the community with the interests of the individual, the applicants' interests were given little weight since they had been able to change first names and official documents, which was a situation more favourable than in some other countries. On the other side of the scale, the Court considered that the United Kingdom could not be required to alter its entire birth registration system to a record of civil status as found in other Contracting States. It accepted the Government's argument that amendments to the register were not possible, save in the cases of clerical or medical mistake, since the system was based on recording facts at the time they occurred and that any subsequent changes would amount to a falsification of the record. It also accepted that measures protecting transsexuals from disclosure of the gender re-assignment would have adverse effects, namely, an alleged risk of confusion and complication in family and succession matters, as well as apparently depriving third parties and government bodies of information which they might have a legitimate interest to receive.

---

[1] *Rees*, para. 44; *Cossey*, para. 40; *X, Y and Z*, para. 44.
[2] See Part IIB: Private life; 3. State obligations; Part I: Convention Approach and Principles; 12. Positive obligations.

The *Sheffield v. United Kingdom* and *Horsham v. United Kingdom* cases,[3] now pending before the Court, raise further challenges to the lack of legal recognition of gender re-assignment which is connected to the inability to amend the birth certificate.[4] In these cases, the Commission has sought to argue that there have been significant medical and legal developments, in particular the findings of the European Court of Justice upholding the rights of transsexuals under discrimination provisions in employment. It has also emphasised the importance in private life of the stigmatisation of transsexuals due to the lack of full legal recognition, which causes significant detriment even in the absence of daily practical difficulties. The approach of the Commission gives more weight to the private life interest as opposed to the interests of the State in maintaining the current practices in birth registration, in particular, in view of the possibility of amending the register prospectively which would avoid secrecy or misrepresentation.

However, in light of the negative approach of the Court in *X, Y and Z*, a family life case (below) these cases are unlikely to be successful. The Court has accepted the United Kingdom's biological approach to the attribution of gender and its exclusion of the element of "psychological sex" as relevant in attributing sex. The Court is unlikely to change its stance until European society and medical science swing firmly towards acceptance of the transsexual phenomenon as being a medical condition (where external or biological criteria are in conflict with a psychological development itself caused by physical or chemical processes in the brain) rather than what is popularly conceived as a wilful perversion of nature.[5]

3. Ability to change name and official documents

While in *Rees* and *Cossey*, the Court did not find that transsexuals experienced a disproportionate amount of prejudice from the failure to allow change of birth certificates in the United Kingdom, it agreed with the Commission that a violation of Article 8 arose in the case *B v. France*, where the applicant (male to female transsexual) was unable to obtain a rectification of the civil status register, with the result that her name remained as before and recorded on all official identity papers, sometimes accompanied by the indication that she was of the male sex. These included documents which were in frequent use (*e.g.* cheque books, national insurance no., driving licence, voting card etc.). This placed the applicant daily in a situation incompatible with the respect due to her private life. Impliedly, in a civil status system, the obstacles posed by the United Kingdom birth register (historical accuracy and lack of secrecy) were inoperative and had no features which outweighed the inconvenience to the applicant.

4. Right to marry

An individual who has received gender re-assignment cannot derive a right from Article 12 to marry a person of the biological sex opposite to that with which he or she was attributed at birth.[6] The Court considers that the right to marry guaranteed by Article 12

---

[3] 22985/93 and 23390/94, (Reps.) January 21, 1997.
[4] The Registrar adopts the biological approach without regard to surgical intervention as in *Corbett v. Corbett* [1971] P. 83.
[5] In *B v. France*, the Court noted the arguments that biological criteria were not always infallible (*e.g.* rare chromosomal conditions) and that there might indeed by a physical explanation for the transsexual phenomenon. While attitudes had undeniably changed, it considered that questions still remained as to the legitimacy in some cases of surgical intervention and that complex problems arose of an anatomical, biological, psychological and moral nature. There was still insufficiently broad consensus between Contracting States to persuade the Court to change its views in *Rees* and *Cossey* on the general, wider issues of transsexualism.
[6] *Rees; Cossey.*

refers to the traditional marriage between persons of opposite biological sex, which interpretation was supported by the reference to the founding of a family and which may be defined by States with reference to biological criteria evident at birth. Further, Article 12 expressly states that the exercise of the right is subject to the national laws of Contracting States. The legal impediment on marriage of persons not of the opposite biological sex imposed by national law was not considered to have such an effect as to impinge upon the essence of the right to marry.[7]

Where however a State does provide for legal recognition of change of gender, including for the purposes of marriage, a transsexual cannot complain under Article 12 of the resulting inability to marry a person of the same legal sex.[8]

5. Family life

In *X, Y and Z v. United Kingdom*, the Court agreed with the Commission that *de facto* family life falling within the scope of Article 8 existed where X, (female to male transsexual) had been in a stable relationship with a woman Y for over 15 years and Y, with his support and involvement, had undergone AID treatment which resulted in the birth of a daughter Z. However, while the inability of X under domestic law to have his name registered as the child's father was found by the Commission to disclose a lack of respect for their family life, emphasising the interests of the child and the family unit to security and legal protection, against which it saw no convincing countervailing public interest, the Court differed. It seem influenced by what it perceived to the controversial nature of the AID treatment and found that while it had not been established that legal recognition would harm any public interest it had neither been established that it was in the interests of the child. Since the applicants were able to live together as a family, the elements of practical detriment arising from the lack of legal relationship between X and the child Z, such as succession rights, rights of support, transmission of nationality or tenancy, were not considered to be significant, since they were either not currently relevant to the applicants' situations or steps could be taken to remedy them.[9]

In the absence of any weight given to emotional and psychological elements, further complaints concerning family life stand little prospect of success without proof of concrete practical prejudice.

6. Discrimination

It is doubtful whether many issues will be found to arise here. If a violation is established under substantive provisions, such as Article 8, no separate issue is likely under Article 14. Conversely, if there is no lack of respect under Article 8, it is likely that any difference in

---

[7] Since apparently the transsexual is still able to marry a person of the opposite sex to his birth sex. This manifestly overlooks the fact that a male to female transsexual would not presumably want to marry another woman or vice versa. Though the Commission found a violation in *Cossey*, on the basis that the applicant had a partner whom she was prevented from marrying, following the Court's rejection of her claims, the Commission has followed its line in later case. See however the dissenting opinions in *Sheffield* and *Horsham* (Reps.), see n.3.

[8] *Eriksson and Goldschmidt v. Sweden*, (Dec.) November 9, 1989, unpublished. Here, Sweden did recognise legally the changed gender of a transsexual but in this case the transsexual (male to female) wanted in fact to marry another female. Whereas in the United Kingdom biological criteria would have permitted such a union, Sweden attributed to the applicant transsexual the gender of re-assignment and did not permit marriage to a person of that same gender. The Commission found that the Swedish law was not lacking in respect of the right to marry since pursuant to its provisions both were legally of the same sex and Art. 12 covered only the right to marry someone of the opposite sex.

[9] In relation to the lack of legal recognition of relationships between parents and their children born out of wedlock, the ability to make *inter vivos* dispositions etc. was not considered as remedying the disadvantages *e.g. Johnston v. Ireland*, December 18, 1986, Series A, No. 112; 9 E.H.R.R. 203.

treatment will be found to be based on objective and reasonable justification. Where there is most obviously scope for complaints by transsexuals of a difference in treatment (*e.g.* pensions and employment, retirement age), such matters will fall outside the scope of the provision if they do not concern substantive Convention rights.

Cross-reference

Part IIB: Discrimination
Part IIB: Marriage and founding a family
Part IIB: Private life

Welfare benefits

Key provision:

Article 6, paragraph 1 (fair hearing guarantees); Article 1 of Protocol No. 1 (right to property); Article 14 (prohibition against discrimination).

Key case law:

Feldbrugge v. Netherlands,. May 29, 1986, Series A, No. 99; 8 E.H.R.R. 425; *Deumeland v. Germany*, May 29, 1986, Series A, No. 100; 8 E.H.R.R. 448; *Salesi v. Italy*, February 26, 1993, Series A, No. 257–E; *Schuler-Zgraggen v. Switzerland*, June 24, 1993, Series A, No. 263; 16 E.H.R.R. 405; *Schouten and Meldrum v. Netherlands*, December 9, 1994, Series A, No. 304; 19 E.H.R.R. 432; *Gaygusuz v. Austria*, September 16, 1996, R.J.D., 1996–IV, No. 14; *Duclos v. France*, December 17, 1996, R.J.D., 1996–VI, No. 25; *Van Raalte v. Netherlands*, February 21, 1997, R.J.D., 1997–I, No. 39.

1. General considerations

The omission of social and economic-type rights from the Convention previously gave the impression that complaints about welfare benefits fell outside its scope. Gradually, however, the developing case law on the scope of civil rights under Article 6, paragraph 1 and the approach to property rights in conjunction with Article 14 (discrimination) have eroded the validity of this assumption. Generally, a complaint that a welfare benefit is not granted or that it is of a particular level will not be considered by the Commission. However, as soon as eligibility criteria appear to single out persons unjustifiably on grounds of status (sex, nationality) or the proceedings dealing with disputes of entitlement show failure to conform to Article 6 requirements, the picture becomes problematic.

2. Applicability of Article 6 and compliance with procedural guarantees

To attract the procedural guarantees of Article 6, there must be a dispute about a civil right or obligation. Whether a claim to a particular benefit or concerning levels of contributions concerns such right or obligation depends on a consideration of the nature and characteristics of the benefit concerned. The Court refers in this examination to public and private law features, and assesses which have greater significance.

Disputes concerning entitlement to benefits were first found to fall within the scope of "civil rights" in *Feldbrugge v. Netherlands* and *Deumeland v. Germany*. In *Schouten and Meldrum v. Netherlands*, the Court had to consider a dispute about contributions to the social security scheme. It found the approach would not necessarily be the same since in previous cases concerning claims to benefits the most important consideration had been the fact that the applicant had suffered "an interference with her means of subsistence" and was claiming an individual economic right, which did not apply automatically to disputes about contributions.[1] Also the fact that the obligation was "pecuniary" in nature would not be of the same decisiveness since pecuniary obligations exist *vis-à-vis* the State in public law, as taxes or part of other civil duties. However, the examination of public and private law features was still the appropriate method of analysis.

In *Feldbrugge*, the Court referred briefly to the principle in *Engel v. Netherlands*,[2] concerning the relevance of the categorisation of the right in domestic law, but stated that

---

[1] *Schuler-Zgraggen*, para. 46.
[2] June 8, 1976, Series A, No. 22: section Fair trial, General considerations: Criminal charge.

this was only a starting point and not conclusive unless corroborated by other factors. It noted that there was no common approach in Europe.[3] In *Salesi v. Italy* and *Schuler-Zgraggen v. Switzerland* seven years later it considered that the development in law and the principle of equality of treatment warranted taking the view that the general rule was that Article 6, paragraph 1 did apply in the field of social insurance, including even welfare assistance.

(a) *Public law features*

Public law features include the character of the legislation; the compulsory nature of the social security scheme and the assumption by the State or other public institution of full or partial responsibility for ensuring social protection. However, the existence of public law features has tended not to be decisive.

Regarding the character of the legislation, in *Feldbrugge*, the fact that the State intervened to regulate health insurance was not enough in itself to bring the matter within the sphere of public law; and the same view was taken in *Schouten and Meldrum v. Netherlands* concerning the obligation under statute to pay contributions to health insurance.

In relation to the compulsory nature of the scheme, in *Feldbrugge*, the Court noted that in other spheres such as car or housing insurance, insurance was compulsory by law but the entitlement to benefits could not be qualified as public law and it did not see that the obligation to belong to a health insurance scheme should alter the nature of the corresponding right. It finds an analogy between contributions to social security schemes and premiums for compulsory insurance.[4]

Regarding the assumption of responsibility by the State or public institutions, the Court noted that the operation of schemes by public or semi-public institutions, supervised by a public law body implies prima facie an extension of the public law domain. But it again gave weight to the affinities of social security schemes with insurance under private law. In *Schouten and Meldrum* it noted that private insurance covering largely the same risks was available in the Netherlands to those not compulsorily affiliated to or entitled to benefit from those schemes primarily intended to benefit those likely to find private insurance beyond their means.

In *Schuler-Zgraggen*, the Government pointed out that sickness benefit did not derive from a contract of employment since affiliation was compulsory also for self-employed and unemployed, that the amount of pension depended entirely on degree of incapacity with no relation to amount paid in or level of income, and that the Swiss system operated on a mixture of pay as you go, solidarity and drawing on tax revenues. The Court emphasised that State intervention was not decisive but that the most important consideration was that the applicant suffered an interference with her means of subsistence and was claiming an individual, economic right flowing from specific rules laid down in a statute. It found no distinction therefore between the applicant's right to an invalidity pension and the rights to social insurance benefits claimed by Mrs Feldbrugge and Mr Deumeland.

In *Schouten and Meldrum*, the Court found no significance in the Government's arguments that the rules governing the deduction and payment of contributions corresponded to those governing the deduction of tax from wages, considering it inevitable that means used by government agencies to ensure payment bore such a resemblance.

---

[3] *e.g.* in the Netherlands it was regarded as public, in other States as private or mixed while in Belgium it was predominantly public law but the domestic courts had still found Art. 6, para. 1 applicable.
[4] *Schouten and Meldrum*, para. 53.

The Commission has rejected claims based on benefits which it has considered to be essentially public law in character.[5] Where a claim of a previously self-employed person to unemployment assistance was based on a scheme wholly paid out of State funds without direct contributions from the workforce and which was available to persons who did not qualify for the benefit paid to unemployed persons who had contributed to the statutory scheme, the Commission distinguished *Feldbrugge* on the basis this did not involve any insurance relationship between the beneficiary and the body paying the benefit or any direct contribution by beneficiaries to the unemployment insurance scheme, nor was there any connection with an employment contract. Thus public law features predominated notwithstanding the personal and economic nature of the right flowing from specific rules laid down by the legislation in force.[6] It might be considered that this approach is overruled by *Schuler-Zgraggen* which gave no weight to the contributions aspect but put emphasis on the effect on means of subsistence, moving away from contract link factors.

(b) *Private law features*

These include the individual, personal and economic nature of the right; the link between social insurance schemes and the contract of employment and the similarity between social security schemes and private insurance.

Insofar as the private and economic nature of the right is concerned, the Court considers whether there has been an interference with a means of subsistence and whether the applicant is claiming a right flowing from specific rules laid down by the legislation in force.[7] It has regard to the significance of the right: in *Feldbrugge* it found that it was of crucial importance where the employee, unable to work, had no other source of income and it was found to be "personal, economic and individual".

As to the link between social insurance schemes and the contract of employment, in *Feldbrugge*, the Court found that although the insurance schemes were derived directly from statute and not from an express clause in a contract, the provisions were in a way grafted onto the contract and formed one of the constituents of the relationship between employer and employee.

Concerning the similarity between social security schemes and private insurance, the Court considered in *Feldbrugge* and *Schouten and Meldrum* that the occupational associations used risk covering techniques and management methods inspired by those in the insurance market and conducted their dealings in a similar way. Private insurance was available to cover largely the same risks and optional extensions of cover were available privately to those who participated in the schemes. This similarity was found more important in *Schouten and Meldrum* rather than the Government point that there was no direct connection between the payment of contributions and entitlement to benefits.[8]

---

[5] 8341/78, (Dec.) July 9, 1980, 20 D.R. 161 where the payment of "military insurance" to soldiers injured on duty was regarded as a purely unilateral initiative, with no payments from beneficiaries.

[6] 10855/84, *Germany*, (Dec.) March 3, 1988, 55 D.R. 51; 11450/85, *Sweden*, (Dec.) March 8, 1988, 55 D.R. 142 where a claim for higher level sickness benefit was found to fall outside Art. 6 since the public law features were predominant, *i.e.* the scheme was governed by public law; managed by public authorities; based on automatic affiliation; financed by Government and contributions taken from the self-employed alone. While the Commission noted that the claim related to a personal economic and individual right, the connection with employment was more remote than *Feldbrugge* and without affinities to insurance (financing was separate from the implementation; assessment and collection conducted by the tax authorities in same legal framework as tax).

[7] *e.g. Feldbrugge*, para. 37.

[8] para. 59.

The public features have generally been insufficient when weighed against the private elements.[9] The Court has generally taken the approach that the State has been intervening in an area of private law allied closely to employment and acting as a form of insurance company. But in light of statements in *Schuler-Zgraggen* and *Salesi v. Italy* and the emphasis given to the effect of subsistence, it would appear likely that Article 6, paragraph 1 will be found to apply to most key benefits.[10] In the recent *Duclos v. France* case, there was no dispute that Article 6, paragraph 1 applied to the applicant's various disputes with the social security authority about the daily allowance for his disablement benefit; and with the family allowance body as to whether his drop in his earnings on unemployment should effect the calculation of the allowance.

(c) *Application of the procedural guarantees*

Once Article 6, paragraph 1 is applicable, in theory the usual guarantees as to, for example, independence and impartiality, length[11] and fairness[12] apply. The application of procedural guarantees may however be affected by the nature of social security proceedings.

In *Schuler-Zgraggen*, an exception appeared to be established to the general principle of providing a hearing. The Court found that the applicant could have asked for a hearing and since she did not, she waived her right unequivocally. Whether nonetheless the nature of the proceedings required an hearing before a court, it found that the highly technical nature of the issues rendered proceedings in writing more effective and it was legitimate for national authorities to have regard to demands of efficiency, economy and the need for particular diligence in social security cases, in which context systematic oral hearings would be an obstacle.

3. Property rights

In *Gaygusuz v. Austria*, for the first time, welfare/social security benefits were treated as falling under Article 1 of Protocol No. 1. While this was only in the context of Article 14, nonetheless the Court found that the right to emergency assistance was pecuniary in nature and linked to the payment of contributions to the unemployment insurance fund, which brought it within the scope of Article 1 of Protocol No. 1.

---

[9] Article 6 was applicable in *Feldbrugge* (dispute as to whether the applicant was no longer entitled to sickness allowance: insurance was compulsory for persons bound by contracts of employment and in case of unfitness entitlement to allowance flowed from an Act, as a substitute for salary); in *Deumeland* (claim by widow for supplementary pension on death of husband from accident covered by compulsory industrial accidents insurance, closely linked to fact that he was an employee and an extension of his salary payable under the contract); in *Salesi* (a refusal of disability allowance, a compulsory welfare benefit funded entirely by the Government but under the jurisdiction of the labour magistrates court); in *Schuler-Zgraggen* (cancellation of invalidity pension following birth of child, initially granted on the basis of incapacity to work); and in *Schouten and Meldrum* (dispute about payment of contributions under health and unemployment insurance schemes in respect of persons alleged to be employees).

[10] It is less apparent whether the considerations adverted to would apply to auxiliary benefits, such as mobility allowances, attendance allowances etc.

[11] *e.g. Deumeland*, concerning litigation over 11 years where particular diligence was found to be required in social security cases (para. 90); *Duclos* where the Government argued that the distinctive features of French social security cases had to be taken into account (*i.e.* tribunals had no power to give directions, the parties had full control over the proceedings), the Court stated that tribunals were subject to the same code of civil procedure as civil cases and the reasonableness of the proceedings length had to be judged in the same way as before ordinary civil courts — there was no mention of special diligence.

[12] *e.g. Feldbrugge*, where the Court found that the procedure did not allow the applicant proper participation *e.g.* the President of the Appeals Board neither heard applicant or asked her to file written pleadings, nor did he give her the opportunity to consult the evidence in the case-file and to formulate her objections thereto.

The Commission had hitherto doubted the applicability of Article 1 of Protocol No. 1 to State benefits. Even assuming contributors to a social insurance system could derive a right to receive benefit, the Commission held that it could not be interpreted as giving a right to a pension of a particular amount.[13] Co-ordination by the State of pensions in light of benefits received from the social insurance system did not thereby deprive the applicant of any property right which he previously had. A claim to a disability pension was also not a "possession" for the purpose of Article 1 of Protocol No. 1, where the social security benefits in issue were part of general insurance system based on the principle of social solidarity, without any direct link between the level of contributions and benefits awarded and consequently a person did not have at any given moment an identifiable and claimable share in the fund.[14] Whether a claim to unemployment benefit constituted a property right was left open in *Claes v. Belgium*,[15] since in any event the Commission found that the applicant still had to satisfy domestic legal requirements governing the right to the benefit. There was thus no deprivation of possessions where the applicant was deprived of benefit for 13 weeks when it was assessed that she left her job without lawful grounds.

4. Discrimination

Differences in entitlement or in obligations to pay contributions may disclose discrimination in conjunction with Article 6 or Article 1 of Protocol No. 1. Differences based on sex require very weighty reasons by way of justification given the importance of the goal of equality of the sexes. In *Schuler-Zgraggen*, such reasons were not discerned by the Court where a decision as to entitlement to sickness pension was based on the assumption that women gave up work when they had children. A violation was found in conjunction with Article 6, apparently on the basis that matters concerning the court's reasoning fell within the scope of Article 6. In *Van Raalte v. Netherlands*, the obligation on the applicant, a man over 45, to pay a contribution to a child benefits scheme was discriminatory where women over 45 were not so obliged. The obligation to pay contributions to the social security system was found to fall within the scope of Article 1 of Protocol No. 1 as part of the right of the State to "secure the payment of taxes or other contributions".

Where in *Gaygusuz v. Austria*, the difference in entitlement was based on status as a foreigner, the Court decided the case under Article 14 in conjunction with Article 1 of Protocol No. 1. Since the applicant, of Turkish nationality, was lawfully resident in Austria, had worked and paid contributions on the same basis as Austrian nationals, there was no objective and reasonable justification to refuse emergency assistance exclusively because of his nationality.

Cross-reference

Part IIA: General Principles, Civil rights and obligations
Part IIB: Discrimination
Part IIB: Pensions

---

[13] 10671/83, (Dec.) March 4, 1985, 42 D.R. 229.
[14] 10971/84, (Dec.) July 10, 1985, 43 D.R. 190.
[15] *Belgium*, 11285/84, (Dec.) December 7, 1987, 54 D.R. 88.

PART III: JUST SATISFACTION

A. BEFORE THE COURT

1. General principles

The grant of just satisfaction is dependent on the finding of a violation and the absence of total reparation in domestic law. Where only partial reparation is given, as in the *Barbera Messegué and Jabardo v. Spain* case, where the domestic courts quashed the applicants' convictions, the Court may still award just satisfaction.[1] It applies to violations based on omissions, notwithstanding the reference to "decision or a measure taken by a legal authority where the applicant is an 'injured party' ".[2]

Just satisfaction is generally awarded at the same time as the finding of violation. Where however difficult questions of assessment arise it may be adjourned for further consideration.[3] Where just satisfaction is adjourned and the parties reach agreement the damages to be paid, the Court will verify the "equitable nature" of agreement between the Government and applicant and then, if acceptable, strike the case out.[4]

Just satisfaction cannot be claimed by an applicant as a right: just satisfaction is only to be granted if necessary and the matter falls to be determined by the Court at its discretion, having regard to what is equitable.[5] The Court will also not raise any just satisfaction issue of its own motion.[6]

The Court has no jurisdiction under Article 50[6a] to issue directions to Contracting States on the measures or steps which they should take to rectify violations. It considers that it is not empowered to do so under the Convention, responsibility for supervising the execution of judgments lying with the Committee of Ministers under Article 54. It will not therefore issue any requirement to, for example, quash a conviction.[7] In property cases however (see below) it has stated that the return of the property would constitute *restituo in integrum*[8].

Just satisfaction is awarded under three heads: pecuniary loss, non-pecuniary loss and costs and expenses. The governing principles in all three heads is the notion of "equity". An applicant must detail his claims: the Court will not examine possible damage of its own

---

[1] (Art. 50). June 13, 1994, Series A, No. 285–C. The Court rejected the Government's arguments that the quashing was total reparation since it did not compensate for the damage suffered from the real loss of opportunity to defend themselves at the original trial.

[2] *Airey v. Ireland*, February 6, 1981, Series A, No. 41, para. 9; "injured party" is synonymous with victim for the purposes of Article 25 in the sense of a person directly affected by the failure to observe the Convention.

[3] *e.g.* large pecuniary losses are allegedly involved which raise difficulties of value assessment as in *Papamichalopoulos v. Greece*, June 24, 1993, Series A, No. 260–B.

[4] Rule 54, para. 4 of Court's Rules of Procedure A.

[5] *Sunday Times v. U.K.*, (Art. 50) November 6, 1980, Series A, No. 38: see *X v. U.K.*, October 24, 1981, Series A, No. 46 where the applicant died — while noting that he may have suffered distress from the breach of Art. 5, para. 4, the Court found that it was not necessary to award a sum to his estate, as it would not advance the cause of justice.

[6] *e.g. Lombardo v. Italy*, November 26, 1992, Series A, No. 249–B, para. 25.

[6a] This will become Art. 41 when Protocol No. 11 comes into force on November 1, 1998.

[7] *Schmautzer v. Austria*, October 23, 1995, Series A, No. 328–A, p.16, para. 44. Also *Oberschlick v. Austria*, May 23, 1991, Series A, No. 204 (violation of Article 10 for conviction for defamation), where applicant requested the judgment to be set aside; *Vocaturo v. Italy*, May 24, 1991, Series A, No. 206 as regarded a request for judgment to be published in the Official Gazette; *Idrocalce v. Italy*, February 27, 1992, Series A, No. 229–F request for declaration that State adopt legislative measures to ensure effective protection of the human rights violated in the case.

[8] *Papamichalopoulos, op. cit,* n.3; *Hentrich v. France*, September 22, 1994, Series A, No. 296, para. 71.

motion.[9] The Court has not proved unduly generous in its approach to awarding compensation under any of the heads. The emphasis is not on providing a mechanism for enriching successful applicants but rather on its role in making public and binding findings of applicable human rights standards.

2. Pecuniary loss

There must be a causal link between the violation and the loss. Where the nature of the breach allows of *restituo in integrum*, it is for the State to effect it but if this does not occur the Court will award just satisfaction.[10] Loss must have actually been incurred.[11]

Where Article 6, paragraph 1 violations are concerned, it is rare that a procedural failing is seen as causative of pecuniary loss following upon the subsequent conviction or sentence or from the decision affecting civil rights or obligations.[12] The Court usually finds itself unable to speculate on the outcome if the breach had not occurred. In rare cases, it may find than there has nonetheless been a real loss of opportunity which requires an award. In *Barbera*, following a finding of violation in a criminal trial in a number of fundamental aspects, the Court considered that there was a real loss of opportunity for the applicants to defend themselves in accordance with the requirements of Article 6 and thus a clear causal connection between the damage claimed and the violation. It did not however accept the calculations of loss of earnings and career prospects during their period of detention, awarding a sum on an equitable basis together with non-pecuniary damage.[13]

In cases of unreasonable length of proceedings, pecuniary loss may be granted where it is attributable to the delay rather than the fact that proceedings were instituted or brought.

Fines imposed and costs incurred in domestic proceedings directly linked to the violation are covered.[14]

Applicants cannot be required to exhaust domestic remedies to obtain compensation for pecuniary loss in light of the Court's judgment since this would prolong the procedure before the Convention organs in a manner incompatible with the effective protection of human rights.[15]

---

[9] *e.g. Kostovski v. Netherlands,* November 20, 1989, Series A, No. 166; 12 E.H.R.R. 434, para. 46; *Huvig v. France,* April 24, 1990, Series A, No. 176–B, para. 37.

[10] In *Papamichalopoulos v. Greece,* October 31, 1995, Series A, (Art. 50) No. 330–B the Court held that return of the expropriated land with award for loss of enjoyment would constitute *restituo in integrum* but if the land was not returned within six months, the State was to pay for the value of the land.

[11] *e.g. Ozturk v. Germany,* October 23, 1985, Series A, No. 85, para. 8 (breach of Art. 6, para. 3(e): the applicant's insurance company had paid the interpretation fees.

[12] *e.g.* claims were unsuccessful in *Findlay v. U.K.,* February 25, 1997, 1997–I, No. 30 (lack of independent and impartial court martial) claim for loss of salary/pension following army discharge; *Saunders v. U.K.,* December 17, 1996, R.J.D., 1996–VI, No. 24 (breach of privilege against self-incrimination) claim of over 3 million loss of salary etc; access to court cases where no causal link found with loss of trade, fees etc. *e.g. Tre Traktorer v. Sweden,* July 7, 1989, Series A, No. 159 (revocation of license to sell alcohol); *Hakansson and Sturesson v. Sweden,* February 21, 1990, Series A, No. 171–A (refusal of sale permit for land); *Fredin v. Sweden,* February 18, 1991, Series A, No. 192 (revocation of permit to exploit gravel pit).

[13] It accepted the original claim based on the minimum salary for their respective fields of employment for the period held in closed prison plus one million pesetas for loss of career prospects, plus increase by retail price index: eight million pesetas in total for two applicants, four million for the third. It rejected the later claim based on daily rates awarded by Spanish courts for incapacity for work (7,000 pesetas per day).

[14] *e.g.* where journalists were fined, required to pay costs or incur costs of publishing in defamation proceedings found in breach of Art. 10 (*Lingens v. Austria,* July 8, 1986, Series A, No. 103; *Oberschlick v. Austria,* May 23, 1991, Series A, No. 204; *Jersild v. Denmark,* September 23, 1994, Series A, No. 298; *Oberschlick No. 2 v. Austria,* July 1, 1997, R.J.D. 1997–IV, No. 42, *De Haes* and *Gijsels v. Belgium,* February 24, 1997, R.J.D., 1997–I, No. 30.

[15] *Papamichalopoulos,* (Art. 50) *op. cit.* n.10, para. 40; *Barbera,* see n.1, para. 17.

Court's findings of pecuniary loss

Main Issues	Case	Just satisfaction awards
ARTICLE 6		
Lack of fair trial — criminal — (the applicants had been detained and suffered a real loss of opportunity to defend themselves)	*Barbera, Messegue and Jabardo v. Spain*	8 million pesetas for two applicants, 4 million for the third for both pecuniary and non-pecuniary loss[16]
Lack of access to court (designation of land preventing development)	*De Geoffre de la Pradelle v. France*	100,000 FF for loss of opportunities
Length of proceedings (civil — recovery of debt)	*Union Alimentaria v. Spain*	1.5 million pesetas for depreciation of the value of the debt
Length of proceedings (civil — welfare benefits)	*Salesi v. Italy*	7 million lira (where the court decision on her entitlement was eventually upheld on appeal)
Length of proceedings (constitutional court)	*Probstmeier v. Germany*	15,000 DM for real loss of opportunity from the effect of court's delay on applicability of rent provisions
Length of proceedings (constitutional court)	*Pammell v. Germany*	15,000 DM (as in *Probstmeier* above)
ARTICLE 10		
Prohibition of pregnancy counselling service	*Open Door Counselling v. Ireland*	Applicant claimed £62,172 IR for loss of earnings. The Government objected. The Court awarded £25,000 IR on equitable basis
ARTICLE 11		
Dismissal from jobs due to closed shop	*Young, James and Webster v. U.K.*	£17,626, £45,215 and £8,706 for loss of earnings and travel privileges
ARTICLE 14		
(in conjunction with Art. 1 of Protocol No. 1) denial of legal standing to pursue proceedings to protect property rights	*Canea Catholic Church v. Greece*	5,000,000 drachmas in respect of the losses incurred due to the dismissal of the actions

[16] See n.13 above.

399

Main Issues	Case	Just satisfaction awards
ARTICLE 14-*cont.*		
(in conjunction with Art. 4) obligation on men to pay fire service levy	*Karl-Heinz Schmidt v. Germany*	225 DM for levy paid over 2 years[17]
(in conjunction with Art. 6) sex discrimination in benefits decision	*Schuler-Zraggen v. Switzerland*	25,000 CHF for interest over eight years which passed until the domestic courts granted her claims
(in conjunction with Art. 8) lack of rights for child born out of wedlock	*Vermeire v. Belgium*	22,192,511 BEF for loss of inheritance on death of grandfather to which applicant would have been entitled if legitimate
(in conjunction with Art. 1, Protocol No. 1) liability to pay church tax	*Darby v. Sweden*	8,000 SEK for the tax paid plus interest
(in conjunction with Art. 1, Protocol No. 1) race discrimination in unemployment assistance	*Gaygusuz v. Austria*	The applicant claimed 800,000 AS for benefit over six years. The Court awarded 200,000 AS
(in conjunction with Art. 1, Protocol No. 1) discriminatory lack of validation of planning permission	*Pine Valley v. Ireland*	£1,200,000 IR in respect of the value of the land if it had been immediately developed, taking into account a reduction for rental value and difficulties in development attached to the land
ARTICLE 1, Protocol No. 1		
transfer of ownership of monastery lands	*Holy Monasteries v. Greece*	F.S. (Friendly Settlement). The Government amended the law, annulling previous measures
expropriation permits in force on property for 8–23 years — combined with violation of Article 6 for lack of access to court	*Sporring and Lönnroth v. Sweden*	800,000 SEK to one estate 200,000 to the other for prolonged uncertainty and lack of opportunities during the period
legislative annulment of arbitration award for contract debt	*Stran Greek Refineries v. Greece*	116,273,442 drachmas; US $16,054,165 and FF 614,627 as the amount recognised by arbitration court plus 6 per cent simple interest from date of award to Court judgment

[17] However, in *Van Raalte v. Netherlands* (sex discrimination in benefit contribution obligations) the Court did not find that the applicant was entitled to retrospective exemption for contributions under the scheme.

Main Issues	Case	Just satisfaction awards
ARTICLE 1, Protocol No. 1—*cont.*		
expropriation of land	*Papamichalopoulos v. Greece*	4,200 million drachmas for the land (if not returned) and 1,351 million for buildings erected on the land as award for the loss of enjoyment
pre-emption by tax authorities on purchase of land	*Hentrich v. France*	FF one million, in absence of return of land, for current market value less sums received on pre-emption
length of tenancy eviction proceedings — combined with violation of Article 6 for unreasonable delay	*Scollo v. Italy*	13 million lira for bailiffs' and lawyers' fees for the enforcement proceedings
retrospective annulment of liability of State for pilots' negligence in shipping accidents	*Pressos Compania Naviera v. Belgium*	The 25th applicant claimed 9,686,039 BEF — the amount of the court judgment against him. The Court, on an equitable basis apportioned one-half of the damage from the accident
long-term restrictions on use of land combined with violation of Article 6 for unreasonable delay	*Matos E Silva v. Portugal*	10 million escudos for pecuniary and non-pecuniary loss on equitable basis
delay in paying compensation for expropriation	*Akkuş v. Turkey*	TRL 273,916 (or approximately US $48) as the difference between the amount actually paid in February 1992 and the amount she would have received if the sum of TRL 576,097 she was owed had been adjusted to take account of depreciation over a period of at least 14 months (inflation rate of about 70 per cent p.a.)
ARTICLE 2, Protocol No. 1—*cont.*		
suspension from school — refusal of corporal punishment	*Campbell and Cosans v. U.K.*	£3,000 for pecuniary and non-pecuniary together on equitable basis. While the applicant claimed loss of education and employment prospects, the Court accepted some effect but found that the breach was not the principal cause of his subsequent material difficulties

401

3. Non-pecuniary loss

An award for non-pecuniary damage may be made in respect of pain and suffering and physical or mental injury, including feelings of anxiety, helplessness or frustration. The latter has led to damages in child care cases for example but not in respect of many procedural breaches of Article 6 cases or where terrorist suspects have been involved.[18] The Court makes awards on an equitable basis without any explanation of its quantification or more than brief reasoning. It often appears to take a moral stance, as in the cases of terrorist suspects and reacts with evidently more sympathy to certain applicants or where there has been a clearly arbitrary use of power. In length of proceedings cases, it may award non-pecuniary damage or none, rarely indicating why it distinguishes between applicants, although it shows some regard to significant hardship or effect on employment and career.[19]

The Court also considers whether there has been a loss of real opportunity from a breach, in the absence of any strict causal link, for example, lack of access to court in child care cases where it could not be established that an application for custody would have successful but the loss of the opportunity to apply is given weight. It has in certain cases referred to the effect on reputation or damage to career.[20]

In the absence of any of the above features, the Court generally finds that a finding of a violation in itself constitutes just satisfaction.

The Court may award a sum in respect of pecuniary and non-pecuniary loss together, on an equitable basis, without distinguishing the proportion.[21] It has expressed doubts that a company could suffer non-pecuniary damage.[22]

Even where Court judgments are binding on domestic courts, an applicant cannot be expected to bring new proceedings for compensation on the basis of a judgment of violation. The Court thus awarded non-pecuniary damage to *Philis v. Greece* for length of proceedings, notwithstanding the Government argument that the applicant could apply for compensation to the domestic court on the basis of the Court's finding of violation.[23]

---

[18] See Art. 8, child care cases below. Terrorist cases: see *McCann and others v. U.K.*, February 24, 1995, Series A, No. 324 (breach of Art. 2); *Brogan and others v. U.K.*, May 30, 1989, Series A, (Art. 50), No. 152–B, (Art. 5, para. 3); *Fox, Campbell* and *Hartley v. U.K.*, March 27, 1990, Series A, (Art. 50), No. 190–B (Art. 5, para. 1(c)).

[19] *e.g. Triggiani v. Italy*, February 19, 1991, Series A, No. 197–B.

[20] *e.g. Darnell v. U.K.* October 26, 1993, Series A, No. 272 (Art. 6 length case): £5,000 for damage to career during length of legal battles; *Helmers v. Sweden*, October 29, 1991, Series A, No. 212–A, where the applicant university lecturer's claims of discrimination and defamation were rejected but he nonetheless received 25,000 Kronor for lack of public hearing.

[21] As in *Allenet de Ribemont v. France*, where the applicant and Commission unsuccessfully sought interpretation of the Court's judgment awarding two million FF for both heads. It was relevant to the applicant's claims in domestic proceedings for the award to be immune from attachment in respect of other liabilities. The Court explained that it did not feel bound to identify proportions in making aggregate awards and that it was often difficult or impossible to make distinctions — August 7, 1996, R.J.D., 1996–III, No. 12.

[22] *Manifattura v. Italy*, February 27, 1992, Series A, No. 230–B.

[23] *Philis v. Greece (No. 2)*, February 27, 1997, R.J.D. 1997–IV, No. 40, para. 59. See however, *Clooth v. Belgium*, December 12, 1991, Series A, No. 225 where the Court reserved Art. 50 as it wished to take into account the award which he might receive in domestic proceedings for the breach of Art. 5, para. 3.

Court's findings of non-pecuniary loss

(F.S.: friendly settlement)
(FOVJS: finding of violation was just satisfaction in the circumstances of the case.)

Principal issues	Case	Findings/settlements
ARTICLE 2		
Killing of three IRA terrorists	*McCann and others v. U.K.*	No pecuniary or non-pecuniary damages granted. It was not appropriate since the three suspects had been intending to plant a bomb in Gibraltar terrorists
Ill-treatment and death in custody	*Diaz Ruano v. Spain*	F.S. 6 million pesetas (including costs)
ARTICLE 3[24] **Assaults and ill-treatment**		
Ill-treatment in custody combined with excessive length of detention on remand	*Tomasi v. France*	700,000 FF, for undoubted pecuniary and non-pecuniary damage, combined with breach of Article 5, para. 3
Assault in custody	*Ribitsch v. Austria*	ATS 100,000
Corporal punishment	*Y v. U.K.*	F.S. £8,000 plus costs
Ill-treatment in custody	*Hurtado v. Switzerland*	F.S. 14,000 CHF
Rape in gendarme custody	*Aydin v. Turkey*	£25,000 plus costs
Risk from proposed expulsion/extradition	*Soering v. U.K., Chahal v. U.K. and Ahmed v. Austria*	Finding of a violation was just satisfaction ("FOVJS")
Ill-treatment in police custody	*Sur v. Turkey*	F.S. 100,000 FF plus legal costs
Risk from proposed expulsion to Peru	*Paez v. Sweden*	Struck out when the applicant was granted permanent residence in Sweden
ARTICLE 5 **(Para. 1: No lawful or Convention basis for arrest or detention)**		
See above	*Lukanov v. Bulgaria*	115 days: 40,000 FF
See above	*Tsirilis and Koloumpas v. Greece*	13 months: 8 million drachmas (pecuniary and non-pecuniary together) 12 months: 7.3 million drachmas (pecuniary and non-pecuniary together)

[24] No claims were made in *Ireland v. U.K.*, January 18, 1978, Series A, No. 25 or *Tyrer v. U.K.*, April 25, 1978, Series A, No. 26.

Principal issues	Case	Findings/settlements
See above	*Amuur v. France*	20 days for asylum seekers in airport holding area: FOVJS
Delayed release from mental hospital	*Johnson v. U.K.*	£10,000 for over three years delay in release, taking into account the applicant's own negative attitude to the authorities
See above	*Ranineu v. Finland*	10,000 FM for 2 hours unlawful arrest. Same moral damage
See above	*Engel v. Netherlands*	2 days: token 100 guilders (detention was taken into account in later proceedings)
Disguised extradition	*Bozano v. France*	100,000 FF, with strong comments on the arbitrary nature of the police action and abuse of procedure causing substantial non-pecuniary damage. (Once expelled to Switzerland the applicant was extradited to Italy where he served a life sentence imposed pursuant to a conviction in absentia)
para. 1(c): Standard of suspicion on arrest	*Fox, Campbell and Hartley v. U.K.*	FOVJS
para. 1(d): 119 days placement of minor in prison rather than educational establishment	*Bouamar v. Belgium*	150,000 BF by agreement of Government and applicant
para. 1(e): Absence of registrar at hearing	*Wassink v. Netherlands*	FOVJS
para. 1(f): Violation of lawfulness and length	*Quinn v. France*	Continued detention 11 hours (no legal basis): 10,000 FF Length of detention (almost 2 years): 50,000 FF
para. 2:	*Van der Leer v. Netherlands*	15,000 guilders for all three heads together, including frustration and fear of return to hospital
para. 3: Pre-trial detention:		
Excessive length of dentention on remand. Breach of Article 6, para. 1 for delay also	*Kemmache v. France*	75,000 FF: while eight months detention was taken into account in his sentence the applicant must have suffered non-pecuniary damage for which this did not constitute adequate redress

Principal issues	Case	Findings/settlements
para. 3: **Pre-trial detention:**		
Excessive length of detention on remand. Breach of Article 5, para. 4 also	*Toth v. Austria*	FOVJS as entire period deducted from sentence
Excessive length of detention on remand	*Scott v. Spain*	FOVJS in view of extradition on condition that time in detention would count towards eventual sentence
Excessive length of detention on remand. Breach of Article 6, para. 1 also	*Yağci and Sargin v. Turkey*	30,000 FF per applicant
Excessive length of detention on remand. Breach of Article 6, para. 1	*Mansur v. Turkey*	30,000 FF
Excessive length of detention on remand	*Muller v. France*	FOVJS
Speed requirement for appearance before judge:	*De Jong, Baljet and Van Den Brink v. Netherlands*	300 guilders per applicant for as they must have suffered some prejudice not wholly compensated by deduction in sentence in loss of opportunity of "prompt" judicial control
Delay in appearance before judge	*Koster v. Netherlands*	FOVJS: any feeling of frustration did not warrant award
Prevention of terrorism provisions — suspects held for over four days without appearing before a judge	*Brogan and others v. U.K.*	FOVJS — although some prejudice was not to be excluded regard was had to the finding that there was no violation of Article 5, para. 1(c), the arrests being based on reasonable suspicion
Detention of former Parliamentarians	*Sakik and others v. Turkey*	25,000 FF to applicant held for 12 days without judicial intervention; 30,000 FF where held 14 days
Lack of "judicial" officer:	*Pauwels v. Belgium; Huber v. Switzerland; Brincat v. Italy*	While in *Pauwels* and *Huber* there was no causal link with damage claimed: FOVJS, in *Brincat*, 1,000 maltese lira was awarded with reference to undoubted adverse effects on reputation (lawyer) and feelings of insecurity

Principal issues	Case	Findings/settlements
para. 4: **Lack of review:**		
Mental health detention	X v. U.K.	Even assuming any distress attributable to the breach, the applicant had died and no award required to be made to his estate for an injury of a purely personal nature
Recidivist case	Van Droogenbroeck v. Belgium	20,000 BEF for some loss from absence of guarantees.
	De Wilde, Ooms and Versyp v. Belgium, Thynne, Gunnell and Wilson v. U.K., Hussein v. U.K. and Singh v. U.K.	The Court found that there was no indication that the applicants would have been released earlier if there had been a review nor found that any feeling of anxiety, helplessness or frustration required additional award: FOVJS
Procedural defects		
Absence of lawyer at hearing — mental health case	Megyeri v. Germany	5,000 DM for feelings of isolation and helplessness
Lack of access to file	Lamy v. Belgium	FOVJS
Lack of appearance at hearing	Kampanis v. Greece	FOVJS
Breach of speed requirement:		
See above	Luberti v. Italy; Koendjbiharie v. Netherlands; Bezicheri v. Italy and E v. Norway	FOVJS (In Luberti, the applicant's own dilatory conduct was taken into account)
Violations also of Articles 8 and 10 for correspondence restrictions	Herczefalvy v. Austria	100,000 ATS (including legal costs)
Pre-trial detention	R.M.D. v. Switzerland	50,000 CHF for undoubted non-pecuniary damage
Para. 5:		
Right to compensation for arrest and detention	Ciulla v. Italy; Brogan and others v. U.K.; Fox, Campbell and Hartley v. U.K.; Thynne Gunnell and Wilson v. U.K.	Generally, no awards made: FOVJS

Principal issues	Case	Findings/settlements
ARTICLE 6		
Para. 1		
Lack of fair hearing	*Barbera, Messegué and Jabardo v. Spain*	See pecuniary damage section above: real loss of opportunities from conviction
Fairness: right to silence		
Customs fine for failure to disclose documents combined with breach of Article 8 for search of home	*Funke v. France*	50,000 FF
Use of incriminatory materials obtained by compulsion	*Saunders v. U.K.*	FOVJS
Equality/adversarial principle:		
Criminal: inequality of status of expert witness	*Bonisch v. Austria*	700,000 AS — prolonged uncertainty and feelings of inequality
Civil: proceedings not adversarial	*Feldbrugge v. Netherlands*	10,000 guilders
Civil — documents not made available to applicants	*Kerojärvi v. Finland*	No awards FOVJS
Civil — inability to obtain opinion of Att.-Gen's department	*Lobo Machado v. Portugal*	No awards FOVJS
Civil — unable to reply to avocat general's department	*Vermeulen v. Belgium*	No awards FOVJS
Civil — inequality vis-à-vis court expert report	*Mantovanelli v. France*	No awards FOVJS
Civil — not informed of lower court's comments on appeal	*Niderost-Huber v. Switzerland*	No awards FOVJS
Inability to reply to procureur's submissions	*Van Orshoven v. Belgium*	No awards FOVJS

Principal issues	Case	Findings/settlements
Lack of public/oral hearing:		
See above	*Le Compte and others v. Belgium;* *Ekbatani v. Sweden* and *Diennet v. France*	No awards FOVJS
See above	*Helmers v. Sweden*	25,000 SEK noting allegations of discrimination and defamation
Combined with breach of Article 6 lack of access to court	*Fredin (No. 2) v. Sweden*	15,000 SEK
Lack of public hearing and inadequate reasoning	*H v. Belgium*	250,000 BEF
Lack of public hearing/reasons	*De Moor v. Belgium*	400,000 BEF
Lack of public rendering of judgment		
See above	*Werner v. Austria* and *Szücs v. Austria*	FOVJS
Lack of reasons:		
See above	*Ruiz Torija v. Spain;* *Hiro Balani v. Spain* and *Georgiadis v. Greece*	No awards made FOVJS
Mistake of fact in reason for decision	*Fouquet v. France*	F.S. 150,000 FF (including costs)
Independence and impartiality:		
See above	*De Cubber v. Belgium*	100,000 BEF — legitimate misgivings on judge who participated
See above	*Ben Yaacoub v. Belgium*	F.S.: 100,000 BEF
See above	*Hauschildt v. Denmark;* *Langborger v. Austria;* *Demicoli v. Malta;* *Pfeiffer and Plankl v. Austria;* *Holm v Sweden;* *Findlay v. U.K.* (lack of independence of court martial); *De Haan v. Netherlands*	No awards FOVJS

Principal issues	Case	Findings/settlements
Length of proceedings[25]:		
Criminal plus 17 and 10 years	*Eckle v. Germany*	FOVJS: the sentence had been mitigated and some proceedings had been discontinued due to length and it was taken into account that the applicant had been convicted of serious fraud offences
Doctor/disciplinary plus over 10 years	*Konig v. Germany*	30,000 DM — prolonged uncertainty, effect on professional opportunities
Doctor — disciplinary 9 years	*Darnell v. U.K.*	£5,000 — some effect on career. Public apology by the Government not enough
Airport nuisance plus three years	*Zimmerman and Steiner v. Switzerland*	FOVJS
Personal injury plus 8 years	*Martins Moreira v. Portugal*	2 million escudos — uncertainty and anxiety, effect on health and finances
Divorce plus 9 years	*Bock v. Germany*	10,000 DM — highly detrimental: element of mental health being persistently put in doubt
Civil plus 6 years	*Neves e Silva v. Portugal*	500,000 escudos — undoubted element of mental stress
Hospital negligence plus 7 years	*H v. France*	50,000 FF for prolonged distressing uncertainty and anxiety
Criminal plus 8 years	*Moreira de Azvedo v. Portugal*	2 million escudos (pecuniary and non-pecuniary loss)
Land consolidation plus 9 years	*Weisinger v. Austria*	200,000 AS for stress and anxiety
Criminal plus 4 years	*Abdoella v. Netherlands*	FOVJS
Criminal plus 3 years	*Bunkate v. Netherlands*	No award
Criminal plus 12 years	*Dobbertin v. France*	200,000 FF
Civil plus 11 years	*Silva Pontes v. Portugal*	1.5 million escudos (pecuniary and non-pecuniary)
Criminal almost 6 years	*Mitap and Müftöglu v. Turkey*	80,000 FF per applicant

[25] Due to the large number of cases, only selected judgments are included.

Principal issues	Case	Findings/settlements
Length of proceedings—*cont.*		
3 sets social security proceedings: plus 8–9 years	*Duclos v. France*	100,000 FF
Expropriation plus 14 years combined with breach of Article 1, Protocol No. 1	*Guillemin v. France*	250,000 FF
Administrative 6–7 years	*Pashkalidis v. Greece*	500,000 drachmas
Criminal plus 5 years/disciplinary plus 7 years	*Philis v. Greece (No. 2)*	1.5 million drachmas
Civil 5–13 years plus breach of Article 1, Protocol 1 property restrictions	*Matos e Silva v. Portugal*	10 million escudos (pecuniary and non-pecuniary)
Civil pension plus 9 years	*Stamoulakatos (No. 2) v. Greece*	3 million drachmas
Civil (costs) procedure plus 4 years	*Robins v. U.K.*	FOVJS
AIDS cases (compensation proceedings):		
plus 2 years	*X v. France*	150,000 FF to parents (the applicant had died) in respect of the sum claimed by him in respect of improvement the compensation would have made to his life psychologically
plus 4 years	*Vallée v. France*	200,000 FF
plus 4 years	*Karakaya v. France*	200,000 FF
4–6 years	*A and others v. Denmark*	100,000 DKK (on the basis that the Government had made *ex gratia* payments and the applicants had significantly contributed to the delays)
ITALIAN CASES		
Civil:		
plus 7 years	*Scopelliti*	FOVJS (her claim of non-authorised occupation of her land to improve a road)
plus 8 years	*Terranova*	20 million lira (inclusive of costs)

Principal issues	Case	Findings/settlements
ITALIAN CASES—*cont.*		
Civil/enforcement plus 18 years	*Di Pede*	15 million lira
Civil/enforcement plus 23 years	*Zappia*	24 million lira (including costs)
Civil bankruptcy: plus 10 years	*Ceteroni*	50 million lira to one applicant: 25 million to two others
Criminal plus civil party procedure nearly 18 years	*Torri*	15 million lira
Criminal:		
Plus 12 years	*Triggiani*	150 million lira for clear pecuniary and non-pecuniary loss (dismissed from employment during proceedings)
plus 5 years	*Pugliese I*	FOVJS (criminal procedure of regulatory nature)
Plus 7 years	*Alimena*	10 million lira (Court noted the acquittal was only on grounds of insufficient evidence)
Plus 13 years	*Adiletta and others*	15 million lira
Lack of access to court:		
Prisoner	*Golder v. U.K.*	FOVJS
Lack of legal aid	*Airey v. Ireland*	£3,000 IR as offered by Government, *inter alia,* for anxiety, frustration etc.
Refusal of licence for fuel installation	*Benthem v. Netherlands*	FOVJS
Revocation of taxi licence	*Pudas v. Sweden*	20,000 SEK
Expropriation permit	*Boden v. Sweden*	FOVJS
Revocation of licence to exploit gravel pit	*Fredin v. Sweden*	10,000 SEK
Building restrictions	*Matts Jacobsson v. Sweden*	10,000 SEK
Building prohibition	*Skarby and others v. Sweden*	30,000 SEK (for 6 appts.)
Engineer's contract fee claims	*Philis v. Greece*	1 million drachmas: frustration and anxiety at financial position

Principal issues	Case	Findings/settlements
Lack of access to court—*cont.*		
AIDS compensation case	*Bellet v. France*	1 million FF for pecuniary and non-pecuniary (real loss of opportunities)
Austrian administrative offence cases:	*Schmautzer, Umlauft, Gradinger, Pramstaller, Palaoro, Pfarrmeier and Mauer*	FOVJS, No award
Access to court in childcare cases: (see also under Article 8)	*O v. U.K.*	£5,000 granted; though it could not be said that without the procedural deficiencies of access the applicant would have obtained access, the deficiency was intimately linked with interference with fundamental right (family life) and it could not be said that he would not have derived benefit if defect had not been there. There was some loss of a real opportunity and also certain feelings of frustration and helplessness warranting monetary compensation
Lack of hearing:		
Conviction inabsentia	*Colozza v. Italy*	6 million lira for loss of real opportunities
Conviction inabsentia	*FCB v. Italy*	FOVJS
Excluded from attending trial court	*Zana v. Turkey*	40,000 FF
Para. 2: Presumption of innocence		
Order to pay costs on termination of proceedings	*Minelli v. Switzerland*	FOVJS
Statements of guilt to press plus criminal length violation	*Allenet de Ribemont v. France*	2 million FF: statements widely reported: Court commented as to lack of restraint and discretion on the part of the authorities being reprehensible
Rascist remarks of juror	*Remli v. France*	FOVJS
Combined with violation of Article 6, para. 3(b)	*Brozicek v. Italy*	FOVJS

Principal issues	Case	Findings/settlements
Para. 3(a):		
See above	*Chichlian and Ekindjian v. France*	F.S.: 100,000 FF (including legal costs)
Para. 3(b):		
Denial of access to criminal file	*Foucher v. France*	FOVJS
Para. 3(c):		
1 year without lawyer	*Artico v. Italy*	3 million lira Distressing sensation of isolation, confusion and neglect
No lawyer at appeal	*Pakelli v. Germany*	FOVJS No indication of distress from isolation, confusion or neglect
Absence of own lawyer at appeal	*Goddi v. Italy*	5 million lira for loss of real opportunities (*i.e.* the benefit of a practical and effective defence might have made a difference)
Lack of private consultation with defence counsel (5 months)	*Can v. Austria*	F.S.: 100,000 AS and undertaking to change law and communication of Commission report to courts and prosecution authorities
No notification to lawyer of appeal hearing	*Alimena v. Italy*	FOVJS
No legal aid for investigation and trial	*Quaranta v. Switzerland*	3,000 CHF — the Court seemed to agree with Commission that even though the applicant received a partial pardon, he had suffered anxiety and bitterness from lack of representation
No lawyer to assist him at appeal hearing on complex issue which he could not fully comprehend	*Granger v. U.K.*	£1,000 (isolation and confusion)
Lack of free communication with counsel	*S v. Switzerland*	2,500 CHF (claim for frustration from surveillance of visits)
No lawyer at appeal on complex issues	*Pham Hoang v. France*	No award FOVJS
No lawyer at appeal hearing	*Boner v. U.K./ Maxwell v. U.K.*	No awards FOVJS

Principal issues	Case	Findings/settlements
para. 3(c)—*cont.*		
No access to solicitor after arrest	*John Murray v. U.K.*	No awards FOVJS
No legal aid for committal proceedings	*Benham v. U.K.*	No awards FOVJS
Legal representation refused due to applicant's absence in court	*Poitrimol v. France*	No awards FOVJS
Counsel barred due to absence of applicant	*Lala v. Netherlands/ Pelladoah v. Netherlands*	No awards FOVJS
Para. 3(d):		
Principal witnesses not appear at trial	*Unterpertinger v. Austria*	100,000 AS — 6 months in prison as a result of guilt established in manner not complying with Article 6.
Lack of confrontation with party claiming damages	*Bricmont v. Belgium*	FOVJS
Anonymous witnesses	*Kostovski v. Netherlands*	150,000 guilders by agreement
Anonymous witnesses	*Windisch v. Austria*	FOVJS: There had been a rehearing with the witnesses and detention taken into account in sentence
Witnesses not examined by the court	*Delta v. France*	100,000 FF for real loss of opportunity
Court's failure to call witnesses	*Vidal v. Belgium*	250,000 BEF for real loss of opportunity
Lack of confrontation with principal witnesses	*Saidi v. France*	FOVJS
Conviction based on anonymous police witness	*Van Mechelen and others (Article 50) v. Netherlands*	25,000 NLG to Van Mechelen (difficult personal circumstances) 20,000 NLG to others [25a]
ARTICLE 7		
Retrospective penalties	*Welch v. U.K.*	FOVJS

[25a] The Government argued unsuccessfully that the release of the applicants, ordered after the Court's finding of a violation, was just satisfaction enough.

Principal issues	Case	Findings/settlements
ARTICLE 7—cont.		
See above	*Jamil v. France*	FOVJS
ARTICLE 8		
Childcare:		
Breach under Articles 6 and 8 for unreasonable delay	*H v U.K.*	£12,000: while the outcome may not have been different without the delay, the deficiency was intimately linked with interference with a fundamental right (family life) and it could not be said that the applicant would not have derived benefit if speedier. There was some loss of a real opportunity and also certain feeling of frustration and helplessness warranting monetary compensation
Lack of consultation combined with breach of Article 6 — lack of access to court	*W v. U.K.*	£12,000 (anguish and distress)
6 and 8 as in *W v. U.K.*	*B v. U.K.*	£12,000
6 and 8 as in *W v. U.K.*	*R v. U.K.*	£8,000 (serious distress)
Breaches of Articles 6 and 8 lack of procedural rights for natural father	*Keegan v. Ireland*	£10,000 IR for trauma, anxiety, feelings of injustice
Breaches of Articles 6 and 8: procedural defects	*McMichael v. U.K.*	£8,000 for evident trauma, anxiety, feelings of injustice, (despite U.K. Government argument that no link with removal of children or loss of real opportunity in this case as compared with other child care cases)
Placement of children at long distances	*Olsson v. Sweden*	200,000 SEK (considerable anxiety and distress and inconvenience)
8 alone	*Nyberg v. Sweden*	F.S. 225,000 SEK plus costs
Breach of Article 6 (access to court) and 8 (delay in returning child)	*Eriksson v. Sweden*	200,000 SEK to mother; 100,000 SEK to child
Restriction on contract	*Margareta and Roger Andersson v. Sweden*	50,000 SEK to mother and child

Principal issues	Case	Findings/settlements
ARTICLE 8—*cont.*		
Childcare—*cont.*		
Breaches 6 (access to court) and 8 (prohibition on removal from care)	*Olsson No. 2 v. Sweden*	50,000 SEK
Uncle's lack of access to nephew	*Boyle v. U.K.*	F.S.: £15,000 plus legal costs plus reference to Children Act 1989 giving procedural rights
Lack of rehabilitation efforts	*Hokkanen v. Finland*	100,000 FIM for distress
Lack of legal recognition of family links out of wedlock:	*Marckx v. Belgium; Johnston v. Ireland; Kroon v. Netherlands*	No awards made FOVJS
Expulsion/family life:		
Proposed expulsion to Algeria	*Djeroud v. France*	F.S. 150,000 FF including legal costs plus revocation of expulsion and 10 year residence permit
Applicant expelled from Belgium	*Moustaquim v. Belgium*	100,000 BEF
Expulsion following divorce form Dutch spouse	*Berrehab v. Netherlands*	20,000 guilders. The applicant had meanwhile been granted a residence permit
Proposed expulsion to Algeria	*Beldjoudi v. France*	FOVJS: The applicant had not left the country
Applicant expelled for time to Morocco	*Lamguindaz v. U.K.*	F.S.: revocation of deportation order and indefinite leave to remain plus costs
Private life:		
Lack of protection in criminal law for rape/assault	*X and Y v. Netherlands*	3,000 guilders
Non-disclosure of local authority records concerning childhood in care	*Gaskin v. U.K.*	£5,000: some emotional distress and anxiety from absence of independent procedure
Criminalisation of adult homosexual acts	*Dudgeon v. U.K.* (Art. 50); *Norris v. Ireland; Modinos v. Cyprus*	No awards FOVJS
Transsexual, lack of ability to change name	*B v. France*	100,000 FF

Principal issues	Case	Findings/settlements
ARTICLE 8—cont **Private life—**cont.		
Police taking of personal details/ photographs plus Article 13 complaint	*Friedl v. Austria*	F.S.: 148,787.60 AS including costs plus destruction of photographs
Disclosure of HIV status	*Z v Finland*	200,000 FIM
Environmental nuisance — health and home	*Lopez Ostra v. Spain*	4 million pesetas — distress, anxiety for child's health
Correspondence:		
Restrictions/ interference with prisoners' correspondence	*Silver v. U.K.; Schonenburger and Durmax v. Switzerland; McCallum v. U.K.; Golder v. U.K.; Campbell v. U.K.; Domenchini v. Italy* and *Calegoro Diana v. Italy*	No awards FOVJS
See above	*Messina v. Italy*	5 million lira for breach of length 6 para. 1 and breach of 8 on lack of delivery of mail
Telephone tapping:		
See above	*Malone v. U.K.*	Agreement of parties: costs paid and money confiscated returned
See above	*Kruslin v. France*	FOVJS
See above	*A v. France*	FOVJS
See above	*Halford v. U.K.*	£10,000 — interception to use material against her in sex discrimination proceedings was a serious infringement of her rights
Home:		
Refusal of residence permit for house on Guernsey	*Gillow v. U.K.*	£10,000 for claims of stress, anxiety etc.
Customs search of home	*Cremieux v. France*	50,000 FF

Principal issues	Case	Findings/settlements
ARTICLE 8—*cont.*		
Home—*cont.*		
Customs search and seizure	*Miailhe v. France*	50,000 FF (one applicant), 25,000 to wife and mother
Search of lawyer's office	*Niemietz v. Germany*	FOVJS
ARTICLE 9		
Convictions for pros-elytising	*Kokkinakis v. Greece*	400,000 drachmas
Conviction for using place of worship without authorisation	*Manoussakis v. Greece*	FOVJS
Lack of authorisation to use place of worship	*Pentidis v. Greece*	F.S.: authorisation granted
ARTICLE 10		
Sanctions imposed on, *inter alia*, journalists and politicians	*Goodwin v. U.K.;* *Oberschlick v. Austria;* *Castells v. Spain;* *Schwabe v. Austria;* *Weber v. Switzerland;* *Jersild v. Denmark;* *De Haes and Gijsels v. Belgium;* *Vereinigung demokratischer soldaten osterreichs v. Austria;* *Piermont v. France* and *Grigoriades v. Greece*	Generally, no awards have been made for cases concerning injunctions or measures or convictions for allegedly defamatory, damaging or insulting statements: FOVJS
Fine for refusal to give incriminating evidence	*K v. Austria*	F.S.: 18,000 schillings plus costs plus proposals for draft law provided
Suspension of teacher for political views	*Vogt v. Germany*	117,639.55 DM by agreement as compensation for loss of salary and terms as to her pension and grading plus costs
Ban on advertising:		
See above (vet)	*Barthold v. Germany*	FOVJS
See above (doctor)	*Colman v. U.K.*	F.S.: £12,500 total plus changes in rules on professional advertising

Principal issues	Case	Findings/settlements
Broadcasting:		
Refusal of licence — State broadcasting monopoly	*Telesystem Tirol v. Austria*	F.S.: 200,000 ATS all claims (reference in text to Constitutional Court ruling following Court's judgment in previous case Informatsverein Lentia which found a violation of Article 10)
ARTICLE 11		
Loss of jobs due to closed shop	*Young, James and Webster v. U.K.*	£2,000, £6,000 and £3,000 agreed by Government for harassment humiliation, stress in obtaining other employment
Disciplinary sanction for lawyer's participation in demonstration	*Ezelin v. France*	FOVJS
Dissolution of political party	*United Communist Party and others v. Turkey*	FOVJS for two individual applicant members of the party
ARTICLE 12		
Prohibition on marriage	*F v. Switzerland*	FOVJS — prohibition only effective for period of 8 months of cohabitation
ARTICLE 13		
See above	*Chahal v. U.K.; Valsamis v. Greece* and *Camenind v. Switzerland*	No awards made FOVJS
ARTICLE 14		
In conjunction with Article 6:		
Sex discrimination	*Schuler-Zgraggen v. Switzerland*	FOVJS
In conjunction with Article 8:		
Sex discrimination in immigration entry rules	*Abdulaziz and others v. U.K.*	FOVJS: while may have been some distress and anxiety, the applicants knew they had no right of entry at time of marriage and they were able to live elsewhere
In conjunction with Article 1 of Protocol No. 1		
Lack of inheritance rights — birth out of wedlock	*Inze v. Austria*	150,000 AS for loss of real opportunities
Liability to church tax	*Darby v. Sweden*	FOVJS

419

Principal issues	Case	Findings/settlements
In conjunction with Article 1 of Protocol No. 1—*cont.*		
Discrimination on sex in contribution obligation	*Van Raalte v. Netherlands*	FOVJS
Discriminatory planning refusal	*Pine Valley v. Ireland*	£50,000 on equitable basis, finding that the inability to proceed with the development compounded one applicant's personal and financial difficulties
Article 1, Protocol No. 1		
Length of expropriation proceedings — breach of Article 6	*Erkner and Hofauer v. Austria*	350,000 AS by agreement plus costs
Same as *Erkner*	*Poiss v. Austria*	450,000 AS by agreement plus costs
Length of tenancy eviction proceedings 6 and lack of enforcement of property rights	*Scollo v. Italy*	30 million lira — with reference to effect on his own living conditions
Delay in paying compensation for expropriation	*Akkuş v. Turkey*	USD 1,000 for hardship, practical difficulties
Article 2 Protocol No. 1:		
Suspension from school	*Campbell and Cosans v. U.K.*	For parents: FOVJS For boy: £3,000 on equitable basis for disproportionate nature of punishment, mental anxiety, deprivation of some opportunity to complete schooling
Article 2 of Protocol No. 4:		
Combined with violation of property rights	*Raimondo v. Italy*	5 million lira

4. Legal costs and expenses

This head potentially covers not only the cost of proceedings before the Commission and Court but expenses incurred in domestic proceedings in order to prevent the violation or to obtain redress.[26] The Court applies the test whether the costs and expenses were

---

[26] *Le Compte v. Belgium*, October 18, 1982, Series A, No. 54 (Art. 50), where the appeal proceedings against the disciplinary sanctions were not part of process to obtain redress for the lack of public hearing but their application to the Court of Cassation where the lawyers pleaded the Convention as part of the process of exhaustion was taken into account and costs awarded. However in *Sunday Times v. U.K.*, (Art. 50), November 6, 1980, No. 38 where the parties in the domestic proceedings agreed to bear their own costs, the Court made no award in this respect.

actually[27] and necessarily incurred in order to prevent, or obtain redress for, the matter found to constitute a violation of the Convention and were reasonable as to quantum.[28] The Court does not consider itself bound by domestic scales and practices in assessing what is reasonable by way of fees, although it may derive assistance from them.[29] It has resisted the invitation by the Commission to impose a uniform approach to the assessment of fees since there is too great disparity between the rates applicable in Contracting States.[30]

Where the Court finds one or more of the applicant's complaints of violation unfounded it may reduce the amount of costs awarded.[31] It will not do so where a violation is found on the principal matter in issue as in *Soering v. United Kingdom,* where the essential concern and bulk of argument was on Article 3, although complaints under Articles 6, paragraphs 3(c) and 13 were rejected.[32] Where an applicant's claims for pecuniary and non-pecuniary damage are rejected in Article 50 proceedings, the legal costs for that part may not be granted.[33]

Awards are made subject to deduction of any sums granted by way of legal aid from the Council of Europe, unless stated otherwise.

The United Kingdom Government is active in querying fees which exceed domestic norms or which appear excessive. The Court has shown itself responsive to its objections to the level of fees or hours claimed, or the number of representatives involved.[34] In *Young, James and Webster v. United Kingdom,* the Court noted high litigation costs might themselves constitute an impediment to effective human rights protection and considered it wrong to give encouragement to such a situation in costs awards under Article 50.[35] High costs claims have almost always been subject to reductions, on an equitable basis. The highest awards in United Kingdom cases for the Strasbourg proceedings have been in the *Observer and Guardian, Sunday Times No. 2, Saunders* and *Tolstoy* cases (see below).

---

[27] Fees to be paid on a contingency basis have been discounted as they were not legally enforceable, *e.g. Dudgeon v. U.K.,* February 24, 1983, Series A, No. 59 (Art. 50); also *McCann and others v. U.K.,* September 27, 1995, Series A, No. 324, where legal representatives acted free of charge in inquest, the applicants could not claim to be under obligation to pay the solicitor and costs of the inquest proceedings could not be said to be "actually incurred".

[28] *e.g. Sunday Times v. U.K.,* November 6, 1980, Series A, (Art. 50), No. 30, para. 23.

[29] *e.g. Silver v. U.K.,* October 24, 1983, Series A, No. 67, para. 20. See also *Abdulaziz v. U.K.,* May 28, 1985, Series A, No. 94, where Government contested rate of fees for junior counsel as higher than the domestic rate but the Court found the amount claimed reasonable as to quantum. *Hadjianstassiou v. Greece,* December 16, 1993, Series A, No. 252 where Court discounted Greek Government's complaints that fees claimed exceeded domestic rates.

[30] *Tolstoy v. U.K.,* July 13, 1995, Series A, No. 316–B, para. 77.

[31] *e.g. Le Compte,* see n.26, reduced where most of the complaints rejected; also reductions in *Benham v. U.K.* June 10, 1996, R.J.D., 1996–III, No. 10 and *Tolstoy v. U.K.,* July 13, 1995, Series A, No. 316–B where claims only partly successful. However the Court rejected in *Sunday Times* the Government claim to reduce amounts due to the fact that not all the submissions on Art. 10 were successful, namely, criticising the length and detail of applicant's case. The Court noted that a lawyer must present his case as fully as he is able and may not anticipate what arguments will convince.

[32] Also *Observer* and *Guardian v. U.K.,* November 26, 1992, Series A, No. 216 and *Sunday Times (No. 2) v. U.K.,* November 26, 1992, Series A, No. 217, where no reduction though no violation of Arts. 13 and 14, since bulk of argument was on Art. 10.

[33] *Welch v. U.K.,* (Art. 50) February 26, 1996, R.J.D., 1996–II, No. 5.

[34] The Court accepted the Government objections to claimed hourly rates in *Fox, Campbell* and *Hartley v. U.K.,* (Art. 50) March 27, 1991, Series A, No. 190–B and *Gaskin v. U.K.,* July 7, 1989, Series A, No. 160.

[35] The Court awarded £65,000 offered by the Government, finding the applicant's claims of 342,349 FF for use of a French legal firm debatable and criticising the applicant's refusal of the Government's reasonable offer to have the costs taxed domestically.

Awards of legal costs and expenses
Recent selected United Kingdom and Ireland cases

Case	Court Awards (A: applicant; G: government; Ct: court)
Halford	A: claimed £119,500 for solicitors (£239 rate for 500 hours) and £14,875 for counsel's fees
	G: objected to rate (£120–150 applicable in domestic proceedings) and excessive hours considering narrow range of issues and that the applicant chose to put in submissions of 200 pages of irrelevant annexes). Proposed £25,000
	Ct: awarded £25,000 as it was not satisfied all costs claimed necessarily incurred or reasonable as to quantum
D v. U.K.	A: claimed £49,443 plus 13,811 FF;
	G: objected as excessive (unreasonable number of lawyers involved) — proposed: £29,000 plus 9,194 FF
	Ct: £35,000 plus VAT
Findlay	A: claimed £23,956
	G: objected to inclusion of Divisional Court application costs of £1,250 (solicitor and counsel):
	Ct: found it reasonable to make application seeking redress for violation and granted claim in full
Saunders	A: claimed over £336,000
	G: objected as excessive and to amounts claimed for advisers beyond solicitor and junior and leading counsel
	Ct: not satisfied necessarily incurred or reasonable as to quantum: £75,000 on equitable basis
Chahal family:	A: claimed £77,700 VAT incl.
	G: proposed £22,000
	Ct: found applicant's claim excessive: £45,000 VAT incl.
Benham	A: claimed £26,000
	G: objected — excessive
	Ct: granted £10,000 *e.g.* applicant only partly successful

Case	Court Awards (A: applicant; G: government; Ct: court
Goodwin	A: claimed £49,500
	G: proposed £37,595
	Ct: considered sum conceded by Government to be adequate in the circumstances
Hussain	A: claimed £32,459 (VAT included)
	G: objection as excessive
	Ct: granted £19,000
Singh	A: Claimed £22,058 (VAT included)
	G: objection as excesive
	Ct: £13,000 granted
McCann and others	Court awarded £22,000 solicitor, £16,700 counsel
Tolstoy	A: claimed £149,000 and 70,000 CHF approx.
	G: objected as excessive
	Ct: was not satisfied all costs necessarily incurred and applicant only partially successful on the merits: awarded £70,000 and 40,000 CHF on an equitable basis
Welch (Art. 50)	A: claimed £13,852
	G: no objection
	Ct: granted in full
Campbell	A: claimed £9,257.69
	G: no objection
	Ct: granted in full
Keegan v. Ireland	A: claimed IR £42,863 supported by costs accountants' view of reasonableness
	G: proposed reduction without substantiation of its basis
	Ct: awarded claim plus VAT

Case	Court Awards (A: applicant; G: government; Ct: court
Open Door Counseling v. Ireland	A: Open Door claimed for domestic and Convention proceedings: £68,985 IR Well Woman claimed £63,302 for domestic proceedings; £21,084 and £27,116 for Strasbourg
	G: accepted domestic costs for both. For Strasbourg proceeding, it made no objection to Open Door's claim but considered it excessive to pay Well Woman's costs for this same proceeding.
	Ct: granted Open Door's claims in full. Awarded IR £100,000 in total to Well Woman, finding its claim excessive in light of the similarity of the cases
Pine Valley Developments v. Ireland (domestic proceedings)	A: claimed £42,655
	G: thought inflated
	Ct: found it was not contested that sums actually and necessarily incurred and considered interest was warranted: granted in full
Pine Valley (Strasbourg proceedings)	A: claimed IR £406,760 for Strasbourg
	G: objection as excessive (proposed IR £80,455)
	Ct: agreed with Government that claims excessive: £70,000 paid after legal aid deduction
Observer and Guardian (Domestic proceedings)	A: claimed: £137,825
	G: objected
	Ct: not agree with Government that applicants should have instructed the same solicitors since they were free to choose own representatives. But since their interests were the same, the number of fee earners involved was not "necessarily" incurred and agreed with the Government that solicitors' fees not reasonable as to quantum. Discounted period where found no violation. Granted £65,000

Case	Court Awards (A: applicant; G: government; Ct: court)
Observer v. Guardian (Strasbourg proceedings)	A: claimed £74,605
	G: objection to size of fees
	Ct: reduction made for finding of no violation for one period and solicitors' fees unreasonable: granted £35,000
Sunday Times No. 2 (Domestic proceedings)	A: £84,219 claimed
	G: objected to solicitors costs over £30,000
	Ct: agreed that solicitors' costs not reasonable and doubted all items necessarily incurred; also counsel's fees not reasonable (£30,590). Granted £50,000
Sunday Times (Strasbourg proceedings)	A: claimed £140,120
	G: objection
	Ct: granted £50,000

5. Default interest

Interest in default of payment of awards after three months from the date of judgment is set according to rate applicable in State concerned. Currently, in United Kingdom cases, the Court is applying the statutory rate of interest of 8 per cent per annum.

B. Before the Commission

Before admissibility, there is no formal settlement mechanism, but cases may settle after communication to the respondent Government, where the parties agree to do so. The initiative usually comes from the Government, who may offer redress, for example, by way of leave to remain in expulsion cases or a sum of ex gratia compensation, which tends to reflect the Court's level of damages in similar cases.

After admissibility, there is a formal approach from the Commission to the parties with a view to achieving a friendly settlement. It may intervene to recommend a basis of settlement. Governments in making offers for settlement will have regard to previous awards made by the Court in similar cases and are unlikely to offer considerably more in the absence of special features. Payment of reasonable legal costs is generally included in offers. The Commission in making proposals may suggest sums above the likely Court award, having regard to the fact that the applicant in settling will not have receive the benefit of a public finding of violation. A refusal by an applicant to accept this proposal may, if the cases is decided by the Committee of Ministers rather than the Court, lead to the Commission proposing a lesser sum.

C. Before the Committee of Ministers

Where, in cases not referred to the Court, a violation is found by the Committee of Ministers, the Committee refer to the Commission who invites the applicant's submissions on the three heads of damages (pecuniary, non-pecuniary, costs) and the Government's comments on those claims before submitting to the Committee its proposals, which are generally accepted. As above, the governing criteria are the likely award from the Court in similar cases, the factor that the applicant will not obtain a Court judgment and, where relevant, any prior refusal of Commission settlement proposals.

APPENDICES

The 1950 European Convention for the Protection of Human Rights and Fundamental Freedoms

The governments signatory hereto, being Members of the Council of Europe,

Considering the Universal Declaration of Human Rights proclaimed by the General Assembly of the United Nations on December 10, 1948;

Considering that this Declaration aims at securing the universal and effective recognition and observance of the rights therein declared;

Considering that the aim of the Council of Europe is the achievement of greater unity between its Members and that one of the methods by which that aim is to be pursued is the maintenance and further realisation of human rights and fundamental freedoms;

Reaffirming their profound belief in those fundamental freedoms which are the foundation of justice and peace in the world and are best maintained on the one hand by an effective political democracy and on the other by a common understanding and observance of the Human Rights upon which they depend;

Being resolved, as the governments of European countries which are like-minded and have a common heritage of political traditions, ideals, freedom and the rule of law, to take the first steps for the collective enforcement of certain of the rights stated in the Universal Declaration;

Have agreed as follows:

Article 1

The High Contracting Parties shall secure to everyone within their jurisdiction the rights and freedoms defined in section 1 of this Convention.

SECTION 1

Article 2

1. Everyone's right to life shall be protected by law. No one shall be deprived of his life intentionally save in the execution of a sentence of a court following his conviction of a crime for which this penalty is provided by law.

2. Deprivation of life shall not be regarded as inflicted in contravention of this Article when it results from the use of force which is no more than absolutely necessary:

   (a) in defence of any person from unlawful violence;
   (b) in order to effect a lawful arrest or to prevent the escape of a person lawfully detained;
   (c) in action lawfully taken for the purpose of quelling a riot or insurrection.

Article 3

No one shall be subjected to torture or to inhuman or degrading treatment or punishment.

Article 4

1. No one shall be held in slavery or servitude.

2. No one shall be required to perform forced or compulsory labour.

3. For the purpose of this Article the term "forced or compulsory labour" shall not include:

    (a) any work required to be done in the ordinary course of detention imposed according to the provisions of Article 5 of this Convention or during conditional release from such detention;

    (b) any service of a military character or, in case of conscientious objectors in countries where they are recognised, service exacted instead of compulsory military service;

    (c) any service exacted in case of an emergency or calamity threatening the life or well-being of the community;

    (d) any work or service which forms part of normal civic obligations.

Article 5

1. Everyone has the right to liberty and security of person. No one shall be deprived of his liberty save in the following cases and in accordance with a procedure prescribed by law:

    (a) the lawful detention of a person after conviction by a competent court;

    (b) the lawful arrest or detention of a person for non-compliance with the lawful order of a court or in order to secure the fulfilment of any obligation prescribed by law;

    (c) the lawful arrest or detention of a person effected for the purpose of bringing him before the competent legal authority on reasonable suspicion of having committed an offence or when it is reasonably considered necessary to prevent his committing an offence or fleeing after having done so;

    (d) the detention of a minor by lawful order for the purpose of educational supervision or his lawful detention for the purpose of bringing him before the competent legal authority;

    (e) the lawful detention of persons for the prevention of the spreading of infectious diseases, of persons of unsound mind, alcoholics or drug addicts or vagrants;

    (f) the lawful arrest or detention of a person to prevent his effecting an unauthorised entry into the country or of a person against whom action is being taken with a view to deportation or extradition.

2. Everyone who is arrested shall be informed promptly, in a language which he understands, of the reasons for his arrest and of any charge against him.

3. Everyone arrested or detained in accordance with the provisions of paragraph 1(c) of this Article shall be brought promptly before a judge or other officer authorised by law to exercise judicial power and shall be entitled to trial within a reasonable time or to release pending trial. Release may be conditioned by guarantees to appear for trial.

4. Everyone who is deprived of his liberty by arrest or detention shall be entitled to take proceedings by which the lawfulness of his detention shall be decided speedily by a court and his release ordered if the detention is now lawful.

5. Everyone who has been the victim of arrest or detention in contravention of the provisions of this Article shall have an enforceable right to compensation.

Article 6

1. In the determination of his civil rights and obligations or of any criminal charge against him, everyone is entitled to a fair and public hearing within a reasonable time by an independent and impartial tribunal established by law. Judgment shall be pronounced publicly but the press and public may be excluded from all or part of the trial in the interest of morals, public order or national security in a democratic society, where the interests of juveniles or the protection of the private life of the parties so require, or to the extent strictly necessary in the opinion of the court in special circumstances where publicity would prejudice the interests of justice.

2. Everyone charged with a criminal offence shall be presumed innocent until proved guilty according to law.

3. Everyone charged with a criminal offence has the following minimum rights:

    (a) to be informed promptly, in a language which he understands and in detail, of the nature and cause of the accusation against him;

    (b) to have adequate time and facilities for the preparation of his defence;

    (c) to defend himself in person or through legal assistance of his own choosing or, if he has not sufficient means to pay for legal assistance, to be given it free when the interests of justice so require;

    (d) to examine or have examined witnesses against him and to obtain the attendance and examination of witnesses on his behalf under the same conditions as witnesses against him;

    (e) to have the free assistance of an interpreter if he cannot understand or speak the language used in court.

Article 7

1. No one shall be held guilty of any criminal offence on account of any act or omission which did not constitute a criminal offence under national or international law at the time when it was committed. Nor shall a heavier penalty be imposed than the one that was applicable at the time the criminal offence was committed.

2. This Article shall not prejudice the trial and punishment of any person for any act or omission which, at the time when it was committed, was criminal according to the general principles of law recognised by civilised nations.

Article 8

1. Everyone has the right to respect for his private and family life, his home and his correspondence.

2. There shall be no interference by a public authority with the exercise of this right except such as is in accordance with the law and is necessary in a democratic society in the interests of national security, public safety or the economic well-being of the country, for the prevention of disorder or crime, for the protection of health or morals, or for the protection of the rights and freedoms of others.

Article 9

1. Everyone has the right to freedom of thought, conscience and religion; this right includes freedom to change his religion or belief and freedom, either alone or in community with others and in public or private, to manifest his religion or belief, in worship, teaching, practice and observance.

2. Freedom to manifest one's religion or beliefs shall be subject only to such limitations as are prescribed by law and are necessary in a democratic society in the interests of public safety, for the protection of public order, health or morals, or for the protection of the rights and freedoms of others.

Article 10

1. Everyone has the right to freedom of expression. This right shall include freedom to hold opinions and to receive and impart information and ideas without interference by public authority and regardless of frontiers. This article shall not prevent States from requiring the licensing of broadcasting, television or cinema enterprises.

2. The exercise of these freedoms, since it carries with it duties and responsibilities, may be subject to such formalities, conditions, restrictions or penalties as are prescribed by law and are necessary in a democratic society, in the interests of national security, territorial integrity or public safety, for the prevention of disorder or crime, for the protection of health or morals, for the protection of the reputation or rights of others, for preventing the disclosure of information received in confidence, or for maintaining the authority and impartiality of the judiciary.

Article 11

1. Everyone has the right to freedom of peaceful assembly and to freedom of association with others, including the right to form and to join trade unions for the protection of his interests.

2. No restrictions shall be placed on the exercise of these rights other than such as are prescribed by law and are necessary in a democratic society in the interests of national security or public safety, for the prevention of disorder or crime, for the protection of health or morals or for the protection of the rights and freedoms of others. This Article shall not prevent the imposition of lawful restrictions on the exercise of these rights by members of the armed forces, of the police or of the administration of the State.

Article 12

Men and women of marriageable age have the right to marry and to found a family, according to the national laws governing the exercise of this right.

Article 13

Everyone whose rights and freedom as set forth in this Convention are violated shall have an effective remedy before a national authority notwithstanding that the violation has been committed by persons acting in an official capacity.

Article 14

The enjoyment of the rights and freedoms set forth in this Convention shall be secured without discrimination on any ground such as sex, race, colour, language, religion, political or other opinion, national or social origin, association with a national minority, property, birth or other status.

Article 15

1. In time of war or other public emergency threatening the life of the nation any High Contracting Party may take measures derogating from its obligations under this Convention to the extent strictly required by the exigencies of the situation, provided that such measures are not inconsistent with its other obligations under international law.

2. No derogation from Article 2, except in respect of deaths resulting from lawful acts of war, or from Article 3, 4 (paragraph 1) and 7 shall be made under this provision.

3. Any High Contracting Party availing itself of this right of derogation shall keep the Secretary General of the Council of Europe fully informed of the measures which it has taken and the reasons therefore. It shall also inform the Secretary General of the Council of Europe when such measures have ceased to operate and the provisions of the Convention are again being fully executed.

Article 16

Noting in Articles 10, 11 and 14 shall be regarded as preventing the High Contracting Parties from imposing restrictions on the political activity of aliens.

Article 17

Nothing in this Convention may be interpreted as implying for any State, group or person any right to engage in any activity or perform any act aimed at the destruction of any of the rights and freedoms set forth herein or at their limitation to a greater extent than is provided for in the Convention.

Article 18

The restrictions permitted under this Convention to the said rights and freedoms shall not be applied for any purpose other than those for which they have been prescribed.

Article 24

Any High Contracting Party may refer to the Commission, through the Secretary-General of the Council of Europe, any alleged breach of the provisions of the Convention by another High Contracting Party.

Article 25

1. The Commission may receive petitions addressed to the Secretary-General of the Council of Europe from any person, non-governmental organisation or group of individuals claiming to the victim of a violation by one of the High Contracting Parties of the rights set forth in this Convention, provided that the High Contracting Party against which the complaint has been lodged has declared that it recognises the competence of the Commission to receive such petitions. Those of the High Contracting Parties who have made such a declaration undertake not to hinder in any way the effective exercise of this right.

2. Such declarations may be made for a specific period.

3. The declarations shall be deposited with the Secretary-General of the Council of Europe who shall transmit copies thereof to the High Contracting Parties and publish them.

4. The Commission shall only exercise the powers provided for in this article when at least six High Contracting Parties are bound by declarations made in accordance with the preceding paragraphs.

Article 26

The Commission may only deal with the matter after all domestic remedies have been exhausted, according to the generally recognised rules of international law, and within a period of six months from the date on which the final decision was taken.

Article 27

1. The Commission shall not deal with any petition submitted under Article 25 which

    (a) is anonymous, or

    (b) is substantially the same as a matter which has already been examined by the Commission or has already been submitted to another procedure or international investigation or settlement and if it contains no relevant new information.

2. The Commission shall consider inadmissible any petition submitted under Article 25 which it considers incompatible with the provisions of the present Convention, manifestly ill-founded, or an abuse of the right of petition.

3. The Commission shall reject any petition referred to it which it considers inadmissible under Article 26.

Article 28

In the event of the Commission accepting a petition referred to it:

    (a) it shall, with a view to ascertaining the facts undertake together with the representative of the parties and examination of the petition and, if need be, an investigation, for the effective conduct of which the States concerned shall furnish all necessary facilities, after an exchange of views with the Commission;

    (b) it shall place itself at the disposal of the parties concerned with a view to securing a friendly settlement of the matter on the basis of respect for Human Rights as defined in this Convention.

Article 29

After it has accepted a petition submitted under Article 25, the Commission may nevertheless decide by a majority of two-thirds of its members to reject the petition if, in the course of its examination, it finds that the existence of one of the grounds for non-acceptance provided for in Article 27 has been established.

In such a case, the decision shall be communicated to the parties.

Article 30

1. The Commission may at any stage of the proceedings decide to strike a petition out of its lists of cases where the circumstances lead to the conclusion that:

    a. the applicant does not intend to pursue his petition, or

    b. the matter has been resolved, or

    c. for any others reason estabished by the Commission, it is no longer justified to continue the examination of the petition.

However, the Commission shall continue the examination of a petition if respect for Human Rights as defined in the Convention so requires.

The Substantive Protocols to the Convention

PROTOCOL No. 1
MARCH 20, 1952

The Governments signatory hereto, being Members of the Council of Europe,

Being resolved to take steps to ensure the collective enforcement of certain rights and freedoms other than those already included in section 1 of the Convention for the Protection of Human Rights and Fundamental Freedoms signed at Rome on November 4, 1950 (hereinafter referred to as "the Convention"),

Have agreed as follows:

Article 1

Every natural or legal person is entitled to the peaceful enjoyment of his possessions. No one shall be deprived of his possessions except in the public interest and subject to the conditions provided for by law and by the general principles of international law.

The preceding provisions shall not, however, in any way impair the right of a State to enforce such laws as it deems necessary to control the use of property in accordance with the general interest or to secure the payment of taxes or other contributions or penalties.

Article 2

No person shall be denied the right to education. In the exercise of any functions which it assumes in relation to education and to teaching, the State shall respect the right of parents to ensure such education and teaching in conformity with their own religious and philosophical convictions.

Article 3

The High Contracting Parties undertake to hold free elections at reasonable intervals by secret ballot, under conditions which will ensure the free expression of the opinion of the people in the choice of the legislature.

PROTOCOL No. 4
SEPTEMBER 16, 1963

The Governments signatory hereto, being Members of the Council of Europe,

Being resolved to take steps to ensure the collective enforcement of certain rights and freedoms other than those already included in Section I of the Convention for the Protection of Human Rights and Fundamental Freedoms signed at Rome on November 4, 1950 (hereinafter referred to as "the Convention") and in Articles 1 to 3 of the First Protocol to the Convention, signed at Paris on March 20, 1952,

Have agreed as follows:

Article 1

No one shall be deprived of his liberty merely on the ground of inability to fulfil a contractual obligation.

Article 2

1. Everyone lawfully within the territory of a State shall, within that territory, have the right to liberty of movement and freedom to choose his residence.

2. Everyone shall be freed to leave any country, including his own.

3. No restriction shall be placed on the exercise of these rights other than such as are in accordance with law and are necessary in a democratic society in the interests of national security or public safety, for the maintenance of *ordre public*, for the prevention of crime, for the protection of health or morals, or for the protection of the rights and freedoms of others.

4. The rights set forth in paragraph 1 may also be subject, in particular areas, to restrictions imposed in accordance with law and justified by the public interest in a democratic society.

Article 3

1. No one shall be expelled, by means either of an individual or of a collective measure, from the territory of the State of which he is a national.

2. No one shall be deprived of the right to enter the territory of the State of which he is a national.

Article 4

Collective expulsion of aliens is prohibited.

PROTOCOL No. 6
APRIL 28, 1983

The Member States of the Council of Europe, signatory to this Protocol to the Convention for the Protection of Human Rights and Fundamental Freedoms, signed at Rome on November 4, 1950 (hereinafter referred to as "the Convention"),

Considering that the evolution that has occurred in several Member States of the Council of Europe expresses a general tendency in favour of abolition of the death penalty,

Have agreed as follows:

Article 1

The death penalty shall be abolished. No one shall be condemned to such penalty or executed.

Article 2

A State may make provision in its law for the death penalty in respect of acts committed in time of war or of imminent threat of war; such penalty shall be applied only in the instances laid down in the law and in accordance with its provisions. The State shall communicate to the Secretary General of the Council of Europe the relevant provisions of that law.

PROTOCOL No. 7
NOVEMBER 22, 1984

The Member States of the Council of Europe signatory hereto,

Being resolved to take further steps to ensure the collective enforcement of certain rights and freedoms by means of the Convention for the Protection of Human Rights and Fundamental Freedoms signed at Rome on November 4, 1950 (hereinafter referred to as "the Convention").

Have agreed as follows:

Article 1

1. An alien lawfully resident in the territory of a State shall not be expelled therefrom except in pursuance of a decision reached in accordance with law and shall be allowed:

    (a) to submit reasons against his expulsion,

    (b) to have his case reviewed, and

    (c) to be represented for these purposes before the competent authority or a person or persons designated by that authority.

2. An alien may be expelled before the exercise of his rights under paragraph 1(a), (b) and (c) of this Article, when such expulsion is necessary in the interests of public order or is grounded on reasons of national security.

Article 2

1. Everyone convicted of a criminal offence by a tribunal shall have the right to have his conviction or sentence reviewed by a higher tribunal. The exercise of this right, including the grounds on which it may be exercised, shall be governed by law.

2. This right may be subject to exceptions in regard to offences of a minor character, as prescribed by law, or in cases in which the person concerned was tried in the first instance by the highest tribunal or was convicted following an appeal against acquittal.

Article 3

When a person has by a final decision been convicted of a criminal offence and when subsequently his conviction has been reversed, or he has been pardoned, on the ground that a new or newly discovered fact shows conclusively that there has been a miscarriage of justice, the person who has suffered punishment as a result of such conviction shall be compensated according to the law or the practice of the State concerned, unless it is proved that the non-disclosure of the unknown fact in time is wholly or partly attributable to him.

Article 4

1. No one shall be liable to be tried or punished again in criminal proceedings under the jurisdiction of the same State for an offence for which he has already been finally acquitted or convicted in accordance with the law and penal procedure of that State.

2. The provisions of the preceding paragraph shall not prevent the reopening of the case in accordance with the law and penal procedure of the State concerned, if there is evidence of new or newly discovered facts, or if there has been a fundamental defect in the previous proceedings, which could affect the outcome of the case.

3. No derogation from this Article shall be made under Article 15 of the Convention.

Article 5

Spouses shall enjoy equality of rights and responsibilities of a private law character between them, and in their relations with their children, as to marriage, during marriage and in the event of its dissolution. This Article shall not prevent States from taking such measures as are necessary in the interests of the children.

APPENDIX 2

Dates of Recognition of the Right of Individual Petition

STATE	CONVENTION	PROTOCOL No. 1	PROTOCOL No. 4	PROTOCOL No. 6	PROTOCOL No. 7	PROTOCOL No. 9
Albania	02.10.1996	02.10.1996	02.10.1996	—	01.01.1997	—
Andorra	22.10.1996	—	—	01.02.1996	—	—
Austria	03.09.1958	03.09.1958	12.03.1970	01.03.1985	01.11.1988	01.10.1994
Belgium	05.07.1955	05.07.1955	30.06.1971	—	—	01.12.1995
Bulgaria	07.09.1992	07.09.1992	—	—	—	—
Croatia	—	—	—	—	—	—
Cyprus	01.01.1989	01.01.1989	01.08.1992	—	—	01.01.1995
Czech Republic	01.01.1993	01.01.1993	01.01.1993	01.01.1993	01.01.1993	01.10.1994
Denmark	13.04.1953	18.05.1954	02.05.1968	01.03.1985	01.11.1988	01.06.1996
Estonia	16.04.1996	16.04.1996	16.04.1996	—	01.07.1996	01.08.1996
Finland	10.05.1990	10.05.1990	10.05.1990	01.06.1990	01.08.1990	01.10.1994
France	02.10.1981	02.10.1981	02.10.1981	02.03.1986	01.11.1988	—
Germany	05.07.1955	13.02.1957	01.06.1968	01.08.1989	—	01.11.1994
Greece	20.11.1985	20.11.1985	—	—	—	—
Hungary	05.11.1992	05.11.1992	05.11.1992	01.12.1992	01.02.1993	01.10.1994
Iceland	29.03.1955	20.03.1955	02.05.1968	01.06.1987	01.11.1988	—
Ireland	25.02.1953	18.05.1954	18.10.1968	01.07.1994	—	01.10.1994
Italy	01.08.1973	01.08.1973	01.01.1983	01.01.1989	01.01.1997	01.10.1994
Latvia	—	—	—	—	—	—
Liechtenstein	08.09.1982	14.11.1995	—	01.12.1990	—	01.03.1996
Lithuania	20.06.1995	24.05.1996	20.06.1995	—	01.09.1995	—
Luxembourg	28.04.1958	28.04.1958	02.05.1968	01.03.1985	16.01.1990	01.10.1994
Malta	01.05.1987	01.05.1987	—	01.04.1991	—	—
Moldova	—	—	—	—	—	—
Netherlands	28.06.1960	28.06.1960	23.06.1982	01.05.1986	—	01.10.1994
Norway	10.12.1955	10.12.1955	26.09.1969	01.11.1988	01.01.1989	01.10.1994
Poland	01.05.1993	10.10.1994	02.02.1995	—	—	01.02.1995
Portugal	09.11.1978	09.11.1978	09.11.1978	01.11.1986	—	01.02.1996
Romania	20.06.1994	20.06.1994	20.06.1994	01.07.1994	01.09.1994	01.10.1994
Russia	—	—	—	—	—	—
San Marino	22.03.1989	22.03.1989	22.03.1989	01.04.1989	01.06.1989	01.10.1995
Slovak Republic	01.01.1993	01.01.1993	01.01.1993	01.01.1993	01.01.1993	01.10.1994
Slovenia	28.06.1994	28.06.1994	28.06.1994	01.07.1994	01.09.1994	01.10.1994
Spain	01.07.1981	27.11.1990	—	01.03.1985	—	—
Sweden	04.02.1952	18.05.1954	02.05.1968	01.03.1985	01.11.1988	01.08.1995
Switzerland	28.11.1974	—	—	01.11.1987	01.11.1988	01.08.1995
TFYR, Macedonia	10.04.1997	10.04.1997	01.01.1998	01.05.1997	01.01.1998	—
Turkey	28.01.1987	28.01.1987	—	—	—	—
Ukraine	—	—	—	—	—	—
United Kingdom	14.01.1966	14.01.1966	—	—	—	—

APPENDIX 3

Article 63 Declaration

Reservations/Declarations
ETS No. 5

Declaration contained in a letter from the Permanent Representative, dated November 8, 1983, registered at the Secretariat General on November 9, 1983 — Or. Engl.

I have the honour to refer to Article 63 of the Convention for the Protection of Human Rights and Fundamental Freedoms, under which the Convention was extended to the Leeward Islands (including St. Kitts-Nevis) in 1953.

On instructions from Her Majesty's Principal Secretary of State for Foreign and Commonwealth Affairs, I now have the honour to inform you that since the independence of St. Kitts-Nevis from September 19, 1983, the Government of the United Kingdom is no longer responsible for this territory.

Declaration contained in a letter from the Permanent Representative, dated April 3, 1984, registered at the Secretariat General on April 3, 1984 — Or. Engl.

I have the honour to refer to Article 63 of the Convention for the Protection of Human Rights and Fundamental Freedoms, under which the Convention was extended to Brunei on September 12, 1967.

On instructions from Her Majesty's Principal Secretary of State for Foreign and Commonwealth Affairs, I now have the honour to inform you that since Brunei Darussalam resumed full international responsibility as a sovereign and independent State on December 13, 1983, the Government of the United Kingdom is no longer responsible for her external affairs.

List of territories for whose international relations Her Majesty's Government in the United Kingdom are responsible and to which the European Convention on Human Rights has been extended:

Anguilla	Guernsey
Bermuda	Isle of Man
British Virgin Islands	Jersey
Cayman Islands	Montserrat
Falkland Islands	St. Helena
Gibraltar	Turks and Caicos Islands

April 1984

APPENDIX 4

Protocol No. 11 to the Convention for the Protection of Human Rights and Fundamental Freedoms, Restructuring the Control Machinery Established thereby

The Member States of the Council of Europe, signatories to this Protocol to the Convention for the Protection of Human Rights and Fundamental Freedoms, signed at Rome on November 4, 1950 (hereinafter referred to as "the Convention").

Considering the urgent need to restructure the control machinery established by the Convention in order to maintain and improve the efficiency of its protection of human rights and fundamental freedoms, mainly in view of the increase in the number of applications and the growing membership of the Council of Europe;

Considering that it is therefore desirable to amend certain provisions of the Convention with a view, in particular, to replacing the existing European Commission and Court of Human Rights with a new permanent Court;

Having regard to Resolution No. 1 adopted at the European Ministerial Conference on Human Rights, held in Vienna on March 19 and 20, 1985;

Having regard to Recommendation 1194 (1992), adopted by the Parliamentary Assembly of the Council of Europe on October 6, 1992;

Having regard to the decision taken on reform of the Convention control machinery by the Heads of State and Government of the Council of Europe Member States in the Vienna Declaration on October 9, 1993,

Have agreed as follows:

Article 1

The existing text of sections II to IV of the Convention (Articles 19 to 56) and Protocol No. 2 conferring upon the European Court of Human Rights competence to give advisory opinions shall be replaced by the following section II of the Convention (Articles 19 to 51):

"Section II — European Court of Human Rights

Article 19 — Establishment of the Court

To ensure the observance of the engagements undertaken by the High Contracting Parties in the Convention and the protocols thereto, there shall be set up a European Court of Human Rights, hereinafter referred to as "the Court". It shall function on a permanent basis.

Article 20 — Number of judges

The Court shall consist of a number of judges equal to that of the High Contracting Parties.

Article 21 — Criteria for office

1. The judges shall be of high moral character and must either possess the qualifications required for appointment to high judicial office or be jurisconsults of recognised competence.

2. The judges shall sit on the Court in their individual capacity.

441

3. During their term of office the judges shall not engage in any activity which is incompatible with their independence, impartiality or with the demands of a full-time office; all questions arising from the application of this paragraph shall be decided by the Court.

Article 22 — Election of judges

1. The judges shall be elected by the Parliamentary Assembly with respect to each High Contracting Party by a majority of votes cast from a list of three candidates nominated by the High Contracting Party.

2. The same procedure shall be followed to complete the Court in the event of the accession of new High Contracting Parties and in filling casual vacancies.

Article 23 — Terms of office

1. The judges shall be elected for a period of six years. They may be re-elected. However, the terms of office of one-half of the judges elected at the first election shall expire at the end of three years.

2. The judges whose terms of office are to expire at the end of the initial period of three years shall be chosen by lot by the Secretary General of the Council of Europe immediately after their election.

3. In order to ensure that, as far as possible, the terms of office of one-half of the judges are renewed every three years, the Parliamentary Assembly may decide, before proceeding to any subsequent election, that the term or terms of office of one or more judges to be elected shall be for a period other than six years but not more than nine and not less than three years.

4. In cases where more than one term of office is involved and where the Parliamentary Assembly applies the preceding paragraph, the allocation of the terms of office shall be effected by a drawing of lots by the Secretary General of the Council of Europe immediately after the election.

5. A judge elected to replace a judge whose term of office has not expired shall hold office for the remainder of his predecessor's term.

6. The terms of office of judges shall expire when they reach the age of 70.

7. The judges shall hold office until replaced. They shall, however, continue to deal with such cases as they already have under consideration.

Article 24 — Dismissal

No judge may be dismissed from his office unless the other judges decide by a majority of two-thirds that he has ceased to fulfil the required conditions.

Article 25 — Registry and legal secretaries

The Court shall have a registry, the functions and organisation of which shall be laid down in the rules of the Court. The Court shall be assisted by legal secretaries.

Article 26 — Plenary Court

The plenary Court shall

(a) elect its President and one or two Vice-Presidents for a period of three years; they may be re-elected;
(b) set up Chambers, constituted for a fixed period of time;
(c) elect the Presidents of the Chambers of the Court; they may be re-elected;
(d) adopt the rules of the Court; and
(e) elect the Registrar and one or more Deputy Registrars.

Article 27 — Committees, Chambers and Grand Chamber

1. To consider cases brought before it, the Court shall sit in committees of three judges, in Chambers of seven judges and in a Grand Chamber of 17 judges. The Court's Chambers shall set up committees for a fixed period of time.

2. There shall sit as an *ex officio* member of the Chamber and the Grand Chamber the judge elected in respect of the State Party concerned or, if there is none or if he is unable to sit, a person of its choice who shall sit in the capacity of judge.

3. The Grand Chamber shall also include the President of the Court, the Vice-Presidents, the Presidents of the Chambers and other judges chosen in accordance with the rules of the Court. When a case is referred to the Grand Chamber under Article 43, no judge from the Chamber which rendered the judgment shall sit in the Grand Chamber, with the exception of the President of the Chamber and the judge who sat in respect of the State Party concerned.

Article 28 — Declarations of inadmissibility by committees

A committee may, by a unanimous vote, declare inadmissible or strike out of its lists of cases an individual application submitted under Article 34 where such a decision can be taken without further examination. The decision shall be final.

Article 29 — Decisions by Chambers on admissibility and merits

1. If no decision is taken under Article 28, a Chamber shall decide on the admissibility and merits of individual applications submitted under Article 34.

2. A Chamber shall decide on the admissibility and merits of inter-State applications submitted under Article 33.

3. The decision on admissibility shall be taken separately unless the Court, in exceptional cases, decides otherwise.

Article 30 — Relinquishment of jurisdiction to the Grand Chamber

Where a case pending before a Chamber raises a serious question affecting the interpretation of the Convention or the protocols thereto or where the resolution of a question before it might have a result inconsistent with a judgment previously delivered by the Court, the Chamber may, at any time before it has rendered its judgment, relinquish jurisdiction in favour of the Grand Chamber, unless one of the parties to the case objects.

Article 31 — Powers of the Grand Chamber

The Grand Chamber shall

(a) determine applications submitted either under Article 33 or Article 34 when a Chamber has relinguished jurisdiction under Article 30 or when the case has been referred to it under Article 43; and

(b) consider requests for advisory opinions submitted under Article 47.

Article 32 — Jurisdiction of the Court

1. The jurisdiction of the Court shall extend to all matters concerning the interpretation and application of the Convention and the protocols thereto which are referred to it as provided in Articles 33, 34 and 47.

2. In the event of dispute as to whether the Court has jurisdiction, the Court shall decide.

Article 33 — Inter-State cases

Any High Contracting Party may refer to the Court any alleged breach of the provisions of the Convention and the protocols thereto by another High Contracting Party.

Article 34 — Individual applications

The Court may receive applications from any person, non-governmental organisation or group of individuals claiming to be the victim of a violation by one of the High Contracting Parties of the rights set forth in the Convention or the protocols thereto. The High Contracting Parties undertake not to hinder in any way the effective exercise of this right.

Article 35 — Admissibility criteria

1. The Court may only deal with the matter after all domestic remedies have been exhausted, according to the generally recognised rules of international law, and within a period of six months from the date on which the final decision was taken.

2. The Court shall not deal with any individual application submitted under article 34 that

(a) is anonymous; or

(b) is substantially the same as a matter that has already been examined by the Court or has already been submitted to another procedure of international investigation or settlement and contains no relevant new information.

3. The Court shall declare inadmissible any individual application submitted under Article 34 which it considers incompatible with the provisions of the Convention or the protocols thereto, manifestly ill-founded, or an abuse of the right of application.

4. The Court shall reject any application which it considers inadmissible under this Article. It may do so at any stage of the proceedings.

Article 36 — Third-party intervention

1. In all cases before a Chamber or the Grand Chamber, a High Contracting Party one of whose nationals is an applicant shall have the right to submit written comments and to take part in hearings.

2. The President of the Court may, in the interest of the proper administration of justice, invite any High Contracting Party which is not a party to the proceedings or any person concerned who is not the applicant to submit written comments or take part in hearings.

Article 37 — Striking out applications

1. The Court may at any stage of the proceedings decide to strike an application out of its list of cases where the circumstances lead to the conclusion that

    (a) the applicant does not intend to pursue his application; or
    (b) the matter has been resolved; or
    (c) for any other reason established by the Court, it is no longer justified to continue the examination of the application.

However, the Court shall continue the examination of the application if respect for human rights as defined in the Convention and the protocols thereto so requires.

2. The Court may decide to restore an application to its list of cases if it considers that the circumstances justify such a course.

Article 38 — Examination of the case and friendly settlement proceedings

1. If the Court declares the application admissible, it shall

    (a) pursue the examination of the case, together with the representatives of the parties, and if need be, undertake an investigation, for the effective conduct of which the States concerned shall furnish all necessary facilities;
    (b) place itself at the disposal of the parties concerned with a view to securing a friendly settlement of the matter on the basis of respect for human rights as defined in the Convention and the protocols thereto.

2. Proceedings conducted under paragraph 1(b) shall be confidential.

Article 39 — Finding of a friendly settlement

If a friendly settlement is effected, the Court shall strike the case out of its list by means of a decision which shall be confined to a brief statement of the facts and of the solution reached.

Article 40 — Public hearings and access to documents

1. Hearings shall be public unless the Court in exceptional circumstances decides otherwise.

2. Documents deposited with the Registrar shall be accessible to the public unless the President of the Court decides otherwise.

Article 41 — Just satisfaction

If the Court finds that there has been a violation of the Convention or the protocols thereto, and if the internal law of the High Contracting Party concerned allows only partial reparation to be made, the Court shall, if necessary, afford just satisfaction to the injured party.

Article 42 — Judgments of Chambers

Judgments of Chambers shall become final in accordance with the provisions of Article 44, paragraph 2.

Article 43 — Referral to the Grand Chamber

1. Within a period of three months from the date of the judgment of the Chamber, any party to the case may, in exceptional cases, request that the case be referred to the Grand Chamber.

2. A panel of five judges of the Grand Chamber shall accept the request if the case raises a serious question affecting the interpretation or application of the Convention or the protocols thereto, or a serious issue of general importance.

3. If the panel accepts the request, the Grand Chamber shall decide the case by means of a judgment.

Article 44 — Final judgments

1. The judgment of the Grand Chamber shall be final.

2. The judgment of a Chamber shall become final

   (a) when the parties declare that they will not request that the case be referred to the Grand Chamber; or
   (b) three months after the date of the judgment, if reference of the case to the Grand Chamber has not been requested; or
   (c) when the panel of the Grand Chamber rejects the request to refer under Article 43.

3. The final judgment shall be published.

Article 45 — Reasons for judgments and decisions

1. Reasons shall be given for judgments as well as for decisions declaring applications admissible or inadmissible.

2. If a judgment does not represent, in whole or in part, the unanimous opinion of the judges, any judge shall be entitled to deliver a separate opinion.

Article 46 — Binding force and execution of judgments

1. The High Contracting Parties undertake to abide by the final judgment of the Court in any case to which they are parties.

2. The final judgment of the Court shall be transmitted to the Committee of Ministers, which shall supervise its execution.

Article 47 — Advisory opinions

1. The Court may, at the request of the Committee of Ministers, give advisory opinions on legal questions concerning the interpretation of the Convention and the protocols thereto.

2. Such opinions shall not deal with any question relating to the content of scope of the rights or freedoms defined in Section I of the Convention and the protocols thereto, or with any other question which the Court of the Committee of Ministers might have to consider in consequence of any such proceedings as could be instituted in accordance with the Convention.

3. Decisions of the Committee of Ministers to request an advisory opinion of the Court shall require a majority vote of the repesentatives entitled to sit on the Committee.

Article 48 — Advisory jurisdiction of the Court

The Court shall decide whether a request for an advisory opinion submitted by the Committee of Ministers is within its competence as defined in Article 47.

Article 49 — Reasons for advisory opinions

1. Reasons shall be given for advisory opinions of the Court.

2. If the advisory opinion does not represent, in whole or in part, the unanimous opinion of the judges, any judge shall be entitled to deliver a separate opinion.

3. Advisory opinions of the Court shall be communicated to the Committee of Ministers.

Article 50 — Expenditure on the Court

The expenditure on the Court shall be borne by the Council of Europe.

Article 51 — Privileges and immunities of judges

The judges shall be entitled, during the exercise of their functions, to the privileges and immunities provided for in Article 40 of the Statute of the Council of Europe and in the agreements made thereunder."

Article 2

1. Section V of the Convention shall become section III of the Convention; Article 57 of the Convention shall become Article 52 of the Convention; Articles 58 and 59 of the Convention shall be deleted, and Articles 60 to 66 of the Convention shall become Articles 53 to 59 of the Convention respectively.

2. Section I of the Convention shall be entitled "RIGHTS AND FREEDOMS" and new section III of the Convention shall be entitled "MISCELLANEOUS PROVISIONS". Articles 1 to 18 and new Articles 52 to 59 of the Convention shall be provided with headings, as listed in the appendix to this Protocol.

3. In new Article 56, in paragraph 1, the words ", subject to paragraph 4 of this Article," shall be inserted after the word "shall"; in paragraph 4, the words "Commission to receive petitions" and "in accordance with Article 25 of the present Convention" shall be replaced by the words "Court to receive applications" and "as provided in Article 34 of the Convention" respectively. In new Article 58, paragraph 4, the words "Article 63" shall be replaced by the words "Article 56".

4. The Protocol to the Convention shall be amended as follows:

    (a) the Articles shall be provided with the headings listed in the appendix to the present Protocol; and

(b) in Article 4, last sentence, the words "of Article 63" shall be replaced by the words "of Article 56".

5. Protocol No. 4 shall be amended as follows:

   (a) the articles shall be provided with the headings listed in the appendix to the present Protocol;
   (b) in Article 5, paragraph 3, the words "of article 63" shall be replaced by the words "of Article 56"; a new paragraph 5 shall be added, which shall read:

   "Any State which has made a declaration in accordance with paragraph 1 or 2 of this Article may at any time thereafter declare on behalf of one or more of the territories to which the declaration relates that it accepts the competence of the Court to receive applications from the individuals, non-governmental organisations or groups of individuals as provided in Article 34 of the Convention in respect of all or any of Articles 1 to 4 of this Protocol."; and

   (c) paragraph 2 of Article 6 shall be deleted.

6. Protocol No. 6 shall be amended as follows:

   (a) the Articles shall be provided with the headings listed in the appendix to the present Protocol; and
   (b) in Article 4 the words "under Article 64" shall be replaced by the words "under Article 57".

7. Protocol No. 7 shall be amended as follows:

   (a) the Articles shall be provided with the headings listed in the appendix to the present Protocol;
   (b) in Article 6, paragraph 4, the words "of Article 63" shall be replaced by the words "of Article 56"; a new paragraph 6 shall be added, which shall read:

   "Any State which has made a declaration in accordance with paragraph 1 or 2 of this Article may at any time thereafter declare on behalf of one or more of the territories to which the declaration relates that it accepts the competence of the Court to receive applications from individuals, non-governmental organisations or groups of individuals as provided in Article 34 of the Convention in respect of Articles 1 to 5 of this Protocol."; and

   (c) paragraph 2 of Article 7 shall be deleted.

8. Protocol No. 9 shall be repealed.

Article 3

1. This Protocol shall be open for signature by Member States of the Council of Europe signatories to the Convention, which may express their consent to be bound by

   (a) signature without reservation as to ratification, acceptance or approval; or
   (b) signature subject to ratification, acceptance or approval, followed by ratification, acceptance or approval.

2. The instruments of ratification, acceptance or approval shall be deposited with the Secretary General of the Council of Europe.

Article 4

This Protocol shall enter into force on the first day of the month following the expiration of a period of one year after the date on which all Parties to the Convention have expressed their consent to be bound by the Protocol in accordance with the provisions of Article 3. The election of new judges may take place, and any further necessary steps may be taken to establish the new Court, in accordance with the provisions of this Protocol from the date on which all Parties to the Convention have expressed their consent to be bound by the Protocol.

Article 5

1. Without prejudice to the provisions in paragraphs 3 and 4 below, the terms of office of the judges, members of the Commission, Registrar and Deputy Registrar shall expire at the date of entry into force of this Protocol.

2. Applications pending before the Commission which have not been declared admissible at the date of the entry into force of this Protocol shall be examined by the Court in accordance with the provisions of this Protocol.

3. Applications which have been declared admissible at the date of entry into force of this Protocol shall continue to be dealt with by members of the Commission within a period of one year thereafter. Any applications the examination of which has not been completed within the aforesaid period shall be transmitted to the Court which shall examine them as admissible cases in accordance with the provisions of this Protocol.

4. With respect to applications in which the Commission, after the entry into force of this Protocol, has adopted a report in accordance with former Article 31 of the Convention, the report shall be transmitted to the parties, who shall not be at liberty to publish it. In accordance with the provisions applicable prior to the entry into force of this Protocol, a case may be referred to the Court. The panel of the Grand Chamber shall determine whether one of the Chambers or the Grand Chamber shall decide the case. If the case is decided by a Chamber, the decision of the Chamber shall be final. Cases not referred to the Court shall be dealt with by the Committee of Ministers acting in accordance with the provisions of former Article 32 of the Convention.

5. Cases pending before the Court which have not been decided at the date of entry into force of this Protocol shall be transmitted to the Grand Chamber of the Court, which shall examine them in accordance with the provisions of this Protocol.

6. Cases pending before the Committee of Ministers which have not been decided under former Article 32 of the Convention at the date of entry into force of this Protocol shall be completed by the Committee of Ministers acting in accordance with that Article.

Article 6

Where a High Contracting Party had made a declaration recognising the competence of the Commission or the jurisdiction of the Court under former Article 25 or 46 of the Convention with respect to matters arising after or based on facts occurring subsequent to any such declaration, this limitation shall remain valid for the jurisdiction of the Court under this Protocol.

Article 7

The Secretary General of the Council of Europe shall notify the Member States of the Council of

    (a) any signature;

    (b) the deposit of any instrument of ratification, acceptance or approval;

    (c) the date of entry into force of this Protocol or of any of its provisions in accordance with Article 4 and

    (d) any other act, notification or communication relating to this Protocol.

In witness whereof the undersigned, being duly authorised thereto, have signed this Protocol.

Done at Strasbourg, this 11th day of May 1994 in English and French, both texts being equally authentic, in a single copy which shall be deposited in the archives of the Council of Europe. The Secretary General of the Council of Europe shall transmit certified copies to each Member State of the Council of Europe.

APPENDIX 5

APPENDIX 5

> Voir Notice explicative
> See *Explanatory Note*

COMMISSION EUROPÉENNE DE DROITS DE L'HOMME
EUROPEAN COMMISSION OF HUMAN RIGHTS

Conseil de l'Europe — *Council of Europe*
Strasbourg, France

REQUÊTE
APPLICATION

présentée en application de l'article 25 de la Convention européenne des Droits de l'Homme, ainsi que des articles 43 et 44 du Règlement intérieur de la Commission

under Article 25 of the European Convention on Human Rights and Rules 43 and 44 of the Rules of Procedure of the Commission

IMPORTANT: La présente requête est un document juridique et peut affecter vos droits et obligations.
This application is a formal legal document and may affect your rights and obligations.

451

I— LES PARTIES
THE PARTIES

A. LE REQUÉRANT
THE APPLICANT

(Renseignements à fournir concernant le requérant et son représentant éventuel)
(*Fill in the following details of the applicant and any representative*)

1. Nom de famille .... 2. Prénom(s) ....
Name of applicant *First name(s)*

3. Nationalité .... 4. Profession ....
Nationality *Occupation*

5. Date et lieu de naissance ....
Date and place of birth

6. Domicile ....
Permanent address

.... 7. Tel. No ....

8. Adresse actuelle ....
At present at

....

Le cas échéant, (*if any*)

9. Nom et prénom du représentant* ....
Name of representative *

10. Profession du représentant ....
Occupation of representative

11. Adresse du représentant ....
Address of representative

.... 12. Tel. No ....

A. LA HAUTE PARTIE CONTRACTANTE
THE HIGH CONTRACTING PARTY

(Indiquer ci-après le nom de l'Etat contre lequel le requête est dirigée)
(*Fill in the name of the Country against which the application is directed*)

13. ....

---

* Si le requérant est représenté, joindre une procuration signée par le requérant en faveur du représentant.
A form of authority signed by the applicant should be submitted if a representative is appointed.

II— EXPOSÉ DES FAITS
STATEMENT OF THE FACTS

(Voir chapitre II de la note explicative)
(See Part II of the Explanatory Note)

14.

III— EXPOSÉ DE LA OU DES VIOLATION(S) DE LA CONVENTION ALLÉGUÉE(S) PAR LE REQUÉRANT, AINSI QUE DES ARGUMENTS À L'APPUI
STATEMENT OF ALLEGED VIOLATION(S) OF THE CONVENTION AND OF RELEVANT ARGUMENTS

A. (Voir chapitre II de la note explicative)
See Part III of the Explanatory Note

15.

Si nécessaire, continuer sur une feuille séparée
Continue on a separate sheet if necessary

IV— EXPOSÉ RELATIF AUX PRESCRIPTIONS DE L'ARTICLES 26 DE LA CONVENTION
STATEMENT RELATIVE TO ARTICLE 26 OF THE CONVENTION

(Voir chapitre IV de la note explicative. Donner pour chaque grief, et au besoin sur une feuille séparée, les renseignements demandés sous ch. 16 à 18 ci-après)
(See Part IV of the Explanatory Note. If necessary, give the details mentioned below under points 16 to 18 on a separate sheet for each separate complaint)

16. Décision interne définitive (date et nature de la décision, organe — judiciaire ou autre — l'ayant rendue)
Final decision (date, court or authority and nature of decision)

17. Autres décisions (énumérées dans l'ordre chronologique en indiquant, pour chaque décision, sa date, sa nature et l'organe — judiciaire ou autre — l'ayant rendue)
Other decisions (list in chronological order, giving date, court or authority and nature of decision for each one)

18. Le requérant disposait-il d'un recours qu'il n'a pas exercé? Si oui, lequel et pour quel motif n'a-t-il pas été exercé?
Is any other appeal or remedy available which you have not used? If so, explain why you have not used it.

V— EXPOSÉ DE LA REQUÊTE
STATEMENT OF THE OBJECT OF THE APPLICATION

(Voir chapitre V de la note explicative)
(See Part V of the Explanatory Note)

19.

VI— AUTRES INSTANCES INTERNATIONALES TRAITANT OU AYANT TRAITÉ L'AFFAIRE
STATEMENT CONCERNING OTHER INTERNATIONAL PROCEEDINGS

(Voir chapitre VI de la note explicative)
(See Part VI of the Explanatory Note)

20. Le requérant a-t-il soumis à une autre instance internationale d'enquête ou de règlement les griefs énoncés dans la présente requête? Si oui, fournir des indications détaillées à ce sujet.
Have you submitted the above complaints to any other procedure of international investigation or settlement? If so, give full details.

VII— PIÈCES ANNEXÉES
LIST OF DOCUMENTS

(PAS D'ORIGINAUX, UNIQUEMENT DES COPIES) (*NO ORIGINAL DOCUMENTS ONLY PHOTOCOPIES*)

(Voir chapitre VII de la note explicative. Joindre copie de toutes les décisions mentionnées sous ch. IV et VI ci-avant. Se procurer, au besoin, les copies nécessaires, et, en cas d'impossibilité, expliquer pourquoi celles-ci ne peuvent pas être obtenues. Ces documents ne vous seront pas retournés.)
(See Part VII of the Explanatory Note. Include copies of all decisions referred to in Parts IV and VI above. If you do not have copies, you should obtain them. If you cannot obtain them, explain why not. No document will be returned to you.)

21. a) . . . .

b) . . . .

c) . . . .

Si nécessaire, continuer sur une feuille séparée
Continue on a separate sheet if necessary

455

VIII— LANGUE DE PROCÉDURE SOUHAITÉE
STATEMENT OF PREFERRED LANGUAGE

(Voir chapitre VIII de la note explicative)
(*See Part VIII of the Explanatory Note*)

22. Je préfère recevoir la décision de la Commission en: anglais/français*
     I prefer to receive the Commission's decision in: *English/French**

IX— DÉCLARATION ET SIGNATURE
DECLARATION AND SIGNATURE

(Voir chapitre IX de la note explicative)
(*See Part IX of the Explanatory Note*)

23. Je déclare en toute conscience et loyauté que les renseignements qui figurent sur la présente formule de requête sont exacts et je m'engage à respecter la caractère confidentiel de la procédure de la Commission.
     I hereby declare that, to the best of my knowledge and belief, the information I have given in the application is correct and that I will respect the confidentiality of the Commission's proceedings.

24. S'il n'est pas indiqué clairement ci-après que le requérant désire garder l'anonymat à l'égard du public, il sera considéré qu'il n'a pas d'objection à ce que son identité soit révélée:
     It will be assumed that there is no objection to the identity of the applicant being disclosed unless it is stated here in unambiguous terms that the applicant does object:

Lieu/*Place* .... Date/*Date* ....

....
(Signature du requérant ou du représentant)
(*Signature of the applicant or of the representative*)

* Biffer ce qui ne convient pas.
Delete as appropriate.

456

Explanatory Note

for persons completing the Application Form
under Article 25 of the Convention

Introduction

These notes are intended to assist you in drawing up your application to the Commission. **Please read them carefully before completing the form**, and then refer to them as you complete each section of the form.

The completed form will be your application or "petition" to the Commission under Article 25 of the Convention. It will be the basis for the Commission's examination of your case. It is therefore important that you **complete it fully and accurately even if this means repeating information you have already given the Secretariat in previous correspondence**.

You will see that there are nine sections to the form. You should complete all of these so that your application contains all the information required under the Commission's Rules of Procedure. Below you will find an explanatory note relating to each section of the form. You will also find at the end of these notes the text of Rules 43 and 44 of the Commission's Rules of Procedure.

Notes relating to the Application Form

I. The Parties — Rule 44, para. 1(a), (b) and (c)
(1–13)

If there is more than one applicant, you should give the required information for each one, on a separate sheet if necessary.

An applicant may appoint a lawyer or other person to represent him. Such representative must be resident in a Convention country, unless the Commission decides otherwise. When an applicant is represented by another person, relevant details should be given in this part of the application form, and the Secretariat will correspond only with the representative.

II. Statement of the facts — Rule 44, para. 1(e)
(14)

You should give clear and concise details of the facts you are complaining about. Try to describe the events in the order in which they occurred. Give exact dates. If your complaints relate to a number of different matters (for instance different sets of court proceedings) you should deal with each matter separately.

III. Statement of alleged violation(s) of the Convention and of relevant arguments — Rule 44, para. 1(d) and (e)
(15)

In this section of the form you should explain as precisely as you can what your complaint **under the Convention** is. Say which provisions of the Convention you rely on and explain why you consider that the facts you have set out in Part II of the form involve a violation of these provisions.

You will see that some of the articles of the Convention permit interferences with the rights they guarantee in certain circumstances — (see for instance sub-paras. (a) to (f) of Article 5, para. 1 and para. 2 of Articles 8 to 11). If you are relying on such an article try to explain why you consider the interference which you are complaining about is not justified.

IV. Statement relative to Article 26 of the Convention — Rule 44, para. 2(a)
(16–18)

In this section you should set out details of the remedies you have pursued before the national authorities. You should fill in each of the three parts of this section and give the same information separately for each separate complaint. In part 18 you should say whether or not any other appeal or remedy is available which could redress your complaints and which you have not used. If such a remedy is available, you should say what it is (*e.g.* name the court or authority to which an appeal would lie) and explain why you have not used it.

V. Statement of the object of the application — Rule 44, para. 1(d)
(19)

Here you should state briefly what you want to achieve through your application to the Commission.

VI. Statement concerning other international proceedings — Rule 44, para. 2(b)
(20)

Here you should say whether or not you have ever submitted the complaints in your application to any other procedure of international investigation or settlement, If you have, you should give full details, including the name of the body to which you submitted your complaints, dates and details of any proceedings which took place and details of decisions taken. You should also submit copies of relevant decisions and other documents.

VII. List of documents — Rule 44, para. 1(f) (No original documents, only photocopies)
(21)

Do not forget to enclose with your application and to mention on the list all judgments and decisions referred to in sections IV and VI, as well as any other documents you wish the Commission to take into consideration as evidence (transcripts, statements of witnesses, etc.). Include any documents giving the reasons for a court or other decision as well as the decision itself. Only submit documents which are relevant to the complaints you are making to the Commission.

VIII. Statement of preferred language — Rule 44, para. 2(c)
(22)

The official languages of the Commission are English and French. Although the Secretariat conducts correspondence in a number of other languages as well, documents such as the Commission's decision will be communicated to you in one of the two official languages. Indicate which you prefer.

IX. Declaration and signature — Rule 44, para. 2(d) and (e)
(23–24)

The declaration includes an undertaking to respect the confidentiality of the Commission's proceedings. Under Article 33 of the Convention the Commission meets *in camera*. This means that the contents of all case-files, including all pleadings, must be kept confidential. The Commission's decisions on the admissibility of your case may, however, be made available to the public. If you have any objection to your name being made public, you should inform the Secretariat of this.

If the Application is signed by the representative of the applicant, it should be accompanied by a form of authority signed by the applicant himself (unless this has already been submitted) — Article 43, para. 3.

Rules 43 and 44 of the Rules of Procedure of the Commission

Institution of Proceedings

Rule 43

1. Any application made under Articles 24 or 25 of the Convention shall be submitted in writing and shall be signed by the applicant or by the applicant's representative.

2. Where an application is submitted by a non-governmental organisation or by a group of individuals, it shall be signed by those persons competent to represent such organisation or group. The Commission shall determine any question as to whether the persons who have signed an application are competent to do so.

3. Where applicants are represented in accordance with Rule 32 of these Rules, a power of attorney or written authorisation shall be supplied by their representative or representatives.

Rule 44

1. Any application under Article 25 of the Convention shall be made on the application form provided by the Secretariat, unless the President decides otherwise. It shall set out:
   (a) the name, age, occupation and address of the applicant;
   (b) the name, occupation and address of the representative, if any;
   (c) the name of the High Contracting Party against which the application is made;
   (d) the object of the application and the provision of the Convention alleged to have been violated;
   (e) a statement of the facts and arguments;
   (f) any relevant documents and in particular the decisions, whether judicial or not, relating to the object of the application.

2. Applicants shall furthermore:
   (a) provide information enabling it to be shown that the conditions laid down in Article 26 of the Convention have been satisfied;
   (b) indicate whether they have submitted their complaints to any other procedure of international investigation or settlement;
   (c) indicate in which of the official languages they wish to receive the Commission's decisions;
   (d) indicate whether they do or do not object to their identity being disclosed to the public;
   (e) declare that they will respect the confidentiality of the proceedings before the Commission.

3. Failure to comply with the requirements set out under paragraphs 1 and 2 above may result in the application not being registered and examined by the Commission.

4. The date of introduction of the application shall in general be considered to be the date of the first communication from the applicant setting out, even summarily, the object of the application. The Commission may nevertheless for good cause decide that a different date be considered to be the date of introduction.

5. Applicants shall keep the Commission informed of any change of their address and of all circumstances relevant to the application.

APPENDIX 6

European Commission of Human Rights

Authority

I, ...

....

(*name and address of applicant*)

hereby authorise ....

....

....

(*name and address of representative*)

to represent me in the proceedings before the European Commission of Human Rights, and in any subsequent proceedings under the European Convention on Human Rights, concerning my application introduced under Article 25 of the Convention against

....

(*respondent State*)

.... on ....

(*date of letter of introduction*)

.... (*place and date*)

....

(*signature*)

APPENDIX 7

Scale of Legal Aid Fees

1. The following scale of fees is applicable as from January 1, 1998 on proceedings before the *Commission*.

Item

A. *Fees and expenses*

Preparation of case	2,000,- FF
Written observations — R.48(2)(b) or 53(2)	1,700,- FF
Supplementary observations — R.50(a)	800,- FF
Appearance at hearing (incl. preparation)	2,000,- FF *per diem*
Friendly settlement (written proposals)	800,- FF
Attending settlement negotiations	950,- FF *per diem*
Out-of-pocket expenses	up to 400,- FF

B. *Allowances for hearings before the Commission*

Daily allowance

Lawyer	996,- FF *per diem*
Applicant	817,- FF *per diem*

2. Legal aid in proceedings before the *Court* is handled by the Registrar of the Court. The fees normally fixed by the Registrar in accordance with Rule 6 of the Addendum to the Rules of Court are as follows:

Item

Memorials	1,900,- FF
If appropriate, observations — Art. 50 (R.50 R.C.)	1,000,- FF
Hearings before the Court (incl. preparation)	2,000,- FF *per diem*

INDEX